Transactions and Strategies

Economics for Management

Transactions and Strategies

Economics for Management

ROBERT J. MICHAELS

Mihaylo College of Business and Economics

California State University, Fullerton

Australia • Brazil • Japan • Korea • Mexico • Singapore • Spain • United Kingdom • United States

Transactions and Strategies: Economics for Management
Robert J. Michaels

Vice President of Editorial, Business: Jack W. Calhoun

Publisher: Joe Sabatino

Sr. Acquisitions Editor: Steve Scoble

Supervising Developmental Editor: Jennifer Thomas

Editorial Assistant: Lena Mortis

Sr. Marketing Manager: John Carey

Marketing Coordinator: Suellen Ruttkay

Marketing Specialist: Betty Jung

Content Project Manager: Cliff Kallemeyn

Media Editor: Deepak Kumar

Sr. Art Director: Michelle Kunkler

Frontlist Buyer, Manufacturing: Sandee Milewski

Internal Designer: Juli Cook/ Plan-It-Publishing, Inc.

Cover Designer: Rose Alcorn

Cover Image: © Justin Guariglia/Corbis

Library of Congress Control Number: 2009940356

ISBN-13: 978-0-538-78609-6
ISBN-10: 0-538-78609-4

South-Western Cengage Learning
5191 Natorp Boulevard
Mason, OH 45040
USA

Cengage Learning products are represented in Canada by Nelson Education, Ltd.

Printed in the United States of America
1 2 3 4 5 6 7 13 12 11 10

Brief Contents

Contents

PART 5 Applications and Extensions

Announcing Robert J. Michaels,

author of *Transactions and Strategies: Economics for Management*

Robert J. Michaels is Professor of Economics at California State University, Fullerton, and Daniel Haan Research Fellow in Law and Economics. He is also an independent consultant to the electricity and natural gas industries. He holds an A.B. from the University of Chicago and a Ph.D from the University of California, Los Angeles, both in economics. His past positions include Staff Economist at the Institute for Defense Analyses and Senior Advisor to Hagler Bailly Consulting (now PA Consulting). He is an Adjunct Scholar at the Texas Public Policy Foundaton, the Cato Institute, the Institute for Energy Research and the National Center for Policy Analysis.

Michaels' research on electricity and gas restructuring, measuring and constraining market power, vertical integration, and renewable energy requirements has appeared in industry and scholarly journals including ***Public Utilities Fortnightly, The Electricity Journal, Regulation, Antitrust Bulletin, Review of Industrial Organization,*** and ***Energy Law Journal***. He is also Co-Editor of ***Contemporary Economic Policy***, a peer-reviewed journal of the Western Economic Association. He has advised state commissions, electric utilities, power marketers, natural gas producers, pipelines, public interest groups, and governments on regulatory and antitrust matters. Additionally, Robert Michaels has testified before the Federal Energy Regulatory Commission, the California Public Utilities Commission, the Illinois Commerce Commission, and the U.S. House Subcommittee on Energy and Power.

Preface

"Over all, I think the main thing a musician would like to do is give a picture to the listener of the many wonderful things that he knows of and senses in the universe ... That's what I would like to do. I think that's one of the greatest things you can do in life and we all try to do it in some way. The musician's is through his music."

John Coltrane

To Students

Your Big Questions: Why This Class? Why Me?

I teach managerial economics to undergraduates and MBA students at a mid-level university six miles from Disneyland. Like many of them you may have landed in this course at gunpoint. Were it not a degree requirement you would surely have picked a class that looked more relevant to your career, whether marketing research or organizational design. This is your reality, and it leaves me with a big job: to convince you that economics matters for your upcoming business lives and that your time spent with this book will more than cover its opportunity cost.

You have probably taken or will soon take a course in managerial accounting. You might like it or hate it, but from day one you know the point of taking it: managers need the information contained in accounting reports if they are to make sound business decisions. Few employers would interview a business graduate whose work did not include managerial accounting, and for good reason. It satisfies a universal need of employers for comparable numerical information about the conditions of their companies. If you do not know in advance what a balance sheet looks like you will probably not get a job offer.

But what good does it do an employer to hire a fresh BBA or MBA whose transcript includes managerial economics?

A Quick History Lesson

For as long as business degrees have existed they have required the familiar two-term economic "principles" sequence. Sad to relate, but for much of the twentieth century universities viewed the business major as a dumping ground for substandard students. In the 1960s business schools finally responded by upgrading themselves to higher academic standards. Most of them began to require a third economics course that stressed business applications. The obvious people to teach it were PhDs in economics who already had advanced courses for their own majors. Business faculties never reached a consensus on the content of that course, and the economists responded by teaching their business students the same microeconomics they already taught to economics majors. It goes without saying that the business experience of many economists ended on the customer side of the cash register.

Not much has changed in forty years. The basic layout of most managerial economics texts still strongly resembles the economics majors' books of the 1960s. Ours have a few more examples, often about businesses that never existed, and lots more math problems.

The star students are often those who are best at math and memorization rather than those who genuinely understand the economics. It is no wonder that neither you nor most employers have much interest in your abilities at managerial economics.

Escaping the Problem

It does not have to be this way. While managerial economics was stagnating economists were expanding their research into areas well beyond those covered in the texts they were using. We developed new ways of thinking about business (and for that matter, about life) that will matter for all of our futures. I wrote this book because yesterday's managerial economics tells you so little about the economics we know today and serves you so poorly. (I also did it for the money.) Economics is about more than markets (but it still has a lot to say about them). Today's economics brings insights into subjects often taught by other specialists – from organization charts to long-term contracts to the structure of the human mind. It's not a question of who is "right" – the reason you take so many different classes is that each of them can give you new and different insights into the many aspects of business life. Come out of an up-to-date managerial economics class, and I contend that both you and your employer will see the value it has created.

And What's In It For You?

When I say that economics matters I mean it. Economics books and professors all too often treat their subject like a parlor game, full of concise graphics and stories that are enjoyable for their own sake. If you are not already in it you should realize that you will soon step into a world that looks less like a Tuesday night bridge game and more like a nonstop poker tournament for real money –yours. Business is a highly competitive place (and so is work for governments or nonprofit organizations). Luck and innate talent are always there, but your success and even survival ultimately depend on your ability to think rationally, often about highly personal things. Treat the ideas in this book as components of a survival kit you can use to think in ways that will improve your chances of competitive success against other smart people. Economic reasoning is quite possibly the best way humans have ever devised to separate sense from nonsense. If you are going into battle carry the best armaments you can.

Incidentally, you might even have a good time for the next few months. I hope you do, because all too many textbooks are easy to mistake for implements of torture. Some of the stuff is hard, but I think I can make it bearable by bringing in some bedrock principles and seeing the remarkable assortment of things to which we can apply them. You will learn why South Africans use high-voltage electrical cables that look like no others in the world, and about how engagement rings came to be (it wasn't the diamond industry). We get a look at the biggest machine in the world, and later find out why jewelers who buy diamonds in bulk are not allowed to see them in advance. You will soon have good reason to distrust books that promise to tell you the secrets of successful companies (not because they are lying), and you will understand why Ireland is now the world's largest exporter of software. We will find out why the organization charts of the Green Bay Packers and a giant electric utility look so similar, and why both differ greatly from General Motors'. We will meet employees of large Japanese companies who are well paid for spending their working lives doing nothing, and find out why a smog-check garage in my neighborhood accepts discount coupons issued by others. After we look at the logic of NASCAR drivers choosing to join or abandon draft lines we will see that it also explains arrangements that allow producers to recover more oil from underground pools.

We will meet a woman who calls herself "a refiner of animals" (she never sees them) and visit some of the world's scarcest real estate—25,000 miles above the equator. All this and a survival kit too.

For Instructors

Our Common Life Histories

I studied economics for the same reasons many of you probably did. I liked the logic, the applied math and econometrics, and that economists talked about things everyone could see. At the time, both of us probably had only minimal experience in business. No boss ever asked me how to go about maximizing profit. Probably also like you I couldn't have given a numerical answer and even the best explanation of marginal revenue and cost would have been dismissed as unreal.

The annoying questions were those I was asking myself. "What should students be learning?" had an all-purpose answer, handed down among generations: how to think like an economist, i.e. like I did – build models of firms and markets, optimize and (judging from the class time allocated to them) solve problems involving linear demand curves, Cobb-Douglas functions and 2 X 2 matrices. Assume that you enter the business world after you take a course like this. Answer honestly: Did what you learned in it give your company any advantage over a competitor whose decision maker dropped out after a year of principles of eocnomics? If you cannot give a convincing answer, and quickly, how do you justify the existence of the course you are teaching?

Learning The Economics That Matters

It was my good fortune to learn from experience, and better yet to be paid for it. Some time ago I was a consultant to a major law firm in a dispute between two electric utilities over a contract that allocated rights to use and pay for an extra-high voltage transmission line. My job was to put dollar figures on how different settlements would affect the firm's client and competitive conditions in its markets. At the time I was experimenting in class with material on contracts and organizations to see if it might elicit students' attention. And here I was billing lawyers for letting me apply the same ideas to a real problem. My report looked so simple I wondered if they would actually pay for it. The big meeting took place in a mahogany-paneled 40th floor conference room with a table full of expensive lawyers. I was nervous beyond belief, and then I saw them taking notes and nodding agreement. I learned that my work had pointed them to a resolution that was worth millions to both parties.

I was on the Santa Monica Freeway at San Pedro Street, and that's where it hit me. Much of the economics that makes a difference in business is about nonmarket phenomena like contractual governance. Real businesses with real problems, in a dispute with economically plausible cases on both sides. My job was to run through the logic and stick in some numbers. The economics of real business was without many of the theoretical subtleties that so excited me in school. Instead some simple economics gave me logic and perspective that I could use to help two parties with opposed interests to create new wealth they would eventually share. From that experience ultimately came this book.

What's In It, And Why

My purpose is straightforward: to bring managerial economics into the new century, to convince you that your changeover costs will be small relative to the benefits, and to make a bunch of money in the process. There is probably no course in the business curriculum whose content and texts have changed so little in forty years. It is doubly strange that they have remained in stasis while both economics itself and the world beyond the classroom are undergoing epochal changes. If you don't think so compare the table of contents of today's typical text with one from the 1960s or 1970s. There are some differences: chapters on externalities, uncertainty, asymmetric information, and game-theoretic strategy have appeared over the editions. Hardly any subjects have vanished, excepting occasionally material on demand estimation and linear programming that are better taught by others. Save for some material on games, the near-uniform experience of my colleagues is that all they ever teach are the same neoclassical models of firms and markets as always.

Teachers are left to shop in a market of managerial books that fit them comfortably, loaded with neoclassical basics and a few almost random addenda. Economics itself has moved on. Over the past forty years economists have extended and reformulated the basic models to cover transactions and organizations, producing a body of theory and empirics that has revolutionized our insights into how businesses actually function. A semester *can* be usefully filled with marginal equalities and Nash equilibria. But the omitted economics is about equally deep questions, and often more relevant ones. We claim to teach managerial decision making and competitive strategy, but most existing texts treat vertical integration as an afterthought. Many of the most important decisions for managers at all levels are about choices between putting an activity in-house or outsourcing it. The scope of a firm is a critical determinant of its costs, and therefore its competitive future. The newer economics explains the general trend to vertical deintegration while many management experts continue to favor it on strategic grounds. If the decision is to outsource what determines the contractual terms that best govern the firm's relationship with its supplier? Competition takes place both inside and outside of markets and students ought to learn both. How many students can give a coherent explanation of any of this, and what are they learning instead of it?

The Book

Transactions and Strategies is organized around the governance of transactions, the institutional backdrop against which they take place. Its perspective is grounded in the familiar neoclassical models, filtered through what we now often call (somewhat inaccurately, in my opinion) the new institutional economics. Acknowledging (and oversimplifying) Oliver Williamson's basic formulation, transactions take place in markets, by contract ("hybrid" arrangements), and within organizations (hierarchies).[1] Approximately the first 40 percent of the material is the familiar economic theory of firms with neoclassical production technologies that operate in markets where transactions are standardized, repetitive and do not require long-term commitments (transaction-specific investments) by the parties. Where commitments can create more benefits for the parties than spot transactions they will choose to organize their relationships under enforceable contracts that detail how their responsibilities will unfold over time. In situations too complex or uncertain to be well-governed by such agreements their place will be taken by authority relationships within organizations. Four capstone chapters on show the value of combining market and non-market approaches in analyzing vertical relationships, employment arrangements, option values and conflict. All of the chapters are heavy with business examples and summaries of research.

What you do with the book is up to you. It depends on the topics your school expects you to teach, your own preferences and the interests of your students. An Instructor's

[1]A concise introduction appears in Williamson's "Comparative Economic Organization: The Analysis of Discrete Structural Alternatives," *Administrative Science Quarterly* 36 (June 1991), 269–296.

Manual will tell you more about how to approach individual chapters and organize class material and discussions (I hope that you will be able to extend these recommendations and detect errors and inadequacies). The book is organized to help you to better cope with a problem we all encounter: time runs out a lot sooner than text. Wherever possible I have structured chapters so that more important material precedes less important. This will help you to allocate X days of class for a particular chapter, put it into perspective at the end of day X and start the next class day with the next topic. Students should be suspicious of instructors who stress the importance of optimization but end the term only partway through the promised material.

Most texts separate theory from applications, usually by putting the applications off to the side in boxes with the implication that they are secondary. My experience is that students take you a lot more seriously if your examples are integral to your narrative. There are two basic interruptions to the flow of this book. "Checkpoints" are intended to be simple stops for students to make certain that they understand the basics. "For Further Thought" items are questions I want the student to mull over for twenty seconds and only come back later to think about in greater depth. End-of-chapter questions have the same range of difficulty. Warning: some questions have several plausible answers, and there are others to which I cannot give a good answer and would therefore appreciate your suggestions.

Three Possible Course Outlines

Like the shipping containers on the book's cover, there are a lot of ways to unpack this material. Here are three possibilities, and I would appreciate hearing about your own experiences and ideas.

1. Traditional, But With Excursions Beyond The Market. This is designed for economists who are comfortable with their belief that neoclassical firms and markets remain by far the most important templates for managerial thinking. Devote the first 2/3 of the course to the familiar materials in Chapters 1 through 7. (If you like to emphasize strategies you can dwell on Chapters 6 and 7 for some time and possibly extend them.) Spend several hours on Chapter 8, where students can translate everyday notions of competition into microeconomic language and see how our model of a firm generalizes into the resource-based model popular in other business school departments. With markets mastered your students can spend the final weeks of the term elsewhere. First do Chapter 9 on the basics of contracts and the choice between them and market transactions ("market failure" enthusiasts can integrate high transaction costs into their classes) Then do Chapter 12, the introduction to hierarchies and organizations. Finally, go through one of capstone Chapters 14 (vertical relationships) or 15 (employment relationships), both if you have the time.

2. A Little Less Theory, A Little More Reality. Some instructors may be interested in more applications than would appear in the above course. Try spending about the first half of the course on Chapters 1 through 7 (remember about truncating them), followed by a week and a half of Chapter 8. Introduce nonmarket relationships (perhaps in less depth) using Chapter 9 and continue with the explanations of contract structure, damages, and incompleteness in Chapter 10. (If you think it important, make a quick detour to asymmetric information in Chapter 11.) Run through some of the logic of organization in Chapter 12 and spend more time in Chapter 13 reviewing some principles of organizational design. Do one of either 14 or 15 in depth, and give a shallow introduction to the other.

3. Tomorrow's Course Today. If you already feel at home with the book's viewpoint and organization, spend about half the term on Chapters 1 – 8. (Please let me know which topics you chose to drop, and why.) Chapters 9 through 13 are the next third of the course (again, what would you drop?), and finish with both 14 and 15 in some depth. This is the structure in which my classes have evolved.

You may have noticed that none of the three suggest going into Chapter 16 (time, risk and options) or 17 (conflict and negotiation). Make room for 16 (your choice about which parts of the rest to jettison) if you or your students have a particular interest in financial economics or risk and uncertainty. I have at times turned to 16 to give students a better appreciation of contracts that allocate risk, and to show examples of how option markets aggregate information (futures are already in Chapter 3). Chapter 17 may be useful for instructors who want to discuss negotiation in more detail, and for those who want to expand their lectures on games to include cores.

Supplements

This test is supported by a full range of supplements to help facilitate the course and learning for students.

The **Instructor's Manual** (ISBN 0538467037), written by the author, is available online at www.cengage.com/economics/michaels and also available on the Instructor's Resource CD-Rom. It includes more tips for possible course outlines as well as answers (where appropriate) to the end-of-chapter Questions and Problems.

The **Test Bank** (ISBN 0538466561) is available both in print and on the IRCD in Word files. It includes multiple choice, true false, and short answer problems with careful coverage of all the topics in the text. The Test Bank is also available in **ExamView** Testing Software on the IRCD. ExamView Computerized Testing Software contains all of the questions in the printed test bank. This program is an easy-to-use test creation software compatible with Microsoft Windows. Instructors can add or edit questions, instructions, and answers and select questions by previewing them on the screen, select them randomly, or select them by other criteria (diffculty level, topic, etc.) Instructors can also create and administer quizzes online, whether over the Internet, a local area network (LAN) or a wide area network (WAN).

The **Instructor's Resource CD-Rom** (ISBN 0538466553) includes all of the resources listed above as well as **PowerPoint presentation slides**. The PowerPoint slides incorporate all key figures from the text as well as providing suggested lecture outline points, and are fully customizable.

Please also consider visiting the book website www.cengage.com/economics/michaels for access to all of these resources for Instructors (Instructor's Manual, Test Bank available for download in Word, PowerPoint), as well as data sets and online quizzing for students.

Thanks

Until electronics catches up, a single textbook must be many things to many instructors. All too many texts appear to have been designed and assembled by committees. The book you are holding is in every relevant way the same book I proposed to Cengage's predecessor company several years ago. Never did anyone from Cengage tell me "XYZ is going to be hot next year, so be sure to add material on it." I thank everyone there for their faith that this book would be finished, and that after it was finished it would matter. At the top were my Senior Acquisitions Editor, Steve Scoble, Developmental

Editor Jennifer Thomas, Marketing Specialist Betty Jung, Designer Michelle Kunkler, and Content Project Manager Cliff Kallemeyn. Above and below them were many other contributors, too numerous to acknowledge even if I could remember their names. Before Jennifer, Susan Smart was my editor, and before all of them was Mike Mercier. This project would never have been started without his encouragement, and never have been finished had he not convinced the company to do the book. I really can't thank any and all of them enough.

Thanks also to a dozen years of students who had to suffer through the many expositions and examples that weren't good enough for this book. Among many, I thank Ken Feldman, Dane Morrison, Aileen Peek, and Gennie Shucard. I particularly thank Aaron Beck, whose voice-activated computer picked up so many classroom examples and expository tricks that I would otherwise have forgotten before I could write them down.

Thanks also to current and past faculty colleagues who generously read drafts, checked details, tried excerpts in class, and listened to and argued with me about my approach. A partial list would include Vic Brajer, Andy Gill, Mira Farka, Chiara Gratton-Lavoie, Brian Moehring, Mort Rahmatian, Denise Stanley, David Wong, and the members of the Mihaylo College of Business and Economics MBA Committee.

And thanks to assortment of teachers, in particular Robert Fogel, Sam Peltzman, Michael Intriligator, the late Jack Hirshleifer, and Armen Alchian. His *University Economics*, long out of print, is an exposition of price theory that was years ahead of its time and still is. It was the inspiration for important parts of this book.

Thanks also to a number of consulting clients and business associates who learned a little economics from me while I learned a lot from them. Academic economics is a lot like the dark side of the moon. Thanks to them I crossed over and learned that I too could shed light on a remarkable world, just like John Coltrane said.

And finally thanks to my wife Victoria, always and for everything.

Acknowledgments I and the Cengage team would also like to extend our thanks and appreciation to the following group of reviewers who generously gave their time and feedback to help ensure that this book could be its best.

Klaus Becker, *Texas Tech University*

Tom Cate, *Northern Kentucky University*

Christopher Colburn, *Old Dominion University*

Chad Cotti, *University of South Carolina*

Dakshina G. De Silva, *Texas Tech University*

David Figlio, *University of Florida*

Dan Gerlowski, *University of Baltimore*

John Hayfron, *Western Washington University*

Steven Hinson, *Webster University*

Stella Hofrenning, *Augsburg College*

David Kalist, *Shippensburg University*

Tom K. Lee, *California State University Northridge*

Vincent J. Marra, *University of Delaware*

Catherine Matraves, *Michigan State University*

Katherine McCann, *University of Delaware*
Edward Millner, *Virginia Commonwealth University*
Joseph Morrison, *Webster University*
Hasan Murshed, *LeMoyne College*
Jamal Nahavandi, *Pfeiffer University*
Hong Y. Park, *Saginaw Valley State University*
Juliette Roddy, *University of Michigan Dearborn*
Matthew Roelofs, *Western Washington University*
Sy Sarkarat, *West Virginia University, Parkersburg*
Bansi Sawhney, *University of Baltimore*

Part One

Creating Economic Value

Chapter 1

Reasoning with Economics: Models and Information

This book is about economics and management, but the opening picture comes from a hospital emergency department. It is the flowchart of a procedure doctors often use to diagnose whether a newly arrived patient is having a heart attack. After taking some

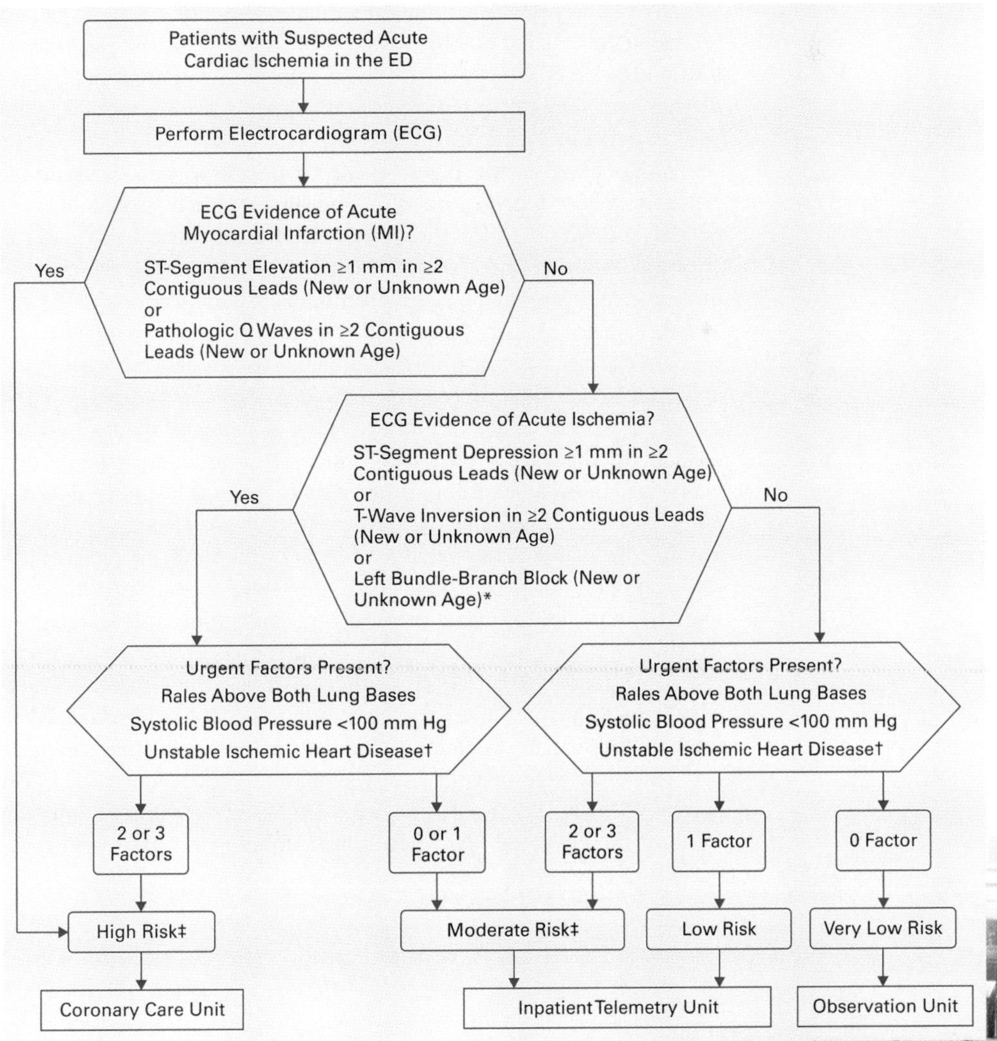

A Model to Diagnose Heart Attacks

routine measurements, the doctor asks the patient 13 questions that have yes or no answers. The doctor is not allowed to ask any more questions. A mathematical formula combines the answers, and patients who exceed a certain score begin heart attack treatments.[1] Those who score lower are held for further observation, given a prescription, or sent home. The Figure shows a very different and far less personal version of care than most patients expect. Doctors often take pride in their abilities to see the uniqueness of each patient—to explore symptoms and investigate conditions those symptoms might suggest. Their diagnostic styles depend on experience, training, and sometimes gut feelings about what is really happening. If asked to choose between a personalized diagnosis by a doctor and a diagnosis based on 13 questions you might strongly prefer a doctor who can explore the details of your case, ask about your personal symptoms, and run additional tests if necessary.

Choose the doctor over the diagram and you are more likely to die. Extensive research has shown that the 13 questions identify patients who are having heart attacks more accurately than almost any doctor.[2] The questions work because they do *not* allow the doctor to think of you as an individual. Rather the doctor is forced to compare your symptoms with those known to be the most common indicators that a heart attack is actually taking place. The chart presents a *model* of what happens to most patients who are having heart attacks—the location of the pain, its timing, where the sense of touch is lost, and so on. When you arrive at the hospital you are a random sample from the population, and the best way to diagnose you is to see how representative you are of people who have actually had heart attacks.

The flowchart in the Figure is Step 1 on the way to thinking like an economist. We economists base much of our thinking on simplified models of reality that neglect many details, and we do so for the same reason emergency department doctors use the flowchart. Without a model of what matters in competitive situations and what does not, businesspeople are in the same position as experienced doctors trying to make a personalized diagnosis. When faced with important decisions both doctors and businesspeople reach back selectively into their experience for guidance on what information to seek out and what to do once they have it. Someone who has worked in a certain industry for many years indeed knows more about that business than an economic or management consultant who uses a more basic model that can analyze many different markets.

Today, an understanding of business requires a lot more than facts about the present and experience from the past. Markets that were once local or national now extend around the planet. They change constantly in ways no one could have foreseen just a few years go. No matter how good your feel for your current business environment, it may become unrecognizable tomorrow, and your accumulated wisdom may become worthless. Models that apply to a broad range of situations must be simple, but they can help you think logically no matter what happens in your market. Detailed knowledge is still worth having—after the heart attack patient is hospitalized the doctors must deal with his particular problems. After you get your bearings in a changed market your detailed knowledge of your business may again become useful. You are more likely to get your bearings right with the help of economic reasoning than without it. This chapter explores the how and why of economic thinking:

---

[1]The chart is called the Goldman algorithm. A diagram and discussion appear in John Field and Michael Bresler, *The Textbook of Emergency Medicine and CPR* (New York: Lippincott Williams & Wilkins, 2008), 30–1.

[2]This example appears in Malcolm Gladwell, *Blink: The Power of Thinking Without Thinking* (New York: Little, Brown, 2005), 125–39. Doctors who did not use the model sent between 2 and 8 percent of patients with actual heart attacks home immediately.

- Why abstract and relatively simple models are often better guides than elaborate factual descriptions in analyzing economic choices and business strategies
- How economists model choices, and why they often start by assuming that people act rationally
- How a model of choice must account for a person's objectives and the constraints that limit the ability to attain those objectives
- Why economists sometimes assume that people are selfish and other times view them as caring about the well-being of others
- Why it matters to think "at the margin" rather than about all-or-nothing choices
- Why economists usually assume that people are imaginative, particularly in competitive situations
- How the costs of obtaining and processing information limit attainment of objectives, and why simple economic models are often most valuable when information is scarce.
- Why people often reason poorly in experiments involving logic and probability, although other experiments show that they have remarkable abilities to improve the quality of their decisions
- Why people often use clearly inappropriate data in analyzing problems, and how to avoid falling into that trap.
- Why groups make more accurate predictions than individuals in a wide range of situations
- Why thinking like an economist can be of great value outside business life

Explanations, Predictions, and Models

Why Be Abstract When You Have Facts?

In ancient times there were no weather maps or barometers. People who wanted an explanation of today's weather or a forecast of tomorrow's, usually turned to leaders who claimed to know the answers. Perhaps the leaders consulted oracles or made their predictions by judging the shapes of clouds, which even today can be helpful. The leaders might explain a recent flood as the work of higher beings who were upset about peoples' behavior. Cloud watching and messages from superior beings were the best models of weather available at the time. We are not sure about superior beings, but a good observer of clouds can often predict tomorrow's weather quite well.

Today, we understand weather because scientific logic and experience have given us a generally accepted model of near-term atmospheric change. A model simplifies reality so we can better understand important aspects of it. Reality is so complex and our mental capacities so limited that we must be selective in what we think about. Models can take many different—today's weather forecast is based on equations solved by a computer, while the model of heart attacks was a flowchart of questions. You might already have encountered the economic model of supply and demand, a graphic with math behind it. Models can improve as we gain additional understanding. Models of weather have progressed to the point that meteorologists can attach numbers to their uncertainty. Weather forecasters are almost unique among experts who make predictions: in a large sample of forecasts that predict a 30 percent chance of rain, approximately 30 percent of the time it actually does rain.[3] In many areas of their research economists are far from this level of accuracy, but in the chapters to come you will encounter fairly simple models that can markedly improve your understanding of the commercial world. This chapter presents a basic model of choice and its extensions.

Q. Look up the difference between weather and climate. Using the reasoning of the previous paragraph, explain why you expect that experts will be in greater agreement about tomorrow's weather than about long-term trends of global warming or cooling.

Q. Thirty years ago small computers and spreadsheet software barely existed. Nowadays almost everyone has access to them. Does their greater availability mean economists should construct more complex models than they did 30 years ago? Give an example of a situation in which using the computer is probably appropriate and an example of one in which it is probably not.

Modeling Choice

Is Economics a Science? In 1968, the Nobel Foundation of Sweden added a prize for research in economic science to those in the natural sciences, literature, and peace.[4] The term "economic science" rather than the more familiar "economics" may better describe how most economists try going about their work. They attempt to use the same principles that guide research in so-called hard sciences like physics and chemistry. Economists combine their factual knowledge, data, and logic to build models and derive hypotheses from them that can be tested against reality. Economics is indeed an inexact science—measuring important concepts can be difficult, and some phenomena are still beyond our understanding. But by those standards all sciences are inexact—measurements are always subject to human and instrumental errors, and we still know virtually nothing about the dark matter that accounts for more than 80 percent of the weight of the universe.

Economists are human, and they have values and beliefs that might render their objectivity suspect. Economists keep this in mind by distinguishing the positive and normative aspects of their work. *Positive economics* describes and analyzes things as they are (or as objectively as they can be seen). *Normative economics* is about how things ought to be—it explicitly acknowledges the researcher's values.[5] The line between positive and normative can be hard to draw in practice. For example, positive economic theory sets out the principles of profit maximization by a seller and the purchase decision of a consumer, whether their transaction is legal or illegal. That theory generally leads to a conclusion that a voluntary transaction between them benefits both sides. Whatever positive theory might say, an economist's normative views on prostitution or the drug trade might lead her to recommend that these activities remain illegal.

---

[3]James Surowiecki, *The Wisdom of Crowds* (New York: Doubleday , 2004), 34.

[4]A list of laureates in economic science, along with summaries of their work, appears at http://nobelprize.org/economics/laureates/index.html

[5]Milton Friedman, "The Methodology of Positive Economics," in *Essays in Positive Economics* (Chicago: University of Chicago Press, 1953), 3–43.

Q. Later in this book you will learn how you and a competitor might make and enforce an illegal agreement to fix prices that will increase your profits at the expense of consumers. Is this analysis positive or normative?

Rationality Economics studies the choices people make in the face of constraints that limit their options. According to another definition, economics studies the allocation of scarce resources among competing goals. Underlying both definitions is an assumption that people act *rationally*, with an eye toward attaining objectives they have chosen. Rationality does *not* mean people are computers with fingernails. People may not perfectly understand their own preferences. They often do not know how best to overcome the obstacles that stand between them and their goals. Some of their choices are mistaken when viewed in retrospect, and their powers of calculation and foresight are limited. What rationality offers is a place to start the analysis. The math and graphics in economics textbooks are there to help us better understand the logic of rational choice, and they can often help us to avoid some mistakes of purely verbal reasoning. They can also suggest hypotheses to test against the data—for example, our theory says that a rise in A implies a fall in B, but do the numbers show it? With math and graphics we might better understand analogies that allow us to extend the theory and show the connections between situations we formerly believed had little in common. Once we understand theoretically rational outcomes we will be better able to analyze the behavior of people with less perfect minds—like yours and mine.

The abstractness of a model's assumptions may not matter if its predictions closely approximate reality.[6] Physicists often assume that objects in their models of gravity take up no space or move without friction, neither of which can be perfectly true. Simplifications like these are good enough to predict the path a newly launched satellite will take but are poor approximations for other problems. If we assume away air resistance, we will erroneously predict that feathers on earth fall as quickly as steel balls. Some mathematical models are too complex for the human mind to work with in real time, but they still might help to predict people's behavior. A baseball outfielder, for example, takes only a fraction of a second to determine where to run and how fast to catch a fly ball. He takes roughly the same path as if he had actually solved the complex equations that determine the ball's trajectory. In reality he solves no equations but acts as if he is doing so, which can help to predict his behavior.[7] An expert pool player might seem to have a computer-like grasp of the laws of motion but in reality be a dropout.[8] She also improves her chances of victory by rationally thinking ahead to her opponent's best response so as better to plan her next shot. Both the outfielder and the pool player may be unfamiliar

---

[6]Some of the greatest economists disagree about the importance of realism in a model's assumptions. Friedman, "The Methodology of Positive Economics," strongly defends the proposition that predictive ability is more fundamental than realistic assumptions. For alternative views, see Paul Samuelson, "Problems of Methodology: Discussion," *American Economic Review* 53 (May 1963): 231–36; Stanley Wong, "The 'F-Twist' and the Methodology of Paul Samuelson," *American Economic Review* 63 (June 1973): 312–25, and Donald McCloskey, *The Rhetoric of Economics* (Madison: University of Wisconsin Press, 1985).

[7]Psychologists have found that the outfielder's motion is determined by a relatively simple mental formula (a "heuristic," as described later in this chapter) that a person can work with in real time. See Peter McLeod and Zoltan Dienes, "Do Fielders Know Where to Go to Catch the Ball or Only How to Get There?", *Journal of Experimental Psychology: Human Perception and Performance* 22 (June 1996): 531–43. The outfielder's options for simplification are nevertheless limited. His thinking must, for example, take into account the fact that wind can change the horizontal distance a batted ball travels by up to 40 percent.

[8]This is the example from Friedman, "The Methodology of Positive Economics," 21.

with Isaac Newton's laws of motion and gravity, but useful models of their behavior often spring from those laws. Such models even work for animals. We can use calculus to determine whether a dog can retrieve an object on the other side of a pond more quickly by swimming or walking on the shore. Real dogs instinctively make the right choice, as if they knew the math.[9] That choice often entails walking part of the distance and swimming the rest.

Rationality is a positive rather than a normative concept. At midnight on some Saturday you may have the misfortune of seeing an unexpectedly rational person in the form of a drunk driver traveling slowly and sometimes drifting out of his lane. His open windows create a sobering breeze and a loud radio keeps him from dozing off. By anyone's normative standards he is a danger to himself and others and should be off the road. Unfortunately, no one took his keys, and he set himself a goal of getting home without an accident or arrest. Drunk he may be, but he does understand that the rational way to drive in that state is to avoid calling attention to himself and to minimize the likelihood of falling asleep. As positive economics his behavior is rational, given that he foolishly insists on trying to drive home. This case is on the wrong side of a bright normative line, but it is not all that distant from more common behavior. Most people make cell phone calls from cars, for example, despite evidence that drivers who use them are as impaired as drunks in their perceptual abilities and reaction times.[10]

Q. Scientists have found little difference between the impairment of drivers using handheld phones and those using hands-free equipment.[11] Laws in California and some other states prohibit the former but allow the latter. If the research findings are true, is it rational for you to abandon all phone conversations while driving? Whether your answer is yes, no, or uncertain, explain why you chose it.

Q. How can your choice of enrolling in this course possibly be rational, when you have no advance knowledge of what you are going to learn? If you learn beforehand that much of the material taught in it will be worthless, are you still rational to take it? What if you already know with certainty that the degree you seek will not improve your earnings at all?

Opportunity Cost and Forward-Looking Decisions The economy's productive resources are limited, and a decision to use them in one place is also a decision not to use them elsewhere. When things are scarce any action one takes is costly. Spending two dollars of a limited income on Good A means the two dollars are no longer available to be spent on some other good. The fact that you voluntarily spent the money on Good A probably indicates that by your standards it was the best use of the funds. In the classic example from elementary economics, if the only two goods in the world are guns and

[9]Timothy Pennings, "Do Dogs Know Calculus?" *The College Mathematics Journal* 34 (May 2003): 178–82.

[10]David L. Strayer, Dennis J. Crouch, and Frank A. Drews, "A Comparison of the Cell Phone Driver and the Drunk Driver," working paper 04-13, AEI-Brookings Joint Center, 2004, http://www.hfes.org/Web/PubPages/celldrunk.pdf.

[11]Jason McCarley et al., "Conversation Disrupts Change Detection in Complex Traffic Scenes," *Human Factors* 46 (2004): 424–36.

butter, then the cost of an extra gun is the amount of butter forgone when the economy's resources make the switch to producing it. This is true even if no money changes hands, for instance, if the gun workers had been drafted rather than attracted by the pay. If there are more than two goods in the world the gun's *opportunity cost* is the most valuable alternative lost when resources move into the production of it instead of the alternative. Opportunity costs assume that there are market prices that can measure the relative values of the different goods. We will have a lot to say about them in future chapters.

If you cannot possibly undo a decision you made in the past, you have incurred a *sunk cost*. To do the best for yourself, you will rationally orient your thinking around those costs that you still have a choice about. It would indeed be nice to make enough over the future to cover the sunk cost, but whether you manage that or not is irrelevant for any business decisions you are making today. Those should be forward-looking decisions based on *marginal costs*, which are defined as those you can avoid if you make some other decision. Marginal costs are at the heart of many models of business decisions.

Q. To perform a day-long job-related assignment your employer gives you the option of using a company car or using your own car. If you use your car, you will be reimbursed 35 cents per mile. Gas costs you 20 cents per mile, depreciation (the decrease in the car's value due to driving) is 8 cents per mile, and insurance (assuming you drive 10,000 miles per year and have a $1,000 policy) is 10 cents per mile. Should you use your car or the company car?

Q. The owner of a business who must borrow to finance it is surely at a cost disadvantage relative to a business owner who uses his own funds that are already in the bank. Yes or no? Explain.

Thinking at the Margin A robber offers you the unpleasant choice of "your money or your life." It makes sense to hand her the money, because even if you die she will take it. This is as clear a choice between two alternatives (a binary choice) as one ever sees. Bank tellers and convenience store clerks facing a holdup are trained to give up the money and cooperate. In everyday situations of money and life, however, most of us generally choose some degree of death. Real decisions are almost always more complex than choices between continued life or instant death. Economists are more likely to examine choices at the margin, like those between the chances of a little more money (or some other desirable thing) and the chances of a little less life.[12] If your drive to work takes 10 minutes on the freeway and 40 minutes on streets, is the freeway a rational choice? Picking it roughly doubles your odds of dying in an accident. When you choose the freeway you are accepting a higher risk of death in exchange for 30 minutes more sleep or an extra cup of coffee. Every day you balance the value of staying alive against other enjoyments. Some people walk when the sign says "don't walk," and others wait. Economics says the decision is made after examining, however fleetingly, its costs and benefits. On cold days in Chicago an extra minute outdoors is so unpleasant that people

[12]Chapter 16 will use probability theory to examine this choice more rigorously. For now we are only trying to learn about thinking at the margin.

cross against red lights if an intersection is clear of cars. In temperate San Diego people nearly always wait for the walk sign, perhaps also because California enforces its jaywalking laws. People who move slowly and people with children who have more than one life to protect are more likely to wait. We know that "when you've got your health, you've got everything," but if someone offers you $5,000 to suffer a head cold for three days you might consider taking the deal.

"There is no such thing as a free lunch" is the now-stultifying slogan of economics teachers around the world. By itself the statement does not get us very far. The follow-up line has yet to be coined, but it might be "forgone opportunities make all lunches costly, and economics is about choosing the one option that is best for you." You may choose to take the freeway, trading a small amount of saved time for a small increase in accident risk, but I might not. A discount coupon on a grocery item might not change my menu plans, but it might change yours. Both big choices and small choices can be viewed marginally. Do you buy a new house or stay in the old one and invest your money elsewhere? Should you go back to college and major in economics this time? What does a household give up by having a third child? The next chapters will say a lot more about costs and margins.

Q. Assume that your employer offers you a choice of health insurance plans, and those with more complete coverage carry higher annual premiums. Because your life is so valuable it is surely rational for you to take the plan with the best coverage, right? Might the rational choice of a 24-year-old to this menu of plans differ from that of a 60-year-old? How about that of a person whose hobby is motorcycle racing compared with one whose hobby is stamp collecting?

Q. The time you spend informing yourself about candidates and casting your vote carries an opportunity cost. The only situation in which you can possibly determine the outcome of a presidential election is if your one vote among millions changes the outcome from one candidate to another. Because this situation is extremely unlikely, is it rational to go through the bother of voting?[13]

Objectives and Constraints

Maximizing Utility Sometimes one's objectives reduce easily to dollars and cents. Buyers usually prefer low prices and sellers usually prefer high ones, all else equal. Many choices, however, inherently include multiple dimensions. Consumers value both price and quality, and investors look at both the returns and the riskiness of stocks they are considering. The cheapest supplier of a good may at times be unable to deliver, and your valuation of low price against delivery risk depends on their relative costs and benefits to you. Likewise, your decision whether to work a second job depends on your valuation of more income relative to more leisure.

A model of choice starts by assuming that people want to make themselves as well off as possible. Economists say that a person attempts to maximize his *utility*, a subjective

[13]Avoid an answer like, "if nobody votes, then the country is in big trouble," as all we are considering in the question is your personal decision rather than those of other people.

measure of well-being unique to that person. It is an *ordinal* measure, that is, situations can be ranked as in "I prefer living in Houston to living in Cleveland," or "I prefer this bundle of goods to that one." We generally do *not* assume that a person's utility is *cardinal,* that is, that she can say "I am 1.24 times better off living in Houston than I was in Cleveland." Utility bears no necessary relation to income. Most people will say they are better off if they receive a higher income, but not all will feel that way if they must work for it. If you can earn $30 for each hour you choose to work, increasing the wage to $40 will probably affect your hours. Whether they increase or decrease depends on your preferences. If you enjoy skydiving (a costly activity that happens quickly) you might choose to work more hours to get a few more dives per week. If you prefer knitting (an activity that requires inexpensive materials and lots of time) you might choose to work fewer hours. Regardless of whether you are a skydiver or a knitter, however, the higher wage cannot possibly make you worse off.

Selfishness, Altruism, and Fairness Your utility probably depends on more than just the goods and services you enjoy. Almost everyone cares about the well-being of others, such as family members. Married couples often pool their incomes and spend them in ways they agree on. Sharing particularly matters for children, who cannot survive independently. Parents receive utility from their children. They choose how many to have and invest in the children's quality of upbringing through education, health, religion, and numerous other activities.[14]

People may also care for those beyond the family, as can be seen from their participation in community activities and contributions to charities. Volunteering to serve at a soup kitchen for the needy sacrifices time, but seeing hungry people smile can make the volunteer feel the time was well spent. Some people have other motives—someone who personally dislikes hungry people may nevertheless still think he has discharged an obligation to the community. Peoples' sympathies extend beyond humans when they send funds to organizations seeking to save endangered animal species. Contributors may feel good even if their funds might have been better allocated on scientific grounds. Big, charming animals like tigers, pandas, and whales receive large donations, while insects and weeds that are ecologically important often attract few contributions.[15] Distinguishing altruism from self-interest is not always easy, however. Homeowners who want to maximize their property values sometimes file environmental lawsuits in hopes of stopping nearby construction. If successful they both increase their wealth and protect an endangered species.[16]

"Fairness" might best be described as a normative term to describe a distribution of goods and opportunities with which a person agrees. It is easy to construct examples in which most observers would find an equal distribution of income less fair than an unequal one, for example, if some recipients were capable of work but chose not to and received their funds from taxes on the incomes of those who did work. People's views on fairness change with their situations. Full-time day students often think it is fairer to have classes allocated by waiting in line, but night students whose cost of time is higher

[14]For an introduction to the economic theory of the family and tests of that theory, see Gary S. Becker, *A Treatise on the Family* (Cambridge, MA: Harvard University Press, 1981). Becker won the Nobel prize for this and related work.

[15]See Andrew Metrick and Martin Weitzman, "Conflicts and Choices in Biodiversity Preservation," *Journal of Economic Perspectives* 12 (Summer 1998): 21–34. The common term for animals like these is "charismatic megafauna."

[16]On the other side, some landowners who want development take steps to make their property undesirable as a habitat for endangered species. See Dean Lueck and Jeffrey A. Michael, "Preemptive Habitat Destruction Under the Endangered Species Act," *Journal of Law and Economics* 46 (April 2003): 27–60.

often prefer that personal merit be used as the standard. People often think that lotteries are fair, but most of us probably prefer that desirable jobs be allocated on the basis of merit rather than randomness. Intensity of preference can matter—hardly anyone would like a lottery that gave equal chances at World Series tickets to fans and non-fans alike.

Q. During class discussion of utility maximization a student tells an instructor that she never makes choices using such numerical comparisons. To prove it she shows the class a shopping list of things she will buy later that day. It contains just the names of items to be bought and no hints about the amounts she might purchase at different prices. Does the absence of numbers that could change her decisions indicate that she is not maximizing utility? Link your reasoning to the earlier discussion of an outfielder going after a fly ball.

Q. After the 2005 Gulf Coast hurricanes the media ran numerous stories about how stores like Wal-Mart and Home Depot incurred substantial costs to rush relief supplies into hard-hit areas, often in advance of deliveries by government. Further, the companies did not raise prices on these goods. Is their behavior better described as self-interested or altruistic? Explain your choice.

Constraints Many different types of constraints put limits on our choices, and differences in the constraints different people face may lead them to different choices. Some important constraints include the following:

- *Physical constraints:* There is a limit to the useful energy that one can get by burning a barrel of oil or the work you can perform on 1,500 calories a day.
- *Time constraints:* The day has only 24 hours, life has a finite length, and we cannot make time flow in reverse.
- *Financial constraints:* People's incomes are limited, their abilities to borrow differ, and liquidity can constrain them—for instance, assets like houses cannot be quickly sold for predictable prices.
- *Contractual constraints:* If you have contracted to sell me something at a fixed price, our agreement may not allow you to cut me off just because you have received an offer from someone willing to pay you more than the contract price.
- *Organizational constraints:* Owners, workers, and managers have different rights and responsibilities in different forms of businesses like corporations and professional groups.
- *Informational constraints:* Some information is intrinsically unknowable with certainty (say, the weather in Pittsburgh next April 4), and we must balance the benefits and costs of lowering our uncertainty.
- *Psychological constraints:* Your ability to process valuable information is limited, and emotional attachments, like those to your family or church, may limit your choices.
- *Societal and ethical constraints:* The law forbids embezzling funds from your employer or failing to pay income tax. You are expected to wear clothes in public and have table manners at home.

Accepting and Altering Constraints Many economic models simplify a complex situation by treating constraints as unalterable. In one basic model of a business firm we will assume that its management cannot improve on the technology that transforms inputs like labor and energy into output. Doing so will help us better understand the choice of input levels that minimizes cost. Sometimes routine actions can alter a constraint, as when a manager cuts electricity costs by installing motion sensors that turn out lights in unoccupied areas. More drastic innovations and inventions can greatly change constraints or even eliminate them. The economics of business is about adapting to constraints and exploiting the possibilities to alter them. One characteristic of entrepreneurs is an ability to recognize constraints and incur the costs of altering them if possible.[17]

People often work to make all types of constraints less binding on their decisions. Air travel and telephones reduced physical constraints on movement and communication, as did Sears Roebuck's nineteenth-century mail-order catalogs. Development of these technologies also affected time constraints, and so did electric lighting, which allowed work and play to spill over from the day into the night. Bank cards gave people new abilities to manage their finances, establish their creditworthiness, and cope with emergencies. New types of contracts, like automobile insurance in the early twentieth century, allowed people to benefit from driving while cutting their exposure to disastrous lawsuits from accidents. The rapid growth of organizations like franchises and limited liability corporations allows hitherto unseen coordination between different businesses. Large libraries and the Internet have cut the costs of accessing information, and new types of futures and options contracts on commodities (derivatives) reduce uncertainty about prices next year. Spreadsheet software and coffee both help people extend their mental abilities, while improved mobility and communications allow them to live in places more to their liking.

Competition

The great golfer Arnold Palmer once said, "if you aren't competing, you're dead."[18] His point was not just about golf. Almost everything worth having is scarce—not enough is available to satisfy everyone's desires for free.[19] Whenever a good or service is scarce, people compete to determine who gets how much of it. Part of our competitiveness may be inherent in our genetic makeup, and some social scientists go further and claim that the institutions of society cause people to be competitive. I do not take a stand on these questions of causation.

Competition takes many forms, and its relative importance differs among societies. People everywhere compete by trading with others, the winners being those who make more attractive offers to prospective counterparties. In the former Soviet Union, many goods carried extremely low prices, and competition to obtain them often took the form of long waiting lines. Political competition allocates important goods and services in the form of public budgets for activities ranging from education to police protection to Medicare. Federal guidelines allocated the short supply of flu vaccine in 2004 to the elderly and other vulnerable groups, but members of Congress were able to obtain shots

[17]Theodore W. Schultz, "The Value of the Ability to Deal with Disequilibria," *Journal of Economic Literature* 13 (September 1975): 823–46.

[18]Quoted in Armen Alchian and William Allen, *University Economics*, 3rd ed. (Belmont, CA: Wadsworth 1972): 11.

[19]Air was once a textbook example of a free good, but nowadays breathing cleaner air entails sacrifices that range from buying pollution-control equipment to living far from a city.

for themselves and their staffs without charge.[20] Government officials themselves compete for access to favorable exposure in the news media.

Some human competitions look like those seen in other species. Individuals often fight over property or a mate, and groups of people wage wars to obtain territory or forcibly spread their ideas. Beauty decides the allocation of many valuable things. A person's earnings in a profession will depend on his or her training, specialty, experience, location, and other factors. After these have been accounted for, more attractive people earn more than less attractive people with the same characteristics.[21] Likewise, college students give higher evaluations to professors who are younger and more attractive.[22]

Q. Your instructor probably gets to park in a lot that is more convenient to classrooms than your parking space but pays the same price as you for her parking permit. Is this evidence that professors have somehow succeeded in winning a competition against students for these spaces? If not, give an alternative explanation.

Q. Economists studying the former Soviet Union discovered an interesting fact when comparing the living standards of otherwise similar families: those that had a grandparent living with them had higher standards of living than those that did not. Provide an explanation.

Information and Choice

Relevant Information

Much of the information that most matters for our lives is never seen in classrooms or textbooks, and this book will be no exception. Its purpose is to show you the remarkable usefulness of thinking like an economist. It will not (knowingly) provide any specific recommendations on how to get rich. You cannot know today exactly what information will matter for your personal future, and the best any text can do is to help you distinguish information that may be worth having from information that is probably not worth having. There are important differences between the facts and principles communicated in classrooms and those that are relevant for business decisions. Economics Nobelist F. A. Hayek summarized the difference:

> *...[T]here is beyond question a body of very important but unorganized knowledge which cannot possibly be called scientific in the sense of knowledge of general rules: the knowledge of the particular circumstances of time and place. ...We need to remember only how much we have to learn in any occupation after we have completed our theoretical training, how big a part of our working life we spend learning particular*

[20]"No Flu Vaccine Shortage at Capital," *Washington Post*, October 20, 2004, http://www.washingtonpost.com/wp-dyn/articles/A46325-2004Oct19.html.

[21]Daniel Hamermesh and Jeff Biddle, "Beauty and the Labor Market," *American Economic Review* 84 (December 1994), 1174–94.

[22]Surprisingly, attractiveness has a significantly larger percentage effect on women's ratings of men than on men's ratings of women. Daniel Hamermesh and Amy Parker, "Beauty in the Classroom: Instructors' Pulchritude and Putative Pedagogical Productivity," *Economics of Education Review* 24 (June 2005): 369–76.

jobs, and how valuable an asset in all walks of life is knowledge of people, of local conditions, and special circumstances. To know of and put to use a machine not fully employed, or somebody's skill which could be better utilized, or to be aware of a surplus stock which can be drawn upon during an interruption of supplies, is socially quite as useful as the knowledge of better alternative techniques. And the shipper who earns his living from using otherwise empty or half-filled journeys of tramp-steamers, or the [real] estate agent whose whole knowledge is almost exclusively one of temporary opportunities, or the arbitrageur *who gains from local differences of commodity prices, are all performing eminently useful functions based on special knowledge of circumstances of the fleeting moment not known to others.*[23]

One of the best questions you can ask any professor is "If you're so smart, why aren't you rich?"[24] An economist might be among the few who can produce a reasonable answer: "I know the *kinds* of facts you should look for and use, and I have models and data to show you why they make sense. I can give you a way of thinking, but only you can implement it in your business or life. You are far more likely than I am to have access to information that will advance your personal interests."

Q. The professor who teaches the basic geography course at your author's university often appears in the media. On the first day of class he gives each student an outline map of the world and asks for the locations of places in the news such as Washington, D.C., Iraq, Venezuela, and so on. Year after year the great majority get most locations wrong, and some cannot even find their home state of California. The professor shows the results to reporters and recommends that students be required to take more geography courses. Are students acting rationally when they choose to remain ignorant of these locations? Do you recommend that the professor spend much of the course time teaching students where particular cities or countries are located? If not, what do you recommend?

Acquiring Information

Economists often take their first shot at a business problem by assuming that all the information that might matter for a good decision is readily at hand, and that the decision maker has a model that can produce valid conclusions. This is not as bad a starting point as it first seems, as otherwise one would have to make assumptions about what is and is not known and would have to guess at how people would reach decisions when they are without important information. To understand how to maximize profit it might be best to first model a hypothetical manager who knows all about the demand for and cost of her product. Grinding through the graphics and math in a simplified problem often provides conclusions that are themselves insightful, and a simple model can be the starting point for a more realistic analysis.

Say a decision maker wants information that can minimize his ignorance about the consequences of different choices. Blackjack players who count cards do not know

[23] F.A. Hayek, "The Use of Knowledge in Society," *American Economic Review* 35 (September 1945): 521. Arbitrage is discussed in Chapter 3.

[24] Donald McCloskey, *If You're So Smart: The Narrative of Economic Expertise* (Chicago: University of Chicago Press, 1990). McCloskey is serious about why you should actually ask this.

the next one they will get, but studying the cards already dealt can help them determine whether the remainder of the deck contains cards that make winning hands more likely. Better information can (but does not always) improve the quality of choices to be made. Substitutes for information include experience—direct interaction with a person might be better for you than unearthing more about her in cyberspace. The ability to postpone a choice can also substitute for information today, because you can sometimes benefit by keeping your options open while you acquire more knowledge.[25]

In some ways information is a good like many others—it has value but is costly to obtain. If so, there will be a time to stop hunting out information and make a choice based on what you have learned. If you already have a make and model car in mind, shopping for a car is really a search for information about price that you undertake by visiting dealers or Web sites. Contacting another dealer gets you one more price, but what matters is the likelihood that it beats the former best offer. A model that tells you the best number of dealers to see involves relatively complicated math, but its economic logic makes clear why most people stop shopping after seeing only a fraction of all nearby dealers. If you have seen only one dealer, seeing a second is relatively likely to yield you a lower price.[26] If there are 20 dealers and you have seen 19, the odds are very high that you already know the lowest price in town.

We can learn more by extending our model of how a producer maximizes profits to apply to consumer decisions—how many dealers should this consumer see to maximize his savings (net of shopping costs) on the car? This number will vary with some underlying conditions, and we will be able to show that (1) a given person will see more dealers, other things equal, the greater the wealth that is at stake (average price of the car), and (2) for a given car, people whose cost of time is low will see more dealers than those with high time costs. Differences in the opportunity cost of time may explain why haggling over the prices of everyday items is common in poor countries. A simple model of information acquisition through shopping has some less obvious predictions—the larger the percentage of dealers seen by the typical shopper, the smaller will be the dispersion (standard deviation) of the prices the dealers quote relative to their average.[27]

Q. Do you expect that people will shop more dealers for a given car than they will for a given piece of furniture? Explain.

Making Information Known

Economics can also help explain differences in the ways sellers inform potential buyers about their offerings. A car dealer paints prices on the windshields of cars in its lot, advertises on TV, owns a Web site, sponsors a Little League baseball team, and hires salespeople to bargain with individual customers. Sellers typically cannot identify which shoppers can be turned into buyers or determine beforehand what a given person is

[25]This reasoning is the basis of option value, which is discussed in Chapter 16.

[26]For reasons that will be detailed in Chapter 17, it is unlikely that I can spot a dealer that offers consistently lower prices on the basis of information I have on hand at the start of the search.

[27]Meir Kohn and Steven Shavell, "The Theory of Search," *Journal of Economic Theory* 9 (October 1974): 93–123.

willing to pay.[28] Economics can help explain how a dealer will disseminate information, however. One located downtown will probably advertise more heavily in the city than the suburbs. Any dealer is more likely to advertise cars that are hard to sell rather than highly desirable models that seem to sell themselves at premium prices.[29]

Understanding the value of information and the nature of opportunity costs can help us understand the economic value of advertising. Because advertising is costly it can raise the price a buyer pays. Here, however, a higher price does not necessarily harm the buyer. That person's full cost of obtaining the good may fall because advertising saves time spent searching for price quotes or other information about it.[30] Characteristics of the product and its market affect how sellers inform buyers. A highly technical product (e.g., a pharmaceutical only understood by doctors) or one that must be customized to meet a particular buyer's requirements (e.g., a mainframe computer installation) is more likely to be sold face-to-face than by mass advertising.[31] Some advertising for mass-market consumer goods (e.g., musical superstars appearing in commercials for soft drinks) may signal to consumers that the product is of dependable quality.[32]

Q. Recently, there has been a large increase in television advertising of pharmaceuticals that consumers cannot purchase without a doctor's prescription. Which types of drugs are likely to be advertised this way and which types are unlikely?

Errors and Biases in Information Processing

Limited Capabilities and Bounded Rationality

There are almost as many models of the human mind as there are researchers who have studied it. Economic models of decision makers whose choices are perfectly rational can provide valuable insights and predictions. No economist or psychologist has ever gone on record as saying that peoples' thought processes are so simple. Simple models of rationality may yield general predictions about behavior, but the accuracy of the predictions might increase if we knew more about how people reason. This section examines how poorly people process information at times, and the next one is about how well they do the same job as other times. Understanding decision making requires that we understand both our weaknesses and our powers.

The human mind's abilities to reason and imagine are facilitated by the great volumes of facts and experiences it can recall from memory. But even with these capabilities few people can attend to more than a handful of concepts at one time and fully analyze their

---

[28]Exactly what price should a salesperson choose to quote to a given customer or set as a target when bargaining? Game theory and negotiation are covered in Chapters 7 and 1717.

[29]Dealers have started using the Internet auction site eBay (which most of them would view as a rival in the used car market) to list cars they are having particular difficulty moving off their lots. "Improbably, Ebay Emerges as a Giant in Used Car Sales," *Wall Street Journal*, February 7, 2003.

[30]Isaac Ehrlich and Lawrence Fisher, "The Derived Demand for Advertising," *American Economic Review* 2 (June 1982): 366–88.

[31]Thus, the ratio of advertising expense to sales is higher for goods bought primarily by consumers than it is for goods bought primarily by producers, and the ratio of sales force expense to sales is correspondingly greater for producer goods than consumer goods. See Ehrlich and Fisher, "The Derived Demand for Advertising."

[32]This is explained in more detail in Chapter 11.

interrelationships. Very few people can consistently make error-free calculations in their heads or navigate through complex logic to correct conclusions. Computers increase our ability to crunch numbers and to store and retrieve data, but our basic reasoning abilities are probably little changed from those of the cave dwellers. We may wish to make perfectly rational choices (at least in our business lives), but mental limitations make that an impossible standard. Thus, economists often treat decision makers as *boundedly rational*, trying their best for rationality but constrained by limited information and limited processing abilities.[33]

The more limited our abilities the more important it is to have a model that will help us to discern the information that matters for a problem and what to do with it. The model should also indicate what sorts of information are *not* worth collecting. We pay trustworthy sources for both the information they bring us and for their services in destroying and suppressing information that is false or unlikely to be of value. *California Energy Markets*, for example, is that state's most important newsletter for producers, marketers, and large consumers of electricity and natural gas.[34] Its accuracy and insightfulness are well-known in those industries. One year its April Fool issue contained an amazing special offer:

> *Some readers have complained about our high subscription prices [$1,500 per year], and we have chosen to respond by offering an alternative. Each week our reporters see literally thousands of pages of press releases, government regulations, research reports, and other documents, as well as many pages of their own notes from interviews and investigations. Instead of a regular subscription you may now buy copies of all this paper at the unbeatable price of only $10 per pound.*[35]

Scattered through that inexpensive pile is all of the information regular subscribers pay $1,500 for. There is also a lot of information that is untrue, unimportant, or impossible to verify. The editors of *California Energy Markets* operate with an unwritten model that helps them select the information that readers in their industry are likely to find valuable.

How Rational Are People?

People's calculating abilities are indeed limited, and their foresight is far from perfect. Because models often assume that people are rational, however, we should ask whether they actually use their information and capabilities effectively. It would be reassuring if people always took advantage of opportunities to make themselves better off. Missed opportunities could be good situations they bypass in favor of poor ones, or prospects they never notice at all. Likewise, do past mistakes teach people how to make better choices in the future? Because information is costly (or perhaps impossible) to obtain, bad outcomes are not necessarily evidence that people are irrational. But what if a person repeatedly makes the same error and fails to learn from experience?

Economists have a catch-phrase for systematically missed opportunities: "dollar bills left on the sidewalk." Anyone walking past can pick them up, but for unknown reasons no one does. Publicly available data on production costs and box office revenues show clearly that year after year Hollywood producers could earn more by producing fewer

---

[33]This is the definition of bounded rationality introduced by Nobel Prize winner Herbert Simon, in *Models of Man* (New York: Wiley, 1957), Chapters 5 and 6.

[34]Summaries of the week's top stories can be found at the Energy NewsData Web site, http://www.newsdata.com/cem/thisweek.html.

[35]"California Empty Markets," *California Energy Markets*, April 1, 1997, 1.

R-rated movies and more with G and PG ratings.[36] R-rated movies, on average, do not collect enough from theaters and the aftermarket (home videos, television showings) to cover production and distribution costs. Family-rated movies are on average profitable. Readers of *Variety* or *The Hollywood Reporter* (the two leading trade newspapers) know these facts, but there is still no good explanation for why profit-seeking investors persistently bankroll movies that are likely to take losses and shun those that are likely to be profitable. Investors in R-rated movies sometimes take risks to make artistic or political statements, but most movies with that rating do not make such statements.

In another possible instance of money left on the sidewalk, overconfident small investors often make poor stock-trading choices and fail to learn from experience. Terrance Odean of the University of California, Davis, examined several years of transactions by 10,000 individual investors. They often traded excessively and unwisely and failed to change their behavior as they learned about their actual performances.[37] Returns on their stocks did not even cover brokerage costs, and the stocks they sold generally outperformed those they subsequently bought. After eliminating other explanations Odean concluded that these investors were too confident in the information they used to make their choices. It may have been generally known (and thus already factored into share prices as we will see later) or possibly just incorrect. Many investors in the sample seemed unable to learn that their frequent trades of poorly chosen stocks were part of a long-term losing pattern.[38] Again, there is no easy explanation of why people trying to become wealthy would err so persistently. It is not known how often episodes like this and the R-rated movie story actually occur, but it seems clear that some observed behavior cannot easily be explained by models of rationality.

Q. Assume that you have a choice among several actions. You make that choice and find that you are not as happy as you would have been had you chosen differently. In what situations would it be rational for you to make a different choice next time, and in what situations would it be rational for you to make the same choice as before?

Q. Between 35 and 65 percent of all prices on consumer goods end in the digit nine. Give a possible explanation that does not depend on consumer irrationality.[39]

[36] Arthur S. De Vany and W. David Walls, "Does Hollywood Make Too Many R-Rated Movies? Risk, Stochastic Dominance and the Illusion of Expectation," *Journal of Business* 75 (2002): 422–37.

[37] Terrance Odean, "Do Investors Trade Too Much?" *American Economic Review* 89 (December 1999):1279–98.

[38] Odean's relatively young sample of small investors may have been more overconfident than the general population, but other investors may also have learning problems. Some index mutual funds just buy and hold all stocks on the market and are not actively managed. Other funds that specialize in certain types of stocks (e.g., large company growth stocks) or certain industries are actively managed by brokers who charge large commissions. There is abundant evidence that most specialized funds return investors less than index funds over the long term. See Burton G. Malkiel, "Returns from Investing in Equity Mutual Funds, 1971-1991," *Journal of Finance* 50 (June 1995): 545–72.

[39] For several possible explanations and tests among them, see Eric Anderson and Duncan Simester, "Effects of $9 Price Endings on Retail Sales: Evidence from Field Experiments," *Quantitative Marketing and Economics* 1 (March 2003): 93–110.

Reasoning with Probabilities

Decisions must be made without complete information, and we often cannot process that information in ways that lead to correct conclusions. A substantial body of research has shown that even professionals often make avoidable errors in reasoning. They can also fail to use all of the available data or draw conclusions on the basis of irrelevant data. Instead of thinking rigorously, people often use rules of thumb derived from experience or illogical shortcuts that economize on their mental capabilities. Rules of thumb and shortcuts (both logical and illogical) are called *heuristics.*[40]

Imagine you are given the following description of a person:

> *Jones is tall and not very muscular. He wears wire-rim glasses, has very precise handwriting, likes to help others, and enjoys reading. Is Jones more likely a truck driver or a librarian?*

Before you said librarian (as almost everyone does), did it cross your mind that there are 30 times more truck drivers in the United States than there are librarians? That 82 percent of all librarians are women?[41] Assume that half of all male librarians look like Jones and only 2 percent of truck drivers do. If truck drivers so outnumber librarians, then a lot more truck drivers than librarians resemble Jones. Your mistake was to use a *representativeness heuristic,* one that evaluates the probability of an event (Jones is a librarian) by looking at how representative your sample is of the population of interest (Jones has these characteristics) instead of the entire population. If your stereotypes are correct (and they may not be—have you checked your local library?), Jones indeed looks more like a typical male librarian than a typical truck driver. The problem is that you so trusted that image of librarians that you chose not to concern yourself with any other data.

In another experiment a researcher reads a list of 30 randomly mixed names of public figures to a group of subjects. It contains equal numbers of men and women. If the women are relatively more famous than the men, both male and female subjects guess that there are more women on the list (and vice versa if the men are more famous). In the same vein, people surveyed shortly after major air crashes estimate higher probabilities that a given flight will crash than people surveyed during intervals without any. (Interestingly, both estimates are too high.) People in these experiments err by using an *availability heuristic*; they are making judgments based on what they can remember (i.e., what is salient) rather than on actual probabilities. Recognizing more women leads to a belief that the list contains more of them, and seeing a recent crash raises beliefs about their likelihood.[42] Psychologists and economists have identified a number of other commonly used heuristics that often lead to errors in reasoning.

---

[40]All of these examples and terminology are from Amos Tversky and Daniel Kahneman, "Judgment Under Uncertainty: Heuristics and Biases," *Science* 185 (September 27, 1974): 1124–31. Kahneman was co-awarded the 2002 Nobel Prize in Economic Science for this work. For applications of heuristics to bargaining and law, see Russell Korobkin and Chris Guthrie, "Heuristics and Biases at the Bargaining Table," *Marquette Law Review* 87 (2004): 795–808.

[41]Rachel Singer Gordon, "NextGen: The Men Among Us," *Library Journal* 129 (June 15, 2004), 49.

[42]Evolution may account for some biases like this one. When prehistoric hunters saw one mammoth they might have had good reason to suspect more—mammoths traveled in herds. It is possible (but not proven) that this mode of thought became hard-wired into our brains because hunters who correctly inferred the presence of herds were more likely to survive than those who did not. For an economic analysis of such biases, see Paul H. Rubin, *Darwinian Politics: The Evolutionary Origin of Freedom* (New Brunswick, NJ: Rutgers University Press, 2002).

Q. People asked to estimate the percentage of smokers who actually die of lung cancer generally give a far higher number than the true value.[43] Surveys taken before and after California passed a law that prohibited all smoking in restaurants and bars showed that the average guess was higher after the law than before. What kind of heuristic may be at work here?

Selection Bias

We often hear that dolphins are playful and smart. Some researchers believe they can learn to speak and behave in other "human" ways, but others question these claims. There are, however, verified stories of drowning people who were pushed toward shore by helpful dolphins. Unfortunately, these stories tell nothing about whether dolphins are smart, or even whether they are nice. The only people who lived to tell them are those who were pushed toward shore. The ones who were pushed out to sea never turned up again. It is, of course, possible that dolphins always do help drowning people, but hearing accounts from survivors indicates nothing about non-survivors.

By themselves, reports of kindly dolphins tell us nothing about typical dolphins, just as reports of murder tell us nothing about typical humans. However many stories we hear from swimmers we still cannot estimate the percentage of kindly dolphins. The dolphins exemplify the widespread problem of *selection bias,* in which the method used to collect a sample biases any conclusions that might be drawn from it. Here the only people who can possibly be sampled are survivors. For a business application, Figure 1-1

FIGURE 1-1
Selection Bias

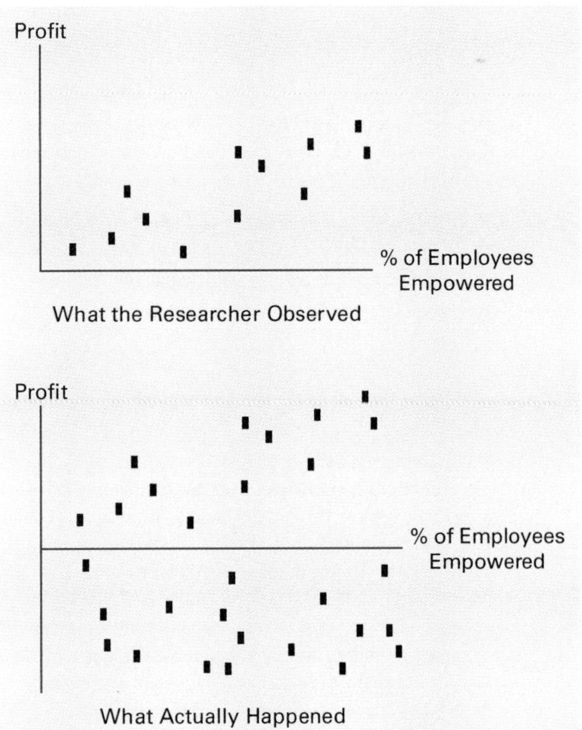

[43]W. Kip Viscusi, *Smoking: Making the Risky Decision* (New York: Oxford University Press, 1992): 75–85.

shows the results of a hypothetical empowerment program that gives employees a greater say in management decisions. The program is risky, and some businesses that adopt it may take losses or be forced into bankruptcy. A researcher examines companies that are using it and obtains the data shown in Figure 1-1. Each data point in the top half of the graph shows the percentage of employees who were empowered employees and the profit of their employer. There appears to be a positive association between empowerment and profit. The lower graph shows that there is no reason to believe in this association, because a researcher today cannot possibly see what happened in all of the companies that tried empowerment. The full story is that a lot of companies that adopted empowerment either went out of business or abandoned the program because it failed to raise profits. Unfortunately for the researcher, only the companies that stayed with empowerment and survived are available to be examined today. Unless researchers are very fortunate, they can only gather data on businesses that still exist.

Selection bias can turn up in more subtle ways. Assume that you somehow know that all of the firms adopting the employee empowerment program survived and none abandoned it, and that those with the programs were more profitable than non-adopters. Even after you account for other factors that influence profitability you cannot conclude that empowerment is worth adopting. Businesses that adopted it may have characteristics we cannot observe that make them inherently more profitable on average than non-adopters. As one possibility, managers of adopting firms may be more open to all types of innovations than managers of non-adopting firms. There are, however, no available psychological measurements of this trait in managers. If businesses that are receptive to innovation are more likely to make high profits *and* to adopt this practice, they are likely to be winners whether or not they adopt it. The researcher needs to somehow determine whether firms with the unobserved characteristics of winners do even better after they adopt it than those with the same characteristics who do not.[44]

Any business student (or instructor) should be constantly on the lookout for selection bias in classroom discussions, textbooks, and advice from consultants. Some authors unmistakably signal that the companies they discuss are handpicked. Their books carry titles like *Lessons from America's Best-Run Companies* and *Successful Habits of Visionary Companies*.[45] A count of case studies in business textbooks will probably turn up considerably more successes than failures. Because new businesses (and many established ones) often fail or are acquired, there is a problem of balance.[46] Unrepresentative case studies may be particularly risky in business schools, because many business students are already optimistic about their likelihood of success. Self-confidence can skew our perceptions if it biases us in favor of accepting stories about success and rejecting stories of failure

[44]Many other types of research must account for selection bias. Assume that we have a large data set consisting of many individuals and want to estimate the effect of illegal drug use on their earnings. Unobserved characteristics, such as chronic depression or poor social skills, might make some people more likely to use drugs, but these same psychological factors may also lower one's earnings regardless of drug use. It is possible to account statistically for unobservable factors like these, and doing so brings new insights into the relationship between drugs and earnings. See Andrew M. Gill and Robert J. Michaels, "Does Drug Use Decrease Earnings?" *Industrial and Labor Relations Review* 45 (April 1992): 419–34.

[45]James C. Collins and Jerry I. Porras, *Built to Last: Successful Habits of Visionary Companies* (New York: Harper Business, 1997); Thomas J. Peters and Robert H. Waterman Jr., *In Search of Excellence: Lessons from America's Best-Run Companies* (New York: Warner Books, 1984).

[46]For a more general discussion of selection bias in business education, see Jerker Denrell, "Vicarious Learning, Undersampling of Failure, and the Myths of Management," *Organization Science* 14 (May–June 2003): 227–44.

without paying attention to their underlying probabilities.[47] Thinking clearly is not always pleasant, but success may depend on how well we detect selection bias in our reasoning and that of others.

Q. A firm rewards new employees who have made risky decisions that turned out well by promoting them quickly to upper management, fires those whose decisions turned out poorly, and leaves those who chose not to take risky decisions on slower career paths. If you are a new employee, why are you likely to overestimate the probability of quick promotion if you choose to make a risky decision?

Simplicity and Accuracy in Information Processing

Smart Shortcuts

The findings just discussed may lead you to doubt that many people are even boundedly rational. Other researchers, however, believe such biases and errors are not as important as they first appear to be. People can blunder on problems contrived to test their limits and at the same time manage complex everyday decisions. Maybe the difficulties are specific to our times—our knowledge of probability and statistics is less than two centuries old, but our reasoning abilities have developed over tens of thousands of years. Recent research on fast and frugal heuristics shows that people have abilities to devise shortcuts in reasoning that can be surprisingly effective.[48] These heuristics often produce results nearly as accurate as methods that require more information, involve complex calculations, or tax our memories. Full rationality may be impossible to attain, but simple methods sometimes closely approach its results.

Recognition Heuristics

Is San Diego or San Antonio the larger city?[49] It might surprise you that nearly 100 percent of students surveyed at an elite German university correctly chose San Diego, but only 62 percent of students at a similar American university got it right. Geography coursework is not why. All of the Americans were about equally familiar with both cities, but full-text databases show that San Antonio makes it into the German media far less frequently than San Diego. When facts are at issue the correct answer is often the one people recognize, and the incorrect answer is the one they do not. Put another way, because Americans were familiar with both cities they were not *ignorant* enough to know the answer. In a larger experiment, subjects were given a list of the 20th through 40th

[47]Some degree of unreality in our outlooks, however, may not be all bad. Psychological research has shown that depressives who lack self-confidence often perceive reality more accurately than persons who display the optimism and resiliency that many believe are indicators of mental health. If the alternative to over-optimism is depression, it is understandable that most of us prefer to hear about success. See Shelley E. Taylor and Jonathon D. Brown, "Illusion and Well-Being: A Social Psychological Perspective on Mental Health," *Psychological Bulletin* 103, no. 2 (1988): 193–210.

[48]Gerd Gigerenzer, Peter M. Todd and the ABC Research Group, *Simple Heuristics That Make Us Smart* (New York: Oxford University Press, 1999).

[49]San Diego is currently America's eighth largest city, and San Antonio is tenth.

largest U.S. cities in random order and asked which they recognized. They were then given pairs from the list and asked which was larger. When they could use a recognition heuristic (because they were familiar with one city but not the other), they correctly chose the larger city 93 percent of the time.[50]

In another experiment, ordinary people using a recognition heuristic chose investments that outperformed the recommendations of financial experts. The researchers gave groups of Americans and Germans a list of large U.S. companies and asked members to mark those they recognized. The two groups also marked a list of large German companies that they recognized. The researchers then assembled four portfolios consisting of each group's ten most recognized stocks on each list and tracked their values. Over the next six months, all four portfolios beat their countries' market averages. They outperformed randomly chosen stocks and portfolios selected by well-performing mutual funds.[51] More surprisingly, the ten German companies most recognized by Americans outperformed the ten most recognized by Germans, and vice versa for the American companies most recognized by Germans. The German companies known by Americans predominantly include those that are successful enough to be written up in American media or produce products (e.g., BMW, Bayer Aspirin) purchased by U.S. households. The typical German would recognize these companies, along with many mediocre ones well-known at home but not in America.

Elimination Heuristics

For another fast and frugal exercise, assume that you wish to rank the 41 largest U.S. metropolitan areas (central cities and their suburbs) by size, and assume that you know all of their names so that a recognition heuristic will not work. You do, however, know three facts about each of them: (1) the number of professional sports (football, baseball, and basketball) franchises it contains, (2) the presence or absence of a Federal Reserve bank or branch,[52] and (3) whether the city is located in the Sunbelt of the southern and southwestern states. Given two of these areas, we wish to determine which is more populous.[53] An *elimination heuristic* makes the choice on the basis of the first category in which the cities differ. Start with sports franchises (or one of the other two categories) and pick the area with the most. If the two areas are tied, choose the one with a Federal Reserve office, and if they are still tied, choose the one in the Sunbelt. Of the 820 pairs that can be chosen from the 41 largest areas, this technique ranks 677 (82.5 percent) of them correctly, ranks 94 (11.5 percent) of them incorrectly, and leaves 49 (6.0 percent) of them undetermined. Thirty-five of the errors involve areas within three ranks of each other, and 30 more of them involve two particular cities.[54] Even if all you know is the number of sports franchises, you will be correct in 94.8 percent of the 672 rankings that you can make using only these numbers.

---

[50]Gigerenzer et al., *Simple Heuristics That Make Us Smart*, 55.

[51]Gigerenzer et al., *Simple Heuristics That Make Us Smart*, 65. The author of that book and his colleagues did what all too few professors do: they invested a substantial amount of their personal funds in these portfolios, leaving them with a really good answer to anyone who asks "if you're so smart, why aren't you rich"?

[52]There are 12 regional Federal Reserve Banks, which have a total of 25 branches, http://www.federalreserve.gov/generalinfo/listdirectors/default.cfm.

[53]You might, for example, be thinking about the alleged financial disadvantages of professional sports teams located in small market areas and need to guess market sizes.

[54]New Orleans and Charlotte are 34th and 35th but both have two sports franchises. Five of their erroneous rankings are against cities three or fewer ranks from them. Because it is not located in a state, San Juan, Puerto Rico (20th on the overall list) was excluded from all rankings.

Economists and psychologists may have devoted more research than is warranted to people's failures in reasoning, and less than is warranted to people's abilities to devise powerful heuristics. Results of this research shed new light on our assumptions about rationality. Only a person with too much spare time will memorize the ranks of the 41 metropolitan areas. If for some reason you want a complete ranking you can easily find it. But if you are like most people, and want to check just a few pairs, an elimination heuristic makes sense. At the outset, how did I know the number of sports franchises was so well correlated with population? I guessed.[55] Someone with other interests or data might choose a quite different set. If you are an educator, for instance, you might know the sizes of school budgets, or if you are a geographer, you might know the square mileage each area covers. And, of course, if you are an economist you might have thought of the Federal Reserve System.

Q. In another experiment, portfolios consisting of stocks that were most recognized by the general population outperformed those consisting of stocks most recognized by graduate students in economics and finance.[56] Why do you expect this outcome?

Can Groups Be Smarter than Their Members?

Jelly Beans and Hollywood An instructor brings a jar of jelly beans to class and asks each student to guess how many it contains. They cannot talk it over or see each others' estimates. Almost every time the class average is within 3 percent of the actual number, despite the fact that many individual guesses are less than half or more than twice the true amount.[57] Why does the group so often outperform so many of its members? Look at a second example: anyone can join the Hollywood Stock Exchange Web site for free.[58] Each week members receive play money that they can bet on the box office grosses of new movies or on who will win TV reality shows like *Survivor* and *American Idol*. For movies they bet the play money by bidding on fictitious shares of stock whose value rises with the gross. The winners get the losers' play money and can use it in the future. The average of the box office grosses bet on the exchange is usually closer to the real figure than the predictions of highly paid experts. In recent years, Hollywood Stock Exchange members have shown remarkable abilities to predict Academy Award winners, getting at least five of the six major categories (e.g., best actor) correct every year. This group's wisdom also exceeds that of its individual members, even though the winners get nothing more than bragging rights.

---

[55] These three criteria (and sequence) were set arbitrarily.

[56] This reasoning might help explain why the small investors discussed earlier performed so poorly and never changed their ways. Perhaps they preferred obscure stocks that they learned about through online rumors, mistakenly believing they would become rich because they had information that would raise prices after the rest of the market learned it. This may be a hard belief to shed if the alternative is to buy stocks in companies with which everyone is already familiar.

[57] Jack L. Treynor, "Market Efficiency and the Bean Jar Experiment," *Financial Analysts Journal* 43 (May–June 1987): 50–3.

[58] See the Hollywood Stock Exchange Web site at www.hsx.com. The exchange currently has about 400,000 registered members, but a far smaller number are likely to vote on any particular question. For a discussion of the exchange's accuracy, see David Pennock et al., "The Real Power of Artificial Markets," *Science* 291 (Feb. 9, 2001), 987–88.

Racetrack Bettors

Some unlikely crowds perform well when real money is at stake. Before discussing horse races we need to review some basics of odds-making. The odds of a horse winning a race are calculated from the actual amounts bet on it and on other horses. In a two-horse race assume that $1,000 total is bet on Seabiscuit and $3,000 on Mel. If Seabiscuit wins, each $1 bet is returned to those who bet on him, along with $3 from the total bet on Mel. If Mel wins, someone who bet a dollar on him gets the dollar back plus 33 cents. The odds on Seabiscuit are 3 to 1, and those on Mel are 1 to 3.[59] Now assume that the bettors see Mel limping on his way to the track, while Seabiscuit looks healthy. Some who already have bets on Mel will hedge by betting on Seabiscuit, and others who did not previously bet will be confident enough in Seabiscuit to bet on him. Assume that no one places any additional bets on Mel, so $12,000 is now riding on Seabiscuit and only $3,000 on Mel. Seabiscuit becomes the favorite at odds of 1 to 4, and Mel is now a long shot at 4 to 1.

Now let's say there is a long record of races between the two horses (Mel limps to the track every time): Seabiscuit wins 80 percent of them and Mel takes the remainder. If bettors lay down their money in a 4 to 1 ratio, their relative wagers correctly predict the actual probability that each horse will win a given race, and all bettors, on average, break even.[60] Economists have found that this outcome is close to what actually happens. Many bettors have little horse sense as they go for entertainment rather than income, but their aggregate bets are often good estimates of the true probabilities of winning, placing, and showing.[61]

Q. Economists have also learned that amounts bet are farther from the correct odds for long shots than for favorites and for bets that a horse will win rather than place (i.e., come in second or better) or show (i.e., come in third or better).[62] Why might you expect these outcomes?

Event Markets

At election time voter surveys, like the Gallup and Roper polls, are common. They ask a scientifically selected sample about their intentions (the likelihood they will vote and the candidate they will choose) to estimate the election's outcome. In addition, Web sites hold event markets, at which people can bet on the outcomes. Each dollar bet on the winner goes back to the bettor, along with that person's share of the losing bets. Among widely used event markets are the Iowa Electronic Markets, operated by the University of Iowa Business School, and Tradesports, a commercial betting site in Ireland.[63] Only small bets are permitted (Iowa's ceiling is $500). In most elections (inside and outside the United States), these markets are superior to the polls at predicting winners, whether on the eve of

[59]This disregards the percentages of the total bet (i.e., the handle) that go to the racetrack, taxes, and so on.

[60]When more than two horses are running the calculation must account for the odds on each rank in the finish of the race.

[61]For a summary, see Raymond Sauer, "The Economics of Wagering Markets," *Journal of Economic Literature* 36 (December 1998): 2021–64.

[62]Richard Thaler and William Ziemba, "Anomalies: Parimutuel Betting and Racetrack Markets," *Journal of Economic Perspectives* 2 (Spring 1988): 161–74.

[63]For more information on the Iowa Electronic Markets, see http://www.biz.uiowa.edu/iem/; see http://www.tradesports.com/ for information on Tradesports. Nevada regulations do not allow betting on political events.

an election or weeks before it.[64] The 2004 presidential election was one of the closest in history, but bettors at Tradesports.com correctly guessed the winner in every state, outperforming every known poll and recognized expert.[65] The recently founded American Civics Exchange is an online venue where businesses and individuals can hedge their uncertainty (bets are in units of $10,000) about whether legislation that affects them will be enacted.[66]

Which Crowds Are Smart? Not every event market forecasts accurately. Smart groups often have four underlying characteristics:

> *...diversity of opinion (each person should have some private information, even if it's just an eccentric interpretation of the known facts), independence (people's opinions are not determined by the opinions of those around them), decentralization (people are able to specialize and draw on local knowledge), and aggregation (some mechanism exists for turning private judgments into a collective decision).*[67]

All the crowds in our examples probably had some of these characteristics. In future chapters we will encounter smart crowds and not-so-smart crowds. A smart crowd might turn up in a commodity market where prices are set by trades based on the diverse information held by individual buyers and sellers. If so, today's price will reflect both today's supply and demand conditions and traders' expectations of future supply and demand. By contrast, some committees may be not-so-smart crowds. If the members are part of a common organization, each might understand that her personal future with it depends not just on her actual opinion but also on her relationships with others in the group. Sometimes people whose knowledge could further the organization's objectives might have good reason to stay quiet to avoid conflict, divulge only part of their knowledge, or agree with people they differ with in reality.

Q. If groups are often smarter than their members, why are decisions in families with children often made by the parents without any input from the children?

Economics, Business, and Life

When computers were introduced in the 1950s, science writers called them "electronic brains." At the same time researchers examining the brain were saying that it resembles a computer. We now know that both were wrong. The brain can indeed add and subtract, but it is a poorly designed computer that gets distracted, feels emotions, loses memories, and sometimes stumbles on simple logic. Neuroscientists today work with a very different model that promises to improve our understanding of both economics and people in general. Instead of being a computer, the human mind consists of a

---

[64]See Joyce Berg et al., "Results from a Dozen Years of Election Futures Markets Research," at the Iowa Electronic Markets archives, http://www.biz.uiowa.edu/iem/archive/BFNR_2000.pdf. Markets for betting on U.S. elections have existed since the nineteenth century and have consistently given predictions that are about as accurate as today's markets. See Paul Rhode and Koleman Strumpf, "Historic Presidential Betting Markets," *Journal of Economic Perspectives* 18 (Spring 2004): 127–42.

[65]See Emile Servan-Schreiber, "Presidential Reality Check: An Assessment of Newsfutures' 2005 US Election Prediction Markets," Newsfutures.com Web site, http://www.newsfutures.com/pdf/Presidential_Reality_Check.pdf.

[66]See the American Civics Exchange Web site at www.amciv.com. Signing up to inspect the site does not obligate you to any further activities or payments.

[67]James Surowiecki, *The Wisdom of Crowds* (New York: Doubleday, 2004), 10.

network of specialized tools whose functions and interconnections we are only beginning to understand. Computers far outshine humans at error-free arithmetic and logical reasoning that many people think of as rationality. But the human mind is also competent at activities computers can only do poorly, if at all. Every day people engage neural circuits that outperform the fastest computers at tasks like recognizing objects, inferring the emotions of others, and acquiring language and grammar.

Cognitive scientists are learning how peoples' brains actually function when they are making choices and interacting with one another. Understanding these processes can help explain some aspects of economic life that we do not yet understand well. Earlier we saw experiments that showed the many difficulties people face when they attempt to reason about probabilities. But other experimenters have shown that our talents for quick and accurate pattern recognition give us remarkable abilities to detect cheating, understand and respond to threats, infer the attitudes of others, and convey information about ourselves.[68] A mind with these abilities is more able than any computer on the horizon to think innovatively and devise heuristics to cope with problems as they emerge. It is well-equipped to distinguish situations when cooperating with others is best from situations where a person should compete. Economics is about people who are neither computers nor ignoramuses. A human logic machine that is unable to relate to others is as poorly suited for survival in a competitive world as a gullible and passive person who is kind to everyone. Each one of us is an interesting mix of selfishness and kindness. In a lot of ways we are "better than rational."[69]

This gives us one final take on how economists view life. Models that use economic reasoning can help you think more clearly about the behavior of others, and perhaps your own behavior as well. Experience has already taught you a lot about economics, even if you call it something else. You rationally assume that a supplier or a customer is as smart and self-interested as you are, but at the same time you understand that the give-and-take of a long-lasting relationship may be valuable to both of you. A new employee has some interest in the survival of your business and his job, as well as some personal interests that run counter to yours. Economic thinking can help you approach the design of a pay and compensation package that best harnesses his beneficial motives and minimizes the impact of those that conflict with yours. It can sometimes help you identify behavior that others use to signal that they are (or are not) to be trusted. Economics is about far more than choices that can be reduced to math. It sheds light on the remarkable richness of human relationships.

The Questions Ahead

Now that you understand the ground rules, let's look at some questions that economics can help you to analyze more insightfully. Some of them will be about actions in the market:

- What factors should you consider when determining how to price the goods or services your company produces? When might it pay to charge different prices to different customers?
- When should you sell a group of goods as a bundle and not let consumers buy them separately, and when does it make sense to give them the option to purchase a bundle or purchase them separately?

[68]Colin Camerer, George Loewenstein, and Drazen Prelec, "Neuroeconomics: How Neuroscience Can Inform Economics," *Journal of Economic Literature* 48 (March 2005): 9–64.

[69]Leda Cosmides and John Tooby, "Better than Rational: Evolutionary Psychology and the Invisible Hand," *American Economic Review* 84 (May 1994): 327–32.

- When should you expand your business, and if you do expand is it better to build a new facility of your own or acquire one owned by someone else, possibly by merger?
- Should you rush to be the first in your industry to begin selling in a new country or wait until you have learned from the experiences of others?

Economics can also help you model relationships with suppliers and competitors:

- When is it better for you to buy all of a raw material your firm uses from a single seller than to share your orders among competing suppliers? What kind of price assurance should a supply contract give you, and what rights should one or both of you have to terminate it? (These are not just questions for lawyers, as we will see.)
- You are in the market for an executive position and have offers from two possible employers. Why do their packages differ substantially in base pay, bonuses, stock options, and so on? What factors should determine the components of the package that you bargain for most aggressively?
- The average time an employee spends working for a single employer in the United States is shrinking. In what businesses does this pose a bigger problem for you as a manager, and what strategies might help you keep employees longer? When will you prefer employees who expect a longer-term relationship with your company, and when will you not?

We will also use economics to examine organizational design and choice:

- At the inception of the automobile industry, Ford had a top-down organization while General Motors was divisionalized into several brands of cars. Why did it make sense for each to choose a different organizational design? Why does the organization chart of the Green Bay Packers look totally unlike that of Microsoft?
- Why do most high-tech companies have relatively short chains-of-command between their highest and lowest levels? In what types of businesses is it better to have a long chain of command?
- When do you organize your business venture as a corporation and when do you organize as a partnership? Why is the corporation the dominant form of business organization everywhere it is legal, but some professionals, such as doctors and lawyers, continue to work in partnerships?
- How can you explain the growth of outsourcing over the past 50 years, and how can you best determine which functions your company should keep in-house and which it should obtain from others?
- What are the best ways to pay workers in different parts of your organization? What about the work environment explains why lower-level workers are usually paid by the hour, middle managers get monthly salaries, salespeople get commissions, tenant farmers get a share of the crop they produce, and restaurant servers get mostly tips?

We have begun a journey that will help us think more clearly about these and countless other questions, some quite distant from business. How, for example, might you explain the origin of engagement rings and how the percentage of married couples who purchase one has fluctuated with time?[70]

---

[70]Hint: We can definitively show that the answer is unrelated to the advertising of diamonds.

Chapter Summary

- Economics is a way of thinking about the many aspects of human activity that involve choice and exchange.
- Economists analyze the world by constructing simplified models of the phenomena that interest them. Models help us to better understand the structure of a problem and often provide predictions about what will (and will not) happen if circumstances change.
- The basic model of economic choice is one of rational (goal-oriented) behavior, in which a person tries to make choices with the intent of attaining that goal.
- Economic rationality is a positive rather than a normative concept. Rational behavior is not necessarily self-centered and can consider the interests of others.
- Choices are made subject to different types of constraints that limit what a person can attain. Attempting to lighten or remove these constraints by innovation is an important economic activity.
- Because goods are scarce and peoples' wants have few limits, they must compete to obtain things and services that they value. Competition takes many forms, including politics, trading, beauty contests, waiting lines, and violence. Different types of competition produce different winners and losers.
- The appropriate economic model to use depends on what we intend to analyze. Sometimes it will be best to proceed as if decision makers have on hand all the information they require, and at other times we must acknowledge that obtaining more information entails costs but can also improve the quality of decisions.
- Information is costly to acquire and disseminate, and some information is intrinsically unknowable. The human mind's abilities to process information have some important limits that influence the quality of some decisions.
- Because information is hard to process, people can make errors in reasoning that lead them to incorrect conclusions. They can make erroneous generalizations, fail to use important data, or choose on the basis of irrelevant data. Sometimes they adjust to changes in their environments too slowly, and other times too quickly.
- Peoples' mental capabilities are limited, but they often devise heuristics, or shortcuts in reasoning, that allow them to economize on intellectual capacity while still reaching decisions that are nearly correct.
- Selection bias due to data samples that are incomplete in particular ways often leads to unreliable conclusions. Selection bias is frequently encountered in research on the success of business practices because successful firms are more likely to survive.
- The quality of a decision sometimes improves if it is made by a group of independent individuals with access to different types of information. In other situations a group's decision will be of lower quality (e.g., accuracy of an estimate) than an individual's.
- The human mind is not a computer, and humans are not entirely selfish. Both of these facts greatly increase the potential scope for beneficial interactions among people.

Questions and Problems

1. Can impulse buying ever be a rational choice? Explain. For what types of goods might it be rational?
2. When discussing the maximization of utility, regardless of whether you chose to work more hours or fewer when offered a higher hourly wage, you could not be worse off than you were at a lower hourly wage. Can you show this?
3. A common economic experiment is called the "ultimatum game." Subject A receives a small amount of cash, say \$10. She can give some whole dollar amount to subject B, a stranger whom she cannot see and who cannot see her. If subject B approves of the amount he receives, both keep their portions of the \$10. If subject B disapproves, they both get nothing.[71]
   a. Can you show that if subject A is interested only in herself, her rational strategy is to give subject B \$1 (Why not nothing?), and subject B's rational response is to accept that amount?
   b. How might you explain the fact that in actual experiments the average amount offered by subject A (who is chosen at random) is an average of \$3, and subject B (also chosen at random) usually accepts it?
   c. What do you think happens to the average amount transferred by subject A and the probability that subject B will accept it if the setup is changed so that subject A wins her place as the giver by outscoring B on a short test of general knowledge? Explain.
   d. What do you think happens to the average amount transferred and the probability of acceptance if subjects A and B are told they might be matched with each other to play the game again at some date in the future but do not know in advance who will be the donor and who the recipient?
   e. If, instead of \$10, subject A gets \$200 to give away, what do you expect will happen to the amount she offers subject B? Why?
4. One of the most fact-filled publications you can buy is the *Daily Racing Form.*[72] For every horse running that day it contains about 30 facts about each of its last ten races, including the name of the jockey, location of the race, track condition, odds on the horse at post time, the winner of the race, position at the halfway mark, and so on. The reader will have hundreds of facts in hand about every horse in a particular race.
   a. Experiments show that experienced bettors who use the *Daily Racing Form* outperform equally experienced bettors who have not been allowed to use it. Why?
   b. Experiments have also shown that casual bettors who are given the *Daily Racing Form* and told to study it before making their bets underperform similar people who are told to choose their horses however they prefer to. Why?
   c. Link your answers to these questions with what you have learned about models and heuristics.
5. An acquaintance once thumbed through this textbook and remarked "I don't believe it. Theories may be rational, but people are not." Do you agree with him? Why or why not?
6. Surely we would agree that it is rational to attempt to stay alive (while taking reasonable risks), because every day we all do just that. Are suicidal terrorists rational? Why or why not?

---

[71]Richard H. Thaler, "Anomalies: the Ultimatum Game," *Journal of Economic Perspectives* 2 (Autumn 1988): 195–206.

[72]See the *Daily Racing Form* Web site at http://www.drf.com/.

7. Jones graduated college a few years ago and can't find a good job. When I suggested she go back and major in economics this time around, she responded that she couldn't because she had already spent so many years in school. Is this behavior rational?
8. Different areas of endeavor allow different forms of competition. What kinds of competition are allowed for getting into college that are not allowed for getting an A in this class? What kinds of competition are allowed in business but not in campaigns for political office and vice versa?
9. You see a bicycle on special sale for $300. After thinking it over you decide you are unwilling to pay that much and walk away. Just before you go you turn the price tag over and see that it was originally selling for $450. You change your mind and choose to buy it. Are you acting irrationally? Why or why not?
10. Would people be better off if they were not selfish? How do you know this for a fact?
11. The Dalai Lama is an inspirational figure to millions who incur substantial travel and time costs to attend his lectures and absorb his wisdom. When he won the Nobel Peace Prize in 1989, he gave most of the money to religious and charitable organizations. Are you sure he was acting altruistically rather than self-interestedly? When he goes on lecture tours, he generally flies first class, although coach would be far cheaper. Are you sure he is acting self-interestedly rather than altruistically?
12. A newscaster interviewed a senator about a proposed fence along the Mexican border. He said not to build it because some illegal entrants would still manage to climb it or cut through it. Assume for now that the senator is correct, and also assume that there are good reasons to exclude illegal entrants. Does his reasoning lead you to conclude that the fence is a bad idea? Would it be a bad idea if it stopped 95 percent of illegal crossings? 70 percent? 10 percent? How would an economist decide on the critical percentage at which the fence should not be built?
13. A local business owner tells you economics is wrong because people do not respond to incentives. She tells you that she increased all of her employees' pay by 10 percent and they did not work any harder. Is her conclusion justified? Why? Would economics be wrong if she cut all their pay and they did not try to get away with more loafing on the job?
14. You are an economist who wants to know how risk of on-the-job injury affects peoples' wages. Studying construction workers (who have a substantial risk exposure), you discover that they earn very little more than otherwise similar people with equivalent skills and training in low-risk jobs. You conclude that people only require a small wage premium to induce them into risky lines of work. How does selection bias make your conclusion doubtful?
15. Shopping for prices is a common form of information gathering. Researchers have found that for a given good the prices paid by middle-aged, upper-income, and large households average as much as 10 percent less than those paid by retired, low-income, and small households, respectively. Construct a model of shopping behavior that explains these facts.[73]
16. Between 1992 and 2002, the University of California's stock market holdings underperformed market averages by $2.3 billion. Officials pointed out that the loss was unimportant because they actually grew by $20 billion over that period.[74] Identify the economic error in their reasoning.

---

[73]Mark Aguiar and Erik Hurst, "Lifecycle Prices and Production," Public Policy Discussion Paper 05-3, Federal Reserve Bank of Boston (July 2005), http://www.bos.frb.org/economic/ppdp/2005/ppdp053.pdf

[74]"UC Missed Out on Extra Stock Gains, Records Say," *Los Angeles Times*, January 15, 2004.

17. People join tennis clubs for a fixed fee per year, which entitles them to play as much as they want without charge. Because people who pay these fees play more tennis than others (who can use free public courts), this means sunk costs matter for decisions. Right?

18. Maybe people have too many choices. According to one political science professor, "choices proliferate beyond our pleasure in choosing and our capacity to handle the choices."[75] One West Los Angeles supermarket has a sign that says, "724 produce varieties available today, including 93 organics." What sorts of heuristics do people use to avoid the difficulties of choosing among so many vegetables when they shop? How about when they go through the 2 million book titles on Amazon.com?

19. Perhaps surprisingly, field experiments have shown that strangers who encounter one another on the street (e.g., to ask directions) are friendlier around 4 a.m. than in similar encounters that take place during the day or evening. Also surprisingly, in both rich and poor neighborhoods street crime falls during those hours.[76] Are people acting rationally when they are friendlier at these odd hours?

20. "Economic models help us to distinguish evidence from coincidence." Explain.

21. On the television show *Jeopardy* contestants in the final round must choose some part of their winnings to bet on their answer to an upcoming question, and the winner's bet is added to the amount he has already won on that day. Only the winner takes home cash, and the other contestants get prizes like vacation trips that they cannot trade for their cash values.[77]

   a. Why would the producers not allow losers to make themselves better off when there is no extra cost to them of allowing it?

   b. Is your answer to the previous question consistent with the following fact: Scattered through the earlier rounds are Daily Doubles, on which a contestant can bet any amount up to her then-current winnings. The typical contestant gets a Daily Double question right about 80 percent of the time. Nevertheless, the average bet is usually only about 30 percent of the amount possible.

22. Most applicants win admission to selective colleges on their academic skills. Prestigious universities do, however, admit some less qualified people whose parents have promised large donations. (In 2002, Duke University admitted between 110 and 120 such legacy applicants.)[78] As a normative proposition, do you object to this practice? Why or why not?

23. [Project]Consider the following six causes of death: Lung cancer, vehicle accidents, emphysema, homicides, tuberculosis, and fires. Guess the total number of persons dying annually in the United States from each and then look up the actual figures.[79] Almost everyone makes several mistakes in their rankings. Can you find evidence that your mistakes may have resulted from your use of an availability heuristic? As one possibility, try looking for media mentions of health hazards in a full-text data service like Nexis or Factiva.

---

[75]Robert Lane, *The Loss of Happiness in Market Democracies* (New Haven, CT: Yale University Press, 2001).

[76]These and other fascinating facts appear in Murray Melbin, "Night as Frontier," *American Sociological Review* 43 (February 1978): 3–22.

[77]Your author was once on the show. He lost in the final round because he knew nothing about Broadway musicals.

[78]"'Buying' Your Way into College," *Wall Street Journal*, March 12, 2003.

[79]See "Deaths: Final Data for 2006," *National Vital Statistics Reports* 57 (April 2009), Table 9. http://www.cdc.gov/nchs/data/nvsr/nvsr57/nvsr57_14.pdf.

Chapter 2

Transactions and Institutions: The Building Blocks

Below is a satellite photo, quite possibly doctored for maximum impact. It is almost identical to one used in advertising by Eskom, the Republic of South Africa's major power producer.[1] Africa is almost entirely dark, while to the north, electric light makes Europe luxuriantly bright. The implied message is that something has gone wrong, but

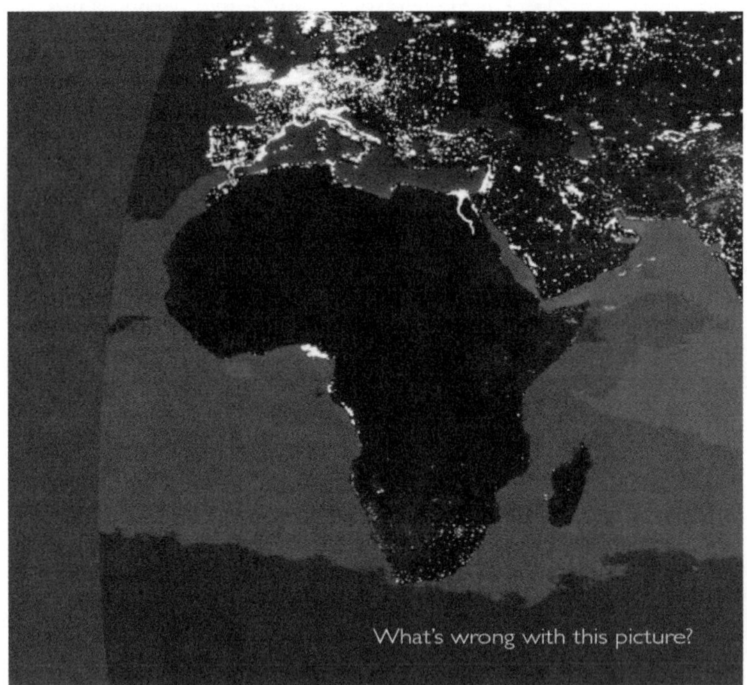
What's wrong with this picture?

Millions have been denied a privilege considered by most as a basic human right; electricity. But it's a scenario we're changing. With the introduction of low cost electricity; at a rate of a thousand new homes a day. Eskom, through its specialised subsidiaries, and with business partners throughout Africa, is paving the way for stimulating regional economic opportunities and reinvestment. And thus helping to unleash this continent's true potential.

Eskom
Unleashing Africa's Energy
www.eskom.co.za
Global Power Company of the Year: 2001

[1]ESKOM's home page is at http://www.eskom.co.za/.

the photo itself is of little help in figuring out why the difference is so stark. Africans are on average poorer than Europeans. Poor people also want electricity, but only in small quantities because their budgets are lower and their appliances are fewer. Instead of small amounts of power, many Africans get none at all. Why is Africa so dark instead of just dimmer than Europe?

An important part of the difference lies in the cost of setting up an exchange of power that benefits both the producer and the consumer. In this chapter we will look at how Eskom has lowered the costs of power transactions for poorer South Africans. Electricity is so unfamiliar to some of them that Eskom prints brochures telling them how to change light bulbs.[2] Between 1991 and 2008, Eskom brought electricity to 3.6 million homes.[3] An important part of what kept South Africans in the dark for so long was the high cost of transacting small amounts of power.

All of us spend a lot of time planning and making exchanges with one another. Often we do this indirectly by selling our work skills to obtain incomes and buying goods and services with them. Yet most of us probably cannot explain why a voluntary exchange benefits both the buyer and seller. (Go ahead. Write down your own explanation before reading on.) Here we model the simplest possible transactions. We need to understand exchange between two persons before we can analyze the more complex transactions encountered in business situations. Models of two-person exchange can be generalized to trade between nations and the choices of what they will import and export. This chapter addresses the following:

- Why a voluntary exchange between two persons leaves them both better off, even if no new goods are produced
- Why economics is less concerned with the price a buyer and seller agree on than on the fact that they both benefit from the transaction
- How the costs of arranging a transaction can change the benefits the parties receive and how those benefits are distributed between them
- Why people have incentives to reduce the cost of transacting, how lower transaction costs make new types of exchanges possible, and how people compete to reduce those costs
- How people determine the goods they will specialize in producing, and why specialization engenders transactions that leave both sides better off
- Why people can gain from specialization and trade regardless of their relative sizes and productivities, a principle that also applies to trade between wealthy and poor nations
- Why specialization and exchange in a society with many people and many goods lower the costs of information and planning
- How economic institutions define the environment in which people can arrange and settle transactions; the range of trades they can devise and the distribution of their benefits will depend on these institutions
- How three basic modes of governance are central to the study of institutions and business decisions: transactions may take place in markets, be arranged by contracts, or reflect the authority relationships of an organization

---

[2]That brochure is found at http://www.eskom.co.za/live/content.php?Category_ID=566.

[3]See page 65 of Eskom's 2006 Annual Financial Report at http://www.eskom.co.za/annreport06/downloads.htm and page 5 of Eskom's 2008 Financial Profile at http://www.eskom.co.za/annreport08/ar_2008/downloads/profile.pdf.

THE LOGIC OF ECONOMIC VALUE

The Benefits of Exchange

Start with you, me, and a single object that might be any product or service. Assume that it is an *economic good*, one that both of us would prefer more of rather than less. My goal is to make myself as well off as possible, and yours is to do likewise for yourself. I will not make myself worse off just to see you happier, and vice versa. Any deal we reach must make both of us better off. It must be voluntary on both sides—you cannot force me to hand you the object against my will, and I cannot keep the object after accepting your money.

Figure 2-1 portrays the initial situation. Assume that I am the potential seller and you are the potential buyer. My opportunity cost is $7. As defined in Chapter 1, I forgo the dollar value of the best alternative if I part with the object. Maybe I think that continuing to own and enjoy it is worth $7. If you pay me $7 perhaps I can buy goods from others that make me feel just as well off as when I had the object. Or maybe I already know someone who will buy it for $7, so I will not accept a lower offer from you. If you offer me $8 I will be better off, because this is more than my best alternative of $7. I can buy $7 of other goods (which leaves me as well off as before) and still have $1 to do with as I please.

Because you are the potential buyer we must also explore your limits. Your *valuation* of the object is the highest price you will voluntarily pay for it. As Figure 2-1 shows, you will refuse an exchange if I insist on more than $11. The fact that your valuation is $11 rather than some other amount reflects your personal preferences and your other opportunities: $11 can buy a bundle of goods that leaves you just as well off as if you had bought the object from me, or you might know someone who can sell you the same good or service for $11. To understand how you benefit from the exchange start by assuming that some very nice person gave you the object for free. You now have it, along with the $11 you would have been just willing to pay for it. Your benefits from the gift are $11. If the lowest price available from a seller is $2 you will take it. Making the deal leaves you with an object worth $11 along with $9 you can spend elsewhere.

The difference between the seller's opportunity cost and the buyer's valuation is known as the *economic value* the transaction can create. Here, $4 in economic value will materialize if we can reach an agreement. Any agreed-upon price between $7.01 and $10.99 benefits both of us. An $8 deal leaves me $1 better off than my next-best opportunity, and you are $3 better off than in your next-best opportunity. In a very real sense, both of us are wealthier. The goods I can now buy with the $8 in cash leave me better off than I was before the trade, and you have an object that is worth more to you than what you paid for it. The benefits also arise if one good is bartered for another instead of using money. Such trades often occur in professional sports. Assume that the Chicago Cubs have an outstanding pitching staff but could greatly benefit from an additional power hitter, and the Boston Red Sox have weak pitchers and strong hitters. The Cubs' ability to win improves if they trade one of their pitchers for a Red Sox hitting

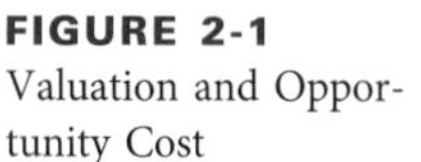

FIGURE 2-1
Valuation and Opportunity Cost

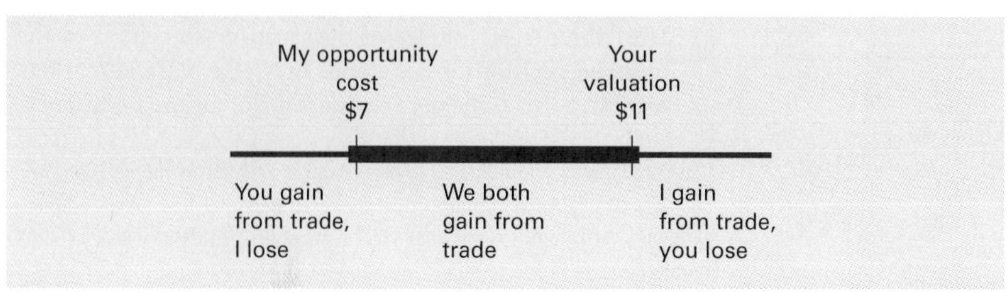

star, and so will the capability of Red Sox. The fact that there is a fixed amount of goods (in this case, talented players) between the parties does not bar them from both becoming better teams by trade. After the trade fans of both teams will feel better off, at least until playoff time.

Q. Explain why no mutually beneficial exchange will occur when the buyer's valuation is less than the seller's opportunity cost.

Q. If trading one hitter for one pitcher benefits both teams, why isn't a trade of two hitters for two pitchers even better? Try to frame your answer in terms of opportunity costs and valuations.

What Matters and What Doesn't

To make a mutually beneficial trade both parties must settle on a price. In this example the exact amount greatly interests both of us, because a low price bestows relatively more of the benefit on you (the buyer) and less on me. Most economists, however, will have little interest in the exact outcome. In terms of positive economics we are both human beings looking out for ourselves. Normative economics has no formula to determine which of us deserves more of the benefits. As long as the trade takes place, a nickel of benefits gained by you is a nickel less of benefits for me. Some observers might be concerned about how I can feed my family if all I get is a low price, while others might worry about the amounts of other goods you are sacrificing if you pay a high one. There is simply no clear standard for such comparisons, so economists wash their hands of the problem and leave it to philosophers. Personal experiences and emotions often make it hard to understand the underlying economics of a transaction. I often think I get paid too little when I sell my services and I pay too much for the goods I buy with the income. You might think the same about what you sell and buy. Because my expenditure is your income and vice versa our feelings tell us nothing about who is really better or worse off.

What does matter is that an exchange takes place at all. If you and I have the opportunity we will probably reach an agreement because the cost of not reaching one is that both of us will be needlessly worse off. The price depends on our bargaining abilities, and neither of us necessarily holds all the cards. Similarly, when I shop for a car the first dealer I visit may offer me a price that is less than my valuation, but I will probably go on to see a second dealer. Visiting the second one is in effect a gamble that I will get a better offer than the one I have in hand. When we bargain the dealer has no reason to tell me the least she will settle for, and I have no reason to honestly report the offers I already have.[4] Some customers will get lower prices than others, and some dealers will thrive as others fail. What matters for economics is not how the buyer and seller split the gains but rather the fact that transactions actually take place.

The parties to an exchange need not bargain face-to-face. Buying a good with a non-negotiable price tag still benefits both if the price is between the buyer's valuation and the seller's opportunity cost. In many parts of the world, price tags are rarely seen, and

[4]Chapter 1717 examines how and why dealer price quotes vary.

both parties expect to bargain before settling on a price. Because haggling has a higher opportunity cost if peoples' time is more valuable, one would expect to see more tagged goods in wealthy countries than poor ones. If language barriers forestall verbal negotiation between strangers, then price tags lower the cost of a transaction. Price tags in fact first appeared on a large scale in northeastern U.S. cities during the era of mass immigration late in the nineteenth century. They made transactions possible that would have otherwise required businesses to hire multilingual clerks.[5]

Q. Why do you expect that price tags will be more common in large stores than in smaller ones that sell the same products?

Q. Why is the sticker price (which by law must appear on a new car) usually just a starting point for bargaining while the tagged price of an item at the supermarket is nonnegotiable?

Transaction Costs

Why Include Transaction Costs?

Our straightforward transaction took place in an unreal world where neither of us incurred any costs to make it. Each of us apparently knew the other all along, so you did not have to look for me, and I did not have to advertise to make you aware of me. We did not need to incur the cost of travel to our meeting, and when we met it took only a split second to bargain to the price (time has an opportunity cost). We just assumed that you were aware of the true quality of the good I was offering, and that I had no reason to check your credit or whether your money was counterfeit. The fact that *transaction costs* were zero allowed the two of us to share the entire $4 of benefits.

Now assume that we speak different languages and need an interpreter to help us reach agreement. That person charges the going rate of $2, which leaves us with $2 in net benefits to share after our exchange. The trade remains worthwhile, but the transaction cost of hiring the interpreter shrinks the gains. In Figure 2-2, part of the line measuring benefits is blocked by a red rectangle whose length corresponds to the $2 interpreter's fee. Either of us could be paying the interpreter, or we might have devised a way to split the bill. If we can find a competent interpreter who charges only $1 we can both gain. If one of us can hire an interpreter more cheaply than the other, the gains potentially available to both of us increase.

FIGURE 2-2
Transaction Cost and the Gains from Exchange

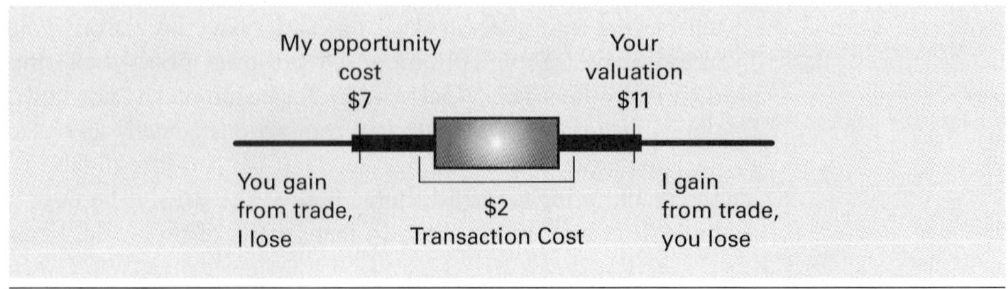

[5]"How Technology Tailors Price Tags," *Wall Street Journal*, June 21, 2001.

Who Hires the Interpreter? Longo Toyota East of downtown Los Angeles, the suburbs of the San Gabriel Valley have become home for upwardly mobile Hispanic and Asian families who have left the central city. The area is also home to many recent immigrants from the Middle East, the Near East, India, and elsewhere. For the past 20 years, Longo Toyota of El Monte has been the country's largest Toyota dealer. (In some years it was the largest dealer in any make of car.) Sixty members of Longo's 80-person sales force are multilingual. On a typical weekend, they can deal with customers in 30 different languages, from Amharic (Ethiopia) to Bengali (India and Bangladesh) to Tagalog [Philippines].[6] All of course also speak English.

Longo lowers transaction costs by hiring multilingual salespeople. But why does Longo bear the cost of having them available rather than leaving non–English speakers to find their own interpreters? If Longo did not employ them each customer who did not speak English would have to incur the cost of finding and paying a personal interpreter, probably on a weekend (friends and relatives have opportunity costs, too). Some might choose not to shop at Longo rather than bearing these costs. Once the negotiations begin customers must somehow make sure their chosen interpreters act in their interest and bargain aggressively. Added up over all customers, the transaction costs are almost surely lower when Longo keeps salespeople on the payroll who can work with both English and non–English speakers as they turn up. It is cheaper for Longo to hire a bilingual sales force than to use monolingual employees and call for an interpreter in the event a non–English speaker comes by. Someone must compensate an interpreter for being on call, regardless of whether any customers arrive that day.

Many transactions are less standardized than the sale of a Toyota where Longo faces thousands of potential buyers. A foreign firm purchasing a large U.S. business, for example, will probably hire its own interpreter rather than using an available employee. The U.S. firm will probably do likewise because it has little reason to expect that an interpreter employed by the foreign firm will act in the U.S. firm's interest. The risks of a poor translation are greater to both parties, particularly in a transaction that is much larger and more complex than the sale of a car. Each side will probably seek out an interpreter with special skills in comparing and translating financial terms. The costs of this one-of-a-kind transaction will probably be minimized if both sides hire their own special-purpose interpreters.

Making Transactions Materialize

Cutting transaction costs increases the benefits available to the parties and might also enable them to make exchanges that were previously impossible. If the interpreter in Figure 2-2 costs $5 our transaction will not be worth making because the cost of arranging it exceeds the total benefits we can share. If instead the interpreter charges $2 (and costs nothing to find) our transaction becomes worth making. The lower the cost of a transaction the more likely it will take place. An innovator can make a fortune not just by inventing some good or service but also by finding a way to lower the transaction costs incurred by others. That person could be the producer, the buyer, or a third party. Longo makes itself and its customers better off by using a multilingual sales force. It eases the movement of cars to buyers who place higher values on them. We sometimes call the dealer a middleman, all too often implying that if only dealers did not exist, both

[6]The Longo Toyota Web site shows the different languages spoken at http://www.longotoyota.com/en_US/f_MiscPage_6.chtml#. (Click on the individual languages to be greeted in them.) See also, "Toyota Dealership a Laboratory for Diversity," Associated Press, May 26, 1998 (available on Factiva).

manufacturers and customers could capture more benefits. From here on the dealer will get a less emotive name—"intermediary."

If a lower-cost intermediary (perhaps an Internet buying service) replaces a higher-cost intermediary both the producer and consumer can gain. Sometimes people with lower opportunity costs of time transact without an intermediary and those with higher opportunity costs use one. For example, cities often close off a street one morning a week for a farmers' market where local growers sell vegetables, sometimes still covered with dirt. Direct dealing between consumers and farmers does not eliminate an intermediary—people simply become their own intermediaries. Both the farmer and the consumer give up time they might have spent earning or relaxing. Farmers' markets are heavily frequented by students whose free time is flexible and retired people whose opportunity costs of time are low. For customers like these the benefits of being their own intermediaries cover the time costs. Others prefer supermarkets that charge more but are open 24 hours and located on the route between work and home. The total cost of a good is the dollars paid for it plus the opportunity cost of time spent shopping. Even if all sellers charge the same price, opportunity cost varies from one person to another.

Sears Early in the twentieth century, farm families in the upper Midwest often bought most of their goods in towns too small to support more than a single general store. Car ownership was still in the future, and roads were primitive. A growing railroad network allowed farmers to sell their crops in a nationwide market, but the typical farm family rarely went to the big city. Because most farmers had only poor alternatives, local stores had more power over prices than they would have had in competitive markets. General stores had other drawbacks. Few customers meant small inventories with little variety, and special orders to distant suppliers took time. Stockouts were a chronic problem because the local store was at the end of a long chain of wholesalers, warehousers, and distributors.

In 1887, a general store in North Redwood, Minnesota, refused a shipment of watches from a Chicago jewelry manufacturer and intended to send them back. Along the way a railroad employee named Richard Sears chose to buy and pay for them. Sears advertised and sold them in railroad towns, later opening a watch business with Alvah Roebuck.[7] It may have taken a railroad employee to envision coordinating with workers at other train stations and communicating by telegraph. Sears and Roebuck later moved to Chicago, then and now the nation's most important railroad junction. There, and elsewhere along railroad lines, they acquired warehouses and stocked them with a wide range of consumer goods (including, for a while, prefabricated houses). Local advertising and face-to-face transactions gave way to a mail-order catalog that had already reached 500 pages by 1894. Sears became the world's biggest retailer, a position it held until Wal-Mart took over almost a hundred years later.[8]

Sears lowered a host of transaction costs, bringing profits to its shareholders and lower prices to its customers. Other forces were also operating. A mail-order business

---

[7]Trading along railroad lines was relatively common at the time, and railroad employees were uniquely situated to be intermediaries. Daniel Boorstin, *The Americans: The Democratic Experience* (New York Random House, 1973), 118–129. For more on Sears, see B. Emmet and J.E. Jeuck, *Catalogues and Counters* (Chicago: University of Chicago Press, 1950) or go to the Sears company Web site at http://www.sears.com/sr/misc/sears/about/public/history/history_main.jsp?vertical=SEARS.

[8]Sears was also one of the first to understand how broadcast advertising could lower transaction costs. Sears owned Chicago radio station WLS, whose powerful signal could (and can still) be heard at night more than 1,000 miles away (WLS stood for "world's largest store"). As America suburbanized, Sears moved from catalog sales to malls, where it could not duplicate the success of the mail-order system. (Think of some possible reasons why.) In 2004, Sears merged with Kmart, another poorly performing mass merchandiser. The merged company's performance has improved little.

would have been impossible before railroads lowered the costs of shipping goods and catalogs. The catalog itself lowered transaction costs. It allowed rural families to learn about new products and brands without ever leaving home. The catalog also offered more varieties of most products than local stores could carry and eased the job of comparison shopping. The catalogs were a landmark in publishing, with illustrations that allowed goods like apparel to sell themselves. Printing catalogs by the millions justified the costs of producing elaborate ones. Sears also cut transaction costs by lowering uncertainty—the catalog's prices and shipping charges were good for the entire year. The company's track-side warehouses lowered the probability that an item would be out of stock or delayed in shipment. Sears's very size lowered transaction costs—management science and statistics show that inventory costs per dollar of sales will often be less in larger firms. Perhaps most importantly, Sears cut transaction costs by eliminating intermediaries. It replaced the entire chain of wholesalers, distributors, and shippers—and the general stores themselves—with an organization that used the cutting-edge technologies of its time.

Q. Sears made its fortune with a catalog of consumer goods aimed at isolated farmers. It did not, however, offer other things they needed, like farm implements and seeds. Give some reasons why Sears might choose to restrict itself to consumer products.

Eskom Like Sears, South Africa's electricity supplier, Eskom, uses the technologies of its day to cut transaction costs. Its power plants produce some of the world's cheapest electricity. Middle- and upper-income South Africans buy their power like most Americans. They use as much as they want and pay monthly for the amounts read off their meters by Eskom employees.[9] The amounts used by consumers like these are unpredictable, but their incomes are steady and large enough that they can budget the funds to cover any bill within an expected range. People with low and unsteady incomes are quite different. Both they and Eskom face high transaction costs in delivering and paying for power, sometimes so high that transactions between them are too costly to make. Eskom has taken actions and invented ways to cut some important transaction costs:

- *Interior wiring:* Poorer areas around large cities (e.g., Soweto, outside Johannesburg) have only rudimentary housing, and the cost of installing safe wiring inside their walls is prohibitive. Eskom devised a new delivery system consisting of an insulated cable attached to a power line and dropped through the roof. At its end are several outlets.
- *Small quantities and limited ability to pay:* The budgets of low-income people limit their power use. Even if consumers were always sure to pay monthly, billing and meter reading would be expensive relative to revenue per house.[10] Eskom's prepayment system only allows power to flow if a magnetic-stripe card has been inserted into the outlets.[11] Consumers can add desired amounts of money to their cards at convenient vending machines. A home display shows the amount remaining on the card.

---

[9]In reality, Eskom only produces the power and then sells it to others (usually local governments) who resell it to ultimate users. For simplicity, the text disregards the role of these intermediaries. (Why might using intermediaries be superior to direct dealing between users and Eskom?)

[10]Like utilities in the United States, those in South Africa are restricted to sell at prices that cover their prudently incurred costs and give investors a reasonable return on their funds.

[11]Details of Eskom's prepayment system are at http://www.eskom.co.za/electrification/index.htm.

- *Theft of cards:* Poor areas are often high-crime areas, and stealing an unprotected power card would be almost as good as stealing money. Eskom lowers the transaction costs of avoiding theft by encoding a user's number on the card. Power will only flow if the card matches its owner's outlet code, making it almost worthless to a potential thief.
- *Theft of power:* Power theft using unauthorized connections or bypassed meters is a major problem in poor countries.[12] An unskilled worker can directly tap an ordinary line in minutes. Because either the producer or the legal users must pay for stolen power, their transaction costs are higher. To deter theft Eskom has reengineered its wires so specialized tools and training are required to tap them.

The Box The electrical and electronic technologies of the twentieth century changed peoples' lives everywhere. A list of the century's most important inventions should probably also include one that appears far simpler—the standardized shipping container. The first "box" went to sea in 1956. Our front cover shows the world 50 years later, with containers as far as the eye can see at the port of Singapore, today the world's largest container terminal. Even if you live a thousand miles from an ocean you see them every day stacked on railroad flatcars, hauled as truck trailers, or parked at warehouses. The box cut so many transaction costs that it forever changed the way the world does business.[13]

Think not? For many years there was one way to see the world if you lacked money or education: join the crew of a freighter ship. Sailors enjoyed free time in port while longshoremen with grappling hooks took weeks to wrestle with heavy, irregularly shaped cargoes. A typical trans-Pacific ship spent more time loading and unloading than it did in motion. Today tourists enjoy the old port of San Francisco, while across the bay in Oakland four miles of gantry cranes can each load and unload more than a thousand containers a day. Bar codes coordinate the boxes with rails and trucks so precisely that many never touch the ground before they move overland.

An inland Asian manufacturer can fill a container, seal it, and truck it to a railroad from which it is loaded onto a ship. After the crossing similar transfers move it to the actual customer. Before containerization each transfer could require days of waiting and worker time. Now they often take minutes and entail far smaller risks of theft. As use of the box reduced transaction costs, it also expanded the scope of markets. People around the world gained potential trading partners. Some once-strategic locations became less important, and for many businesses the advantage of locating near customers or suppliers shrank.[14] Containers full of once-unprofitable commodities, like South African coal, could now economically reach Europe.[15] Twenty years after the introduction of the box

---

[12]It is estimated that between 10 and 20 percent of all electricity in Mexico is stolen, and 20 to 40 percent in India. "Thieves Lurk—The Sizable Problem of Stolen Electricity," *Electrical World T&D*, September/October 2000, http://www.platts.com/engineering/issues/ElectricalWorld/0009/0009ew–theft.shtml. South Africa's power-theft monitoring organization is found at http://www.sarpa.co.za/.

[13]Marc Levinson, *The Box: How the Shipping Container Made the World Smaller and the World Economy Bigger* (Princeton, NJ: Princeton University Press, 2006).

[14]The Panama Canal is an example of a once-vital location that lost importance. Containers moving from Asia to Europe no longer have to travel through the canal. Today, containers are often delivered to the West Coast and transported by rail to Gulf or East Coast ports from which other ships take them to Europe.

[15]For more on the causes of increased international commerce, see Paul Krugman, Richard Cooper, and T.N. Srinivasan, "Growing World Trade: Causes and Consequences," *Brookings Papers on Economic Activity* 25, no. 1 (1995): 327–77.

ocean-borne commerce doubled to and from the United States. The previous doubling took 60 years.

Choosing What to Produce: Specialization and Comparative Costs

How do people choose what to produce, and what do they get in return? In our last transaction when you gave me money in exchange for the object I did not ask where it came from. Disregarding robbery, your only possible source was payment from others for something you sold them. But that left a deeper question. When people decide what to produce and what to acquire by trade, how do they avoid leaving some valuable goods unproduced? Is it possible to coordinate our choices without a dictator who assigns specific persons to produce specific goods? Exactly who produces which goods is important, because peoples' competencies differ. As you will see, some possible assignments of production leave the society with more of *all* goods than other assignments. What happens if instead of being assigned to certain tasks people choose their specializations based on what they think is best for themselves?

Production Sets and Marginal Costs

Again we start in an unreal world and slowly make it more real. There are only two people, you and I, but now there are two goods, anchovies (A) and bananas (B). Each of us has certain skills and other productive assets—physical strength, mental ability, landholdings, and our own toolboxes. Over a day my resources can produce some combination of A and B that lies on the line shown in Figure 2-3a. If all I do is tend my banana trees I get three bananas and no anchovies. If I spend all day fishing I can catch six anchovies but get no bananas. Assume further that I can effortlessly and instantly switch between A and B and do not value the leisure time I would get by producing neither.

The line on Figure 2-3a is the outer boundary of my *production set,* the shaded triangle below the line and above the axes. It shows both my possibilities and my limits—with my available resources I cannot produce four anchovies and two bananas, but I can produce one of each. But instead of (1A, 1B), I can produce a combination like (2A, 2B) that has more of both goods. At (1A, 1B) I may be using all my resources but not as productively as possible—trying to pick bananas with my anchovy fishing net and trying to capture anchovies with my banana-picking knife. Using the net to catch anchovies and the

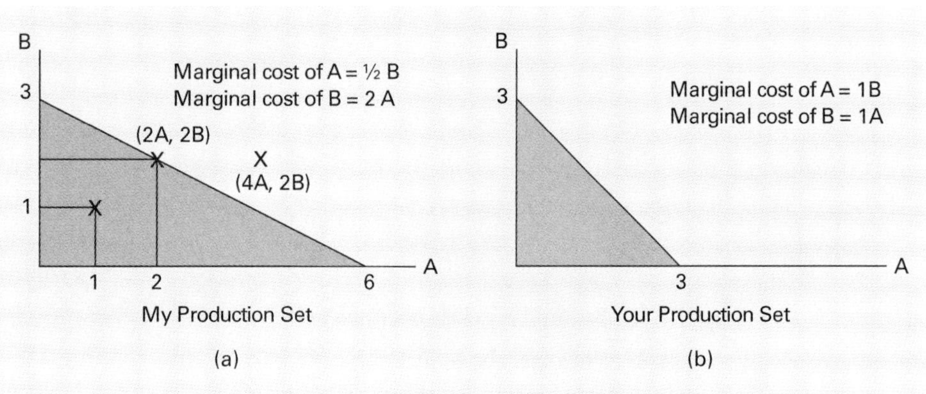

FIGURE 2-3
Production Sets and Marginal Costs

knife to cut bananas off the tree gets me more of both goods. We call a point inside the production set like (1A, 1B) *economically inefficient.*

Points on the set's boundary are *economically efficient.* If there only two goods, a combination of A and B is efficient if for a given output of A I am producing the most possible B (or vice versa). Equivalently, the combination is efficient if producing more A requires that I reduce my output of B. Either definition says I am on the boundary of my production set. I want to produce efficiently (remember, I don't value leisure time) but can choose from many combinations of A and B. If I work only for myself I will choose the combination that makes me best off, given my personal preferences and opportunity costs.

The costs that matter are those I can avoid by making a different choice. They are known as *marginal costs.* With only two goods the marginal cost of an anchovy is the number of bananas I forgo when I choose to produce it. The slope of the boundary shows that the marginal cost of an anchovy is half a banana, and the marginal cost of a banana is two anchovies. If there are more than two goods, we will need to look at their dollar prices, as we do in a later chapter. For now, just having two goods forces us to remember that any choice entails forgone alternatives. Everything we just said about production sets applies to yours as well. Figure 2-3b shows that in absolute terms you are less productive than I am. With the exception of a specialization at three bananas your set lies inside mine. Our differing resources explain the differences between our production sets. If you produce only for yourself you will probably enjoy fewer of both goods than I do. Your marginal cost of an anchovy is one banana, and that of a banana is one anchovy.

Efficiency by Command

With just two of us economic efficiency depends on who specializes in which good. Assume that you and I produce all of our outputs to satisfy the desires of another person, called a boss. (How you and I survive is left to our imaginations.) Figure 2-4 shows the combinations we can produce under different specializations. As a starting point assume that both of us specialize in anchovies. I produce six and you produce three for the boss, shown on the diagram as (9A, 0B). The next day our boss wants variety, in the form of one banana. Because the boss enjoys both goods, he wants us to produce as many anchovies as possible along with the banana. Marginal costs determine the efficient pattern of specialization. If I produce the first banana, the boss forgoes two anchovies, but if you produce it only one anchovy is lost. You are less productive in an absolute sense, but you are the lower marginal cost producer of bananas. In Figure 2-4, this means starting from (9A, 0B) and moving northwest to (8A, 1B). Assigning me to produce the first

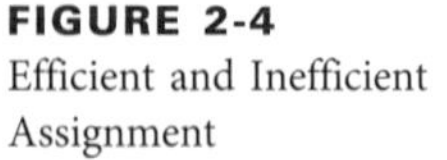
FIGURE 2-4
Efficient and Inefficient Assignment

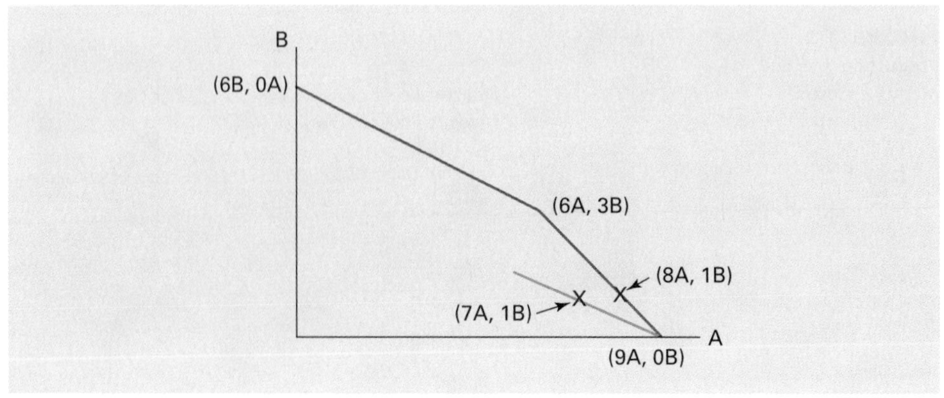

banana is a big mistake, as we now move up the dotted line to an inefficient mix of (7A, 1B). If the boss reassigns us we will produce more of both goods, as shown by the arrow pointing northeast.

If the boss wants a second or third banana a day those too should be your responsibility. When three are produced our output is six anchovies and three bananas. There is no alternative to having me produce the fourth banana, because you already specialize in them. That one (and the fifth and sixth, if wanted) comes at a higher marginal cost—two anchovies rather than just one. The production set for the entire economy is bowed outward.[16] If we both start as specialists in bananas, efficient production has me making the first anchovies, because I am the lower marginal cost producer of them. Not producing according to the marginal cost rule brings inefficiency; reassigning us according to it brings more of both goods. If there were more than two people to produce the two goods, we could still rank them by marginal cost and use the same rule.

Q. Is it possible for one person to be the lower marginal cost producer of both goods? Explain why or why not.

Efficiency by Trade

Restart the story. You and I are the only people on earth and neither of us is aware that the other exists. I produce my most desired mix of A and B, and you do the same for yourself. Assume that when I produce for myself I choose a bundle of two anchovies and two bananas, but your preferred production is two anchovies and one banana. (These are just starting points—we could have chosen any other combinations on the boundaries of their production sets.) One day we meet. Luckily we speak the same language, but neither of us knows anything about the other's production set or consumption habits. We have a rather stilted conversation:

Me: I like both anchovies and bananas (that's why I currently produce some of each), but whenever I produce a banana I give up two anchovies. If I could get that banana and lose fewer anchovies I'd be better off.

You: I've got a different problem. I'd like another anchovy but producing it means I lose a whole banana. If I gave up a banana and got more than one anchovy for it I'd be better off.

Me: Looks like we can make a deal. You're better off selling me the banana if you get more than one anchovy for it, and I'm better off getting it from you as long as I pay fewer than two anchovies for it.

You: How about you giving me 1.5 anchovies and I give you a banana.

Me: Done. Let's deliver to each other at 5 p.m. tomorrow.

In real life we would probably never tell each other about our marginal costs and valuations of the goods. Even if you did I would have no good reason to believe you and

[16]This reasoning may help solve a mystery from your first economics class. Early in that course you may have been introduced to the economy's production set (guns versus butter). Opportunity cost explained why its boundary sloped downward, but it was harder to see why it was bowed outward. Our reasoning in this section explains why.

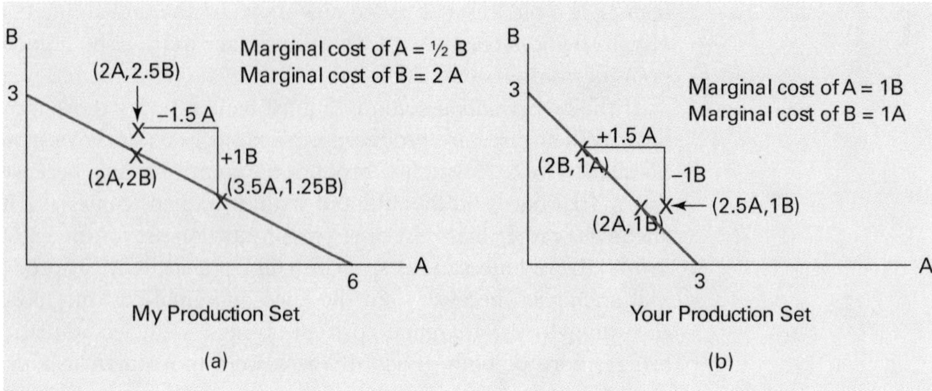

FIGURE 2-5 The Gains from Exchange

vice versa. You might start by asking for a lot of anchovies, and I might counter by offering very few. Where we will finally wind up (between one and two anchovies for the banana) is anybody's guess. The one thing we can be almost sure about is that a deal will go down. If we walk away we will both be worse off than if we had traded.

Figure 2-5 shows how the trade benefits the two of us. First, my production set shows that I will continue producing two anchovies for myself like before, along with the 1.5 that I will trade. I will also continue to produce 1.25 bananas. (Check this as you read along.) Break the trade into two steps shown by the arrows. If the banana you produce arrives first, I temporarily have 3.5 anchovies and 2.25 bananas. After shipping you the promised 1.5 anchovies I end up with 2 anchovies and 2.25 bananas. After trade, I can consume a bundle of goods that my production set does not allow me to produce for myself. All of this reasoning also holds for you, as can be seen by looking at your production set. After the goods change hands you have 2.5 anchovies and 1 banana, a combination you cannot produce on your own.[17]

Q. Using a diagram like Figure 2-5, show that you and I will be unable to reach a mutually beneficial agreement that has me sending bananas to you and you sending anchovies to me.

Q. A natural disaster occurs that shifts your production set downward but parallel to itself, while leaving mine unchanged. Show that we can both still benefit from an exchange like the one we discussed.

Why the Example Matters

If this story generalizes it also tells us a lot. I give you the anchovies not because I care about your well-being, but because I care about mine, and you have no charitable

[17]In this example I consume two anchovies both before and after trade, and you continue to consume one banana. This is not necessary and is only done to make the exposition easier. After trade opens up I may well want to produce more anchovies to go with the additional bananas, and you may want to produce a few more bananas.

feelings toward me that lead you to send out the banana. Caring only about our individual selves looks like a sure recipe for chaos and poverty. Here it It is not. When we trade we make each other wealthier. Both of us are able to consume bundles of goods that we could not produce as individuals. The pattern of specialization is efficient: the lower marginal cost producer of each good concentrates on it and trades for some of the other good. We do not require a boss to order us into the efficient specialization. Instead, we fall into that pattern out of self-interest.

Trade benefits both of us but does not necessarily make us more equal—my standard of living is higher than yours both before and after. But both of us are better off than if we had not traded at all. Some factor that we did not specify gives me a larger production set. Maybe I am better educated, am stronger, or own more tools. Maybe you have less of those resources, or maybe you just prefer to work fewer hours. In the language of Chapter 1, that our living standards both improve is a positive statement, one about what has actually happened. Your like or dislike for our remaining differences is a normative judgment.

Our spontaneous trade and choice of specializations has another interesting property. When we made our agreement neither of us needed to know anything about the other's costs or valuations or about other aspects of the other person's life. (The earlier conversation mentioned costs and valuations purely for your benefit.) Chapter 1 showed that information is a scarce and costly resource. To efficiently assign us to anchovies and bananas the boss had to somehow find out our individual marginal costs and the sizes of our production sets. With two people and two goods this sounds simple, but if there are ten people and ten goods, and each person produces only one of them there are 3.6 million ways to make the assignment. Planning is not costless—the people and computers who construct and supervise plans are unavailable to produce other valuable goods and services.

Q. Assume that there are five persons and five goods, and each person specializes in one of them. Show that there are 120 possible assignments of persons to goods.

Q. I like to eat zucchini and hate to eat turnips. Why might I nevertheless devote part of my garden to turnips?

NATIONS AND PERSONS

Early in the nineteenth century, the English economist David Ricardo first explained the benefits of specialization and trade using relative marginal costs. In his words you had a *comparative advantage* as the low marginal cost producer of bananas and I had one in anchovies. The fact that I had an *absolute advantage* by being more productive in both still meant we could both benefit from trade. Now we will apply this reasoning to the question Ricardo first approached—how nations and people benefit from specialization and trade.

Ireland: What Happened to the Potatoes?

The potato originated in the Americas and was a staple food of the Peruvian Incas. In the 1700s, it came to Ireland, where the damp climate and boggy terrain were suited to its cultivation. The potato is one of the very few foods that includes all known necessary human nutrients. By the early 1800s, 90 percent of Ireland's rapidly growing population ate only potatoes, an amazing total of 8 to 14 pounds per adult every day.[18] Then came disaster. Every year from 1845 to 1849 a severe blight destroyed most of the crop. The resulting famine killed approximately 2 million of Ireland's 9 million people, and more than a million of the survivors emigrated to the United States and Canada. A century after the famine Ireland was northern Europe's poorest nation, still producing more potatoes per person than any other on earth.

Fast forward to the twenty-first century. Ireland has replaced the United States as the world's largest exporter of software, mostly to Europe but also to the United States.[19] Between 1990 and 2003, employment in Ireland's information technology industry rose from 19,000 to 90,000.[20] Land planted in potatoes fell from 1.8 million acres in 1867 to 30,000 in 2007.[21] Ireland now imports most of its potatoes from the United States. As for the United States, it is still a net exporter of software, but imports have been rising rapidly relative to exports. Between 1998 and 2008, programmers employed in the United States fell by 31.3 percent.[22] The United States never imported many potatoes, but by 2004 it had become the world's largest exporter of them.[23]

Think of Ireland and the United States like you would think of persons. Each has a variety of skills and productive assets that give them differently sized production sets and different marginal costs. In reality both produce and exchange many goods with many countries. To model the basics of the switch in specialization, for now we will assume that there are no other countries and no other goods. In Figure 2-6, Ireland's production set in 1990 (before the changes began) is the lower line in the top graph. The country has relatively abundant land suited for potatoes, little skilled labor, few computers, and limited opportunities to trade with Europe. At that time it is a high marginal cost producer of software and a low marginal cost producer of potatoes relative to the United States, and it produces the combination labeled "1990." Relative to Ireland, the United States has low marginal costs of software and high marginal costs of potatoes. Its output mix favors software at the point labeled "1990" on its production set.

After 1990, both countries' production sets shift, in different ways and for different reasons. A nation with more resources has a larger production set but not all resources are equally productive in both of the goods. Ireland gained two important resources that raised its productivity in software but not in potatoes. First, U.S. companies, including Intel and

---

[18]These and other fascinating facts appear in John E. Davies, "Giffen Goods, the Survival Imperative, and the Irish Potato Culture," *Journal of Political Economy* 102, no. 3 (1994): 547–65.

[19]I Accenture Consulting, *ICT – The Indispensable Sector in the Knowledge Based Economy* (2004), unnumbered. http://www.ictireland.ie/Sectors/ICT/ICTDoclib4.nsf/wvICSS/26103E439DEC7B9680256F6D00587A3C/$File/Accenture+report-final-+Nov04.pdf.

[20]*Ibid.*

[21]Central Statistics Office, Statistical Yearbook of Ireland 2008, p. 196, http://www.cso.ie/releasespublications/documents/statisticalyearbook/2008/Statistical%20Yearbook%202008%20for%20web%20complete.pdf. Figures on pounds produced are not directly available.

[22]The drop has been from 574,000 to 394,000 programmers. See U.S. Bureau of Labor Statistics, Occupational Employment and Wages, 2002 at http://www.bls.gov/news.release/archives/ocwage11192003.pdf and Occupational Employment and Wages, 2008 at http://www.bls.gov/news.release/pdf/ocwage.pdf.

[23]U.S. Department of Agriculture, *Track Records, United States Crop Production, March 1998*, http://www.usda.gov/nass/pubs/track98d.htm#Potatoes; U.S. National Agricultural Statistics Service, Agricultural Statistics Data Base, http://www.nass.usda.gov:81/ipedb/.

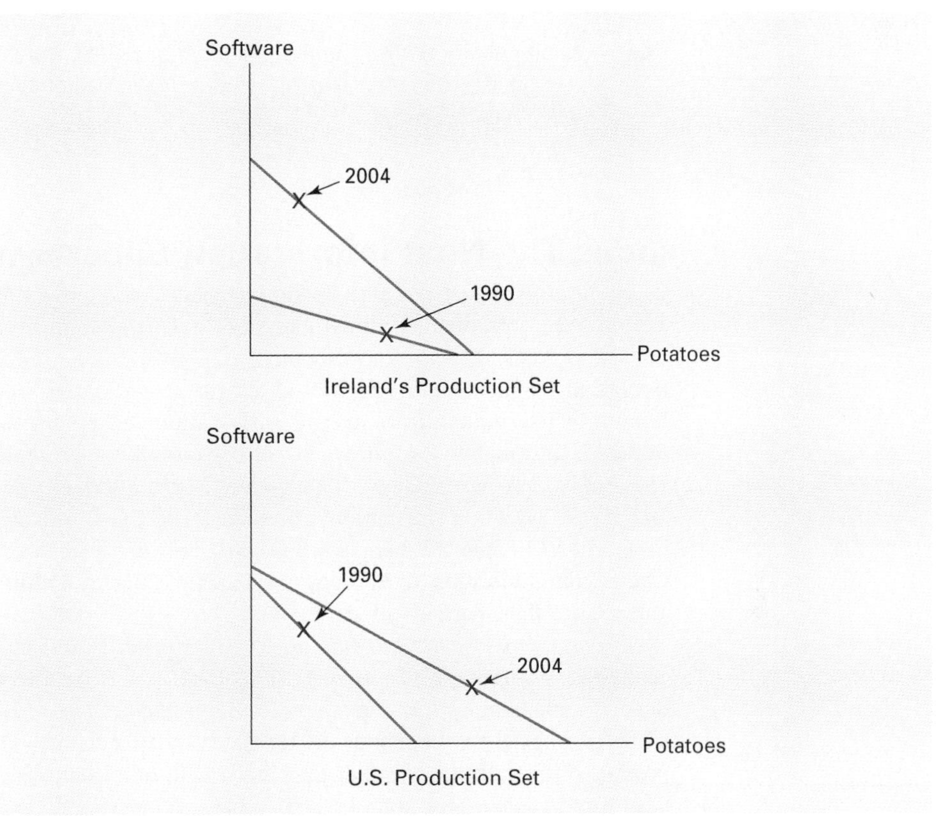

FIGURE 2-6
Changing Specializations: Ireland and the U.S.

Microsoft, opened large operations in Ireland, hoping to take advantage of its relatively low wages and closeness to continental Europe. Their modern plants increased Ireland's productivity in software and other information technology products but not in potatoes. Second, after English-speaking Ireland became a member of the European Union all of its barriers to trade with the continent fell. Ireland responded by going beyond the duplication and resale of U.S. software. The technology base of U.S. plants spurred the growth of Ireland's own software industry, which could better tailor its products to the newly accessible European markets.[24] Ireland's production set today is the upper line, with a lower marginal cost of software. It produces fewer potatoes and more software than it did in 1990.

Productivity in the U.S. software industry changed little over the 1990s; there were no cost-shifting innovations the size of Ireland's new plants and its improved access to markets. On the other hand, Ireland's potato industry changed little, while America's was transformed. Potato culture moved from Maine to Idaho, where new varieties of plants and harvesting equipment allowed output per acre to double. Other new U.S. technologies greatly lowered the costs of cutting, drying, packaging, and freezing the frozen french fries and powdered mashed potatoes that are replacing home-cooked potatoes almost everywhere. Ireland's potato imports (and most American exports) are almost entirely frozen or dried products. In Figure 2-6, the U.S. production set has shifted outward, and the lower slope indicates that its marginal cost of potatoes has fallen relative to software and relative to Ireland. As the marginal cost principle predicts, the United States moves toward a specialization in potatoes and away from software.

---

[24]Between 1992 and 2003 software writers in Irish companies rose by 600 percent, from 3,000 to 18,000. Dennis O'Hearn, *Inside the Celtic Tiger* (London: Pluto Press, 1998), 74–8.

Q. A small country whose people are often at risk of starvation would probably be better off if it concentrated on growing food rather than weaving high-quality textiles. Right? Explain.

India: The Next Information Superpower

Economists used to have a fairly simple model of international trade. They started by assuming that productive inputs like labor and land were immobile between countries, but the outputs they produced could easily cross borders. Those assumptions are still important for manufactured goods and farm products, but the twentieth century's revolutions in telecommunications and information technology have forced us to rethink things. If information can flow cheaply between countries their patterns of employment and production will change. The skills of workers today produce valuable information and ideas that can cross national boundaries at the speed of light. If information and ideas are so mobile the people who create and use them can reside almost anywhere. Cheap communication technology is a resource that can shift national production sets and change their patterns of trade.

The stereotype of India is one of desperate poverty, and many of its billion-plus citizens fit that stereotype all too well. But India also has colleges and universities that produce 260,000 engineers and many more math and science graduates every year, virtually all fluent in English.[25] For four decades after independence in 1947, India's governments promoted self-sufficiency rather than trade with other nations. Recent governments have been more hospitable to international trade and investment, and telecommunications has brought the country into the rest of the world. Almost overnight the south Indian city of Bangalore became a home or branch office to 1,180 information technology (IT) companies. Some carry familiar American names, like Dell, Intel, and Yahoo. Others are Indian, like Wipro and Cognizant, whose stocks already trade on NASDAQ. Indian software exports are currently rising at 35 percent per year, and 75 percent of them go to the United States.[26] Bangalore has more IT engineers (150,000) than California's Silicon Valley (120,000).[27] The opening of trade and modern telecommunications allowed India's engineers to create more value than they could before.[28] Their wages were low relative to wages in countries whose businesses had access to broader markets. Economic openness has allowed Indian engineers to move into IT and away from the domestic industries they formerly served.[29]

---

[25]"The Rise of India," *Business Week*, December 8, 2003.

[26]"Bangalore Software Exports Forecast to Soar by 35 Percent," October 29, 2003, SpaceDaily Web site, http://www.spacedaily.com/2003/031029093845.w44ugb1s.html. For comparison, Microsoft Corporation's worldwide revenue is growing at 13.5 percent per year.

[27]"The Rise of India."

[28]Some believe India's former isolation in part explains the high quality of software produced there. Many Indians learned programming on castoff early-generation computers from the United States and Europe, short on memory and slow in processing. The need to economize on calculations and memory turned users into superior writers of code. "Boomgalore," *Wired* 8 (March 2000), http://www.wired.com/wired/archive/8.03/bangalore.html.

[29]In an odd connection with the previous topic, the Irish Software Association is also exploring alliances with India for its members. See Irish Software Association, *Developments in the Software Sector, Annual Review 2005-2006*, 9. http://www.software.ie/Sectors/ISA/ISADoclib3.nsf/dafa0ab2f3f9f3b680256edf004936de/b3da587715db9a48802571c400624b0f/$FILE/ISA%20REVIEW%202006_Sat_1Apr.pdf.

What Are Resources?

Today oil is called a resource, though it took thousands of years before anyone discovered its uses as a fuel and a feedstock for chemicals. Oil became a resource when people invented ways to create value with it. Before then it was largely a nuisance that seeped out of the ground in some locales. The map of the world does not change, but spots on it can become valuable resources. The busiest cargo airport in the world is Hong Kong's. The second busiest is in Anchorage, Alaska, a city that is ten hours or less from almost 80 percent of the industrial world. Some convenience stores prosper because they are on people's routes from home to work, while sellers of luxury goods pay large amounts to locate on Beverly Hills' Rodeo Drive or Tokyo's Omotesando Dori. Bangalore's location thousands of miles from the United States and Europe was once a major detriment, but telecommunications have turned it into a resource. Because Bangalore is ten and a half time zones away from the United States, Americans can work on programming and design projects during their daytime and send them to India for further work during the Indian day.

Telecommunications have increased the value and pay of English speakers around the world. Before the coming of toll-free telephone numbers, telemarketing and call-in services such as travel reservations (since taken over by the Internet) were minor industries.[30] As these services grew in volume during the 1970s, Omaha, Nebraska, became home to the largest number of call centers. Its location became a resource because it was in the center of the country, which was important when rates varied more with distance than they do today. It also had the highest-capacity telecommunications network of any major city because it was adjacent to Strategic Air Command Headquarters during the Cold War. As growth drove up the wages of call-center workers in Omaha, their owners discovered another resource. They set up shop in farm towns where job opportunities were vanishing with population decline.[31] What happened in Omaha is now happening in India, and for the same reason—high-quality telecommunications now make English-speaking call-center workers there an economical alternative to Americans.[32]

Some U.S. companies are developing new resources after discovering that the costs of outsourcing to India are higher than they expected. They see few benefits in the time difference and believe labor in Bangalore has become uneconomically expensive relative to the value of its output. Some are experimenting with outsourcing to South America. They believe South American workers will cost less than Indian workers, and time zone differences cause more problems than they solve. North and South America are in similar time zones, and both have increasingly bilingual workforces that can communicate as problems arise over the working day.[33] You can be almost certain that by the time you have finished this book some people will have begun trying out still other locations.

---

[30]Note to business students: Before the introduction of 1-800 numbers, some AT&T executives expected them to flop. The executives said they could not understand why anyone would pay to receive calls from people unknown to them. "In Business, Good Connections Mean 800 Numbers," *Omaha Times-Herald*, August 2, 1992.

[31]Ibid. See also "Texas Getting the Call / State's Cities Big and Small Get a Nice Ringing in Their Ears from the Hundreds of Jobs Created When Nationwide Phone Banks Set up Shop," *Houston Chronicle*, May 12, 1996.

[32]"Where Your Job is Going," *Fortune*, November 10, 2003. Some Indian call centers train employees to speak with American regional accents, and some post U.S. baseball and basketball news to help them make small talk with customers.

[33]"A New Tide in Offshore Outsourcing," *Business Week*, January 12, 2004.

ECONOMIC INSTITUTIONS

What Institutions Are

Thus far production and exchange have taken place on a rather empty stage, an unreal venue without personal relationships, laws, or social conventions. In the models thus far both you and I have attempted to maximize our individual gains. There was no mention of forces in the background that influenced what we could and could not do. Those forces include our society's laws and *norms* (generally accepted conventions about how to behave). Without these formal and informal rules, one or both of us might have been unwilling to trade, and we would have both forgone some benefits. We abided by the rules even though one of us might have gained even more by violating them. After I handed you the object, you could have run away without handing me the money. Or possibly after you gave me the money I could have given you an object of lower quality than promised. Even if I offer you a warranty I might choose not to honor it.

Economic institutions define the environment in which we can trade. As an example, criminal law is one of many conditions that will affect the trades we can and cannot make. That law limits our opportunities—it threatens me with punishment that may be severe enough to deter me from stealing your goods or offering to sell you something illegal, whether these are goods I have stolen from someone else or some illegal substance. The law also expands our opportunities: If the law makes people less likely to steal what you produce, you can be more confident of earning a return on your investment in a facility to produce them. Institutions differ among societies. Some governments, for instance, allow unrestricted copying of software or refuse to enforce laws against it, while others enforce intellectual property law more vigilantly. Institutions like laws can change with their environment. When equipment to duplicate music and video recordings was costly, few people could make unauthorized copies, and producers seldom initiated lawsuits against them. Now unauthorized copying has so seriously affected the entertainment industry that it is investing large amounts in lawsuits and introducing product designs intended to make copying difficult.[34]

Other Examples of Institutions

Contracting Transactions are often far more complex than an immediate transfer of goods for cash. If you sell hot dogs at the ballpark, both my income as a baker and yours as a vendor depend on a delivery of 5,000 buns four hours before game time. Because you will take a substantial loss if they are too few, too late, or too early, our agreement may specify that you need only pay if I meet delivery conditions exactly. You may own a hotel and contract with me to deliver all of your natural gas requirements, which are large on cold days and small on warm ones. If we have agreed on a price the contract will probably prohibit me from rerouting your deliveries to someone who offers me more on a cold day, and it will not allow you to abandon me for a supplier who temporarily offers you gas for less. I may produce a good custom-built to your specifications that I can only sell elsewhere at a loss if you refuse to take delivery. Our contract (or a court) will probably require you to pay me the difference if you refuse the good. The delivery and payment obligations in these examples are only a small sample of the many commitments that would increase the economic value a transaction creates for both of us.

---

[34]Stan J. Leibowitz, "File Sharing: Creative Destruction or Just Plain Destruction," *Journal of Law and Economics* 49 (April 2006): 1–28; and Alejandro Zentner, "Measuring the Effect of File-Sharing on Music Purchases," *Journal of Law and Economics* 49 (April 2006): 63–90.

The laws of contracts and their enforceability in court will determine the range of transactions that we will find it worthwhile to undertake.

Market Protocols Buyers and sellers often agree to use *market protocols* to propose and make transactions. A protocol may be imposed from above, like the U.S. government's systems for auctioning Treasury bills[35] and telecommunications frequencies,[36] or it may have evolved over time, like the practices automobile dealers use to buy and sell used cars among themselves.[37] Auctions are an institution where the protocols may determine a participant's best bidding strategy and the expected revenue of the seller. Participants in an English auction (like those for high-end works of art) make bids in ascending order. Its protocol may further specify that any new bid must exceed the last by a preset amount or that the highest bidder must pay immediately or lose the item to the next highest. A Dutch auction (originally from wholesale flower markets in Holland) starts with a one-handed clock that initially points to a far higher price than any buyer is willing to pay. As the hand moves it shows lower prices. The first buyer to bid gets the item at that price. A second-price auction is like an English auction, but the high bidder pays only the second-highest bid. The bidder's strategy depends on the auction institution. Later you will see that the best strategy in a second-price auction is to bid your true valuation of the object, but in an English auction you should bid less than that. The different protocols in these three types of auctions lead rational bidders to choose different strategies.

Q. You are a seller who wishes to auction a single item to a group whose individual valuations you do not know. Which of these protocols would you choose to use? What factors are you taking into account?

Etiquette Whether two strangers can arrange a transaction that benefits them both can depend on whether they meet each other's expectations before the transaction. I may need to credibly show that I am likely to deliver as promised, and you must convince me that you are likely to pay the agreed-upon amount. Etiquette is an economic institution that can greatly ease the process by which a transaction moves from proposal to commitment. Parties from different cultures may have particular problems distinguishing behavior that is acceptable from behavior that is not. Some observers have commented that Americans negotiating with Americans often prefer to state their areas of disagreement upfront, whereas Asians negotiating with Asians often wait to air their differences in hopes of achieving a better climate for compromise.[38] If an American and an Asian are unaware of each other's etiquette, a valuable transaction could be lost.

---

[35] Sushil Bikhchandani and Chi-fu Huang, "The Economics of Treasury Securities Markets," *Journal of Economic Perspectives* 7 (Summer 1993): 117–34.

[36] See the Federal Communications Commission Web page at http://wireless.fcc.gov/auctions/.

[37] David Genesove, "Search at Wholesale Auto Auctions," *Quarterly Journal of Economics* 110 (February 1995): 23–49.

[38] See, for example, Scott Seligman, *Chinese Business Etiquette* (New York: Warner Books, 1999). There are almost surely equivalent books in Chinese that explain U.S. business etiquette. The U.S. Government also provides information on etiquette in connection with the Department of Commerce's mission to expand trade. For example, its guide to Middle Eastern business practices and manners is at http://web.ita.doc.gov/ticwebsite/FAQs.nsf/6683dce2e5871df9852565bc00785ddf/1af083a655bca2a085256c870056fe3b!OpenDocument.

THE GOVERNANCE OF TRANSACTIONS

Three Forms of Governance

Transactions are fundamental units, and breaking more complex activities into transactions can be of great help in analyzing them. Transactions take place under *governance* arrangements that describe the opportunities available to the parties and the constraints under which they operate. The concept of governance will often allow us to see common factors in seemingly dissimilar transactions. Many business choices, for example whether to buy a good or produce it yourself, are choices of a mode of governance. This book is centered on three fundamental modes: markets, contracts, and hierarchies.

Markets A household buys vegetables and a business buys office supplies by selecting one of the alternative sellers in a *market*. We will soon define markets more precisely, but for now think of them as facilitating the purchase and sale of standardized goods or services, often in repeated transactions. At market-clearing prices supply equals demand, so participants can usually rest assured that shortages or surpluses will not frustrate their expectations. Each buyer has (and is aware of) many suppliers and can switch among them at very low cost. Each seller has many potential buyers and has low costs of starting or ending a relationship with any one of them. Low switchover costs are more likely for standardized goods and services, particularly if buyers and sellers have little to gain from personalized, extended relationships. In markets, for example, a seller will not invest in a specialized facility whose value is at risk if its relationship with a particular buyer ends. In markets goods are interchangeable, and so are the parties who transact in them.

Contracts A contract is a set of promises intended to create economic value and enforceable by a court or some other agency, such as an arbitrator. Often a buyer and seller can increase the economic value they create by engaging in an unstandardized transaction. The natural gas market, for example, covers North America and contains thousands of producers, marketers, and brokers.[39] A buyer such as a large industrial user often wants deliveries of unpredictable daily amounts. A contract between that buyer and some seller saves the buyer the transaction cost of going to market every day for an unpredictable amount of gas, and it might further specify a predictable price that helps both parties avoid risk in the market.

To make the agreement work, the buyer and seller must make commitments. The seller can only offer flexible deliveries if it builds a storage facility that loses value if this buyer vanishes. This could happen if the buyer is the only large one in the area, and the seller's storage facility cannot be cheaply torn down and moved elsewhere. A contract that protects the seller's investment might run for years and require that the buyer only buy from the seller. The parties get predictable prices and ensured deliveries, but the contract also forecloses them from some benefits of using the market to take advantage of short-term price fluctuations in it. Over the long term, however, both parties can expect that the contract will create more economic value (net of transaction costs) than either could get by taking its chances in the market. The storage facility is a *specific investment,* one that cannot be redeployed into equally valuable uses if the buyer leaves the seller. For the storage to be worth building the parties must agree to a long-term, enforceable relationship memorialized by a contract.

[39]Gas is so standardized that it trades by heat content (millions of British thermal units) rather than volume (cubic feet). In most states homes are supplied by a single utility company that distributes gas to all small customers in the area, and customers do not legally have a choice of supplier. In other areas, large industrial and commercial users can choose to buy gas from a marketer or broker who pays to use the local distributor's pipes.

Hierarchies The determination and payment of prices are fundamental in transactions governed by markets or contracts. By contrast, *hierarchies* are command-based systems in which prices usually play a relatively smaller role. You cannot order a seller in a market to deliver goods without an agreed-upon price, and unless both agree to a change the parties to a contract can trade only at prices specified in it. In a hierarchy, a superior can order a subordinate to do something without determining a price for that service. For instance, each worker on an assembly line receives an hourly wage to perform one of a sequence of tasks that will yield a finished product. If one worker calls in sick it will be too costly to advertise, interview, and select a replacement, that is, to use the labor market. The employer also does not want to fire the sick person and lose the productivity of someone with years of experience. But without someone doing this person's job production will fall to zero. In this hierarchy the supervisor can use judgment to arrive at a temporary fix. She might call in someone from the loading dock for the day or ask people who work near the missing person to make some extra efforts.[40]

It is impossible (too costly) to write a contract that covers all possible situations that might arise in a workplace. There is no way to enumerate all of the possible assignments the person on the loading dock might be given in an emergency, or to reach agreement with that person on specific pay for each of them. Unless the line keeps moving there will be no income for anyone in the hierarchy. Assigning the supervisor the right to cope with the emergency cuts the cost of decision making, which includes the costs of an incorrect fix. If the workers made a group decision on how to fill the vacancy they would lose production time and their individual choices might depend on personal factors rather than an interest in efficient production. (And what if they cannot agree unanimously?) A hierarchy that gives certain persons rights to give orders and others an obligation to follow them resolves the problem without going to market and without the cost of writing a contract. Workers receive predictable wages that are independent of their exact assignments, and these wages are higher because individuals allow themselves to be directed in ways that enhance the group's productivity.

The Dimensions of Governance

Trade-offs Many managerial decisions entail choosing a mode of governance for some activity. The decisions are often about whether the firm itself will undertake certain activities or transact with outsiders for them, that is, they are about the company's *vertical* scope. The firm might own the mine that produces its raw material (hierarchical governance), enter into a delivery agreement with a producer (contract), or buy it in an assortment of short-term transactions (market). Choice of governance matters for many activities. For example, which parts of a firm's legal work will be performed by in-house lawyers and which by outside law firms? Can management better cope with rising health costs by contracting with an insurer that allows employees to choose their doctors or by putting doctors on the payroll and requiring employees to use them? Looking toward customers, when will management prefer to sell the firm's product at wholesale to any retailer who wants to resell it, and when will it prefer to contract with a single retailer and no others? The best choice depends on accurately assessing the costs and benefits of the various modes of governance. The rest of this book is largely about how to analyze that choice.

Mixed Modes of Governance A given transaction can take place under a mix of governance modes. For instance, during a game a professional baseball player is a

[40]Large assembly-line operations often have reserve workers with certain skills available in the plant or on call to fill in these randomly occurring gaps.

subordinate who takes orders from persons above him in a hierarchy. The team's manager announces where he will bat in the lineup, and if he is running the third-base coach tells him whether to stop or try for home plate. A written contract that runs for several years outlines the basics of the relationship between the player and the team's owners. Beyond his pay it will specify such other duties such as showing up in good condition for every game and being available for media interviews. The contract might also provide incentives such as a bonus for exceeding a certain number of home runs. At various points in his career the player participates in a market. Teams initially compete to sign him, and his contract will specify how soon he may become a free agent and negotiate with any interested team. Later, you will see that virtually all employment relationships are a mix of governance arrangements like this one.

Relationships like the baseball player's are based on written contracts that are costly to negotiate and enforce. The costs of contracting over unlikely events (of which there are many in most employment situations) may not be worth the benefits. The parties can, however, get some of the benefits of a contract even without a written one. Long-lived employment relationships have aspects of unwritten or *implicit contracts*. (Notice the rarity of detailed written contracts outside of sports, entertainment, and high-level executives.) Even if the parties could write a contract, it would be costly to engage lawyers to enforce or modify it. The worker and employer might be better off with an ongoing, unwritten understanding that allows both of them to adapt to conditions that can change unpredictably. Understanding the adaptations in such a *relational* agreement will also require a longer look at governance.

Chapter Summary

The benefits of an exchange are determined by the seller's opportunity cost (value of the next-best alternative) and the buyer's valuation (maximum willingness to pay). The difference between these is the economic value that can be created.

- The price at which a buyer and seller should trade is a normative question. We are more interested in positive matters such as the amount of benefits they can share and how those benefits might be increased.
- Transaction costs affect the economic value an exchange can create and the distribution of its benefits between the parties. The innovator who cuts transaction costs potentially benefits both herself and the buyer and seller. Lower transaction costs can make some trades possible that were formerly not.
- Efficient production maximizes the output of one good for any given output of the other(s). Efficient specializations stem from the principle that whoever has the lower marginal cost of each good will produce the first units of it. In unplanned societies, people have incentives to specialize efficiently because doing so maximizes the economic value they can create.
- The principle of marginal costs explains why people gain from specialization and trade, regardless of their sizes, and it applies to trade between both nations and persons.
- Economic institutions define the environment in which people can arrange their transactions, and in some cases they also define the range of feasible transactions and the distribution of their benefits.

- Governance arrangements determine the environments within which transactions take place. We work with three modes—markets, contracts, and hierarchies. Many managerial decisions are about modes of governance that will structure their firm's transactions and define its relationships with outsiders.

Questions and Problems

1. How does the existence of money reduce the costs of making transactions, relative to a society based entirely on barter? English is becoming the usual language for international transactions, even if the language of neither country is English. How does this reduce the costs of transacting?
2. Why does Longo use salespeople instead of price tags? Why not just offer cars at a fixed discount under the sticker price? Or why not be like the General Motors Saturn and advertise a no bargaining policy?
3. My parking permit at the university gives me rights to use a very convenient lot reserved exclusively for faculty. Even if I arrive at a peak hour like 10 a.m. I can almost surely find a space in it. Your student permit allows you to park in an inconvenient lot that is often full by 9 a.m., sometimes forcing you to use an overflow lot and take a bus to campus. We would both be better off after a trade in which you paid me $100 for my permit and in return I used yours. Why might the school's administration make trades like these illegal even though they leave us both better off?
4. The local supermarket offers melons for $1 a pound, but the farmer who grows it receives only 20 cents. The remainder goes for the costs of transport and retailing. Under what circumstances would the farmer prefer to get a larger percentage? When might the consumer prefer that the farmer get more?
5. How is production different from theft? How does it differ from declaration of bankruptcy?
6. Jones purchases medical care from Smith, and the benefits from the exchange are divided between them. Is Smith profiting from Jones's misfortune? Does it matter for economic analysis how the transaction is described?
7. People with non-mainstream sexual preferences are a larger percentage of the population of large cities than small towns. Is this because cities encourage deviant behavior or might there be an economic explanation for this fact?
8. Jones and Smith have identical marginal costs for anchovies and bananas. Explain why mutually beneficial trade cannot take place between them.
9. There are two goods in the economy, anchovies (a fish) and bananas (a farm product). Draw the economy's production possibilities before and after a natural disaster that lowers the banana harvest but does not affect anchovies.

Part Two

Governance by Markets

Chapter 3

Markets

The gestures people are making in Figure 3-1 may not look like those of mentally sound people, and the jackets they are wearing might confirm your suspicions. Whatever they are doing, however, probably looks a lot more interesting than a picture of supply and demand.

In reality, Figure 3-1 *is* a picture of supply and demand. The people are floor traders at the New York Mercantile Exchange (NYMEX), buying and selling futures contracts in crude oil.[1] If you know the code you can read their hand signals and see the prices they are trying for and the amounts they want to trade. NYMEX is an outcry market where buyers and sellers call out prices in hopes of finding a match.[2] Because the pit (i.e., the circular steps they stand on) for a commodity might contain as many as 200 people, the traders use hand signals and find counterparties largely by eye contact. Each holds an

FIGURE 3-1

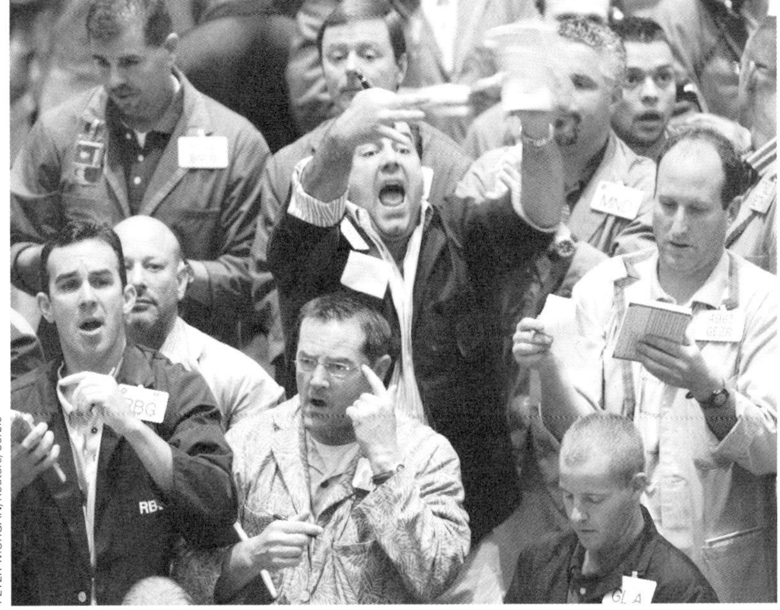
PETER MORGAN/Reuters/Corbis

[1]See the NYMEX Web site at http://www.nymex.com/index.aspx. Among many others, NYMEX contracts include natural gas, gasoline, copper, and aluminum.

[2]For more on the basics of NYMEX trading, see the organization's Web site at http://www.nymex.com/how_exchang_works.aspx?pg=0.

order book that identifies the counterparty and the price when an agreement is reached. Runners take the orders to a central point to be executed.

The man in the lower center is probably saying he wants to buy ten contracts for delivery in July.[3] (Left palm toward the face means buy, one finger means ten units, and pointed at the eye means July. Many trades require a sequence of signals.) His level right hand with index finger extended shows that he wants to pay the current price but with a final digit of 6. The open-mouthed man in the center probably wants to sell at a final digit of 8. As for the funny coats, brokerage firms choose colors for their representatives with an eye toward quick recognition.

The people in the picture are shaping an important part of the future. The trades they make commit their clients to deliver and take delivery in months to come at prices that are being determined today. If a new weather forecast predicts a poor harvest (and people believe it) today's prices for deliveries in future months will rise. The forecast change is an early warning of increased scarcity that everyone can see, and the earlier it comes the more options consumers and producers will have to adjust to it. If the forecast is wrong and prices stay low, those who bought at high prices will take losses. Nobody—including Washington pundits and the media—knows for sure whether or not the new weather forecast is right. And there is no Plan B to invoke if prices change unexpectedly. Because the world has to operate without a safety net, these people's gestures count for a lot.

This chapter is about how prices come to be what they are and how prices convey information. The last chapter was about individual transactions; this one is about how supply and demand help us analyze the effects of large numbers of transactions. We begin by examining markets as places where people trade goods and acquire information, in order to set the stage on which the forces of supply and demand determine prices. After we see how equilibrium is attained and its value as a predictive tool, we go on to examine how prices provide information and how people act on that information. In the process we will see how they link the present and the future, and get a better understanding of what the people in the picture are doing.

Buyers, Sellers, Goods, and Information

Markets are where people make comparisons. When you say you are in the market for a new car you probably mean you are acquiring information. That information might be about the characteristics of various models you are considering, the value of your trade-in, the price a certain dealer will offer you, or the reputation of that dealer. You acquire this information in different ways. Guidebooks or advertising can reveal a car's length or horsepower, but you probably must negotiate face-to-face with a salesperson to get a firm price. Conversations with acquaintances may be your only way to learn about a dealer's reputation. Dealers likewise learn about you. From a conversation they can tell how serious you are about buying. From a test drive they can estimate your current car's trade-in value. From a credit report they can infer your ability to finance the purchase. Markets reduce the transaction costs of making exchanges, and they raise the potential benefits to a seller or buyer by expanding the range of buyers and sellers available as counterparties.[4]

[3]A description of basic hand signals can be found at the Futures Technology Web site at http://www.futurestech.net/hand1.htm.

[4]There is clearly some cost involved in participating in a market (i.e., getting to a dealership and taking the time to bargain). Later you will see that such costs are important determinants of how businesses are organized.

Some markets are geographically centralized. Every large city contains a wholesale produce market, or terminal market, that usually occupies several square blocks. In predawn and early morning hours, the city's grocers, restaurants, and others compare prices and evaluate the quality of the goods being offered by the sellers who rent space. Having all of the sellers in one place lowers transaction costs, particularly for a good like produce that requires hands-on quality comparisons. Sellers in a central location have lower costs of finding buyers, and centralization can also increase the gains from operating as a specialist and further lower the costs of information.[5] The management of San Francisco's market publishes a weekly Internet newssheet on incoming produce, price trends, and newly available items.[6] A national association of produce market operators (who lease space to merchants) publishes detailed daily price data for major cities.[7]

Q. Most terminal markets have a rule that only qualified wholesale buyers can deal with sellers located in them. Why would the operators of a market want to exclude potential buyers, and why would sellers be willing to accept such a restriction as a condition of leasing space in them?

Some markets have standardized rules, often called "protocols," for trading. Every week the U.S. Treasury auctions short-term debt (called "T-bills") to large buyers, who mainly resell them.[8] The auction takes sealed bids under extremely precise rules. The Internet auction site eBay is another example of an auction that has numerous rules, ranging from registration of traders to when an auction will end (often specified by the seller) to how a seller can set a bid level that will close the auction and give the item to the first person bidding over that amount.[9] Bidding for multimillion dollar paintings at art auctions takes place under exceedingly complex rules. Even rejected bids contain information about market conditions that is valuable to the auction house and prospective sellers of other paintings. A seller maintains the option of removing a painting from the auction if bids fail to exceed a minimum reserve price, which is usually not revealed to bidders. Other aspects of the protocols allow bidders to keep their identities unknown to other bidders if they desire. (Why would they want to do this?) The protocols also include rules that ensure a clear transfer of ownership, which is valuable to all parties.[10]

Q. Why might a seller not want the reserve price revealed to potential buyers before the start of an auction?

---

[5]In Adam Smith's words, "the division of labor is limited by the extent of the market." Small cities probably have few specialists in individual vegetables, but you can meet the okra king of Los Angeles at Joel Kotkin, "Sublime Vegetables for a Demanding Niche," *New York Times*, January 21, 2001, http://www.diehardindian.com/news/2001Jan/26.htm.

[6]San Francisco Wholesale Produce Market Web site, http://www.sfproduce.org/news.html.

[7]See the Terminal.com Web site at http://www.terminalmarkets.com/usa.htm.

[8]See the U.S. Treasury's guide, "How Treasury Auctions Work," at http://www.treasurydirect.gov/instit/auctfund/work/work.htm.

[9]See eBay's summary of basic rules for buyers and sellers at http://pages.ebay.com/help/policies/overview.html.

[10]Sotheby's guides for buyers and sellers are at http://www.sothebys.com/help/buy/index.html and http://www.sothebys.com/help/sell/index.html. For description and analysis of many art auctions, see Orley Ashenfelter and Kathryn Graddy, "Auctions and the Price of Art," *Journal of Economic Literature* 41 (September 2003): 731–87.

Other markets are linked electronically and are less standardized. A worldwide network of banks and other financial institutions, for example, trades large quantities of currencies in the foreign exchange, or Forex, market.[11] In the U.S. natural gas industry, the third week of every month is "bidweek." Producers, large users, marketers, and brokers do not meet in any central place. During bidweek they are in contact by telephone and the Internet, negotiating prices for gas that will flow over the following month. The use of one market may entail participation in another—bidweek gas transactions require parties to simultaneously negotiate terms for pipeline transport, and risk management requires the use of specialized financial instruments.[12]

Still other markets are continuously in operation, rather than set in a single venue or restricted to certain dates or times. Houses in an urban area, for instance, change hands at unpredictable times as they are bought and sold, and a comprehensive sampling of all the opportunities is too costly for any buyer or seller to undertake. Wages emerge in markets for labor after limited searching by potential employers and employees. Sometimes one side of the market (usually sellers) does not actively make offers to individual buyers, preferring to give them a take-it-or-leave-it option in the form of a nonnegotiable price tag. Goods change hands in markets, and so does information. Sellers learn about the willingness of buyers to pay, and buyers learn about the prices sellers find acceptable. Sellers may learn about the offers of their rivals, and likewise for buyers. As they trade, some of that information is built into market price, through processes detailed in this chapter.

Markets themselves may increase the confidence traders have in the transactions they make. The parties may pay the market's organizers for the right to use it as a trading venue. Markets compete to attract traders—NASDAQ, the automated stock exchange, has made heavy inroads on the once-dominant role of the New York Stock Exchange, while the American Stock Exchange now handles only a small number of stocks (and now operates under NASDAQ). Beyond transaction services and liquidity, stock exchanges offer dispute resolution services that usually cost the parties far less to use than the courts. Sellers can cooperate to offer additional services through the market venue that would not be worthwhile for them to make individually. In a similar vein, Southern California is home to auto malls that contain as many as 24 competing dealerships. The dealers contribute to advertising that publicizes the mall and to supporting other services that can make visiting any dealer there a more attractive experience for customers.[13]

Demand

Willingness to Pay and Consumer Benefits

Let's generalize the ideas about valuation from Chapter 2. My *marginal valuation* is the maximum I will pay for another (possibly the first) unit of some good or service, all other things equal. If I hold three units of good A and am willing to pay up to $7 for a fourth unit, that amount is my marginal valuation of it. The step graph in Figure 3-2 shows how that valuation varies with the number of units I am consuming. In most situations it is safe to assume that marginal valuation declines with consumption—the first gallon of

[11]The Federal Reserve Bank of New York's useful reference on foreign exchange markets, "All About … The Foreign Exchange Market in the United States," is at http://www.ny.frb.org/education/addpub/usfxm/.

[12]For a description of these markets, see Bruce Henning, Michael Sloan, and Maria de Leon, *Natural Gas and Energy Price Volatility*, Energy and Environmental Analysis, Inc., Oct. 2003, I-5–I-10. See the information and deals offered by a pipeline transportation broker at http://www.capacitycenter.com.

[13]Cerritos Auto Square, for example, offers access to a Web page with Kelley Blue Book prices to help prospective buyers estimate trade-in values. Another page allows a customer to make a service appointment or order parts from any dealer in the group. See http://www.cerritosautosquare.com.

FIGURE 3-2
Marginal Value of A

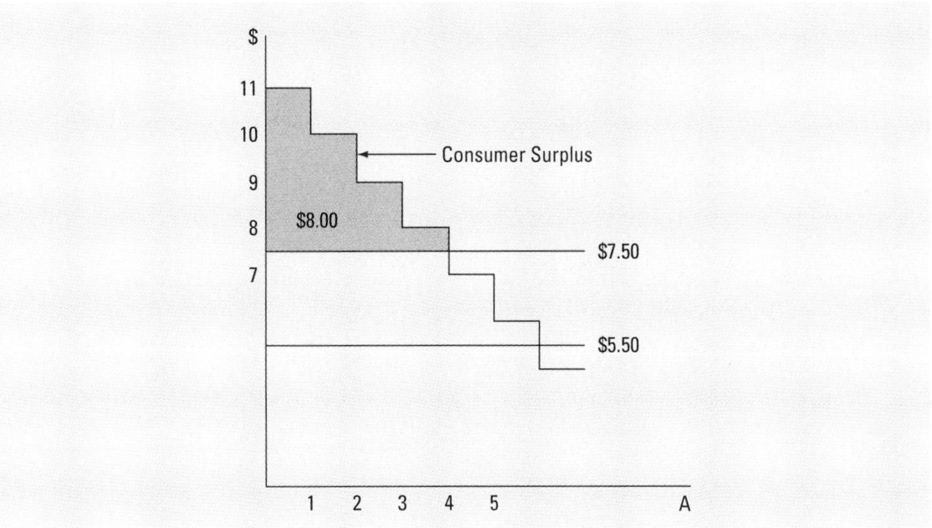

water a day may be the difference between life and death, but the fourteenth gallon allows me to wash my car. Demand always has a time dimension. It is meaningless to discuss my valuation of an eleventh apple unless I know whether the apples are to be consumed over the next day, week, or year. The vertical axis measures cost to the purchaser. For now we simply treat it as a cash outlay that does not include such other costs as those of the time spent searching for a bargain or paying a lawyer to negotiate a delivery contract.

To estimate the benefits of consuming A, assume that I can buy all I want at $7.50 per unit. According to Figure 3-2 I will pay up to $11 for the first unit. If the price is $12 I will buy none—giving up $12 leaves me worse off than having no A at all. Alternatively, if I get the first unit for free I clearly gain, because I have both the good and the $11 I was willing to pay for it. The benefit of getting the first unit for free is $11. If instead I pay $7.50 for it, my benefits from that unit are $11 − $7.50 = $3.50. The same reasoning goes for the second unit, but I value it less highly than the first unit, and my benefits are $10 − $7.50 = $2.50. Doing likewise for the third and fourth units, my total benefits from buying at $7.50 are $8. Benefits measured in this way usually get the confusing name *consumer surplus.* This amount has no relation to surpluses or shortages that might occur if a market is prevented from reaching equilibrium, as described later. It is just an unfortunate coincidence that economists use the same word for two totally unrelated concepts. If market price falls, consumer surplus must increase.

Now let's start the story over but with a market price of $5.50. Each of the first four units now brings me $2 more in consumer surplus, to which we add the gains from the fifth and sixth units for a total of $18. Because step functions like Figure 3-2 are clumsy to work with, we usually treat demand as a continuous function of price, as in Figure 3-3. Consumer surplus is then the shaded triangle above price and below the curve.[14]

Q. For the demand curve in Figure 3-3, can you show that consumer surplus is $32 when market price is $8?

---

[14]Mathematically, because the demand curve represents marginal valuations of the units, its height is the derivative (rate of change) of total value and consumer surplus is the integral under the curve the net of the price being paid.

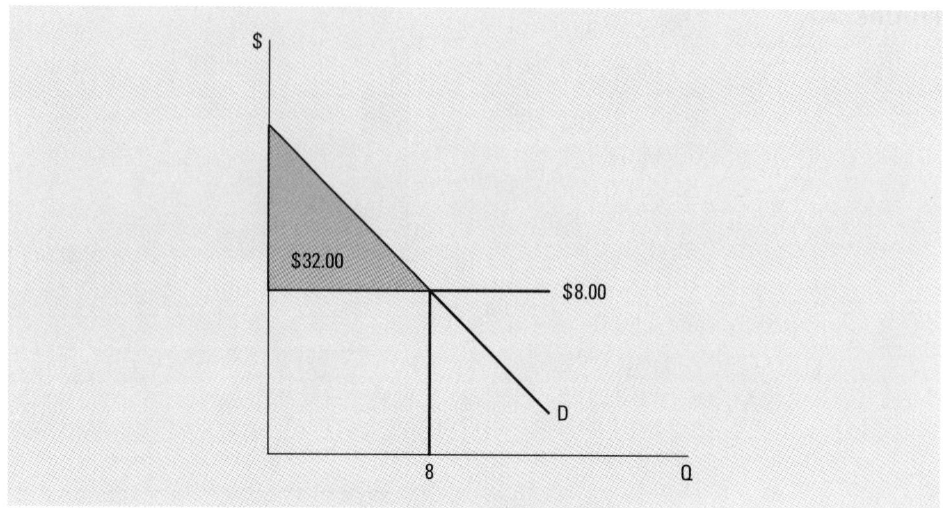

FIGURE 3-3
Consumer Surplus with Continuous Demand
$Q = 16 - P$

Demand and Quantity Demanded

There is an important distinction between quantity demanded and demand. A movement between two points on a given demand curve is called a *change in quantity demanded.* It can only occur in response to a change in the good's own price. Figure 3-4a shows my daily demand curve for coconut macaroons. An increase in price from $4 to $6 lowers my quantity demanded from 12 to 7 macaroons per day. The adjustment comes because I can substitute among various goods to create well-being ("utility") for myself. The rise in the price of macaroons makes other sources of enjoyment (whose prices are held constant) cheaper relative to macaroons, and my best response is to substitute against macaroons and in favor of other goods. In contrast, a *change in demand* is a shift of the entire demand curve. That shift occurs when some change in my economic environment changes my desired purchases at any price. Such changes can include the information available to me, my income or wealth, the price of a substitute for macaroons (say, doughnuts), or the price of a complement to them (coffee).[15]

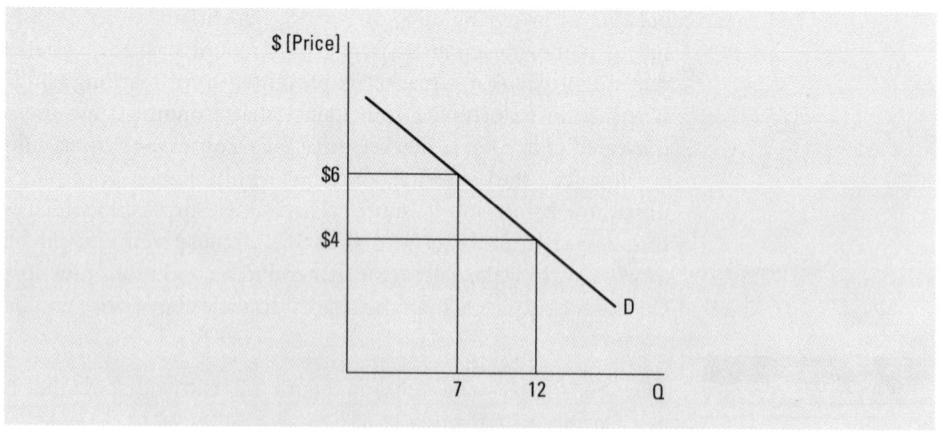

FIGURE 3-4a
Change in Quantiy Demanded

[15]Economists sometimes mention the possibility that demand shifts when a person's underlying preferences (i.e., "tastes") change. It is best to avoid this sort of explanation, because it can explain any imaginable change in a person's behavior. If I become the parent of triplets, for example, my demand curve for baby food will shift. Perhaps it is better to assume that I get utility from children, and that if I actually become a parent my demand for complements to children, like baby food and rattles, will shift.

FIGURE 3-4b
Change in Demand

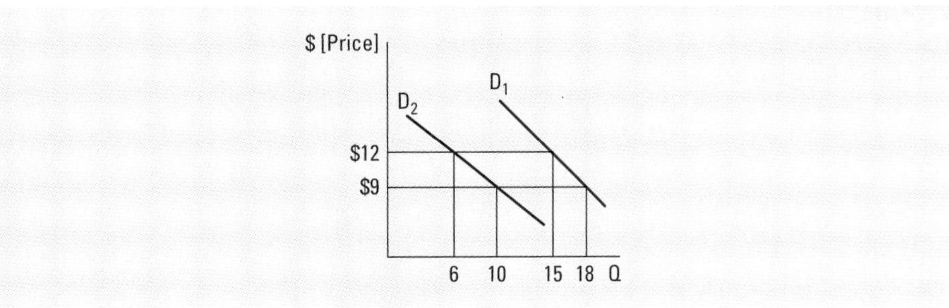

Information In Figure 3-4b, my demand curve (D) for macaroons is originally D_1. One day I learn about medical research that reliably links macaroon consumption to increased risk of a heart attack. This information shifts my demand inward to D_2. At the current price of $12, I formerly wished to consume 15 macaroons per day, but now I only want 6. At a market price of $9, I originally purchased 18 macaroons a day, but after learning about the risk I only buy 10.

Q. Why doesn't learning that macaroons are risky shift my desired purchases to zero at all prices, as doing so would probably cut my chances of a heart attack by even more?

Q. Most people who quit smoking for health reasons reduce their consumption to zero whatever the market price of cigarettes. Give a possible reason for the difference between macaroons and cigarettes.

Income or Wealth We can use the same diagram to examine the effects of changes in other variables that determine demand. In Figure 3-4b, assume that D_1 is my demand curve for macaroons when my income is high. An economist calls macaroons a *normal good* if a decrease in income lowers my demand curve for them to D_2. The lowered income reduces my well-being, but if different goods are substitutes I probably minimize the impact by cutting down on most goods rather than dropping my consumption of a few to zero and leaving the rest the same as before. It is also possible that macaroons are an *inferior good*, one for which my desired consumption rises as income falls. When my income was high I preferred to have expensive desserts in restaurants, but now that it has fallen I make the best of a bad thing by taking home more macaroons from the bakery. If macaroons are an inferior good, D_1 is my demand curve for them when my income is low and D_2 when it is high.[16]

Prices of Substitutes and Complements Later in this chapter we will introduce a measure of substitutability, but for now just use your intuition. Macaroons and doughnuts are *substitutes* because both contain large amounts of sugar and provide similar taste

[16]Inferiority is a positive rather than a normative concept. Eating oatmeal may be better for your health than eating processed cereal, but your demand curve for oatmeal shifts downward with rising income.

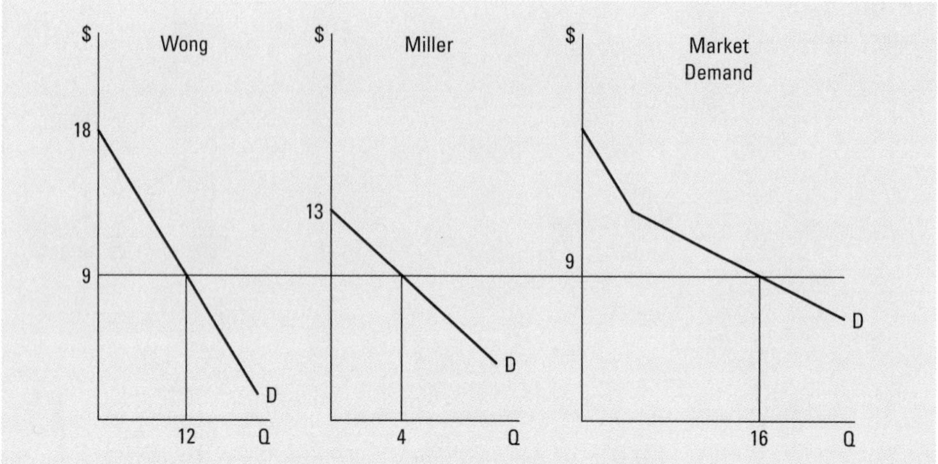

FIGURE 3-5
Summation of Individual Demands

sensations. (Substitutes can vary with the individual—if I am allergic to coconut, then macaroons and doughnuts are not substitutes for me.) When the price of doughnuts rises my demand curve for macaroons shifts upward from D_2 to D_1 in Figure 3-4b. I alter my macaroon–doughnut mix to favor macaroons, which are now relatively cheaper. Two goods are *complements* if I must use both to produce something of value to me. For example, I require both flour and eggs to make a cake, and taking a trip requires both gasoline and tires. A higher price of flour makes a cake more expensive. The fall in my desired consumption of cakes because of their higher price means that my interest in buying eggs (i.e., my demand curve for them) has also fallen. In Figure 3-4b, D_1 is my demand for eggs when the price of flour is low, and D_2 is my demand when the price of flour is high.

From Individual to Market Demand The choices made by individuals are aggregated (totaled) in markets. To find total quantities purchased at different prices, add the demand curves of all buyers horizontally. A real market will have many buyers, but two will suffice to illustrate the principle. The left and center panels of Figure 3-5 show Wong's and Miller's demand curves for macaroons. Start with both of them facing a price of $9, add the quantities that each wishes to purchase (12 for Wong and 4 for Miller) and represent their sum in the right-hand panel. Do the same for all other prices to get the market demand curve. If both persons have downward-sloping demand curves, market demand will also be downward-sloping. Also note that Miller will cease buying at prices above $13, though Wong remains a buyer at prices up to $18. At $13, the slope of the market demand will abruptly change, but it remains negative. As the number of buyers increases, such changes in slope become less noticeable.

Q. Can you show algebraically that if both persons' demand curves are downward-sloping, then so is the sum of their demands?

SUPPLY

The Profit Motive and the Gains to Producers

Production transforms inputs such as labor time, raw materials, and borrowed funds into something more valuable, whether it be batteries or manicures. The underlying commodity can remain unchanged while its value is increased, for example, by opening a sales

TABLE 3-1 MARGINAL COSTS FOR FIVE PLANTS

PLANT	A	B	C	D	E
Marginal cost	$1	2	4	5	7
Capacity/day	5	3	7	5	3

outlet for some particular good that is closer to buyers. Just as opportunity cost determined a seller's choices in the simple transactions of Chapter 2, it is also the foundation of more complex decisions about production. In Chapter 2 a seller traded away a good she held if the buyer offered more than her opportunity cost. That cost might have been the highest price some other buyer was willing to pay, or the value to the seller of keeping it for her own enjoyment. Often market prices and expenses correspond to opportunity costs. Paying the market price for a gallon of fuel you will use in your business is equivalent to bidding it away from whoever values that gallon the next most highly.

Assume that I own five plants, A through E, all capable of producing a certain good. Their marginal costs differ. Some of them may be better managed than others, or some may use technologies that can squeeze more output from a given set of inputs. As in Chapter 2, marginal cost is the cost avoided if a unit of the good is not produced. The plants, marginal costs, and maximum outputs (capacity) each can produce in a day are shown in Table 3-1. It is important to note that the concept of a supply curve presupposes that I am a *price-taker*. I am a seller who is so small a part of so large a market that my production decision cannot possibly affect the price at which I can sell my product. I might, for example, control only a tiny percentage of total production in a market where global supply and demand determine price. In Figure 3-6 the world price is shown as a horizontal line at $3. I operate plants A and B to capacity because that price exceeds their marginal costs, and I leave plants C, D, and E idle. Every unit produced in A (B) adds $3 to revenue and only $1 ($2) to cost. If the world price changes to $6, production in C and D becomes worthwhile. Arranging the plants in order of marginal cost, my production decisions at various prices are points on my supply curve.

The supply curve follows as part of the logic of profit maximization when I am a price-taker.[17] Being able to sell at a higher price makes me better off. The difference between price and marginal cost becomes greater for each unit I was previously producing, and it

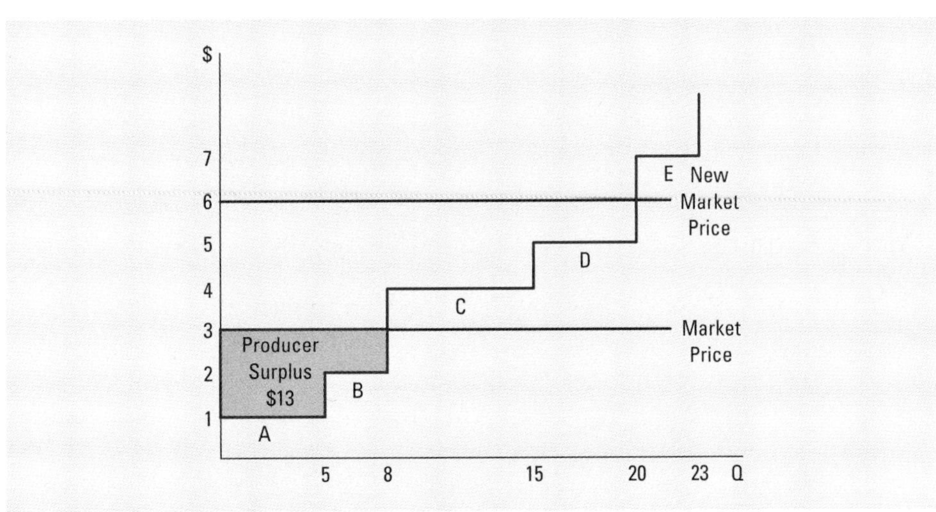

FIGURE 3-6
Supply Curve of Five Plants

[17] In Chapter 5 profit will be considered in more detail and will be linked with forgone opportunities and uncertainty. For now just define profit as revenue minus cost.

changes from negative to positive for the additional ones I produce in response to the higher price. This suggests a measure of benefits analogous to consumer surplus. In Figure 3-6 market price is again \$3, so I operate plants A and B. The marginal opportunity cost of producing a unit in A is \$1. Had the market price been \$1.01 I still would have produced that unit because doing so leaves me one cent better off than choosing my best alternative, which is worth only \$1. Because I can sell at a market price of \$3, each of the 5 units produced in plant A gives me a benefit of \$2 above its marginal cost. The shaded area above \$1 and below \$3 is part of my *producer surplus.* Each of the three units produced in plant B contributes an additional \$1 of benefits, leaving a total surplus of \$13. Because they are still idle, plants C, D, and E provide no benefits. A market price of \$6 increases producer surplus, because the difference between price and marginal cost increases for units produced in A and B, and it changes from zero to positive for C and D.

Q. Calculate the new producer surplus after the market price rises.

Instead of several plants with limited capacities and constant marginal costs, consider a single business whose costs vary continuously with output. Figure 3-7 shows an upward-sloping marginal cost curve.[18] It is still a supply curve, because it shows the most profitable output at each possible market price. As in the previous example, producing every unit whose marginal cost is less than market price increases my profit. My producer surplus is the area above that curve and below the market price. As with demand curves, the market supply curve is the horizontal sum of the producers' supply curves. The left two panels of Figure 3-8 are the supply curves of the Jay and Kay companies, and the right panel shows their sum. The angle in market supply occurs at the price at which Kay begins to produce.

Q. Can you show that if my supply curve is $Q_S = -30 + 1.5P$ (graphed in Figure 3-7) and market price is \$50, my producer surplus is \$750?

FIGURE 3-7
Supply and Procedure's Surplus

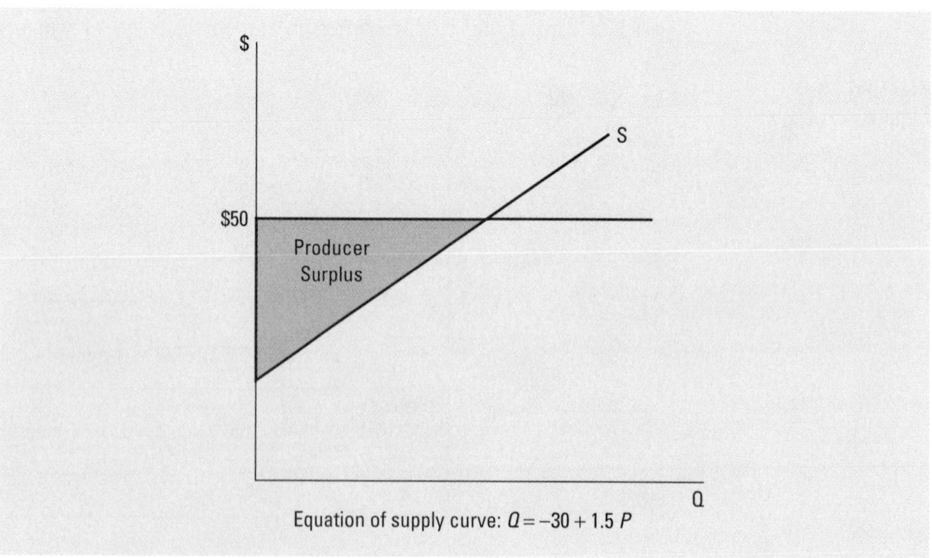

[18]Chapter 4 will cover costs in more depth. There we will see that rational production decisions generally entail operating where marginal cost is increasing.

FIGURE 3-8
Adding Supply Curves

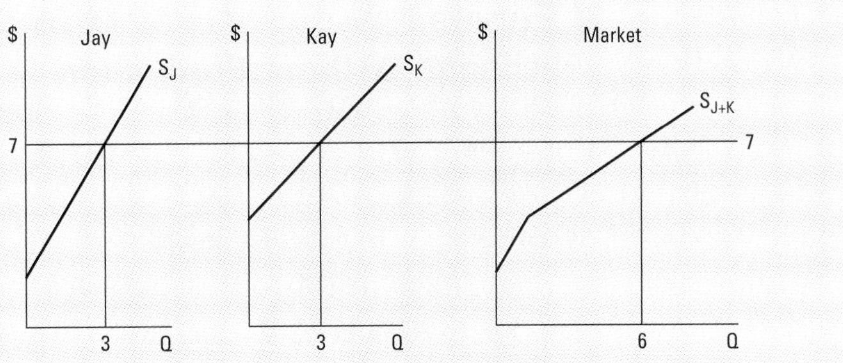

Supply and Quantity Supplied

The distinction between quantity supplied and supply is similar to the distinction between quantity demanded and demand. In Figure 3-9a a firm's profit-maximizing output increases from 15 units per day to 30 when market price increases from $30 to $40. This is a *change in quantity supplied,* and it occurs only in response to a change in market price. Figure 3-9b portrays a shift of the entire curve, known as a *change in supply.* Such a change has two possible causes. First, a decrease in marginal cost shifts the curve downward at all outputs. In the figure, if marginal cost falls by $10 after a variable input (e.g., plant fuel, workers' wages) becomes cheaper, the new supply curve is S′. If market price is still $30, profit is maximized by producing 30 units rather than the previous 15. Second, changing technology can affect marginal cost. In Figure 3-9b, S will shift downward to S′ if the firm buys a new boiler that burns less fuel per unit of output produced.

Q. Explain in commonsense terms why producer surplus rises after the curve shifts from S to S′.

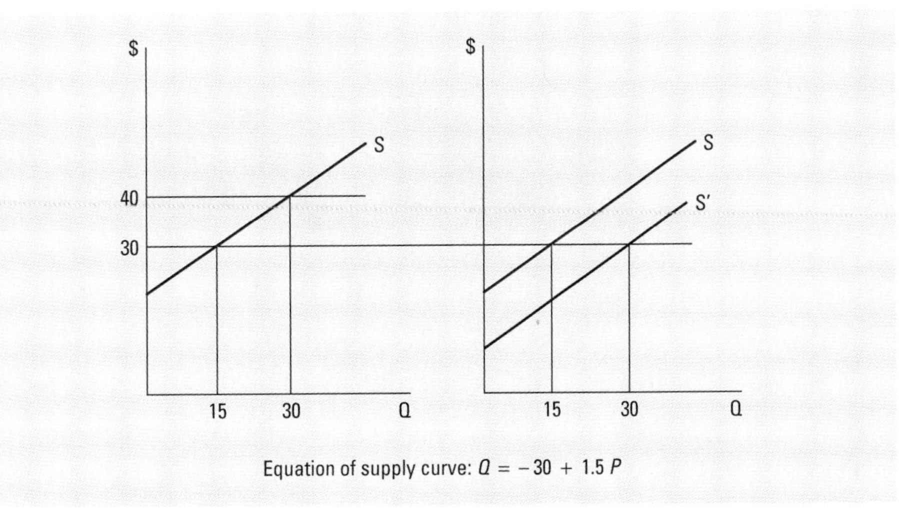

FIGURE 3-9a
A Change in Quantity Supplied

FIGURE 3-9b
A Change in Supply

EQUILIBRIUM

Exchange Without Production

It is easiest to begin studying market behavior in a situation called "pure exchange." There is no production and people only trade money (i.e., purchasing power over other goods) for goods that already exist. In Table 3-2a, each of the five people begins by holding a certain amount of some good. (Enzo starts with none.) The columns of Table 3-2a show their individual demands and the market demand at various prices shown in the leftmost column. Table 3-2b shows their initial holdings and how they change as trade progresses. Many possible sequences of trades could take place. You can probably already guess where price will settle, but the people in the table cannot. Each knows only his personal demand for the good, and no one knows how much anyone else owns. As they did in Chapter 2, they trade at whatever prices they can agree on. For the time being assume that no one has any knowledge of the prices at which others have made deals. Here's one possible sequence of trades:

1. Enzo buys 1 unit from Ahmed for $7.
   This trade works because Enzo has none of the good and will pay up to $8 for a first unit. When offered $7, Ahmed only wants to hold two, that is, he values $7 in cash that can be spent on other goods more highly than the third unit he holds. Depending on their bargaining abilities they could just as well have traded this unit for $8 rather than $7. Next, the following is one of many possibilities:
2. Becky buys 1 unit from Deb for $1.
   Why such a low price? Even at this price, Deb wants to hold only one unit. If offered $1 for one of her two remaining units, she will also take the deal. Resist the temptation to criticize Deb for accepting such a low price. Unlike you, she has none of the information about the others that you can discover just by looking at Table 3-2. Now three more trades might take place.
3. Carl sells 1 unit to Enzo for $3.
4. Deb sells 1 unit to Ahmed for $6. (Note that Ahmed was a seller at $7 and has turned up as a buyer at $6.)
5. Deb sells 1 unit to Becky for $4.

TABLE 3-2A DEMAND CURVES

PRICE	AHMED	BECKY	CARL	DEB	ENZO	MARKET DEMAND	NEW DEB DEMAND	NEW MARKET DEMAND
$10	0	2	0	0	0	2	0	2
9	1	2	0	0	0	3	0	3
8	2	3	0	0	1	6	1	7
7	2	3	0	0	1	6	1	7
6	3	4	0	0	1	8	1	9
5	3	4	1	0	2	10	1	11
4	3	5	1	0	2	11	2	13
3	4	5	1	0	2	12	2	14
2	4	6	2	1	2	15	3	18
1	5	7	2	1	3	18	3	21

TABLE 3-2B HOLDINGS

	AHMED	BECKY	CARL	DEB	ENZO
Initial	3	3	2	3	0
After the first trade	2	3	2	3	1
After the second trade	2	4	2	2	1
After the third trade	2	4	1	2	2
After the fourth trade	3	4	1	1	2
After the fifth trade	3	5	1	0	2
Deb's Demand Increases					
After first trade	3	4	1	1	2
Three Units are Lost					
New holdings	2	3	1	1	1
After the first trade	3	3	1	0	1
After the second trade	3	4	0	0	1

Now check that no more trades are possible that benefit both buyer and seller. None of the five wants to add to his holdings at a price of $4 (or any higher price), and none of them wants to sell a unit they currently own at that price. With no more mutually beneficial trades to be made, the market comes to rest, at a position called *equilibrium.* The price of $4 rations the available supply. At $4 there are no frustrated buyers who cannot find sellers, and there are no frustrated sellers who cannot find buyers. The trades they have made reallocate the good in accordance with the valuations shown on their individual demand curves. Figure 3-10 shows each person's demand curve (labelled by their initial) and their horizontal sum, the market demand D. Because there is no production, the supply curve is a vertical line at 11 units. At the equilibrium price of $4, all of them are holding the amounts they wish to hold at that price, as shown by their individual demand curves. The equilibrium price is sometimes called the *market-clearing price.*

Q. Devise another sequence of trades and show that it ends with the same allocation of the good among these individuals.

FIGURE 3-10
Equilibrium in a Five-Person Market

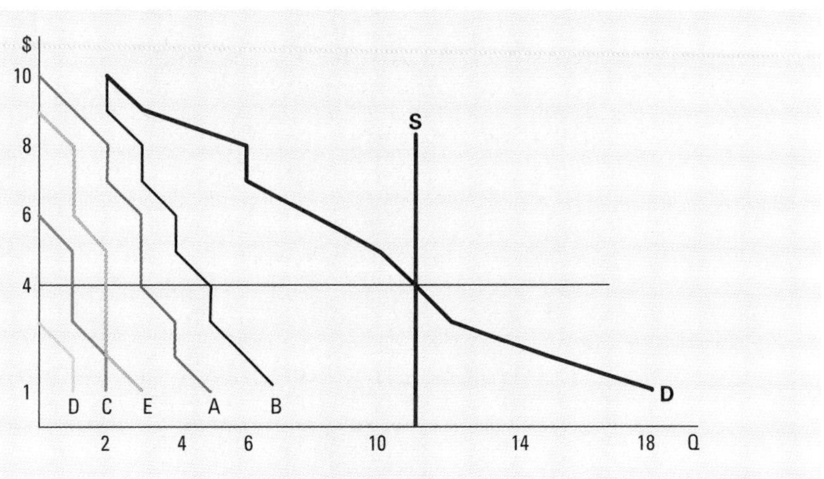

The sequence of trades just described came out of thin air. People simply met at random and discovered whether a trade would benefit them both, much like Jones and Smith in Chapter 2. The sequence could have included meetings between persons whose demands and holdings did not allow them to invent such deals. Instead of depending on random meetings, trade might be governed by other economic institutions. Perhaps an auctioneer quotes prices until the total the five people want to hold equals the amount that exists. Buyers and/or sellers will have to bear the costs of hiring an auctioneer, but the benefits might outweigh the cost of finding trading partners and the risks of uncertain prices for individual trades.[19]

Q. Show that if Ahmed and Becky meet at the start, they will not be able to find any transaction that benefits both of them.

Changes in the Equilibrium

An Increase in Demand Having learned that a sequence of exchanges converges to equilibrium, next see what happens when there is a shift in supply or demand. First, let Deb's demand for the good shift outward to D′ on Figure 3-10, which graphs the second-rightmost column in Table 3-2. Start from the existing equilibrium at \$4. At that price, Deb now wishes to hold two units (she currently holds none) but cannot find a seller. After examining other possible trades, she approaches Becky and offers her \$5 to part with one. (Becky could just as well have approached Deb.) At \$4 Deb wanted two additional units, but at \$5 she prefers to have only one unit and keep her remaining cash to spend on other goods. The change to a \$5 price reallocates the good from Becky, whose valuation is unchanged, to Deb, whose valuation has risen. Ahmed, Carl, and Enzo remain willing to hold what they had after the original set of trades occurred, and they would not have been willing to trade with Deb at \$5. Figure 3-11 shows the outward shift in the market demand and allows us to compare the new equilibrium with that of Figure 3-10.

FIGURE 3-11
Demand Shift in Five-Person Market

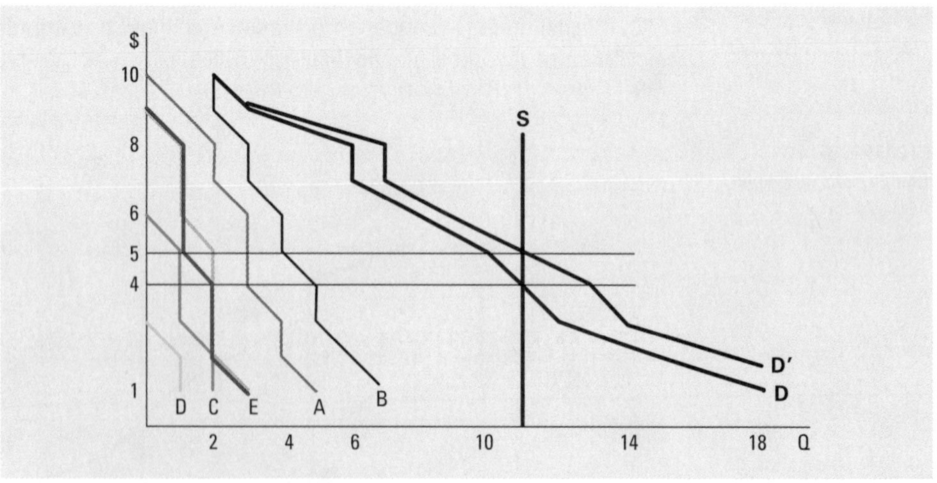

[19]Note that we are not yet considering strategies that could lead one or more persons to increase their gains relative to what they get in this solution. Deb, for example, might have realized early that she was going to be a pivotal seller and priced her goods accordingly.

FIGURE 3-12
Supply Shift in Five-Person Market

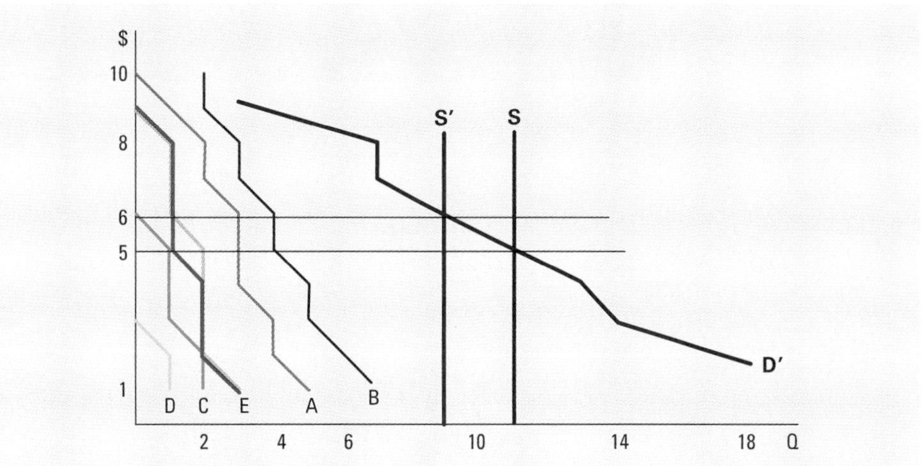

A Decrease in Supply Starting from the equilibrium price of $5 in Figure 3-11, assume that two units of the good are destroyed—one of Ahmed's and one of Becky's. Both would like to replace their destroyed units for $5 or some lower price, but neither can find a seller. They will, however, find sellers if they offer more.

1. Deb sells Ahmed a unit for $6.
2. Carl sells Becky a unit for $6.

After these two trades, no more mutually beneficial exchanges can take place. The good has been reallocated to those who value it more highly relative to their holdings after the losses. At $5 Enzo wants to have two units, but at $6 he is better off hanging on to his remaining unit and $6 in cash than he would have been if he had spent the money. In Figure 3-12 the supply curve shifts two units leftward to S′, which crosses the demand curve at $6.

Exchange with Production

If the economy also produces goods, equilibrium prices will allocate their production among suppliers and allocate the produced units among buyers. The supply curve to this market is given by the marginal costs of the producers shown in Table 3-3, and the demand curve is D' from Figure 3-11. Table 3-4 tabulates them and Figure 3-13 illustrates them. As before, each producer is assumed to have constant marginal costs up to its capacity. The first to produce will be V, whose marginal costs are lowest at $1. Only if V is producing its capacity output of 4 units might it be W, whose marginal cost is $2, to produce. As with pure exchange, many trading sequences that end at equilibrium are possible. The logic of the exchange examples continues to hold, and Figure 3-13 shows that the equilibrium price is $4 and total output is 13 units.[20] This price-quantity

TABLE 3-3 FIVE PRODUCERS AND THEIR COSTS

Producer	V	W	X	Y	Z
Marginal cost	$1	2	3	4	6
Capacity	4	4	2	4	6

[20]This assumes that all producers act as price-takers. In this example, producer Y might under some assumptions have latitude to restrict output by a small amount to raise the market price. This problem will be revisited in Chapter 5.

TABLE 3-4 SUPPLY AND DEMAND WITH PRODUCTION

PRICE	QUANTITY SUPPLIED	QUANTITY DEMANDED
$1	4	21
2	8	18
3	10	14
4	14	13
5	14	11
6	20	9
7	20	7
8	20	7
9	20	3
10	20	2

combination has three properties of interest: (1) The market is in equilibrium at a price of $4, which equates quantities supplied and demanded; (2) all buyers willing to pay $4 or more for a unit are able to find sellers, and all sellers willing to produce for $4 or less can find buyers; and (3) the 13 units of output are produced in the economically efficient manner, that is, at the lowest avoidable cost. They are produced at the smallest sacrifice (in terms of market value) of other outputs the economy might produce. All of these outcomes also occur when price-taking producers have continuous and increasing marginal costs.

The Law of One Price

Now assume that the five people in the pure exchange example fall into two groups that cannot trade with each other. The first group consists of Ahmed and Becky, and the second group includes Carl, Deb, and Enzo. Their initial holdings and demands are those at the start of the exchange example, the first row of Table 3-2b. Ahmed and Becky hold six units between them and will trade to a price between $6 and $7. Carl, Deb, and Enzo hold five units between them and will trade to a price of $2. If the groups become part of the same market rather than smaller isolated ones, there will be additional opportunities for trade. Becky will become a willing buyer from Carl and Deb, who are happy to sell for more than the $2 their product fetched when exchange was confined to their

FIGURE 3-13
Five-Person Market with Production

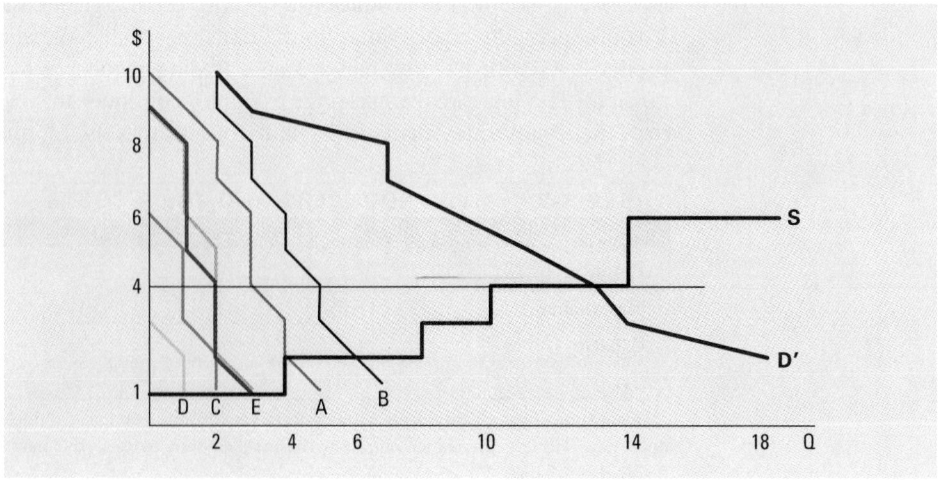

isolated threesome. (Enzo was also a member of that group but does not want to sell at prices as low as Carl and Deb.) Trades will take place and goods will be reallocated until the price moves to $4 as before. If there are transaction costs (e.g., transportation), prices may still differ between the groups but by no more than the transaction cost.[21]

Q. Check that the calculations in the previous paragraph are correct.

Trading to profit from price differences—buying and selling a good simultaneously in two different venues—is known as *arbitrage*. Because prices are clearly visible, the activity is riskless. Adding risk turns the transaction into a *speculation*, which is discussed later in this chapter. Arbitrage unifies a market and brings about a single equilibrium price or price differences that just cover the cost of transacting. This tendency is called the *Law of One Price*. Noneconomists sometimes fail to appreciate its wide applicability and its consequences. In the reality television show *The Apprentice*, two teams of applicants compete for a job with billionaire Donald Trump. Each week the second-place team loses the person Trump determines is its least competent member. In one early episode he gave the teams a day to purchase a list of items in New York at the lowest total cost. On the list were a leg waxing, ten pounds of squid, and an ounce of gold.[22] The law of one price applies with differing force to these items. Arbitrage is difficult for leg waxing (an untradable service) and squid (there are few knowledgeable traders), but it is easy for gold, which is bought and sold at hundreds of places. In one team's strategy meeting a member recalled hearing from an acquaintance that gold was always cheaper late in the day, and the others (some of whom had MBA degrees!) apparently believed him. They waited until the afternoon (the price had actually risen since the morning) to try bargaining, but sellers refused to budge. The team had forgotten the law of one price. If you know with certainty that gold is always more expensive late in the day, you can become rich by buying early and reselling later. As buying and selling take place, price becomes more uniform over the hours. Bargaining was useless in this market as every seller was a price-taker who had no reason to sell below a market price that all of them knew.[23]

Q. Let's reexamine leg waxings. One team was all men and the other all women, and both were headquartered in midtown Manhattan. The women (some of them longtime New Yorkers) took a taxi to Chinatown for their waxings, a relatively distant poor neighborhood with low prices. The men walked to a salon near headquarters (located in a wealthy area) and paid higher prices. Because they paid different prices (assume that the waxings were of the same quality), does this mean the law of one price does not hold for leg waxings in Manhattan? Explain.

---

[21]In Chapter 17 we will investigate why prices often vary over small areas for identical items such as prepackaged foods and new cars.

[22]Week 3 recap, The Apprentice, Season 1, NBC Web site, http://www.nbc.com/nbc/The_Apprentice/weekly_recap/week03a.shtml.

[23]That price is determined in a worldwide market and is publicly known. Even if a seller needs to raise cash at the end of the day, it can resell its gold to other dealers or borrow using it as collateral at a low transaction cost.

Traders in some commodities are in such close contact that a single price almost always prevails. In foreign exchange markets the banks and financial institutions that trade currencies will see price differences erased in a matter of seconds. Transactions are made electronically between these large institutions at minimal transfer cost and risk per unit of currency. Sometimes the breakdown of a legal barrier can unify a market, as happened with natural gas. Before 1984, access to the interstate pipeline system by gas producers and large customers was highly restricted, and it was particularly difficult to arrange long-haul transactions requiring transfers between pipelines. In that year, the Federal Energy Regulatory Commission issued Order 436, which made it far easier for gas producers and large users to arrange for pipeline transportation. After Order 436 they could buy transport from pipelines themselves or from shippers who held unused transportation rights. Before Order 436, markets were fragmented, and a region's gas price was set by local conditions. After it, most of the United States and Canada became a single market in which regional prices seldom differed by more than the cost of transporting gas between them.[24] A cold snap in a consuming area, a hurricane in a producing area, or a pipeline accident now affects prices across the nation in a matter of hours. Figure 3-14 shows the convergence of average prices between East Texas (the solid line) and Oklahoma (the dashed line), two locations hundreds of miles apart, as markets expanded in the aftermath of Order 436.

Q. Assume that 1 euro exchanges for 80 U.S. cents, 120 yen exchange for a dollar, and one euro exchanges for 90 yen. Assuming they are the only currencies in the world, can these possibly be an equilibrium set of exchange rates? If not, what number of dollars per euro would bring about equilibrium, assuming that the other two rates are not allowed to change?

FIGURE 3-14
Texas-Oklahoma Natural Gas Price Convergence

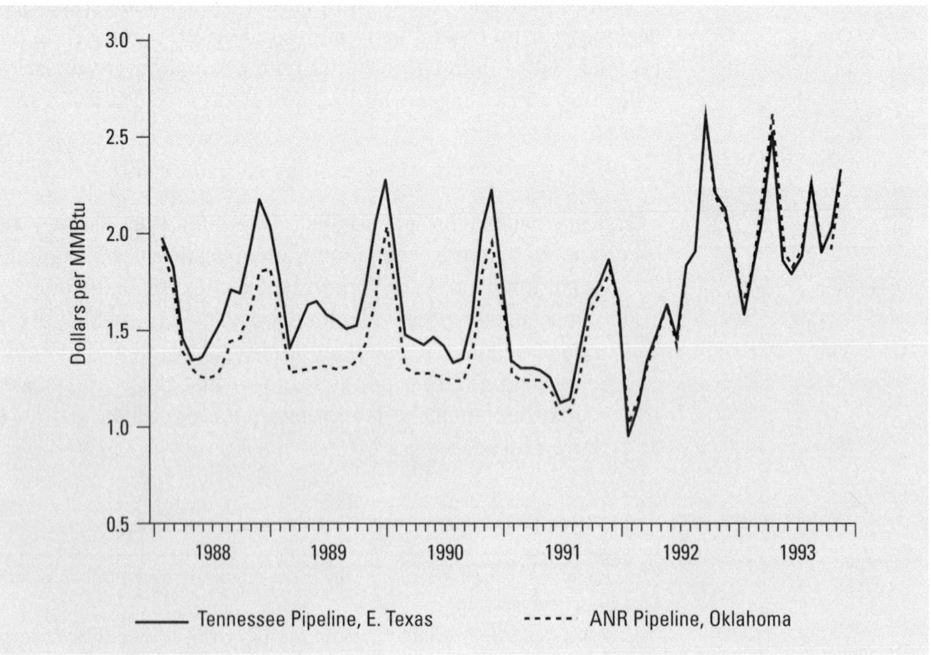

[24]See Robert J. Michaels and Arthur S. DeVany, "Market-Based Rates for Interstate Gas Pipelines: The Relevant Market and the Real Market," *Energy Law Journal* 16, no. 2 (1995): 299–346.

FIGURE 3-15
Effect of Change in Input Price

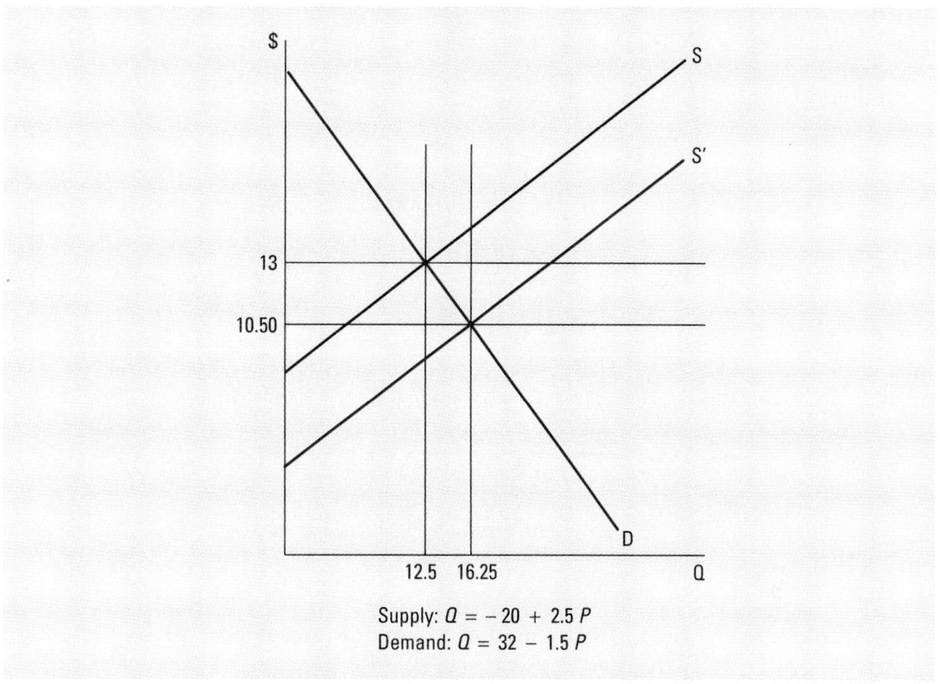

Comparing Equilibria

Figure 3-15 starts our analysis of changes in equilibrium when underlying market conditions change. Initially our market with demand curve D and supply curve S is in equilibrium at a price of $13 and an output of 12.5 units.[25] Now assume a decrease in the price of some input into production (worker wages, fuel costs, etc.) shifts marginal cost downward by $4 for every unit that might be produced. The new supply curve S′ is $4 below S and the new equilibrium is at an output of 16.25 and a price of $10.50. Buyers capture part of the benefits in the form of a $2.50 lower price and a larger volume of purchases, which raises their consumer surplus. Sellers capture the remainder of the $4 lower cost as increased profit.

Q. Explain in commonsense terms why market price falls by less than $4.00. Hint: It may be best to begin by explaining why it falls at all.

Extreme cases may be rare in real markets, but they can provide us with additional insights. If demand slopes downward and the supply curve is horizontal, input and output prices fall by equal amounts. In Figure 3-16a, the demand curve is as before; in the initial situation supply is horizontal at $13, with 12.5 units exchanged. If marginal costs fall to $9, supply shifts downward to S′ by the full $4, and more units will change hands in the new equilibrium than changed hands when the supply curve sloped upward. Consumers capture all of the benefits from the $4 decrease in the input's price, and producers are no better or worse off than before. If all of them broke even (just managed to

[25]The algebraic formulation of this model and derivation of the equilibria are presented in Mathematical Appendix 3-A.

FIGURE 3-16 Effect of Input Price Change Under Extreme Supply and Demand Assumptions

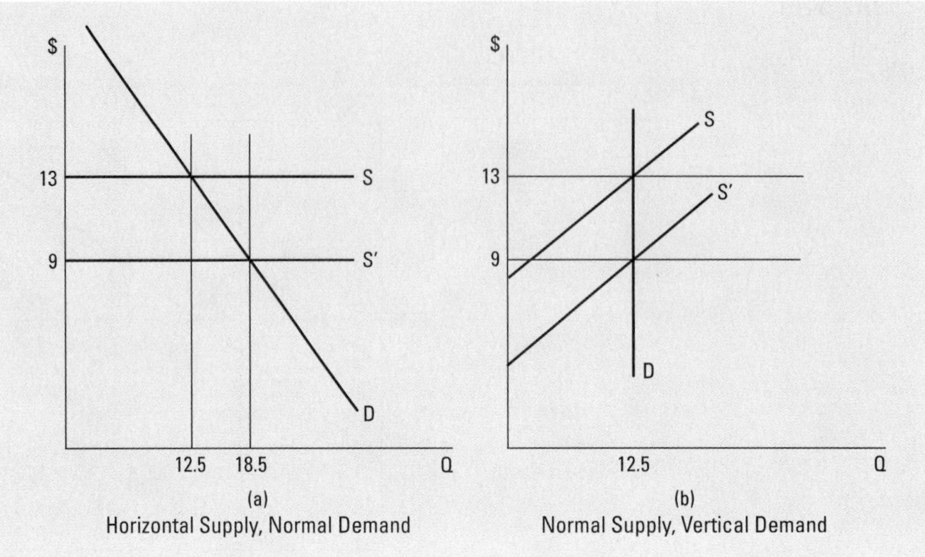

cover their costs) at $13 and if price does not fall by the full $4, competitors will enter the market to the new $9 breakeven level.[26] Figure 3-16b shows the effects of an extreme assumption about market demand—that it is vertical so consumers purchase the same quantity regardless of price. If so, the $4 drop in input price brings an equal drop in output price.[27] If output price fell by less than $4, again the threat of competitive entry would drive it down to that level.

Q. If buyers demand the same amount, regardless of price, why do you expect price to fall at all?

Q. Show graphically that if the demand curve is downward sloping but the supply curve is vertical then all of the benefits of a lower input price go to producers. Then show that this also happens if the supply curve is upward sloping but the demand curve is horizontal.

Beyond these extreme cases, buyers and sellers both gain when the input price falls. Figure 3-15 shows that both consumer and producer surplus increases. Initial consumer surplus benefits are the area bounded by the demand curve, the vertical axis, and the horizontal line at $13. Producer surplus is the area above the supply curve and below $13. Figure 3-15 shows that both consumer and producer surplus increase after the input price falls.

Refer to Appendix 3-A

[26]The possible entry of competitors in response to profit opportunities is discussed in detail in Chapter 5.

[27]The possibility of substitutes for virtually every good means vertical demand curves probably do not exist. However unlikely a vertical demand is in reality, these would be the consequences if one did exist.

Why Equilibrium Matters

Shortages, Surpluses, and the Alternatives to Markets Thus far, we have seen markets move to equilibrium as a result of buyers and sellers making trades that are in their individual interests. There may, however, be legal obstacles to attaining equilibrium. Among the most common of these are laws that prohibit price from reaching its equilibrium point, whether by enforcing a maximum that is below equilibrium (a price ceiling) or a minimum that is above it (a price floor). Figure 3-17a shows the effects of an $11 price ceiling in the market of Figure 3-15. At $11 producers as a group are willing to supply 7.5 units to the market while consumers want to purchase 15.5. The gap between the supply and demand curves at the ceiling is called a *shortage*. Figure 3-17b shows the effects of a $15 price floor. At the lowest allowed price of $15 producers want to supply 17.5 units and consumers wish to buy only 8.75 of them. The gap between the curves at $15 is called a *surplus*.

These definitions do not always match our everyday language. Often we say there is a shortage when the price of something seems abnormally high. A high price that clears the market is simply an indication of the good's underlying scarcity, and people who are willing to pay it can find sellers. A shortage by our definition entails frustrated buyers who are willing to pay the ceiling price but cannot find sellers. Likewise, when a market clears at an abnormally low price (e.g., because of an unexpectedly large farm crop) we sometimes say that there is a surplus. Sellers might have preferred a higher price, but any seller wishing to sell at the equilibrium price can find a buyer. A surplus only exists if there is a binding floor price at which frustrated sellers cannot find buyers. Shortages and surpluses are only defined at particular prices, and they only occur if price is kept from adjusting to equilibrium.

Market price is but one of many ways used to ration scarce goods. If price is not allowed to do the job, some other method must take its place. The many alternatives include hand-to-hand combat, beauty contests, politics, and waiting in lines. Every method of allocating a scarce good runs up against the fact that there is not enough of it to fully satisfy everyone's desires for free. Every scheme discriminates in favor of some persons, and quite often people prefer a method by which they are more likely to win. You might prefer combat to market prices if you are strong, beauty contests to prices if

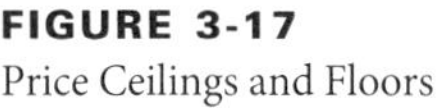

FIGURE 3-17
Price Ceilings and Floors

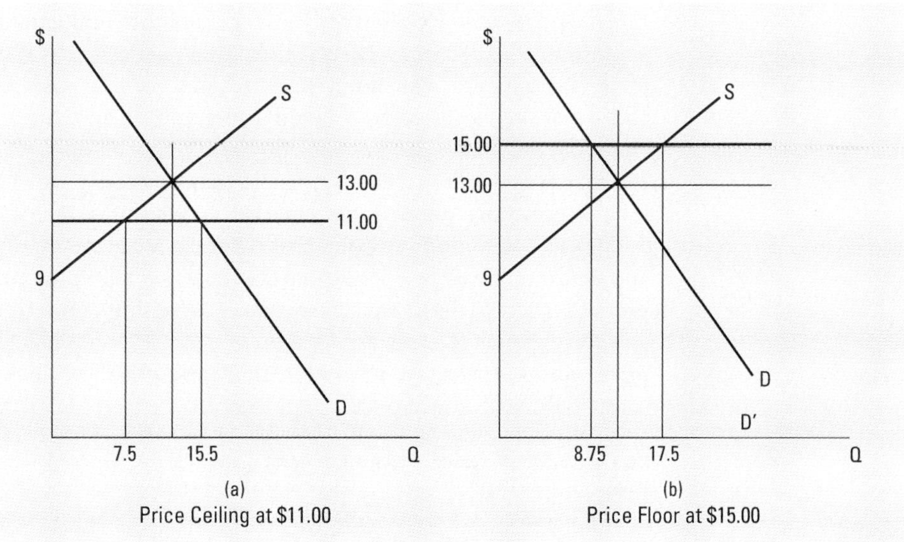

you are beautiful, politics if you have friends in government, and standing in line if you can study while you wait.[28]

Q. In whose favor do market prices discriminate? Why can you not conclude with certainty that they favor wealthy people?

Q. In whose favor does an equal distribution of the good discriminate? What about a lottery that gives everyone an equal chance of obtaining a unit of the good?

An example of the standing-in-line method occurs daily in Washington, DC. Most congressional hearing rooms are very small relative to the number of people who would like to see testimony that will shape important new laws. But Congress allocates seats in hearing rooms on a first-come, first-served basis, that is, at a money price of zero. The line to attend tomorrow's hearing often starts at the close of today's hearing. Many of the people in that line, however, are unlikely to actually attend. Some people who place a high value on attendance (e.g., lobbyists and attorneys for groups the law will affect) also have high opportunity costs—they cannot bill clients while waiting in line. To ensure that they will get seats they hire people (often students or employees of messenger services) to wait in their places. In the morning the overnighters give their permits to the persons who hired them and are paid for their time.

Q. Members of Congress set the rules for allocating seats in committee rooms. They are well aware that allowing overnight waiting in line means people with high values of time can pay their way into hearings by purchasing the rights from people who put lower values on it. Why do they not just sell the rights to high bidders (and possibly use the proceeds to cut the budget deficit), which would get the same result?

Equilibrium Is a Predictive Tool Economists find equilibrium a useful concept not because they expect it to be reached, but because it tells them the directions in which price and quantity will move. Real markets seldom reach equilibrium with the speed and precision suggested by looking at a graph or an equation. Buyers and sellers enter and leave the market, and as they do the supply and demand curves shift. Unpredictable external events take place, and people's actions today can be influenced by changes in their expectations about future market conditions. Assume that the market of Figure 3-18 is in equilibrium at a price of $7 and a quantity of 60 units, with supply curve S and demand curve D_1.[29] Unexpectedly there is a fall in the price of a complement to our product. Theory tells us that the demand curve shifts upward and the supply curve is unaffected. Though $7 was an equilibrium price, it now has characteristics of a shortage price. Forces will be set in motion that raise price and increase quantity. Some buyers

[28]This may explain why full-time students who do not work usually tell instructors that they think waiting in lines is fair, while evening students who work during the day feel differently.

[29]Why start from an equilibrium or someplace near one? In the absence of information to the contrary, we know that forces will move the market there. If we have good reason to believe the market in its original condition was far from equilibrium, we can change the analysis accordingly.

FIGURE 3-18
Movement to a New Equilibrium

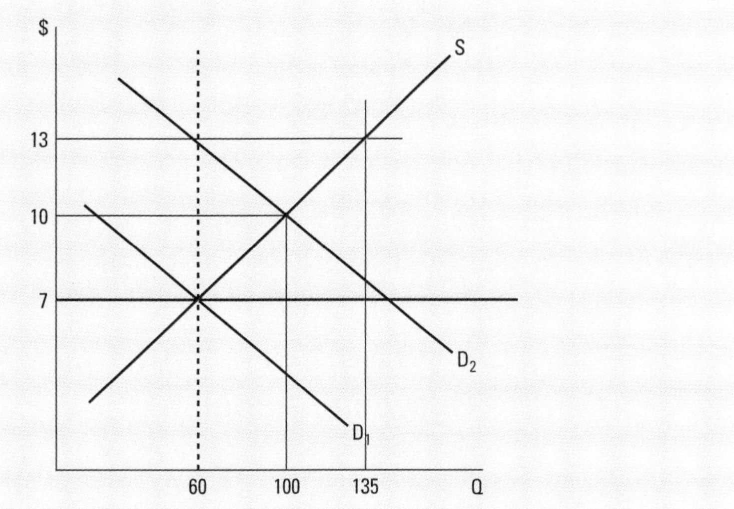

who expected a price of $7 may see sellers whose buffer inventories have run down but do not wish to increase production at that price. Such a buyer might suggest that he is willing to pay $8 (or more) for a unit of the good. If the alternative is the inability to get anything at $7, our buyer might make the best of it by offering $8 and finding a producer whose marginal cost is above $7 but below $8. Alternatively, some producers who see their inventories running down at $7 might successfully raise their asking prices and be able to profitably produce additional units. It does not matter for the new equilibrium whether a buyer or a seller is the first to suggest raising the price. How quickly the transition to a new equilibrium proceeds will depend on the economic institutions that underlie this market.

Q. The speed of adjustment in some markets varies with the direction of price movement. Go to www.gasbuddy.com, click on the state of your choice, explore, and then go to the page that lets you graph prices. Plot the past year or two of prices in any metropolitan area and you will see that they usually rise more quickly than they fall.[30] Why? Try giving an explanation for the difference that does not depend on sellers having the ability to somehow keep prices above market-clearing levels.

Whose Well-being Is It, Anyhow? The positive and normative attributes of equilibrium differ. Positive economics says that if people trade an already produced good, the market-clearing price redistributes it in accordance with their individual valuations. If the good must be produced, the price brings forth the market-clearing quantity at the lowest avoidable cost. In equilibrium there are neither surpluses nor shortages. These attributes of equilibrium do not make it normatively desirable by everyone's standards. Equilibrium must not be confused with a state of general happiness. You may have normative concerns about buyers who appear to be in hardship or sellers you think are profiteering. Some people whom you think deserve more of the good may not get as much at the market-clearing price as you believe they should.

[30]The one important recent exception is a very rapid fall near the end of 2008.

In the example of Table 3-2, assume that the commodity is milk. It is quite possible that Becky uses the four gallons she has after trading to feed her cat, while Carl's five children must survive on only one gallon. This outcome might offend your sense of fairness. You might, however, also note that early in the sequence of exchanges Carl sold one of his two original gallons for $3. You and Carl may have different opinions about how he should allocate his budget and raise his kids, and you may think Becky is wrong to indulge her cat this way.[31] Whether your preferences or Carl's or Becky's should rule is a normative question that goes beyond economics into the realms of politics and ethics. Relative to their initial holdings, all we know is that none of the five people in this market is worse off after trade than before in terms of their own preferences.[32]

USING SUPPLY AND DEMAND

Recycling Paper

Tree acreage responds to changes in the opportunity cost of land. It might surprise you that forests in the New England states occupied more land in 1990 than they did in 1790. For the first hundred of those years, land was more valuable as pasture than as forest and was steadily cleared. Eastern meat and dairy output became noncompetitive as the West opened up, and eastern pastures have been steadily replaced by forests since about 1870.[33] Forested land also responds to increases in the demand for wood, even in unlikely places. Feeding India's massive and growing population requires intensive use of farmland, but since 1960 forested acreage in that country has actually increased by more than 30 percent. Researchers have linked the change to increases in the demand for wood that have come with increasing incomes.[34]

The economics of these two cases is straightforward: if you want to see more land devoted to trees, find a way to make alternative uses of it less valuable (New England cattle ceased to earn premium prices after western grazing lands opened up), or make wood more valuable (rising incomes in India increase demands for furniture and paper). Many people believe more land can be maintained as forests and trees saved if they participate in programs to recycle paper. But supply and demand quickly indicate that recycling is one of the surest ways to *deforest* the world. Most of the trees used in pulpwood and paper production grow on land that has many other uses.[35] (Some forested land is under legal protection that does not allow any other uses. It will remain forested whether people recycle or not.) Figure 3-19 shows demand (D) and supply (S) curves for pulpwood before recycling becomes a popular activity: 100 million cords are produced each year and sold at $70 each. After recycling becomes popular, paper mills get part of their feedstock more cheaply from recyclers, so the market demand for pulpwood shifts leftward to D′. Price falls to $60 and output to 90 million cords. The amount of land devoted to trees that produce this type of wood eventually falls. It is possible that there

[31]Or perhaps there is a deeper problem, discussed in Chapter 9 under the heading of external costs. Malnourished children might be more likely to become sickly or unproductive adults, requiring support from others that would not have been necessary had their childhoods been different. Hence both taxpayers and recipients of the good might win over the long term by coercing taxpayers to pay and recipients to consume.

[32]At $4, Ahmed wants to hold the exact number he began with, so he is no better or worse off.

[33]The West was mostly unsettled until after the Civil War, and between 1790 and 1870 forested acreage in New England fell by more than half. See Andrew Foster and Mark Rosenzweig, "Economic Growth and the Rise of Forests," *Quarterly Journal of Economics* 118 (May 2003): 601–37.

[34]Foster and Rosenzweig, 605.

[35]The trees under discussion are common, fast-growing ones like firs, spruces, and pines that are suited for cultivation and whose wood has many different uses. Thousand-year-old redwoods may be a heritage that uniquely deserves legal protection, and the discussion does not apply to them.

FIGURE 3-19
Recycling Paper

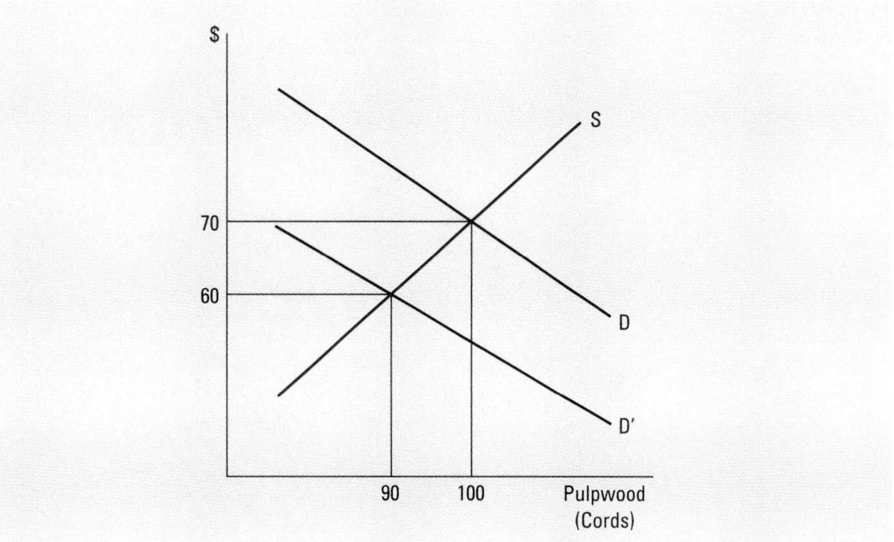

other reasons to encourage an increase in acreage devoted to trees.[36] One way to get that acreage is to raise the reward for growing trees—instead of promoting recycling, tax the activity.

Q. Will a trend toward recycling induce owners of trees to cut them later or earlier than otherwise? Explain your reasoning.

Demand, Cost, or Both?

China's appliance market is booming as economic growth raises household incomes, and stainless steel appliances, particularly refrigerators, have become prestige items there. Increases in their output have increased appliance manufacturers' demands for stainless steel, whose output cannot be quickly increased because of limited production capacity worldwide. Between September 2003 and September 2004 its price rose by 60 percent.[37] Figure 3-20a shows world demand D_R^1 and supply S_R^1 for stainless steel refrigerators before and after the increase in Chinese demand. Assume (as is roughly true) that refrigerator makers have available capacity and workforce skills to increase output with only small increases in marginal costs. The supply curve is relatively flat, and the expansion of Chinese demand has raised the world demand curve from D_R^1 to D_R^2.

At the outset refrigerator manufacturers can increase production by using up inventories of stainless steel that they keep on hand for random fluctuations in it. But if production rises to a permanently higher level the manufacturers will reorder it in larger quantities. In Figure 3-20b the increase in their demand shifts world demand for stainless steel upward from D_S^1 to D_S^2. Steel suppliers, however, are capacity constrained, and

[36]As one possibility, trees might mitigate the effects of global warming that some believe is caused by increased human production of carbon dioxide.

[37]"The Rising Cost of Going Stainless—China's Demand for Steel Makes Stylish Kitchens Pricier," *Wall Street Journal*, September 9, 2004.

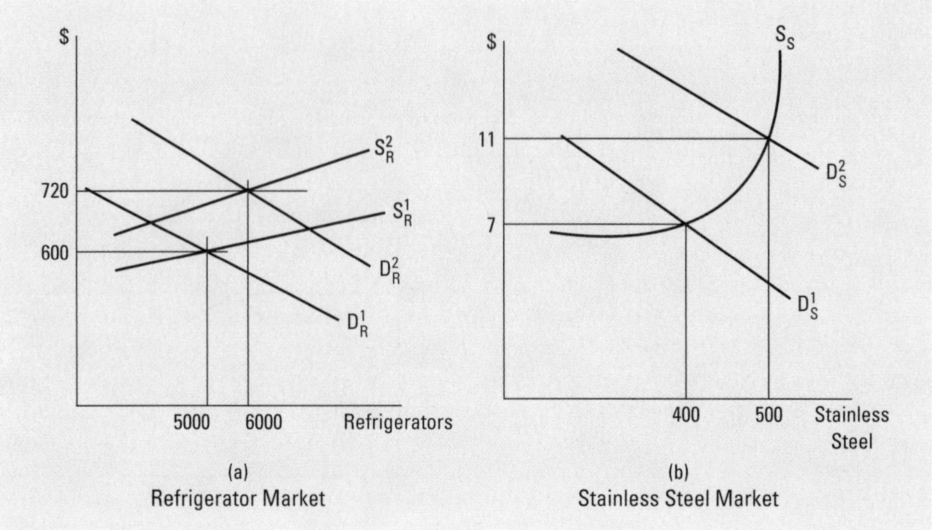

FIGURE 3-20 Cost or Demand?

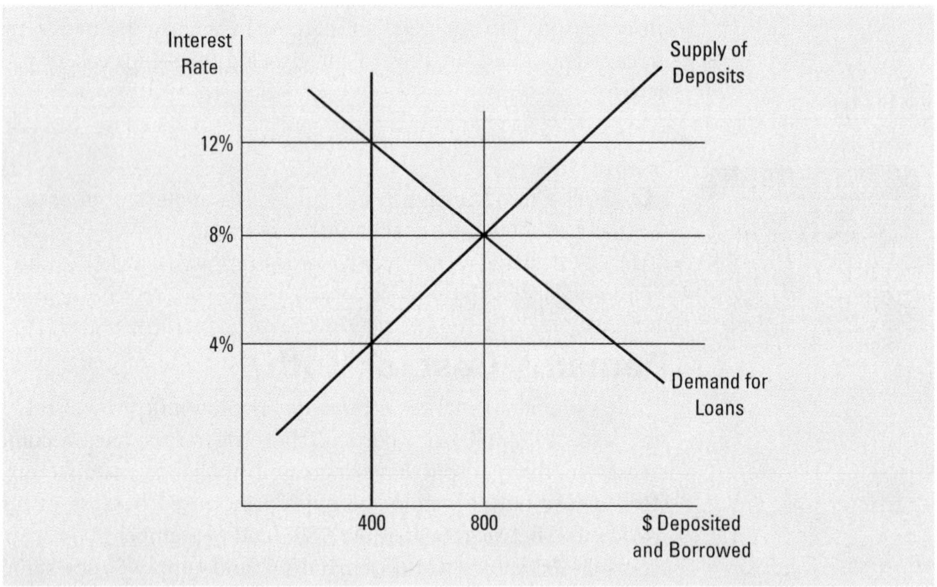

FIGURE 3-21 Interest Ceiling on Deposits but Not on Loans

the increase in demand drives them to produce on a steeper part of their industry's supply curve. Steel increases from $7 to $11 per pound as refrigerator makers bid away production from other industrial users who are unwilling to pay as much for it, perhaps because their technologies allow them to switch to substitute metals when steel prices are high. The higher steel price raises the marginal cost of refrigerators, shifting their supply curve upward from S_R^1 to S_R^2, and the world price of refrigerators increases from $600 to $720. American consumers who were expecting to pay $600 ask sellers why price is higher. The answer they get is that the prices reflect the higher cost of steel. But it is equally true that an increase in worldwide demand for refrigerators raised their prices. Manufacturers could only get the steel for the additional refrigerators by bidding it away from other industrial users whose demands did not increase. As stainless steel becomes more valuable, all those who use it see higher costs.

Who Benefits from a Price Ceiling

Before the deregulation of banks and other savings institutions in the 1980s, federally imposed ceilings limited interest rates payable to depositors. Although savings accounts no longer have such ceilings, interest on business checking accounts is still illegal under the Federal Reserve Board's *Regulation Q.*[38] Before the invention of money market mutual funds and new types of checking accounts, small depositors had little choice but to accept Regulation Q's ceiling rates. Bankers often explained their support for Regulation Q by claiming that interest ceilings lowered their cost of funds, which allowed them to charge lower interest rates on loans. Unlike interest rates on deposits, however, those on loans were largely unregulated.

Figure 3-21 helps in the analysis of the bankers' claims.[39] The supply curve of deposits is upward sloping.[40] At the ceiling rate of 4 percent, depositors put $400 billion into their accounts, and at higher rates they would put in more. Many factors underlie borrowers' demands for loans, but holding these constant they will borrow less when charged higher interest rates. To keep things simple, assume that banks have no important operating costs, face little risk of default, and are price-takers for both loans and deposits. Then interest rates on loans will be above those on deposits by enough to allow bankers to cover their costs. Without rate ceilings for deposits, $700 billion would go into savings, and the same amount would be loaned at a market-clearing rate of 8 percent. (Remember there is no ceiling on loan interest.) The interest ceiling on deposits leaves banks with only $400 billion to lend. The interest rate that rations this amount among borrowers is 12 percent. Less money is deposited, but banks pay depositors only 4 cents of every dollar loaned while receiving 12 cents from borrowers. It is not surprising that they defended the ceilings.

Q. Before the coming of free agency in professional sports, active bidding by team owners for players was rare. A player had to take either the modest salary offered by the team that drafted him or not play at all. Owners defended this scheme by claiming it reduced ticket prices. Does the analysis of deposit interest ceilings apply here? Are there any important differences?

Q. Donors of organs for transplant operations or their heirs are almost never paid for them. Common explanations are that the exchange of body organs is too important to be left to the market or that it is immoral to put a price on them. How is the analysis of a price control (at a price of $0.00) on donated organs similar to that of a ceiling on bank deposit interest rates? How is it different? If you think money should not play a role here, do you object to doctors charging to perform transplants? Why or why not?

---

[38] See "Regulations," Federal Reserve Web site, http://www.federalreserve.gov/regulations/default.htm#q. The regulation prohibits interest payments on demand deposits, which formerly included virtually all checking accounts.

[39] For evidence on the effects of the ceilings, see David Humphrey and Lawrence Pulley, "Banks' Responses to Deregulation: Profits, Technology and Efficiency," *Journal of Money, Credit and Banking* 29 (February 1997): 73–93.

[40] Under fractional-reserve banking, many of the dollars deposited will have been created by loans.

Rationing in an Energy Crisis

Oil trades in a worldwide market, but the Organization of Petroleum Exporting Countries (OPEC) has at times succeeded in limiting production in major countries and raising its global price. As the price of oil rises, so does the price of gasoline. Seeing high prices at the pump, the United States enacted price ceilings in the 1970s that produced long lines of frustrated drivers at gas stations. The lines themselves were short-lived thanks to reductions in world prices and government action to raise U.S. ceilings. As oil prices rose during 2003–2004, some again proposed price controls and possible rationing of gasoline. Proponents of one proposal claimed that it would eliminate lines while keeping prices to motorists at low controlled levels. Under this system of "tradable ration coupons," the government decides who should get coupons and how many of them, then prints and gives them to these users for free. The number of coupons printed equals the number of gallons coming to market. (Assume that amount can be accurately forecast.) A price control is in effect, so to obtain a gallon the consumer must surrender a coupon to a service station *and* pay the ceiling price, which we assume is binding. Those who want more gas than they have coupons for can legally buy additional ones from other holders at whatever prices they can agree on.

Q. Assume that there are oil wells in the United States whose marginal costs are below the price of OPEC oil. Explain why putting a ceiling on the prices their owners can receive for crude oil will not affect the price of gasoline in the United States.[41]

In Figure 3-22, assume that 100 gallons of gas arrive at stations each week, regardless of the price producers receive for it, and that coupons are only valid for that week. The supply curve is thus vertical at 100 gallons. Market demand is D and the market-clearing price for 100 gallons is $8. The ceiling price payable for each gallon is $5. A real market would contain numerous buyers, but assume that here there are only two, Jones (J) and Smith (S). D is the sum of their individual demands, D_J and D_S. Each has been issued coupons good for 50 gallons. Smith's demand shows that she is willing to pay up to $11 to obtain a 51st gallon, while Jones values his 50th gallon at $0.75. Smith will wish to buy coupons from Jones. She is willing to pay up to $6 for the first of them, because she values the last gallon at $11 and must pay the ceiling price of $5 at the station. Jones is willing to sell his first coupon for 75 cents or more. Recalling the pure exchange market example, the last coupon Smith sells to Jones will go for $3. This is the equilibrium price of a coupon. (Again, disregard the complications that stem from there only being two customers.) If it were under $3 the total cost (coupon plus ceiling) of a gallon would be under $8 and gasoline would be in shortage; if above $3, it would be in surplus.

Q. If instead of buying coupons I use coupons that were issued to me, will my cost of gas be $5 instead of $8?

Figure 3-22 shows that after they trade coupons, Jones buys 30 gallons and Smith buys the remaining 70. But these are exactly the amounts they would have bought and consumed if the price at the pump had simply gone to the equilibrium of $8 without rationing or price controls! The only difference is that without the ceiling sellers would get $8 a gallon instead of $5. The price control transfers wealth in the form of valuable gasoline from

---

[41]This topic is discussed in more detail in Chapter 5.

FIGURE 3-22
Rationing with Tradable Coupons

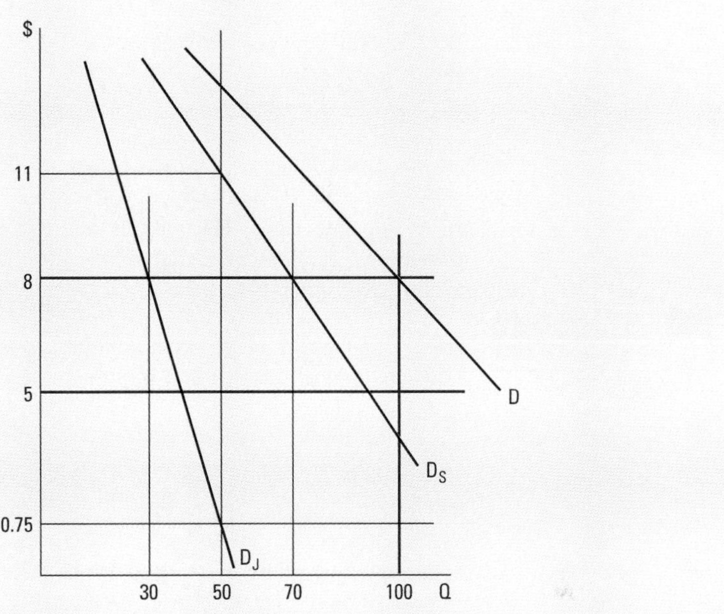

sellers to buyers. Allowing buyers to trade coupons between themselves lets both consume the same amounts they would have bought from sellers at $8. The tickets disguise a transfer of wealth from sellers to buyers in a way that many noneconomists will be unable to see through. There is a more direct (and more obvious) way to implement the transfer that delivers the same outcome as Figure 3-22. Allow the price at the pump to go to $8, so Jones and Smith buy 30 and 70 gallons each. At the end of the week, federal agents go to each station and compel the owners to give up $3 for every gallon they sold. The agents then give that money to Jones and Smith, $3 for each of the gallons they consumed.

Q. Is this situation similar to ticket scalping? Assume that the organizers of some event sell tickets to the public for less than the market-clearing price. (Later we will consider possible reasons why they might do this.) Persons with low opportunity costs of standing in line get them and then resell them at the market-clearing price. In some cities and states the practice is illegal. Who benefits from such a law? California allows unlimited resales of tickets at any price by brokers and others, but they cannot be resold at the event itself. Who benefits from this law, and why prohibit sales at the actual event?

ELASTICITY

Elasticity of Demand

Supply and demand curves can predict how equilibrium will change after some demand or supply shift, but we may also want to know the likely size of the change. For that we require a measure of how quantities demanded or supplied respond to changes in price. Along any demand curve its *elasticity* is defined as:

(3.1)
$$E_D = \frac{\textit{Percentage change in quantity demanded}}{\textit{Percentage change in price}}$$

If we look at two points (P_1,Q_1) and P_2,Q_2 that are close to each other on the demand curve, the percentage changes are approximately $Q/_Q$ and $P/_P$, where $\Delta Q = Q_2 - Q_1$ and $\Delta P = P_2 + P_1$. Then elasticity is

$$E_D = \frac{\Delta Q/Q}{\Delta P/P}.$$

For small changes the percentages will not be very different, depending on which point you call "1" and which you call "2."[42] Because the numerator and denominator have opposite signs, elasticity is actually negative. But because demand curves slope downward, economists usually eliminate the minus sign and treat elasticity as positive.[43]

Q. Explain why elasticity is independent of the units used for prices (e.g., pennies instead of dollars) and quantities (e.g., pounds instead of tons), but slope is not.

Elasticity also allows us to determine whether a change in price raises or lowers the total amount buyers spend on the good (or sellers receive as income). We can show that in a region of the demand curve where $E_D > 1$, a rise (fall) in price lowers (raises) total spending, and where $E_D < 1$, a rise in price lowers it. In a region where $E_D = 1$, spending does not change with price. We usually say that demand is *elastic* if $E_D > 1$, *inelastic* if $E_D < 1$, and *unit elastic* if $E_D = 1$ Elasticity generally varies when moving along a demand curve, even if it is a straight line. For example, Figure 3-23 portrays the demand curve given by the equation $Q = 32 - 1.5P$. Total spending on the good equals price times quantity, shown as the area of the rectangle under the demand curve. (Price is the height and quantity is the base.) An increase in price from \$13 to \$13.50 (a range where elasticity exceeds 1) reduces total spending from \$162.50 to \$158.63. An increase from \$6.00 to \$6.50 (where elasticity is less than 1) increases it from \$138.00 to \$144.63. The rectangle whose height is \$13.50 has a smaller area than the one whose height is \$13.00, but the reverse holds when comparing the rectangle whose height is \$6.50 with the one whose height is \$6.00.

Q. Check all calculations in this paragraph.

Q. The relationship between elasticity and total spending has an interesting consequence. If I have the freedom to choose the price I will sell at, I will always choose to be in the range of the demand curve where elasticity exceeds 1. Explain why.[44]

---

[42]For example, assume that the demand curve takes the linear form. Let price rise from \$13.00 to \$13.50, after which quantity demanded falls from 12.5 to 11.75. If percentage is calculated using the midpoints of price (\$13.25) and quantity (12.12), it is approximately 1.64. If instead the endpoints are used, it is either 1.56 or 1.72.

[43]Because of historical accidents, supply and demand diagrams disregard mathematical convention by putting the dependent variable on the horizontal axis and the independent variable on the vertical axis. Thus, a curve that appears steeper on the graph has a lower (absolute) slope and elasticity.

[44]This statement might be easier to understand using the following reasoning: If I can raise my price and increase revenue, then in addition to the revenue gain I also save on the cost of the lower output. I want to price where customers are on the brink of running away, not where I can increase my profits by raising price.

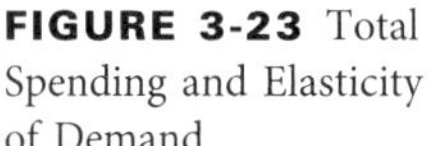
FIGURE 3-23 Total Spending and Elasticity of Demand

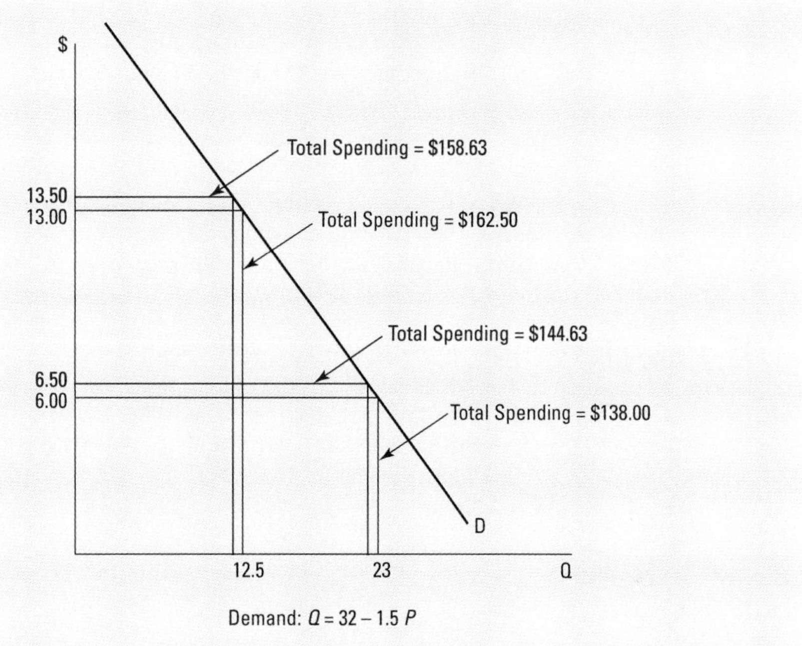

Refer to Appendix 3-B

Elasticity and Substitutes

Any demand curve is drawn on the assumption that the price of a good can change while all other factors that influence quantity demanded (e.g., income, prices of substitutes) remain unchanged. In the future chapters on seller behavior in markets it will be important to define the goods being sold with more precision. If the entire nation is treated as a market, its near-term demand curve for gasoline is relatively inelastic because most people cannot change their commuting and other travel patterns quickly in response to a nationwide change in price. At other times we will examine the demand faced by a single seller (or subset of all sellers), such as that for gasoline at the particular Arco station located at First Avenue and Main Street. That demand is based on the assumption that this station's price is the only one changing, while prices of all other goods (including gas sold at other stations) remain the same. If First and Main's owner chooses to lower prices, it will attract substantial numbers of drivers—from other brands and from Arco stations that did not change their prices. There may be an inelastic demand for gas in the entire city, that is, a relatively small response in the total quantity sold if all stations are charging the same higher price. The demand facing a single station, however, will have a high elasticity because there are so many close substitutes for the gas it sells.

Exactly which goods are substitutes depends on the details. Assume that gasoline of a given octane is uniform in quality (and all buyers know this). At two adjacent stations the lower-priced one should get almost all of the customers.[45] More generally, substitution depends on the prices of the goods, the preferences of buyers, and the information buyers have. If you regularly buy from a station next to your home, you might only view gas a mile away as a substitute if its price is more than three cents less than at your

[45]This assumes that other aspects of quality are the same in the eyes of customers—for example, hours open, courteous staff, and acceptance of credit cards.

station, which makes the extra time to reach the distant station worthwhile. Butter and margarine are a common example of substitutes, but a gourmet chef whose recipes require butter may not think so. His refined taste buds can detect differences that your economics professor's cannot. Whether you view goods as substitutes also depends on your knowledge of the alternatives. If you do not know that a store on the other side of town sells for less than the store you currently patronize, the two stores do not sell substitutes from your standpoint. If you learn about the distant store's prices (perhaps through advertising) that may change. Your demand curve to buy the item *somewhere* will be unchanged, but your demand curve to buy it from the local seller will become more elastic because you now have an alternative.

Q. We assumed that gas of a given octane was the same quality everywhere. If so, why do we often see advertising claiming that one brand is superior to others because it is the only one that contains a certain additive? Relate this to elasticities of demand.

Q. Explain why your demand curve to buy the item from the more distant seller is also more elastic.

Q. Examples of substitutes have thus far been pretty obvious, like butter and margarine. In general, however, people's actual behavior is more imaginative. Explain how a person might think of the following as substitutes: (1) gasoline and goldfish, (2) concert tickets and postage stamps.

Elasticity of demand for a good can also change over time, as experience in using it accumulates, information about substitutes becomes available, and the costs of adjusting your use of it fall. In Figure 3-24 let's begin by assuming that the price of electricity has been 11 cents per kilowatt-hour (kWh) for a long time. At that relatively low price you

FIGURE 3-24
Short-Run and Long-Run Elasticity

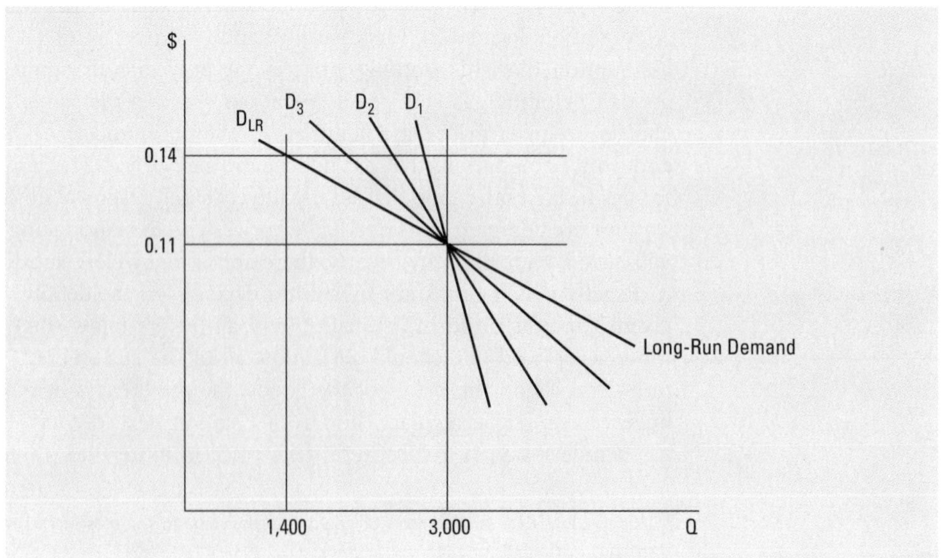

use it heavily, in applications where you would not use it if the price were higher. (In the Pacific Northwest, where prices are low, it heats many homes.) You consume 3,000 kilowatt-hours (kWh) per month and are on your long-run demand curve, D_{LR}, having purchased all of the complements to electricity (appliances) that you found worth buying at their current prices. Unexpectedly, the price of electricity rises to 14 cents per kilowatt-hour. Unless you have a special meter you will probably not even know about the increase until next month's bill arrives. When you do learn about the new price, there is little you can do to economize on power beyond checking for lights that should be turned off. You may choose not to make more costly adjustments because you do not believe the change is permanent. Your consumption adjusts by only a small amount, that is, you are operating on a short-run demand curve like D_1. As time passes you begin to inform yourself of other ways to economize. Before the next cold season you install higher-quality insulation, which cuts your power use to a point on demand curve D_2. Other complements to electricity may remain unchanged for a longer time. You might be able to cut your heating bills by burning oil instead of using electricity, but that changeover will wait until your electric radiators are near the end of their lives. After the change the demand curve will be D_3. Note that your goal is not just to minimize your fuel bill but to minimize your total cost of heating inclusive of the investment in a furnace. When you have fully adjusted your holdings of all the complements to electricity you will again be on your long-run demand curve, consuming 1,400 kWh per month.

There is substantial evidence of increased possibilities for substitution in the long run.[46] In response to the oil price increases that occurred in the 1970s, the use of petroleum products per dollar of gross domestic product fell steadily during the 1980s. This can also be seen by examining some econometric estimates of long-run demand elasticities for various fuels by manufacturers. According to one study, those elasticities were 0.92 for electricity, 2.82 for fuel oil, 1.47 for natural gas, and 1.52 for coal.[47] These are substantially higher than estimates of short-run elasticity found in other studies. In the northeastern United States the short-run elasticity of industrial demand has been estimated at approximately 0.11 for electricity and 0.60 for natural gas.[48] Economists have estimated these elasticities in many different ways, but they often find numbers in these ranges. The longest-run demand curve may still be evolving. Some evidence suggests that inventive activity responds to market conditions. If energy prices increase relative to labor costs, inventors will devote more effort to developing products that save energy and less to products that save on other inputs.[49]

Example: Affordable Housing Laws

Prices of homes have risen substantially faster than the Consumer Price Index in some areas, giving rise to public concerns about affordability. Prior to the 2008 "meltdown" in house prices, in some California counties under 25 percent of families earned enough to make payments on a median-priced home.[50] Some cities in fast-growing areas responded

[46]See Mancur Olson, "The Productivity Slowdown, the Oil Shocks, and the Real Cycle," *Journal of Economic Perspectives* 2 (Autumn 1988): 56.

[47]Robert Halvorsen, "Energy Substitution in U.S. Manufacturing," *Review of Economics and Statistics* 59 (November 1977): 388.

[48]James G. Beierlein, James W. Dunn, and J.C. McConnon, Jr., "The Demand for Electricity and Natural Gas in the Northeastern United States," *Review of Economics and Statistics* 63 (August 1981): 407.

[49]See Richard G. Newell, Adam Jaffe, and Robert Stavins, "The Induced Innovation Hypothesis and Energy-Saving Technical Change," *Quarterly Journal of Economics* 114 (August 1999): 143–75.

[50]Of course, people who currently live in median-price homes often bought them years ago for far less. Others have moved after making large down payments from capital gains on their previous houses.

by enacting affordable housing laws that require developers to set aside a percentage of the land in new subdivisions for affordable houses. In California's Orange County two cities (out of about 30), Irvine and Laguna Beach, have these laws. Easily distinguishable from the suburban sprawl around them, Irvine is a master-planned community with a University of California campus, and Laguna Beach is a cultural island of artists and others who opt for alternative lifestyles. Palo Alto, the home of Stanford University, is the only city in the San Jose area with an affordable housing law. Elasticity helps answer two questions. First, what are the effects of an affordable housing law? Second, why do these laws exist in Irvine, Laguna Beach, and Palo Alto but not in more ordinary cities?[51]

The law has virtually no impact on the price of mid-range houses. The number of affordable homes that have been built in these cities is negligible relative to the regional supply in that price range. Instead, an affordable housing law imposes a per-unit tax on builders of expensive new houses. Assume that a city requires that one of every ten lots in expensive subdivisions contain an affordable house. Instead of receiving $500,000 for each of ten houses, the builder gets that amount for each of the first nine but only, say, $200,000 for the tenth. (All of these figures are hypothetical.) Figure 3-25a looks at the demand and supply of expensive new houses in that city. As happens with any per-unit tax, the law shifts the supply curve upward from S_1 to S_2. The demand curve remains unchanged. Before the law, expensive new homes sold for $500,000 in this city, and after it they are $530,000, but there is also a close substitute for expensive new homes in that city: expensive existing homes in it. Figure 3-25b shows the market for them. Their supply is fixed at the existing number. Before the affordable housing law, demand for them was D_1 and they sold for $470,000. When the law raises the price of expensive new homes, it also shifts the demand curve for expensive existing ones upward to D_2. Their market price rises to $495,000. A city's affordable housing law has no effect on the price or amount of mid-level houses in the region. Its most important beneficiaries are the owners of expensive existing houses in that city. This outcome should not surprise you. Citizens often vote their self-interest while claiming they are doing good for others.

We next determine why these three cities are the only ones in their localities with affordable housing laws. Both the Orange County and San Jose areas contain other cities with lots of expensive homes and some undeveloped land. Southern Orange County,

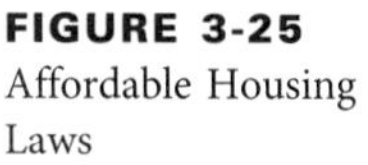

FIGURE 3-25
Affordable Housing Laws

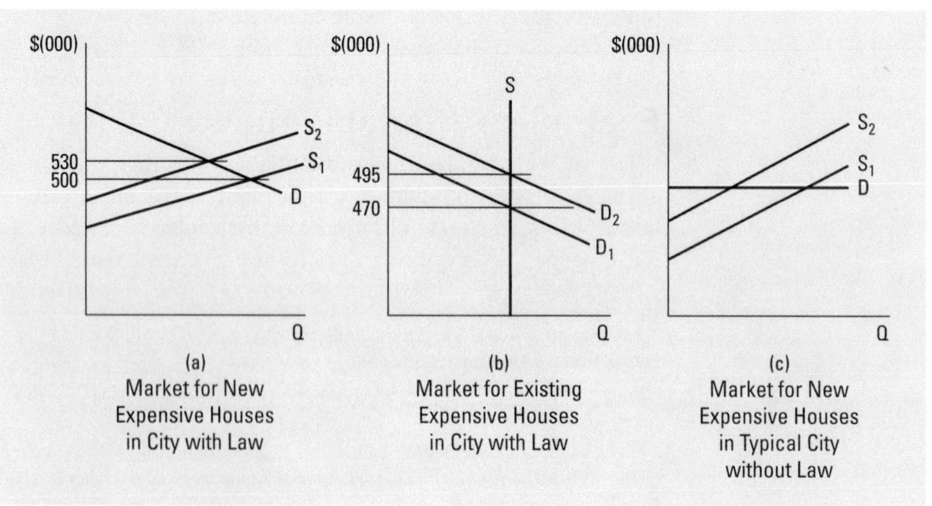

[51]This analysis follows Robert Ellickson, "The Irony of 'Inclusionary' Zoning," *Southern California Law Review* 54 (1981): 1167–1224.

where Irvine and Laguna Beach are located, contains a number of cities with recently built residential areas, all virtually indistinguishable from each other.[52] If one of these look-alike cities passes an affordable housing law it will have little impact on the price of existing expensive houses in it. Few people want to pay a premium for a house in one city over another if their neighborhoods are identical and their governments offer the same quality of public services. High substitutability between houses in these cities means the demand curve for expensive new houses in either city is highly elastic, that is, nearly horizontal. Figure 3-25c shows that if such a city enacts an affordable housing law the price of expensive new houses in it will not change, and the same goes for expensive existing homes. Irvine, Laguna Beach, and Palo Alto are one-of-a-kind places that stand out in the sameness of their regions. Some people are willing to pay a premium to live in Irvine if the alternative is life in an anonymous part of the sprawl, but hardly anybody will pay a premium to live in one look-alike city rather than its look-alike neighbor. The law will only affect a city's house prices if the demand for houses in the city is downward sloping rather than highly elastic. The three cities with these laws probably fill the bill.[53]

Some Other Elasticities

Income Elasticity An economist discussing demand elasticity without any qualifiers will almost surely be talking about own-price elasticity of demand. Demand, however, also depends on other variables whose elasticity we might want to examine. The *income elasticity of demand* for a good is also a ratio of percentages, defined as:

(3.2) $$E_I = \frac{\textit{Percentage change in quantity demanded}}{\textit{Percentage change in income}},$$

or

(3.3) $$E_I = \frac{\Delta Q/Q}{\Delta I/I},$$

where I is the person's income (or possibly wealth). All other determinants of demand, including the good's price, are held constant. Income elasticity can be positive or negative. We call X a *normal good* if the quantity consumed increases with income. If its income elasticity of demand exceeds 1, an increasing proportion of income is spent on X as income rises. If its income elasticity is negative, X is an *inferior good* whose demand curve shifts downward as income rises. For example, laundry done at a laundromat is an inferior good—when your income rises you will buy your own washer and never have to hoard quarters again. Figure 3-26 shows how consumption varies with income for normal goods with elasticity less than 1 (Panel a), greater than one (Panel b), and inferior goods (Panel c).

Cross-Elasticity We may also be interested in how changes in the prices of other goods affect the quantity demanded of some good we are studying, holding all other factors constant. The *cross-elasticity of demand* for X, with respect to the price of Y, is also a ratio of percentage changes:

(3.4) $$E_{XY} = \frac{\Delta X/X}{\Delta P_Y/P_Y},$$

[52]Some are so indistinguishable that they put their names on all street signs to help visitors, police, and fire departments.

[53]In these regions there are also some distinguishable cities that do not have affordable housing laws. All the elasticity analysis says is that distinguishable cities are more likely than look-alike cities to have these laws (not that all such cities will have them), and that nonunique cities are unlikely to enact them.

FIGURE 3-26
Income-Consumption Curves

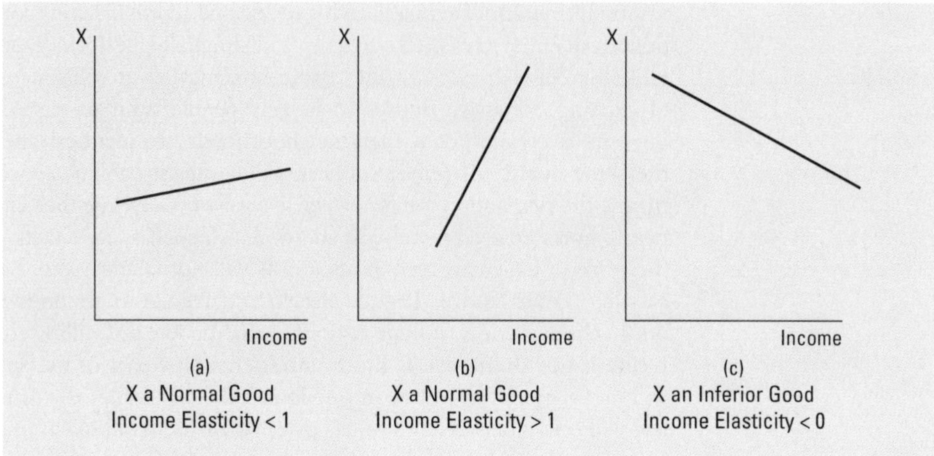

If X and Y are substitutes, $E_{XY} > 0$, that is, an increase in the price of Y shifts the demand curve for X outward. If they are complements, $E_{XY} < 0$. Note that in general $E_{XY} \neq E_{YX}$.

Elasticity of Supply The elasticity of supply of a good is the analogue of own-price elasticity of demand:

(3.5)
$$E_s = \frac{\Delta Q_s / Q_s}{\Delta P / P}$$

where P is the market price of the good and Q_S is quantity supplied. The higher E_S is, the more responsive quantity is to a change in price, that is, the flatter the slope of the supply curve. Because supply curves slope upward, E_S is always positive.

INFORMATION AND MARKETS

How Prices Convey Information

Economists often say that prices are determined in markets, the result of trades like those in the five-person example described earlier. Perhaps it is more accurate to say that prices are *discovered* in markets. No diagram of supply and demand appears when the day's trading opens to show the difference between today's market-clearing price and yesterday's. Participants must weigh the information they have recently acquired (in reality it arrives continuously) to make their own assessments of how events and rumors of events will affect supply and demand.[54] Different traders have different information—the opinions of an expert on weather and those of an expert on grocery marketing trends will both influence the market's determination of the price of wheat. Our next job is to understand the roles prices play in conveying information that influences decisions of producers and consumers.

Adam Smith In Chapter 2, self-interested individuals reached patterns of productive specialization and arranged trades that were economically efficient. Trading, however

[54]Joel Hasbrouck, "One Security, Many Markets: Determining the Contributions to Price Discovery," *Journal of Finance* 50 (September 1995): 1175–99; and Ananth Madhavan and Venkatesh Panchapagesan, "Price Discovery in Auction Markets: A Look Inside the Black Box," *Review of Financial Studies* 13 (Autumn 2000): 627–58.

did not take place in markets. Instead, we saw only extremely simple transactions involving two people and two goods. In real life, however, production requires many individuals and coordinated use of the many different resources they bring with them. When there are millions of people who can produce thousands of different goods and services, the problem of efficiently assigning persons to activities is beyond the reach of computing power. The costs of solving it incorrectly can be very high. Yet the world attacks this problem every day with some success (if not theoretical perfection). The market prices of goods and resources adjust with the discovery of new information, and individual decision makers adjust their production and consumption in turn. Long-lived surpluses and shortages are rarities. Adam Smith, the founder of economics as we know it, first showed the size of the coordination problem and helped us to appreciate the role of markets in resolving it. A few pages into *The Wealth of Nations* (1776), he set the scene.

> *The woollen coat, for example, which covers the day-labourer, as coarse and rough as it may appear, is the produce of the joint labour of a great multitude of workmen. The shepherd, the sorter of the wool, the wool-comber or carder, the dyer, the scribbler, the spinner, the weaver, the fuller, the dresser, with many others, must all join their different arts in order to complete even this homely production. How many merchants and carriers, besides, must have been employed in transporting the materials from some of those workmen to others who often live in a very different part of the country! How much commerce and navigation in particular, how many ship-builders, sailors, sail-makers, rope-makers, must have been employed in order to bring together the different drugs made by the dyer, which often come from the remotest corners of the world! What a variety of labour too is necessary in order to produce the tools of the meanest of those workmen! To say nothing of such complicated machines as the ship of the sailor, the mill of the fuller, or even the loom of the weaver, let us consider only what a variety of labour is requisite in order to form that very simple machine, the shears with which the shepherd clips the wool. The miner, the builder of the furnace for smelting the ore, the feller of the timber, the burner of the charcoal to be made use of in the smelting-house, the brick-maker, the brick-layer, the workmen who attend the furnace, the mill-wright, the forger, the smith, must all join their different arts in order to produce them.*[55]

And that's just for the coat. Smith goes on for another page describing the coordinated efforts that produce the worker's furniture, windows, china, and eating utensils. If he knows any of them at all, the worker knows at most a few of the individuals who produced his coat. But when he buys the coat, he trades indirectly with each of them.[56] We can better understand how the coat comes together by watching these people and others as they adjust to unforeseen changes.

After the Epizootic Take the coat story a step further. Assume that an epizootic (the animal version of an epidemic) suddenly cuts the sheep population by half. The price of wool rises as coat manufacturers bid against one another for the smaller amount available. Thousands of adjustments ensue. As expected, new woolen coats rise in price. Makers of other fabrics that substitute for wool in coats step up production as the prices of their coats also rise. The price of milk rises as some cows become worth more dead than

---

[55]Adam Smith, *The Wealth of Nations* (New York: Modern Library, 1994), orig. 1776, 11–12.

[56]Nowadays, manufacturing a coat still requires almost all of the skills that were required in Smith's day, plus such new ones as software writers and electrical linemen. Just as then, the buyer need not know any of them or the details of their jobs. If you wonder what the carder, the fuller, and the scribbler actually do, you can find job descriptions at the Hat Shapers Web site at http://www.hatshapers.com/Felting_Dictionary.htm.

alive because leather from their hides can be made into coats. So does the price of shoes as coat makers bid leather away from shoe makers. Some people settle for keeping their old coats another year rather than pay the higher prices for new wool coats. Makers of earmuffs (a complement to coats) cut their output, as people economizing on coats spend more time indoors and lose fewer earmuffs outside. Substitutes of all kinds are affected. Makers of playing cards increase output because staying home is an alternative to going outdoors in an unfashionable coat. Coal increases in price with an increase in demand for heating by stay-at-homes. (Or possibly it falls because of decreased demand for heat and power at woolen mills.) Firms that produce substitutes for coats will want more workers, and those producing complements will want fewer. Importers who did not previously handle wool coats will start looking for manufacturers in countries not hit by the epizootic, whose citizens will now also encounter higher coat prices.

With fewer animals to tend, sheep farmers hire fewer workers. Makers of shears used for cutting wool shrink output and cut price. If their plants can also produce scissors, the price of scissors may fall. Some former farm workers make the best of it by moving to the city, where apartment rents rise as they add to demand for living space. Industries that can substitute other materials for wool (socks can also be cotton) will do so. Lenders reallocate their funds in hopes of quick money from people who will import sheep to replenish the flocks. Others expect that imported sheep will not thrive in the local climate and see longer-lived profits in industries that produce substitutes for wool coats. Some people devote themselves to researching new substitutes for wool or inventing ways to manufacture these new products. Others finance them. Insurers realize there is money to be made by drafting a new type of coverage for epizootics and selling policies to sheep farmers.

If the narrative is continued, almost everyone and every price in the economy will adjust in large or small degree to the new price of wool. The price may lead to the invention of new goods and the discovery of new resources. This adjustment process would be impossible to plan, however, because no one person or computer can possibly have knowledge of all its aspects.

Dispersed Knowledge and Informative Prices Market prices solve the planning problem by decentralizing decisions into the hands of people who know only the particulars of their individual situations. They need not know about the epizootic at all to respond to the price changes that result from it. Playing card manufacturers, for instance, do not need to know why people want to buy more of their product this winter than they did last year. Buyers of coats will adjust whether or not they know why their price increased, but someone trying to plan all of the economy's adjustments will need to know how each industry influences the others and by what amount. People adjust in accordance with preferences that are their knowledge alone. Some will balk at the price of new wool coats and buy coats made of other material or make do with older ones, but there is no obvious way for an outsider to calculate how many of them will buy other coats and how many will not. Playing card producers compare their costs of cardboard and workers with the price they can get for cards. Some may have economical sources of cardboard unknown to other manufacturers or to the planning agency.

Prices allow adjustments to changing scarcities of goods and resources to be decentralized. The effective use of plans instead of prices presupposes that planners will get all of the information they require. It also presupposes that the planners will input that information into an accurate economic model that accounts for the numerous interrelationships among markets. Even less realistically, planners will have to be selfless despite being responsible to elected officials who can gain political support if planners make decisions that favor their individual constituents. Bureaucracy and politics make it likely that planners will have problems adapting to unforeseen circumstances, a difficulty that markets may be better equipped to cope with. What if an unexpected flood destroys the transportation facilities needed to fulfill the plan for recovery from the epizootic?

Price controls do more than create shortages and surpluses. If prices become inaccurate measures of scarcity, then consumers' decisions on what to consume and producers' decisions on how to use their resources will be affected in ways that decrease economic value. Assume that politicians respond to rising coat prices by setting a price ceiling on them. A high price says sheep have become scarce. It tells sheep farmers that they can profit by replenishing their flocks, an activity coat buyers value greatly. With a price control, farmers will forsake sheep that are really more valued by consumers in favor of livestock and crops that are not under price controls. Seeing a continuing shortage of wool, government may declare a sheep crisis. It might extend price controls to police profiteering by retail sellers of the coats and then open a new department to allocate coats to those who are believed to need them the most. If substitutes for wool coats rise in price, they too may be put under controls. It may require coat makers with access to inexpensive wool to share their savings with those whose sources are more expensive. Taxes will fund unnecessary research into substitutes for scarce wool, a problem that will worsen as sheep farmers continue to drop out of the market because of poor long-term prospects.[57]

The Present and the Future

Trading with Yourself How can an individual best allocate a good between the present and the future if information about the future is uncertain or unknown? Because most potatoes are harvested at the end of the summer, consumers cannot rely on growers to deliver a steady stream of them to market every week over the year. Some of the harvest must be stored and decisions made daily on how much to release from storage for consumption over the year. Begin with your objectives as a consumer as shown in Figure 3-27. Assume that at the start you have 100 bushels of newly harvested potatoes and that a year must pass before you can purchase any more. Divide the upcoming year into halves and assume that your demand to consume potatoes during the first half is identical to that in the second half.

It helps to think of yourself as two different persons. When you hold some potatoes over from the first half to consume during the second you are making a trade with yourself, one that clearly benefits you. Consuming everything in the first half gives you

FIGURE 3-27
Allocation Between Two Periods

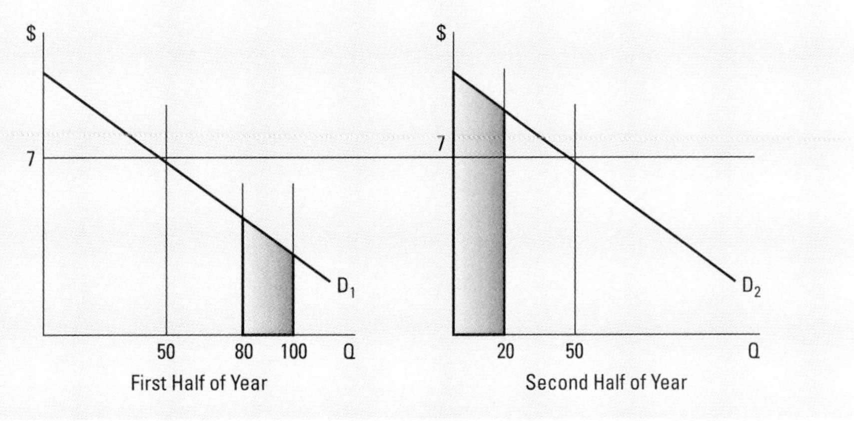

[57]Substituting oil for wool in this paragraph summarizes important parts of the U.S. experience with price controls on oil and oil products during the energy crises of the 1970s. See Joseph P. Kalt, *The Economics and Politics of Oil Price Regulation: Federal Policy in the Post-Embargo Era* (Cambridge, MA: MIT Press, 1981).

consumer surplus equal to the area under the demand curve up to 100 bushels on the left-hand side of Figure 3-27. (Assume you cannot recover your purchase cost, sell what you own, or buy more.) Forgoing 20 of those potatoes loses you the shaded trapezoid of consumer surplus on the left side. Consuming them a half year later brings you larger benefits in the form of the area to the left of 20 units on the other side of the figure. Your total benefits from deferring consumption increase as long as the value of consuming another unit in the second half exceeds the loss of forgoing it in the first half. With identical demands you are best off consuming equal amounts.[58] Had a market price of $7 prevailed throughout, you could simply have purchased 50 potatoes in each half of the year.

Buying the stockpile is costly and holding it is risky. If you are skilled at investing, the potatoes tie up funds that have earning power in investments elsewhere. If you do not acquire information about potatoes while you hold them, you might make mistakes that a potato expert would not. (Maybe the next harvest will be poor and you would be better off carrying some over rather than consuming all 100 of them as planned.) The more commodities you must treat like potatoes, the more severe your information problems. Self-sufficiency in potatoes carries high transaction costs and risks you might rather pay someone else to bear. Fortunately, intermediaries are available.

Speculators Here, the intermediaries are called *speculators.* To understand their role, consider a commodity whose peak harvest occurs in October while smaller amounts come to market in other months. All of each month's production is immediately sold and consumed. (We make this strange assumption only to make the role of speculators clearer.) As before, assume that the demand curve stays constant from month to month. In Figure 3-28, price reaches its low of $3 a pound in October and its peak of $11 in June. Consumers want to avoid this sort of situation, and speculators can help them do so. Consumers buy the commodity to use immediately, while speculators buy when it is abundant and hold it in expectation of gains from being able to resell it later for more money. In October they bid against consumers for current production and, in

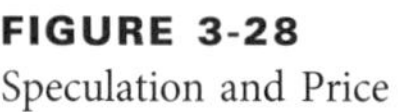
FIGURE 3-28
Speculation and Price

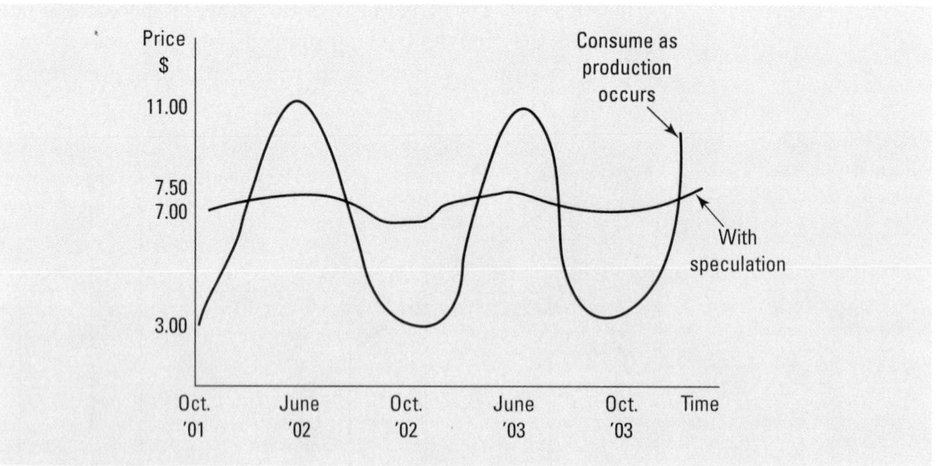

[58]There are many qualifications to this statement, some discussed in later chapters. If you prefer to consume a unit today over an identical one later (a positive time preference), you will eat more potatoes during the first half. We are also assuming that there is no uncertainty about how many potatoes will be available in the future (If not, you might want to buy insurance). There are also no other storage costs such as rental of space in a warehouse. Finally, you might lose willpower and consume more than planned at first, an act you will later regret.

response, that month's equilibrium price goes to \$7. In months like June speculators bring some of their holdings to market, and because they add to the small amount harvested that month, the price settles at \$7.50 rather than \$11. The 50 cent increase from October reflects the opportunity cost of holding the commodity instead of other investments, the costs of storing and insuring it, ad compensation for bearing the risk that the June price will be lower than expected.

Speculators have performed a service that consumers could only do for themselves at higher cost. Equilibrium price is leveled over the year, allowing consumers to enjoy the levels of consumption they prefer. This month's price is determined by both this month's supply and demand and by expected future supplies and demands. Because it reflects both the present and the future the price is a more useful guide to rational consumption and production decisions than it would be if determined solely by today's supply and demand. Speculators do not destabilize prices. Here their actions bring about monthly prices that are more nearly uniform and are also more accurate measures of scarcity. Speculators can only destabilize price (increase the violence of its swings) if they buy when the price is already high (driving it still higher) and sell when it is low (driving it even lower). This is a near-certain recipe for bankruptcy. Speculators who are better predictors will survive, and those who are not will vanish.[59]

Information and Revision of Prices Assume that the market price is \$7.50 in May and speculators expect to deplete most of their inventories before the October harvest. They expect that the harvest will be of normal size and will replenish their holdings for release over the next year. At the end of May, a few market participants learn that one meteorological service predicts very bad weather between May and October. If this forecast is correct, the harvest will be much lower than is generally expected. Market participants can purchase many professional weather forecasts, however, and the other forecasts do not agree with this new and pessimistic one. Knowing that this forecast differs from those of other professionals, not everyone places complete faith in it, but a few do. Those who believe in the more ominous forecast make preparations to profit from higher October prices. Some release less from their holdings onto the market. Others begin buying from persons who are unfamiliar with this forecast or who have chosen to continue believing forecasters who disagree with it.

As the weeks pass a few other forecasters begin predicting bad weather. Some may be held in higher regard than the first forecaster, and some traders start believing weather will be bad because more forecasters now say it will be. As the information accumulates, more of those who hold the commodity cut the amounts they release to market, and some attempt to add to theirs. Not much is harvested in June, but people can add to their holdings by purchasing from others who still believe the weather will remain normal. As a consensus favoring bad weather emerges, fewer people want to sell at the old price and those who wish to increase their holdings will have to offer them higher prices. Today's price will increase until it equals the expected value of the cash price (*spot price*) that will prevail in the future.

By August the price has risen to its expected October level. Even if the bad weather does not happen until September, its expected effects are already embodied in the August price. Because of this, people have more time to adjust to what is starting to look like a sad

---

[59]Many participants in these markets are producers and users of the commodity whose businesses are at stake. They have strong incentives to acquire accurate information and act wisely on it. The Web sites of all commodity exchanges contain guides to trading on them. (The Chicago Mercantile Exchange's is at http://www.cmegroup.com/education/product-specific/the-basics.html.) Traders with hedging (risk mitigation) interests profit more on average than pure speculators. See Michael Hartzmark, "Returns to Individual Traders of Futures: Aggregate Results," *Journal of Political Economy* 95 (November 1987): 1292–1306.

certainty: this year's harvest will be a poor one. The earlier the world recognizes a poor harvest, the more of the commodity it can carry over to replace any shortfall. As in the case of the epizootic, the higher price conveys information that different participants act on in accordance with their individual situations. This time, however, the market gives them the information in advance of the unfortunate events. People who planned on exporting the commodity change plans because high prices make the domestic market more attractive. Those who make other products from the commodity (e.g., bakers make bread from wheat) change their plans and consider concentrating on other products (e.g., rye bread instead of wheat). Of course, weather forecasts are sometimes wrong. If the harvest is good, those who sold at a premium to pessimists will have been right, and the pessimists will suffer losses. Some may leave trading to others who they now realize are better informed.

The market price is affected by information besides that in weather forecasts. For instance, an expert on grocery markets expects that a continuing trend for low-carbohydrate diets will decrease the economy's demand for wheat. An expert on foreign policy hears from informed sources that the government will soon initiate policies to raise wheat exports. Some people believe the information of the grocery researcher or foreign policy expert will move prices, and so begin to trade accordingly. Price changes as different people trade on the basis of information that others do not know and beliefs that others do not hold. There is simply no imaginable way to centralize all of this knowledge in, say, a government agency. Yet the market incorporates it into prices through the actions of dispersed individuals.

Derivatives and Derivatives Markets Our commodity markets have so far offered their participants a range of choices that are far smaller than exist in reality. To make our basic points, we restricted traders to buy-and-hold strategies, where the only possibilities are spot transactions—cash trades for immediate delivery. As a first step beyond these, people might enter into *forward contracts* that fix the price today for delivery of a good at some date in the future. The buyer of the forward contract is "long"—committed to take delivery—and the seller is "short"—committed to deliver it. There is no requirement that the seller actually own the commodity or that the buyer have the necessary cash to pay for it when they make the original agreement. The value of future delivery in a forward contract depends on the market price of the commodity. (The commodity is usually called the "underlying".) Because its value depends on the price of the underlying, the forward contract is an example of a *derivative* or a *derivative asset.*[60] Many forward contracts originate in *over-the-counter* (OTC) markets, which are contact points (possibly electronic) where their terms are set. Some forward contracts may be reassigned or sold, or have specialized provisions that are particularly valued by the parties making them.

A *futures contract* is a standardized forward contract, traded on a *futures exchange.* Like a forward contract, it sets a price today for future delivery. Futures markets exist in several hundred commodity contracts, each of which specifies in detail the properties of the underlying, the delivery process, settlement provisions, and other attributes of the package. As an example, the New York Mercantile Exchange (NYMEX) contract in natural gas specifies its product not by volume but by its heat content. A contract is for 10 thousand million British thermal units (or 10,000 mmbtu, roughly 10 million cubic feet) of gas, to be delivered at the Henry Hub, a pipeline junction in southern Louisiana. It is to flow at as uniform a rate as possible over the month specified in the contract. Contracts are possible for deliveries in every month over the next six years.[61]

---

[60]For a helpful introduction to derivatives and their usefulness, see Rene M. Stulz, "Should We Fear Derivatives?" *Journal of Economic Perspectives* 18 (Summer 2004): 173–92.

[61]Contract specifications are described at the NYMEX Web site at http://www.nymex.com/NG_spec.aspx.

The contract is valuable to both producers and large consumers of gas as a *hedge* that lessens the risks associated with the highly unstable ("volatile") spot price. Being long allows one to lock in the price of a delivery months before it is to occur, and being short allows one to be certain about the price to be received for making a delivery in the contract month. The prime use of the gas contract is as a hedge, and fewer than three percent of such contracts go to delivery in most months. The remainder are settled in cash through the exchange, which acts as a counterparty for buyers and sellers to eliminate the risk of nonperformance (i.e., if you owe money you pay the exchange, and if you are owed money the exchange pays you). In the event of a default the exchange will have sufficient cash from membership dues and insurance to make good any claim. Many other forward contracts exist in gas, with different volumes, timing of deliveries, and locations of delivery. OTC contracts, for example, are frequently used to hedge against unexpected changes in the price difference between two locations.[62]

Table 3-5 shows the October 21, 2004, prices of gas futures for delivery in various months. On that date gas was available for delivery at Henry Hub in February 2005 at $9.15 per mmbtu. Prices behave as one would expect: gas use peaks in January and February, when pipelines are filled to capacity and storage is drawn down to meet heating requirements. When demand falls in the summer, storage is refilled. An electricity producer whose generator burns gas can lock in a $6.95 price for deliveries next July by buying a futures contract today.[63] A gas producer looking ahead can sell a futures

TABLE 3-5 NATURAL GAS FUTURES PRICES (PER MMBTU) FOR OCTOBER 21, 2004

MONTH/YEAR	PRICE
November 2004	$7.65
December	8.69
January 2005	9.18
February	9.15
March	8.68
April	7.27
May	6.99
June	6.96
July	6.95
August	7.05
September	7.02
October	7.04
November	7.35
December	7.63
January 2006	7.82
February	7.89
March	6.54
April	6.50
May	6.30

[62]The difference is usually referred to as the *basis*.

[63]On the table, the May, June, and July prices are very close, as are the August, September, and October prices. This is coincidence and is not a general pattern.

contract today and be certain of receiving $9.18 in January 2005. The futures market thus sharpens predictions of the spot price in different months. The November 2004 price depends on expectations of weather in that month and the rest of the winter. Someone interested in delivering or receiving gas in the summer of 2006 will not learn much from the November futures price.

As information specific to various months is uncovered, the prices of individual futures contracts change. The reasoning is the same as in the buy-and-hold market. If I expect that the February 2005 spot price will exceed $9.15 (possibly I am in possession of a superior weather forecast), I can pay that amount for a futures contract today. If I am right, I can resell the gas in the February spot market for, say, $11.[64] As others in the market come to believe that the winter will be very cold, they too will attempt to purchase the February contract, driving up its price. If expectations about the summer of 2005 are unchanged, little may happen to contract prices for those months as the February price changes.[65] Likewise, if I expect that mild weather will bring low February spot prices, I can sell a futures contract ("short") to deliver then. If the spot price is low, I can buy in the spot market and still resell to my counterparty at $9.15. If belief in a mild winter becomes more general, others will try to imitate me, and the price of the February contract will be driven down today.

Chapter Summary

- Markets are where people acquire information about possible exchanges and where they make the exchanges that they find most attractive. Markets reduce transaction costs by making it easier to discover and compare the offers of counterparties.

- A buyer's demand curve summarizes willingness to pay for a good. Its height is the person's valuation of each unit, and its downward slope reflects substitutability—faced with a high price for the good, a buyer will substitute away from it.

- There is a fundamental distinction between quantity demanded (movement along a fixed demand curve in response to a price change) and demand (a shift of the entire curve due to changes in the buyer's information, income, or changes in the prices of substitutes and complements.) Adding the demand curves of all buyers produces the market demand curve.

- A price-taking producer (one so small relative to the market that its actions alone cannot influence price) wishes to be as profitable as possible. That producer's supply curve shows its most profitable outputs at different market prices, and is the same as its marginal cost curve.

- As with demand, we distinguish a change in quantity supplied (movement along a fixed supply curve in response to a price change) from a change in supply (a shift of the entire curve due to a change in the price of a variable input or a change in technology). Market supply is the sum of the producers' supply curves.

- Market price converges to its equilibrium value as buyers and sellers make transactions that benefit them as individuals. If a prospective buyer meets a prospective seller both can gain from a transaction at a price above the seller's marginal cost

[64]In reality the contract will probably be settled for the cash difference between the spot price and the contract price.

[65]It's not quite so simple: if storage is drawn down beyond expectations in February, demand for gas to refill the storage will be higher in summer, and the summer price may be affected.

and below the buyer's valuation. As exchanges take place, the range of feasible prices shrinks, and at equilibrium all mutually beneficial exchanges have been made.

- The equilibrium price clears the market, leaving neither shortage (frustrated buyers attempting to find sellers) nor surplus (frustrated sellers attempting to find buyers) and allocating the good in accordance with the valuations of individual buyers. When demand or supply shifts, new trades are set in motion that bring the market to a new equilibrium.
- If production is possible at the equilibrium price, the market's output is produced at the lowest possible (avoidable) cost. If trade opens up between two formerly separated markets, arbitrage will take place until the price difference between them is no more than the cost of transferring the good.
- To see the range of problems that supply and demand can handle we examined four applications: how recycling paper will reduce acreage in trees, how a ceiling price on an input can raise the price of output, how cost and demand interact to affect prices, and how gasoline rationing with tradable tickets transfers wealth from sellers to buyers.
- Elasticity of demand is the ratio of the percentage change in quantity demanded of a good to a (small) percentage change in its price. In general the elasticity of demand for a good is greater, the more substitutes buyers perceive for it. Costs of quickly adjusting consumption imply that the longer the time that has elapsed since a good's price change, the more elastic the demand for it will be.
- In a system of interrelated markets prices are essential for the coordination of economic activity. They allow decentralized adjustment of production and consumption to changes in individual markets and to new information. The transaction costs of achieving the same adjustments through central planning are likely to be higher and the outcome less efficient.
- Market prices convey information about present and future supplies and demands. As peoples' information and expectations change, prices change today to more accurately anticipate the future, giving people in markets more time to make adjustments to changed conditions.
- Speculators are intermediaries that make transactions in expectation of future price changes. By doing so they are likely to reduce market price fluctuations. Futures contracts that promise future delivery at a price set today help further improve the ability of markets to anticipate changing conditions.

Appendix 3-A

Mathematics

An Algebraic Approach to Market Equilibrium

A Numerical Example Numbers and graphics are all we need here to understand exchange and market equilibrium. Sometimes additional insights can be obtained by modeling the market as a set of simultaneous equations whose solution is an equilibrium. As an example, let the demand curve be given by

$$Q_D = 32 - 1.5P, \tag{3.6}$$

where Q_D is quantity demanded and P is market price. The supply curve is

$$Q_S = -20 + 2.5P, \tag{3.7}$$

where Q_S is quantity supplied. In equilibrium the two quantities are equal, that is,

$$Q_S = Q_D. \tag{3.8}$$

Substituting, we find $P = \$13$ and $Q_D = Q_S = 12.5$, as shown by the intersection of curves D and S in Figure 3-15.

We can then show how equilibrium will change if the supply or demand curve shifts. Economists call this an exercise in *comparative statics,* which analyzes what will happen if the market is "shocked" (the standard terminology) by some external event. In this market assume that a fall in the market price of some input decreases sellers' marginal costs by $4 for each unit of output. In Figure 3-15 the supply curve shifts downward to S′, becoming

$$Q_S = -10 + 2.5P. \tag{3.9}$$

Q. Derive equation (3.9.)

The demand curve remains as before in equation 3.1. The new equilibrium price is $10.50, and 16.25 units are exchanged. Price has fallen and quantity has increased, with benefits to both consumers and producers. Buyers pay $2.50 less per unit, and sellers get $1.50 of additional revenue per unit.

Q. Show that the previous results are correct. Why does the position of the demand curve not change? For a general system of linear equations with upward-sloping supply and downward-sloping demand, show that if a variable input becomes cheaper, market price will fall and output will rise.

Q. Check that in the initial equilibrium consumer surplus is $52.08 and producer surplus is $31.25. Then check that after the $4 downward shift in supply consumer surplus increases to $88.00 and producer surplus to $52.81.

A Generalization

The earlier linear model is a particular instance of a general formulation that treats quantities supplied and demanded as functions of market price:

(3.10) $$Q_S = S(P)$$

(3.11) $$Q_D = D(P)$$

(3.12) $$Q_S = Q_D$$

There are three equations in three unknowns. If the demand curve slopes downward ($dQ_D/dP<0$) and the supply curve slopes upward ($dQ_s/dP>0$) they will have a solution.[66] That solution only makes economic sense if equilibrium price and quantity are positive. Whether they are depends on the slopes and intercepts of the demand and supply functions.

Using more advanced methods it is possible to show that as long as the slopes (derivatives) of the demand and supply functions have the aforementioned sign pattern, a shock that, for example, shifts the demand curve upward will lead to an increase in price and an increase in market output.

Q. Assume that demand and supply are linear. Given their slopes, what conditions on the intercept terms ensure that equilibrium price and quantity will be positive? First solve the problem using the numerical slopes in equations 3.6 and 3.7, and then generalize the solution to any possible slopes.

Q. Check that the sizes of the shortages in Figure 3-17 are as claimed in the text that accompanies it.

[66]To avoid mathematical complication the text assumes that all functions are differentiable.

Appendix 3-B

Elasticities via Calculus

Using calculus, elasticity of demand is defined as

$$E_D = \frac{dQ}{dP} \cdot \frac{P}{Q}, \qquad \textbf{(3.13)}$$

where dQ/dP is the derivative of quantity demanded as a function of price.

Q. Using this formula, prove the assertions of the text about how the response of total spending to price depends on elasticity of demand.

A straight-line demand curve is often the simplest way to illustrate some economic principle, but the value of elasticity changes as we move along it. In some future applications (e.g., those coming in Chapter 6) it helps to use a demand curve whose elasticity is constant. The equation of such a curve is

$$Q = aP^{-b}, \qquad \textbf{(3.14)}$$

where a and b are positive constants. Using equation 3.13, we can show that its elasticity equals b for all positive prices and quantities.

Q. Graph this equation when a = 10 and b = 2. Then show how the curve shifts with changes in a and b.

Q. Show that if a good's income elasticity of demand exceeds 1, an increasing proportion of income is spent on it as income rises.

Q. Elasticity of supply also varies as we move along a straight-line supply curve, with one possibly important exception. Show that the elasticity of a straight-line supply curve passing through the origin is everywhere equal to 1.

Questions and Problems

1. Markets are where people exchange information about potential transactions. If so, can advertising create economic value? Explain. Identify some other institutions whose effects on lowering information costs are similar to those of advertising.

2. Advertising can inform buyers, but sellers must incur costs to advertise. If so, advertising can result in higher prices to consumers. Does this mean advertising is economically inefficient? If not, explain how it can simultaneously create value and increase market prices.

3. In a barter economy, would you rather be a potato farmer or an avant-garde artist? Why?

4. Say alcohol is strictly illegal in your dorm and any student caught supplying or drinking it faces automatic expulsion from school. As you might expect, some students will not be deterred by the threat. It is, however, more likely that those choosing alcohol will be more likely to consume it in the form of bourbon than beer. Explain why. (Assume that although beer is bulkier and has a lower concentration of alcohol than bourbon, the probability of being caught is the same for both.)

5. Is the demand curve for children downward sloping? Explain, being careful to specify exactly what you mean by the price of children. What is your evidence? How about the demand for high grades in this course? Divorces?

6. Assume that your probability of surviving an accident is greater in a car equipped with certain safety features. If so, what will be the likely effect on the number of accidents? Give a numerical example showing that the safety requirement might actually increase injuries or deaths, and relate your work to the concept of demand elasticity. Now assume no safety features, but instead assume that the government requires every car to be equipped with a dagger in the center of the steering wheel, pointed at the driver. Do you expect that this will reduce injuries or deaths by more than safety equipment? Explain.

7. The U.S. legal system generally requires that each party to a civil dispute be responsible for its own legal fees. In England the loser pays the winner's legal fees as well as its own. Do you expect to see more lawsuits and trials that are long shots for the plaintiff in the United States or England? How about lawsuits and trials where the sides have roughly equal probabilities of prevailing? (Remember that in both countries the parties have an option to reach a settlement rather than going to trial.)

8. In no-fault insurance, anyone involved in an accident is compensated for losses, regardless of who actually caused it. What do you expect will happen to the volume of auto accidents if no-fault insurance replaces the current system in which the driver who causes the accident must pay the victim?

9. In the market for corn the supply curve is $Q_S = -2 + P$ and the demand curve is $Q_D = 10 - P$. Solve these for equilibrium price and quantity. Now assume that producers in Illinois grow 10 percent of that output. One year, however, they have particularly good weather and their crop yields increase by 20 percent, that is, their share of the nation's corn output increases to 12 percent. (Think of this as a 2 percent rightward parallel shift in the supply curve.) What happens to market price and output? In qualitative terms, what happens to the incomes of producers in Illinois?

10. In June of 2009 the U.S. House of Representatives passed H.R. 2454, which introduced a "cap-and-trade" system to reduce carbon emissions associated with global warming. The federal government will issue a fixed number of allowances, each of which permits the holder to emit a ton of carbon dioxide over the next year. As time passes the annual issuance of allowances will fall to reflect declining

carbon emissions targets. An allowance holder may surrender its allowances to government after emitting its quota of carbon dioxide or it may sell them on a market to entities that want the right to emit more of their own. There are two possible ways to allocate the allowances initially. Government can either auction them or give them away.[67]

a. True or false? An economist would expect that regardless of whether the allowances are initially sold or given away their final distribution among firms that emit carbon dioxide will be the same. Explain.
b. Some large emitters (e.g., oil refiners and electricity generators) are on record as favoring giveaways because they consider their products to be necessities. They claim that paying for allowances will raise the prices of their products, but if they get the allowances for free the prices of their products will not be affected. Does this make sense? Explain.

11. Just because a good is scarce does not necessarily mean there is a shortage of it. Explain why.

12. Rent controls that are set below market equilibrium prices can help ensure that poorer people will be able to obtain living space on reasonable terms. Does this make sense?

13. Airlines routinely overbook flights, selling more tickets than seats available. If too many ticketed passengers show up, they offer payments to volunteers who are willing to give up their seats. These take such forms as cash vouchers for future flights and upgrades to first class on the next flight out.
    a. Why is this situation more efficient than a simple rule that prohibits airlines from overbooking? (Be sure to say precisely what you mean by efficiency.)
    b. Why do you (probably) not object to the airline practice of bribing passengers off the plane, but you (probably) would object if you learned that the airline had bribed a local politician to obtain airport gate space that would otherwise have been used by a competitor?

14. Flour and eggs are complements in making a cake. Assume that cakes, flour, and eggs are bought and sold in price-takers' markets. An external event decreases the variable cost of producing flour. Using supply and demand, show what happens to the price and quantity of eggs, flour, and cakes.

15. Assume that popcorn and potato chips are substitutes, and popcorn and cola are complements.
    a. How does a ceiling price (below equilibrium) on popcorn affect the price of cola? Explain.
    b. Start the problem over and assume that there is an effective floor price (above equilibrium) on potato chips. What happens to the price of popcorn?

16. Following are observations on the market price and the quantity of good X produced and consumed in three different years: $10 and 100 units, $4 and 57 units, and $8 and 88 units. Can we conclude that the market demand for X slopes upward?

17. In the example from the Exchange Without Production section, construct a different series of trades among the five people and show that it leads to the same equilibrium price and the same allocation of the good among them.

---

[67]The H.R. 2454 has extremely complex allowance allocation provisions. In the first years 85 percent of allowances will be given away, but by the 20th year all of them will be auctioned.

18. An increase in the demand for steak will reduce the prices of dog food, soap, and shoes. Yes or no? Explain.

19. If the supply curve of cattle is perfectly vertical, invention of a perfect substitute for milk will have no effect on the price of cattle. Yes or no? Explain.

20. Say the New York Stock Exchange average fell by 2 percent yesterday, and commentators spoke of a rush to sell. Because there had to be a purchaser of every share sold, why didn't they talk about a rush to buy?

21. Assume that the elasticity of demand for some good is less than 1 in absolute value. If half of the available supply is destroyed its price will rise, as will the total amount consumers spend on it. Does this mean the economist's concept of value is worthless, because a smaller amount of the good is worth more than a larger one? Explain.

22. Drug law enforcers can concentrate their efforts on reducing supply or demand, removing suppliers or removing demanders.

a. Assuming that your goal is to raise the price of drugs to a prohibitive level, should you pursue suppliers or users? What does your answer assume about elasticities of demand and supply?

b. If instead you want simply to reduce consumption and are uninterested in what happens to price, under what assumptions about elasticities should you target users rather than sellers?

23. Do you expect that the cross-elasticity of demand for Hyundais with respect to the price of Subarus will be positive or negative? Do you expect the cross-elasticity of demand for Subarus with respect to the price of Bentleys to be smaller or larger than their cross-elasticity with respect to the price of Hyundais? Explain.

24. When you choose to buy insurance, are you speculating? When you choose not to buy insurance, are you also speculating? Explain.

25. What's the difference between a futures price and a future price?

26. "Market fundamentals often have little to do with prices. Even if available supplies are unchanged, futures trading can be responsible for pushing prices up." Does this make sense?

27. Short selling in futures markets entails promising to deliver something you have not yet bought or produced. Is it short selling when a publisher promises to deliver you a magazine subscription over the next 12 months?

Chapter 4

Production, Costs, and Supply

Introduction

The Biggest Machine in the World

The people in Figure 4-1 have the awesome responsibility of operating the biggest machine in the world. They work in the control room of the California Independent System Operator (Cal-ISO, or just ISO) in Folsom, California, producing and delivering power to 80 percent of the state's households and businesses.[1] The back wall is a circuit diagram of the state, laid on its side. At any moment the ISO and its computers may be controlling as many as 800 electrical generators and 30,000 miles of high-voltage transmission lines, seeing to it that total power produced always equals exactly the amount people wish to use. If these are not equal (whether over or under) for as little as a quarter of a second,

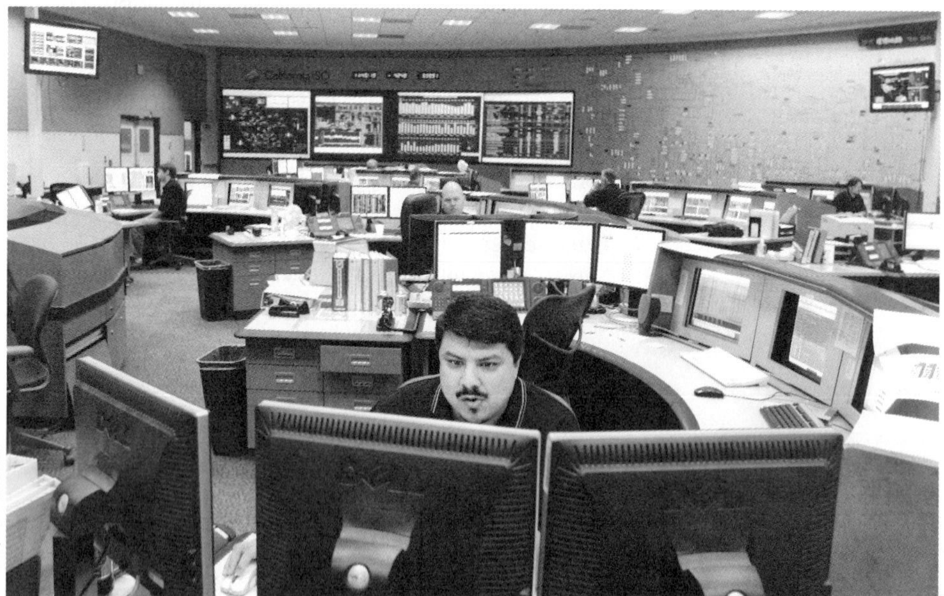

FIGURE 4-1 The California ISO Control Room

AP Photo/Rich Pedroncelli

[1]See the CAISO Web site at www.caiso.com. The photo is found at http://www.caiso.com/14c9/14c9b13039800.html.

most of the western United States is likely to black out. (California both imports power from other states and exports it to them.) The generators and transmission lines are distinct pieces of equipment, but the system is really like a machine—a mistake in operating a power plant near San Francisco can trigger a blackout in San Diego.

That's enough responsibility for almost anyone, but the ISO has an even harder job: to minimize the cost of the power being produced at every instant. It has an almost infinite number of choices about which generators it can order to operate, and literally billions of different combinations will suffice to maintain reliability. Its dispatchers and computers must figure out the lowest-cost combination of all these elements. Their job is similar to (but far more complex than) one of the problems we will see how to resolve in this chapter. Simply using the generators with the lowest operating costs will not do the job for a real electrical system. Some take time to start up and shut down, most importantly nuclear and coal-burning units with low operating costs. They must operate overnight because they must be ready to serve the next day's peak afternoon load, and at 4 a.m. the ISO must figure out how to dispose of their power somewhere in the West (the generators cannot simply be disconnected). Quick-starting high-cost generators that burn natural gas must be on hand to meet air-conditioning load on an unexpectedly hot day, and reserve units must be ready at all times to make up for the outage of a large power plant or major transmission line. Spilling water over dams will create hydroelectric power at no direct expense, but limited reservoir capacity means today's production has opportunity costs that will be felt later. Renewable power sources such as wind generators can produce whenever it blows, but the ISO incurs special costs of quickly curtailing some gas-burning power plants when the wind comes up and putting them back on-line quickly when it goes down.

What's Next

We will touch on almost all of Cal-ISO's cost-related problems in this chapter, which introduces concepts of costs and principles of minimizing them that we will soon apply to concrete business problems.

- We first define production and summarize the basic characteristics of business firms. Although most inputs are heterogeneous (e.g., different types of specialized labor), for now we will treat them as standardized units.
- We reintroduce opportunity cost as the basis of production decisions, while noting that it is sometimes difficult to exactly identify the most valuable forgone alternative. Differences between economists' and accountants' cost concepts reflect the different purposes for which they use them.
- Because inputs are often substitutes a business must choose the lowest-cost mix of them. In the short run some inputs are fixed and others are variable, but a business can alter its output level by changing only the variable inputs. In the long run all inputs can be varied.
- We derive short-run costs from technological relationships between a variable input and its output, paying particular attention to the relationships between marginal and average costs.
- From these cost relationships we can derive the short-run supply curve of a price-taking seller as the part of its marginal cost curve that lies above average variable cost.

- We analyze long-run costs by showing the ways in which two variable inputs can be combined to produce a given output level (isoquants), and the costs associated with those different input combinations (isocosts).
- Long-run cost curves show the minimum cost of each possible output level. Returns to scale determine whether long-run average costs are increasing or decreasing. The shape of long-run average cost determines whether competition is sustainable in a market.
- Problems of management can help explain why most long-run average cost curves eventually turn upward. Management innovations and new technologies lower the entire long-run average cost curve and shift its minimum rightward or leftward. That minimum indicates the least-cost size of firm.
- Learning through actual experience in production can also shift long-run cost curves downward. In general, learning effects are greatest for the first units produced and diminish as cumulated output rises.

Inputs, Outputs, and Decisions

Production

Production is the act of transforming resources into goods and services that are more valuable. It can take many forms:

- Oil is extracted from the ground, refined into gasoline, and used as transportation fuel.
- A hair stylist uses time, scissors, and chemicals to make a customer feel more attractive and self-confident, which is potentially of great value for a job interview.[2]
- An intermediary finds a previously undiscovered low-cost source of a good that allows her to resell it for less than competitors would charge.
- A bank offers savers interest on their funds and lends them to businesses that invest in new plants that produce goods more cheaply.
- An insurer creates a policy that pays claims resulting from car accidents. Absent insurance, people will drive less and get fewer benefits from their cars because they fear the loss of their homes or savings after an accident. As much as Henry Ford, insurers made the automotive age possible.

The oil producer, stylist, middleman, banker, and insurer are all productive by our definition.

Q. Explain why burglary is not productive in the economist's sense.

The theory of production and costs sheds light on some of management's most important decisions: what quantities to produce and how to produce them. If inputs can be substituted for each other, managers must consider both their productivities and their

---

[2]Economists have learned that expenses to enhance a person's attractiveness are often worth the cost. People who look good to others earn more on average than less attractive people with similar qualifications. Spending on self-beautification is the equivalent of an investment with high returns in the form of earnings. See Daniel Hamermesh, Xin Meng, and Junsen Zhang, "Dress for Success—Does Primping Pay?," *Labour Economics* 9 (2002): 361–73. For evidence on beauty and wages, see Daniel Hamermesh and Jeff Biddle, "Beauty and the Labor Market," *American Economic Review* 84 (December 1994): 1174–94.

prices. Additionally, costs can be incurred simply in adjusting the inputs. We will first learn how to produce a given output at lowest cost, and then extend the analysis to show how costs vary with output. This reasoning is the basis for determining the most profitable amounts to produce in different types of markets. Finally, we will see what costs can tell us about the possibilities for competition in a market.

Outputs, Inputs, and Business Firms

It is harder to define a business firm than it appears at first. What characteristics do a family-owned farm and a multinational bank have in common? Are a nonprofit hospital, a mutual insurance company (one that is owned by its policy holders), and a farmers' marketing cooperative firms, or something else?[3] In Chapter 12 we define a firm as a set of written and unwritten agreements among providers of inputs used in production. That definition, however, says little about the input-output relationships that matter for now. In this chapter a firm is just an entity that transforms inputs into output. Figure 4-2 shows inputs like labor, capital, and energy entering a box and produced goods or services leaving it. Economists call the relationship between inputs and outputs the firm's *production function.* Here we use "function" in its mathematical sense: for every bundle of inputs, the production function shows the maximum output they can produce.

A firm combines inputs to produce its output, whether an agricultural crop, a manufactured product, or a personal service. Output can be measured, and all units of output are identical.[4] Some inputs are homogeneous—for instance, any gallon of fuel oil is interchangeable with any other. Here we simplify by treating all inputs as if they were homogeneous. Adding up types of labor that include assembly workers, salespeople, and executives is an apples-and-oranges problem. Here, however, we assume that their skills can be added up into a single total or index of person-hours employed. Adding up *capital goods*, like machinery, inventories, and buildings, is a similar problem, commonly simplified by adding their market values to a single total.

Here we assume that there is a single person who makes all of the decisions on inputs to use and output to produce, one whose only interest is a well-defined objective such as minimizing costs or maximizing profits. This person has authority over all the firm's activities, from finance to production to marketing. Unlike many real managers, this hypothetical manager can be sure that subordinates will obey all orders he gives and that people outside of the box in Figure 4-2—like suppliers and purchasers—will honor their commitments. These simplifications allow us to postpone studying conflicts between managers and workers and between shareholders and managers. We further assume that the decision maker has other knowledge that real managers may not. He knows the production

FIGURE 4-2 The Business Firm: A Box That Turns Inputs into Output (To Be Opened in Future Chapters)

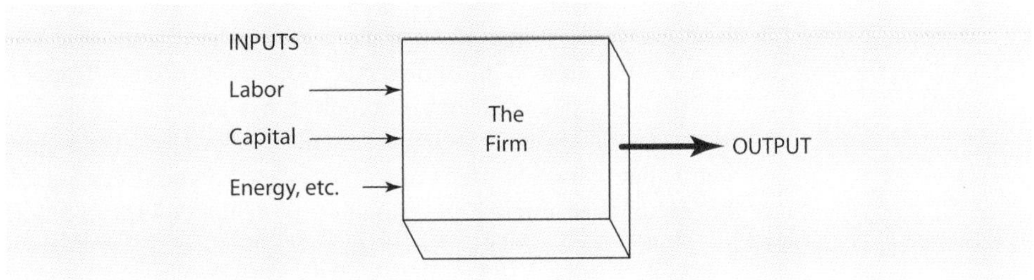

[3]Household names like Sunkist oranges, Land O' Lakes butter, and Ocean Spray cranberries are trademarks of farm marketing cooperatives.

[4]This model is simplified by treating services as identical. In reality, customers want individualized hairstyles and different patients pose distinct challenges to the skills of a dentist.

function well enough to predict exactly how much output any mix of inputs will produce, even if that mix is outside the range of his experience. He also knows a lot about markets for inputs and outputs, including prices and risks that range from deliverability to customer credit. This person initiates and monitors all necessary legal and personal relationships, including financial ones. After all of these relationships with customers and suppliers of inputs are settled, our decision maker pockets what is left or pays any amounts still owed. Our decision maker is also known as the firm's *residual claimant*.

COSTS AND TECHNOLOGY

Opportunity Cost and Its Complications

The Economist, the Accountant, and the Newlywed When economists and accountants discuss costs they sometimes sound as if they come from different planets. The economist calls the cost of some action the most valuable alternative forgone by the decision maker. She is often less interested in a precise dollar figure than in examining how forgone opportunities influence the decisions a business makes. Chapter 2 established that even if money does not exist, peoples' choices will depend on their alternatives. For example, if Jones uses his own funds to finance a business instead of borrowing, he has not avoided paying interest in an economically relevant sense. He explicitly pays interest to a lender, but if he funds himself he forgoes interest that might have been earned on his savings.

Accountants of all types have jobs quite unlike the economist's. A management accountant is concerned more directly with cash flows and is less interested in abstract opportunity costs because cash directly constrains some important operating decisions. Financial accountants must categorize costs in conformity with rules of the Securities and Exchange Commission and the Financial Accounting Standards Board so that investors can better compare the records and prospects of different companies. A tax accountant determines the legally defined costs that minimize her client's payments, whatever their relation to forgone opportunities. The Internal Revenue Service limits her options for a depreciation method and a life span for the client's capital equipment in ways that do not always mirror economic reality. Economists and accountants have different objectives, but they share the misfortune of using the same word—"cost"—to describe what are often quite different concepts.

Opportunity cost reasoning sharpens our understanding of resource allocation. Assume that you have left home to start your own household, but you have not saved enough for the down payment on a house. You ask your parents to lend you the necessary funds. There is no question that you will pay back the amount loaned, but you balk when they further insist that you pay them interest on the money. You tell them that that this is a family, not a bank, all to no avail. They use the logic of opportunity cost to remind you that if all you pay is the amount loaned you are in effect stealing from your brothers' and sisters' inheritances. If your parents do not lend you the money it will remain in investments that will grow over time. If they lend to you everyone forgoes returns that increase the size of their estate and ultimately all of the children's inheritances.[5]

Exactly What Is the Forgone Alternative? The opportunity cost of self-financing your business is the return on your best alternative investment, but what might that

[5]Here the tax code is consistent with economic reasoning. Internal Revenue Service rules allow children to deduct interest payments on loans from their parents in the same way as on an ordinary mortgage, as long as the interest rate is close to the market level and there has been no intent to evade taxes through abuse of provisions on gift giving.

investment be, and what does "best" mean? You clearly cannot examine all the world's business opportunities before making the choice, so the set of alternatives is confined to those you know or can easily learn about. How intensively to search depends on the costs and benefits of acquiring more information. If one of these alternatives had been clearly superior, you presumably would have chosen it.[6] Uncertainty multiplies the problems of identifying opportunity cost because peoples' attitudes toward risk differ, as do their opportunities for combining investments. Few if any of the alternatives will have perfectly predictable returns, and uncertainty carries a price tag—investments with higher expected returns will be riskier. Even if our expectations about the returns from a risky venture are identical, our underlying tolerances of risk may lead us to different investment decisions. Those decisions will also depend on our other investments. If my holdings are well diversified, a small investment in a certain risky stock may nevertheless lower my overall exposure to risk.[7]

Before giving up on the concept of opportunity costs, think of how often they are easy to identify. For many productive inputs, market prices reliably measure opportunity costs. Someone who buys a bag of cement in the market must pay enough to eliminate the next highest bidder for it. Opportunity cost reasoning also helps us understand broader issues. For example, the great increase over the past 70 years in the percentage of married women who work for pay reflects both higher market wages (the opportunity cost of staying at home) and lower costs of housework thanks to cheaper appliances (lower opportunity cost of acquiring them).[8] The rise in obesity over the past 40 years parallels a decrease in the cost of tasty but fat-laden foods and an increase in the opportunity cost of time spent exercising.[9] Opportunity cost even helps explain why higher earners spend less time asleep on average than those who make less.[10]

Q. Propose an explanation for the fact that over the past 20 years married women had a significantly higher average increase in weight than single men.

Substitution: The Short Run and the Long

Consumers buy different bundles of goods as their relative prices change, and producers choose different mixes of inputs. Natural gas and feed, for example, are substitutes in the production of chickens. Colder baby chicks use more of their food to stay warm, leaving less to build weight.[11] If gas is cheap relative to food, it costs less to raise the chick to

[6]For more on the problems of identifying opportunity cost, see James M. Buchanan, *Cost and Choice* (University of Chicago Press, 1979).

[7]See Chapter 16 for details about this point.

[8]Many other facts about women in the workforce can be explained by using opportunity costs. See Dora L. Costa, "From Mill Town to Board Room: The Rise of Women's Paid Labor," *Journal of Economic Perspectives* 14 (2000): 101–22.

[9]David M. Cutler, Edward Glaeser, and Jesse Shapiro, "Why Have Americans Become More Obese?" *Journal of Economic Perspectives* 17 (Summer 2003): 93–118. This reference contains a possible answer to the question immediately below it.

[10]Jeff Biddle and Daniel Hamermesh, "Sleep and the Allocation of Time," *Journal of Political Economy* 98 (October 1990): 922–43.

[11]Feed intake necessary to maintain growth in a chick increases by about 0.5 percent for every 1 degree (Fahrenheit) drop in temperature within normal ranges. http://www.engormix.com/e_articles_poultry_industry.asp?ID=78. Also see Tom Horton, "42-Day Wonders," *Washingtonian* (September 2006): 66–80.

adulthood in a warmer environment. There are limits to substitution, but many possibilities within them. The actual delivery of medical care often requires a physician, but doctors with more nurses and other assistants can see more patients. A doctor with three aides on average sees 40 percent more patients in a week than a doctor with only one.[12] Equipment is also substitutable. A manicurist with electric tools can file, fill, and polish acrylic nails in half the time of one using a cheaper manual file.[13]

What is possible depends on what the firm is free to vary. A manufacturer in a leased building cannot quit producing and stop paying rent without facing serious financial consequences. It is, however, free to vary the fuel it burns in the boiler that provides it with high-pressure steam. The *short run* is defined as the length of time during which the decision maker can vary some inputs, although others remain fixed. In the *long run* all inputs are variable. Inputs are still substitutable in the short run: the firm can change its output level by changing only those inputs that are variable. Long-run substitution is more obvious: the firm can produce a given rate of output using *labor intensive* methods that use a high ratio of worker time to capital (machinery) services, or it can use the opposite mix, a *capital intensive* one.

Short run and long run are not fixed lengths of time. One can lease a storefront, furnish it, and hire staff to open a manicure salon in a matter of weeks. A new power plant can take eight years from siting to operation. In our terminology both are long run. "Fixed" and "variable" are also extremes—you can adjust a fixed input more quickly if you are willing to pay the cost. A new plant might normally take two years to build, but three-shift-a-day construction is faster and more expensive. Or if you are in a bigger hurry you can buy an existing plant from its owner. There may also be costs of altering a variable input. Expanding your workforce quickly gives you little time to interview candidates. With this limited sample you could end up with lower-quality workers than if you had interviewed more. (You could also use the services of a business that certifies the competence of temporary workers.) New workers must be integrated with existing ones and acquire experience before they become fully productive. Employers faced with temporary declines in demand often promise to rehire laid-off workers when business comes back. The promise deters them from seeking jobs elsewhere and allows the employer to avoid the costs of obtaining and training a new workforce.

Short-Run Production, Cost, and Supply

Production with One Variable Input

Marginal Cost Again Start with two inputs, one fixed and the other variable. A large boiler produces steam that heats a building or provides energy for some industrial process.[14] The boiler is fixed—its capacity can only be expanded by buying a new one. Being fixed also means it is indivisible—the owner who wants just a small amount of steam cannot somehow fire up only half of the boiler. Its fuel supply can be freely varied to

[12]Uwe Reinhardt, "A Production Function for Physicians' Services," *Review of Economics and Statistics* 54 (January 1972): 63.

[13]Virginia Postrel, "The Nails File: the Economic Meaning of Manicures," *Reason* 29 (October 1997): 29–32.

[14]In European cities commercial operators or government agencies sometimes deliver steam heat through underground pipes to large buildings whose owners may have the option of self-supply. A worldwide guide to "district energy" can be found at http://www.energy.rochester.edu/deassn.htm.

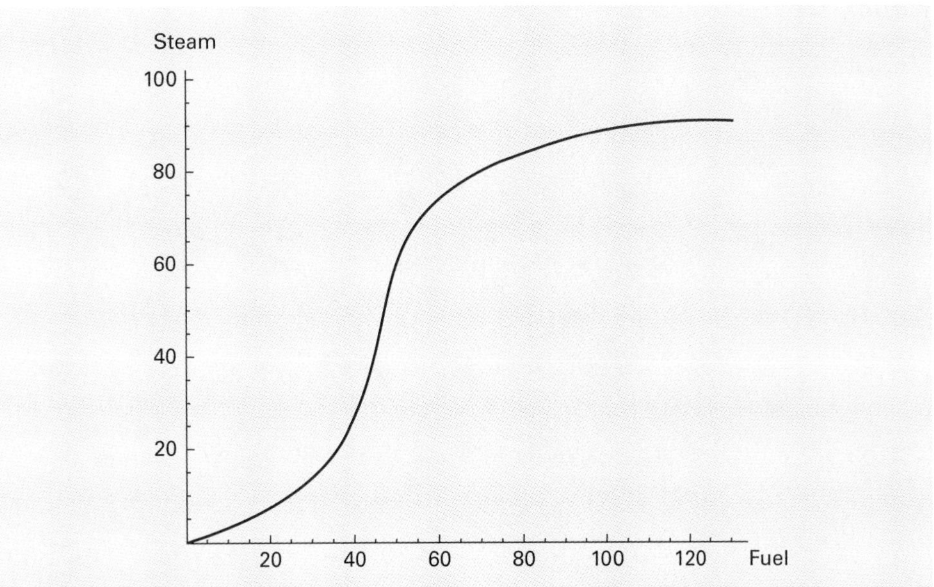

FIGURE 4-3 Total Product

produce steam along the curve shown in Figure 4-3.[15] That steam is called the *total product* of the fuel.[16] Above about 40 gallons per hour steam output continues to increase with a larger fuel burn, but at a decreasing rate.[17] Moving rightward on the curve, the boiler becomes the limiting factor. At 40,000 cubic feet of steam an hour, it takes only a small increment of fuel to produce another cubic foot. At 80,000 that increment must be larger. At low steam outputs we can see the other consequence of a fixed boiler: Only after burning some minimum amount of fuel does it begin to produce any steam at all. A smaller boiler could produce these small amounts of steam with less fuel, but our boiler cannot be subdivided into smaller ones.

To turn total product into total cost, start by reversing the axes of Figure 4-3, because fuel expense (the dependent variable) depends on how much steam (the independent variable, now simply called "Q") we wish to produce. Then convert fuel from physical units (gallons) to dollars. (Just define a unit of fuel as a dollar's worth.) These steps produce the total variable cost (TVC) curve of Figure 4-4. Marginal cost (MC) is the rate of change in TVC, which is equal to the slope of its tangent. Figure 4-3 shows two such tangents. At an output of 24,000 cubic feet (from now on we will just say "24 units") marginal cost is 54 cents, and at 75 it is $1.39. In the lower graph these are two points on the marginal cost curve.[18]

---

[15]The relationship between fuel and steam and the corresponding costs for actual boilers look like the figures in this chapter. See Council of Industrial Boiler Owners, *CIBO Energy Efficiency Handbook* (1997), 30–31, http://www.oit.doe.gov/bestpractices/steam/pdfs/steamhandbook.pdf.

[16]Both boiler and fuel must work together to produce steam, but economists usually call the output the total product of the fuel.

[17]Mathematicallly, the first derivative is positive and the second derivative is negative. Below 40 gallons the second derivative is also positive.

[18]If you wish to check any figures, start with the following equation:

$$TVC = 1.688 \times 10^{-7}Q^5 - 3.553 \times 10^{-5}Q^4 + 3.088 \times 10^{-3}Q^3 - 0.140Q^2 + 3.629Q.$$

Note that this function does not provide a reasonable description of costs outside the range we are examining. All calculations in this chapter were made with Mathematica®.

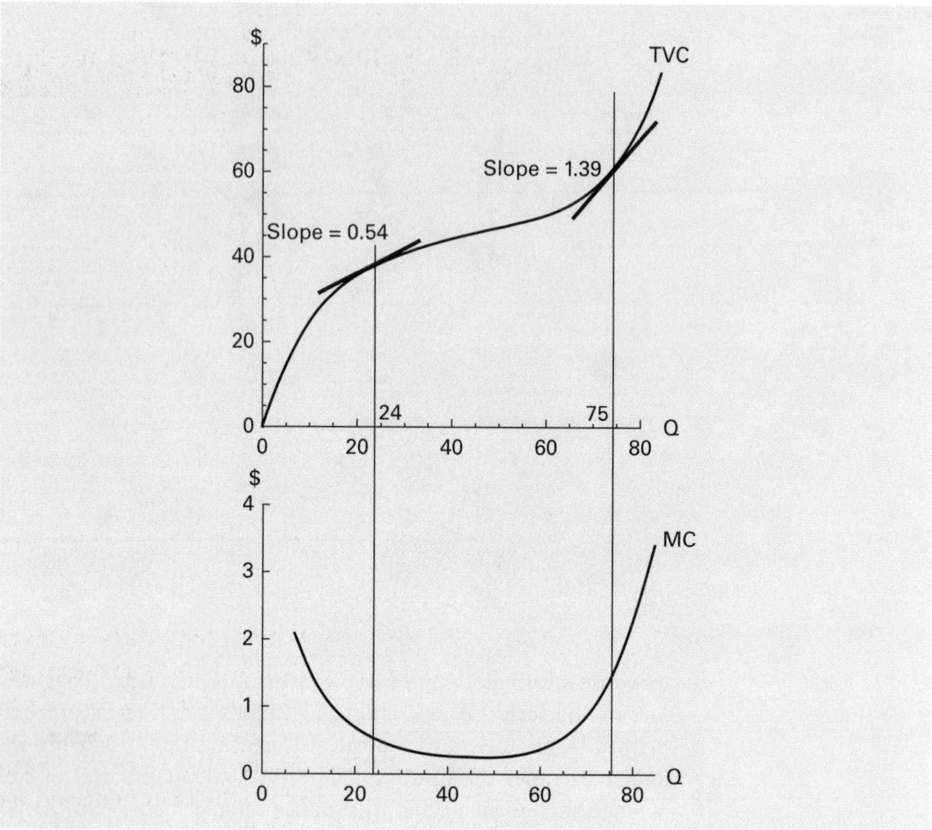

FIGURE 4-4 Total Variable Cost and Marginal Cost

The upward-sloping portion of MC is the only part that matters for production. In Figure 4-5, assume that market price is $1.50. The simple rule to produce where marginal cost equals market price now needs a minor amendment, since they are equal at both 10.9 and 75.8 units. We do not want to stop at the lower output, however, because the marginal cost of every earlier unit exceeds $1.50. In fact, 10.9 units gives us the minimum possible profit (i.e., the biggest loss) we can take at this price. But each unit past the eleventh now benefits the firm because its marginal cost is less than price. In this

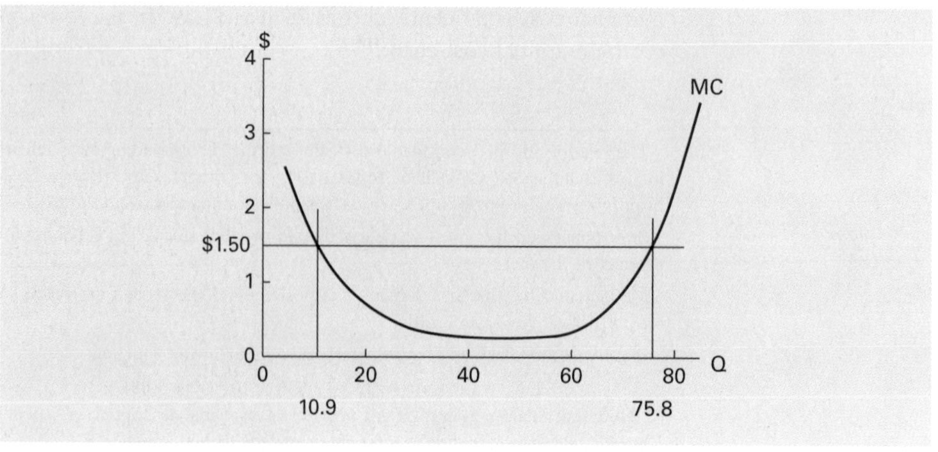

FIGURE 4-5 Marginal Cost Equals Market Price at Two Outputs, but Only One Yields a Profit

example the gains from the extra units eventually exceed the losses from the earlier units and profits become positive. Whether they do become positive depends on market price—if it is 50 cents the firm should never begin production at all, even though there are a few units whose marginal cost is less than 50 cents. Profits are maximized (or losses minimized) by producing the output where marginal cost equals market price, provided marginal cost is rising.

Average Cost and Average Variable Cost The upper portion of Figure 4-6 again shows the TVC curve from Figure 4-4. To calculate average variable cost (AVC) at some output, start with the line from TVC at that output to the origin. For example, at 20 units, total variable cost is $36.00. The slope of the ray from that point to the origin is $36.00/20 = $1.80, which is plotted on the AVC curve in Figure 4-6.[19] Above 7 units the slope of the ray at first decreases, meaning that AVC slopes downward. The curve hits its minimum of $0.79 at an output of 69.2 units. Above that the ray to the origin becomes steeper and average variable costs increase. AVC = $1.02 at two points, one (45 units) on its downsloping branch and the other (86.1 units) on its upslope. Where average variable cost reaches its minimum (69 units) it equals marginal cost, because the slope of the ray

FIGURE 4-6 Total and Average Variable Cost

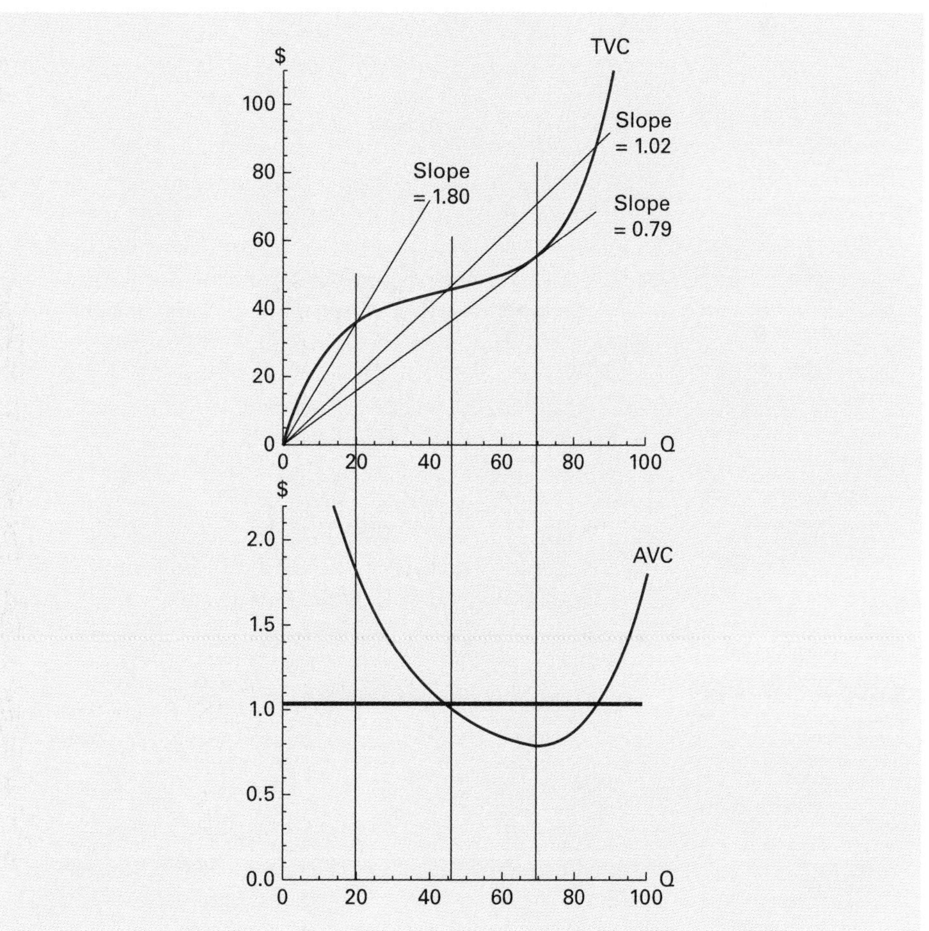

[19]The slope of a straight line is $\Delta Y/\Delta X$, but if the line through x and y goes through the origin the slope also equals y/x.

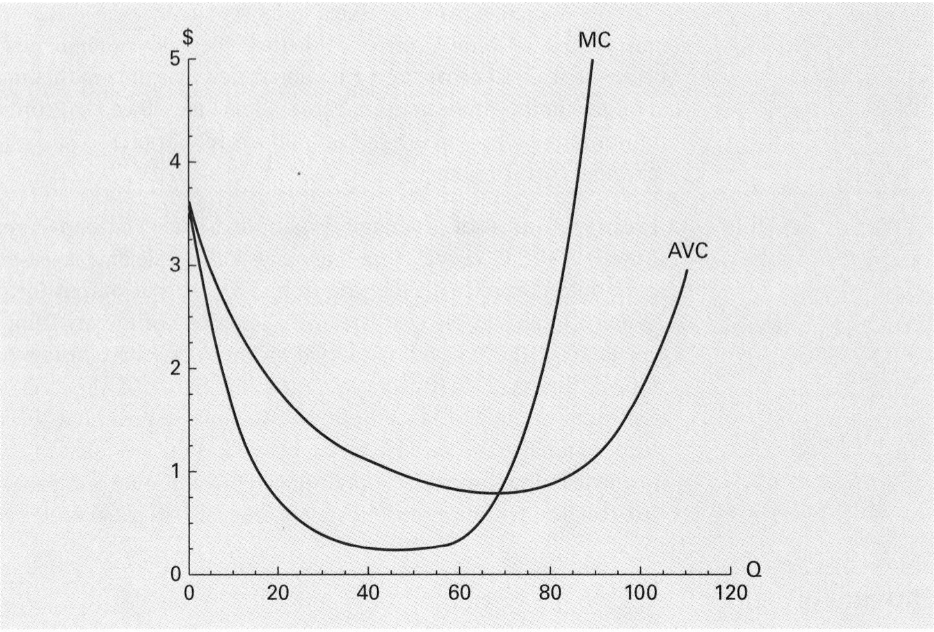

FIGURE 4-7
Marginal Cost (MC) and Average Variable Cost (AVC)

to the origin from TVC (i.e., average variable cost) equals the slope of the tangent to TVC (i.e., marginal cost).

Figure 4-7 superimposes the average variable and marginal cost curves, allowing us to deduce an important relationship between the two. At outputs less than the minimum of average variable cost (i.e., where the AVC curve is falling) marginal cost is less than average variable cost. Similarly, where the AVC curve is rising marginal cost is greater than average variable cost. Finally, if average variable cost is constant (as occurs near the minimum of AVC), it equals marginal cost. Convince yourself that the reverse implications are not necessarily true—immediately to the left of the minimum of AVC, MC is below it but the marginal cost curve itself is rising. For an analogy, assume that you scored 100 on your first exam in this course and 40 on the second (i.e., the marginal) one. Your average falls from 100 to 70. On your third exam you earn 60, a higher marginal score than the second. The average of the three, however, is (100 + 40 + 60)/3 = 66.7, still below your average for the first two exams.

Q. In our example marginal cost is also U-shaped. Why are we seldom interested in determining the output at which it reaches its minimum?

Cost curves also show when a firm should cease production, even in the short run. Assume that fixed costs are $100. Total cost (TC) in Figure 4-8 is the sum of total variable cost and fixed costs. Because marginal costs are avoidable and fixed costs are not, the marginal cost curve is unchanged. To find average total cost (AC), draw rays (not shown) to the origin of Figure 4-8 like those in Figure 4-6. (Try it.) You will see that AC is a U-shaped curve, like AVC. Minimum average cost is $2.24 at an output of 79.5. Because AC includes fixed costs, it is always above AVC. Because fixed costs per

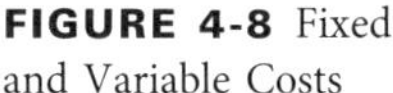
FIGURE 4-8 Fixed and Variable Costs

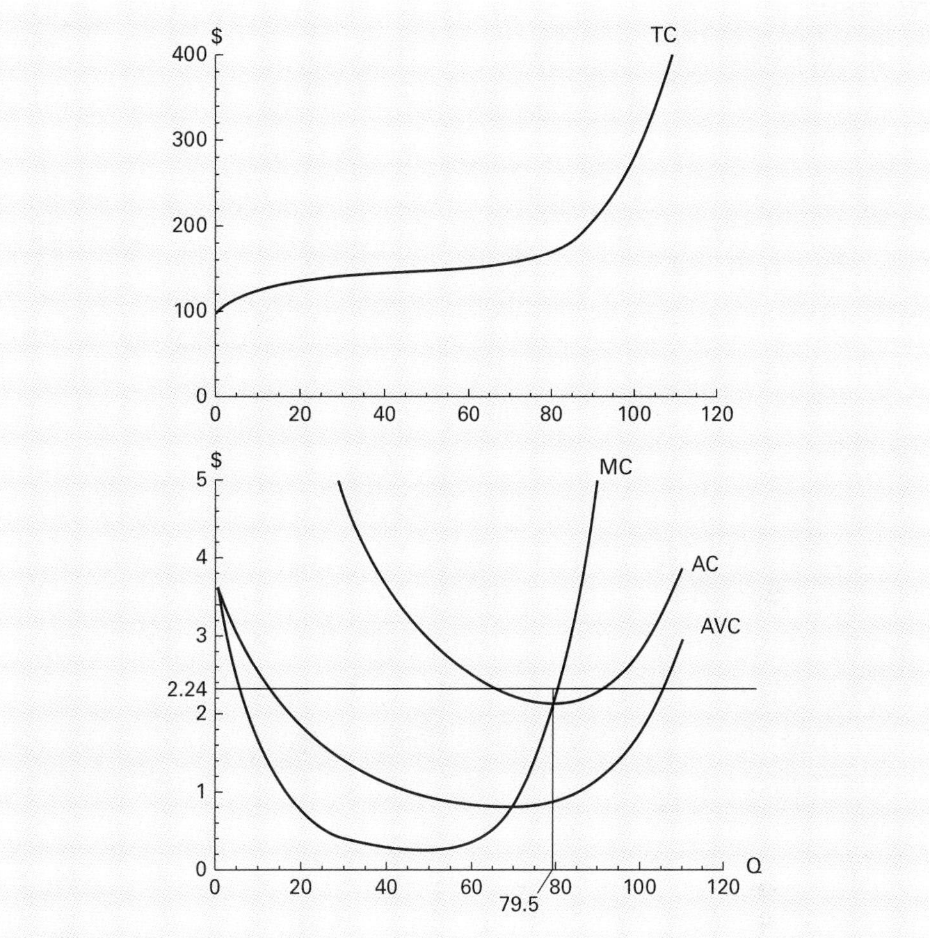

unit are smaller at high outputs, the distance between AC and AVC becomes smaller as output rises. Just like it did for average variable cost, marginal cost also passes through the minimum of average cost.

The Short-Run Supply Curve

Figure 4-9 illustrates the firm's best output decision at three possible market prices. (Remember that it is a price-taker and cannot influence that price.) A seller facing a $3.50 market price maximizes profit by producing 85.3 units, where marginal cost equals that price. Because average cost is below $3.50 we can conclude that it is making a profit (covering all of its opportunity costs) and will stay in business as long as this price prevails. For a second case, start over and assume that market price is $1.50, below the minimum of average cost and above that of average variable cost. Because average cost always exceeds $1.50 there is no output at which it can recover all of its costs. There are, however, outputs whose revenue exceeds variable cost. Because the alternative is to incur the fixed costs in full, the firm minimizes its losses by continuing to produce in the short run. Producing where marginal cost equals price (75.8 units) minimizes its loss. If price is between the minima of AC and AVC, the firm makes the best of a bad thing by operating in the short run and closing in the long run, when its fixed costs are no longer fixed. For the third case, start with a price of $0.50. Although there are outputs at which

FIGURE 4-9
Optimal Outputs at Various Market Prices

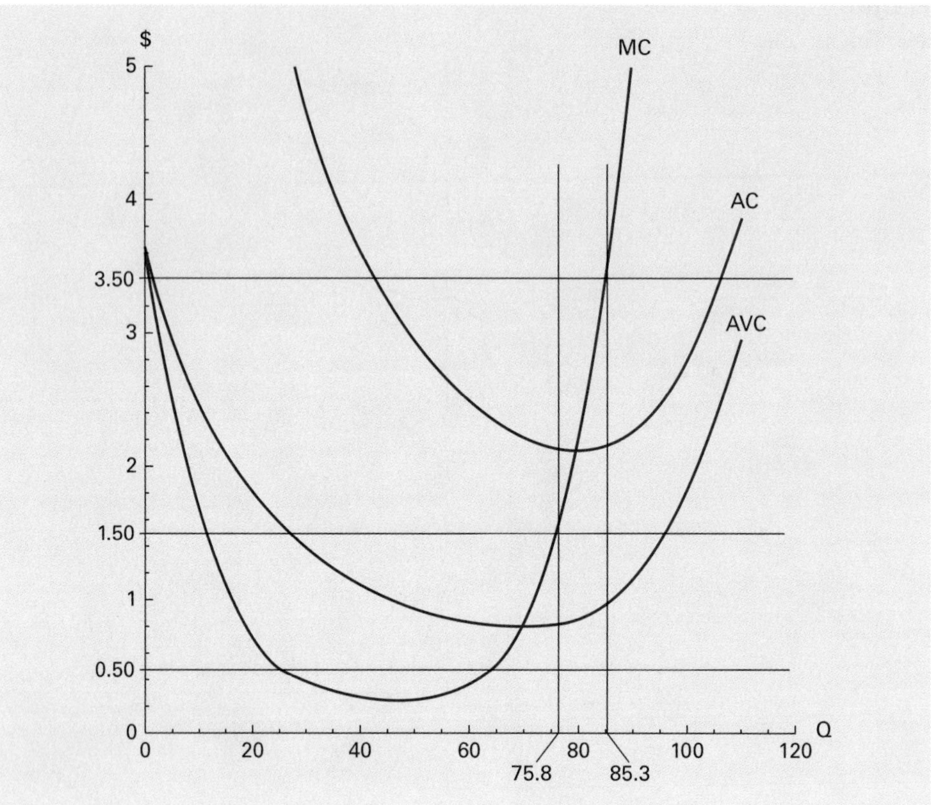

marginal cost is below 50 cents, it is best to produce nothing.[20] Staying in production means losing the fixed costs and not recovering all variable costs, and halting production means losing only the fixed costs.

At the $3.50 market price, profit per unit is the difference between revenue per unit (i.e., the $3.50) and average cost ($2.17 at 85.3 units). Total profit is their difference multiplied by output, or $113.44, equal to the area of the shaded rectangle in the left-side graph of Figure 4-10. If market price is $1.50, lying between average cost and average variable cost, each unit produced incurs a loss equal to the difference between them ($1.25 − 0.82 = 0.43). The firm's loss is that amount times output of 75.8, or $32.59, the area of the shaded rectangle in the right-side graph of Figure 4-10. This is a smaller loss than the $100 in fixed costs the firm would still face if it closed.

In the short run the firm produces the output that maximizes its profits at the market price. If it is covering at least its variable costs, that output is on its marginal cost curve. If fixed costs are not fully recovered, it will operate in the short run and close in the long run. If price is below the minimum of AVC ($0.79), it does not even produce in the short run. Figure 4-11 summarizes this in a short-run supply curve that coincides with the vertical axis (zero output) for prices below minimum AVC, at which point it jumps to the MC curve. We have thus resolved the question from Chapter 3 about why firms

[20]There are actually two such outputs, 25.3 and 64.3 units. By the reasoning used for Figure 4-4, we can reject the first of these. Unlike Figure 4-4, however, even at 64.3 units its gain is not big enough to offset the losses taken on the first 25.3 units.

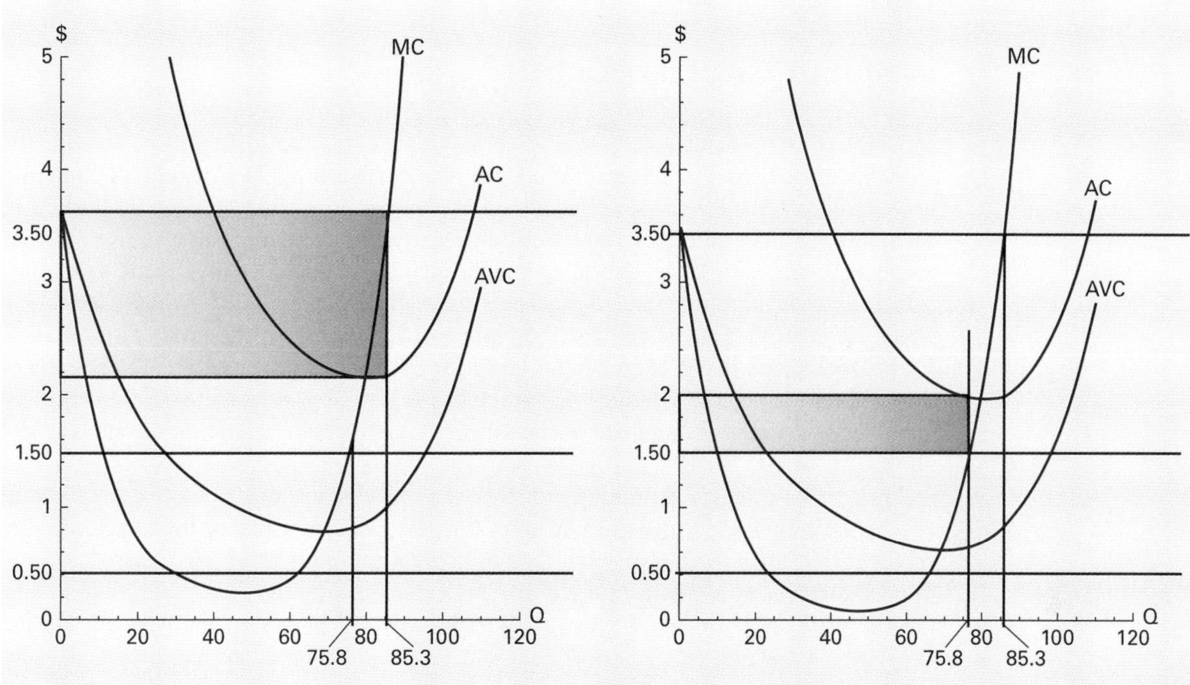

FIGURE 4-10 Profit at Market Price of $3.50 (Left); Loss at Market Price of $1.50 (Right)

do not slowly increase output from zero as prices rise. The next chapter covers the process of competitive entry into profitable markets and exit from unprofitable ones in more detail. Because entry and exit are long-run phenomena, however, we should first examine long-run costs.

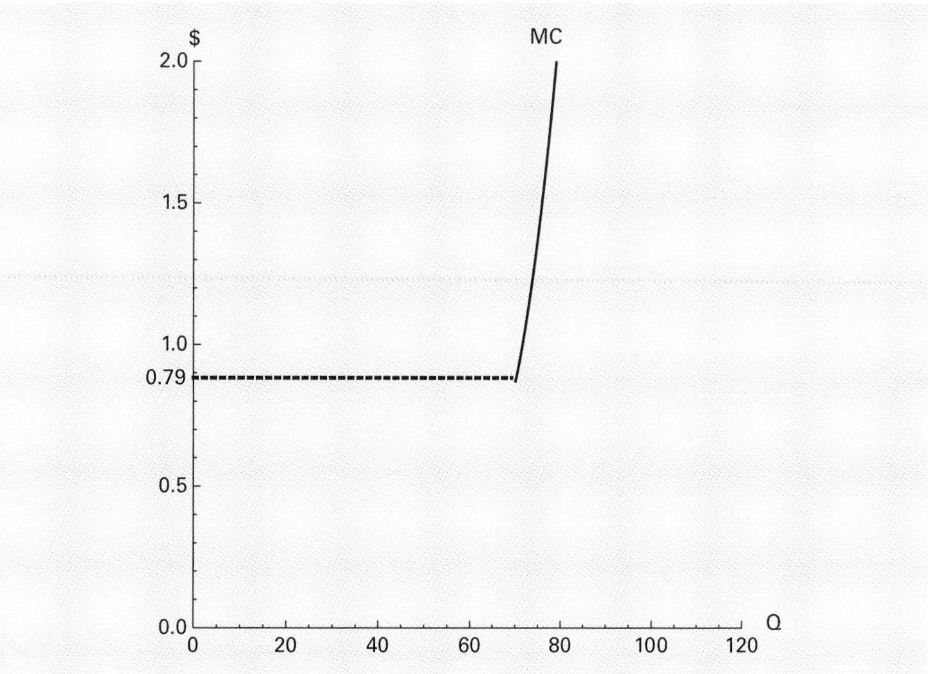

FIGURE 4-11 Firm's Supply Curve Is Marginal Cost (MC) Above the Average Variable Cost (AVC)

The Long Run

Isoquants and Isocosts

Isoquants In the long run a firm can vary all of its inputs. Figure 4-12 uses data from agricultural experiments to show how corn output on an acre of land varies with the amounts of two types of fertilizer applied.[21] The curve labeled "80" shows all combinations of nitrogen and phosphate fertilizer (both in pounds) that will yield 80 bushels of corn on it, and the others correspond to different yields. A farmer can also use different amounts of land and labor, but going beyond two dimensions requires math that is unnecessary to make our points. The curves are called *isoquants,* the first syllable being Greek for "equal." They show that the inputs are substitutes in the production of corn. Figure 4-12 shows that it is possible to produce 100 bushels per acre with 125 pounds of nitrogen fertilizer and 77 pounds of phosphate. We could also reach the 100 bushel isoquant with a nearby combination consisting of slightly more nitrate and slightly less phosphate, or vice versa.

Figure 4-13 extends our example of short-run production to the long run. As before we can vary the fuel burned (F) per hour, but now we can also vary the boiler capacity (K). It is best for now to envision a firm as able to rent a boiler of any desired capacity. This simplification avoids complications that stem from its durability and allows us to put the prices of both inputs on a per-month basis. All points on the isoquant labeled "10" are combinations of F and K that can produce 10,000 cubic feet of steam in an hour, for example, a boiler with capacity 5 burning 5 barrels of fuel can do the job, but so can a capacity 4 boiler with 7.0 barrels and a capacity 6 boiler with 3.8.[22] The isoquant labeled "15" likewise shows ways of producing 15,000 cubic feet an hour. To get this from a capacity 5 boiler requires 13.8 barrels of fuel, and from a capacity 6 boiler,

FIGURE 4-12
Isoquants for Fertilizer Inputs into Corn Production (Bushels/Acre)

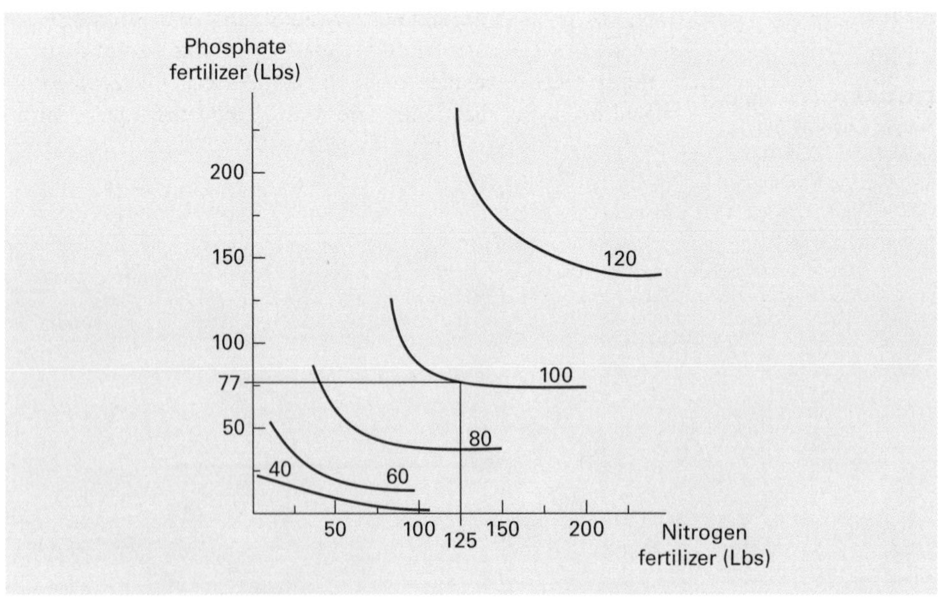

[21]Figure 4-12 is adapted from Earl O. Heady, "An Econometric Investigation of the Technology of Agricultural Production Functions," *Econometrica* 25 (April 1957): 253.

[22]The production function is the Cobb-Douglas form, detailed in the Appendix to this chapter. Its exact form is $Q = 2F^{0.4}K^{0.6}$.

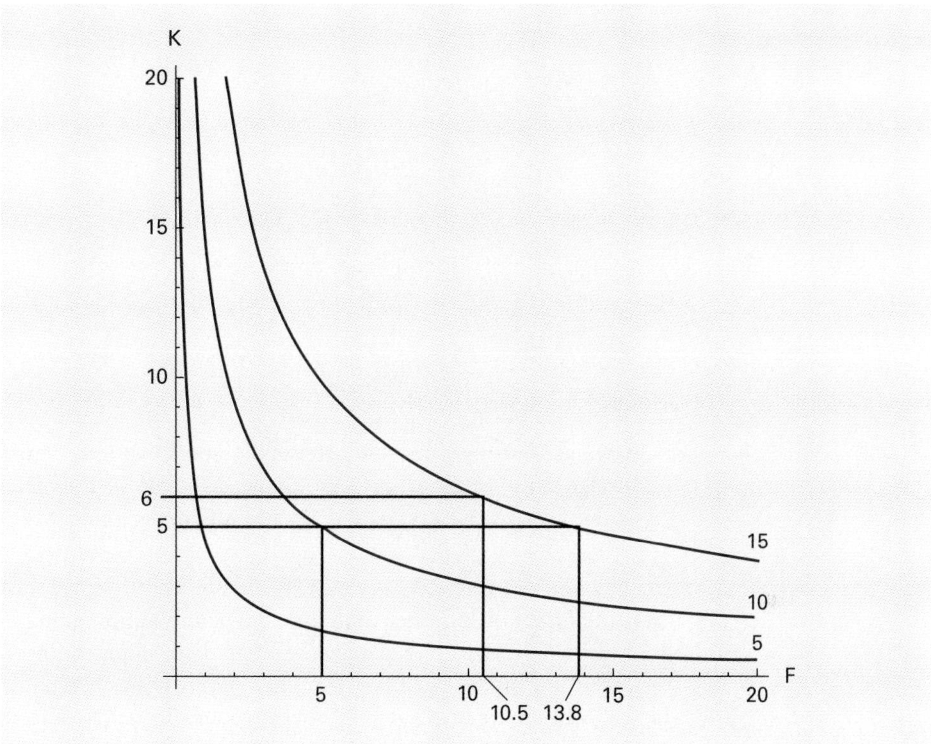

FIGURE 4-13
Isoquants

10.5 barrels. We are implicitly assuming that this firm is *technically efficient*, e.g., 10,000 cubic feet is the maximum output possible from 5 barrels burned in a capacity 5 boiler. There is no slack that a smart manager can eliminate to squeeze more output from this pair of inputs. Producing more than 10,000 cubic feet an hour requires more fuel and/or a larger boiler. Technical efficiency implies that isoquants cannot cross. If they did we would be saying that at the intersection point the same bundle of fuel and capital was capable of producing, say, either 10 or 12 units, which is a contradiction.

An isoquant's slope becomes steeper moving from southeast to northwest. We say that it is *convex* to the origin, bulging outward toward a viewer situated there and looking upward. Convexity reflects changes in the productivities of the inputs as they vary relative to each other. The marginal product of fuel MP_F is the change in output caused by a small change in fuel use, holding boiler capacity constant, and the marginal product of boiler capacity MP_K is correspondingly defined. As shown in the Appendix 4-A, if F is measured on the horizontal axis and K on the vertical, the slope of an isoquant is MP_F/MP_K, prefaced by a negative sign. In the far southeast the isoquant is nearly flat—the boiler is so small and fuel is so abundant that a slightly larger boiler would have a high marginal product. Viewed another way, capital is so scarce relative to fuel that adding more of the latter would produce little additional output.

Isocosts An isoquant shows all of the "recipes" for a certain amount of output if both inputs are variable, but it cannot by itself tell us the lowest-cost way to produce it. We can only find the efficient mix of inputs if we know their prices. We start by showing the ways a given budget can be split between fuel and capital costs. If the firm's budget is \$40, and fuel is available at \$2 per unit and capital at \$4, it can buy any non-negative combination for which

(4.1) $$2F + 4K \leq 40.$$

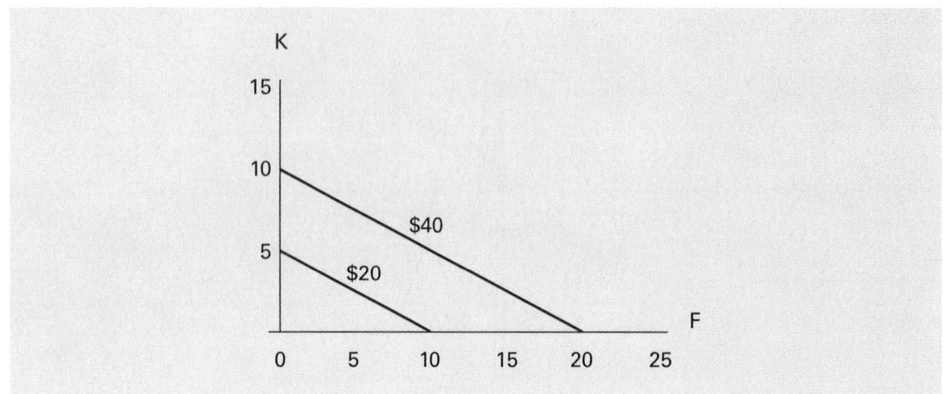

FIGURE 4-14
Isocosts for \$20 and \$40, P_F = \$2, P_K = \$4

If we assume that any budget is fully spent, we can replace the inequality with an equal sign and get a straight line known as an *isocost*, which is shown in Figure 4-14. Algebraically, with prices P_F and P_K and a C dollar budget the isocost is given by

(4.2) $$P_F F + P_K K = C.$$

If the total is \$20 rather than \$40, any combination along the lower isocost in Figure 4-14 is feasible. They are parallel because their slopes both equal the ratio of P_F to P_K (again with a minus sign).[23] If the price of an input changes, so does the isocost's slope. Figure 4-15 shows how the \$40 isocost rotates if fuel rises from \$2 to \$4 a barrel.

Minimizing the Cost of a Given Output

Now combine isoquants and isocosts to minimize the long-run cost of producing 10 units of output, that is, 10,000 cubic feet of steam per hour, when P_F = \$2 and P_K = \$4. Figure 4-16 shows the 10-unit isoquant along with three isocosts. On the lowest of them the firm spends \$20, an amount that cannot buy any input combination capable of producing 10 units. The highest isocost is \$50, more than just enough to get 10 units produced because a portion of the isocost lies above the 10-unit isoquant. Input combinations on the \$50 isocost that are above that isoquant can produce more than the desired 10 units. For the lowest possible cost, imagine shifting the \$50 isocost downward until it is tangent to the isoquant. The tangency is the lowest cost of producing 10 units of output, \$29.71. The funds are spent on 5.95 units of F and 4.46 units of K.

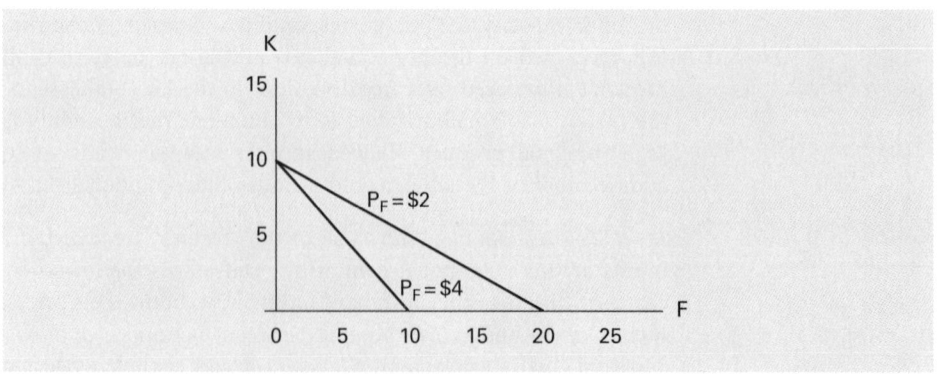

FIGURE 4-15
Isocost Rotates as P_F Increases from \$2 to \$4

[23]To check this, rearrange equation 4.2 to $K = \frac{C}{P_k} - \left(\frac{P_F}{P_k}\right)F$.

FIGURE 4-16
Cost Minimization

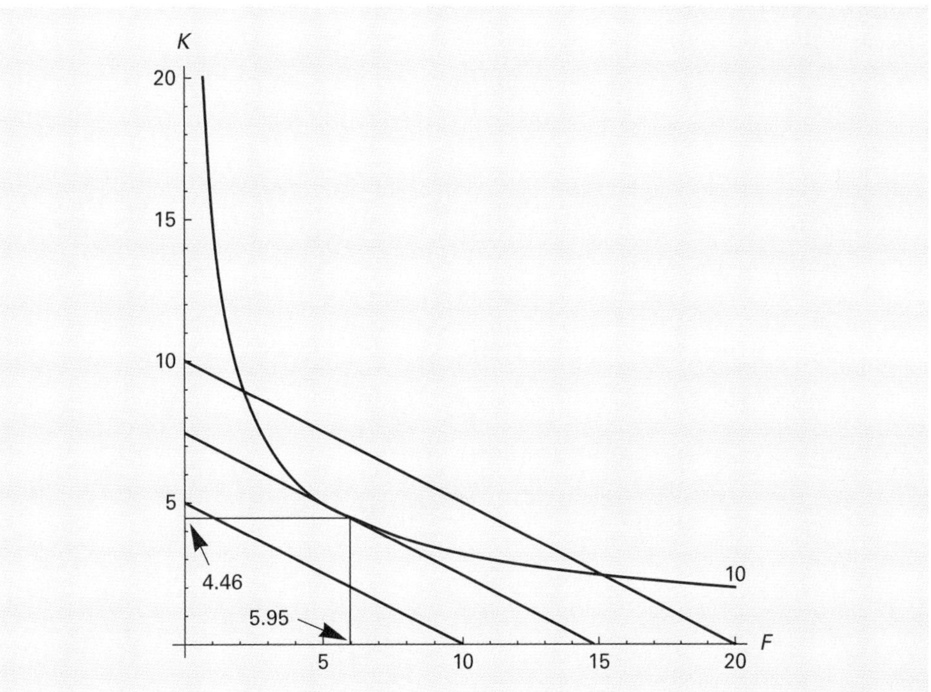

When input prices change, so will the least-cost mix of them. For a given output it will entail using more of the one whose relative price has fallen and less of the other. Figure 4-17 shows the now-familiar isoquant for 10 units along with two isocosts. The flatter one is that of Figure 4-14, with P_F = \$2.00, P_K = \$4.00, and a least-cost input mix of 5.95 F and 4.46 K. On the steeper isocost, P_F = \$4.00 and P_K = \$2.00. With fuel more costly relative to capital, the least-cost input mix will be 2.59 units of F and 7.76 units of K. Total cost will be a lower \$25.88, but whether it rises or falls depends on the details of the situation. Figure 4-17 also makes clear that an isoquant's curvature indicates the degree to which inputs are substitutes. The shallower its curvature, the greater the impacts of a change in their relative prices on least-cost mix of them. The less "L"-shaped the isoquant, the greater are the possibilities for substitution. For example, Figure 4-18 indicates that hay and grain are good substitutes on dairy farms. The isoquants in it are for different "yields" (pounds of milk per month) from a cow.[24] If we start at, say, a 50-50 mix of grain and hay, a small increase in the price of grain could mean a diet of 100 percent hay. We took the trouble to find the slopes of the isoquant and isocost to better explain the logic of the least-cost input mix. At the tangency their slopes are equal, that is,

(4.3)
$$\frac{P_F}{P_K} = \frac{MP_F}{MP_K},$$

which rearranges to:

(4.4)
$$\frac{MP_F}{P_F} = \frac{MP_K}{P_K}.$$

[24]Figure 4-18 is adapted from Heady, "An Econometric Investigation," 259.

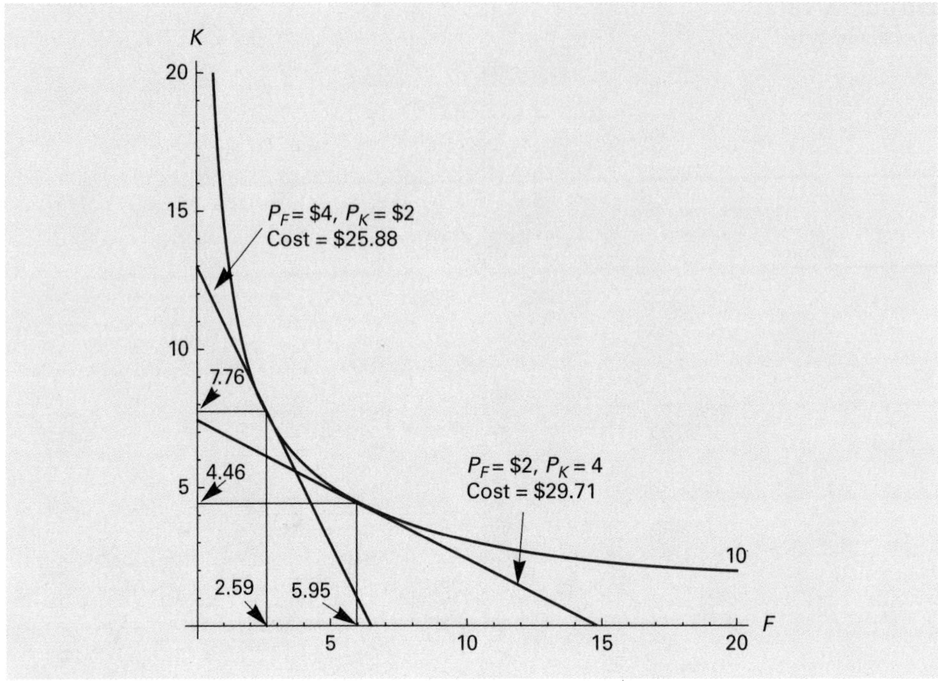

FIGURE 4-17 Cost Minimization at Two Sets of Input Prices

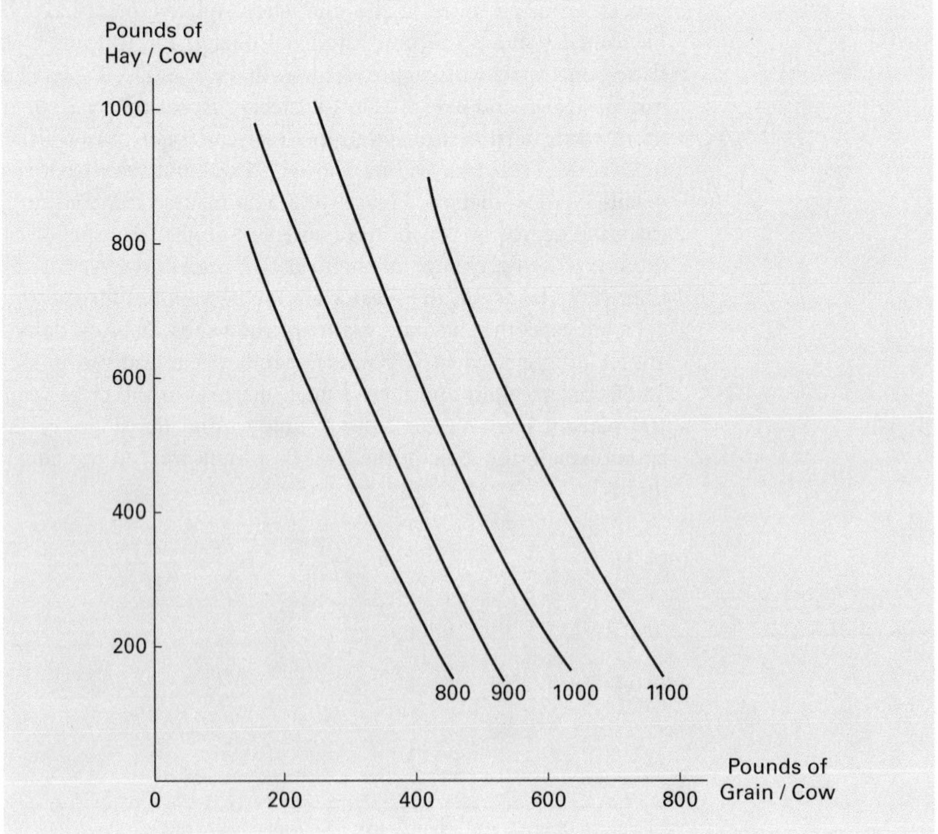

FIGURE 4-18 Milk per Cow (Lbs) and Feed Intake

The marginal product of the last dollar spent on F must equal that of the last dollar spent on K. Figure 4-19 shows what happens when equation 4.4 does not hold. We want to produce the isoquant amount, and (for the sake of clarity) assume that $P_F = P_K = \$1.00$. A rigorous demonstration requires calculus, but imagine that the figure is an extreme close-up of the area around point A. Assume that in the neighborhood of A the marginal product of capital is 3, while that of fuel is 1, so the isoquant's slope is $-1/3$. It is flatter than the isocost line, whose slope is -1. To reduce total cost begin by spending \$1 less on fuel, which cuts output by one unit. By itself this would put us on the lower isoquant (not shown) that passes through B. To restore the old output spend 33 cents of the saved dollar on 1/3 of a unit of capital, which raises output by one unit (i.e., 1/3 of capital's marginal product of 3), back to its old level, at C. Changing the input mix to favor capital saves 67 cents. We are climbing along the isoquant toward the northwest, and it becomes steeper as we climb. More steps like this one lead to where its slope is -1, tangent to the lowest feasible isocost (not shown).

The Expansion Path and Long-Run Total Cost

Thus far all we have done is minimized long-run cost for a single output level. To get the rest of the curve, Figure 4-20 shows isoquants for 5, 7, 10, and 12 units. As before, $P_F =$ \$2.00 and $P_K =$ \$4.00. To produce 5 units the firm will use 2.19 barrels of fuel and 1.64 units of capital, for a total cost of \$10.95.[25] To produce 7 units requires 5.48 barrels

FIGURE 4-19
Adjustment to a Lower-Cost Mix of Inputs

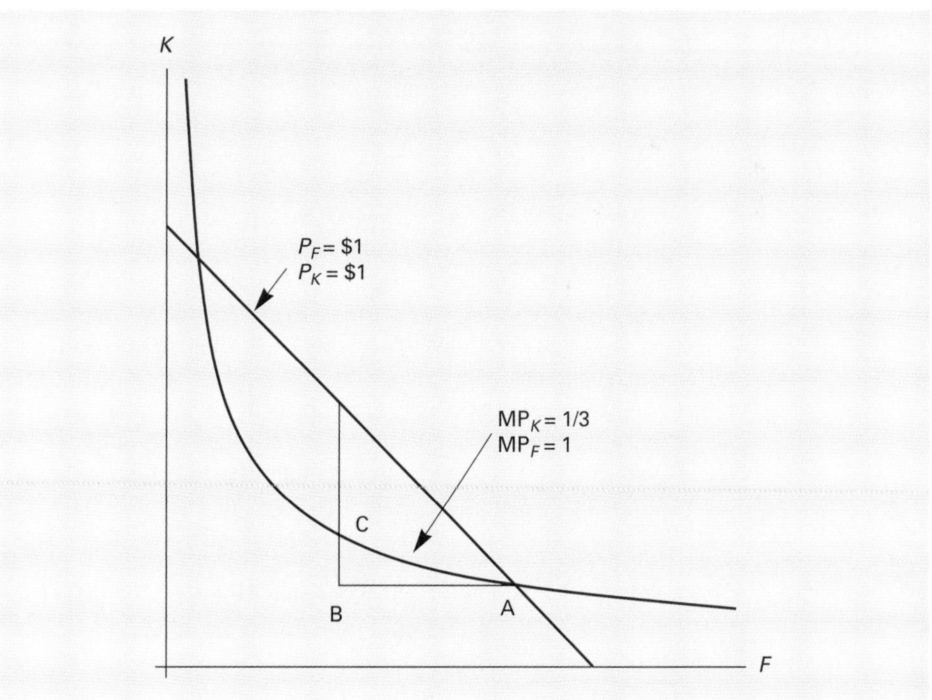

[25]To maintain readability the diagram does not display these input amounts. The isoquants for 5 and 7 units of steam are from the production function $Q = 2F^{0.6}K^{0.9}$. Those for 10 and 12 units use $Q = 2F^{0.36}K^{0.54}$. The Appendix shows the relationship between the sum of the two exponents and the behavior of average costs. Because the ratio of the exponents is the same in both, the expansion path will be a straight line. (Can you show this?)

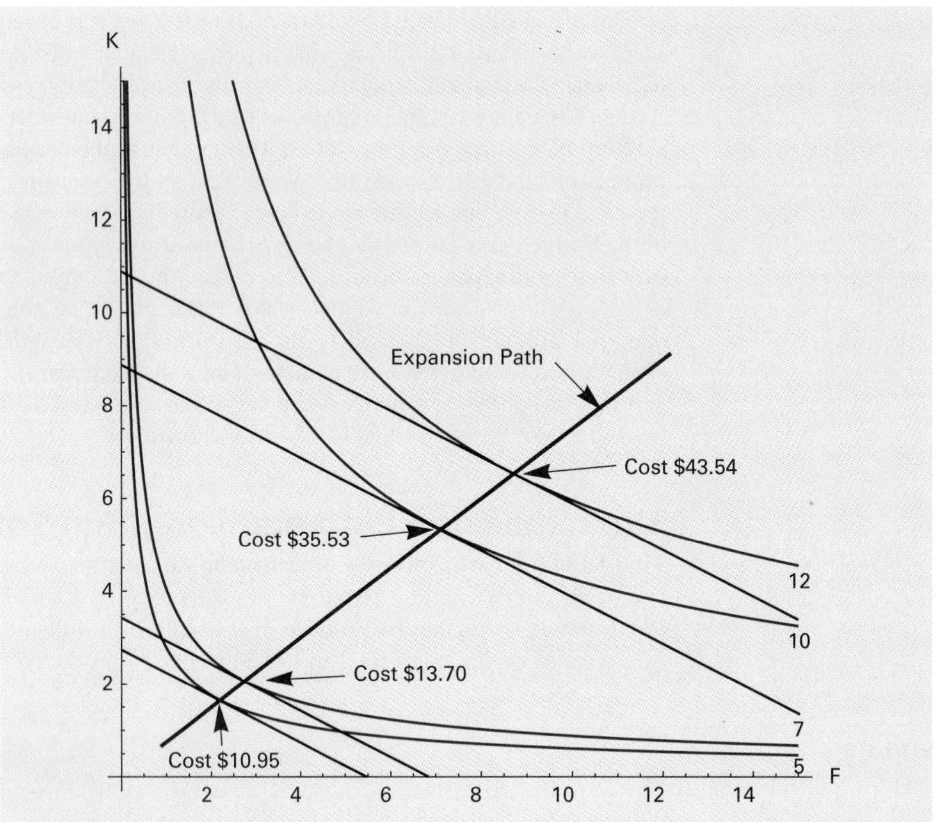

FIGURE 4-20 The Expansion Path and the Behavior of Costs

of fuel and 8.22 units of capital, for a total cost of $13.70. Output has increased by 40 percent and costs have increased by only 25 percent. Saying it another way, long-run average cost is falling in this range of output. We can also produce an output of 10 at a cost of $35.53 using 7.11 units of F and 5.33 of K. Twelve units require spending $43.54 on 8.70 units of F and 6.53 units of K. Here 20 percent more output comes at a 22.5 percent higher cost, and we conclude that long-run average cost is increasing in this neighborhood. The line passing through all of the tangency points shows how the optimal long-run combination of inputs changes with output. We call it the firm's *expansion path*. Here it is a straight line through the origin, but other shapes are possible.

Q. Explain in commonsense terms why the isoquants in Figure 4-20 for 5 and 7 units of output are closer together than those for 10 and 12 units.

Q. Can you draw a set of isoquants whose expansion path is curved? Can you give a (perhaps hypothetical) example of a production process whose expansion path would probably not be a straight line?

Figure 4-21 allows us to compare short-run and long-run costs. Its three isoquants are for outputs of 5, 10, and 13.[26] In the short run capital is fixed at 5.33 units, but fuel use can be varied at will. Earlier we found that the cost of producing an output of 10 was minimized by buying 7.11 barrels of fuel and 5.33 units of capital. If capital is fixed at 5.33 the short-run and long-run total costs of 10 units are equal. Even if the firm can change its capital, it will have no reason to do so as long as it wants to continue producing an output of 10. Figure 4-21 further shows that if capital is fixed at 5.33 the firm will need to combine it with 14.72 barrels of fuel if it wishes to produce 13 units, making for a short-run total cost of $50.76. The isocost for that amount would pass through the point (14.72,5.33), but is not shown to keep the diagram readable. The lowest-cost way to produce 13 units if both inputs are variable is at the usual tangency with an isocost, using 9.51 units of F and 7.13 of K for a lower long-run total cost of $47.54. The difference is a consequence of our inability to increase the fixed input in the short run. The same argument holds in the event we wish to change our output from 10 units to 7, but now our problem is an inability to decrease the fixed input. In the short run we must keep paying for the 5.33 units of capacity, and the cheapest way to produce 7 units will entail purchasing only 0.66 units of fuel for a total cost of $22.63. When both inputs are variable we burn 2.74 barrels of fuel in a boiler with capacity of 2.06, yielding the lower long-run total cost of $13.70.

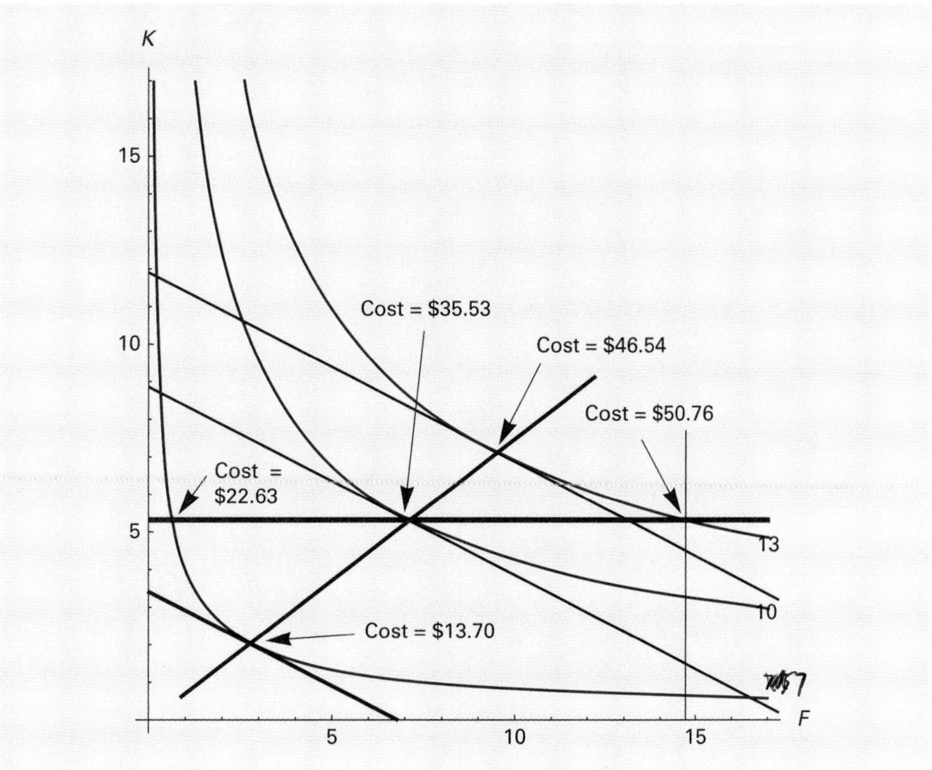

FIGURE 4-21 Short-Run and Long-Run Input Choices and Costs

[26]The expressions for the isoquants are the same as in the previous footnote. Those for 10 and 13 units both use the second one.

Long-Run Average Cost and Returns to Scale

The Shape of Long-Run Average Cost

Figure 4-21 tells us that at all outputs but one, short-run total costs, exceed long-run total costs. If so, the same holds for short-run and long-run average costs. To see this, assume that a firm can choose from only three possible types of plant, labelled A, B, and C in Figure 4-22. Its choice of plant will depend on the output it expects to produce. For outputs below 14 units a Type A plant produces at the lowest average cost, between 14 and 27 a Type B, and above 27 a Type C. If a Type B plant is built its cost will be above that of A for outputs below 14 and above that of C for outputs above 27. The bottom parts of the three curves show the firm's minimum long-run costs.

Figure 4-23 generalizes this reasoning to a large number of possible plant sizes. $SRAC_1$, $SRAC_2$ and $SRAC_3$ are three representative short-run average cost curves, each tangent to the long-run average cost curve LRAC at a single point. For every other output level there is also an optimal plant size that minimizes the long-run average cost for producing that quantity. If we hypothetically drew all of their short-run curves their "lower envelope" would be the LRAC curve. Each possible plant size would correspond to the lowest long-run average (and total) cost for some particular output.

The long-run average cost curve of Figure 4-23 is a shallow "U," but there is no obvious reason for it to look that way. In particular, if all inputs are variable why would we expect to see the LRAC curve rising at high outputs? The question matters because whether competition can survive in an industry will depend on the behavior of long-run costs. We first define *returns to scale.* If all inputs are raised by equal percentages and output increases by a larger percentage, there are *increasing returns to scale.* If increasing all inputs by the same percentage increases output by a smaller percentage, there are *decreasing returns to scale.* If output changes by the same percentage as the inputs, there are *constant returns to scale.*[27] Increasing returns to scale mean that long-run average costs are falling, as happens near the lower outputs in Figure 4-21. Increasing output from 10 to 12 in the region of decreasing returns to scale will mean long-run average costs rise with the higher output.

It is important to remember that the concept of returns to scale applies only in the long run. If other inputs are fixed (i.e., in the short run), increasing a variable input

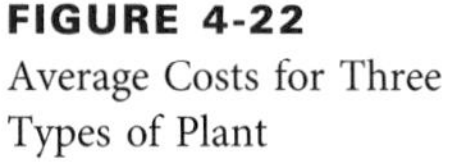
FIGURE 4-22
Average Costs for Three Types of Plant

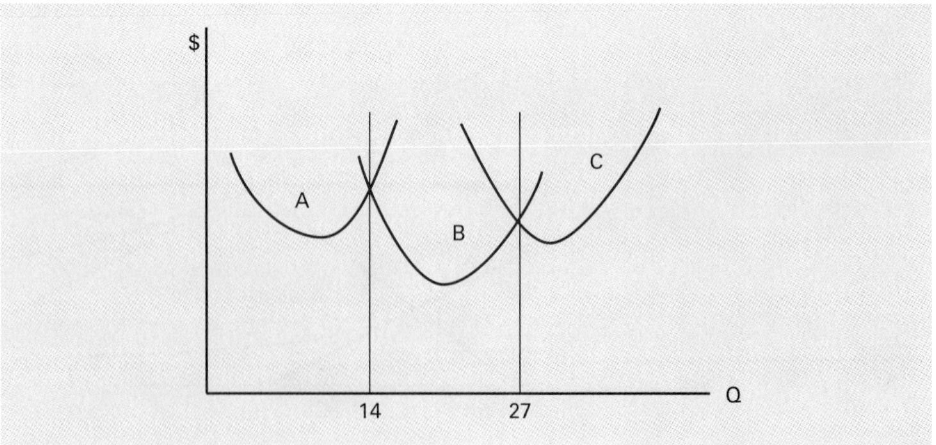

[27]The Appendix to this chapter discusses returns to scale for the Cobb-Douglas function. The cost curves in Figure 4-23 illustrate general principles and are not derived from earlier isoquant diagrams.

FIGURE 4-23 Long-Run and Short-Run Average Costs

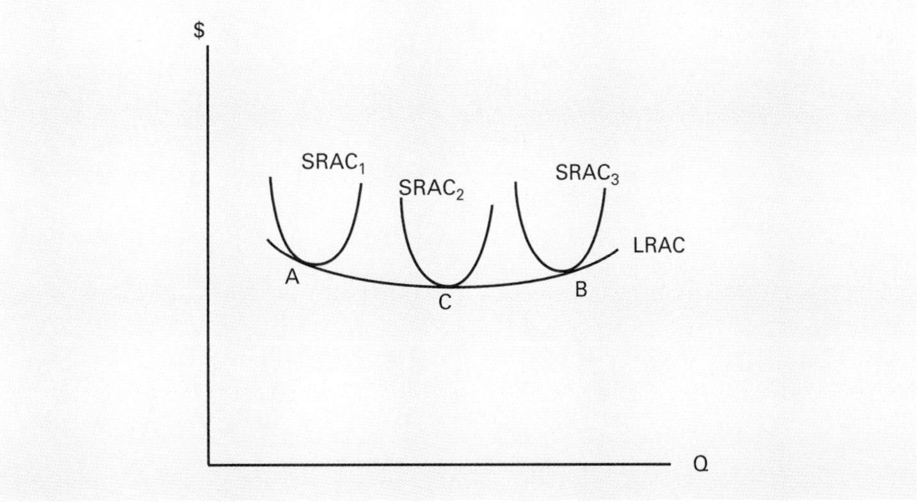

ultimately leads to increasing marginal costs and average variable costs. This will occur regardless of how returns to scale behave. Where returns to scale are constant, long-run total cost is an upward-sloping straight line and long-run average cost is horizontal. Short-run average cost curves, however, are U-shaped as usual and tangent to long-run average cost at their minima, as shown in Figure 4-24.

Q. Explain why long-run total cost is an upward-sloping straight line when returns to scale are constant.

Long-Run Average Cost and Competition

The Extreme Case of Natural Monopoly To better understand when competition is possible in the long run we start with a situation where it is not. Figure 4-25 portrays isoquants estimated from data on U.S. natural gas pipelines. It shows the combinations

FIGURE 4-24 Average Costs with Constant Returns to Scale

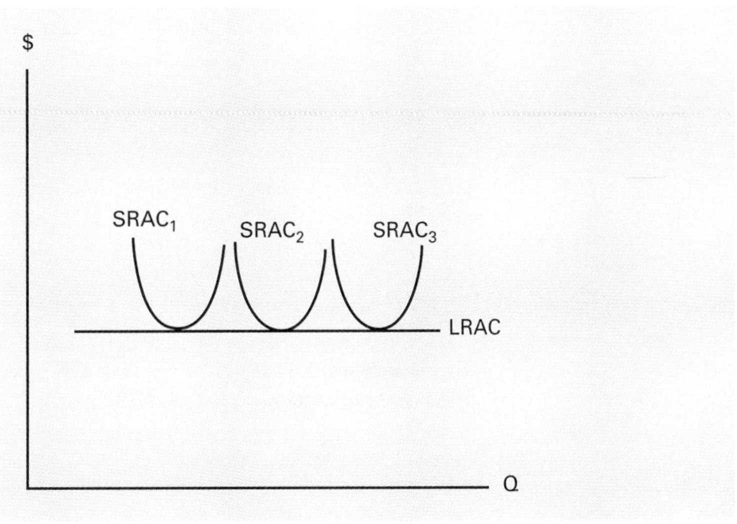

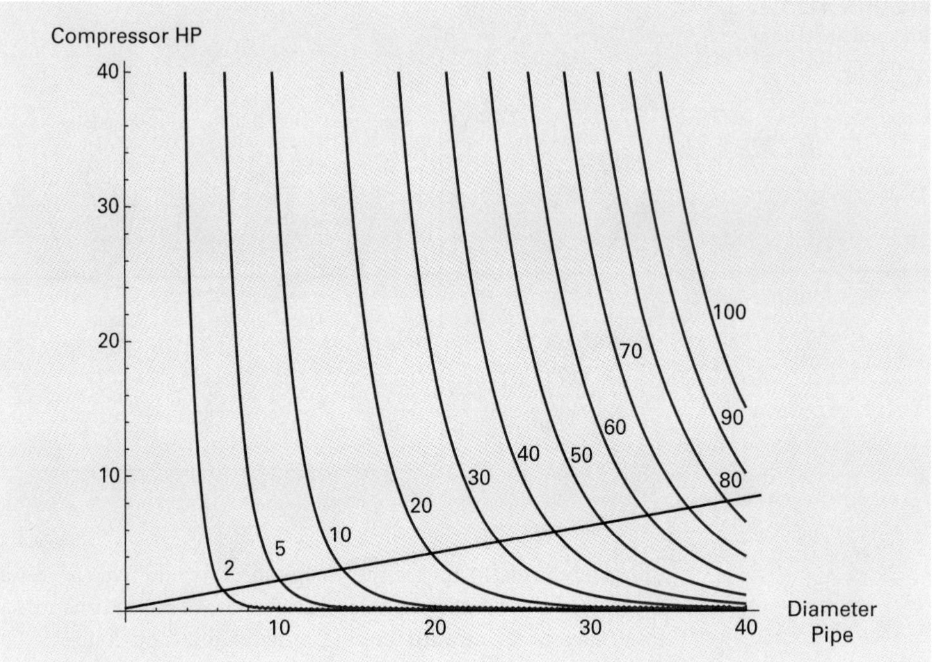

FIGURE 4-25 Isoquants for Natural Gas Transportation

of pipeline diameter and compressor horsepower (in hundreds) that can move various amounts (millions of cubic feet) of natural gas 100 miles in a day.[28] The spacing between them may indicate that a pipeline displays increasing returns to scale over a long range. Almost all of the isoquants correspond to outputs that are multiples of 10, and along the ray from the origin their slopes are equal. Higher isoquants are closer to their neighbors—it takes a larger increase in cost to increase output from 20 to 30 than from 60 to 70, and this appears to be the case for all pipeline sizes but the smallest.[29] Decreasing long-run average cost is in part a consequence of geometry. A pipeline's carrying capacity is approximately proportional to its cross-sectional area—i.e., that of a circular slice through it. A pipeline made of twice as much metal as another (the biggest part of cost) will have about twice the circumference. Doubling the circumference, however, more than doubles its cross-section, which reduces its cost per cubic foot of gas transported.

Figure 4-26 shows a long-run average cost curve that declines all the way up to the size of the market.[30] In a case like this competition among pipeline owners will not be possible in the long run. In Figure 4-26, assume that the delivery area consumes 2 billion cubic feet of gas per day (bcfd) and customers are not very sensitive to price. (Total U.S. consumption averages 80 bcfd.) Any existing pipeline has a U-shaped short-run average cost curve: it can carry more than its rated capacity for a short time, but operating costs are higher and its life span is shorter. Let's start with several independently owned pipes, each with costs given by $SRAC_1$. The builder of a new line with greater capacity, such as

[28]This is a plot of equation A1 in Jeffrey Callen, "Production, Efficiency and Welfare in the Natural Gas Transmission Industry," *American Economic Review* 68 (June 1978): 319.

[29]The largest U.S. pipelines are 42 inches in diameter.

[30]Many large consuming areas are served by more than one pipeline—Southern California has six and Chicago has five. Total consumption in such large areas (market size) exceeds the carrying capacity of the largest pipelines, additional lines increase reliability, and more pipelines give large consumers the ability to shop among different producing areas.

FIGURE 4-26 Natural Monopoly

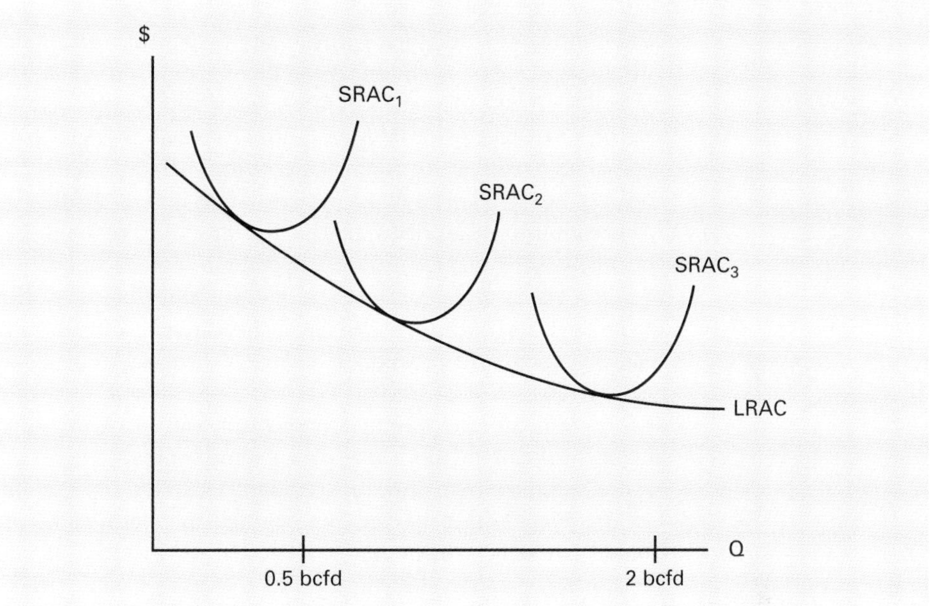

one with costs given by $SRAC_2$, can underprice any existing owner and still cover all of its own costs. The first to build a line with costs like $SRAC_3$ will be able to serve the entire market at a lower cost than the owner of any line with lower capacity. This situation in which technology makes long-run competition impossible is called *natural monopoly*, that is, decreasing long-run average costs are inherent in the industry's technology. Competition is not just impossible here, it is also inefficient—a single line is the lowest-cost way to deliver 2 bcfd. If the efficiently sized pipeline is a monopoly, its owner will quickly realize that it can charge users considerably more than the costs of building and operating it. To keep rates reasonable while ensuring that lines are efficiently sized, state and federal governments in the United States regulate the rates they can charge so the owner can realize no more than what is considered a fair return on it.

Where Is Competition Feasible? Only a small fraction of economic activity falls into the category of natural monopolies that are regulated (or sometimes operated by governments). Most other industries are potentially competitive to greater or lesser degrees. In those industries long-run average cost begins to slope upward at outputs small enough relative to market size that two or more firms can coexist as competitors. In Figure 4-23 a firm with a small plant and short-run costs $SRAC_1$ is inefficiently small, and one with $SRAC_3$ is inefficiently large. Both could lower their costs in the long run by resizing themselves to have cost curves like $SRAC_2$. Whether it is too large or too small, a higher-cost firm is less likely to be a competitive survivor. In some industries a typical firm's cost curve begins to slope upward at an output that is very small relative to the market, meaning that a large number of competitors can coexist in the long run. The next three chapters will show the importance of the number of competitors for industry analysis and managerial decision-making.

Why Might LRAC Slope Upward? Long-run average costs have long interested economists because they determine whether competition is possible in a market. Around 1900, the English economist Alfred Marshall provided what remains the standard textbook explanation for why LRAC curves reach a minimum and turn upward. He asserted that larger firms placed such demands on management that even the most talented executives would eventually lose the ability to control costs.[31] Marshall reasoned that a single manager or a small group of them would ultimately be unable to monitor the performance of a large workforce or to efficiently coordinate the many different activities that take place in a large firm. Marshall thought that even managers who delegate some decisions to subordinates would have problems communicating with them and motivating them to make decisions that benefit the firm's owners.

Attention to detail helps explain the structures of some industries. Very few top-tier gourmet restaurants, for instance, operate in more than one or two venues. Their success or failure depends on constantly monitoring the quality of ingredients and operations in the kitchen, and authority over details like these is difficult to put into the hands of more than one person. In practice, a financier often bankrolls a chef and gives the chef final authority over all food-related decisions. By contrast, fast-food outlets are better viewed as factories than as restaurants. Franchising puts decisions about purchasing, advertising, and menu items in the hands of a parent company, leaving local operators the job of assembling these ingredients in standardized ways and keeping their stores clean.[32] The fact that New York City contains hundreds of McDonald's while renowned chef Daniel Boulud has only a single outlet reflects the difficulties of managing the latter. On the other hand, prestige steak houses, like Morton's and Ruth's Chris, operate nationally and are mostly franchises. Their simple recipes facilitate quality control and their standardized menus allow the parent companies to buy ingredients of uniform quality for all of their outlets.

In many other cases, however, Marshall's reasoning is harder to apply, particularly in the twenty-first century. Marshall primarily observed British firms, which were usually smaller than their foreign counterparts and were often still controlled by their founding families several generations later. At the same time manufacturing, chemical, and metals processing firms in America and Germany were growing to sizes never before seen. New organizational structures were devised to manage their many activities, some of which crossed national boundaries.[33] The twentieth century saw developments in information technology, law, communications, and organizational design that greatly increased the sizes to which firms might grow and the scopes of activities they might undertake. Unlike managers in Marshall's time, today's are often trained as professionals in general principles that can be applied in almost any type of business.[34]

Shifts in LRAC Changes in technology and organization shift the LRAC curve. The first commercially successful computer was Remington Rand's Univac, which sold in 1959 for $350,000, equivalent to $2.03 million today.[35] Only a large business could own one (or lease it for $7,000 a month), and the rudimentary telecommunications of the time made it usable in only one location. The huge fixed costs of a computer meant that the LRAC curve of its owner decreased over a large range of output, as shown by $LRAC_1$ on Figure 4-27. The computers of the 1990s were cheaper, and their efficient sizes were far smaller than the Univac. Even a small business could purchase any

[31]Alfred Marshall, *Principles of Economics*, 8th Variorum ed. (London: Macmillan and Co., Ltd., 1920), 267–313.

[32]We discuss franchise arrangements in detail in Chapter 14.

[33]Alfred Chandler, *Strategy and Structure: Chapters in the History of the Industrial Enterprise* (Cambridge, MA: MIT Press, 1962).

[34]The University of Pennsylvania's Wharton School, generally acknowledged as the world's first degree program for professional managers, opened in 1881.

[35]Unisys History Newsletter, http://wiki.cc.gatech.edu/folklore/index.php/Main_Page.

FIGURE 4-27
Changing Technology Shifts LRAC Downward and Shifts Its Minimum Leftward

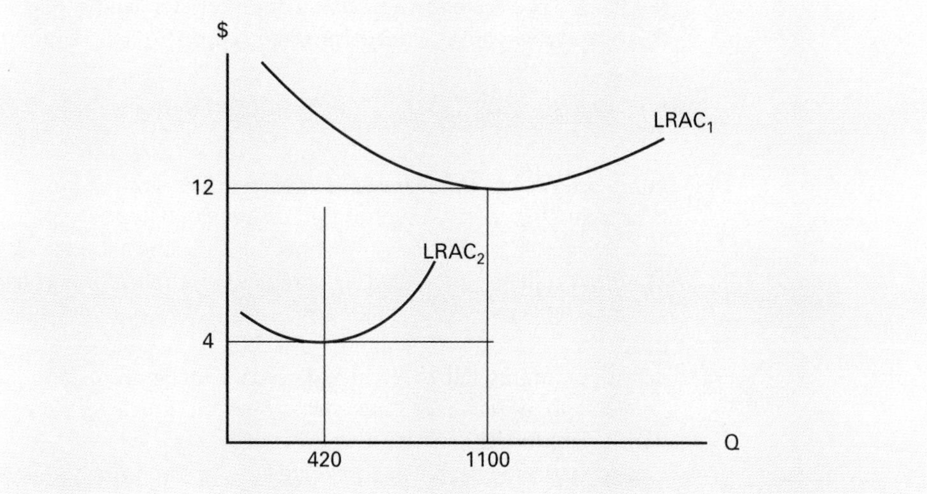

number of personal computers and workstations, and link them through local networks and long-distance telecommunications. The firm whose costs were $LRAC_1$ in 1959 would be somewhere on $LRAC_2$ in 2000, and attain minimum unit cost at a lower output. In Chapter 14 we will see in detail how changing technologies are decreasing firm sizes in many industries.

Figure 4-28 shows the effects on LRAC of the organizational changes discussed above. A firm with a traditional internal organization operated along a curve like $LRAC_1$, with high average costs that reached their minimum at a low output. New types of organization developed around 1900 and facilitated the effective management of much larger firms. Long run average cost would shift downward (in part because the larger firms used more efficient technologies) and reach its minimum at a higher output, as happens on $LRAC_2$. Technologies and organizational forms have changed, but there are still limits to the size most firms can attain before LRAC begins increasing.[36] The effects of these changes vary among industries. In some, average sizes of firms and plants are rising

FIGURE 4-28
Changing Organization Shifts LRAC Downward and Minimum Rightward

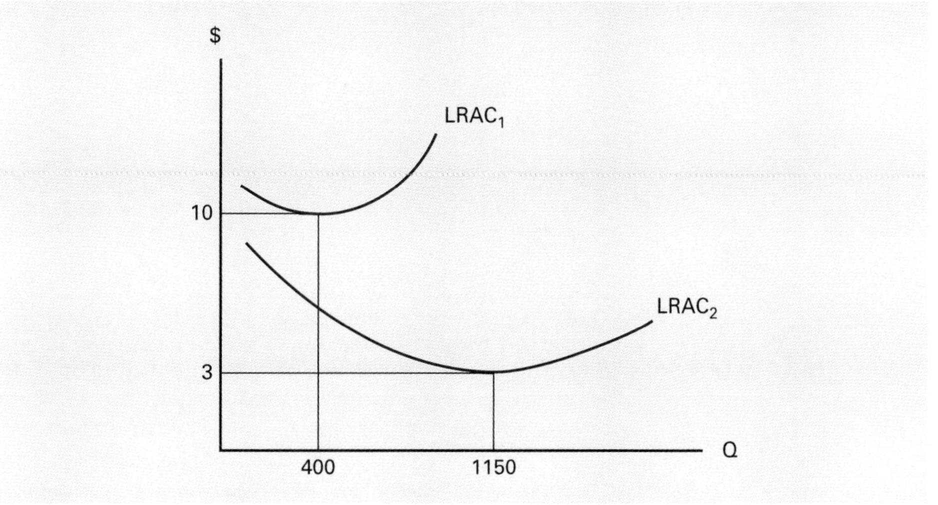

[36]Chapters 12 and 13 will discuss these limits in more detail.

(e.g., mass-market brewing); in others, they are falling (e.g., steel); and in still others, they are converging to an intermediate range (e.g., oil refining).[37]

Learning

"Experience is a great teacher" is one of those rare proverbs that we can document with numbers. We have previously seen cost curves shift downward with falling input prices, new technologies, and organizational changes. They can also shift as production experience accumulates. Figure 4-29 shows the decline in direct labor hours to produce an advanced military aircraft as its cumulated output rose through the 1980s.[38] Experience also pays off in services—success rates of new surgical procedures follow similar paths as doctors perform more of them.[39] Machinery also gains productivity with experience, as defective outputs fall over time. The data in Figure 4-29 trace out a *learning curve* or *progress curve*. Its shape is a typical one; the greatest improvements come in the early days of production.[40]

Experience comes in many varieties. Workers learn to coordinate their activities and handle everyday problems expeditiously. They can better adapt themselves to the capital goods they work with and can better serve individual customers as they gain familiarity

FIGURE 4-29
Learning Curve for Aircraft Production

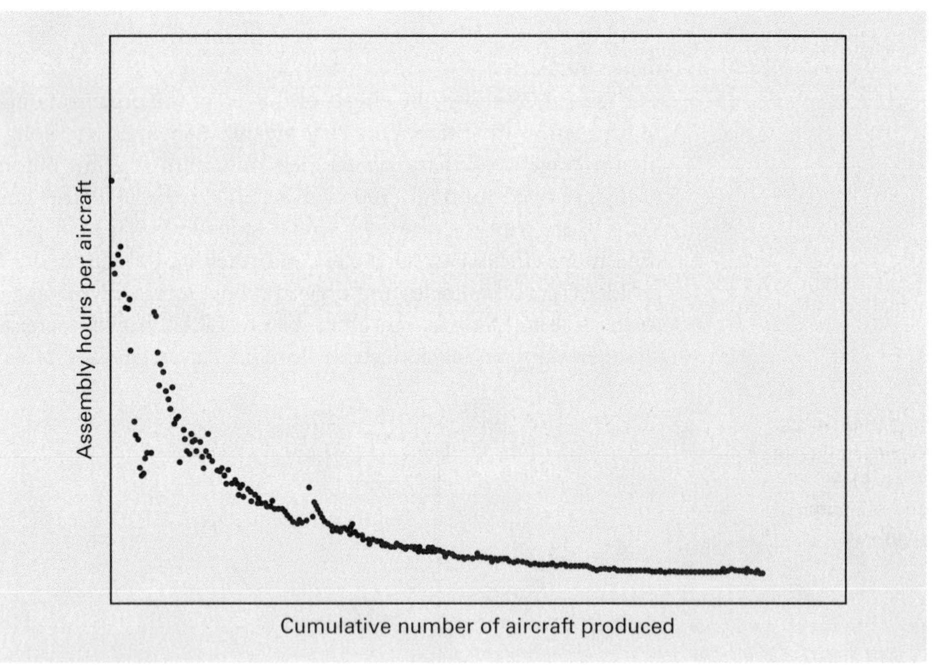

[37]Bela Gold, "Forces Tending to Reduce Concentration Levels in U.S. Industries," *Managerial and Decision Economics* 10 (June 1989): 115–119; Dennis W. Carlton and Jeffrey M. Perloff, *Modern Industrial Organization*, 4th ed. (Upper Saddle River, NJ: Pearson Addison Wesley, 2004), 40–44. In the case of refineries, firms that own them are becoming larger while individual refineries are becoming smaller.

[38]Linda Argote and Dennis Epple, "Learning Curves in Manufacturing," *Science* 247 (February 23, 1990): 920–24.

[39]Sheryl F. Kelsey et al., "Effect of Investigator Experience on Percutaneous Transluminal Coronary Angioplasty," *American Journal of Cardiology* 53 (1984): C56–C64.

[40]The most commonly estimated learning curves are of the form $C = aX^{-b}$, where X is total output from the start of production.

with their particular desires. Productivity also rises with the experience of managers as their accumulated learning allows them to better adapt their organizations to the environments in which they operate. They can experiment with new methods to monitor and evaluate worker productivity and new techniques to elicit and reward effort. Learning curves also have strategic uses. Managers can (and have) used them to estimate the costs of competitors and to determine which activities are better performed by subcontractors than in-house employees.[41]

Learning curves do not just happen—management practices and work environments determine how quickly the effects of experience appear, or whether they exist at all. Those effects can also disappear.[42] A firm with high employee turnover may see less learning than one with a more stable workforce, as happened when Lockheed (now part of Lockheed Martin Corporation) left airliner manufacturing. During its five initial years of building the L-1011 in the 1970s, costs fell as a learning curve would predict. Orders then fell for three years as a recession hit the airlines and Lockheed greatly reduced its workforce. When customers finally returned, the company was unable to produce at the low costs it had enjoyed three years earlier.[43] Experience in related goods or services can improve productivity elsewhere, but the degree of relatedness matters. For example, Lockheed's experience building military aircraft did not translate into lower airliner costs.[44]

Learning can be specific to a single firm, or it can reflect the experience of an entire industry.[45] Firms with similar technologies can learn from their competitors, sometimes by observation and sometimes by hiring away the right workers. As costs fall the structure of the industry itself can change as specialists take over activities from firms that formerly performed them in-house.[46] For example, individual manufacturers of personal computers initially made many components themselves, but as the industry grew specialists emerged in mass memories (e.g., EMC and Network Appliance), disk drives (e.g., Seagate Technologies), assembly (e.g., Celestica), and other activities. A firm's costs can decrease as it ceases production of components and purchases them from others who can supply them more economically. These need not be material components—such functions as maintenance and sales are also outsourced when the market becomes large enough to support specialists.

Chapter Summary

- Production transforms resources into more valuable goods and services. It takes place in profit-seeking firms that attempt to minimize their costs of producing the output quantities they choose.

---

[41]Bruce D. Henderson, "The Application and Misapplication of the Experience Curve," *Journal of Business Strategy* 4 (December 1984): 3–9.

[42]Argote and Epple, 922.

[43]Argote and Epple, 922.

[44]U. E. Reinhardt, "Breakeven Analysis for Lockheed's Tri-Star: An Application of Financial Theory," *Journal of Finance* 28 (September 1973): 831–38.

[45]For an analysis that estimates both firm- and industry-level effects on the costs of wind-driven electricity generation, see M. Junginger, A. Faaij, and W. C. Turkenburg, "Global Experience Curves for Wind Farms," *Energy Policy* 33 (January 2005): 133–50.

[46]George J. Stigler, "The Division of Labor Is Limited by the Extent of the Market," *Journal of Political Economy* 59 (June 1951): 185–93. It is worth a look just to read about the incredible degree of specialization in the nineteenth-century British firearms industry.

- The relationship between inputs and outputs exhibits possibilities for substitution in both the short run (not all inputs being variable) and long run (all inputs being variable). In the short run, changing only the variable inputs can change output.
- Fixed inputs constrain the firm in two ways. When desired output is low the amount of the fixed input will be excessive, and when it is high the fixed input is a bottleneck. These input–output relationships allow the derivation of the marginal and average cost curves.
- A price-taker firm maximizes profit or minimizes losses in the short run by producing where marginal cost equals market price. If market price is below average variable cost, however, ceasing production in the short run minimizes its loss.
- Isoquants summarize how inputs can be substituted in the long run. They are downward sloping and convex when viewed from the origin. Isocosts show input bundles that have the same total costs. Total cost of a given output is minimized by finding the lowest isocost that is tangent to the isoquant for that output. When the relative prices of inputs change, the least-cost mix changes to favor the one that has become relatively cheaper.
- Each possible quantity of a fixed input generates unique short-run total and average cost curves, and long-run total cost is the lower envelope of the short-run curves. Each of the short-run curves is tangent to the long-run curve at a single output and above it at all others.
- The shape of the long-run average cost curve determines the possibilities for competition in an industry. Increasing returns to scale mean that LRAC is falling, and decreasing returns to scale mean that it is rising. If increasing returns to scale prevail everywhere, an industry is a "natural monopoly," in which competition results in higher costs than monopoly and cannot be sustained.
- Long-run average cost curves can eventually slope upward if there are limits on management's ability to operate large firms efficiently but organizational innovation and technological change can affect the output at which its minimum occurs. The long-run average cost curve can also shift downward as a firm gains experience in production.

Appendix 4-A

Calculus

The Cobb-Douglas Function

The isoquants graphed in Figures 4-12 are level curves of the Cobb-Douglas production function, whose general form is

(4.5) $$Q = AF^{\alpha}K^{\beta}.$$

Q represents output, and F and K are amounts of the two inputs. A is a constant that increases with the efficiency of production, and α and β are so-called share parameters, which are usually taken to lie between 0 and 1. The marginal products of F and K are

(4.6a) $$\frac{\partial Q}{\partial F} = \frac{AQ}{K}$$

and

(4.6b) $$\frac{\partial Q}{\partial K} = \frac{\beta Q}{K}.$$

Q. Derive these two expressions.

Q. Derive expressions for the slopes of the two marginal product curves and show that they are downward sloping for any output level above zero.

If $\alpha + \beta < 1$, we can show that production displays decreasing returns to scale; if $\alpha + \beta > 1$, returns to scale are increasing; and if $\alpha + \beta = 1$, they are constant.

Q. Show that the previous definitions are consistent with the usual definitions of increasing, decreasing, and constant returns to scale.

Isoquants and Their Slopes

Let the production function be given by

(4.7) $$Q = G(F, K).$$

Then the equation of a particular isoquant is

(4.8) $$Q^{*} = G(F, K),$$

Where Q^{*} is the output level of interest. Its total differential is

(4.9) $$dQ = (\partial G/\partial F)dF + (\partial G/\partial K)dK,$$

that is,

(4.10) $$dQ = MP_F dF + MP_K dK.$$

Along an isoquant, however, quantity is constant, that is, $dQ = 0$. Rearranging, the slope of the isoquant is

(4.11) $$\frac{dK}{dF} = -\frac{MP_F}{MP_K}.$$

Minimizing the Cost of a Given Output

Start from equation 4.2 and rearrange to find that it has slope

(4.12) $$\frac{dK}{dF} = -\frac{P_F}{P_K}.$$

At the tangency between the isoquant and isocost the slopes are equal, that is,

(4.13) $$\frac{MP_F}{MP_K} = \frac{P_F}{P_K}$$

or

(4.14) $$\frac{MP_F}{P_F} = \frac{MP_K}{P_K}.$$

Questions and Problems

1. Are shareholders residual claimants in a publicly traded corporation? Why or why not? In some industries, like hospitals, for-profit producers compete with nonprofit ones. Who is the residual claimant in a nonprofit organization?
2. Developing a new product has taken longer and required more work than was expected at the time the decision to develop was first made. Should the firm raise the price of the product above what it originally planned to sell it for because the costs are higher than before?
3. Explain in more detail the claim about burglary in the section on Production (page 114).
4. Find average variable cost and average cost for each of these total cost curves:
   a. $TC = 10 + 2Q$
   b. $TC = 5 + 3Q^2$
   c. $TC = 20 - Q + 2Q^2$
5. A firm's marginal cost of production is constant at \$5 per unit, and its fixed costs are \$20. Draw its total, average variable, and average cost.
6. For the supply curve shown in Figure 3-6, what does the corresponding total variable cost curve look like? How about marginal cost?
7. Assume that the marginal product of a server in a restaurant equals the number of customers he can wait on per hour. The restaurant owner currently uses one server and is considering adding a second to work alongside the first. Why might the marginal product of the second server be higher than that of the first?

8. New producers in a market naturally have an advantage over preexisting producers because they can buy the newest equipment while the others must make do with older, higher-cost equipment. Yes or no? Explain.
9. Using calculus, try showing that average variable cost and marginal cost have the relationship discussed in this chapter.
10. Average cost contains both fixed and variable costs, but marginal costs are only variable costs. Therefore marginal cost must always be less than average cost. Right? Explain.
11. What is the shape of average *fixed* cost? Give a commonsense explanation for why the minimum point of AVC occurs at a lower output than the minimum of AC.
12. An electricity producer owns two plants (fixed in size) but can burn different amounts of fuel in each of them to produce electricity. It must produce a certain amount of electricity or the area will be blacked out. What conditions hold when the total cost of that amount is minimized? (Hint: think of each plant as an input in an isoquant diagram.)
13. Provide an alternative explanation to the one given in the text for why isoquants cannot cross.
14. In Figure 4-14, what does an isocost look like if the firm can buy capital at a constant price but gets a discount for buying larger quantities of fuel?
15. In Figure 4-16, the example, check that 10 units of output are being produced (use the production function from footnote 22) and that $29.71 is spent on the inputs.
16. Reproduce the reasoning about the tangency in Figure 4-19 when the relative prices of the inputs are P_F = $2.00 and P_K = $4.00. Assume the marginal products are the same as in that example.
17. What happens to a firm's expansion path if one of its inputs permanently falls in price while the price of the other remains constant?
18. What do isoquants look like if there are no substitution possibilities at all, for example, if making a one-pound cake requires precisely three eggs and three cups of flour?
19. Check the computations used to derive the numbers in the text accompanying Figure 4-21.

Chapter 5

Extreme Markets I: Perfect Competition

INTRODUCTION

The Ethanol Upheaval

Iowa was always corn country, but visit today and you will see even more corn than just ten years ago. Since then a substantial number of operations like the one in the photo have turned up in the fields. The plant in the background turns corn into ethanol that will be blended with gasoline. In 2005 federal law began requiring that refiners add "renewable" ethanol into the nation's gasoline supply. This requirement raises the demand for corn, and its impact will grow as more ethanol plants open for business. By 2011, ethanol will use 30 percent of the U.S. crop. The supply/demand analysis of Chapter 3 gives a straightforward prediction: The upward shift in the demand curve for corn will raise its price, and output will rise as producers slide up their supply (marginal cost) curves in response. Before 2006, corn usually traded at about $2 per bushel on

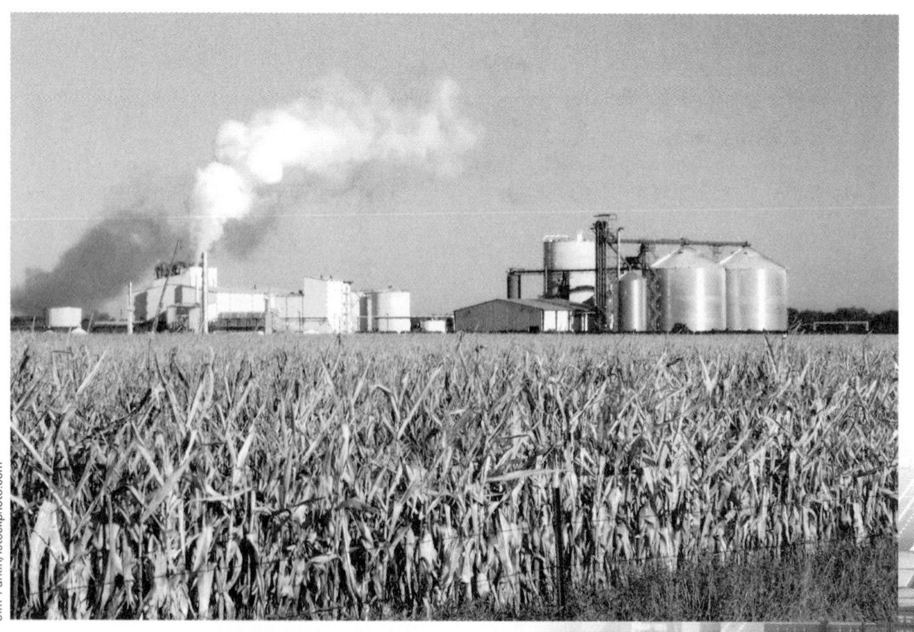
Jim Parkin/istockphoto.com

commodity exchanges, but by the end of that year its price had more than doubled.[1] Since then it has fallen, but not to its former level.

Economics can tell us more about the response to rising corn prices. First, farmers already growing corn can further increase their profits by increasing the acreage they plant in it, or they can attempt to raise yields through more intensive cultivation. Second, some of those who are not growing corn will switch to it. When the price of corn is low their land is better suited to other crops, but when it is high they will divert some acreage to it. Some land formerly not worth cultivating (e.g., pasturage or woodlots) might now be better put into corn production. And these adjustments are occurring. In 2004, just before the new law, U.S. corn production was 11.8 billion bushels on 80.9 million acres. By 2009 the figures would grow to 12.9 (up 9 percent) billion bushels and 87.0 million acres (up 7.5 percent). Acreage of all types grew over the period, but acres in soybeans grew more slowly than corn – by only 3.3 percent.[2] Corn and soybean prices moved closely together, reflecting their substitutability as livestock feeds.

Extending the basic market model to include adjustments in the numbers of producers and outputs of individual producers might provide still more useful insights. Why might we expect that corn prices will never fully return to their pre-2006 levels? What can we say about whose corn consumption would shrink, and why? Might U.S. ethanol policy have destabilized Mexican politics? And why have retail prices of many food items increased, rather than just those of items that use corn as an input, such as beef?

What's Ahead

This chapter is about *perfectly competitive* markets, in which individual producers are so small relative to the market that each of them is a price-taker that cannot affect price by changing its output. Perfectly competitive markets are at one extreme of a spectrum of supply structures. At the other extreme is a single seller that has enough market power to choose from a wide range of possible prices, to be encountered in Chapter 6. The market for corn approximates a perfectly competitive market, and understanding these markets is fundamental for all of economics. We will cover the following:

- Identifying exactly who competes in a market is not as obvious as it may seem. Goods are substitutes in the eyes of buyers, and the presence of substitutes limits any one seller's power over price.
- Each seller in a perfectly competitive market produces a perfect substitute for the output of any other seller. All sellers are price-takers who produce an identical good or service, new competitors can easily enter the market, and it is easy for buyers and sellers to learn about market conditions and potential transactions.
- The perfectly competitive model is valuable for two reasons. First, some actual markets fit its assumptions quite closely. Second, it is an anchor for our thoughts, a starting point for analyzing markets that do not perfectly satisfy its assumptions.
- Our conceptual distinction from Chapter 4 between the short run (some inputs are fixed) and long run (all inputs are variable) is also useful here. In the short run, the only response to a change in demand or cost conditions comes from firms already

---

[1]The text only discusses the effect of increased demand due to ethanol. Weather and related factors also led to a lower 2006 yield per acre than expected, but its effects on the supply curve were small relative to ethanol's effects on demand.

[2]U.S. Department of Agriculture, National Agricultural Statistics Service, "Field Corn" and "Soybeans." http://www.nass.usda.gov/QuickStats/index2.jsp.

in the market. In the long run, profits will attract new entrants (who can collect all the necessary inputs) and losses will induce unprofitable firms to leave the market.

- If all firms in a perfectly competitive market (including those that might begin operating in response to new profit opportunities) have identical costs, short-run market supply increases with price. All sellers, however, enjoy no economic profit in the long run, that is, the long-run supply curve is horizontal. If firms have dissimilar cost curves, the long-run market supply curve will slope upward but show greater responsiveness than short-run supply.
- Our model predicts how sellers enter and leave markets, but the adjustment process in real markets is more complex than it is in the model.

Defining the Market

Substitutes and Competition

Preferences and Prices In Chapter 3, we said that a market was a venue (possibly an electronic one) where buyers and sellers compare offers and choose their transactions. Price is discovered as they acquire information and make transactions. The previous discussion was incomplete, however, because it did not specify in detail the alternatives buyers and sellers could choose from. There was a reason for the omission: the market to examine depends on the problem you are tackling.

If you are thirsty, your choices include tap water, bottled water, diet cola, cola with sugar, milk, or champagne, but few people think them perfect substitutes for one another. What you think are substitutes depends on your preferences and their prices. Some people will pay a lot for cola if the alternative is a fruit drink, and others would only buy cola if it sold at a discount. Substitutes help determine competition. A set of producers is competitive if each supplies a good substitute for what the others produce. They might produce perfect substitutes—corn produced by Farmer Jones is so similar to corn from Farmer Smith that neither ever sells at a premium over the other. Producers may compete even if only some buyers view their products as perfect substitutes. Every brand of coffee contains caffeine, but flavor and price (and for some the prestige of being seen consuming a certain brand) determine the choices of individual customers.

Who Competes with Coke? The Coca-Cola Company is the only entity that can legally use that brand name. In that sense it has a monopoly, but if most people view a range of other beverages as good substitutes for Coke it is not a particularly valuable one. If substitutes are abundant at attractive prices, the market's demand for Coke is highly elastic and the company may be unable to profit by raising price. If an important competitor vanishes or Coke acquires it, the company's power over price will change. If there are only a few producers of substitutes, a merger between Coca-Cola and one of them could significantly decrease the elasticity of demand for Coke.

In 1985, Coca-Cola announced its intent to purchase the Dr. Pepper Company, maker of a carbonated non-cola drink. Antitrust law requires that the U.S. government examine mergers of this size before they take place to evaluate their impact on competition.[3] Coke

[3]*FTC v. The Coca-Cola Company*, 641 F. Supp 1128 (1986). An economic analysis of the case appears in Lawrence J. White, "Application of the Merger Guidelines: The Proposed Merger of Coca-Cola and Dr. Pepper," in John Kwoka and Lawrence White, *The Antitrust Revolution*, 2nd ed. (New York: Oxford University Press, 1994), 76–95; also available at http://www.oup.com/us/pdf/kwoka/0673383776_03.pdf.

and the Federal Trade Commission (FTC) both presented market analyses based on substitution and elasticities. The FTC's economists produced a study purporting to show that the merger would increase Coke's share of carbonated soft drink production by enough that the merged company could profitably raise prices by 5 to 10 percent. If true, this finding would have met the law's standard for rejection of the merger or imposition of other conditions (e.g., divestitures of some assets) before it could take place.[4] Coke's economic experts responded that the FTC had analyzed the wrong market. Their research purported to show that over the past 30 years sales of Coke had responded substantially to prices of other soft drinks and those of beverages that ranged from fruit juice to bottled water. With so many substitutes available, Coke argued that acquiring Dr. Pepper would give it little additional power over prices because the merged company would still be a small part of this large market.[5] As a final alternative, Coke argued that competition from most other soft drinks was of little concern to its management, which concentrated on its long-term rivalry with second-ranked Pepsi-Cola. There might be only two big brands, but Coke claimed that strong competitive threats from Pepsi would constrain its pricing whether or not it owned Dr. Pepper.

All three of of the market definitions are believable, and each can help us analyze a different problem:

1. Someone interested in the long-term evolution of the soft drink industry (and industries producing other beverages) would probably use a study like Coke's to discover how carbonated soft drinks grew to their present-day status and what the future might hold for them. Here Coke has all sorts of actual and potential competitors.
2. Someone interested in the effects of the merger on near-term soft drink prices and on other soft drink makers would look to the FTC analysis, which covers the most important competitors Coke is likely to face over the next few years. The FTC turned down the merger largely on the basis of its staff's research.
3. A marketing analyst or management strategist advising Coke or Pepsi on near-term strategy might reasonably concentrate on just those two companies. It is unlikely that newcomers or smaller producers will grow enough over the next year to affect the underlying relationship between Coke and Pepsi or that consumers' preferences will change radically.[6]

Price-Takers and Monopolies

Market conditions constrain any producer's pricing decisions, and the most important of those conditions is the availability of substitutes. For almost any good, however, we can envision a range of substitutes from near-perfect to very poor. All substitutes put some limits on a seller's power over price, but there is usually no clear way to determine which

---

[4]The government's standards for acceptance or rejection appear in its *1992 Horizontal Merger Guidelines,* at http://www.ftc.gov/bc/docs/horizmer.htm.

[5]The FTC also questioned the merger on grounds that Coke's contracts with its bottlers would make it difficult for new producers of carbonated soft drinks to enter the market.

[6]As an example of rivalry between the two, during the Communist era Pepsi was the only cola sold in the Soviet Union. Other countries, like Poland, allocated exclusive sales territories to Pepsi and Coke. After the Soviet collapse, Coke had to evaluate the pros and cons of entering a large market dominated by its arch-rival and decide on a strategy if in fact it chose to enter. Other drinks played virtually no role in Coke's strategic plans. For a discussion of Coke's choices see Prajit K. Dutta, *Strategies and Games* (Cambridge, MA: MIT Press, 1999), 162–170. Coke in fact chose to enter and currently outsells Pepsi in every former Soviet Bloc country.

goods or sellers are to be included in a market and which are not.[7] The lesson of the Coke/Dr. Pepper case is that competitors are not defined once and for all. Instead, the competitors to study depend on the problem we are attacking. Ultimately the FTC's decision in the Coke/Dr. Pepper case depended on its determination of which entities Coke competed with and which it did not, over the future time period specified by the law. Managements face the same problem the FTC did. Whatever you produce, your strategies are constrained by customers' abilities to substitute and the abilities of rivals to expand or enter the industry. Your tactics to obtain an advantage next month may center on one subset of these factors, while a very different group of factors will help determine your strategy for the next decade.

As for economics, if substitutes are everywhere and vary by degrees it is hard to tell exactly what monopoly means. Coca-Cola is the only seller of drinks with its brand name, but this by itself says nothing about its ability (or lack thereof) to profit by charging high prices. What does matter is the elasticity of demand that a producer faces for sales of its own product. This chapter is about producers who unlike Coke are price-takers and have no power as individuals to affect their markets. Price is at the intersection of market supply and demand, and each seller's profit possibilities are limited by its inability to alter that price by its own actions. Another way to say this is that a price-taker perceives the demand for its own output as horizontal at the market price—it can produce as much or as little as it wants without affecting that price.

Q. Explain how market demand for a good can be inelastic while at the same time demand for a particular producer's output is extremely elastic. Why is this not an impossibility?

Perfectly Competitive Markets

What We Assume, and Why

Four conditions define a *perfectly competitive* market:

1. There are many sellers, all of whom are price-takers. No seller is large enough to affect market price by its own actions.
2. Each seller produces a good or service that is perfectly interchangeable with the output of any other; in other words, the product is *homogeneous.*
3. Firms are not restricted from entering or leaving the industry in response to profits or losses.
4. There are no important transaction costs. In particular, information is available to all participants at no cost. Without cost, buyers can learn the asking prices of sellers and sellers can compare the bids of buyers.

Economic terminology differs from everyday use of the term "competition." The preceding four assumptions rule out many activities usually called competitive. No seller

[7]In some antitrust cases, economists have attempted to delineate competition by calculating cross-elasticities of demand, as defined in Chapter 3. Goods with high and positive cross-elasticities will be good substitutes for the good in question and should be included in the market. Cross-elasticities are often difficult to estimate with available data, and high values can sometimes be evidence of market power rather than competition. See Richard A. Posner, *Antitrust Law: An Economic Perspective* (Chicago: University of Chicago Press, 1976), 126–29.

needs to discount price to attract buyers, because each can sell its entire output at a market price everyone knows. Producers in many markets compete by differentiating their product designs or the quality of service they offer, but the assumption of homogeneous products rules out this type of competition. If information is costless there is no reason for advertising or other promotions. Some of the most common forms of competition are ruled out of a model called "perfectly competitive," for reasons buried in the history of economics.[8]

The perfectly competitive model is one of our most important analytical tools. We did not say so at the time, but its assumptions underlaid our familiar diagrams of supply and demand. Economists have three main uses for the model.[9] First, its assumptions are reasonably close to actual conditions in some markets—those for many farm and forest products, some securities markets, foreign exchange markets, and others. Second, if a market satisfies some but not all of the assumptions, we often start from perfect competition and then see what happens when we replace the usual assumptions with more realistic ones. Third, the perfectly competitive market is a standard for analyzing consumer and producer benefits. (In Chapter 3 we showed that the sum of consumer and producer surpluses is maximized in equilibrium.) We will soon compare markets where competition is less than perfect against this benchmark and will be able to see how various economic events might affect those benefits. The treasury might, for example, want to determine which type of tax on a market (e.g., sales, excise, profit) minimizes lost benefits, or the antitrust authorities might analyze a wave of mergers in a once-competitive industry.

The Short Run and the Long Run

In Chapter 4 we imposed a helpful but fictitious time dimension into production and costs. In the short run, all firms in the market have some fixed inputs that must be paid for, regardless of whether they are producing. In the long run all inputs are variable, and fixed costs need no longer be incurred. Using this terminology, firms only enter or leave a market in the long run, when they can amass all the inputs necessary to open for business or divest them all before closing down. The short-run/long-run distinction is helpful when some external event (e.g., a demand shift or a change in costs) upsets a preexisting equilibrium.

We gain insight by treating the market's adjustment in two phases. First, we examine short-run changes in the outputs of existing firms. In the new short-run equilibrium some of them may be making profits or taking losses. Second, in the long run we watch the number of firms change. Newcomers enter if there are profits to be made, and existing firms close if they are taking losses. In a long-run equilibrium (1) there are no firms outside the market that can earn an economic profit by entering it, and (2) no firms that are taking losses remain in the market. Comparison of long-run equilibria also requires that we specify how (if at all) the costs of firms inside and outside the market differ. Each of the following examples starts at a long-run market equilibrium. Real markets may never settle down to long-run equilibrium, but they tend to move in that direction. If we know the market was far from long-run equilibrium when the shock happened, we can change the analysis accordingly.

---

[8] George J. Stigler, "Perfect Competition, Historically Contemplated," *Journal of Political Economy* 65 (February 1957): 1–17.

[9] There are others that are not important for our purposes, such as general equilibrium analyses of entire economies that contain many perfectly competitive markets.

Market Adjustment

Identical Firms

A Shift in Demand Begin with the simplest possible assumption about firms in this market: they are all identical. All those in operation have identical cost curves, and any outsider can open one just like the others. We first examine a shift in market demand. At the start the typical firm on the left side of Figure 5-1 is in long-run equilibrium, producing an output of 10. It and all other firms are at the lowest point on their average cost curves, earning zero economic profits at a market price of $7. For simplicity we assume that only one size plant is possible, so we need not graph both its long-run and short-run cost curves.[10] With 1,000 identical firms, total output is 10,000 units and no one wishes to enter or leave the market. At that output market demand D_1 intersects short-run market supply curve SRS_{1000}.

Now assume that demand permanently shifts to D_2. In the short run, any change in output can only come from firms that already exist; thus $7 is now a shortage price, and each firm can profit by increasing production. In the new short-run equilibrium each firm increases output to 11 units, and the market clears at $16, where 11,000 units change hands. Because each existing firm earns an economic profit and new firms with the same costs can enter, they will do so in the long run. On the market graph, the effect of entry by 100 new firms is shown by the SRS_{1100} curve. The short-run supply curves of the additional firms are added horizontally to those of the preexisting ones, and price begins to fall below $16. But as long as price is above $7, new producers will want to enter the market. When 500 of them have done so, both the newcomers and the preexisting producers once again break even at a market price of $7. In the new long-run equilibrium, 15,000 units are traded. The long-run supply curve to this market is the thick horizontal line at $7. If there were another shift in demand, the initial response by producers would be a movement along SRS_{1500}.

Q. Perform the same analysis for a leftward shift in demand, being sure to describe the process by which firms leave the industry.

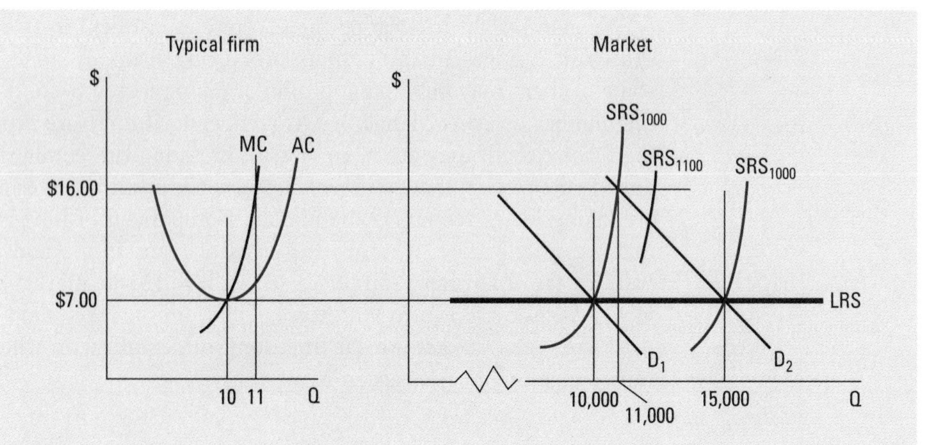

FIGURE 5-1 Firm and Market Response to Change in Demand

[10]Without this assumption we would also need to examine adjustments in the plant sizes of existing firms as they adjust to a new long-run equilibrium. Because we are more interested in comparing equilibria than studying transitions between them, we neglect this complication.

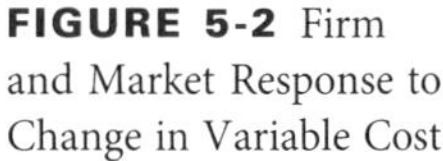

FIGURE 5-2 Firm and Market Response to Change in Variable Cost

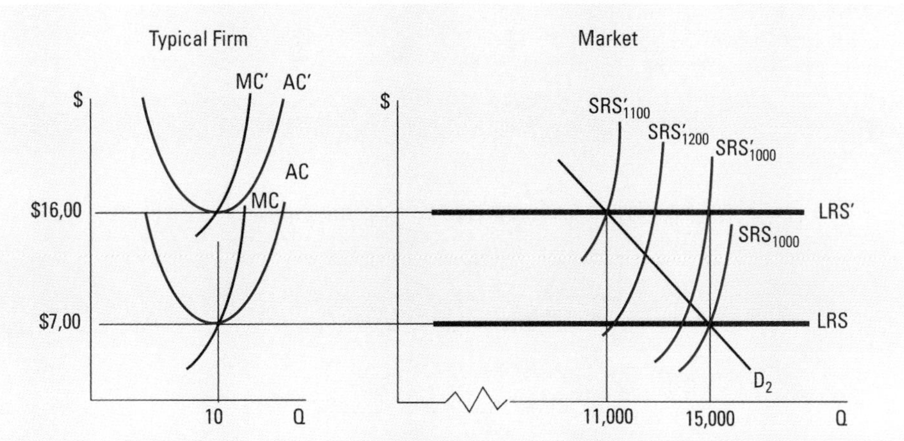

An Increase in Variable Costs Now assume that an increase in the price of a variable input shifts all of the firms' marginal and average costs upward by \$9. On the left side of Figure 5-2, the typical firm's curves shift upward to AC′ and MC′. Assume that there are 1,500 firms in the initial long-run equilibrium, producing 15,000 units of output at the market-clearing price of \$7, along demand curve D. The short-run supply curve is shifted upward by \$9, from SRS_{1500} to SRS'_{1500}. That curve crosses demand at a price between \$7 and the new breakeven price of \$16. All firms are now taking losses. As some drop out of the market, their output is subtracted from SRS'_{1500}. After 200 firms close, the remainder are operating on SRS_{1300}, which intersects demand at a price closer to \$16 but still below it. When 400 have made their exit, the remaining 1,100 firms will break even at a market-clearing price of \$16, and long-run equilibrium will have been restored along SRS_{1100}. By the same reasoning that we used for a demand shift, we can conclude that the new long-run supply, LRS′, is a horizontal line at \$16.

Q. Show algebraically that a given change in the price of the variable input shifts marginal and average costs by the same amount.

Q. Perform the analysis in the preceding paragraph for a fall in the price of the variable input.

Q. Investigate how a rise in the price of a fixed input will affect long-run supply.

Dissimilar Firms

A Shift in Demand Until now almost all the supply curves you have seen sloped upward, but in the previous examples long-run supply was horizontal. To give it a more familiar positive slope all we need is for producers to have differing costs. The left and center panels of Figure 5-3 show two types of firms, denoted A and B. There is some

FIGURE 5-3
Response to Change in Demand with Two Types of Firms

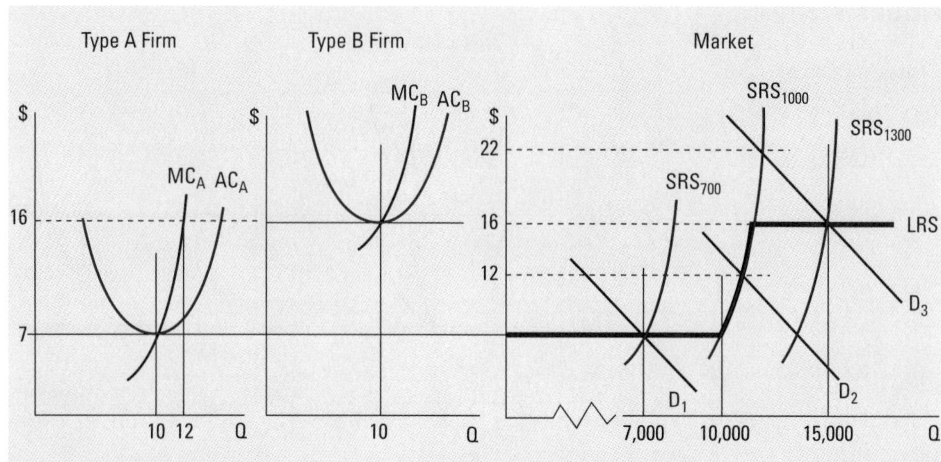

resource (e.g., quality land that requires little fertilizer or labor) in such limited supply that at most 1,000 Type A firms can exist. Their average costs reach a minimum at $7 and an output of 10 units. There are also large expanses of low-quality land that can support an unlimited number of Type B firms, whose average costs reach a minimum of $16 at 10 units. (Again we assume there is only one possible size of firm.) This time we will consider two possible shifts in demand. Begin with low demand curve D_1, along which 7,000 units are demanded at a price of $7. In the initial long-run equilibrium there are 700 Type A firms, each breaking even at 10 units. Their short-run supply curve is SRS_{700}. If we consider only Type A firms their long-run supply curve is horizontal at $7.

Next assume that demand shifts rightward to D_2. All 1,000 potential Type As will be operating and short-run supply will be SRS_{1000}. The market-clearing price of $12 is still low enough that any Type B firm that opened would take losses, so each Type A firm maximizes profit at that price by producing approximately 11 units. Each Type A receives an economic profit of slightly less than $5 per unit. Because no Type Bs will enter at that price, their profit persists, reflecting the scarcity of Type A land and the productivity gap between it and the low-quality land available to Type B firms. Finally, let demand shift outward still further to D_3. If only Type A firms exist in the short run, their short-run supply SRS_{1000} will intersect D_3 at $22. At this price, Type Bs can profitably enter the market. They continue to do so until 300 have entered and price has fallen to $16. At $16 each of the Type Bs breaks even by producing 10 units and the market is again in long-run equilibrium. If price is $16 each type A maximizes profit by producing 12 units, and total output of the As and Bs is 15,000 units.

Q. Why is the economic profit of the Type As slightly less than $5 per unit, rather than exactly $5?

The heavy line labeled "LRS" is the long-run supply curve. Because firms in the industry have different costs, market price must pass the $16 threshold to induce the high-cost Type Bs to begin operating. To turn LRS into a more familiar smoothly sloping curve, all we need do is allow more types of firms with finer differences between their costs. If there is one firm whose minimum cost is $7, a second and third with $7.01, a fourth at \$7.02, and so on, the step-like appearance of LRS becomes far less noticeable. The principle of long-run equilibrium, however, remains the same. The highest-cost firm in operation just breaks even, and all firms with lower costs are also operating. If we wanted to stretch opportunity cost reasoning a bit we could say that all of the firms just cover their costs in the long-run equilibrium, because the owners of those with \$7 costs could sell them at high prices but choose not to. Anyone wanting to buy a Type A firm would have to pay a price that left him indifferent between buying it and a Type B firm. Although formally correct, this reasoning does not provide many additional insights into the process of competitive adjustment, so to maintain clarity we continue to treat profits as we have up to now.

Q. Starting from a long-run equilibrium, assume that the demand curve in Figure 5-3 shifts downward from D3 to D1. Analyze the adjustment to the new equilibrium.

A Change in Variable Cost Figure 5-4 examines the effects of a \$5 rise in variable costs for both Type A and Type B firms. Two cases are worth a closer look: when both types of firms operate and when only one type operates.

Both types of firms operate after the change. To keep things uncluttered Figure 5-4 does not show the cost curves of Type A and Type B firms. As before, however, their minimum average costs are \$7 and \$11, both at outputs of 10, and there can be at most 1,000 Type As. The initial long-run supply curve LRS is the same as in Figure 5-3. If demand is D_1 then the long-run equilibrium price is \$11 and both types of firm operate. All 1,000 Type As produce 12 units each, and 900 Type Bs each produce 10, for a market output of 21,000. Type As earn approximately \$4 per unit produced and Type Bs break even. After the input price rises, long-run supply shifts upward from LRS to LRS.' Price rises from \$11 to \$16 and all Type A's remain in operation profitably. 500 Type Bs close and only 400 of them remain to break even, the entire \$5 increase in variable costs is paid by consumers as a higher price.[11] All of the Type As also make the same profit margins per unit as they did before the cost change.

FIGURE 5-4
Response to Change in Variable Cost with Two Firm Types

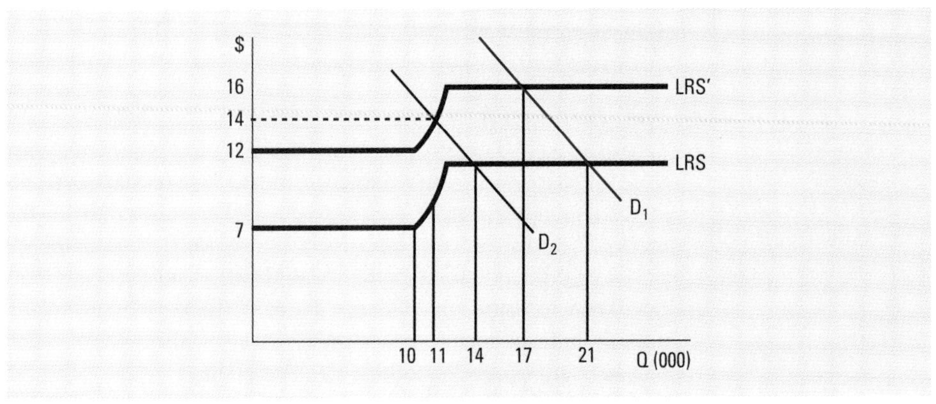

[11]The Type Bs that drop out are also no better or worse off than in their next-best alternatives, save for any possible costs of transitioning to them. Their economic profits are zero both before and after.

Only type A firms operate. Now we start from a long-run equilibrium where demand curve D_2 crosses LRS at \$11, with 200 Type Bs in operation demand curve. After costs rise by \$5, equilibrium price falls and Type Bs begin taking losses. But this time all of the Type Bs drop out, but all Type As continue to operate. At the new long-run equilibrium price of \$14, all Bs will have left the market. All of the As survive, but the cost increase impacts them and their customers. The Type As' profit margin per unit has fallen from \$4 to \$2, and the price paid by buyers has risen from \$11 to \$14. The sum of these \$2, and \$3 changes accounts for the entire \$5 rise in costs. Economists say that in this case the *incidence* of the higher cost falls partially on buyers as higher prices and partially on sellers as lower profit.

Q. If the market supply curve is horizontal, what is the incidence of an increase in variable costs?

Case Studies

Ethanol Again

Long-Run Adjustment We can now tell a simplified version of the ethanol story using Figure 5-3. Say there are a small number of low-cost Type A producers and a limitless potential number of high-cost Type Bs. For reasons discussed later, we assume that the supply curve becomes vertical when all available land is dedicated to corn. We start in 2005 along demand curve D_1 at long-run equilibrium of 7,000 (million) bushels at a price of \$7. An ethanol requirement then shifts the demand curve for corn up to D_3. In the short run, only farms already producing corn can increase production, along SRS_{700}. In the long run, the remaining Type A farms switch to corn and some Type B farms also open for business. As long as price is above \$16, additional Type Bs will enter. Price falls until they once again break even at \$16. Figure 5-5 plots the price over time as predicted by the model. Before the law, it is \$7. When demand shifts upward, the short-run equilibrium price rises to \$22. As new producers enter, it shifts back to \$16, lower but not as low as before the law. After demand shifts the final units can only be produced at higher costs, and the price received by all producers rises.

Project: Go to http://www.indexmundi.com/commodities/ and plot average monthly corn prices from 2002 to the present. In what ways does the graph resemble Figure 5-55-5? In what ways is it different? Next, do the same exercise and answer the same questions for soybeans, which were discussed at the start of this chapter.

The Tortilla Effect The rising price of U.S. corn affects its neighbors. The North American Free Trade Agreement (NAFTA) has eliminated barriers that previously foreclosed Mexico from exporting corn to the United States. As corn leaves Mexico the cost of tortillas there rises. Figure 5-6 shows how trade unifies the U.S. and Mexican corn markets. Rising exports raise its price in Mexico, and increased imports bring lower prices in the United States than would otherwise prevail. (The diagram assumes that all prices are measured in dollars.) To ease the exposition, assume (as was not true) that initially both countries are a single market with a single price of \$10 per bushel.[12] (All numbers are purely hypothetical.) The ethanol program raises U.S. demand from D^1_{US} to D^2_{US}, eliciting an increase in production from 30 to 50 (billion) bushels, while price rises to \$16. At any U.S. price over \$10, Mexicans will have incentives to export. As this

[12]Prior to the coming of ethanol policy the U.S. exported corn to Mexico.

FIGURE 5-5
Adjustment of Corn Prices

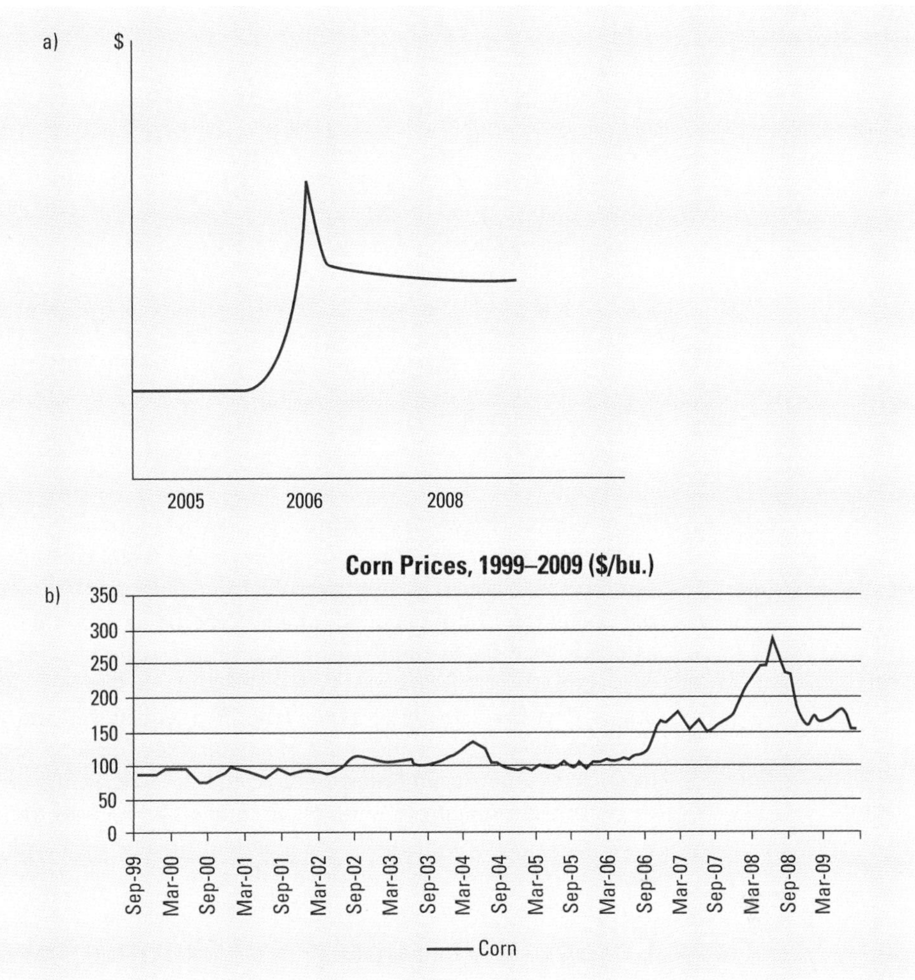

happens, prices converge. At $13, U.S. firms produce 40 bushels for themselves and import 30 more. Mexican firms increase output by 20 bushels, from 65 to 85, and Mexican consumers purchase 10 fewer bushels. The sum of Mexico's production increase and consumption decrease (30) equals the number of bushels imported by the United States. Lower-income Mexicans protest the higher tortilla prices (as indeed they did) and create political difficulties for their government.

Q. Mexicans are debating whether the government should impose price controls to benefit poor people for whom tortillas are a staple. Using Figure 5-6, show what will happen if a price ceiling is imposed on corn. Will poor people necessarily be the beneficiaries of the ceiling?

Q. What happens if, instead, a ceiling price is imposed on tortillas rather than corn?

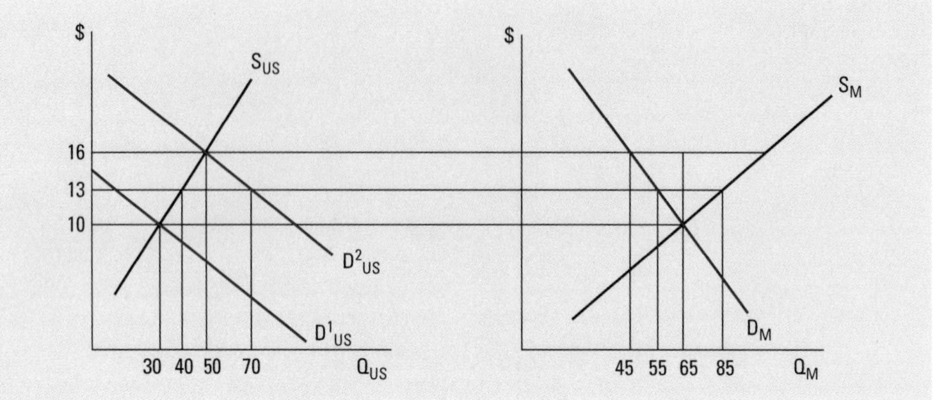

FIGURE 5-6 U.S. – Mexico Corn Trade

Why Other Prices Are Rising Finally, let's explain why other farm product prices are rising, along with those of foods made from corn. In Figure 5-3 we implicitly assumed that the total land available was unlimited—if market conditions warranted the opening for business of additional Type Bs, they could obtain the same quality land as other Type Bs. Figure 5-7 brings in limits on usable land. In it the national demand curve for land D_1 is the sum of the demands of farmers, homeowners, businesses, and others. The fixed supply of usable land, SRS, equals demand at $7 per acre. The ethanol program shifts the demand curve of corn farmers for land upward. Market demand rises to D_2 with a new equilibrium price of $11 an acre. In the long run some land becomes worth transforming from unusable to usable—perhaps by draining a swamp or irrigating a desert. The long-run supply, LRS, of land suitable for farming will be more elastic than the short-run supply, and its price will settle between $7 and $11.

Competitive Supply and Competitor Entry

Agriculture The ethanol story shows that the supply response to a price change may be substantial when firms face low costs of altering the types or amounts of output they

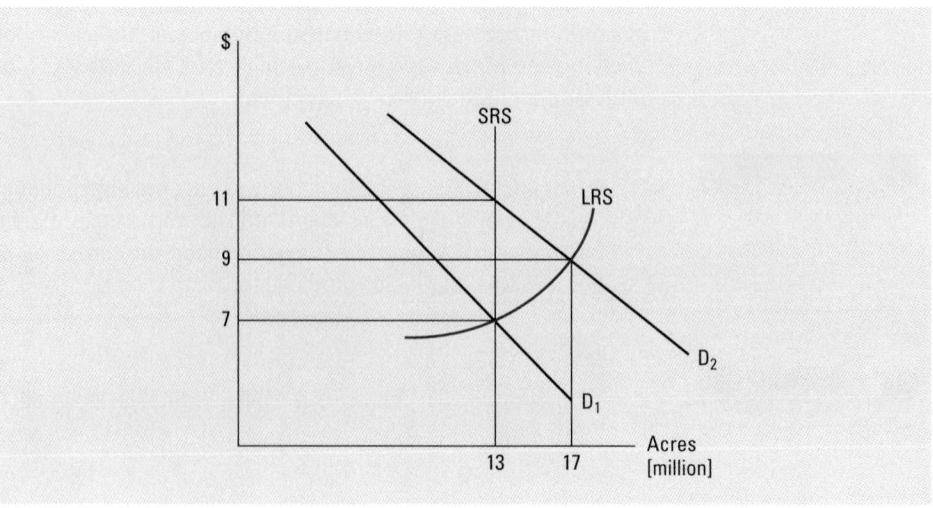

FIGURE 5-7 The Supply of Land

produce. Changing farm acreage from one crop to another is often easy, and agricultural economists have often found high own-price elasticities and cross-elasticities of supply for specific crops. The response is usually even greater over several years than over a single year.[13] Existing growers of a crop whose price has risen allocate more acreage to it, and over the longer run others also begin production. Long-run adjustment takes longer for livestock than for crops because years must pass between the birth of some animals and the time they are ready for market. Short-run responses of livestock to higher prices are low (most estimates of supply elasticity are under 0.10), and long-run responses are considerably higher (elasticities as high as 3 over ten years).[14]

New Products Other research has examined how the numbers and sizes of suppliers change in markets for new products. New sellers enter in response to rising product demand, but the model of long-run costs does not directly predict the shakeouts that are sometimes important parts of the market adjustment process. One study of 47 new products (including outboard motors, electric blankets, penicillin, and zippers) found that in almost every case the number of firms rose sharply after introduction, as output and demand increased with knowledge of the product and the spread of technology to produce it.[15] With almost all of these products, the number of producers peaked within a few years, followed by a fast and substantial elimination of lesser competitors. On average, 52 percent of producers who were operating at the peak vanished, and the highest shakeout rate was 80 percent. After the drop-off, the number of producers becomes relatively steady or grows slowly with the market for the product.

These markets for new products do not strictly satisfy the assumptions of a perfectly competitive model. The sellers are not pure price-takers, and they often produce distinguishable products or use advertising. Still, the perfectly competitive model predicts entry of new firms if demand shifts outward, and the survival of these newcomers after demand growth stops. It does *not* predict that so many producers will enter around the start of the product's life cycle only to drop out soon afterward. Are new producers just overly optimistic (and why are they that way in so many different industries?), or is there some other reason for the outcome? If they are indeed overly optimistic, can economics account for this seeming departure from rationality? In Chapters 7 and 8 we go beyond this model to look at interactions among sellers and the strategies they might choose to deal with rivals.

Oil and Gasoline

Same Story, Different Sellers To analyze U.S. markets for crude oil and refined products like gasoline, try a variation on our model of Type A and Type B firms. Figure 5-8 is a simplified picture of the market for crude oil in the United States. The nation's demand for crude oil that will ultimately become gasoline is shown as D. The details of refining are not of interest here, so let's simplify and assume that a barrel of crude oil yields a barrel of gasoline and nothing else; no other inputs are required and there is no waste.[16]

[13]David R. Lee and Peter G. Helmberger, "Estimating Supply Response in the Presence of Farm Programs," *American Journal of Agricultural Economics* (May 1985): 193–203.

[14]For a summary of literally dozens of supply response estimates, see Hossein Askari and John Cummings, "Estimated Agricultural Supply Response with the Nerlove Model: A Survey," *International Economic Review* 18 (June 1977): 256–92.

[15]Steven Klepper and Elizabeth Graddy, "The Evolution of New Industries and the Determinants of Market Structure," *RAND Journal of Economics* 21 (Spring 1990): 27–44.

[16]In reality the barrel can produce many other compounds, including naphtha, kerosene, diesel fuel, lubricating oil, and petroleum coke, to name a few.

FIGURE 5-8
Domestic and Imported Oil

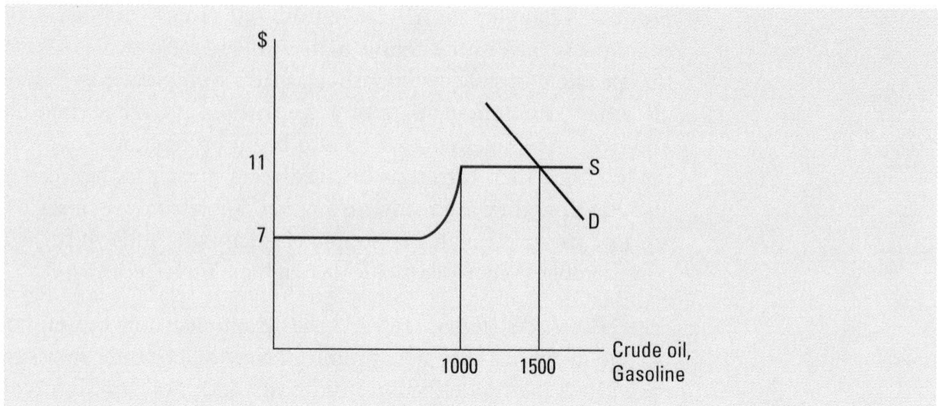

These assumptions allow us to measure both barrels of oil and gasoline in the same units on the horizontal axis. We are also uninterested in the costs of refining oil and marketing gasoline so assume both are zero—just wave a magic wand over the crude oil and gasoline appears at your corner station. The crude oil comes from two sources. The first is domestic production at a marginal cost of $7 a barrel. There are only a limited number of domestic oilfields (we disregard exploration and new discoveries), and long-run supply from them is horizontal at $7.[17] There is also a world crude oil market, in equilibrium at $11 a barrel. Disregarding transport and other transaction costs—anyone anywhere can buy at this price.[18] The United States is small enough relative to the world that shifts of its demand curve cannot move the world price away from $11.[19]

Our earlier reasoning once again tells us that the price of crude oil to Americans will be the world price, where U.S. demand crosses long-run supply. (This analysis neglects many interesting short-run phenomena.) In equilibrium, the U.S. consumes 1,500 barrels per day, 500 imported and 1,000 produced at home. The law of one price holds true. If U.S. producers were receiving only $9 per barrel, it would be a bargain relative to imports, and we would expect buyers to bid it up to the world price. Likewise, refiners will not pay domestic producers more than the world price because they can buy all of

[17]We also disregard any complications stemming from the fact that production takes place over calendar time—the opportunity cost of extracting oil today is in part determined by the forgone revenue that comes from not producing it in the future.

[18]The production decisions of some large suppliers, such as Saudi Arabia, can and do influence the world price. Likewise, the Organization of Petroleum Exporting Countries (OPEC) has at times been able to coordinate production to move the world price. But even if these producers can influence world price Americans will still be able to buy all they want at whatever that price is.

[19]Looking at the numbers this may be a reasonable assumption. Total world oil consumption in 2007 was 87 million barrels per day, 21 million by the United States; U.S. production averages 5 million barrels per day, and crude oil imports are 10 million. The remainder is imported petroleum products, converted to barrel equivalents. In addition, 2.5 million a day come from Canada, 1.5 million from Mexico, and 6 million from various countries in OPEC. Middle Eastern OPEC members, which include Saudi Arabia, send only 2 million barrels per day to the United States. Most other imports from OPEC originate in Nigeria, Venezuela, Indonesia, Angola, and Brazil. See U.S. Department of Energy, Energy Information Administration, *Petroleum Basic Statistics*, http://www.eia.doe.gov/basics/quickoil.html; and *Crude Oil and Petroleum Imports Top 15 Countries*, http://www.eia.doe.gov/pub/oil_gas/petroleum/data_publications/company_level_imports/current/import.html.

their requirements at that price. Downstream, gasoline prices in the United States and other countries move with the world price.[20]

The Effects of Government Policies *Taxing away domestic profits.* Disregarding fixed costs, domestic crude oil suppliers in Figure 5-8 can sell oil at $11, while their marginal costs are only $7, for approximately $4 profit per barrel. Assume that the U.S. government sees the profits as an undeserved windfall and imposes a $4 per barrel tax on domestic producers but not on imports. This tax will not affect what Americans pay for crude oil or gasoline. As long as domestic producers break even they will continue to sell their output at the world price. Money that formerly flowed to domestic producers will now go to the government and ultimately to the beneficiaries of government spending. Domestic producers could even be taxed out of existence. The only effect is that imports replace their entire output, while gas prices remain unchanged. Instead of a windfall tax, the government could impose a price ceiling of $7 on domestic crude oil output and somehow allocate the shortage among refiners. The marginal barrel of oil in the United States would still come from the world market, and gasoline prices would not be affected. World prices would also not be affected if the $7 price control were abolished. Events proved this true in 1981, when the crude oil price controls and windfall profits taxes enacted in the 1970s were abolished without any effect on the price of gasoline.[21]

Q. We just said that U.S. refiners will have to pay the world price to U.S. producers for crude oil. Might the refiners be able to get a better bargain if they were vertically integrated and also owned their oil wells?

Q. Assume that the world crude oil price is set by the Organization of Petroleum Exporting Countries (OPEC) cartel, and the U.S. government taxes away the profits of domestic producers. If OPEC decides to further restrict production in order to raise world prices, the U.S. government will have little interest in trying to bring prices down. Right?

Q. What happens to domestic gasoline prices and crude oil output if the United States imposes a $3 tariff (tax) on every barrel of imported oil.

Political Platforms and Prices The previous reasoning also shows what will happen in the event policies or events change the amount of domestic oil production capacity. In Figure 5-9 assume that some domestic oilfields have been destroyed or that a new law prohibits production from them. The new supply curve of oil to the United States is the red line, which partially coincides with the former supply curve. At a world price of $11, domestic production is 700 barrels per day and imports are 800 barrels per day.

[20]In reality, the price of gasoline does not fluctuate with daily movements in oil prices, but over longer periods it does track the world price. For further explanations and evidence see Joseph P. Kalt, *The Economics and Politics of Oil Price Regulation* (Cambridge, MA: MIT Press, 1983). Most of the differences in retail prices between, say, the United States and Europe are due to taxes. After accounting for transport costs, the price of a newly refined barrel of gasoline before taxes is almost the same everywhere in the world.

[21]See Kalt, *The Economics and Politics of Oil Price Regulation.*

FIGURE 5-9
Reduction in U.S. Production Capacity

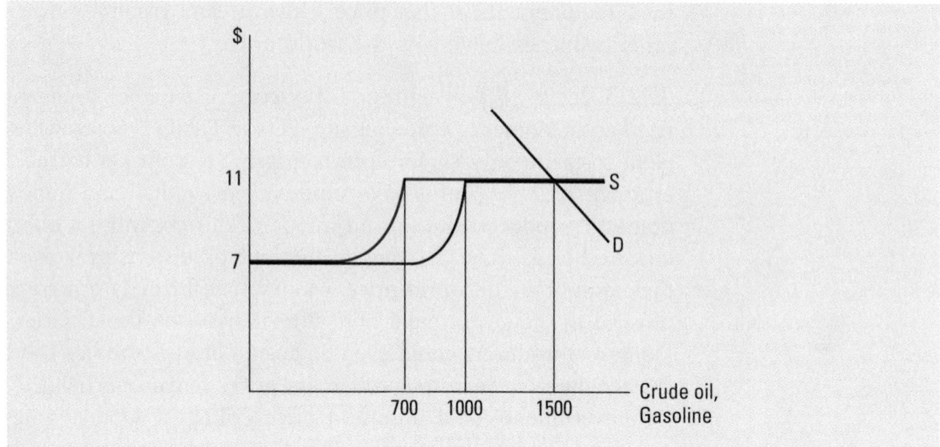

Because the loss in domestic production capability does not affect the world price of oil, it will not affect the price of gasoline.

Increased domestic exploration. In a typical presidential election one party (in the U.S., typically the Republicans) attempts to convince voters that environmentalists (mostly Democrats) are responsible for high gasoline prices because they have obtained legislation closing off some oil-bearing lands from exploration. To see if this makes sense, run Figure 5-9 in reverse. Assume that the red supply curve, which shows limited domestic production, is replaced by the black curve, which shows more of it after formerly outlawed areas begin producing oil. (Here, assume for convenience that their marginal costs are the same those of existing production areas.) As long as there are any imports at all, the prices of domestic crude oil and gasoline will continue to be set by world prices and opening the lands will have no effect on prices. The price of gasoline is not determined by the cost of crude oil averaged over domestic and foreign sources. Instead, it is the cost (world price) of the last barrel.

Q. Assume that the pro-exploration policy is so successful that it reduces U.S. imports to zero and turns the country into an exporter. Explain why this too will not bring about lower gasoline prices.

Policies to reduce demand. The other major political party (in the United States, the Democrats) currently proposes that reducing demand will bring down the price of gasoline. If new laws, for example, raise mileage requirements for new cars, the U.S. demand curve for gasoline will shift leftward. In Figure 5-10 this is a shift from D1 to D2. Once again, as long as the country imports any oil at all, the cost of the final barrel of oil it uses will be the world price. Policies to limit demand will not change the price of gasoline. Notice that even if the program is so successful that it reduces imports to zero, the price of gasoline will remain at $11. The United States will indeed be self-sufficient in oil, but it will be exported until the domestic price again equals the world price. It might surprise you to know that in 2008 the United States exported 1.4 million barrels of oil and refined products a day.[22]

[22]See *Petroleum Basic Statistics.* http://www.eia.doe.gov/basics/quickoil.html

FIGURE 5-10 Effect of Demand Shift

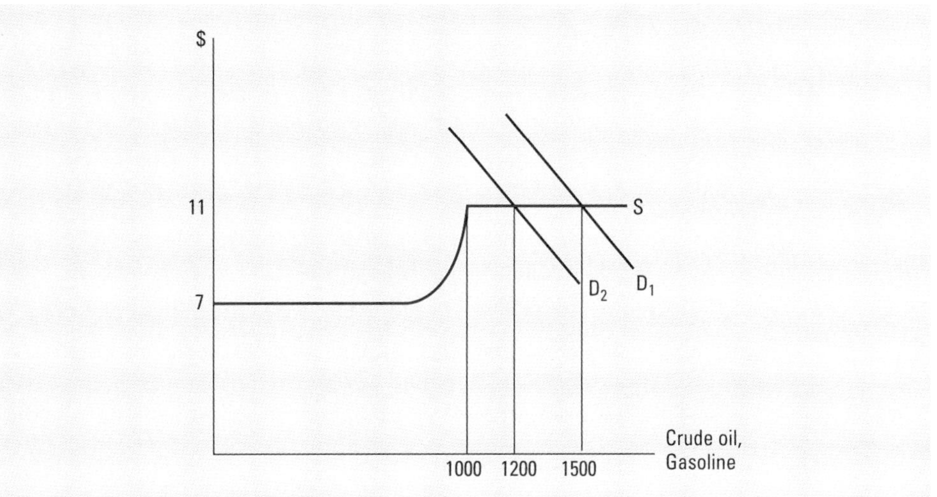

Q. Figure out where the exports are produced and where they go.

Q. Can the simultaneous import and export of oil by the United States be consistent with an efficient pattern of international specialization and trade?

Q. Evaluate claims that the U.S. policy should aim at zero oil imports so that the nation can enjoy energy independence. Assume that the government of the oil-producing country of Slobovia dislikes the United States so intensely that it prohibits all exports of oil to it. Why do you expect that the policy's only effect will be to change the origins and destinations of some shipments, and there will be no effect on world prices or the availability of oil in the United States?

Chapter Summary

- The competitiveness of a market is defined by the range of substitutes for products in it. If buyers can easily switch among substitutes, any individual seller will have less latitude in which to profitably alter the price of its goods. Different economic problems may require the analysis of differently defined markets.
- The model of a perfectly competitive market starts by assuming a large number of price-taker suppliers, each with no power to influence market price. All suppliers sell identical goods, there are no barriers to the entry of new competitors, and buyers and sellers can obtain information about market conditions at very low cost.
- The perfectly competitive model admittedly has extreme assumptions. While they apply in some actual markets, the model itself is often useful as a jumping-off point for analyzing markets where the assumptions do not hold perfectly. Perfect

competition is also sometimes the starting point for analyzing the benefits buyers and sellers receive from being able to participate in markets.

- Our basic supply-demand model assumed a perfectly competitive market. Before now, we analyzed only short-run equilibria, where the only responses to change in market conditions came from already existing sellers. This chapter introduces long-run equilibria in which the number of sellers responds to profits and losses.
- The long-run supply curve to a market depends on characteristics of firms that currently operate in it and firms that could potentially form. Because the number of firms changes, the long-run supply curve is more elastic than the short-run.
- If both current sellers and potential sellers all have identical cost curves, long-run market supply will be horizontal. Firms may make economic profits in the short-run, but entry of new competitors in the long run will drive their returns to the opportunity cost of capital.
- If firms of different types have different cost curves, long-run market supply will be upward-sloping, but output will be more responsive to price in the long run than the short because the number of sellers can change over the long run.

Questions and Problems

1. A firm in a perfectly competitive market invents a new method of production that lowers its marginal costs. What happens to its output? What happens to the price it charges?
   a. The firm has an employee who threatens to tell all other firms in the industry about how to implement this new technique. Will it be possible to bribe the employee not to do this? Explain why or why not.
   b. Why should this employee probably choose to tell only some of the other firms rather than all of them?
   c. What factors will determine the best number of firms to sell the secret to? (Assume that those who get the information keep the secret instead of selling it to still others.)
2. In a certain market demand is

$$Q = 2000 - 100P.$$

   Each of 100 producers has marginal costs of \$2 for outputs of 10 units or less and cannot produce more than 10 units. No other sellers may enter the market.
   a. Draw the demand and supply curves and find the equilibrium price, quantity, and profit per producer.
   b. [Requires calculus] What is the elasticity of market demand at the equilibrium price and quantity?
3. According to the definition, a perfectly competitive firm cannot affect the market price by any changing only its own output. Producer No. 27 in problem 2 decides to experiment by producing only 8 units.
   a. What happens to the market price?
   b. Calculate the elasticity of demand facing Producer No. 27 for its own output.
   c. What happens to Producer No. 27's revenue as a result of cutting output?
   d. Experiment to find the approximate number of firms that must agree to cut their output by 2 units apiece before it becomes profitable for them to do so as a group. Might the reduction in output fail to raise profits even if all firms in the market agree to make such a cut? Explain.

4. Explain why a perfectly competitive firm generally does *not* maximize its profit by producing the output at which average cost is minimized.
5. If the perfectly competitive firm produces the output at which its marginal cost equals market price, it receives no profit (or a very tiny one) on the last unit it produces. Doesn't it make sense to produce fewer units because the difference between price and marginal cost on the last unit it produces will then be bigger?
6. Jones is one of 100,000 corn farmers in a perfectly competitive market. What will happen to the price she can charge if:
   a. The rental price on all farmland increases as urbanization turns increasing amounts of it into home sites?
   b. The price of fuel for tractors falls?
   c. The price of fuel for Jones's, and only Jones's, tractor falls because Jones is a special friend of some politician?
   d. Scientists find that hogs (important consumers of corn) have a disease that is deadly to pork eaters?
   e. Jones loses part of her land as a result of default on a mortgage?
   f. Aliens land in Jones's field (and nowhere else) and the crop circles from their spacecraft destroy part of Jones's crop?
   g. A law is passed that requires all corn farmers to cut their acreage by half?
   h. A per-acre property tax is instituted on all farmland?
   i. A per-acre property tax is instituted only on land that currently grows corn? (What if switching from corn to some other crop does not allow you to avoid the tax?)
   j. Scientists discover that Jones's corn, and only Jones's of all the farmers' corn in the world, cures deadly diseases?
7. Assume that X is produced in a perfectly competitive industry where firms that currently operate and potential competitors both have identical cost curves. Current output is 1 million units a year. What happens to industry equilibrium if a public agency competes with existing producers of X and gives away 100,000 units per year to randomly selected people who would otherwise have purchased X. Does the output of X fall in the short run? In the long run?
8. Good X is produced in a perfectly competitive market using a single input, Y, which is itself also supplied by a perfectly competitive industry. If the government imposes a price ceiling on Y, what happens to the price of X?
9. The price of licenses for tractors owned by farmers who grow X falls. The cost of a license is independent of how many days the tractor is used. Will profits on the typical farm increase by more than, less than, or the same as the saving in the license fee? Explain.
10. [Requires calculus] A perfectly competitive firm faces a market price of $10 for its output X. It owns two plants, A and B, whose total costs are

$$TC_A = 10 + 2X + .25X^2$$

$$TC_B = 15 + .4X + .1X^2.$$

    How many units should each plant produce to maximize profit at that price?
11. You are a perfect competitor facing a market price of $20 for your output Q. Your total costs are

$$TC = Q + .2Q^2.$$

    Your current output is 40 units. What is your profit?

12. [Requires calculus] In the above problem show that 40 units is not the profit-maximizing output and compute profit there. Then find the profit-maximizing output and calculate profit.
    a. Find the percentage differences between actual and maximum profits, and actual and profit-maximizing levels of output. Are you surprised that profit is close to its maximum value for so large a range of outputs?
    b. What might the above problem suggest about using rules of thumb, that is, relatively rough estimates, as opposed to exact calculations?
13. Your company is considering whether to retain the highest-quality raw materials supplier available. Assuming that it really is the best supplier, does this ensure that you will make an economic profit? Explain.
14. A law is passed that requires every firm in a perfectly competitive industry to give six months' notice before it closes. What effect, if any, will this law have in the short run? In the long run?
15. A perfectly competitive industry has a large number of identical firms whose short-run costs are a follows:

Q	TC	FC	VC	MC
1	14	$5	$9	
2	15			$1
3	16			
4	18			
5	24			
6	29			
7	35			
8	42			
9	50			
10	60			

Q is the firm's output, TC its total cost, MC its marginal cost, FC its fixed cost, and VC its variable cost. Fill in the empty spaces and then find the profit-maximizing output and the level of profits when market price is $4.00. Then do the same if market price is $6.50. What is the lowest price at which this firm will supply any output at all to the market? Explain.

16. There are 100 Type A firms in existence with marginal cost curves

$$MC = 10 + .5Q_i,$$

where Q_i is the output of an individual firm. These firms have no fixed costs. Demand is

$$Q = 1000 - 50P,$$

where P is market price.
    a. Assuming that all of these firms are currently in operation, what will be the market price? How much will each firm produce?
    b. Assume that it is not possible to open any more firms of the first type, because they use an input that is fixed in supply. It is, however, possible to open an unlimited number of Type B firms with supply (marginal cost) curves

$$MC = 20 + .8Q_i, \text{ for } Q_i \geq 4 \text{ units.}$$

How many of them will enter the industry?

c. What will be the long-run equilibrium price? What happens to the profits of the type As?
d. Draw the supply curves to this market before and after entry of the Bs.
e. Now assume that there is another alternative to buying from Type A and Type B firms, a world market in which X is available at $30. What will be the equilibrium price and the outputs of the two types of firms?
f. The U.S. government next prohibits all imports of X. Does this make Type A firms better off than before the prohibition? How about Type Bs?

Chapter 6

Extreme Markets II: Monopoly

Introduction

Surely you already know what it means to have a monopoly. With no competitors, you can charge just about whatever price you want, a sure way to make your fortune. Probably the best monopoly of all might be one that is protected by law from competitors, like one (and only one) of the two institutions whose drop boxes are shown below. Since 1863, the U.S. Postal Service (USPS) has had a monopoly on light, sealed correspondence known as first-class mail. It has become a monopoly that barely breaks even, one that must routinely raise its first-class rates if it hopes to stay afloat in the face of shrinking volume.[1] The USPS is a monopolist in first-class mail, but it has no monopoly on the delivery of messages. An industry of overnight shippers like FedEx and UPS have taken

Greg Whitesell/Getty Images

[1]Postal rates are actually set by the U.S. Postal Rate Commission, a government agency that must consider political and economic factors when setting rates for different classes of mail. The combination of these factors means analyzing the actual behavior of the USPS requires more than a simple model of profit-maximizing monopoly.

away most of its package trade, while telecommunication and e-mail services of all types continue to fall in price. In 2004, the USPS reached an agreement with FedEx—It would use FedEx's fleet of planes for long-distance package movement, while FedEx gained the right to install drop boxes on USPS property.[2]

We first encountered problems distinguishing monopoly from competition in Chapter 5, when we tried to identify exactly which companies and products competed with Coca-Cola. As another example, state and local governments license electric utilities to be the only sellers of power in their areas, but your local light company also faces competitors—producers of other forms of energy (e.g., gas for cooking) and producers of fluorescent bulbs and efficient motors that help people economize on electricity. If you have electric heating the electric company also competes with makers of flannel shirts. Local governments often select a single cable television supplier for their cities, but viewers continue to migrate to satellite carriers that are beyond local control. Even seemingly ironclad monopolies face competition, but this chapter's model of pure monopoly will be useful for the same reasons the model of perfect competition was in Chapter 5. In some markets a single seller is so dominant and substitutes for its product are so poor that we can treat that seller as having no competitors who can respond quickly to its choices. Just as we did in studying perfect competition, we will see what happens when we change some of the assumptions that underlie the basic model of monopoly. Specifically, we will explore the following concepts:

- Monopolies and perfectly competitive firms operate under different demand conditions. A perfect competitor faces a demand curve for its own output that is horizontal at the market price, able to sell any amount it can produce without affecting that price. Because a monopolist is the only seller, the demand for its product or service is market demand.
- There are important differences between a monopolist who can only sell at a uniform price and one that can charge different prices to different customers. Downward-sloping demand means that a single-price monopolist can only sell more units per day if it lowers the price on all of them. The net effect increased output and decreased price is called "marginal revenue."
- A single-price monopolist maximizes profits by producing all units that add more to revenue than they do to cost, setting output where marginal revenue equals marginal cost and setting price from the demand curve.
- Perfectly competitive and single-price monopoly markets have important differences. At a moment in time, a monopolist produces an inefficiently small output relative to the perfectly competitive market, but over longer intervals monopolists may have stronger incentives to devise cost-cutting innovations.
- A monopoly can arise from exclusive ownership of a resource, which might be physical property like a unique location, or intellectual property like a patent. Monopolies may also exist because the law prevents competitors from operating in a market they might otherwise enter.
- If a monopolist can charge different prices to customers with different elasticities of demand (price discrimination), profits will increase and consumers will also benefit. Success, depends on being able to separate customer groups and to keep them from reselling the good among themselves.

[2]Montgomery Research, "USPS-FedEx Agreement Delivers First-Class Service," (May 15, 2004), http://www.postalproject.com/documents.asp?d_ID=2487.

- Price discrimination helps to explain cover charges and service charges that a customer must pay before being able to purchase any quantity of a good. It also helps explain when and why a monopolist can profit by requiring customers to buy other goods as a condition of buying the monopolized one.

One-Price Monopoly

Some Ground Rules

The most basic distinction between monopoly and perfect competition is that a monopolist has some choice about its selling price but a perfect competitor is a price-taker. Put another way, the demand curve that a perfect competitor perceives for its own output is a horizontal line at the market price. The firm can produce as much or as little as it wants without affecting that price. A price-taker has no reason to discount below the market, and no buyer will accept a price above the market when so many alternatives are available. A monopolist, however, has no market price to "take." The downward-sloping market demand curve is also the demand this firm faces. Its management's task is to choose price and output that maximize profits, and our first job is to find them. Other assumptions made at the outset include the following:

- *Product definition*: The monopolist produces a single, homogeneous, divisible product or service.
- *Certainty*: The firm knows with certainty the demand and cost conditions it faces.
- *Ignorance or disregard of rivals*: The monopolist attempts to maximize its immediate profit. In particular, it does not consider the possible reactions of future competitors or firms that produce close substitutes for its output.
- *Single price*: The monopolist must charge all customers identical prices at all times.

Maximizing Revenue and Maximizing Profit

If you face a downward-sloping demand curve for your output, you most likely envision yourself as choosing a price and seeing how many units customers will buy. Of course, if you really knew the exact demand curve, you could first decide how much to produce and then go back to the graph and determine the highest price at which you could sell that amount. Picking the output and then finding the price sounds a bit unreal as a business practice, but doing so here will help us make some important comparisons between monopoly and competition.

In Figure 6-1, assume that you can only sell integer units of your product. To make things still easier, assume that marginal costs are zero so that maximizing revenue is the same as maximizing profit. If you want to sell one unit per day, it will find a buyer at $12. Two units can be sold for at most $11 each, and likewise on down to 12 units, for which you can charge $1 apiece. It is easy to find the output that maximizes your revenue—just calculate it for every price-quantity pair and pick the best. Here you produce either seven units and sell them at $6 apiece or six units at $7. Either gives a revenue rectangle under the curve whose area is $42. This sort of calculation, however, is worse than boring—it does not suggest any general principles to follow either in theory or practice.

But stick with the numbers another minute. Producing one more unit a day is only worthwhile if it increases revenue. Under the single-price assumption, however, you can only sell more units a day if you cut the price of all of the units. Figure 6-1 also shows the effect on revenue of changing from three to four units of output per day. You can sell three units for $10 each for total revenue of $30, the area of a rectangle with a base of

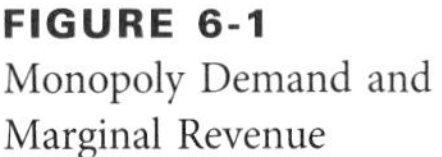

FIGURE 6-1
Monopoly Demand and Marginal Revenue

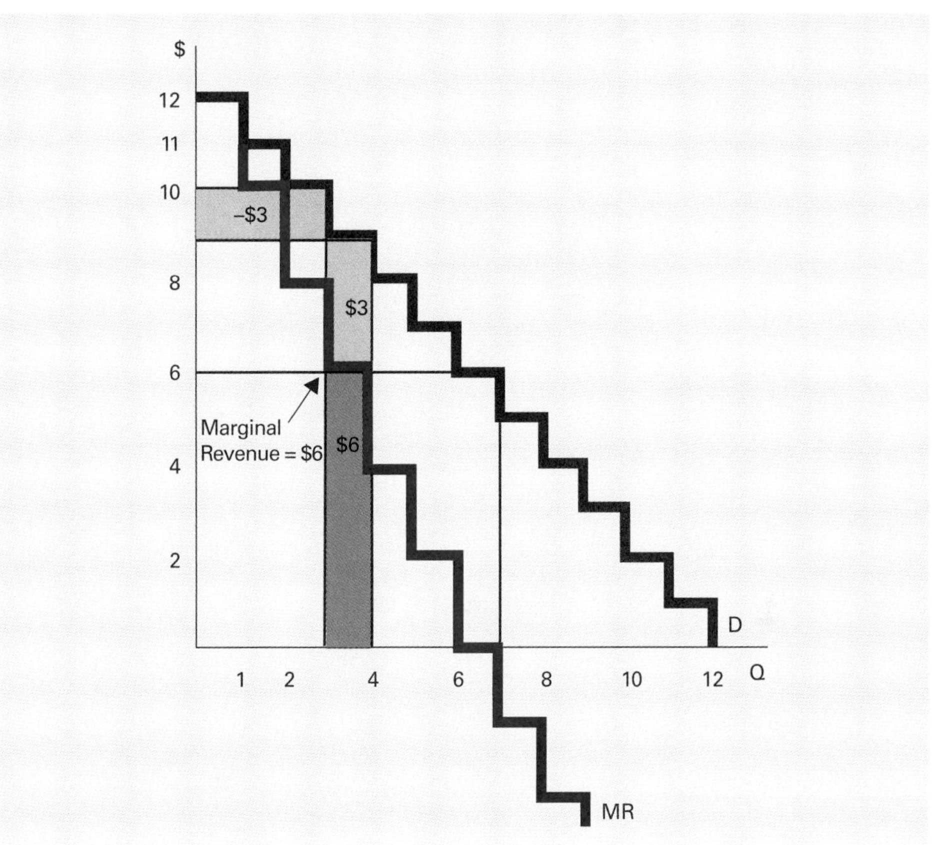

three and a height of ten. You can also sell four a day for $9 and make $36 in revenue. The net contribution of the fourth unit is the extra $9 from selling it minus the $3 lost by cutting price on the first three, that is, $6. This is called *marginal revenue.* If we subtract $3 from the top of the narrow rectangle above the fourth unit, marginal revenue of $6 is the height of what remains. Repeating this exercise for every output gives the MR line of Figure 6-1. For outputs over seven units a day it becomes negative; in other words, total revenue decreases when another unit is produced.

Q. Check the preceding claim by graphing total revenue on a duplicate of Figure 6-1.

Q. Must marginal revenue slope downward? Can you give a numerical example of a downward-sloping demand curve whose marginal revenue is increasing over some range of output?

To maximize revenue, just choose the output at which marginal revenue is zero. Each unit to the left of it increases your profit, but going beyond it decreases profit. The top half of Figure 6-2 shows a monopolist's demand and marginal revenue as smooth lines. If its marginal costs are zero, profit maximization occurs where output is six units a day and price is $7, the maximum at which each of the units can be sold. If the monopolist has costs, maximizing profit requires that they be considered. The upper half of

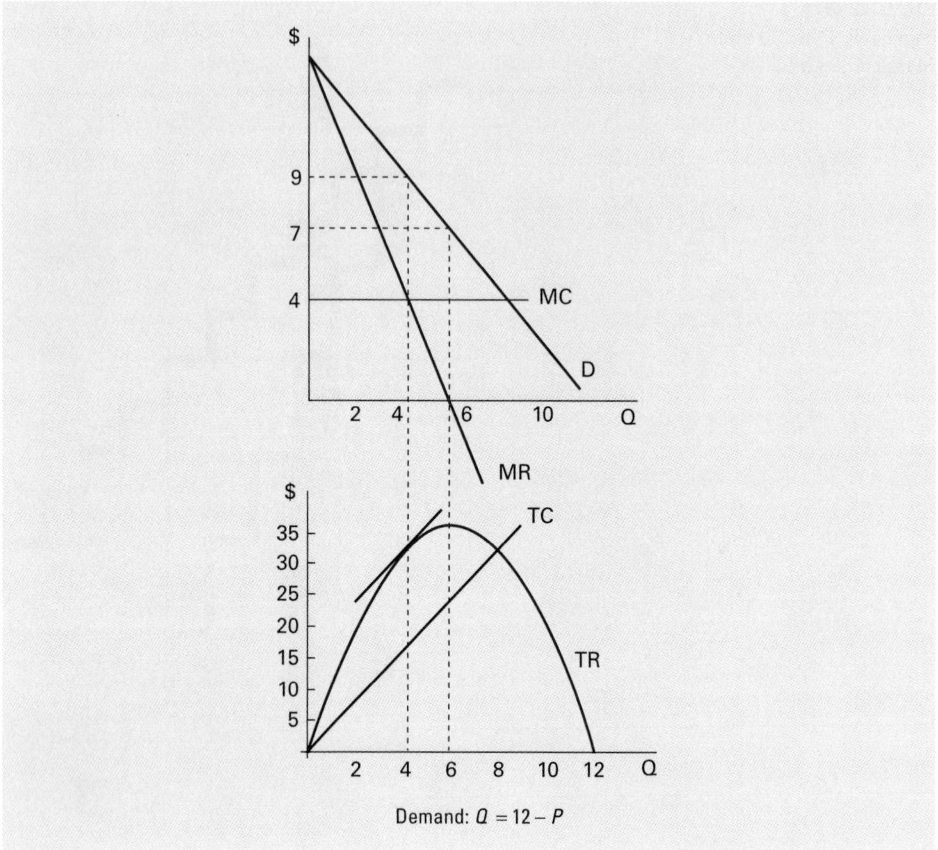

FIGURE 6-2
Revenue and Profit Maximization for a Single-Price Monopolist

Figure 6-2 also shows a constant marginal cost of $4 per unit. Now the extra profit from an extra unit of output is the difference between its marginal revenue and marginal cost. The monopolist produces where the two are equal: 4 units in the top half of Figure 6-2 to be priced at $9 each. The bottom panel of Figure 6-2 shows total revenue, which increases with output as long as marginal revenue exceeds zero. (Note the different vertical scales on the two graphs.) If the monopolist has no costs, profit is maximized where marginal revenue equals zero. If marginal cost is constant, profit is maximized at 4 units, where the slope of total cost (i.e., marginal cost) equals the slope of the tangent to total revenue (marginal revenue).

Comparing Monopoly and Perfect Competition

Replacing Competition with Monopoly Let us assume a market for mineral water that contains 110 competing sellers rather than one monopolist. Each firm owns a single spring that has a marginal cost of zero (the water flows naturally) and can produce at most a tenth of a gallon per day. The market demand curve is the same one as in Figure 6-2, and it is also shown on Figure 6-3. In the perfectly competitive equilibrium, each gallon sells for $1, and each spring owner gets 10 cents for its tenth of a gallon.[3] No owner acting alone can profit by keeping part of its output off the market. One day Merger Woman turns up. (Instead of being an outsider, she could just as well be an

[3]Each of the 110 sellers could have a tiny impact on price by changing its own output, but neglect the algebra and assume that each is a true price-taker.

FIGURE 6-3
Comparing Monopoly and Competition

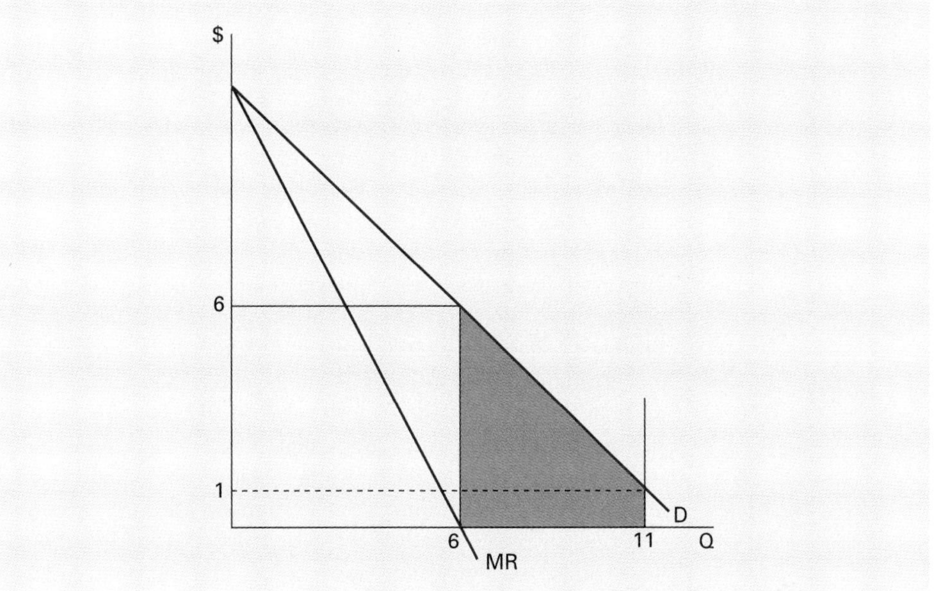

enterprising spring owner.) She makes each owner an offer that sounds hard to refuse: "Give me control over your spring and I will pay you 20 cents every day." Assume that there are no holdouts and every owner takes the offer. Merger Woman is now a monopolist whose opportunities are shown in Figure 6-3—the market demand curve is now the demand she faces. Operating along marginal revenue curve MR she abandons 50 of the springs and sells the 6 gallons still being produced at $6 each. From the revenue of $36, she pays each of the 110 owners 20 cents and pockets the remaining $14.

Q. Why was it important to assume that there were no holdouts? What might happen if there are a number of holdouts?

Q. What will likely happen if several competing people are trying to set up a merger of all the spring owners?

Merger Woman and the spring owners are better off than when competition prevailed but consumers are not. Each of the 6 gallons they still buy sells for $6 instead of $1. This change taken by itself, however, does not necessarily matter to an economist. It is a redistribution of some benefits that also existed before the monopolization. Consumers who were willing to pay up to $11 for the first gallon obtained it for only $1 in the competitive market.[4] They enjoyed $10 in consumer surplus from the first gallon, and spring owners got $1 in producer surplus. After the monopolization, the buyers still get the gallon, but the new $6 price shrinks their consumer surplus to $5. Their lost $5 is a newly gained $5 benefit to Merger Woman and the spring owners. Just like the purchasers,

[4]Because the demand curve in the diagram is continuous the first tenth of a gallon is valued more highly than the second tenth and so on. Statements about the value of the first gallon are thus not strictly accurate, but they do get the point across.

they are also human beings, and there is no normative reason to favor one side over the other. If you think consumers deserve a larger fraction of the benefits, you may of course criticize the monopolization on normative grounds.[5]

Deadweight Loss and Other Possible Losses The problem with this monopoly is not the 6 gallons that still change hands. It is the 5 gallons that are no longer produced and exchanged. Before the Merger Woman came along, gallons 7 through 11 changed hands to the benefit of both sellers and buyers. The Merger Woman, however, can only maximize her profit if she throws them away. Marketing more than 6 gallons a day cuts her profit, as does marketing fewer than 6 gallons. The gallons that go unexchanged engender what economists call a *deadweight loss*—a loss of benefits to consumers and/or producers that is gained by no one. The water from 50 springs flows back into the ground unused. The Merger Woman leaves the world a poorer place because both she and her potential customers forgo any possible benefits from those 5 gallons. In the competitive market that formerly existed, all of those gallons did change hands. Deadweight loss is the shaded area in Figure 6-3, below the demand curve between 6 and 11 gallons. Buyers value gallon number 7 at $5, and we assume it is costless to produce. Throwing it away deprives the world of those benefits, and neither the seller nor anyone else gains. Throwing the eighth gallon away means that a bit more than $4 in benefits is lost. Adding up the lost benefits of gallons 7 through 11, that is, calculating the area under the demand curve, gives a deadweight loss of $17.50.

Q. Check the previous calculation for deadweight loss.

The same logic holds if the good is costly to produce, but here we must also account for resources the monopolist does *not* use that would have been used in a competitive market. Assume that the springs no longer flow naturally and the $4 marginal cost in Figure 6-2 is for fuel used to pump water up to ground level. In a competitive market, production would have been 8 gallons a day, where marginal cost (competitive supply) cuts the demand curve, and price would have been $4. A monopolist who does not produce units 5 through 8 does not have to burn the fuel required to make the units. That fuel can now go to some other use where it is worth $4 (the price reflects its opportunity cost). Four dollars per unit is recoverable, because the fuel is not thrown away. The deadweight loss is thus the triangle bounded by $4, the demand curve, and the vertical line at four units. It equals $10.

Q. Check the previous computations about deadweight loss when the spring no longer flows naturally.

The diagrams tell nothing about actual deadweight losses that might exist. Just changing the scales of the axes can make the triangles look big or small. Most estimates by economists have been quite small relative to the size of the affected markets

[5]Most of us probably identify with consumers, but it is easy to invent stories that make us feel sorry for the sellers. Possibly before Merger Woman came along the price of water was so low that spring owners lived on the edge of starvation. Or we might assume that the merged operation is a publicly traded company. Spring water is consumed by wealthy people who use it solely to flaunt their status. Widows and orphans hold most of the company's stock and, thanks to the monopoly's high dividends, they can pay the rent on their tiny rooms and avoid being thrown out on the street.

or the entire economy. At one end are figures like 0.1 percent of gross national product for the entire economy in 1954 and 0.4 to 0.7 percent in U.S. manufacturing in the 1960s.[6] At the other end are figures of 4 to 13 percent of the value of sales for large manufacturers in the United Kingdom in 1968.[7] Researchers have criticized both the low and high estimates, and no general agreement on the size of deadweight loss has been reached.[8]

Monopoly might also bring other losses. The term *x-inefficiency* refers to the use of excessive quantities of inputs relative to best-practice methods. It raises the monopolist's costs and leaves the economy with fewer resources free to produce other goods. X-inefficiency could exist if the monopolist monitors its costs less closely than a firm that faces competition, because inattention is less of a threat to a monopolist's survival than to a competitor's. Economists disagree on the relevance and detectability of x-inefficiency.[9] The late British economist (and Nobel Prize winner) John Hicks once said, "[t]he best of all monopoly profits is a quiet life," that is, one spent with few concerns about competition or x-efficiency.[10] But this superficially plausible statement may disregard corporate reality. Managers who choose the quiet life impose costs on their shareholders, who can (and sometimes do) replace the managers or allow the firm to be taken over or acquired.[11]

In some markets—such as cable television—competition is possible, but government suppresses it and allows only one provider to serve a city or region. The firm with the monopoly is insulated from direct competition, but we may still see a competition to obtain the monopoly, a process known as *rent-seeking*. Cable television providers compete for monopoly franchises to serve a city, but this competition is costly. Prospective providers often hire lobbyists, lawyers, and economists to convince the city's government that they are better suited to run the system than rival applicants, or they incur other expenses to gain political favor.[12] (Sometimes bribes will do the job just as well.) A cable company uses these people and resources to help it gain a monopoly. Used for this purpose, these resources are unavailable to produce other goods and services that consumers value. Because data on rent-seeking expenses are hard to obtain (and not all applicant expenses are necessarily wasteful) our information about losses from the activity is sparse. One study of the deadweight loss from competition to obtain cellular phone

---

[6]Arnold Harberger, "Monopoly and Resource Allocation," *American Economic Review* 44 (May 1954): 77–79; Dean A. Worcester Jr., "New Estimates of the Welfare Loss to Monopoly, United States: 1956–1969," *Southern Economic Journal* 40 (October 1973): 234–45.

[7]Keith Cowling and Dennis Mueller, "The Social Costs of Monopoly," *Economic Journal* 88 (December 1978): 727–48. One expects that an estimate restricted to large manufacturers would be high as a percentage of their sales, because these are among the firms most likely to have substantial pricing power.

[8]Abram Bergson, "On Monopoly Welfare Losses," *American Economic Review* 63 (December 1973): 853–70 (this author is critical of low estimates); Dean A. Worcester Jr., "On Monopoly Welfare Losses: Comment," *American Economic Review* 65 (December 1975): 1015–23 (this author is critical of high estimates).

[9]Harvey Leibenstein, "Allocative Efficiency vs. X-Efficiency," *American Economic Review* 56 (June 1966): 392–415; George J. Stigler, "The Xistence of X-Inefficiency," *American Economic Review* 66 (March 1976): 213–16.

[10]In "Annual Survey of Economic Theory: the Theory of Monopoly," *Econometrica* 3 (January 1935): 1–20.

[11]Michael C. Jensen, "The Modern Industrial Revolution, Exit, and the Failure of Internal Control Systems," *Journal of Finance* 48 (July 1993): 831–80.

[12]The firm that won the franchise in Fullerton, California, gained important support by promising to build a state-of-the-art television studio on the local state university campus. In neighboring Anaheim the eventual winner thought it important that the city council see one of its systems in operation. It sent the council members and their spouses for an expense-paid week in Honolulu, where it held the franchise.

franchises in smaller cities in the 1970s estimated it at 20 percent of expected profits from winning.[13]

Do Monopolies Raise Prices?

Some Historical Cases The story of Merger Woman predicts that turning a competitive market into a monopoly lowers output and raises price. In many cases on record the opposite happened—under monopoly output rose and price fell.

- *Standard Oil of New Jersey*: Between 1880 and 1895, John D. Rockefeller's company controlled between 82 and 88 percent of U.S. refining capacity. A gallon of refined oil in the barrel that sold for 9.33 cents in 1880 had fallen to 5.91 cents by 1897.[14] Over that period, Standard Oil increased its output of kerosene by 74 percent and lubricating oil by 82 percent. (Gasoline was unimportant before the automobile.) In 1892, Standard Oil refined 39 million barrels of crude oil, which grew to 99 million barrels in 1911, the eve of the company's breakup by federal authorities.[15]
- *American Sugar Refining Company*: Mergers between competitors in the late 1880s gave American Sugar 95 percent of U.S. sugar-refining capacity in 1893.[16] Wholesale refined sugar sold for 9.60 cents a pound in 1880, 6.17 cents in 1890, and 4.97 cents in 1910. Because the wholesale price of refined sugar is heavily influenced by the price of raw sugar, the margin per pound between the raw and refined products may be more informative. It fell from 1.44 cents in 1882 to 0.50 cents in 1899.[17]
- *American Tobacco Company*: In 1880 (long before health concerns arose), cigarettes were a minor part of tobacco product output, which was mostly cigars and bagged tobacco for pipes and handmade cigarettes. Manufactured cigarettes became popular, but the growth of sales was hindered by high production costs. In 1890, James B. "Buck" Duke (benefactor of Duke University) merged 90 percent of U.S. cigarette-making capacity into the American Tobacco Company, which dominated the industry until its forced breakup in 1911. American's engineers designed and built the first reliable, low-cost cigarette-making machines and continuously improved them. Its cigarettes sold for $2.77 per thousand in 1895, and $2.20 per thousand in 1907. This decline is remarkable because over those years the price of leaf tobacco rose by 40 percent, from 6 cents to 10.5 cents per pound.[18]

Innovation or Inefficiency? All of these episodes have one common factor: After combining a group of competitors into a single firm, each monopolist devised ways to cut costs and passed some of these cuts on to buyers. Figure 6-4 shows that a monopolist whose marginal costs fall will increase its profits by raising output and lowering price, but not by the full drop in cost. With the same demand curve as Figure 6-2 and a marginal cost of $8, the profit-maximizing output is 2 units sold for $10 each. Disregarding

---

[13]Thomas W. Hazlett and Robert J. Michaels, "The Cost of Rent-Seeking: Evidence from Cellular Telephone License Lotteries," *Southern Economic Journal* 59 (January 1993): 425–35. More on the theory of rent-seeking and estimates of losses due to the practice is in Richard A. Posner, "The Social Costs of Monopoly and Regulation," *Journal of Political Economy* 83 (August 1975): 803–28.

[14]Ida Tarbell, *The History of the Standard Oil Company* (Gloucester, MA: Peter Smith, 1950), 385. The percentage fall in price exceeded the drop in average prices due to deflation that was occurring over some of the period.

[15]Ralph and Muriel Hidy, *Pioneering in Big Business: History of the Standard Oil Company (New Jersey)*, (New York: Harper and Row, 1955), 289.

[16]*Sugar Institute et al* v. U.S., 297 U.S. 533 (1936), 565.

[17]Elliot Jones, *The Trust Problem in the United States* (New York: Macmillan, 1923), 117.

[18]Richard B. Tennant, *The American Cigarette Industry* (New Haven, CT: Yale University Press, 1950), 53.

FIGURE 6-4
Monoply and Innovation

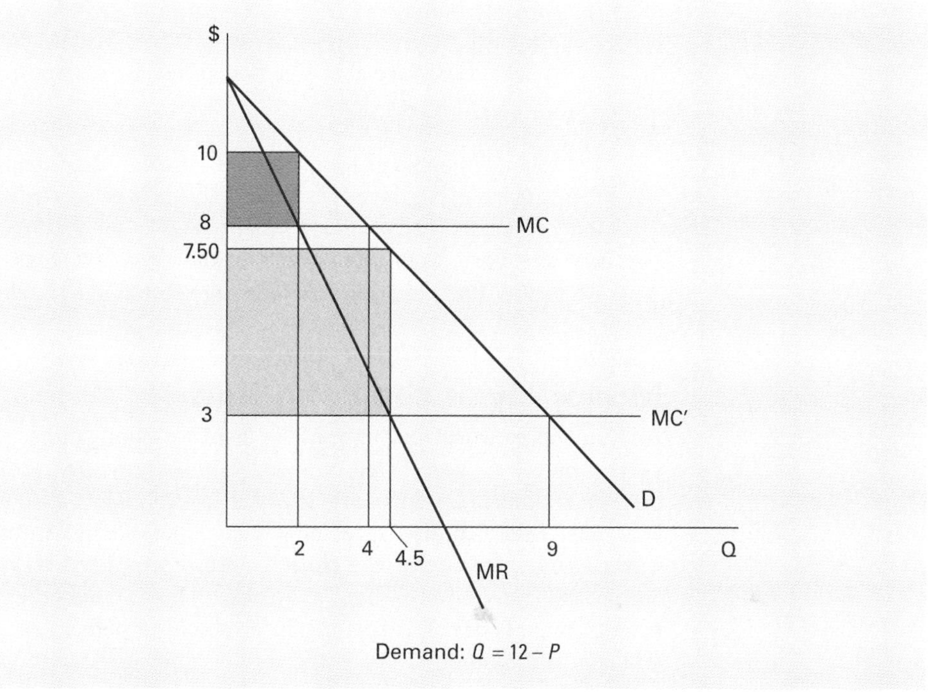

any fixed costs, profit is $4, the area of the small red rectangle. If the monopolist finds a way to reduce marginal cost to $3, its marginal revenue at the old output now exceeds marginal cost. Its new best output is 4.5 units, which will sell for $7.50 each and yield profits of $20.25, the area of the large blue rectangle.

Q. Check that the above calculations are correct.

The invention profits the monopolist, and the lower prices benefit its customers. Of course, they would gain even more if some inventor had given all of the sellers in a perfectly competitive market rights to use it. If the market of Figure 6-4 had been perfectly competitive with a horizontal supply curve at $8, sellers as a group would have produced 4 units of output and each would break even at the equilibrium price of $8.[19] If the invention reduces each firm's marginal cost to $3, output will be 9 units and price $3. Producer surplus is zero before and after the invention, and all of the gains go to consumers.

Innovation and invention can be costly and risky. Not all innovations can be patented, and those that can must be defended against infringement. If you have a monopoly, however, these intellectual property problems diminish because you face fewer competitors (possibly none) who might steal it. American Tobacco's monopoly meant it would enjoy the profits of automated cigarette manufacturing without competitors to share them. Our study of monopoly leaves us with a dilemma. Looking at a snapshot of the market, the monopolist might create a resource-wasting deadweight loss that would not exist under perfect competition. Looking at behavior over a longer horizon, the monopolist may be more likely to innovate cost reductions than would a perfect competitor. Of course, this

[19]We are assuming that each competitor's marginal cost is unchanged after all of them go under a single management.

might mean some number of sellers between monopoly and perfect competition is even better. The firms as a group would bring a lower deadweight loss than monopoly, and their rivalry would produce a greater flow of inventions and innovations.[20]

Q. We said that people in a price-takers' market—like farmers—would be unlikely to innovate much, but in fact farm productivity has risen steadily and rapidly for more than a century. If individual farmers have little incentive to invent, where do the changes come from? (Hint: Are farm implement and seed companies perfect competitors? What about publicly funded research at agricultural universities?)

Monopoly in the Long Run

Any monopoly worth having must be hard for competitors to erode quickly. Some important ones have been based on ownership of a resource with few good substitutes. For example, the DeBeers company achieved its dominance of the diamond industry in the late nineteenth century by gaining control of South Africa's Kimberley "pipe," the world's largest source at the time. DeBeers responded to new discoveries in Russia, South America, and elsewhere in Africa by buying into them or becoming their marketing agent. Today, DeBeers produces about 40 percent of the world's raw diamonds and controls another 30 percent, carefully limiting the amount it releases into the market.[21] DeBeers is a singular case. More often, a monopolist's profits promise wealth to those who can find and produce substitutes. In 1890, Standard Oil controlled more than 80 percent of oil production in the Northeast and Midwest. In 1901, the discovery of oil on Spindletop Hill near Beaumont, Texas, opened up the Southwest to oil exploration, with production and reserves in volumes that even Rockefeller could not attempt to control.[22]

An exclusive resource can also take the form of intellectual property, like the inventions discussed earlier. The U.S. Government's Patent and Trademark Office grants inventors of provably original and useful items a 20-year right to be monopolists. The patent holder obtains exclusive control of the invention and can sue to prevent unauthorized use or infringement by producers of items believed to be the same as the protected one.[23] Similarly, trademarks allow exclusive use of an identifier, such as a brand name, and can be renewed indefinitely. A copyright currently gives the creator of a literary, musical, or artistic work protection against unauthorized use for 70 years.[24]

Technological innovations ranging from laser copiers to the Internet have greatly expanded the reach of intellectual property law and the difficulties of enforcing it. Patents can now be issued on keystroke patterns (e.g., Internet bookseller Amazon.com's

---

[20]See Morton I. Kamien and Nancy L. Schwartz, "On the Degree of Rivalry for Maximum Innovative Activity," *Quarterly Journal of Economics* 90 (May 1976): 245–260

[21]An introduction to DeBeers and the diamond industry appears at "The Diamond Pipeline—From the Rough to the Polished," Keyguide Directory Portal, http://www.keyguide.net/rough/, and in Lisa Bernstein, "Opting Out of the Legal System: Extralegal Contractual Relations in the Diamond Industry," *Journal of Legal Studies* 21 (January 1992): 115–157. DeBeers's corporate Web site is at http://www.debeersgroup.com/debeersweb.

[22]"Oil in Southeast Texas," Spindletop-Gladys City Boomtown Museum Web site, http://www.spindletop.org/history/index.html. Texas conveniently passed a law prohibiting the Rockefeller interests from exploring there, but other western oil states Oklahoma, Louisiana remained open and competitive. A few years before Spindletop, the U.S. government's Geological Survey predicted that there was no oil to be found in Texas.

[23]The U.S. Patent and Trademark Office's Web site is found at http://www.uspto.gov/.

[24]The U.S. Copyright Office is operated by the Library of Congress; for more information see the Web site at http://www.copyright.gov/.

"one-click" ordering) and on new forms of life (e.g., bacteria that have been developed to eat up oil spills in the ocean).[25] The rationale for all of these protections is the same—if inventors and artists cannot secure the returns from successful projects fewer new inventions and works of art will be produced.[26]. Some artists, however, believe the publicity that comes with free copying ultimately gives them higher incomes. The balance between rewards for creative activity and monopoly profit is a complex one that we cannot address in more detail here.

Finally, some monopolies exist because competitors are legally unable to challenge them. Even legal restrictions, however, may become irrelevant as the example of the USPS and FedEx makes clear. Sometimes government prohibits the entry of competitors for reasons that are entirely political, but in others the theory of natural monopoly from Chapter 4 provides a potential justification for laws excluding them. Most Americans today prefer the many channels cable and satellite television can deliver and have abandoned free over-the-air broadcasters with their small number of network stations. Cable first became a viable technology in the 1960s, but for the next 20 years ABC, CBS, and NBC successfully lobbied Congress and the Federal Communications Commission to suppress it and protect their local monopolies.[27] Since then, direct broadcast satellite dishes have attracted an increasing number of former cable customers.

Multiple-Price Monopoly

Separating Markets by Demand Elasticity: Price Discrimination

Say there are ten potential buyers of my product, each of whom will buy either one unit or none. Because their valuations differ, charging each the same price will not maximize my profit. First, different prices allow me to extract more revenue from those who did purchase at the uniform price. Second, those who did not buy at that price may have been willing to pay smaller amounts that still covered my costs. If I could somehow learn each buyer's valuation I could maximize profit by offering that buyer a personalized price just below it. Buyers, however, have few good reasons to reveal their valuations. If I can somehow obtain that information I can increase my profit by practicing *price discrimination*. Here discrimination is on the basis of willingness to pay and bears no relation to such illegal practices as discrimination by race, gender, or age.

Figure 6-5 shows the daily market demand curve (the same as in Figure 6-2) for sparkling mineral water that only you produce. Assume that your fixed costs are zero and marginal cost is $2 a gallon. If you must charge only one price, you maximize profit by selling 5 gallons at $7 each for a profit of $25. To make the logic clear, assume unrealistically that you sold all 5 gallons before noon to prestigious restaurants for expense-account lunches. They are the only customers willing to pay $7 or more. Further assume that they must buy in the morning (if they keep the water overnight it goes flat). Later in the day you see another opportunity to sell to buyers with lower valuations. You set an afternoon price of $4 per gallon for people to take home and drink with dinner. These customers buy an additional 3 gallons, and your profit rises to $31. Note that this

---

[25]See the U.S. Supreme Court's 1980 decision in *Chakrabarty v. Diamond*, 447 U.S. 303. As this book goes to press, the Supreme Court is reviewing a case which may remove patent protection in cases like Amazon's. "High Court Considers Whether Business Methods Can Be Patented," *Washington Post*, Nov. 10, 2009.

[26]Another class of intellectual property is the trade secret, where the owner risks the loss of value simply by providing a public description of that secret. The most notorious of these has long been the secret formula for Coca-Cola.

[27]Stanley Besen and Robert Crandall, "The Deregulation of Cable Television," *Law and Contemporary Problems* 44 (Winter 1981): 77–124.

FIGURE 6-5 Price Discrimination

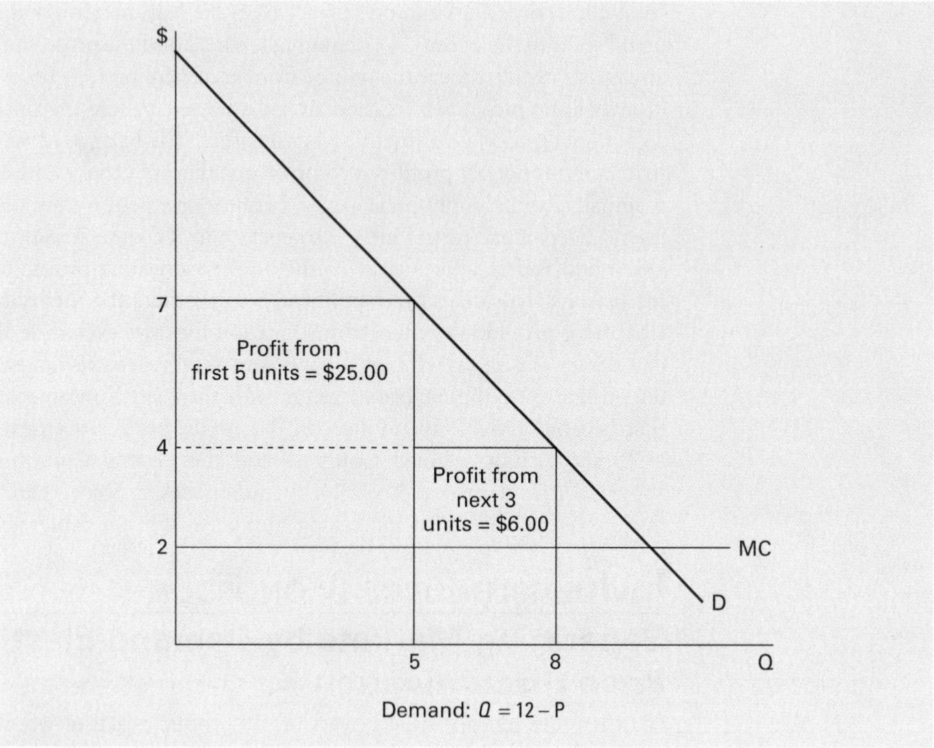

strategy only works if you can prevent the afternoon buyers from stocking up and reselling to restaurants in the morning for under $7. (That's why we ruled out the possibility of overnight storage.) Price discrimination makes marginal revenue irrelevant, because you are no longer selling at a uniform price. Discriminating more finely makes you even better off. If downtown restaurants value water more than suburban restaurants you might be able to sell the first 2 gallons at $10 each downtown, the next 3 gallons at $7 each in the suburbs, and the final 3 gallons at $4 each to home users for a profit of $37.

Q. Show that if you must charge a uniform price your best choice is $7.

A single-price monopoly created a deadweight loss—to maximize profit your best strategy was to throw some water away (if marginal cost is zero) or to not extract some water that consumers would have paid you more than $2 to pump to the surface (if marginal cost is $2). A single-price monopoly produces only 5 units, but a multiple-price monopoly generally produces more. The production and sale of gallons six through eight at $4 makes both you and your customers better off. You get $6 more profit, and the new buyers, who got no benefits under a single price, now get $4.50 in consumer surplus. Restaurants still pay $7 for the first five gallons and are as well off as when $7 is the uniform price. A discriminating monopolist makes more profits while producing an output closer to the competitive level. If a firm like this one is up for sale, a buyer who sees possibilities for price discrimination will outbid a buyer who does not see them.

Q. Show that the buyers of gallons 6 through 8 get a total of $4.50 in consumer surplus.

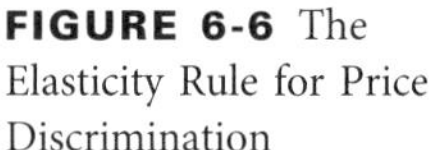

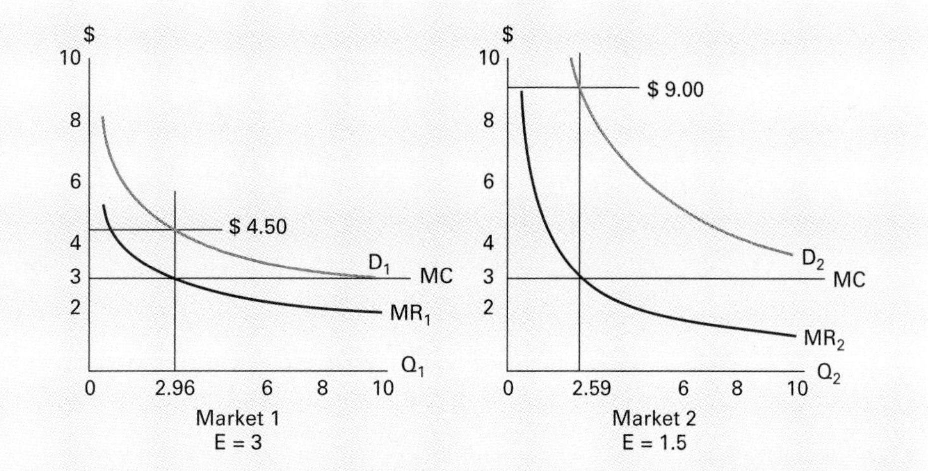

FIGURE 6-6 The Elasticity Rule for Price Discrimination

Figure 6-6 sets forth the general principle of price discrimination (the algebraic details are found in Appendix 6-A): charge a higher price in the market with the more inelastic demand. Market 1 has a demand elasticity of 3 everywhere on its demand curve, and Market 2 has an elasticity of 1.5.[28] Marginal cost in both markets is \$3. Marginal revenues in the markets are MR_1 and MR_2. The profit-maximizing output is 2.96 units for Market 1 and 2.59 units for Market 2. Price will be \$4.50 in Market 1, which has the higher elasticity of demand, and \$9 in Market 2. The percentage markup of price over marginal cost is twice as high in Market 2, where elasticity of demand is half that of Market 1.

From this discussion we distill three principles for successful price discrimination.

1. The seller must be able to group buyers by their willingness to pay for the good (elasticity of demand).
2. The seller must be able to prevent low-price buyers from reselling their purchases to those who would otherwise pay high prices.
3. Barriers to entry must be set for competitors who produce good substitutes and do not price discriminate, because they could take away the seller's high-price customers.

Other Forms of Price Discrimination

As the following examples illustrate, price discrimination can take many different forms that satisfy the three conditions.[29]

The Chevette The first Japanese cars exported to the United States in the 1960s were luxury models that sold poorly. The real competition with domestic producers began in the early 1970s, when more economical models became popular as buyers responded to the gasoline shortages that occurred during that decade's energy crises. In 1975, General Motors (GM) introduced the Chevette, a tiny, no-frills Chevrolet that promised fuel economy comparable to that of Japanese cars. GM assembled Chevettes at several locations, and the costs of delivering them to dealers were roughly uniform throughout the

[28] The relevant equations are $Q_1 = 270P_1^{-3}$ and $Q_2 = 70P_2^{-1.5}$.

[29] Some economists attempt to distinguish three degrees of price discrimination that depend on its fineness. Because all price discrimination follows the same principles, these classifications provide few insights.

country. GM, however, charged dealers in the Northeast higher wholesale prices than dealers in California for identical Chevettes. Eastern dealers complained to the Federal Trade Commission, which filed suit against GM.[30]

In Figure 6-6, let Market 1 be the market for Chevettes (*not* the market for small cars!) on the West Coast, and Market 2 the East Coast. Marginal costs of assembly and delivery are the same in both, but West Coast demand is more elastic than East Coast demand. Japanese manufacturers concentrated their initial marketing efforts in the West, and by 1976, they dominated small car sales there. In the East, the Japanese achieved a smaller market penetration. The West had more Japanese dealerships and the early sales success of the Japanese cars there made it easier for westerners to learn about them from dealers and neighbors. Thus, it appears that western demand for Chevettes was more elastic than eastern demand. The elasticity rule says GM should charge a higher markup in the East, and it did.

Q. Why is the market for small cars the wrong market in which to analyze the Chevette case?

Parking Garages Price discrimination does not require actually quoting different prices to customers. The Wells Fargo Bank Tower in downtown Los Angeles displays this sign at its parking entrance: "First hour \$8, second through fourth hours \$5 each, park all day for \$25." Everyone sees the same sign, but customers staying for only an hour pay \$8. Those who stay 3 hours pay an average of \$6 per hour (\$8.00 + 2 × \$5.00)/3, and those who stay for 8 hours pay an average of \$3.12 per hour. Charging less per hour for longer stays is consistent with the elasticity rule. A document courier whose customers want quick pickup and delivery is probably an inelastic demander of space in this particular building and wants to stay for only the short time required to visit a customer's office. Even if a cheaper lot is only a block away, there will be a 15-minute round-trip walk to Wells Fargo. Further, the messenger's parking bill is small relative to the value of quick service (e.g., delivering documents to court during a trial) and is sometimes paid directly by clients. Couriers are inelastic demanders of space at the Wells Fargo Tower, and most are likely to spend less than an hour on business in the building.

Now consider someone who expects to spend the entire day in the building. Two-block walks at the start and end of his day can produce a big saving at a relatively small time cost. To attract his business, the operator of Wells Fargo's parking service (a company called Parking Concepts) offers a low hourly price conditional on staying the entire day. Some office buildings attempt to select more elastic demanders by allowing anyone who enters the garage before 8:30 a.m. to spend the entire day at a flat, discounted rate. Finally, price discrimination can explain the substantial discount on monthly passes available to the building's tenants. The lot operator offers them for \$250 per month, half the price of a month of parking at daily rates. Tenants will be familiar with alternatives in the area and conscious of the savings, that is, they will be more elastic demanders of space in the Wells Fargo Tower.[31]

---

[30]The FTC issued its complaint under laws that prohibit wholesalers from charging different prices to retailers unless the difference is cost-justified. Court decisions have made such claims hard to prove, and the FTC dismissed its complaint. See In the Matter of General Motors Corporation, FTC Docket No. 9114, June 21, 1984.

[31]The requirement that each person exiting the lot use either a monthly permit or a ticket issued at entry discourages arbitrage by trading tickets. People who use the building's valet parking option will find trading virtually impossible.

Discount Coupons About once a week many households receive large envelopes in the mail containing discount coupons from such local businesses as carpet cleaners, gardeners, and grocery stores. Coupon users can save an average of 30 percent on each item offered, but some people throw the envelope away unopened. To check whether this is price discrimination, recall that the total cost of an item is more than just the cash paid at the store. There is a cost of keeping and remembering to use the coupons, and possibly there is lower enjoyment from consuming a substitute instead of the item one usually buys. People with high opportunity costs of time—particularly if they spend relatively little on groceries—are less likely to make these efforts. Coupons attract people who can be enticed into buying items for a small cash discount, that is, those with more elastic demands for particular products. People identify their elasticity of demand by choosing to save or not to save coupons, because saving them requires flexibility and a minor effort that non-savers do not find worthwhile.

Closely related to coupons are the contests and games often seen at fast-food outlets. For example, on each visit a customer gets a stamp showing half of a picture of a cheeseburger, which may be pasted on a game card. The customer who collects both halves of the stamp turns in the game card and gets a free cheeseburger. Other stamps are far less common, and the lucky person who matches them can win a first prize of $1 million. The structure of prizes in these contests indicates that their main purpose is price discrimination—first prize is $1 million, second prize is half a million, and then there are 20 million third prizes of a free cheeseburger. A regular customer who makes several visits and saves the stamps has a high probability of getting a free cheeseburger. In effect, that customer gets a quantity discount. Buying five cheeseburgers for $2 and winning the sixth yields an average price of $1.67 for all six. The elasticity rule is the same as for grocery coupons. Someone who saves game cards is a more elastic demander, for whom a small discount covers the cost of keeping track of the card and pasting the stamps.

Q. A local garage performs the smog checks that are required every 2 years to re-register a car in California. The garage accepts both its own discount coupons and coupons issued by any other smog checker. Does this make sense as price discrimination?

Free Furniture Delivery A store that offers free delivery is only saying that it will pay for a truck to come to your home. Most free deliveries also require investment of time by the recipient. When you buy the item, the store may inform you that their delivery service only goes to your part of town on Thursdays. You will be told to call early Thursday morning to learn the 4-hour window in which the truck is expected to arrive at your house. Someone with a lower opportunity cost of time (or who lives with someone who stays at home) will be more willing to bear the cost of an uncertain wait on a workday. Someone who wants delivery at a specific time must pay extra for it. That person is a more inelastic demander, because she chooses to forgo a discount that takes the form of free delivery during hours with a high opportunity cost.

Department Store Sales Stores occasionally do overstock some goods, but many sales are better understood as price discrimination. Some are predictable, like January white sales of bedsheets and towels. The store's intent is to attract price-sensitive customers who expect such a sale and are willing to postpone their purchases until January. Those who do not inform themselves about the sale or are unwilling to postpone their purchase are less elastic demanders. Some uninformed customers will of course get lucky, turn up in January, and get the same discount as the informed ones. Other types of sales also discriminate between informed and uninformed buyers, such as promotions for a single brand of apparel in which many items with that label are discounted. Finally, some sales take the form of "one day only, five percent off everything in the store," and are only announced a few days in advance. These sometimes include other forms of price discrimination, such as larger discounts for customers arriving very early in the morning (sometimes the store opens earlier than usual) or additional discounts for those who use or apply for the store's credit card.

Q. Why are credit cards sometimes a form of price discrimination? Why might you expect that buyers who use the store's credit card are more elastic demanders of merchandise that it sells?

Two Trips to the Restaurant Many restaurants have "early bird specials" that offer discounted dinners before, say, 7 p.m., when most people arrive for dinner after workdays. Here again the difference may be explained as price discrimination. Afternoon customers (often retirees) have greater freedom to choose their dinnertimes than those who work and are more elastic demanders of space in the restaurant. In a variation on this, a southern California restaurant offers a special on Monday nights only: At the end of your dinner the waiter comes by and flips a coin. Call it correctly and your dinner is free; otherwise, you pay menu prices (alcohol is not included).[32] In effect this amounts to a 50 percent discount on Mondays, a day on which few people are interested in dining out.

Q. The restaurant also restricts the coin flip to parties of four or fewer. Why?

Discrimination by Service Quality Men's business suits are usually major purchases, not bought casually like leisure wear. Subtle differences in fabric and design can mean that a store must make efforts to sell a particular suit, particularly if it is an expensive one. Different customers, however, will require different amounts of sales effort, some of which are a type of price discrimination. Customer Jones might fall in love with a particular suit as he walks past it, try it on without the help of a salesperson, buy it at the tagged price, and leave. Customer Smith might look at the same suit and wonder if it is right for him and worth its price. A salesperson makes small talk with Smith, explains why the price is reasonable, tells him how good he looks in it, picks out a shirt and tie that match it, and arranges for quick tailoring. Smith also pays the tagged price for the suit itself. Jones was a relatively inelastic demander of that particular item—he took care of himself and received no special services. Smith was a relatively elastic demander who had to be "sold" on the same suit. He received a number of other valuable services (including small talk and flattery) and could be confident that the suit and tie were well-coordinated, while paying the same as Jones for the suit itself.

Price Discrimination or Different Costs? Why does a newspaper cost the same at the airport and the city newsstand, while a ham sandwich often costs more at the airport

[32]Advertisement for Commonwealth Lounge and Grill, Fullerton CA, *OC Weekly*, Sept. 4, 2009, 13.

than at an outlet of the same chain downtown? Price discrimination for the sandwich is a reasonable possibility. There are few food sellers in airports, and it is costly for most flyers to go off the premises or to wait until an inferior dinner—or a bag of peanuts—is served on their outgoing flight. But the newspaper requires a bit more thought. Most newspapers and magazines sell between 80 and 90 percent of their press runs to subscribers, who obtain each issue at a price well below the one printed on it. If you forgot to bring reading matter along there are few alternatives to the newsstand, so selling at the cover price is consistent with the elasticity rule. The price difference, however, might also reflect the cost of serving different customers. Subscriptions allow the publisher to better plan production and inventories because it can predict its press runs with greater certainty. The publisher can also present subscriber data to advertisers who will pay higher rates for exposure to a guaranteed readership. Newsstand sales, by contrast, are uncertain. Big news days come unexpectedly, and the publisher may need to print enough copies to ensure that few casual purchasers will be frustrated because newsstands have sold out. Most publishers also pay newsstands some or all of the costs of unsold magazines that are returned to them. In short, the cost of serving occasional buyers may be substantially higher than that of serving prepaid subscribers, but occasional buyers might also have lower demand elasticities than subscribers.

Variations on Price Discrimination

Cover Charges

Some of the principles underlying price discrimination apply to other pricing practices. Electric utilities often include a fixed service charge in their bills that applies regardless of how much power is taken.[33] You also pay for each kilowatt-hour consumed. Clubs with live entertainment often collect a cover charge from all patrons before they enter. After paying it, you can stay as long as you want and buy as many drinks as you want. Figure 6-7 shows your personal demand curve for drinks at this club, again the same as in Figure 6-2. If drinks are $5 you will buy seven (maybe not all for yourself). You spend $35 but still enjoy consumer surplus benefits of $28, the area of the triangle below the demand curve and above $5. This is the value you place on being in this club (net of expense on drinks); in other words, it is the most you will pay for the right to be there relative to your best alternative. The cover charge takes away some (in the diagram, barely less than all) of your consumer surplus but does not affect the price of drinks, so you purchase the same number of them with or without it.[34]

The maximum cover charge the club can impose before you choose to go elsewhere depends on the price per drink, which is in other contexts called the "commodity charge." If all buyers are identical its best policy is to price the drinks at their marginal cost. If, for example, that cost is $4 the club can take away everyone's consumer surplus in full with a cover charge of $36. If instead it charges $5 for drinks, it still collects the rectangle between $4 and $5, but there is also a deadweight loss. Neither the club nor the customer captures the value of the triangle below the demand curve between 8 and 9 drinks—the customer does not buy a drink that she values at more than its marginal cost, and the club does not collect any cash for it. There can be extreme combinations of cover and commodity charges—in 2009, for example, Disneyland charged a $72 single-day entrance fee, which lets customers ride all the rides they want for no additional payment.

[33]The service charge often covers both the costs of keeping you on the system and other costs, such as contributions to a fund that helps pay the bills of low-income persons.

[34]Economists will note a few qualifications involving "income effects" that we neglect.

FIGURE 6-7 Cover Charges and Drink Prices

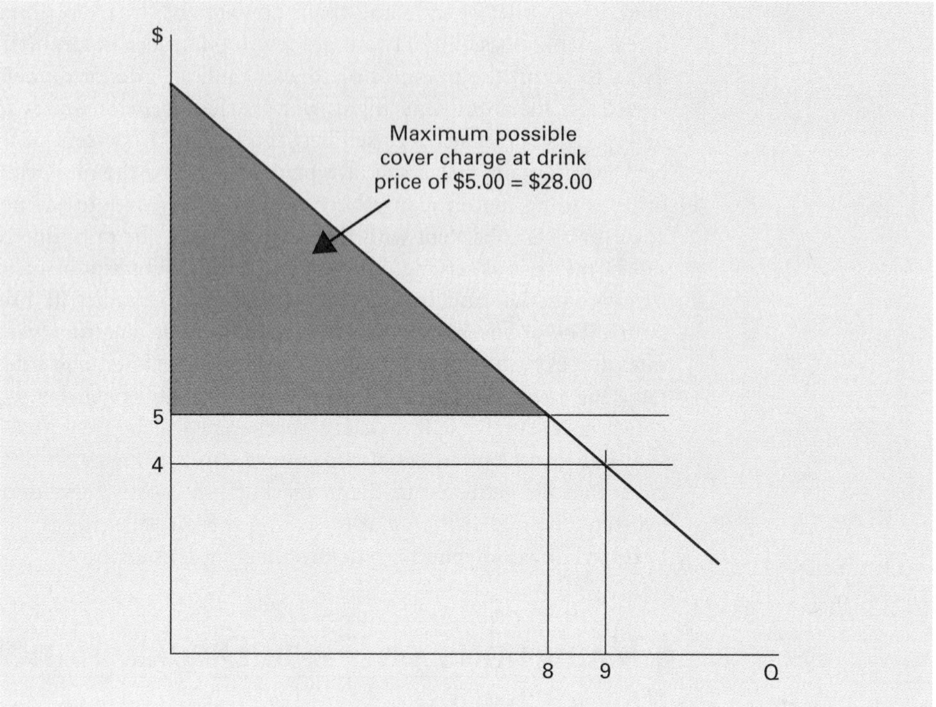

Real clubs (and Disneyland) face a more complex problem because customers have different demand curves. Let the only two customers, Type A and Type B, have the demand curves shown in Figure 6-8. Pricing drinks at marginal cost, the club can induce both to come in by setting a cover charge of $9. This choice, however, does not maximize the club's revenue because it forgoes the $36 cover charge that Type A will hold still for while Type B chooses to go elsewhere. Of course, if there are 20 Type B customers and only one Type A, it is best to charge $9. If there are several types of customer it can be more profitable for the club to charge more than the marginal cost per drink while imposing a smaller cover charge.[35]

Q. Can you give a graphic example with two types of buyers in which charging more than marginal cost for drinks and cutting the cover charge is more profitable than charging marginal cost and then the maximum cover charge possible?

Q. How does the analysis change if part of Type A's willingness to pay the cover charge is due to the fact that Type B will also be in the bar, a fact that is known to the owner?

[35]The pricing choices are detailed in Walter Y. Oi, "A Disneyland Dilemma: Two-Part Tariffs for a Mickey Mouse Monopoly," *Quarterly Journal of Economics* 85 (February 1971): 77–96. Oi also shows an odd case in which it pays for the bar to charge less than marginal cost for drinks.

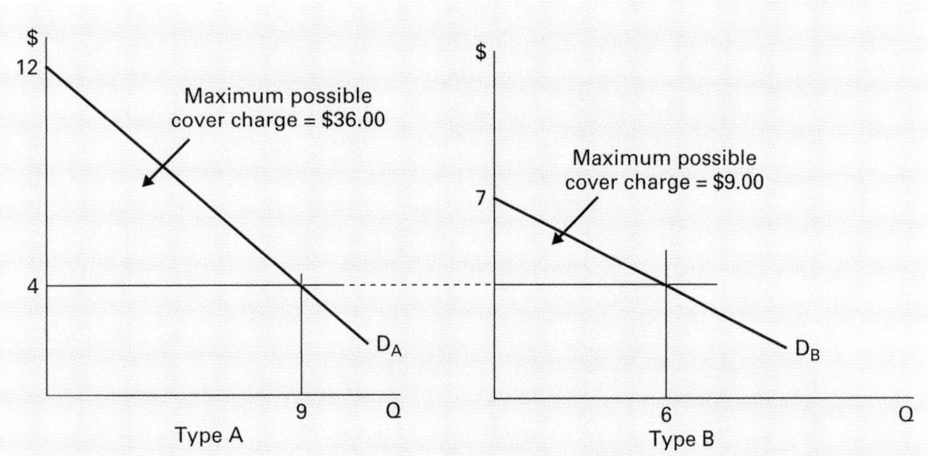

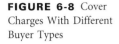

FIGURE 6-8 Cover Charges With Different Buyer Types

Self-Selection

Some sellers let customers choose from a menu of cover charge/commodity charge combinations. Where this is possible the seller can better utilize the characteristics of different customers' demand curves. A supplier of cell phone service might do this by offering two options: (1) a low service (cover) charge and a high price per minute of use (commodity charge), or (2) a high service charge and a low price per minute.[36] The seller may be unable to tell whether it can profit more from a given customer by offering a plan like the first one or like the second. By properly designing a group of plans, however, the seller can induce that customer to choose the one that will maximize the seller's profit.

Figure 6-9 shows the demands of individual Type A and Type B customers. Type As are small users with relatively inelastic demands, and Type Bs are large users with more

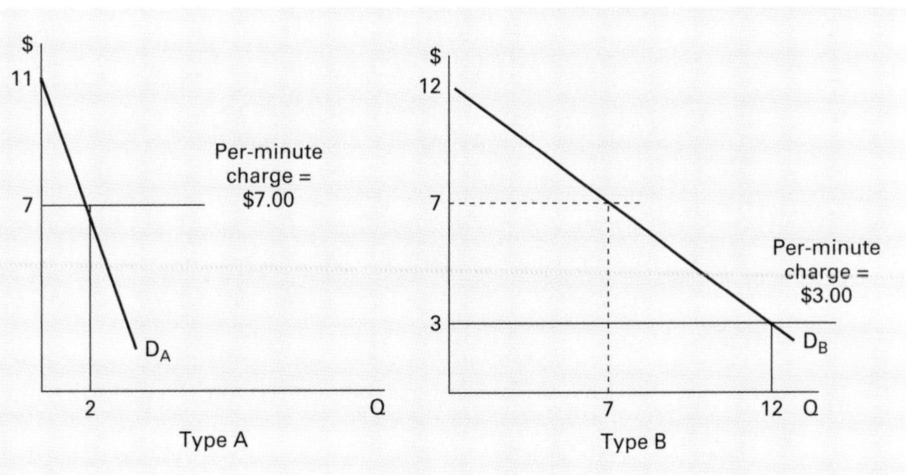

FIGURE 6-9 Self-Selection by Customers

[36]Many providers of cellular service offer a fixed charge followed by several hundred free minutes with per-minute charges for those over the free amount. In practice, competition can undo these arrangements. Complaints about charges incurred for excess minutes (particularly if accompanied by threats to switch suppliers) can often lead to cancellation of the excess and offers to replace the calling plan with a more economical one, even if the original plan required a year's participation.

elastic demands. Plan 1 has a $4 per month service charge and a $7 per-minute commodity charge, and Plan 2 has a $40.50 per month cover charge and $3 per-minute charge.[37] To see where the $40.50 came from, calculate the benefits a Type B customer would get from using Plan 1. A customer with demand curve D_B who uses Plan 1 receives $17.50 in consumer surplus at the Plan 1 per-minute charge of $7, from which that plan's $4.00 service charge must be subtracted. If Plan 2 offers more than $13.50 in consumer surplus, the customer with D_B will choose it. If Plan 1 was not available, a Type B customer with a $3 per-minute charge would be willing to pay a service charge of $54. Because Plan 1 *is* available, the biggest service charge Type B will pay is $54.00 – $13.50 = $40.50. Type As choose Plan 1 and Type Bs choose Plan 2, but because Plan 1 is an alternative for Type Bs, the seller cannot capture all of their consumer surplus in a service charge.

Tying and Bundling

The Consumer Benefits of Bundling Goods or services are often sold as packages of potentially separable components. Customers gain in several ways when GM gives them no choice but to buy cars with preinstalled engines built by the company. If left to choose, many people would buy the same engines but each would have to bear the costs of shopping and installation. Non-engineers might make costly errors when choosing, and almost everyone would have to hire a specialist to perform an installation that the factory could do more cheaply. A manufacturer who puts the same engine into every car can better design the engine, drive train, and body as an integrated unit and assemble them more economically. A prepackaged engine inconveniences only a handful of customers, such as racers and custom-car buffs.

By comparison, most boats are sold without engines. The buyer of a hull can easily install an outboard motor just by clamping it on, and the right motor depends on the customer. A fisherman will choose a small, quiet motor, unlike someone who wants to tow water skiers at high speed. Larger boats that use inboard engines are often designed to take a range of engines as the owner prefers, and specialist installers are easy to find around water. Other examples of economical bundling point up its many disguises. Warehouse discount stores like Costco and Sam's Club sell only bulk goods, which are easier to inventory and handle, to customers who are willing to bear the cost of holding larger amounts at home. The bulk package is really a bundle of moderately sized packages that must be bought as a unit.[38]

Q. Why might Costco and Sam's Club charge annual membership fees, while discounters who sell smaller packages do not?

Price Discrimination by Tie-Ins A seller can also tie two goods together in a single package to facilitate price discrimination, a potentially profitable strategy if their demands are interrelated. In the early and mid-twentieth century, for example, International Business Machines Corporation (IBM) dominated the market for punch-card

[37]Assume that the per-minute charges reflect marginal costs of serving large and small customers.

[38]For a more thorough discussion of bundling and its treatment by the courts, see Stan Leibowitz and Stephen Margolis, "Bundles of Joy: The Ubiquity and Efficiency of Bundles in New Technology Markets," *Journal of Competition Law and Economics* 5 (June, 2009), 1–47. The cases they analyze include the iPod's linkage with iTunes.

tabulating equipment used for accounting and other record-keeping purposes.[39] IBM did not sell the machines; it only leased them. The lease contract allowed IBM to terminate a customer without notice if it did not use IBM-made punch cards, although numerous producers made cards of equivalent quality. In 1949, the U.S. Department of Justice filed an antitrust lawsuit claiming the tie-in was an illegal attempt by IBM to monopolize the card market. The reasoning was questionable because the cardboard industry was large and relatively competitive, and IBM's machines used only a tiny fraction of total production. The tie-in was better viewed as a tool to facilitate price discrimination. IBM leased its equipment by the month rather than the hour (meters were primitive and ingenious customers could bypass them), so tying the cards to the lease allowed the company to charge a premium to more intensive users in the form of a higher price for cards.[40]

Q. If IBM wanted to price discriminate on the basis of use, why not just put meters (which were available at the time) into its machines?

Bundling Unrelated Products Is a Losing Strategy A monopolist might try other types of tie-ins. What if you require anyone who purchases a unit of your monopolized good to also buy (from you) a unit of a good produced in a perfectly competitive market? If demands for the two goods are independent, this strategy cannot possibly raise your profits and more likely will lower them.[41] The axes of Figure 6-10 are both in dollars, measuring costs (C), prices (P), and valuations (V) for anchovies (A) and bananas (B). There are numerous buyers, each of whom will purchase nothing, one of either, or both, depending on their values relative to prices. Anchovies are produced in a perfectly competitive market and sell for \$3 apiece (P_A), equal to their marginal cost C_A. You are the banana monopolist, who produces at a marginal cost of \$3 (C_B). Because your (mistaken) strategy is to bundle, your sole offering is a package of one anchovy and one banana, whose price you have set at \$8 (P_P).[42] Consumers whose valuations of the two goods are to the east and south of the pink boundary consume only anchovies, which they purchase at \$3 in the competitive market. They value anchovies at more than \$3 and bananas at less than $P_P - C_A$ (i.e., \$5). Someone who values a banana at more than \$5 is better off buying the package. You sell the package to everyone whose valuations are north and east of the maroon line. They value B at more than $P_P - C_A$ and either (1) value an anchovy at more than C_A (\$3) or (2) value an anchovy at less than that amount, but they value a banana highly enough that purchasing the package for \$8 leaves them better off. Compare this with your revenue from selling unbundled bananas. Offering them at $P_P - C_A$ (\$5) leaves you with the same profit as the package, keeps all the customers in the area that lies above the maroon boundary, and allows you to gain

[39]The case is detailed in Franklin M. Fisher, James W. McKie, and Richard B. Mancke, *IBM and the U.S. Data Processing Industry: An Economic History* (Santa Barbara, CA: Praeger, 1983).

[40]The fact that IBM only leased equipment also indicated its interest in price discrimination. Offering equipment for sale would in effect have put owners and other resellers into competition with the company, ready to offer superior terms to those paying IBM the most. The settlement of the case required IBM to offer a purchase option and to abandon the tie-in with cards.

[41]Richard Schmalensee, "Commodity Bundling by Single-Product Monopolies," *Journal of Law and Economics* 25 (April 1982): 65–71; William James Adams and Janet L. Yellen, "Commodity Bundling and the Burden of Monopoly," *Quarterly Journal of Economics* 90 (August 1976): 475–98.

[42]How you set that price depends on your costs and on what you know about how customers' valuations of the two goods are scattered over the quadrant. Here you can assume that \$8 is the most profitable choice if you offer customers no choice but the bundle.

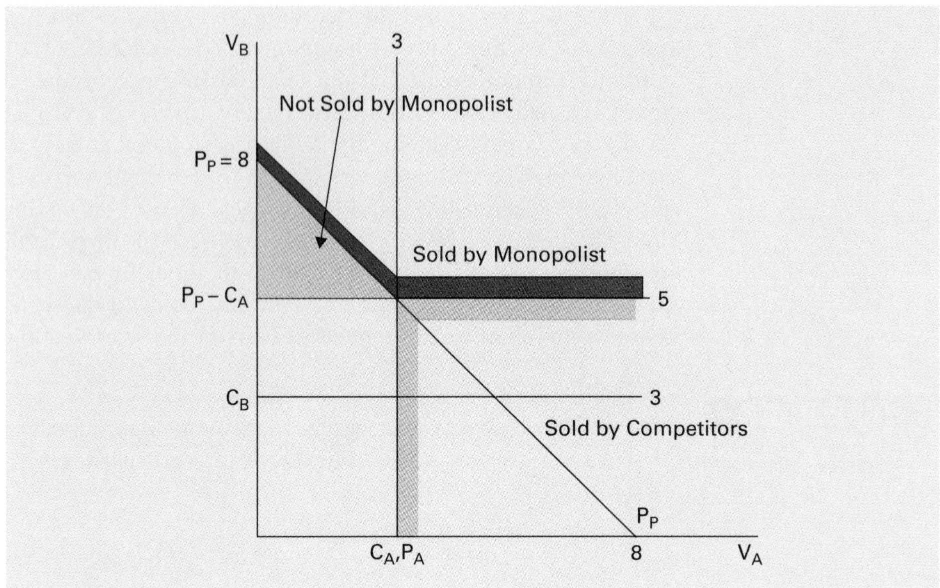

FIGURE 6-10 Bundling Monopoly and Competitive Goods

those customers whose valuations are in the solid triangle. Their low valuations of anchovies meant that they would not buy the bundle, despite the fact that bananas were worth more than \$5 to them. Offering only the bundle deprives you of potential profits.

Bundling Two Monopolized Products Next, you are a monopolist who sells two products with interrelated demands. Your amusement park has two rides, a roller coaster and a kiddie car. Your customers are either people on dates or families with children, and there are equal numbers (one) of each. Because the graphic gets more complicated, an example will suffice. Table 6-1 shows that those on dates value the roller coaster at \$15 and the kiddie car at \$3, while families value the roller coaster at \$4 and the kiddie car at \$13. Assume that your marginal cost of operating either ride for one customer is \$1. If you sell separate tickets for individual rides, you make the most by charging \$15 for the roller coaster (only selling to people on dates) and \$13 for the kiddie car (only selling to families). Your profits are \$13.00 + \$15.00 – (2 × \$1.00) = \$26.00. Now try requiring customers to buy a single ticket that is good for both rides, with no single-ride alternative. Each customer will pay at most \$17 for that ticket. After subtracting the costs of the four rides your profit is \$30. Bundling works because demands for the rides are negatively correlated—families will pay a high price for the kiddie car but only a low one for the roller coaster, while people on dates have the opposite preferences.

Bundling becomes less profitable, or possibly unprofitable, if the valuations of both customers are positively correlated. In Table 6-2, the marginal cost of a person's ride is again \$1. Unbundled ticketing allows you to charge \$7 for the roller coaster and \$5 for the kiddie car (which people on dates do not buy), for profit of (2 × \$7.00) +

TABLE 6-1 VALUATIONS WITH PROFITABLE BUNDLING

RIDE	PEOPLE ON DATES	FAMILIES
Roller coaster	\$15	\$ 4
Kiddie car	\$ 3	\$13

TABLE 6-2 VALUATIONS WITH NO GAIN FROM BUNDLING

RIDE	PEOPLE ON DATES	FAMILIES
Roller coaster	$7	$8
Kiddie car	$2	$5

$5.00 – (3 × $1.00) = $16.00. The best price you can get for a bundled ticket is $9, which nets you only (2 × $9.00) – (4 × $1.00) = $14.00. Keep in mind that ticketing strategies can change. Before instituting its single-admission charge in 1982, Disneyland strongly encouraged customers to buy books that contained two tickets in each of five classifications: "A" tickets were good for children's rides and "E" tickets were for the most adventurous.[43] There was no change in customer demographics or the mix of Disneyland's rides that can easily explain why the changeover took place when it did. Disneyland may have been motivated by other considerations. Ticket books may have made lines for different rides a bit more equal and possibly left guests (Disney's name for customers) with more time to explore, shop, and eat, but a single entry charge may have been cheaper to implement.[44]

Offering the Option of a Bundle Table 6-3 shows yet another set of valuations for two rides. This time assume that the marginal cost for each person riding is $5. Your best strategy now is to offer both bundled and unbundled tickets. If you sell only unbundled tickets, you should charge $9 for the kiddie car (which only families buy) and $10 for the roller coaster, bought by both. Your profits are $9.00 + (2 × $10.00) – (3 × $5.00) = $14.00. If you sell only bundled tickets, you can charge $17 to each customer, with profit of $34.00 – (4 × $5.00) = $14.00, coincidentally the same as before. But if you offer a choice between the bundle and single tickets you should charge $14 for a single roller coaster ticket, any amount higher than $5 for a single kiddie car, and $19 for a bundled ticket. People on dates buy only the roller coaster for $14, and families buy the bundle at $19. Your profit is now $14.00 + $19.00 – (3 × $5) = $18.00. Dates do not buy the bundle because its price exceeds their willingness to pay for the two rides together. Families do buy it because the $19 price just equals their total valuation.

TABLE 6-3 VALUATIONS WITH GAIN FROM MIXED BUNDLING WHEN MARGINAL COST OF RIDE IS $5

RIDE	PEOPLE ON DATES	FAMILIES
Roller coaster	$14	$10
Kiddie car	$ 3	$ 9

[43]See "The A-B-C's of Disneyland Tickets," Yesterland Web site, http://www.yesterland.com/abcde.html. Extra tickets could be bought individually inside the park. This is the genesis of the still popular Southern California phrase "E-Ticket ride."

[44]Standing in line at Disneyland is as much a deadweight loss as elsewhere. To help shrink that time, Disneyland recently introduced a system that allows customers to obtain priority admission to rides an hour or two in advance. See "Disney's FASTPASS® Service," Disneyland Web site, http://disneyland.disney.go.com/disneyland/en_US/help/gsDetail?name=FastPassGSDetailPage.

Chapter Summary

- A model of monopoly helps us understand markets that are dominated by a single firm, but customers can often economize on the monopolized good. The important distinction between monopoly and perfect competition is the demand facing a single seller. A perfect competitor sees faces a flat (perfectly elastic) demand at the market price, and a monopolist serves the entire market's downward-sloping demand curve.
- Marginal revenue of a monopolist is the net extra revenue from the sale of an additional unit when prices must be reduced on all units sold. To maximize profit, the monopolist sets output where marginal revenue equals marginal cost.
- Relative to an otherwise identical perfectly competitive market, a monopolized market produces a under the same cost conditions, a deadweight loss. The economy produces a less valuable bundle of outputs than if the monopolized market been perfectly competitive. Most estimates of deadweight loss in the economy appear relatively small, but monopolies may result in other inefficiencies as well.
- Over the longer term it is possible that monopolistic markets see greater levels of innovation and cost reduction than perfectly competitive ones because monopolists can be more secure that their ideas will not be appropriated by competitors. At least some historically important monopolies were characterized marked by decreasing prices and rising outputs.
- A monopolist that can separate its customers by elasticity of demand may be able to implement price discrimination that increases its profits and increases output relative to a single-price policy. Doing so requires that low-price customers be unable to resell their purchases to high-price ones.
- Price discrimination can take many forms, including take, including non-uniform price schedules, coupons or other selective discounts, and quality of service. We also see Time of purchase (e.g., air tickets) discrimination, and discrimination that favors informed customers (e.g., department store sales).
- Price discrimination can be generalized to service charges a customer must pay before being able to buy any amount of the product. The model also shows when it is profitable to "tie" or "bundle" a monopolized good with some other one, and when it pay to offer customers the option of purchasing a bundle.

Appendix 6-A

Calculus

Maximizing Revenue and Maximizing Profit

Here we use calculus to restate and generalize the graphic analysis of a monopolist constrained to charge a uniform price. The equation of the demand curve in Figure 6-2 is

(6.1) $$Q = 12 - P.$$

where Q is quantity demanded and P is price. If your marginal costs are zero you seek the quantity that maximizes total revenue R.

(6.2) $$R = PQ.$$

Now solve (6.2) for P and substitute into (6.1)

(6.3) $$R = 12Q - Q^2.$$

Next, differentiate it, set the derivative to zero, and solve for Q.

(6.4) $$\frac{dR}{dQ} = 12 - 2Q = 0.$$

So the revenue-maximizing $Q^* = 6$. Read the optimal price, $P^* = 7$, off the demand curve and compute total revenue of $42. Because marginal revenue is dR/dQ, it is given by (6.4). If demand is linear, marginal revenue lies halfway between the demand curve and the vertical axis, that is, it is twice as steep as demand. The two appear in the upper portion of Figure 6-2. The lower part of the figure shows how total revenue (labeled TR) varies with output, that is, it contains a plot of equation 6.3. Total revenue rises, reaches its maximum where marginal revenue is zero, and then declines at outputs where marginal revenue is negative.

Q. Prove that for any linear demand curve, marginal revenue is also linear and lies halfway between it and the vertical axis.

Q. For a general demand function Q = F(P), with F′(P) < 0, find an expression for the slope of the marginal revenue curve. Show that the slope need not be negative.

To maximize profit with the demand curve in Figure 6-2, we must bring in cost. For simplicity assume that total cost C is linear in output,

(6.5) $$C = 4Q.$$

Marginal cost is constant, because $dC/dQ = 4$. Disregard fixed costs, which in any case have no bearing on the profit-maximizing (or loss-minimizing) output choice. Profits π equal total revenue minus total cost.

(6.6) $$\pi = 12Q - Q^2 - 4Q.$$

Maximize them by differentiating and equating to zero

(6.7) $$\frac{d\pi}{dQ} = 8 - 2Q = 0,$$

that is, set marginal revenue equal to marginal cost and find $Q^* = 4$, $P^* = \$9.00$, and $\pi^* = (4 \times \$9) - (4 \times \$4) = \$20.00$. With no fixed costs and constant marginal cost, profit is the area of the rectangle above MC in the top half of Figure 6-2. Its lower half shows total cost (TC) as a straight line through the origin. Profit is maximized at 4 units, where marginal cost equals marginal revenue, that is, the slope of total cost equals the slope of total revenue.

Q. Check all of the calculations that appear after equation 6.7.

Q. Figure 6-4 also uses the demand curve of equation 6.1. Show that if marginal cost is $8, the profit-maximizing output and price are 2 units and $10, respectively. Then show that if marginal cost falls to $3, the corresponding figures are 4.5 units and $7.50, respectively.

Separating Markets by Demand Elasticity: Price Discrimination

To approach problems in price discrimination, generalize the analysis we just performed for a monopolist that was constrained to charge a uniform price. The demand curves for Markets 1 and 2 in Figure 6-6 are given by the following equations:

$$Q_1 = 270P_1^{-3}$$

$$Q_2 = 70P_2^{-1.5}$$

To get to the text answer work through the following questions:

Q. Using the calculus formula from Chapter 3, show that their respective elasticities are 3 and 1.5.

Q. Find expressions for total revenue and marginal revenue in each market as functions of quantity demanded.

Q. Then show that if marginal cost in each market is $3, the profit-maximizing output and price in Market 1 are 2.96 units and $4.50, and in Market 2 they are 2.59 units and $9.

Q. Derive the general formula relating marginal revenue, price, and elasticity of demand

$$MR = P(1 - 1/E).$$

Then show that the price discriminator's markup is inversely proportional to the elasticity of demand in each market.

Questions and Problems

1. A monopolist's demand curve and total costs are given by:

Q	P	TC	TR	MR	MC	Π
1	$20	$22				
2	18	31				
3	16	39				
4	15	49				
5	14	60				
6	13	74				
7	12	92				
8	10	115				
9	8	144				
10	6	180				
11	4	224				
12	2	277				

Q is the quantity demanded at each price P, TC is total cost, TR is total revenue, MR is marginal revenue, MC is marginal cost, and π is profit. Fill in all the blanks and determine the optimal output and price.

a. If marginal cost falls by $5, find the new profit-maximizing output.

b. Since the firm is a monopolist and can set any price it wants, why does price fall at all?

2. A single-price monopolist whose marginal costs are zero receives a government subsidy of $1 for every unit of output it produces, but it is free to choose its price. Will the monopolist now produce an output at which elasticity of demand is less than 1? Explain why or why not.

3. (Requires calculus) The demand facing a monopolist is

$$Q = 50 - 2P$$

and total cost is

$$TC = Q + 4Q^2.$$

Find the monopolist's optimal price, quantity, and profit. Graph the solution.

a. If this were instead a perfectly competitive market with a supply curve the same as the monopolist's marginal cost, what would output and price be? Graph the solution.
b. What would be the total profit made by competitors? Why would there be no deadweight loss?
c. The price of the monopolist's only input doubles, which doubles total cost to

$$TC = 2Q + 8Q^2.$$

What happens to output, price, and profit? Graph the new solution and compare it with the old one. Why is the rise in input costs not passed on in full to customers as a higher price?

4. (Requires calculus) A monopolist has two plants A and B, with total costs

$$TC_A = 10 + 0.2Q_A + 0.25Q_A^2$$

and

$$TC_B = 20 + 0.25Q_B + 0.1Q_B^2.$$

Find its profit-maximizing output and price. How will that output be shared between the plants? Why do the plants operate at the same marginal cost for their last units of output?

5. Give a numerical example to show that a monopolist's marginal revenue can be upward-sloping over part of its range. Hint: The price on the demand curve is the producer's average revenue. Think of the graphic in Chapter 4 that showed the possibility of declining average costs while marginal costs were increasing.

6. If marginal cost is constant and marginal revenue can slope upward, the firm will never operate at an output where marginal revenue cuts marginal cost from below. Explain why.

7. For linear demand and constant marginal cost, explain in commonsense terms why the deadweight loss of monopoly is greater the flatter (more elastic) the demand curve.

8. The monopolist in Figure 6-4 who invents a way to reduce marginal costs becomes more profitable, but in that figure we can also see that the deadweight loss has grown. Does this mean the invention should never have been made at all? Explain.

9. You are producing a new play that will open next week. You are happy because advance purchasers have bought enough tickets that you will have a full house every night for the next year. Have you maximized your profits? Explain why you might not have.

10. You run a tutoring service for economics students. On half of all days the demand for your service is high, with

$$Q_H = 10 - 0.2P.$$

Q_H is the number of hours you will work if you choose price P. On the remaining days, demand is low:

$$Q_L = 5 - 0.2P.$$

High and low days arrive at random with probabilities of 0.5 each. Your marginal opportunity cost is \$10 per hour on all days. You want to choose a price that maximizes your average profit per day, but that price must be the same on all days. Find that price.

a. Show that this price leaves you with a smaller profit than if you can announce different prices early in the morning of each day, after you have learned whether demand will be high or low.

11. (Requires calculus) A monopolist with constant marginal costs of \$20 serves two separate markets, where demands are

$$Q_A = 100 - P_A$$

and

$$Q_B = 140 - 2P_B.$$

Add the demands and find the optimal output and uniform price if the markets cannot be separated. What is elasticity of demand at this price and quantity? Graph the total demand, marginal costs, and marginal revenue, and explain the shape of marginal revenue. (Note that demand has an angle in it at a price of \$100.)

Now allow the seller to set different prices in A and B. Find those prices, along with the quantities sold and elasticities of demand. Is total output greater than in the case of a single price?

Using the previous demand curve from Market A, find an example in which the demand curve in Market B is low enough and elastic enough that it does not pay a single-price monopolist to sell any output at all in Market B, but it does pay a price discriminator to do so. Now is the discriminating monopolist's output greater than if it had charged a uniform price?

12. Only a competitor would offer its customers personalized discounts, because a monopolist can always insist that all of its customers pay full price. Right?

13. The National Park Service charges visitors to a certain monument a \$5 per car admission fee and an additional fee of \$5 per camera. Is this necessarily price discrimination or might it be based on costs? If it is price discrimination, is it consistent with the elasticity of demand rule? Give a possible cost-based explanation.

a. Now assume, as seems reasonable, that the government is not trying to maximize its profit from operating this monument. How might its per-car and per-camera prices change if it wants to maximize its revenue from visitors? How about if it is interested in maximizing the number of visitors, subject to covering its cost of operation?

b. On a graph, show the two outcomes you derived for part a

14. A monopolist has two types of customers. There are 100 of Type A, who will each pay up to \$10 for a single unit of the good, and 50 of Type B, who will each pay up to \$8. Neither is willing to purchase additional units at any price. If it must charge a uniform price, find that price.

a. Assume that spending \$80 on advertising will attract 100 more Type B customers. Should the monopolist advertise? If so, what will happen to price?

15. Your personal demand curve for a good sold by a monopolist is depicted in the following table:

Q	P
1	$10
2	9
3	8
4	7
5	6
6	5
7	4
8	3
9	2
10	1

a. The salesperson first quotes you a price of $6, and you respond by buying 5 units. Just as you are about to leave he offers you a sixth unit for $5. Why do you accept this offer? Again, you are about to leave and he offers you a seventh unit for $4. You also take this offer, right? Why?

b. Next week you return to the monopolist and see a sign: "New pricing policy: pay a $21 admission charge and then you can buy all you want for $4 per unit." Why are you willing to pay the admission charge rather than walk away? After you pay, you buy 7 units. Why are you willing to pay $21 + $28 = $49 for 7 units this week, when last week you paid only $39 for them?

16. Assume that the maximum amounts members of the two groups in Table 6-1 are willing to pay at the amusement park are now:

RIDE	PEOPLE ON DATES	FAMILIES
Roller coaster	$13	$ X
Kiddie car	$ 9	$15

a. For what range of X is the ticket book more profitable than separate tickets for each ride?

b. Consumer advocates have criticized ticket books because they force consumers to buy things they don't really want. Does this reasoning make sense?

17. A soap producer has two types of customer, A and B. Each will buy at most 1 pound per week. Type A customers will pay at most $6 for it, and Type B will pay at most $4. Production cost is $2 per pound. Using a discount coupon costs a Type A customer $1.50 to keep track of the coupon, and a Type B customer nothing.

a. What price should the producer charge the Type As?

b. At this price, how large must a coupon discount be before Type Bs choose to use them?

c. What is the maximum discount a coupon can offer before Type As begin using them?

Chapter 7

Between the Extremes: Interaction and Strategy

INTRODUCTION

Some important markets do not fit into the extreme categories of perfect competition or monopoly. An *oligopoly* (from the Greek term for "few") is a market containing only a small number of sellers. Unlike buyers served by monopolies, those in oligopoly markets can go to alternative suppliers. Unlike price-taking sellers in perfectly competitive markets, each oligopolist has some ability to affect price by its own actions. These two characteristics make the analysis of oligopoly markets particularly challenging. Oligopolies pose new problems because a seller that can affect price must be able to anticipate how other sellers will react to its choices. Interactions among sellers mean each must look further ahead to the consequences of its decisions than sellers in perfectly competitive or monopoly markets need to. The fact that sellers must look ahead greatly complicates the analysis of oligopoly equilibrium. The methods we develop to attack oligopoly, however, will also help us think more clearly about many interactions that do not take place in markets.

Figure 7-1 shows an oligopoly moving at 190 mph. In the top picture, two NASCAR drivers are only inches apart in a "draft line" of several cars whose other members are not shown.[1] At this distance they can both go faster than if they are separated. A car at high speed leaves a vacuum in its wake, which is surrounded by a zone of turbulence

FIGURE 7-1A
This figure demonstrates what can happen to an eager driver who is in a tight draft.

Stephen A Arce/Icon SMI/Icon Sports Media/Corbis

[1]The photo is from Corbis, DWF15-592233 (rights managed). NASCAR stands for the National Association of Stock Car Auto Racing, which operates all races for the national championship. See NASCAR's Web site at www.nascar.com. For a more detailed discussion of drafting, see NASCAR's glossary.

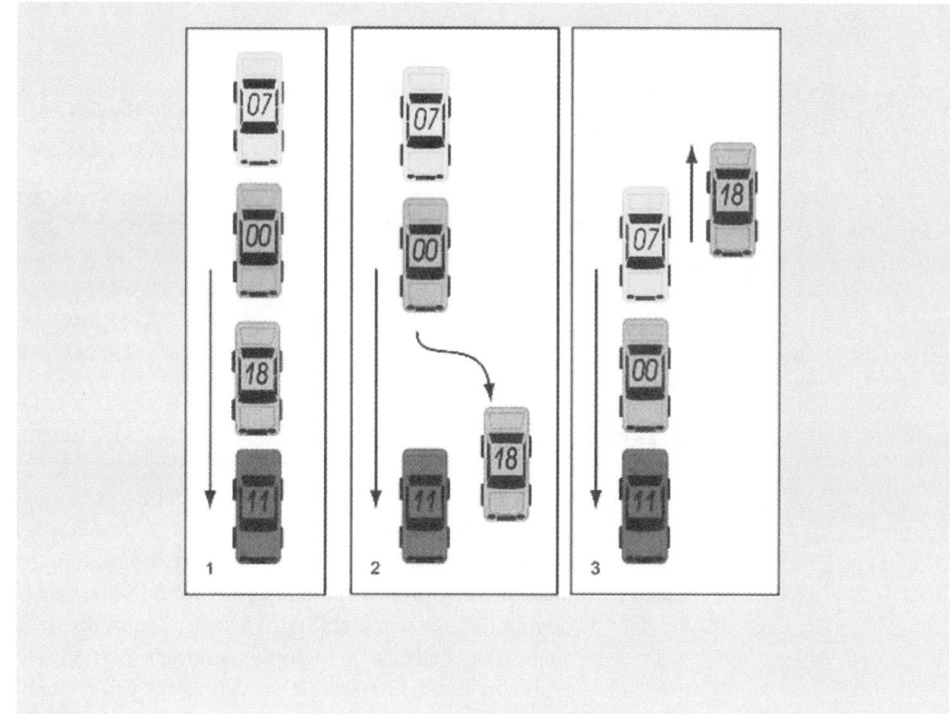

FIGURE 7-1B

a) shows the tight draft on a track like Talladega or Daytona.
b) shows the second car in line (18) stepping out in an attempt to pass the first car. The problem is, unless others go with him it will lead to Figure 3, the cars behind the leader closing the gap.
c) when the gap is closed, the eager driver (18) has been hung out to dry–the draft train passes him and shuffles him to the back of the pack. If, on the other hand, the (18) car stepped out and had help, then the leader (11) would be the one shuffled to the back of the pack.

that slows it down. A car that follows very closely lessens the drag on the front car due to turbulence, and the vacuum lowers the air resistance for the follower. Lines containing more cars can often go faster than lines with only a few, but two cars suffice to create the basic effect. NASCAR's tight design and engineering rules give all cars nearly the same top speed, so drivers have little choice but to draft for a few extra miles per hour. A driver who wants to win must attempt to pass any cars ahead of him. (Most NASCAR drivers are men.) One who leaves the line by himself, however, loses about 10 mph and soon falls behind everyone remaining in the line. The driver who wants to pass needs companions to move with him and form a new draft line parallel to the old one. (See the bottom half of Figure 7-1.) The drivers' interactions are like those of oligopolists. Being in a draft line improves the position of any member, but a driver who wants to win the race must eventually leave the relative safety of the line. A driver who establishes a reputation for trustworthiness is more likely to attract others to move out and form a new line, but one who wants to win must ultimately violate the trust of the others. A winner must be both cooperative and devious, each at the appropriate time.

The economics of oligopoly is about relationships like those between the drivers, whom we will revisit later in this chapter. Specifically:

- We will examine the wide range of outcomes that occur in oligopoly markets and the difficulty of attributing different outcomes to specific market characteristics. We illustrate that range by comparing the U.S. automobile, personal computer, cigarette and airline industries.
- Oligopoly outcomes depend on sellers' beliefs about how other sellers will respond to their decisions. Our starting point is a market in which a dominant firm faces a fringe of small competing sellers. The dominant firm's profitability depends on how the fringe responds to its choices.

- The interactions become more complex when each seller understands that it can change market conditions by acting alone. To illustrate, we examine a hypothetical price-fixing agreement, in which each seller's best strategy is to break it, leaving both of them worse off than if they could have enforced the agreement.
- The price-fixing model is our introduction to the theory of games and the Nash equilibrium, in which each player makes the best choice possible given the choice of the other. We go on to study more complex games, and to examine commitment strategies that can sometimes advantage a player.
- In some games the best play requires probability-based choices known as mixed strategies. Games in which mixed strategies can be optimal include certain types of auctions.
- This background in game theory allows us to examine equilibria under a range of assumptions about sellers' beliefs regarding each other. Assuming that other sellers will not change their outputs leads to a very different equilibrium than a superficially similar assumption that they will not change their prices.
- It is often difficult to examine practices in an industry and and reach a firm conclusion about whether sellers are competing or attempting to coordinate their activities to raise group profits.

Oligopoly: Many Outcomes, Few Explanations

The easiest way to appreciate the range of possible outcomes in oligopoly markets is to examine a few. These examples have some common characteristics: they contain only a few sellers and large size is necessary to achieve low-cost production. Our job in this chapter will be to try making some headway in explaining why these seemingly similar markets have developed so differently.

Automobiles

In the 1950s and 1960s, the "Big Three" automobile manufacturers (General Motors [GM], Ford, and Chrysler) had U.S. sales almost entirely to themselves, and their market shares changed little over those years. Two possible reasons suggest themselves. Might they have had an unwritten understanding not to compete aggressively, or might they have been so evenly matched as competitors that their rivalrous efforts largely cancelled each other out?[2] Instead of aggressive pricing and design innovations, competition among the Big Three often took the form of annual model changes that were largely cosmetic.[3]

There is no agreed-upon explanation for the lack of aggressiveness among the Big Three. Japanese imports only became a force in the 1970s, as price and quality-based competition became stronger and the Big Three's once-steady profits became memories.

[2]Most studies show that cooperation rather than competition prevailed before the 1970s. See Stanley Boyle and Thomas Hogarty, "Price Behavior in the American Automobile Industry, 1957–71," *Journal of Industrial Economics* 24 (December 1975): 81–95; and Timothy Bresnahan, "Competition and Collusion in the American Automobile Industry: The 1955 Price War," *Journal of Industrial Economics* 35 (June 1987): 457–82.

[3]For an estimate of the costs of annual model changes during the 1950s, see Franklin M. Fisher, Zvi Griliches, and Carl Kaysen, "The Cost of Automobile Model Changes Since 1949," *Journal of Political Economy* 70 (October 1962): 433–51.

Why could the U.S. firms not arrive at an understanding with the new sellers like they once had among themselves? All three of them already owned production facilities overseas, but the scope of competition grew in the 1990s as Ford acquired a controlling interest in Japan's Mazda, GM bought Sweden's Volvo, and Chrysler merged with Germany's Daimler-Benz. Mergers and acquisitions sometimes produce superior competitors, but they did not help the Big Three. Why? Long before the twenty-first century's global financial crisis the Big Three's competitive skills had weakened, perhaps fatally. By 2009 many believed their best solution was bankruptcy, and GM and Chrysler received bailout funds from Washington. At the same time, Japan's Toyota replaced GM as the world's largest auto maker. Again, why?

Personal Computers

A small number of large producers dominate U.S. personal computer (PC) sales. Aggressive competition in price and technology has left profit margins persistently low for all except Apple. As of 2004 (second quarter), Dell sold 32.9 percent of PCs; Hewlett-Packard (HP), 19.3 percent; IBM, 5.6 percent; Gateway, 5.6 percent; Apple, 3.8 percent; and others (including retailer brands), 32.9 percent.[4] Only four years later, in the third quarter of 2008, Dell's share had fallen only slightly, to 29.5 percent, but HP's was up to 25.7 percent and Apple had risen to 9.5 percent. Gateway had been absorbed by Taiwan's fast-growing Acer (8.9 percent), and Toshiba resurrected itself from the ranks of "others" to gain 5.6 percent of the market. Giant mainframe manufacturer IBM's PC brand vanished after its 2004 purchase by China's Lenovo, whose low sales still left it among the "others."[5] It was an unexpected fate for the company that in 1981 had introduced the first PCs based on Microsoft software and Intel processors.[6] If IBM ever had a first-mover advantage it ended a year later when Compaq introduced less expensive clones that used the same parts and software. Compaq went on to lead the market for a few years, but by the mid-1990s it had run out of counterstrategies to defeat Michael Dell's innovative Internet marketing and efficient manufacturing logistics. At first Compaq's 2002 merger with HP seemed to show that large size was no cure-all, but by 2008 the combined company had achieved profitability and a market share just behind Dell's. Why have some makers that dominate other markets, like Japan's Sony, achieved only tiny shares of PC sales? Why has the continuing shakeout not weakened competition among the survivors, whose quality-adjusted prices continue to fall rapidly? Unlike autos prior to the 1970s, a relatively small number of PC producers have competed aggressively since the birth of their industry.

Cigarettes

Since the early twentieth century between four and six manufacturers have dominated the U.S. cigarette industry. All of them have enjoyed steady and generally high profits through good times and bad. Like the automobile manufacturers in the 1950s, price competition has been less important than new "models" (brands) produced in response

---

[4]See the Web site of data service Gartner, Inc. http://www.gartner.com/it/page.jsp?id=777613.

[5]"Lenovo-IBM Deal a Giant Step for China," *Associated Press Newswires*, December 8, 2004. Globally, Dell accounts for 17 percent of PC sales, HP 15 percent, and IBM 5.6 percent. In Chapter 15 we examine IBM's problems in more detail.

[6]Mary Bellis, "Inventors of the Modern Computer: The History of the IBM PC – International Business Machines," About.com, http://inventors.about.com/library/weekly/aa031599.htm.

to market changes (e.g., menthol, low tar, and less expensive generics). Tens of millions of smokers have quit after learning of health hazards, new laws restrict the venues where people can smoke, and a multibillion dollar settlement of some major lawsuits have all had little impact on the profits of cigarette makers. As the domestic cigarette market shrinks, price competition remains unaggressive in all segments of the industry except generics.[7] Why has this industry never seen aggressive competition since its inception? Why has price competition been restricted to generics? Might restrictions on advertising actually be helping producers to maintain their profitability?

Q. Explain how restrictions on advertising could help cigarette producers maintain their profitability.

Airlines

From the 1940s to 1978, the federal Civil Aeronautics Board (CAB) restricted the U.S. skies to a handful of airlines. The CAB invariably refused applications by new entrants to fly interstate routes that were already served by existing airlines. It fixed fares at high levels and regulated service quality down to such details as the sizes of sandwiches that could be served in flight. Legislation brought an end to all of these controls in 1978. New airlines opened for business, price competition strengthened, and incumbent airlines transformed their route structures to hub-and-spoke systems. Some airlines were able to keep fares high in and out of hubs they dominated, and they introduced new forms of price discrimination such as advance purchase ticket restrictions and frequent-flyer mileage programs.

Nevertheless, in the 1980s and 1990s attempts by some airlines to introduce uniform (high) pricing for all air trips came up short. Almost as soon as new higher fares were announced, airlines began offering discounts on them.[8] Competition turned the industry into such a low-margin business that between the 1980s and today all but two of the old major airlines underwent bankruptcy reorganizations. Now the major airlines face new competition for their long-haul and short-haul passengers. New airlines like Jet Blue with no "legacy costs" (e.g., high union wages inherited from the days of regulation) have been able to underprice the major airlines almost everywhere, and so have efficiently managed carriers like no-frills Southwest airlines.[9] The older airlines now face competition on 80 percent of routes between the 1,000 largest U.S. city pairs. Airlines started their lives protected from competition by regulators. After deregulation they became a low-price, low-profit industry, with little certainty that today's competitors will stay in business.

---

[7]William B. Burnett, "Predation by a Nondominant Firm: the Liggett Case," Case 10 in *The Antitrust Revolution,* 3rd ed., ed. John E. Kwoka Jr. and Lawrence J. White, 239–63 (New York: Oxford University Press, 1999).

[8]"Airline Fare Wars Far from Over," *Reuters,* August 6, 1992.

[9]Shawn Tully, "Why the Big Boys Won't Come Back," *Fortune*, June 1, 2004, http://money.cnn.com/magazines/fortune/fortune_archive/2004/06/14/372607/index.htm; Barney Gimbel, "Southwest's New Flight Plan," *Fortune,* May 6, 2005, http://money.cnn.com/magazines/fortune/fortune_archive/2005/05/16/8260158/index.htm.

Why the Differences?

In all of these examples each seller's pricing and production decisions depend in important ways on decisions other sellers are making. GM chooses the price of Chevrolets with an eye toward market conditions, and perhaps the most important is its expectation of the prices Ford and other manufacturers will charge for their cars. Ford's pricing choice, however, similarly depends on its expectations about GM. Both of their decision rules will probably change if highly competitive imports show up in markets they formerly shared. This sort of interdependence, along with other industry characteristics, may help explain why outcomes in oligopoly markets are so diverse.

DOMINANT FIRMS

The Dominant Firm with a Competitive Fringe

One attribute common to perfectly competitive firms and to monopolists allowed us to greatly simplify the analyses of their markets. In neither market did a firm's managers need to consider the responses of other firms to their decisions. A perfect competitor was such a small part of the market that its production choice could not possibly influence price. Whether that firm closed down or doubled its output, the resultant shift in market supply was so imperceptible that price was unaffected. To make the distinction between monopoly and perfect competition clear, we assumed that a monopolist only looked at currently existing demand and cost conditions. Even though the monopolist loomed very large in its market, we assumed that it did not consider the reactions of new market entrants or producers of close substitutes for its good. To better understand the actions and reactions, we start with a dominant firm that faces a fringe of small competitors.

The Dominant Firm in the Short Run In the 1960s and 1970s, IBM earned approximately 70 percent of all U.S. revenue from the sale and lease of mainframe computers and peripheral equipment such as printers and tape drives.[10] The remainder of sales were divided among five or more other manufacturers, known at times as the "Bunch."[11] Members of the Bunch were not perfect competitors—each had some latitude to set the prices of its own products, particularly because it was costly for an existing user of one maker's equipment to switch to another's.[12] The decisions of each Bunch member would, however, be influenced primarily by its competitive situation against IBM. That company clearly cared about the Bunch's responses to its policies (1 percent of the market in 1972 was $120 million), but few of the millions of documents produced in antitrust litigation hinted that IBM made major decisions in response to initiatives by members of the Bunch.[13] In this example, we refer to IBM as the "dominant firm" and the Bunch as

[10]Gerald Brock, *The U.S. Computer Industry: A Study of Market Power* (Cambridge, MA: Ballinger, 1975), 22–23.

[11]So-called because of the initials of the firms: Burroughs, Univac, NCR, Control Data, and Honeywell Corporations.

[12]There was no compatibility between the products offered by any of these suppliers; a Honeywell printer could not be attached to an IBM computer.

[13]Franklin M. Fisher, James McKie, and Richard Mancke, *IBM and the U.S. Data Processing Industry: An Economic History* (New York: Praeger, 1983), 348.

the "competitive fringe" of price-takers responding to IBM. That company in turn knows how the fringe will respond and takes that response into account in its decision making.

In Figure 7-2, D represents market demand for the industry's product. IBM faces a perfectly competitive fringe of price-takers (the Bunch) whose supply curve is S_F. IBM's marginal cost, MC_D, is constant at $4. Its options are limited by the fringe's ability to react. Whatever quantity IBM chooses, the fringe will produce on its supply curve at the market-clearing price. That price is where the sum of IBM's and the fringe's output equals market demand. IBM's options are given by the *residual demand* D_{Res} that it faces, where D_{Res} is the difference between the market demand and the supply that the fringe will produce at each price. The graphic subtraction shown on Figure 7-2 gives us the residual quantity demanded at each possible price. Residual marginal revenue, labeled MR_{Res}, can be calculated from residual demand. As shown in the Appendix to this section, IBM maximizes profit by producing the output (3.69 units) at which its marginal cost equals residual marginal revenue. The corresponding price on the residual demand curve is $6.64, and at that price the fringe produces 1.65 units. Total production is 5.34 units, which equals market demand at $6.64.

The existence of a fringe makes price lower and output higher than would occur without it. Following are some other predictions about the market:

1. The more elastic market demand is, the lower market price will be and the smaller the dominant firm's profits.
2. The smaller the percentage of the market served by the fringe, the higher will be the price the dominant firm chooses and the higher its percentage of market output.
3. The more elastic the supply curve of the fringe, the more elastic residual demand will be and the lower the dominant firm's profits.

FIGURE 7-2
Dominant Firm with a Competitive Fringe

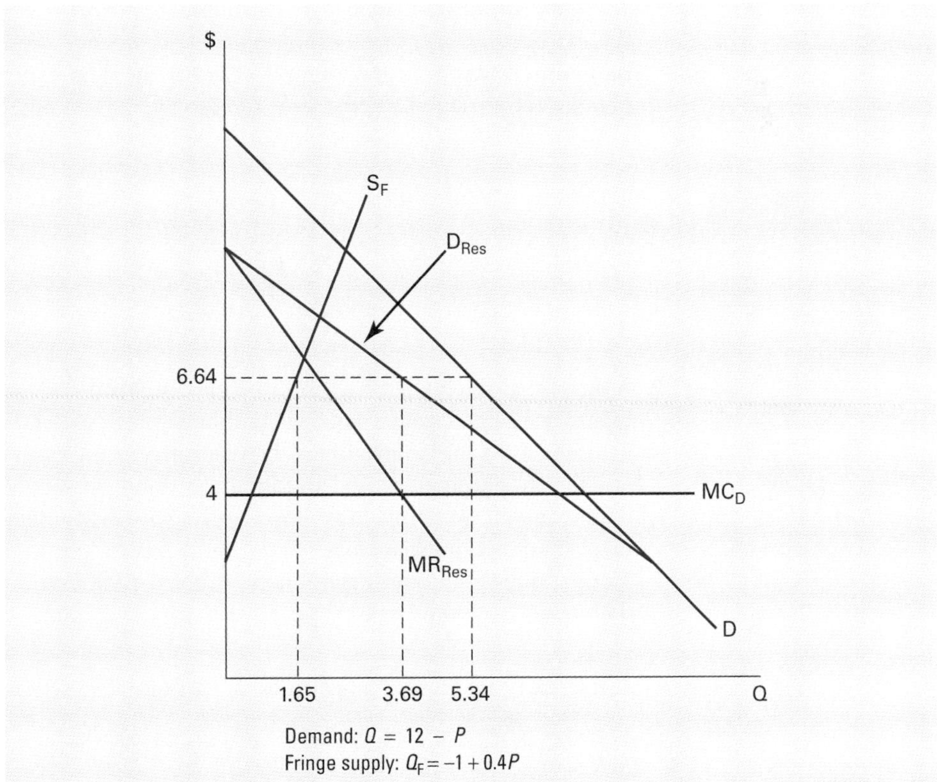

Q. Illustrate the three statements about the market in a figure like Figure 7-1, or better yet try demonstrating them algebraically.

The dominant firm is aware of how the fringe will react to its choices, and it can be confident in that belief because members of the fringe are all price-takers. In this model fringe producers do not, for example, agree to restrict their outputs in hopes of changing market conditions to their advantages. If they were able to do so, the dominant firm's decision problem would be far more complex. Instead of knowing the fringe's response with certainty as it does here, the dominant firm would have to make some assumptions about the fringe's reaction to its potential choices. But if the fringe acts as a group and knows how the dominant firm expects it to react, the fringe might be better off disappointing the dominant firm. And if the dominant firm knows this, each side must go a level deeper into the other side's reasoning. After a few more preliminaries we will examine this reasoning in more detail.

The Long Run What happens to the dominant firm in the long run depends on what we assume about the entry of new competitors. If newcomers can enter with supply curves like those of individual fringe members, there is profit to be made at the initial market price of $6.64. Assuming that it is indeed possible to enter, several possible scenarios might ensue, depending on the beliefs of the dominant firm and potential entrants:

1. Assume that new fringe firms with the same cost structures as existing fringe firms can enter the market as time passes. As they do so the fringe supply will rotate rightward and downward, reducing the dominant firm's abilities to extract profit from the market. If fringe firms can operate at lower total cost than the dominant firm, they will displace it in the long run. Even if the dominant firm's costs are lower the presence of a fringe restrains its market power.

Q. Why will fringe supply rotate rightward and downward as new sellers enter the market?

2. Assume that the higher the profits of the dominant firm and the existing fringe, the higher the rate at which new fringe members will enter the market. The dominant firm might be able to maximize the present value of its future profits by pricing below the simple single-period maximum.[14] Doing so sacrifices immediate profits but might discourage competitive entry so that its discounted future profits are worth more than its immediate loss.
3. The previous point has a possible flaw that we will examine later. Specifically, if the dominant firm threatens a price war, fringe entrants may not take the threat

[14]Present values and discounting are discussed in Chapter 16. A model of this type appears in Darius W. Gaskins Jr., "Dynamic Limit Pricing: Optimal Pricing Under Threat of Entry," *Journal of Economic Theory* 3 (September 1971): 306–322.

seriously. If they look a step ahead they will realize that if they actually open for business the dominant firm's best strategy will usually be to accommodate them rather than sacrifice profits in hopes of bankrupting them.

The Histories of Dominant Firms Dominant firms often see competitors entering their industries and eroding their dominance, but these competitors are typically not small price-takers. Table 7-1 shows some entries from a list of dominant firms in a 1979 textbook.[15] By 2005, most of the listed firms had declined substantially, some had vanished by merger or bankruptcy, and some faced new competitors from other industries. About the only one whose status remained the same was Gerber, which since the 1920s has sold nearly 70 percent of all jarred baby food in the country. As for the others, in mid-2009 GM was surviving on government funds. It had only 18.5 percent of U.S. auto sales, a figure that will fall further in the near future when it ceases producing Saturn, Pontiac, and Hummer.[16] In 2008 Japan's Toyota replaced it as global industry leader.[17] As noted earlier, IBM's PCs failed to duplicate the still-continuing success of its large computers, and typewriters have become historical curiosities. During the days of American Telephone and Telegraph's (AT&T) near-monopoly, Western Electric was a captive of AT&T and the sole manufacturer of telephones and switching equipment for that company. After deregulation Western Electric's successor, Lucent Corporation, failed as a stand-alone operation and is today a small part of France's Alcatel-Lucent. Kodak no longer makes cameras in the United States, and recently ended production of its once-dominant Kodachrome film, a victim of digital photography and camcorders.[18] According to the table, Xerox's original copier patents posed high barriers to the entry of competitors, but Japanese manufacturers (and Kodak!) worked around them to dominate world copier markets by the late 1980s. Campbell still sells the lion's share of canned soups, but any supermarket contains dozens of substitutes, canning is an easy business to enter, and homemade soup is always a possibility. Boeing and McDonnell Douglas merged in 1997 to relieve the latter's financial distress. Their 100 percent share of U.S. passenger jet production, however, has lost much of its meaning because worldwide competition has emerged in the form of Europe's Airbus and Brazil's Embraer. The *New York Times* has lost local market share to the *New York Post* and *Long Island Newsday*, but its real competitors are a mix of new newspapers and new media, including *USA Today*, dozens of news broadcasters, and thousands of Internet sites, including those of newspapers that formerly circulated only in their home cities.

Barriers to entry can delay the arrival of new competitors. If the technologies of existing firms are capital-intensive, or if consumers trust their brands (like Gerber), a newcomer will have to invest large amounts in its plant or in establishing the credibility of its product. High barriers to entry may protect the market power of existing firms, but they also discourage the formation of firms that are inefficiently small and cannot realize economies of scale. There are no objective standards for calling an industry's barriers "high" or "medium," and some of the firms listed in Table 7-1 have declined despite seemingly high barriers. Western Electric declined because the 1982 settlement of the

[15]The table contains entries from William G. Shepherd, *The Economics of Industrial Organization* (Saddle Rive, NJ: Prentice-Hall , 1979), 206. Gerber is not included in Shepherd's table.

[16]"GM Chairman Vows to Defend Market Share," *New York Times*, August 4, 2009.

[17]"Toyota Passes General Motors as World's Largest Car Maker," *Washington Post*, January 22, 2009.

[18]"Kodak Retires Kodachrome Film," *Kodak Corporation News Release*, June 22, 2009; http://www.kodak.com/eknec/PageQuerier.jhtml?pq-path=2709&pq-locale=en_US&gpcid=0900688a80b4e692.

TABLE 7-1 DOMINANT FIRMS IN 1979

FIRM	MARKET	1970 MARKET SHARE	BARRIERS TO ENTRY
General Motors	Autos, buses, locomotives	55%	High
IBM	Computers, typewriters	65%	High
Western Electric	Telecommunications equipment	95%	High
Kodak	Photo supplies and cameras	65%	Medium
Xerox	Copying equipment	75%	High
Campbell soup	Canned soups	80%	Medium
Boeing	Aircraft	45%	High
McDonnell-Douglas	Aircraft	45%	High
New York Times	Newspaper	75%	High
Gerber	Baby food	70%	High

government's antitrust case against AT&T opened telecommunications equipment manufacturing to competition. As noted earlier, Japanese automakers circumvented the U.S. industry's capital barriers by manufacturing at home and forming their initial network through arrangements with U.S. dealers. Computers, photography, newspapers, and copying evolved away from the technologies that allowed dominance by IBM, Kodak, the *New York Times*, and Xerox.[19]

GAMES

A Price-Fixing Example

Problems of Enforcement We previously assumed that after the dominant firm chose its output the members of the competitive fringe individually adjusted to that choice as price-takers. Because the presence of the fringe keeps the dominant firm's profits down, both it and the fringe might consider an agreement. The dominant firm might try acting like the Merger Woman of Chapter 6, who becomes wealthier by paying fringe firms to keep their outputs low. As also noted in Chapter 6, the parties might not reach an agreement. Foresighted members of the fringe could hold out for more of the profits that they know will become available if enough others turn control of their springs over to the Merger Woman. But even if the dominant firm does make deals with most fringe members, the commitments both sides have made will not be self-enforcing. Any fringe member that has agreed to cut output will see that market price is higher than its marginal costs. If so, that member is forgoing profits it could have made by producing more and secretly shading its price to attract customers from others. The promised profits will not materialize for anyone unless the behavior of fringe members can be observed, and punished if necessary. But even if monitoring is feasible new problems loom. If the agreement is profitable the parties must cope with new firms that enter the industry in response to higher profits. Any share for the new firms can only come from profits of

[19]In addition, Xerox's patents were finitely lived assets that were probably more valuable to the company as sources of license royalties than as tools to exclude all competitors. With demand for copiers growing quickly, Xerox probably could not have expanded its own facilities fast enough to reap all of the gains from market growth.

the existing ones. But if the new firms cannot reach agreement with existing ones it pays them to stay on the outside. The dominant firm has little reason to trust the fringe members, and vice versa. If everyone in the fringe keeps its output low the dominant firm too can increase its profits by breaking the agreement.

The Agreement as a Game Relationships like those between the dominant firm and the fringe are like games of strategy in certain ways. Whether the parties enjoy high or low profits depends on their joint choices to adhere to the agreement or to break it. The payoff to each depends both on its own action and the actions of the others. If its rules can be enforced the price-fixing game promises gains to both the dominant firm and the fringe, thanks to consumers who must pay more. To keep things simple let's assume just two identical firms, one owned by you and the other by me. We are the only sellers in the market, and assume that even if our price-fixing collusion succeeds no newcomers will open to compete with us.

There are many ways to break an agreement (a cheater can cut price by any amount), but for now assume that there is only one. Table 7-2 is a matrix of payoffs to each of us for each possible combination of our choices. The matrix is known as the *normal form* of the game. The first number in each cell is your payoff, and the second is mine. Each of us chooses a *strategy*, to either keep or break the agreement. You choose one of the rows and I simultaneously choose one of the columns. If we both keep to the terms of our agreement we each profit by $11. If we both break it, we are back where we started making $7 each.[20] If I alone break the agreement by increasing output and shading my price, I will make $14 and you will make $3. Keeping the agreement means you continue to charge the agreed-on price and lose masses of customers to me, which leaves you worse off than if we had not colluded at all. For symmetry, assume that if I keep the agreement and you break it, you make $14 and I make $3.

Assume that neither of us can observe the other's choice and neither can threaten the other into making a particular choice. Comparing payoffs to the different strategy combinations brings an inescapable conclusion: each of us is better off breaking the agreement than keeping it. In the language of game theory, breaking it is a *dominant strategy*. My best choice is to break the agreement regardless of whether you choose to keep or break it, and the same holds for you. If I keep the agreement, you make $14 by breaking it and only $11 by keeping it. If I break the agreement, you make $7 by breaking it and only $3 by keeping it. The same reasoning holds for your choices. But if each of us chooses the dominant strategy and breaks the agreement, both of us end up worse off than if we had kept it.[21] This reasoning generalizes to more than two players.

Some special aspects of this example help to explain its rather extreme results. Perhaps the most important is that we simply assumed the agreement was unenforceable in a court. Conspiring to fix prices is illegal under U.S. antitrust law, but some such agreements have been successful and have occasionally lasted for years.[22] (And there is no way to know how many have escaped detection.) In some ways a price-fixing

[20]Later we will see that if there are only two of us, only under quite special assumptions will we compete so aggressively that we bid market price down to our costs.

[21]This is an example of a generic game known as the prisoners' dilemma. The psychologist who invented it, the late Anatol Rapoport, told a story of two prisoners, Jones and Smith, who were both accused of conspiring to commit a crime. If neither confesses, they will both receive relatively light sentences. If only Jones confesses and implicates Smith, the police will go easier on Jones than if neither confesses, and harder on Smith than if they both confess. The same holds with the characters reversed.

[22]Peter Asch and J.J. Seneca, "Is Collusion Profitable?" *Review of Economics and Statistics* 58 (February 1976): 1–12.

TABLE 7-2 A PRICE-FIXING GAME

		Me	
		Keep	Break
You	Keep	\$11, \$11	\$3, \$14
	Break	\$14, \$3	\$7, \$7

agreement is like an ordinary transaction, albeit an illegal one that creates deadweight and other losses rather than economic value. In subsequent chapters we will show that contracts that create economic value often have the same structure as price-fixing games, and we will examine alternative ways to enforce such agreements.

Enforcing the Agreement

Repeating the price-fixing game a number of times might give us experience and time to learn, but repetition does not necessarily mean we are more likely to keep to the agreement. If we set a fixed number of plays for the game, no matter how large that number is, breaking the agreement is the dominant strategy for both of us every time. To see why, assume that we play for two, and only two, rounds. To determine our best choices we use *backward induction.* Assume that the first round is over, and each of us is deciding whether to keep to the agreement in the second round. With only one round left we are in effect once again in the one-round game of Table 7-2 and should both break the agreement. Now put both of us back at the start of round one. Because both of us are certain to break the agreement in the second round, the first round is the equivalent of a single-play game, and we should both break the agreement. This reasoning holds regardless of how many rounds we play, as long as their number is unalterable and known to both of us. A finitely repeated price-fixing game collapses to the same outcome as a one-play game, each player breaking the agreement every time.[23]

This scenario of a perennially collapsing agreement lacks realism. The great majority of our encounters and interactions do not have well-defined termination dates that all parties know beforehand. Even if there is such a date for our current game, we might meet again some time later and remember each other's reputations. Many of our relationships extend over the indefinite future, with termination at any given time a matter of probability rather than certainty. Interestingly, if our price-fixing collusion goes on forever or has an uncertain ending date, we may be able to enforce the agreement. It may be rational for a player who is keeping the agreement to punish a player who is violating it. Let's look at one of many possible scenarios for an indefinitely repeated game with payoffs like those in Table 7-2. Assume that before we start you announce your intent to punish any violations on my part. You tell me that if I break the agreement just once, you will initiate an irreversible policy of breaking it for eternity, a strategy game theorists call a *grim trigger.* If I do not break it you commit yourself to keeping the agreement at all times.[24] The first play happens today, and all subsequent choices will occur on its anniversary.

Table 7-3 shows what happens with and without a grim trigger. On the first play you keep to the agreement. I, however, decide to cheat and get \$14 while you get \$3. (For

[23]The argument of the text is a variant of one known as the "chain-store paradox."

[24]We do not consider how you might go about establishing your credibility when you make this threat.

TABLE 7-3 PAYOFFS TO COOPERATION AND THE GRIM TRIGGER

YEAR	TRIGGER ACTUATED		BOTH KEEP TO AGREEMENT	
	YOU	ME	YOU	ME
0	$14	$3	$11	$11
1	7	7	11	11
2	7	7	11	11
3, 4...	7	7	11	11
Present value at 0.25	$42.00	$31.00	$55.00	$55.00
Present value at 2.00	$17.50	$6.50	$16.50	$16.50

simplicity assume that payoffs come at the time a decision is made, so that the first round amounts do not have to be discounted.) You carry out your commitment to perpetually break the agreement, and each of us gets $7 every year thereafter. If the interest (discount) rate is 25 percent per period, your income stream has a present value of $3 + $7/0.25 = $31, and mine is worth $14 + $7/0.25 = $42.[25] Alternatively, if we always cooperate, we each get $11 each year, which has a value of $11 + $11/0.25 = $55. The threat that you will pull the grim trigger keeps me from violating the agreement in the first round.

But if I value immediate rewards highly enough relative to future ones, the grim trigger may not deter me. If my annual discount rate is 200 percent, the present value to me of breaking the agreement and suffering the grim trigger is $14 + $7/2 = $17.50, and the present value of keeping the agreement is $11 + $11/2 = $16.50. (This discount rate is purely for illustration—few people value the present so highly that they are willing to pay back $300 a year from now for a $100 loan today.) At a high enough discount rate the grim trigger fails to deter cheating, and both of us break the agreement in all rounds after the first.[26] Figure 7-3 shows the tradeoffs faced by the cheating party—instead of an $11 per year stream forever this person sees $3 more today as worth a subsequent $4 annual loss that runs into the indefinite future.

Nash Equilibrium

Let's look at the price-fixing game from another viewpoint. Say I think to myself: "I want a strategy that maximizes my profits, given that I confidently expect that you will be trying to do the same for yourself." You think likewise regarding me. When all players are choosing their best strategies on the assumption that their opponents are doing likewise,

---

[25]If you have not yet studied present values Chapter 16 covers the basics. The value of an infinite stream (a perpetuity) of $7 payments can be calculated by asking how much you would have to put into a bank account today to withdraw $7 at the end of every year when the bank pays 25 percent interest. If you deposit $28, it grows to $35 at the end of the first year, of which you withdraw $7 and keep the remaining $28 in the account to earn another $7 over the second year, and likewise for all succeeding years. The text formula is saying that you can put $7/0.25 (i.e., $28) in the bank today to get the perpetual stream.

[26]Other possible sanctions include a "forgiving trigger" that lasts for a predetermined number of years. See Prajit K. Dutta, *Strategies and Games* (Cambridge, MA: MIT Press, 1999), 227–242 for more on trigger strategies and a discussion of the large number of possible equilibria in games like these. For a study of actual pricing in a cartel of U.S. railroads prior to the passage of antitrust laws, see Robert H. Porter, "A Study of Cartel Stability: The Joint Executive Committee, 1880–1886," *Bell Journal of Economics* 14 (Autumn 1983): 301–314.

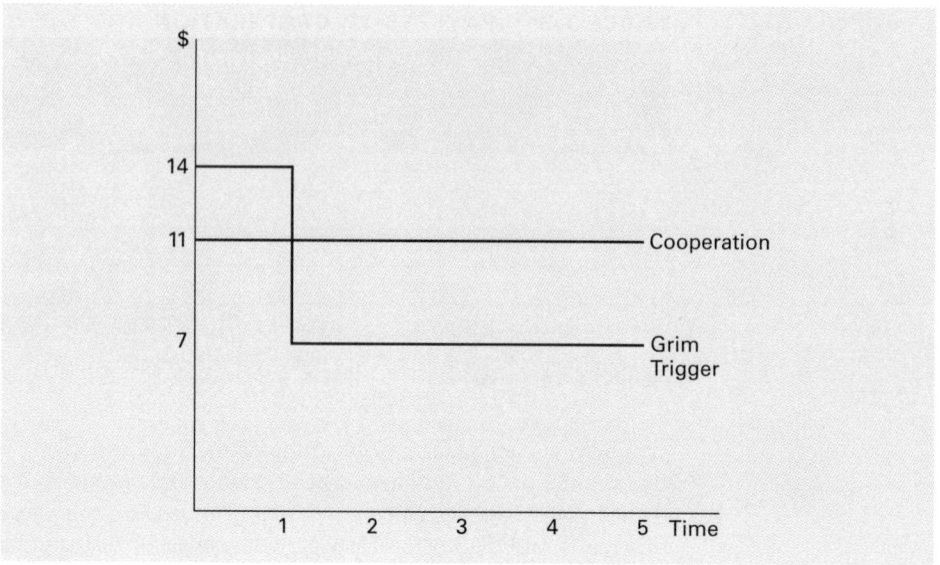

FIGURE 7-3
Cooperation VS. The Grim Trigger

the outcome is called a *Nash equilibrium.*[27] In the price-fixing game, the pair of dominant strategies is a Nash equilibrium. All games with a finite number of strategies have at least one of them.[28] The concept has gained importance as economic models of market interaction become more complex and more general. Its use is growing in other social sciences, and it has become a mainstay of population genetics.[29] Nash equilibrium in actual markets is discussed later.

In games without dominant strategies we can sometimes find the Nash equilibrium using the method called "iterated elimination of dominated strategies."[30] This technique identifies strategies that a player will definitely reject, examines the choices left for the other, eliminates choices the other will reject, and repeats the process until the equilibrium is found. When all of the dominated strategies have been sorted out, however, there may still be more than one, in which case we say that the game is not *dominance solvable.* In the game shown in Table 7-4, you have two strategies, Top (upper row) and Bottom (lower row). I have three, called Left, Center, and Right. First eliminate a dominated strategy of mine. No matter what you choose I will never pick Right because regardless of your choice it pays me less than either Left or Center. Even though your best return ($4) comes when you pick Top and I pick Right, you understand that I always reject right. Your choice between Top and Bottom is clearly Bottom, because it is the

[27]John Nash was co-winner of the 1994 Nobel Prize in Economic Science for proving this. An introduction to his work can be found at the Nobel Prize Web site at http://nobelprize.org/economics/laureates/1994/. The popular movie *A Beautiful Mind* was a dramatized and inaccurate version of Nash's actual life, which was accurately rendered in Sylvia Nasar, *A Beautiful Mind* (New York: Touchstone Books, 1998).

[28]The equilibrium may require the use of mixed strategies, which are defined below. For an informal discussion of Nash's theorem, see Dutta, *Strategies and Games*, 458–60.

[29]For its use in political science, see Stephen Brams, *Game Theory and Politics*, rev. ed. (Mineola, NY: Dover, 2004). For its use in population genetics, see John Maynard Smith, *Evolution and the Theory of Games* (Cambridge, UK: Cambridge University Press, 1982).

[30]Computer algorithms are available for finding Nash equilibriums in certain types of games. For an example that solves two-person zero-sum games, see John Dickhaut and Todd Kaplan, "A Program for Finding Nash Equilibria," in *Economic and Financial Modeling with Mathematica,* ed. Hal R. Varian (New York: Springer-Verlag U.S.,1992), 148–66.

TABLE 7-4 ELIMINATING DOMINATED STRATEGIES

		Me		
		Left	Center	Right
You	Top	1,2	1,3	4,1
	Bottom	2,3	3,2	1,1

dominant strategy over the set of outcomes that remain after I reject Right. But if you have chosen Bottom, my best choice will be Left, because it gives me $3 rather than the $2 I get by playing Center. The Nash equilibrium strategy pair is (Bottom, Left).

Another way to find the Nash equilibrium in Table 7-4 is to first take each of your possible strategies and mark my best response(s) to them. Thus if you pick Top my best response is Center, with payoffs of (1,3), and if you pick bottom it is Left, with payoffs of (2,3). If I choose Left you are best off with Bottom (2,3), if I choose Center you should take Bottom (3,2), and if I choose Right, you should pick Top (4,1). Only one pair (2,3) is on both of our lists. When you pick bottom, Left is my best response, and when I pick Left, Bottom is your best. That combination of strategies is this game's only Nash equilibrium.

Not all games are solvable by iterated elimination of dominated strategies, and a game may have more than one Nash equilibrium. In the game of Table 7-5 you and I are the only manufacturers of a certain product. Either of us can make a Red version or a Blue version, but neither of us can produce both. A person who begins producing a given color cannot reverse the decision. If we choose different colors each of us can earn a profit, and the profits from either choice are the same. Either of the two corners of the matrix with positive profits is a Nash equilibrium. But if we both produce the same color the market will be too small to accommodate both of us. Each of us faces disaster, but communicating our intentions to each other easily solves the coordination problem regardless of who produces which color.

Q. Using iterated elimination of dominant strategies, show that the upper right and lower left entries in Table 7-5 are both Nash equilibria.

Commitments

Conflicts and Chickens Table 7-6 shows a small change in Table 7-5 that drastically changes the possibilities for the players. Now the person who decides to produce Red items earns $7 and the one who produces Blue gets only $4. As before, if we both want to produce the same color we both take substantial losses. Being the first to announce

TABLE 7-5 MULTIPLE NASH EQUILIBRIA

		Me	
		Red	Blue
You	Red	−$9, −$9	$5, $5
	Blue	$5, $5	−$9, −$9

TABLE 7-6 PRODUCT CHOICE WITH ASYMMETRIC PROFITS

		Me	
		Red	**Blue**
You	**Red**	−\$9, −\$9	\$7, \$4
	Blue	\$4, \$7	−\$9, −\$9

that you intend to produce Red does not ensure that you will get the \$7. Even if you have announced your plans, I know that as long as you have not yet begun production I can start producing Red and leave you with no choice but to produce Blue. If I am first to produce Red, it is irrational for you to do the same and take a loss in hopes of inflicting a loss on me, particularly because the more modest profits from producing Blue are still within your reach. In this case, talk is cheap. If you want to produce red you must either be the first to actually begin doing so, or you must make some sort of commitment that will discourage me from trying to beat you to the punch.

To see what sort of commitment that might be, look at Table 7-7. Assume that we both own fast cars and have decided to play a game of chicken. We start at a distance apart and begin driving toward each other at high speed. Each of us can either choose to continue moving forward or to turn away just before a collision would occur. If we collide we both die, losing \$100 apiece (or whatever our lives are worth). If one of us turns away and the other continues moving forward, the one who turns will survive but must spend his or her life marked as a cowardly chicken, a payoff worth minus \$40. The one who keeps going forward enjoys rewards that are worth \$50. If both of us turn away we both spend the future living meaningless lives worth \$0, exempt from being called chicken but not getting invited to many parties.

Chicken has two Nash equilibria, at which our fortunes differ considerably. Once we have begun driving, each of us is completely uncertain whether the other will go straight or turn. If I have reason to believe with certainty that you will turn, my best strategy is to continue moving forward. But even if you are a chicken at heart and really do intend to turn you can only harm yourself by communicating that fact to me. I can, however, gain an advantage using a more radical strategy. As we drive toward each other I very quickly take a wrench and remove my steering wheel. When you are close enough to see me clearly I throw the steering wheel out the window. Because you have no reason to kill yourself just to see me dead (and if you are dead you will not be able to see me anyhow), your only rational choice is to turn away. Even if you have the time, removing your steering wheel after I have removed mine makes no sense. Chicken turns a common belief on its head: We usually think that having more choices cannot possibly make a person worse off, but in Chicken I can guarantee myself a win by limiting my choices and informing you that I have done so. Because you now know I cannot turn away, you face disaster for certain if you fail to turn.

Chicken suggests a way to ensure that I and not you will be the producer of Red. Assume that before either of us makes any announcement I build a very large plant that

TABLE 7-7 A GAME OF CHICKEN

		Me	
		Straight	**Turn**
You	**Straight**	−\$100, −\$100	\$50, −\$40
	Turn	−\$40, \$50	\$0, \$0

can produce Red, and only Red, at a very low marginal cost. The plant is not usable in any other industry and has a scrap value of zero, that is, it is a totally irreversible sunk cost. Building that plant is analogous to throwing away my steering wheel. If you begin producing Red in your existing higher-cost plant, I will be able to underprice you and still cover my marginal cost. My sunk cost is irreversibly sunk, so marginal cost is the only cost that matters to me. I may not recover all my sunk costs if you for some reason insist on producing Red, but you will definitely be taking a loss that you can avoid by resigning yourself to the lower profits of producing Blue. This may be an appealing story, but it is hard to find clear-cut cases where someone made an investment like my Red plant solely to discourage a competitor from entering the business.[31] The story also presumes that it is possible to build a very large and totally specialized plant with very low marginal costs. Even if such a plant could be built, doing so might be a competitive strategy rather than a monopolizing one. If I must compete with you, my best forward-looking choice may be to build a specialized plant that only becomes fully utilized as the demand for its product grows.[32]

It is hard to find clear real-world examples of people voluntarily playing Chicken. The game first appeared as a dramatic device in the classic movie *Rebel Without a Cause*, in which James Dean played a bored teenager for whom adult life held little promise. Few people appear to place such low value on their lives that they will voluntarily play a game that may kill one of them the first time it is played, particularly if the payoff for staying alive is either indifference (if you both turn away) or the admiration of some shallow-minded friends (if you do not). The business situations described previously involve possible financial loss that must be balanced against substantial gains to the winner. A problem at the end of this chapter explores in more detail conditions in which people will voluntarily play Chicken.

How Smart Are People? The theory of games seems to suggest that people must have a high degree of rationality if they are to succeed. Often I must think beyond your immediate response to my choice and examine in advance how I will respond to that response. You of course ought to be thinking about how to respond to that response, and there is no limit to how deep we might go.[33] This vision of mental capabilities is quite different from the one we started with in Chapter 1. There we envisioned individuals with limited access to information and limited abilities to process it, at least in practical situations. It is hard to find real-world situations that allow us to assess exactly how farsighted people really are and how well they can predict and respond to the reactions of others. Economists have, however, run controlled experiments (with cash rewards for the best performers) to examine the depth of peoples' reasoning.

In one such experiment, members of a group must each choose a whole number between 0 and 100. The winner is the person whose number is closest to a constant

---

[31]The only important case in this area is a 1980 Federal Trade Commission (FTC) proceeding that looked into the DuPont chemical company's persistent construction of new plants to make titanium dioxide (which makes white paint white) in anticipation of growing demand. The FTC rejected its staff's analysis, stating that DuPont's behavior could not be distinguished from competitive behavior on the basis of the available facts. See Douglas C. Dobson, William Shepherd, and Robert Stoner, "Strategic Capacity Preemption: *DuPont* (*Titanium Dioxide*) *(1980)*," in *The Antitrust Revolution*, 2nd ed., ed. John Kwoka Jr. and Lawrence J. White, (Oxford, U.K: Oxford University Press, 1994), 157–90.

[32] See Richard L. Smith, "On Strategic Behavior as a Basis for Antitrust Action," *Antitrust Bulletin* 29 (1984): 501–22.

[33]Economists familiar with game theory sometimes do well in experimental game situations in which their opponents come from different backgrounds. There is, however, no firm evidence that economists fare better in real-life gaming situations than noneconomists of similar intelligence and educational attainment.

(e.g., 0.5) times the mean of all the numbers picked.[34] (Before reading on, try to figure out the Nash equilibrium of this game.) Thus, if ten persons pick the numbers 0, 10, 20, 30, 40, 50, 60, 70, 80, and 90, which have a mean of 45, the target number will be 0.5 × 45, rounded downward to 22. Assume that people change their numbers in descending order of their previous choices. The person who picked 90 can reduce her choice to 19 and become the winner.[35] But the person who chose 80 plays next and will reduce his choice to 15. As the players continue doing this they end up at the game's only Nash equilibrium, where everyone chooses zero.

We can also estimate a player's degree of foresight. Assume, for example, that the first nine players either maintain their original choices or pick new numbers at random. The choices of these zero-step players involve no foresight. If the first nine players are zero-step but the tenth can see a step ahead, her superior foresight makes her the winner. A group of perfectly calculating players would all choose zero at the outset. Most experimental subjects are one-step or two-step reasoners. Very few of the experimental subjects appear to foresee the outcome if everyone is perfectly rational, but it does not take perfect rationality to win—all you need is to be a step more foresighted than your opponents.

Q. Verify that if the person who chose 80 plays next (after the person who chose 90) he will reduce his choice to 15.

Q. Verify that if the first nine players can only see zero steps ahead and choose random numbers or maintain their previous choices, a person who can see one step ahead can make herself the winner.

Mixed Strategies

Heads or Tails All the games thus far have had solutions in *pure strategies*, where a player picks a single action and exercises it with certainty. Paradoxically, choosing at random can sometimes be best for a player. In a *mixed strategy* situation one does best by unpredictably mixing one's strategies in accordance with probabilities that depend on the strategies of the others. I maximize my expected (mean) payoff by playing strategies with certain probabilities rather than choosing a single one. Table 7-8 shows the payoffs in a simple game of heads or tails, which we play without a coin. Each of us simultaneously writes "heads" or "tails" on a slip of paper and shows it to the other. If we both write heads or both write tails, you owe me $1. If our choices differ I owe you $1. Neither of us should choose to write "heads" or "tails" using any rule that the other can discover.[36] If you know I will write "heads" every time, you can guarantee yourself a

[34]Rosemarie Nagel, "Unraveling in Guessing Games: An Experimental Study," *American Economic Review* 85 (December 1995): 1313–26. The numerical example in the text is taken from David Sally, "Symposium: Game Theory Behaves," *Marquette Law Review* 87 (2004): 783–92.

[35]This would be a Nash reaction, made on the expectation that all others will maintain their current choices. The mean of the numbers from 0 to 80 plus 19 is 379/10 = 37.9, half of which is 19.

[36]This is an extremely simple variant of the better-known rock-paper-scissors game. A number of Web sites offer tournaments and advice for rock-paper-scissors players. The advice consists of methods that may help you to understand your opponent's mindset on the basis of past plays so you can better predict his choices. Without a table of random numbers or some other randomizing device, a player's choices may have non-random elements that allow a smart opponent to infer his future moves. Try this out by playing rock-paper-scissors at http://www.playrps.com/.

TABLE 7-8 THE HEADS OR TAILS GAME

		Me	
		Heads	**Tails**
You	**Heads**	\$0, \$1	\$1, \$0
	Tails	\$1, \$0	\$0, \$1

steady income by always writing "tails." If we only play once and you know I have already decided what to write down, you can also beat me with certainty. If I constantly alternate between heads and tails or choose some other repeating sequence, sooner or later you will figure out my pattern and be able to beat me. It should be fairly clear that each of us maximizes our income by randomly choosing heads and tails on every play, each with probability of 0.5.

Q. Can you show algebraically that the best heads and tails probabilities are 0.5 for each of us?

Auto Racing Drafting in NASCAR races is a situation where mixed strategies are a clear necessity. Table 7-9 shows one possible representation of the underlying game.[37] Cars A (ahead) and B (behind) are both behind the leader of an existing draft line, and each must decide whether to leave that line and attempt to pass. First, consider the choices in the middle of a race, the upper half of Table 7-9. If both cooperate, then Car A, who is ahead, gains \$4 in improved position, and Car B, who remains behind but ends up closer to the leader, gets \$3.[38] If Car A stays in line and Car B leaves, Car A stays in his existing position, worth \$1, and Car B falls far behind (loses \$5) because he has no partner. If Car B stays and Car A leaves, Car B automatically moves up a spot (worth \$2), while Car A falls behind and loses \$5. If neither of them leaves, assume that their payoffs are both zero because others behind them in line may also be drafting and overtaking them. Neither player has a dominant strategy. If Car B leaves, Car A is better off leaving, but if he stays in line Car A is also better off if he also stays. Car A's best choice depends on Car B's choice, and vice versa. This game has a solution in mixed strategies. Car A should leave the line with probability 0.833, and Car B should leave with probability 0.625.

Q. Can you calculate these probabilities? (Hint: Think Nash equilibrium. Each driver chooses the probability of each strategy to maximize his gains, given the strategy the other is playing. Set up the maximization [you will need to use calculus] and optimize by choosing the probabilities.)

---

[37]This is a variation on an example in David Ronfeldt, "Social Science at 190 MPH on NASCAR's Biggest Superspeedways," *First Monday,* 5, no. 2 (February 7, 2000), http://firstmonday/htbin/cgiwrap/bin/ojs/index.php/fm/article/view/727/636.

[38]Car A also gains because a car at the head of a line is in a better position to escape a wreck than a car farther back. As an alternative possibility, Car B might gain more than Car A from drafting because being behind makes it easier for Car B to set up a slingshot pass of some car ahead, not necessarily Car A's. In addition, Car B can sometimes follow so closely (sometimes purposely tapping his bumper) that Car A loses traction.

TABLE 7-9 DRAFTING

Middle of Race			
		Driver B	
		Leave line	Stay in line
Driver A	Leave line	\$4, \$3	−\$5, \$2
	Stay in line	\$1, −\$5	\$0, \$0
Near End of Race			
		Driver B	
		Leave line	Stay in line
Driver A	Leave line	\$7, \$5	−\$8, \$3
	Stay in line	\$2, −\$9	\$0, \$0

Treating the decision to draft as a game also helps explain other behavior. As a race goes into its final laps almost all of the unwritten agreements that allowed draft lines to persist earlier in the race collapse. The gains to mutual cooperation increase, because an improved position is more likely to last until the end of the race. So too do the gains to staying in the line when the other driver leaves it. The new payoffs might be like those in the bottom part of Table 7-9. There, Car A should leave the line with probability 0.818, almost the same as early in the race, and Car B should leave the line with probability 0.615. The returns to cooperation for both players rise, but so do the losses from discovering that your partner has chosen not to cooperate. When both the gains and losses increase, as happens near the end of the race, the probabilities in our example remain close to the values they took on earlier in the race. You should be able to check that if only the gains to cooperation in the upper left corner increase, cooperative drafting will be more frequent. This example also shows the limits of simple game theory: its structure is not detailed enough to explain why drafting agreements become more short-lived as the end of the race nears.

Auctions: The Format Determines the Strategy Auctions have existed throughout history, but economists only began theorizing about them in the 1970s. Some economists have achieved distinction as designers of multibillion dollar auctions used by the government to maximize its revenue from the sale of rights to use portions of the electronic spectrum.[39] Other economists have used auction theory to design markets for short-term sales of high-voltage electricity and its transmission.[40] Auction sites on the Internet number in the thousands. Giant eBay's \$2.1 billion in revenue is a tiny fraction of the dollar volume it trades, while others like Ariba specialize in designing and administering procurement auctions for businesses.[41]

Anyone bidding (or considering a bid) at an auction is in a game with other bidders. In an *ascending-value auction*, I hope to win a certain object by bidding a price below my valuation (maximum willingness to pay for it) but higher than anyone else's bid. Governments frequently give construction contracts to the winners of *sealed-bid* auctions in which prospective contractors submit written bids in sealed envelopes before a deadline, and no rebidding is allowed. The government may pay more when rebidding is

[39]Paul Milgrom, "Putting Auction Theory to Work: the Simultaneous Ascending Auction," *Journal of Political Economy* 108 (April 2000): 245–72.

[40]Robert Wilson, "Architecture of Power Markets," *Econometrica* 70 (July 2002): 1299–340.

[41]For more information, see the companies' Web sites at www.ebay.com and www.ariba.com.

allowed than when it is not. Procurement, with or without rebidding, is a *first-price auction* where the lowest bidder receives its actual bid as payment for the job. A bidder has no incentive to reveal its actual costs, because being paid that amount leaves it with benefits of zero. Instead, the bidder bids more than its cost, as discussed in more detail in Appendix 7-A. An alternative is the *second-price auction,* in which the winning bidder pays the amount bid by the first runner-up. Appendix 7-A contrasts first- and second-price auctions. It shows that in a first-price auction your best bidding strategy depends on your valuation of the good, and that you might optimally use a mixed strategy to choose your bid. Perhaps unexpectedly, in a second-price auction all bidders have a dominant strategy of bidding their true valuations of the good.

Q. Why might the government pay more when rebidding is allowed than when it is not?

How Relevant Are Mixed Strategies? Mixed strategies maximize a player's expected returns in games like NASCAR drafting and Heads or Tails. Their actual importance in business is less clear. The question matters because many games, particularly complex ones, only have solutions in mixed strategies. However, it is hard to find actual situations in which managers choose their competitive strategies by assigning probabilities to them and letting a random number determine the choice. Mixed strategies may occur so seldom because the choices are usually more numerous than in a simple game, and determining the right probabilities to assign to them requires accurate estimation of their financial consequences, including consideration of risks. Those consequences, however, also depend on the strategies chosen by competitors. Few managers will feel comfortable facing their shareholders and explaining that an unsuccessful year was the result of a random choice among strategies, even if the mixed strategy made sense before events unfolded. All business ventures have degrees of uncertainty, but it is hard to imagine a manager telling investment bankers that the venture she is asking them to fund was chosen at random.

Models of Oligopoly

Quantity-Setting Duopoly

Cournot-Nash Equilibrium In 1838, Augustin Cournot, a French Engineer, published *Researches into the Mathematical Principles of Wealth*, the first important work in economics that was grounded in higher mathematics.[42] Cournot was the first to tackle the complexities of interaction among oligopolists, and he faced the same problems as today's economists. What principles might form a reasonable foundation for a theory of oligopoly? An assumption that each seller has psychoanalyzed the competition and decided how to react in all possible situations is both unrealistic and impossible to incorporate into a usable model. Cournot went in the opposite direction and chose a simplification that remains a mainstay of economics to this day: he assumed that when each seller chooses its own output it believes the others in the market will not respond and will keep their outputs as they were before. In equilibrium, no seller wishes to change output because each of them is individually maximizing profit given the choices

[42]A brief biography of Cournot can be found at the History of Economic Thought Web site, operated by the New School for Social Research; http://cepa.newschool.edu/het/profiles/cournot.htm.

of the others. Each seller's expectation that the others will not change their outputs is fulfilled. This solution concept is a particularization of Nash equilibrium to the market Cournot chose to model—each seller is doing its best given that the others are doing the same for themselves. Nash arrived 100 years later, but today we often call this a Cournot-Nash equilibrium.

We need a bit more detail about market institutions to complete the model. There are only two sellers, A and B, a duopoly that faces no threat of competitive entry. (The model generalizes to any number of sellers.) Assume once again (as Cournot did) that each seller owns a mineral water spring with zero marginal cost that can, if necessary, produce the entire quantity demanded by the market each day. Sellers know the market demand curve for the water, but they are never in contact with each other so that they could, for example, agree to limit output to fix prices. They make their decisions simultaneously, and all of their water is shipped to a central market where each gallon fetches the price at which quantity demanded equals their total production.

Figure 7-4 begins with the same market demand curve that was used in Figure 6-2 and others. Assume that A makes the first choice and she assumes that B will maintain his output unchanged, at zero. A would then be a monopolist, produce 6 units, and market price would be $6. (Six units is where marginal revenue for this demand curve crosses the horizontal axis.) Now B chooses, and he also holds the Cournot assumption that A will continue producing 6 gallons, no matter what B does. In effect this leaves B to optimize against that part of the demand curve to the right of 6 units. B's best choice is to produce 3 units. Now 9 units go to market and price goes to $3. In the next round, A assumes that B will keep his output at 3 units and optimizes against that part of the demand curve to the right of 3 units. A's best choice is 4.5 units. Still assuming that A's output will stay constant, B changes his to 3.75 units. A's output decreases with each move and B's increases, but they appear to be converging to an equilibrium. Appendix

FIGURE 7-4
Comparison of Perfectly Competitive, Monopoly, and Cournot-Nash Equilibria

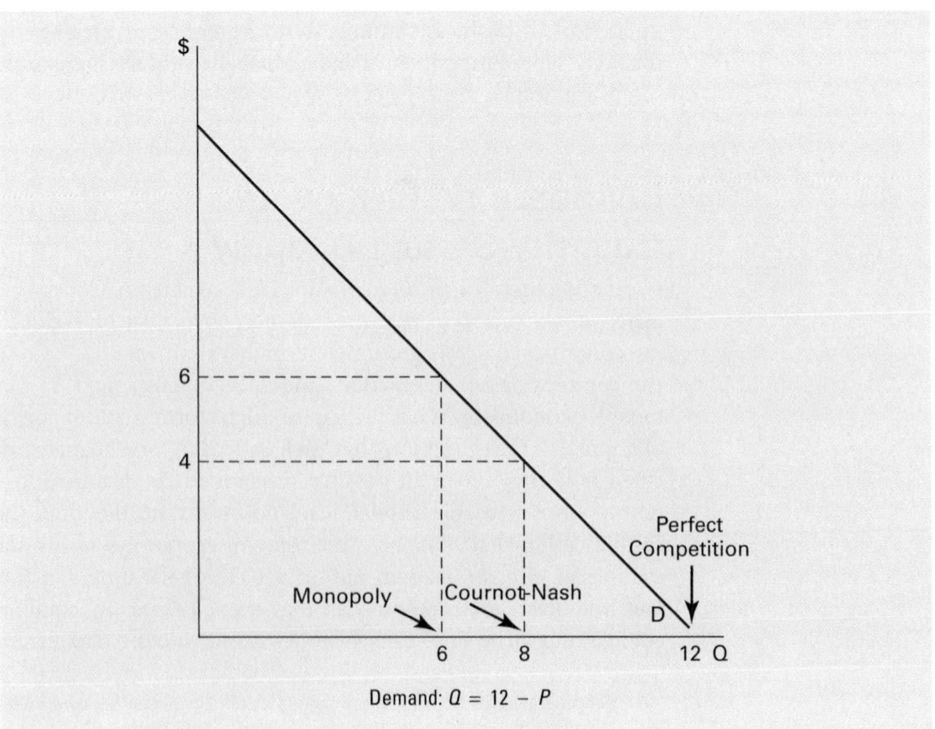

7-B uses calculus to show that in this equilibrium each produces 4 units, and the 8 units sell for $4 apiece. Once that equilibrium is reached, neither has reason to change output and each of their expectations that the other's output will stay constant is fulfilled.

Q. Check that the sequence of outputs calculated for A and B is correct.

Table 7-10 summarizes the sequence of A's and B's production decisions. The market converges to an equilibrium output of 8 and a price of $4, leaving $32 in profit (revenue) for A and B to split. As shown in Figure 7-4, this outcome differs from both monopoly and perfect competition. If A and B were successful price-fixers they would in effect be partners in a monopoly producing 6 units, selling them at $6 each and splitting a profit of $36. Figure 7-3 also shows the outcome in a perfectly competitive market. If A and B act as price-takers they will produce 12 units in total and compete price down to zero (i.e., marginal cost), leaving each of them with profits of zero. In the linear demand case (with constant marginal costs that need not be zero), the monopolist produces half of the perfectly competitive output, and duopolists who operate under the Cournot assumptions produce two-thirds of that output. As the number of producers rises in the Cournot model, the market outcome approaches the perfectly competitive one.[43] With N producers the ratio of the Cournot output to the perfectly competitive output is N/(N+1).

Reaction Functions Plotting each duopolist's best response to the other's decision provides additional insights. Figure 7-5 shows A's and B's *reaction functions* or *reaction curves* for the demand curve shown in Figure 7-4. We can derive them using calculus (see Appendix 7-B), but the logic is understandable without it. At the low end of her reaction curve A is a monopoly. She produces 6 units while assuming that B will always produce zero. At the Cournot-Nash equilibrium, A and B each produce 4 units. On that part of her reaction curve to the northwest of (4,4), A produces her profit-maximizing output for larger outputs by B. She will produce some small amount as long as any demand remains unserved by B and allows her the opportunity to receive a price that exceeds her marginal cost of zero. When demand and marginal cost are linear, so are the reaction curves. We can also plot the approach to equilibrium on Figure 7-5. Start with A producing 6 and B producing zero, followed by B's reaction of 3 units. When A sees B's new output (the upper end of the first arrow) she responds with 4.5 units, after which B changes his output to 3.75 (the left end of the second arrow). They continue to act and react, but changes in their individual outputs soon become very small.

TABLE 7-10 OUTPUT RESPONSES IN A COURNOT DUOPOLY

ROUND	Q_A	Q_B	TOTAL	PRICE
1	6	3	9	$3.00
2	4.5	3.75	8.25	3.75
3	4.125	3.937	8.062	3.94
Equilibrium	4	4	8	4.00

[43]Sellers in the perfectly competitive model also behave under the Cournot assumptions, because each seller assumes that no other seller will respond to a change in his own output.

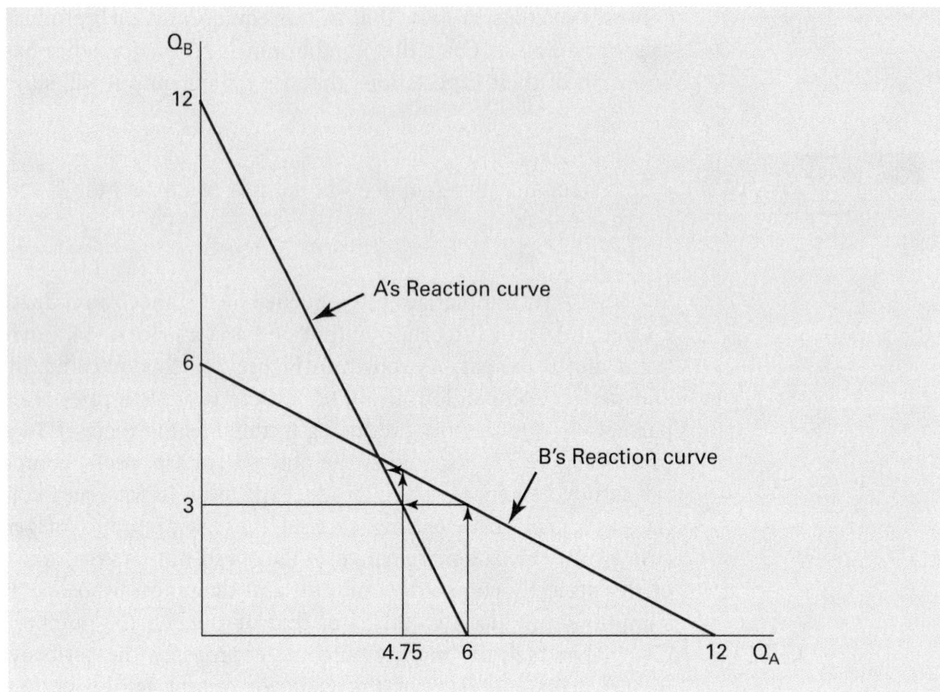

FIGURE 7-5
Reaction Curves

Reaction curves are helpful when analyzing cost and demand changes. Assume, for example, that marginal costs of both sellers rise from zero to a constant \$3. Figure 7-6 shows the inward shifts to the dotted reaction curves and A's and B's new equilibrium outputs of 3 units each. Market price rises to \$6, and their individual profits fall to \$9. Asymmetric changes are also possible, as shown in Figure 7-7. Starting from marginal costs of zero, assume that A convinces the government to enact a \$3 tax on every unit

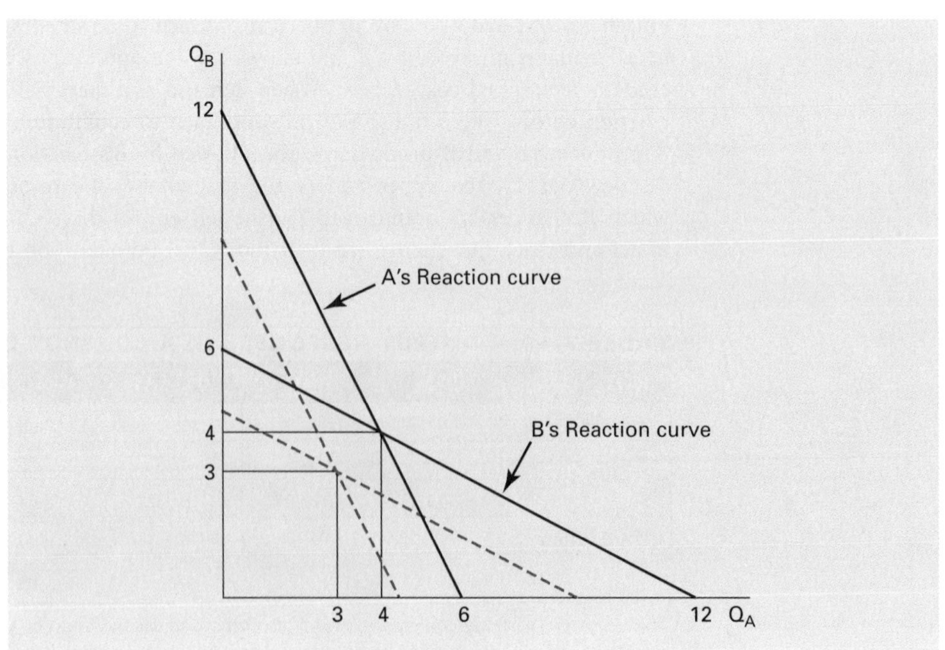

FIGURE 7-6
Reaction Curve Shifts with Cost Increase

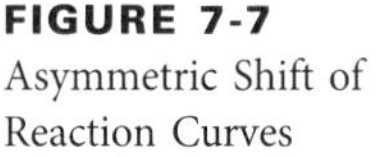

FIGURE 7-7
Asymmetric Shift of Reaction Curves

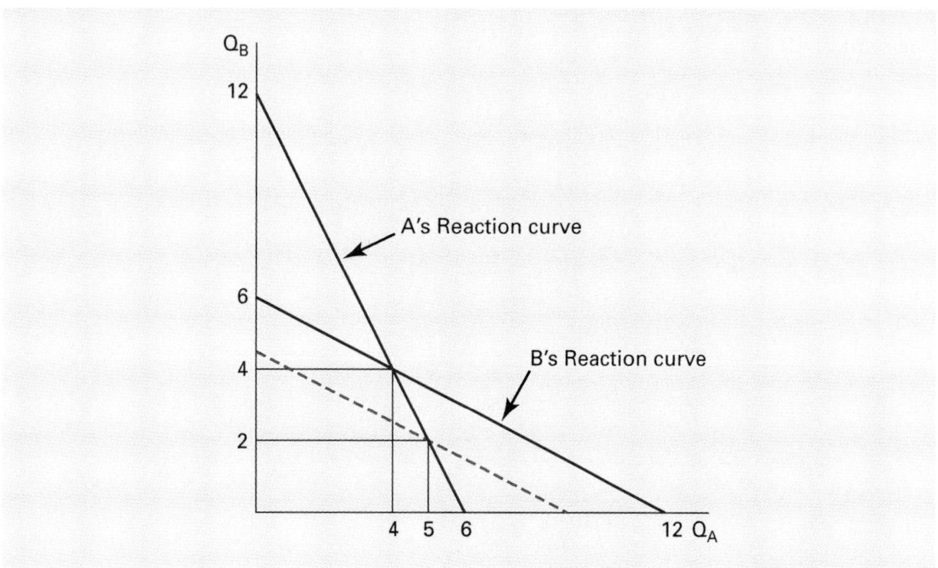

of B's output while leaving her exempt. A's reaction curve is unchanged while B's shifts inward to the dotted line. In the new equilibrium, A's best output is 5 units and B's has fallen to 2. Market price is $5, at which A's profits are $25 and B's are $4. It looks like A would have been willing to pay a substantial bribe to get this law passed.

Q. Verify the calculations in the discussion of Figures 7-6 and 7-7.

Price-Setting Duopoly

The insights Cournot's model provides into duopoly equilibrium depend critically on its assumption that each seller treats the other's output as fixed. To see the consequences we make seemingly small changes in the ground rules and in the sellers' expectations about each other. Instead of choosing quantities to produce, A and B will now choose prices. Each will further assume that the other will not change price in response to his or her decision. We now have the model first devised by Joseph Bertrand, a British critic of Cournot.[44] As before, assume that there are two water producers, each of whom can produce any output level at a marginal cost of zero.

The equilibrium changes drastically. In Figure 7-8, D is the same market demand curve as before. If A is the first to choose a price, she picks the monopoly price of $6 and produces 6 units. B enters the market and charges a price slightly below A's, say $5.50 (the middle line on the graph), with the expectation that A will keep her price at $6. Because A would lose all her customers if she left her price unchanged, she reduces it below B's, perhaps to $5, and reclaims the entire market. A and B continue responding to each other until price is reduced to marginal cost (i.e., zero). A Cournot market's equilibrium output lies between those of monopoly and perfect competition. A Bertrand model with the same number of competitors settles into the same equilibrium that would prevail if there were a large number of price-taker sellers.

[44]His biography is at http://homepage.newschool.edu/het//profiles/bertrand.htm

FIGURE 7-8
The Bertrand Model

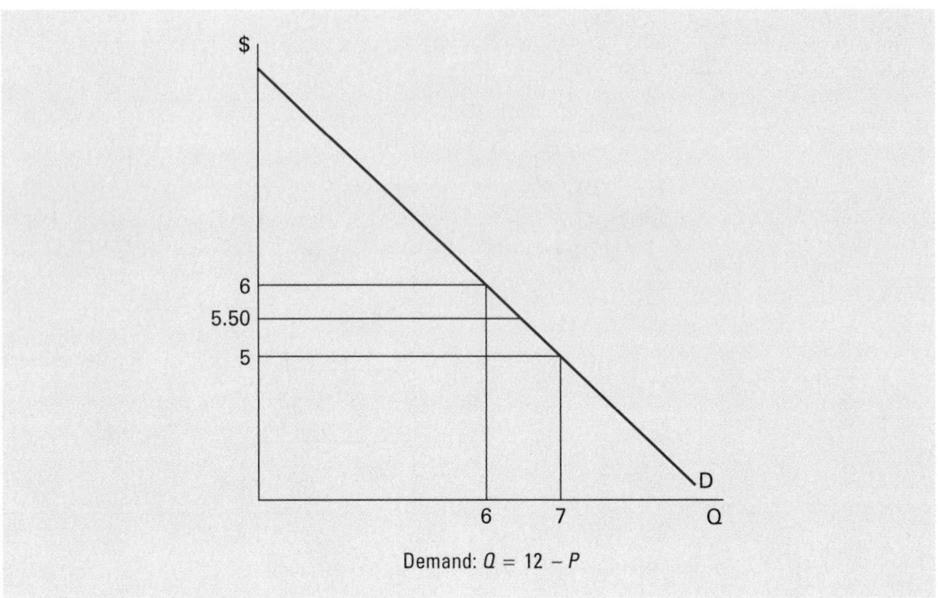

A Leader and a Follower

In both the Cournot and Bertrand models the sellers had identical expectations about each other, and these expectations were fairly naive. In addition, events on the way to equilibrium contradicted their expectations of each other, but they nevertheless continued to hold them. During the adjustment process, A continued to assume that B would keep price or quantity constant but B's response consistently dashed that expectation, and likewise for B's beliefs. In addition, it was not clear why the sellers had identical expectations about each other.

Our final duopoly market starts by assuming a difference in those expectations. In the *Stackelberg model* one seller acts as a leader and the other as a follower. After the leader L chooses her output, follower F makes his most profitable choice in light of L's decision. The Stackelberg model allows the leader to think a step ahead. Specifically, she chooses output with an expectation that the follower will make the most profitable response available to him. L's foreknowledge that F will act this way allows her to make larger profits than F, who in turn is worse off than he would have been if both of them had held identical Cournot assumptions about each other's output. The model and its solution are presented in more detail in Appendix 7-B.

Conclusions: Is Oligopoly Theory Relevant?

Estimating the Beliefs of Oligopolists The outcomes of oligopoly models depend heavily on what is assumed, and sometimes they defy most people's expectations about how equilibrium will vary with the number of sellers. A Cournot market with five sellers will have a higher price and lower output than a Bertrand market with only two sellers. We can question the assumptions about producers' beliefs in any model of oligopoly, and Stackelberg's too is no exception. Because the leader's profits (in the model of Appendix 7-B) are twice the follower's and their costs are the same, it is hard to explain why either firm would accept the role of follower. In that Appendix you can check that if for some unknown reason both sellers act as followers they will arrive at the Cournot-Nash equilibrium, but if they both want to be leaders the model does not provide a usable solution concept.

Q. If both Stackelberg sellers wish to act as leaders, explain why the model does not offer a solution concept.

Oligopoly markets exhibit every imaginable outcome on the line between cutthroat competition and collusion to share the profits of a monopoly. In the current state of their knowledge, economists are simply unable to examine the characteristics of an industry and conclude that its participants will act according to the assumptions of a Bertrand, Cournot, or some other model. (We have a bit more information about price-fixing because a good-size sample of offenders has been caught.) The study of industry behavior requires both knowledge of its institutions and detailed data on the prices and outputs of individual firms, the latter being particularly hard to obtain unless they were produced in litigation.[45] Even with the data, economists can seldom determine exactly which of these oligopoly models (or one of many not discussed here) best describes conditions in a market.

Here's just a sample of findings. In the international rice trade, countries behave more like price-takers (close to the Bertrand model) than like Cournot oligopolists or price-fixers.[46] The three firms that dominate the Japanese plate-glass industry, by contrast, have followed either Cournot or price-fixing behavior and have definitely not been price-takers.[47] Leader-follower relationships have been found in industries as different as chemicals in the United Kingdom and coffee roasting in the United States.[48] Those who are followers in both of those markets appear to react to one another's decisions as if they have Cournot expectations. Two duopolists produce most of the electric power in the United Kingdom and sell it into auction markets. They do not behave like price-takers, but the prices they bid carry smaller markups over marginal costs than they would in a Cournot market.[49] Just about anything that can happen in oligopoly markets appears to have happened somewhere, but explaining why one outcome rather than a different one has occurred remains largely beyond the capabilities of economics. If nothing else, oligopoly theory helps us to appreciate the range of those outcomes.

What Do Industry Practices Mean? The same economic behavior can be consistent with quite different market situations. Uniform prices are seen in perfectly competitive markets and in markets where price-fixing prevails. Models like those of Cournot and Bertrand simply assume that duopolists follow constant rules when reacting to one another and disregard possible motives to fix prices. Price fixing may be illegal, but if it provides more profit than other types of behavior we must assume that oligopolists will weigh its costs and benefits. They need not do so in some illegal meeting, because if they have a common interest in profits an unspoken or tacit collusion might evolve. But if

---

[45]Even in lawsuits, the court usually restricts the availability of company-specific data to those parties with a need to know it. Competitors with access to such data may be able to infer competitive strategies of the litigants that would otherwise be highly confidential.

[46]Larry S. Karp and Jeffrey M. Perloff, "Dynamic Oligopoly in the Rice Export Market," *Review of Economics and Statistics* 71 (August 1989): 461–70.

[47]Gyoichi Iwata, "Measurement of Conjectural Variations in Oligopoly," *Econometrica* 42 (September 1974): 947–66.

[48]Jonathan Haskel and Pasquale Scaramozzino, "Do Other Firms Matter in Oligopolies?" *Journal of Industrial Economics* 45 (March 1997): 27–45; Frank M. Gollop and Mark J. Roberts, "Firm Interdependence in Oligopolistic Markets," *Journal of Econometrics* 10 (September 1979): 313–31.

[49]Catherine Wolfram, "Measuring Duopoly Power in the British Electricity Spot Market," *American Economic Review* 89 (September 1999): 805–26.

they agree to collude they might also agree to use pricing practices that allow violators to be detected. The problem is that some suspicious-looking practices can also be evidence of competition. The following case study can shed some light on the difficulties government enforcers face when they are trying to interpret actual behavior.

The Ethyl Investigation Evidence about the health hazards of lead in the environment accumulated during the 1950s and 1960s. In 1973, the federal government responded with regulations that enforced phaseouts of several lead compounds, most importantly lead tetraethyl, commonly known as ethyl, used as an antiknock additive in gasoline. Four large firms produced all of the ethyl in the United States. The phaseout regulation put their industry under a death sentence, and observers noted that they engaged in very little price competition.[50] Ethyl producers operated in a market whose characteristics matched those of some markets that had seen successful collusion in the past: a handful of producers, declining demand, and a small number of large oil refiner customers. Each buyer purchased quantities substantial enough that all of the producers would notice if any buyer had migrated to a new seller. The FTC thus suspected that it would be relatively easy to monitor and detect those violating even an unwritten agreement. It was particularly interested in three practices: (1) all of the producers notified all of their customers about price changes 30 days before they became effective; (2) all of the producers charged uniform delivered prices, that is, no matter the customer's distance from an ethyl plant it paid the same price as a customer on the plant's doorstep; and (3) all had "most favored customer" clauses stipulating that if one customer was offered a discount from the list price all of that seller's other customers would also receive it.

Q. Earlier in the chapter we argued that if two parties repeatedly play the price-fixing game and both know exactly when it will end, each will choose to break the agreement at every play. The ethyl producers, however, may well have been able to hold an implicit price-fixing agreement together over the final years of their industry's existence. Why might the simple model of a collapsing agreement not predict what happened in their market?

The FTC argued that practices like these three helped enforce an unwritten agreement. One producer's preannouncement of new prices could give the others time to raise theirs, rather than allowing those who continued to charge lower prices a window to gain additional business. Uniform delivered prices simplified pricing in ways that would make it harder for someone violating the agreement to offer a discount in the form of lower transportation charges. Most-favored customer provisions made it impossible for a producer to selectively discount, facilitating the maintenance of uniform prices. Perfectly competitive markets also have uniform prices, but this was a far different market.

The ethyl producers responded by showing that prices were not as uniform as the FTC claimed, and that in any case individual companies provided free services that were the equivalent of competitive price cuts. (For example, one built a dedicated railroad track for deliveries to a customer.) The producers claimed that in a market with large and knowledgeable customers price announcements just speeded information flows that would have occurred anyway. They said uniform delivered prices facilitated

[50]Details of this case are in George A. Hay, "Facilitating Practices: The *Ethyl* case (1984)," in *The Antitrust Revolution*, 3rd ed., ed. John E. Kwoka Jr., and Lawrence J. White, 189–213 (New York: HarperCollins, 1994); http://www.oup.com/us/pdf/kwoka/0195120159_07.pdf.

comparisons and were not significant because transportation was such a small part of costs. Finally, they noted that most-favored customer clauses had been put into contracts at the requests of individual customers, who wanted guarantees that they would not be harmed by discounts given to their competitors. All of the questioned practices had evolved in the days when the industry's only producer was the Ethyl Corporation, rather than being instituted after competitors entered the industry. The FTC ruled against the producers on grounds that the practices facilitated a cartel. The companies took their case to the Court of Appeals, which ruled that the historical development of the practices and the producers' evidence indicated a high probability that these were legitimate business practices of firms in competition with one another. Economic theory and the available evidence both give no clear reason to conclude that the FTC's analysis was right or wrong.

Chapter Summary

- Oligopoly both fascinates and frustrates economists. The interdependent decisions of small numbers of sellers bring aggressive competition in some industries, but in others they settle down to coordinated pricing decisions and minimal rivalry. Theoretical models provide some insight but are by themselves incapable of specifying whether competition in a market will be vigorous or anemic.
- In the model of a dominant firm with a competitive fringe, when making its decisions a large firm must account for the reactions by members of the fringe to its output decisions. If the dominant firm has no cost advantage over fringe firms and entry is possible, its dominance will probably diminish with time.
- The fundamental problem in oligopoly is that each seller understands that the others will respond to any particular decision of his, and he will have to account for those possible reactions when choosing price or output. This makes equilibrium difficult to characterize in general.
- One popular economic assumption is that a Nash equilibrium will prevail. In a Nash equilibrium each player plays his best strategy in light of those being chosen by the others.
- Applying Nash equilibrium to a price-fixing agreement yields a conclusion that it must break down, but an agreement may persist if it is enforceable, whether by legal or illegal means. Related strategies include commitments by one player that change the other's best strategy.
- Strategies may be pure (the same choice is best for me regardless of what you do) or mixed (a strategy is chosen at random but with a given probability). Mixed strategies are also of importance in situations that range from auctions to sports.
- Application of game-theoretic concepts to market behavior is difficult because minor changes in assumptions about sellers' expectations and behavior lead to very different outcomes. A Cournot-Nash model settles to an equilibrium between monopoly and perfect competition, but a Bertrand model generates a perfectly competitive equilibrium. Many other assumptions such as leaders and followers are also possible.
- Oligopoly theory helps us understand the difficulties in interpreting industrial behavior. In the ethyl case, several of the industry's pricing practices could be interpreted as evidence either for or against competitive behavior.

Appendix 7-A

First-Price and Second-Price Auctions

The Second-Price Auction

Bidders will bid their true costs or valuations in a *second-price auction,* where the high bidder pays the auctioneer the highest losing bid (i.e., the second-highest bid if a single item is being auctioned). The second-price auction has a solution in pure strategies. Assume that only two of us are bidding, and we were selected at random from a population in which half of the members (Type 3 or T3) value the item at $3 and half value it at $5 (Type 5 or T5). Neither of us knows the other's type.[51]

If my bid exceeds yours, I receive the object and pay the amount you bid. If our bids are identical, the winner of a coin flip gets the object at that price with a probability of 0.5. Assume that I am a T5. If I bid $5.50 rather than $5, I may win, but if you bid between $5.01 and $5.50 I will end up paying more than my valuation for the good. If your bid was under $5, I also win, but I would also have won had I bid $5. Next, assume instead that I am a T5 who bid $4.50. If your bid was between $4.51 and $4.99, I get nothing. Changing my bid to $5 eliminates this possibility and allows me to benefit because all I have to pay is your bid. If your bid is over $5, you get the object regardless of whether I bid $4.50 or $5.00, but in this case I do not want to win because that would entail paying more for the good than my valuation. Regardless of your bid (and regardless of our types) my best strategy is to bid my true valuation, and the same holds for you. The second-price auction has a solution in pure strategies.

Q. Show that a T3's best strategy is also to always bid her true valuation of the good.

The First-Price Auction

The first-price auction has a quite different outcome, in which T3s play pure strategies and T5s play mixed strategies. If I am a T5 I will never bid $5 or more because if I won I would have to pay that amount, receiving either no benefits or negative benefits. Hence, I will only bid less than $5. Now we have two possibilities: First, if you are also a T5, I must not bid too low because you can beat me by bidding slightly more but less than $5. But you might be a T3, in which case all I need bid is $3.01 (because you too will not voluntarily pay more than your valuation). If I don't know your type, I must balance the likelihood of beating you with a higher bid if you are a T5 against the benefit from winning with a lower bid if you are a T3. My choice will depend on my beliefs about the probabilities that you are a T5 or a T3.

Now assume that you are a T3 and are uncertain about whether I am a T5 or T3. If I too turn out to be a T3, each of us goes to $3, and each wins with a probability of 0.5. If I am a T5 you can only win if I irrationally bid under $3. If I do that, however, a $3 bid

[51]Note that strategy in the second-price auction is independent of the frequencies of T3s and T5s in the population. That is not the case for a first-price auction.

guarantees you the item. You also know that I understand this (even if I am not sure about your type). You will thus bid \$3 with certainty, that is, play a pure strategy, because anything less is certain to yield you nothing. If I am in fact a T5, it can be shown that my best choice is the mixed strategy of a random bid between \$3 and \$4, with an equal probability for every value in that range.[52]

[52]For a proof, see Dutta, *Strategies and Games*, 371–372.

Appendix 7-B

Calculus

The Dominant Firm with a Competitive Fringe

In Figure 7-2, the market demand curve is given by

(7.1) $$Q = 12 - P.$$

Fringe supply is

(7.2) $$Q_F = -1 + 0.4P.$$

IBM's marginal cost, MC_I, is \$4. Residual demand is the difference between market demand and fringe supply, that is,

(7.3) $$Q_{res} = 13 - 1.4P.$$

IBM maximizes profit at the output where residual marginal revenue equals marginal cost. Solving

(7.4) $$9.29 - 1.43Q_{res} = 4,$$

the result is $Q_{res} = 3.70$ units, a market price of \$6.64, a fringe output of 1.65 units, and total output of 5.35.

The Cournot Duopoly

Equilibrium Assume that market demand is again

[7.1) $$Q = 12 - P.$$

Duopolist A chooses first and believes that, whatever her choice, B will not change his output, which is currently zero. She maximizes total revenue by producing $Q_A = 6$ units. B believes A will stay at 6 units and chooses Q_B to maximize

(7.5) $$Q_B + 6 = 12 - P,$$

yielding $Q^*_B = 3$. Total output is 9 units and market price is \$3. Start from here by recalculating A's best output, given her new belief that B will continue producing 3 units. She maximizes

(7.6) $$Q_A + 3 = 12 - P,$$

and chooses to produce 4.5. Then B assumes that A will stay at 4.5 and maximizes

(7.7) $$Q_B + 4.5 = 12 - P$$

by producing 3.75 units. Market output is 8.25 units and price is \$3.75. Maintaining the Cournot assumptions, in round three A will first produce 4.125 and B will react by producing 3.937.

Q. Check all the calculations for the duopoly.

Reaction Functions To get the reaction functions via calculus, remember that A is maximizing its profit π_A given B's output,

(7.8) $$\pi_A = 12Q_A - Q_A^2 - Q_B,$$

and B is doing likewise, with

(7.9) $$\pi_B = 12Q_B - Q_B^2 - Q_A.$$

Take the partial derivative of each with respect to the output under that producer's control, and set each equal to zero. We get

(7.10) $$12 - 2Q_A - Q_B = 0$$

and

(7.11) $$12 - 2Q_B - Q_A = 0.$$

Reaction function 7.10, when rearranged, gives A's best response to B's choice of output, and 7.11 gives B's response to A's. They have a simultaneous solution at $Q^*_A = Q^*_B = 4$. To solve the problem where B has a \$3 tax per unit of output while A remains untaxed, subtract the tax bill from B's profits. Thus, B maximizes

(7.12) $$\pi_B = 12Q_B - Q_B^2 - Q_A - 3Q_B.$$

A continues to maximize (equation 7.8), and the new solution is $Q^*_A = 5$ and $Q^*_B = 2$.

Q. At what per-unit tax does B go out of business?

The Stackelberg Model

To find the solution if market demand is given by equation 7.1, the leader reasons backward. The follower wants to maximize his profit

(7.13) $$\pi_F = PQ_F = Q_F(12 - Q_F - Q_L),$$

where P is market price. He takes Q_L as beyond his control, because L is the leader. Expanding, differentiating, and maximizing equation 7.8, at the optimum we have

(7.14) $$\frac{\partial \pi_F}{\partial Q_F} = 12 - 2Q_F - Q_L = 0.$$

Solve this for $Q_F = 6 - Q_L/2$, which appears in top half of Figure 7-9. The larger is the leader's output, the smaller is the follower's best choice.

Next, the leader maximizes her profits, factoring the follower's best response into her choice. She wants to find Q_L that maximizes

(7.15) $$\pi_L = PQ_L = (12 - Q_F - Q_L)Q_L.$$

Expanding, differentiating, and maximizing gives us

(7.16) $$\frac{\partial \pi_L}{\partial Q_F} = 12 - 6 + Q_L - 2Q_L = 0.$$

The leader's best choice is $Q^*_L = 6$ units, to which the follower responds by producing 3. Market price will be \$3, and total output is greater than in a Cournot duopoly.

FIGURE 7-9
The Stackelberg Model

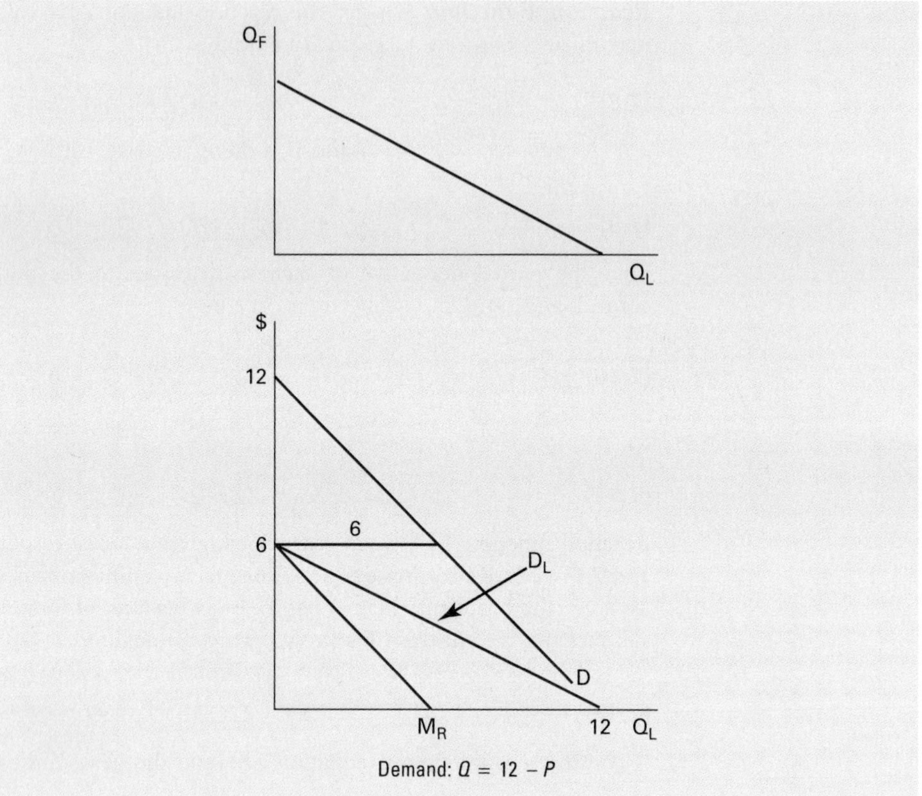

Graphically, in the lower half of Figure 7-9 we first subtract the follower's best response from the market demand curve to get the residual demand curve D_L that the leader faces. She maximizes profit (revenue, because marginal cost is assumed zero) by producing where MR_L, the marginal revenue associated with D_L, crosses the horizontal axis, at 6 units. Adding the follower's response of 3 units gives market quantity of 9 units, which sell for $3 each. The leader makes $18, and the follower makes half that amount.

Q. Check that if both play as followers the equilibrium is the same as in the Cournot-Nash model.

Q. If the leader's cost is higher than the follower's, does it ever pay not to be the leader? Can the Stackelberg leader's profits ever exceed those of a Cournot duopolist?

Q. The Stackelberg leader produces 6 units, the same as the monopoly output. Will this also happen if she has two followers? Why or why not?

Questions and Problems

1. (Requires calculus) In the model of a dominant firm, assume that the fringe supply curve is given by $Q = -1 + 0.2P$, where P is market price and Q is output. Demand is given by $Q = 11 - P$.

   What will price and output be if there is no dominant firm? Now assume that there is a dominant firm, whose marginal cost is constant at \$6. Derive the residual demand curve that it faces and calculate its profit-maximizing output and price.

2. The prisoners' dilemma provides insight into much more than price-fixing, as the next three questions indicate.[53]

   a. People often complain that conversations at cocktail parties (where there is no music) are so loud that they have trouble understanding the conversation they are engaged in. Using a prisoners' dilemma game, show why you would expect this problem to arise.
   b. Jones and Smith are sharing a 2-quart bowl of popcorn. Use prisoners' dilemma logic to show that they will finish the popcorn more quickly than if each of them were given their own 1-quart bowl.
   c. The prisoners' dilemma can also explain the emergence of social conventions, such as driving on the right side of the road. Construct a prisoners' dilemma matrix to show that having everyone drive on one side of the road will be a unanimous choice, but we cannot predict whether it will be the left or right side.

3. In the grim trigger example of the text, show that if the discount rate is low enough it pays the potential cheater to adhere to the agreement for two (or more) periods rather than break it in the first period.

   Extra credit: Calculate the maximum discount rate at which she will keep to the agreement for two periods rather than just one.

   What happens to the incentive to cheat as a person's discount rate approaches zero?

4. The Jones Company produces a deluxe auto that is powerful and stylish. The Smith Company (the only other manufacturer) produces an ugly but equally powerful car. Each must decide whether to charge a low or a high price, with profits given by:

		Smith	
		High Price	**Low Price**
Jones	**High Price**	\$200, \$130	\$130, \$160
	Low Price	\$100, \$50	\$60, \$110

   Show that Smith's dominant strategy is to charge a low price, which forces the solution into the northeast corner, and that Jones would prefer to be in the northwest corner.

   Jones tries to get his way by threatening to charge a low price. Assuming that they play the game just once, explain why he cannot possibly win by using this threat.

[53]They are taken from Donald McCloskey's out-of-print text *The Applied Theory of Price* (New York: Macmillan, 1985), 461.

5. Find the Nash Equilibrium of the game in the following matrix, and explain how you did it:

		Smith	
		Left	Right
Jones	Top	\$7, \$8	\$9, \$3
	Bottom	\$5, \$5	\$6, \$6

6. Show that the Nash equilibrium of the following game is for Jones to play Top and Smith to play Left.

		Smith		
		Left	Center	Right
Jones	Top	\$8, \$6	\$9, \$4	\$6, \$9
	Middle	\$5, \$10	\$4, \$7	\$7, \$8
	Bottom	\$4, \$7	\$1, \$2	\$1, \$9

7. (Requires calculus) The following matrix shows why we may not see many people playing chicken in real life. Assume that Jones and Smith are playing it and the payoffs are:

		Smith	
		Straight	**Turn**
Jones	**Straight**	−\$100, −\$100	\$50, −\$40
	Turn	−\$40, \$50	\$0, \$0

Show that in the Nash equilibrium each goes straight with probability of 0.36 (i.e., 40/110). Then show that the expected payoff for each player is negative.

When the value to each driver of winning is \$50, they will not play the game. How high must this amount be (for each of them) for a driver to want to play because the game now has a positive expected value? (Hint: the probabilities associated with the strategies must change when the numbers change.)

8. The previous problem also helps explain the logic of another classic movie, Stanley Kubrick's *Dr. Strangelove.* At the beginning of the movie, which is set during the Cold War, the audience learns that the Soviet Union has built a doomsday machine, a collection of nuclear warheads that when set off will kill all life on earth. It has been built and programmed to go off if the United States bombs the Soviet Union, whether with a single bomb or a mass attack. Sensors in the doomsday machine will detect the bombing and start its operation. Once it begins no one can take the machine off-line. One minor mistake occurs in the movie: the Soviets have inexplicably delayed announcing the existence of the doomsday machine to the Americans, and during that interval a rogue U.S. general has sent planes to bomb the Russians.

Show that this scenario is roughly equivalent to a game of chicken if both sides know of the machine's existence.

Then show what happens if the doomsday machine's existence is not known to the United States.

9. In this game, assume that Smith may not fully understand the rules or know all of the payoffs to both him and Smith. If so, can it be rational for Jones to play Top? How does the usual definition of rationality (from Chapter 1) change in this situation?

		Smith	
		Left	**Right**
Jones	**Top**	\$100, \$100	\$500, \$300
	Bottom	−\$10,000, \$90	\$900, \$200

10. A selfless person approaches Jones and Smith with a \$100 bill and offers to sell it to the highest bidder, but both the winning and losing bidders must pay her their bids. So if Jones bids \$2 and Smith bids \$1 they pay a total of \$3, but Jones gets the money, leaving him with a net gain of \$98 and Smith with −\$1. If both bid the same amount, the \$100 is split evenly between them. Assume that each of them has only two \$1 bills on hand, leaving three possible bids: \$0, \$1, or \$2. Write out the payoff matrix for this game, and then find its Nash equilibrium.

11. In baseball, a pitcher faces a batter. If hit, the coming pitch will produce the game-winning run, if not the team loses. There are two types of pitch—a fastball and a curve. If the batter swings at the fastball he will hit it out of the park, but if he does not swing it will be strike three. If the batter swings at a curve ball he will likely miss it, but if he lets it go by he will walk and the winning run will come home. (Disregard foul balls.)

    Construct a game that portrays this situation and show that it has a solution in mixed strategies.

    Then ask how the pitcher's and batter's choices will change if (1) instead of the ninth inning it is the first, and (2) if there is only one out, but the next to bat (as in the National League) will be the pitcher. (Assume that a pinch hitter is unavailable.)

12. (Requires calculus) Three Cournot oligopolists, all with constant and identical marginal costs of \$5, serve a market with demand $Q = 15 - P$.

    Calculate their equilibrium output and show that it is three-fourths of the perfectly competitive level. Also show that it is 50 percent above the monopoly level.

    Two of them now consider merging. If they merge they can better coordinate operations, and their marginal costs will fall to \$2 at all outputs. What happens to market output? To the profit of the nonmerging firm? To the profit of the merged firm? Does this outcome seem odd to you?

13. On a diagram whose axes are the quantities produced by two identical Cournot oligopolists and compare them with a perfect price-fixing agreement that splits the monopoly profits between them. Then in the same diagram show the Stackelberg equilibrium output with one firm a leader and the other a follower. Compare it with the previous two situations.

Chapter 8

Competition and Strategy

INTRODUCTION

Another Endangered Species—The Supermarket

On February 21, 2005, Winn-Dixie Stores, Inc. filed for bankruptcy after losing $553 million in its last two fiscal quarters. The nation's eighth largest food retailer, Winn-Dixie intended to survive by closing more than 30 percent of its stores and restructuring its debt obligations.[1] Twenty-six major grocers went bankrupt between 2000 and 2005, some of them familiar regional names like Big Bear and Pathmark. Other financially troubled chains have merged or allowed themselves to be acquired. Size, however, does not always mean success. In May 2006, the shareholders of poorly performing number two chain Albertson's approved its acquisition by a consortium led by Supervalu stores.[2]

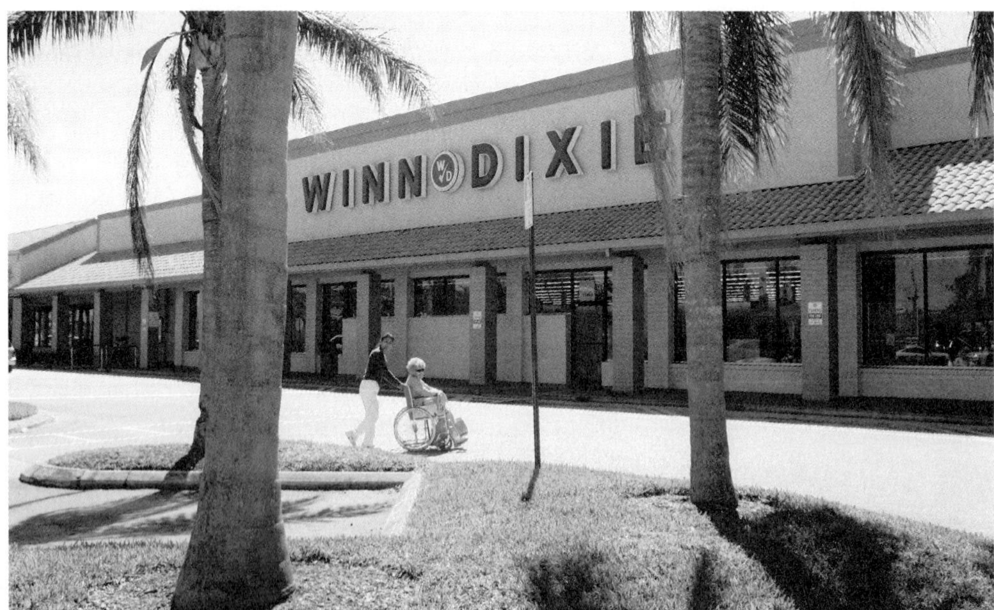

AP Photo/J. Pat Carter

[1]"Big Grocers Under Stress," *Christian Science Monitor*, February 25, 2005. Winn-Dixie had returned to viability by 2008, crediting an ongoing program of major store remodels for the change. See Winn-Dixie 2008 Annual Report to Shareholders, http://library.corporate-ir.net/library/78/787/78738/items/308708/52823WinnDixieARFull.pdf.

[2]"Investors Approve Sale of Albertson's," *Orange County Register*, May 30, 2006.

Supermarkets that dominated grocery retailing in the twentieth century are losing their customers in the twenty-first. Between 1920 and 1970, supermarkets innovated to win customers from small retailers with few locations and smaller inventories, often known (inaccurately) as "mom and pop" stores. Improved highways and cheap refrigeration lowered their cost of managing centralized distribution networks. The industry structure also changed as the chains eliminated intermediaries who repackaged goods into small lots for resale to small stores. Supermarkets thrived with the growth of the suburbs, bringing variety and convenient hours to customers whose time had grown in value. Competition also took the form of service offerings. Customers no longer had to wait for clerks to reach for items on shelves after Clarence Saunders initiated self-service at his Memphis Piggly Wiggly store in 1916. Other stores in the chain introduced the checkout stand.[3]

Q. Most chain-store managers today would not be allowed to install an innovation as radical (and it was at the time) as the checkout stand. Why the difference between today's industry and that of the early twentieth century?

Managements of chains large and small are searching for strategies to restore their former dominance. Customers have changed—households contain fewer persons, and their members are increasingly concerned about health and food quality. Prior to the 2008-2009 recession 33 percent of shoppers were purchasing ready-to-eat foods, a figure that was growing at 4.5 percent per year.[4] Even in the recession 80 percent of supermarket delis continued to record sales growth, as did their wine departments.[5] Supermarkets face new forms of competition and new types of competitors. "Grocers don't know who they are," said one consultant. "They're fighting Wal-Mart on one flank. They have a store within a store to fight the natural foods marketplace. They're doing prepared foods on another flank. They have lost any kind of meaning to a particular customer."[6] Some supermarkets are trying to meet the challenge of convenience stores by extending their hours and selling gasoline, while others are opening smaller outlets. They have not coped well with discounters—Wal-Mart opened 1,700 Supercenters between 1988 and 2005, while major chains were closing stores.[7] Supermarkets may also have problems competing with smaller stores—British retailer Tesco has begun rolling out Fresh & Easy markets in California and the Southwest. These smaller stores devote larger percentages of their space to prepared items and fresh meats and vegetables for upwardly mobile consumers, while deemphasizing commodities like detergent and pet foods.[8] At the other

---

[3]See the Piggly Wiggly Web site at http://www.pigglywiggly.com/about-us. Innovations are not always as obvious as they seem in retrospect. The shopping cart first appeared in the mid-1930s at a Piggly Wiggly in Oklahoma City; Birgit Lohman, "The (All American) History of Shopping (Carts)," Designboom.com Web site, http://www.designboom.com/history/cart.html.

[4]Steve Martinez, *The U.S. Food Marketing System, Recent Developments 1997–2006*, U.S. Department of Agriculture Economic Research Report, 42 (May 2007), http://www.ers.usda.gov/publications/err42/err42.pdf.

[5]"Deli Meals, Comfort Food Drive In-Store Sales," *Progressive Grocer*, September 27, 2009 http://www.progressivegrocer.com/progressivegrocer/content_display/supermarket-industry-news/e3i74b60625ee3a4565fd072742a938a7fc; "U.S. Wine Consumption Still Rising," *Progressive Grocer*, September, 28, 2009. http://www.progressivegrocer.com/progressivegrocer/content_display/supermarket-industry-news/e3ife9d9d88fcefbcdcd3a7811e08b25c1e.

[6]"Big Grocers Under Stress," *Christian Science Monitor*.

[7]Martinez, 8.

[8]See the Rresh & Easy Web site at http://www.freshandeasy.com/.

end, SuperValu subsidiary Save-A-Lot has opened more than a thousand stores in lower-income areas that carry limited inventories. Save-A-Lot announces upfront that it does not have lobster tanks, latte stands, sushi bars, and floral departments.[9] Foreign-owned retailers sold 17.7 percent of U.S. groceries in 2005, up from 6.8 percent in 1988.[10]

Q. Unlike most other grocery stores, 75 percent of Save-A-Lots are franchises rather than under company ownership. Give some possible explanations for the difference between them and more upscale chains.

Individual stores and brands have some market power, but competition rules at all levels of the industry.[11] Food producers vie for space on retailers' shelves. In 1997, in addition to fresh items, 320,000 different packaged foods were available in U.S. grocery stores. A typical supermarket holds 50,000 products, and in 2005 18,722 new products competed with them for shelf space.[12] Competition takes the form of response to changing buyer preferences. Over 4,500 of 2005's new products claimed that they were "natural," "organic," low fat, low sugar, or high vitamin.[13] Fresh food is also competitive—one California wholesaler was first to market kiwi fruit, brown mushrooms, alfalfa sprouts, spaghetti squash, and jicama. It responded to the rise in immigration from Asia by introducing products that range from fuzzy melons to chrysanthemum leaves.[14]

Q. Many chains insist that producers of new products they are considering retailing purchase their shelf space by buying up the store's inventory of the products they are replacing. Explain why this practice is not necessarily evidence of the chain's market power.

The supermarket saga is about competitive reality. Many important facts about competition defy summarization in the simple diagrams that served so well in earlier chapters. Competition is about disequilibrium, and all too often it lacks happy endings. In the perfectly competitive market of Chapter 5 all producers were price-takers selling identical goods. Food retailing is far from this—sellers compete on price (Wal-Mart), hours (7-Eleven), variety (Wegman's, or your local equivalent), organic purity (Whole Foods), snob appeal (Southern California's Gelson's, or your local equivalent), and location, to name just a few attributes that might matter. This chapter builds on earlier models to

---

[9]See the Save-A-Lot Web site at http://save-a-lot.com/shopping-at-save-a-lot.

[10]Besides Tesco they include Holland's Ahold (Stop & Shop, Giant), A&P (originally American, now German), and Belgium's Delhaize (Food Lion, Hannaford).

[11]This does not necessarily mean that prices just cover costs, as in the long-run equilibrium of a perfectly competitive market. Some studies have shown that markets with fewer competing supermarkets have higher markups over cost than markets with more sellers. See Ronald W. Cotterill, "Market Power in the Retail Food Industry: Evidence from Vermont," *Review of Economics and Statistics* 68 (August 1986): 379–386.

[12]Martinez, 34.

[13]Martinez, 37.

[14]See the Frieda's Web site at http://friedas.com/index.cfm.

redirect our thinking about competition and business decisions. Rivalry among the grocers is nearly the polar opposite of the passive price-taking we saw in perfect competition. Each supplier is actively strategizing to earn and protect profits above opportunity cost, and each is subject to constant threats from innovators and imitators. This chapter will cover:

- How competition is rivalry to obtain a distinct advantage—paradoxically, competitive strategy is an attempt to obtain market power that yields profits.
- Why your knowledge of heuristics and selection bias should usually lead you to question popular explanations of why businesses succeed or fail.
- How to categorize and analyze competitive strategies using the tools we developed to study economic value, competition, and market power.
- How both market participants and outsiders can affect the benefits that buyers and sellers realize from their transactions.
- How mergers and lawful agreements among competitors can sometimes increase the economic value that is created in a market.
- How seemingly restrictive "vertical" agreements between manufacturers and dealers or parent companies and franchisees can increase competition and benefit consumers.
- Strategies for protecting profits from competitors and counterstrategies for competitors. They can involve both customer relationships and intangibles like trademarks and patents.
- The costs and benefits of attempting to compete by influencing public opinion or government policy.
- How a business can identify tangible and intangible competitive resources and formulate strategies that make the best use of them.

Competitive Behavior

Competition: A Quest to Be Exceptional

Competitive Ideas Competition starts with ideas. Asked how he had produced so many good ideas over his career, Nobel Prize–winning chemist Linus Pauling responded that "the best way to have a good idea is to have lots of ideas."[15] Even the most original ideas build on a foundation of other ideas.[16] Good ideas are a small subset of all ideas, and so are profitable ones. Successful competitive ideas need not be big, or even very original. Many pathbreaking innovations have failed, while seemingly minor ones have made their originators wealthy. A competitive idea is not necessarily a scientific one—it may be as simple as opening a business in an underserved location, keeping it open all night, or outrightly imitating the success of a competitor. Ideas are only worthwhile in context. An all-night store may make sense in Manhattan, but a 24/7 operation in rural

---

[15]The quote appears at the Quote Lady Web site at http://www.quotelady.com/subjects/ideas.html.

[16]For more on the economics of ideas, see the work of economist Paul Romer. A nontechnical summary appears in Kevin Kelly, "The Economics of Ideas," *Wired,* June 1996.

Maine is probably a loser.[17] Execution matters. Amazon.com and eBay are among the few early Internet marketers that turned the corner on profit while thousands folded without a trace.

No one can know in advance if a particular idea is a winner. Its originator is often understandably optimistic, quite possibly overoptimistic. Those who supply capital (their savings) to implement an idea must make their own evaluations. They too can make errors, as happened in the rush to Internet-related ventures during the dot-com days of 1997 to 2000. An innovator may start a business with her own funds, but some ideas (think FedEx, which can only succeed with nationwide service) are harder to scale down than others. Ideas often exist in an environment of uncertainty, and there may be no objective way to determine their probabilities of success. Ideas that later prove to have been winners may go unsupported while losing ones get funded. Despite these uncertainties, economics allows us to analyze competitive ideas and their implementation, often using the models we have already studied.

The Paradox: Competing to Acquire Market Power When sellers are active rivals the textbook distinctions between monopoly and competition become blurred. Businesses compete to distinguish themselves in the eyes of customers, and by becoming distinctive they acquire some market power. A business implements a risky competitive idea for the promise of high returns on it. A person with no competitive ideas can earn the market average return at low risk just by investing in a diversified stock portfolio. The possibility of high returns induces risk taking, but those returns may be short-lived as imitators and other innovators erode them. Of course, the original innovator might also devise strategies to extend the life of those gains.

The competition that now interests us is quite unlike what we saw in the model of a perfectly competitive market. That market was purposely an extreme case that allowed us to understand equilibrium and see how it depended on certain economic assumptions—price-taking behavior, identical products, easy entry, and abundant information. In actual markets, businesses often compete by discounting prices rather than taking the equilibrium price as given and unalterable. Business try to bind customers to themselves using techniques like frequent-flier miles or other loyalty programs. They can compete by redesigning their offerings rather than selling identical goods or services. Advertising has no role to play if information is free, but in real markets advertising is valuable to buyers who might not know that a business exists or where it is located. The perfectly competitive model still anchors much of our reasoning about markets, but now we must extend it to more realistic situations.

The Risks of Competition Competition is risky, particularly for small startups. Reliable data on the formation and survival of startups are hard to obtain, because many never obtain licenses or pay taxes as incorporated entities.[18] The U.S. Bureau of Labor Statistics reports that 2.9 million businesses involving 4 million persons were founded in 1997. In addition, 700,000 existing businesses were sold to others. More than two-thirds of new businesses start at home. Only about 40 percent of startups show accounting profits over their lifetimes, which may not cover their opportunity costs. Thirty percent break even and 30 percent are losers.[19] Of new businesses started in 1998, 66 percent survived to 2000 and 44 percent to 2002. (Some non-survivors were acquired.) Internet-related

---

[17]Or maybe not. Outfitter L.L. Bean is open 24 hours, 365 days a year in tiny Freeport, a 2.5-hour drive from Boston. See the company's Web site at http://www.llbean.com.

[18]Taxes on their profits are paid with the owner's personal income tax.

[19]Taken from Karen E. Klein, "What's Behind High Small-Biz Failure Rates?" *Business Week Online*, September 30, 1999, http://www.businessweek.com/smallbiz/news/coladvice/ask/sa990930.htm.

businesses started in the dot-com boom years had poorer survival chances: 63 percent lasted for two years and 38 percent for four.[20] The U.S. Small Business Administration provides statistics on trends. Between 1988 and 2003, firms with employees increased from 4.9 to 5.7 million (up 15.0 percent), and sole proprietorships increased from 13.7 to 18.7 million (36.5 percent).[21] Between 1999 and 2006, an annual average of 614,000 firms with employees opened and 561,000 closed.[22]

Competition and Deception

Competitive conditions constrain the freedom of all producers, whether they face many competitors or few. A seller with market power has more choices than a perfect competitor who can only charge the equilibrium price. Sellers who operate in markets that are not perfectly competitive, however, can also devise new ways to create economic value. In this chapter we continue to assume that buyers and sellers act rationally on information that is available to them. In particular we rule out strategies that only succeed if one side can deceive the other.

In one such folktale a retailer sells a loss-leader product below cost to entice customers into the store. After they arrive they overpay for items that are cheaper elsewhere. Of course, suspicious customers will either avoid the store or buy only the loss leader, making the strategy unprofitable. Temporary discounts might reflect overstocks, price discrimination (see Chapter 6), or investments in customer loyalty. A free sample can provide information that induces subsequent purchases, as when a software supplier's free demonstration download informs people about the value of owning it. Razor-blade producers, for example, give away holders to reduce changeover costs. Other strategies, like frequent-flyer mileage programs, raise their members' costs of switching airlines. In cases like these it usually makes more sense to assume that consumers understand the logic and are not fooled.

Q. The law defines "predatory pricing" as selling below cost in hopes of driving a rival out of the market. Are free samples examples of predatory pricing? Explain why or why not.

Pitfalls in Studying Competition

Selection Bias, Again Books about strategy are often written by consultants who recount how managers of major corporations successfully adopted the ideas they are discussing. As noted in Chapter 1, their readers should be on the lookout for selection bias. The only information given the reader is that Company X used Strategy A and

[20]The figures are from the U.S. Bureau of Labor Statistics. See Amy E. Knaup, "Survival and Longevity in the Business Employment Dynamics Data," *Monthly Labor Review*, May 2005, 50–56, http://www.gpoaccess.gov/eop/2005/2005_erp.pdf. We can only collect data like these with a substantial time lag.

[21]These businesses do not include farms. U.S. Small Business Administration, *The Small Business Economy 2004: A Report to the President,* Appendix Table A-1, http://www.sba.gov/advo/stats/sb_econ2004.pdf. During this period, the adult population grew by 20.8 percent, and real gross domestic product grew by 61.5 percent. See U.S. President's Council of Economic Advisors, *Economic Report of the President 2005,* Appendix B, Tables B-2 and B-34, http://www.gpoaccess.gov/eop/2005/2005_erp.pdf.

[22]U.S. Small Business Administration, *The Small Business Economy 2009*, 103, http://www.sba.gov/advo/research/sb_econ2009.pdf. Preliminary data indicate a decrease in openings and an increase in closings with the 2008-2009 recession.

prospered. Absent other documentation the reader should treat Company X as a nonrandom sample of size one, an observation that is handy to make the author's point. Even if the author mentions several firms that succeeded with Strategy A, the reader is likely to remain in the dark about (1) those that used Strategy A and failed, and (2) those that rejected Strategy A and succeeded. Even if these additional data are somehow available, determining that Strategy A is the true source of success requires a deeper analysis. Limits on our abilities to process information can compound the problems of selection bias, as seen in Chapter 1. We also know that people recall successes more easily than failures, and they give more weight to more recent experiences. Our recall is biased, and we must often use data that are not random samples of underlying populations.

What's Wal-Mart's Secret? Today's books on management and economics probably devote more space to Wal-Mart than any other corporation, but they appear unable to agree on the sources of Wal-Mart's success. Like it or not, no one really knows why Wal-Mart has attained its stardom.[23] Let's examine an incomplete list of possible explanations:

- *Decentralized decision-making*: Store managers have authority to stock items and price them to satisfy localized demands, such as apparel that names high school teams.
- *Centralized decision-making*: Wal-Mart is such a large buyer of standard consumer goods that it can aggressively bargain down prices.
- *Decision-making between the center and the stores*: Wal-Mart's warehousing and distribution system cuts costs in ways that are unavailable to even its largest rivals.
- *Regional relationships*: Unlike many other nationwide stores, most of Wal-Mart's regional managers are at headquarters rather than in the field. This allows them easy contact with colleagues, particularly at the company's famed Saturday morning meetings.[24]
- *Relationships with employees*: Wal-Mart rewards ideas from low-level employees and encourages them to be team players, and it has a reputation for merit-based promotions. At the same time it works actively to discourage unionization.
- *Using economics to determine strategy*: Some economics textbooks claim that Wal-Mart pre-empts competitors.[25] It opens large stores with low operating costs in small markets, leaving little room for new competitors to compete with it on price.[26]

With a little research and imagination you can certainly add to this list. However long or short it is, without a far deeper study of Wal-Mart and its competitors (including vanished ones) you will be unable to determine the actual sources of its success. How best to compete against Wal-Mart depends on its resources and yours. Does relatively successful Target use Wal-Mart's practices, or does it have some resource (stylish merchandise

---

[23]If you think you know Wal-Mart's secret (but the rest of us do not), invest in some other firm that faces Wal-Mart's market situation and uses Wal-Mart's strategy. Alternatively, short the stock of one that does not use it.

[24]Brent Schlender, "Wal-Mart's $288 Billion Meeting," *Fortune*, April 4, 2005.

[25]See, for example, William Samuelson and Stephen Marks, *Managerial Economics*, 4th ed. (New York: Wiley, 2003), 464; or James Brickley, Clifford Smith, and Jerold Zimmerman, *Managerial Economics and Organizational Architecture*, 3rd ed. (New York: McGraw-Hill, 2004), 241.

[26]The data show that this strategy generally benefits Wal-Mart's customers, whatever it does for profits. Wal-Mart's opening in a city soon brings price declines averaging 1.5 to 3 percent for basic household items, and in the long run it cuts them by 7 to 13 percent. The effects are greatest in relatively smaller cities. See Emek Basker, "Selling a Cheaper Mousetrap: Wal-Mart's Effect on Retail Prices," *Journal of Urban Economics* 58 (2005): 203–229.

marketed with stylish advertising) that Wal-Mart (whose advertising theme is a smiley face) cannot easily duplicate? If Wal-Mart's massive scale and nonunion wages matter, how has Costco succeeded with only 20 percent of Wal-Mart's sales and unionized workers who average $40,000 a year after four years?[27] The list of reasons also says little about unsuccessful competitors (Sears) or failed ones (Kmart), whose distribution strategies and buying power nearly match Wal-Mart's. Their merger was heavily criticized when announced, and in retrospect the critics appear to have been correct.[28]

Self-Serving Recommendations The structure of corporate business further complicates the analysis of strategy. A corporation's executives and board of directors might make choices that are in their personal interests rather than those of their shareholders, who would prefer decisions that maximize the values of their stock. As will be seen in Chapter 12, managers whose firms produce substantial free cash flows may prefer to spend them on questionable acquisitions that often fail to benefit shareholders. Such acquisitions, however, give managers a larger firm to run, which generally means higher pay and more prestige in the community.

It should not surprise you that management books and consultants often advise executives to grow their companies, a message that many executives will be happy to hear. The books frequently treat CEOs like General Electric's (GE) now-retired Jack Welch as examples worth following. During Welch's tenure, GE indeed performed well for its shareholders (in a generally rising market). The company made many acquisitions, some quite unrelated to its core businesses. In reality, Welch was almost unique—although he succeeded, most corporations with strategies like GE's underperformed stock market averages, and those that invested farthest from their cores did the worst. Welch later said that his vision was to "move away from businesses that were being commoditized toward businesses that manufactured high-value technology products or sold services instead of things," a statement that could rationalize almost any acquisition but might impress superficial readers.[29] A frequent consequence of takeovers that occurred in the 1980s and 1990s was divestiture of poorly performing acquisitions made by the companies' former management teams.[30]

Creating Economic Value

The Basics: One Seller and One Buyer

Buyer and seller both benefit from exchanging some good if the seller gets more than his opportunity cost (i.e., the value of the best forgone alternative), and the buyer pays less than her valuation (maximum willingness to pay for it before going elsewhere). *Economic value* is the difference between the cost and valuation that they share. Figure 8-1a is our starting point. With no transaction costs, buyer and seller will both benefit from a price between the $7 opportunity cost and the $11 valuation. The price they settle on determines how they share the $4 value created. In this section we examine strategies to increase that value.

[27]"The Only Company Wal-Mart Fears," *Fortune*, November 24, 2003, http://www.fortune.com/fortune/subs/article/0,15114,538834,00.html (Subscription required).

[28]For some unfavorable opinions see "Kmart-Sears Deal Won't Pose Much of a Threat to Wal-Mart," *Wall Street Journal*, November 24, 2004. For a retrospective see "Sears Responds to Its Critics," *New York Times*, July 4, 2007.

[29]Jack Welch, "It's All in the Sauce," *Fortune*, April 18, 2005, 138–144.

[30]See Sanjai Bhagat et al., "Hostile Takeovers in the 1980s: The Return to Corporate Specialization," *Brookings Papers on Economic Activity Microeconomics*, no. 1 (1990): 1–84.

FIGURE 8-1
Changing Costs and Valuations to Increase the Benefits of Exchange

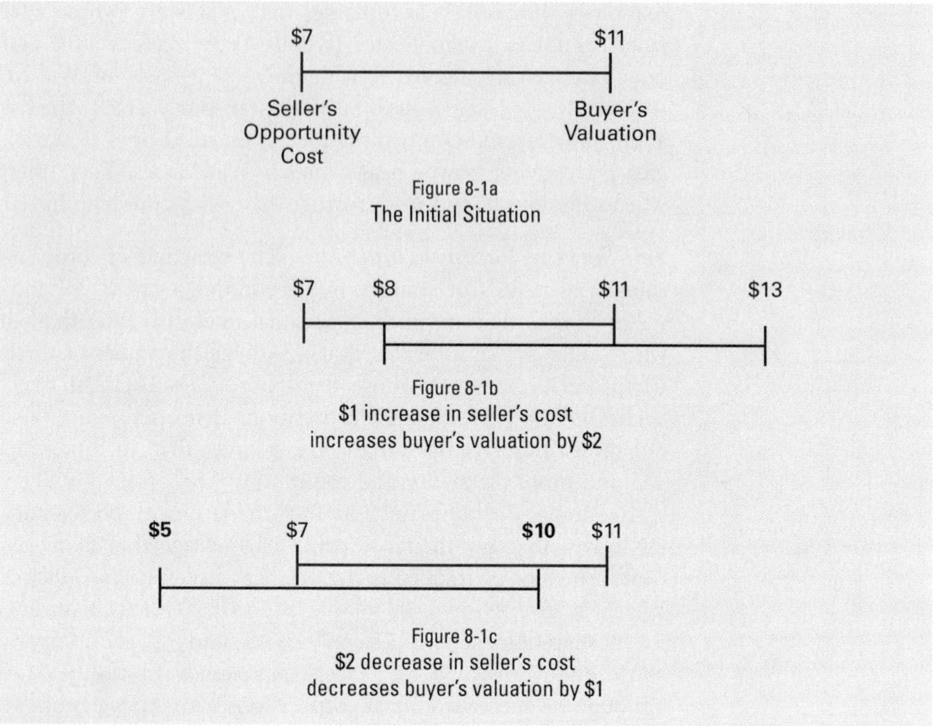

Raising the Purchaser's Valuation In Figure 8-1b, the seller chooses to incur a cost of $1 to alter his good's characteristics, possibly by improving its quality or making it available closer to the buyer's home. If this raises her valuation by $2, an additional $1 of economic value is created net of the seller's cost. If they originally traded at $9, the seller will spend $1 to improve the product, as long as the buyer pays more than $10 for it. Because any price below $11 brings the buyer greater benefits than the old $9 transaction did, both parties benefit from a price between $10 and $11.

Lowering the Seller's Costs Next, let the seller devise a way to cut production costs from $7 to $5 while the buyer's valuation remains $11, so that a transaction now creates $2 more economic value. If they formerly transacted at $9, any price between $7 and $9 leaves them both better off. For a more general example, the seller in Figure 8-1c reduces cost by $2, which in this case lowers quality and reduces the buyer's valuation by $1. If they originally traded at $9, any price between $7 and $8 leaves them both better off. The good's quality may have been lowered, but the seller's activity has created another $1 of value.

Q. Show that if the seller and buyer in Figure 8-1b formerly transacted at $9, any price between $7 and $9 leaves both buyer and seller better off.

Q. Unlike the buyer in Figure 8-1c, Jones places a very high value on the services this retailer formerly offered. Show that if the retailer institutes a discount strategy Jones will probably stop dealing with it.

Lowering Transaction Costs by the Trading Parties Like all costs, transaction costs involve forgone opportunities. Figure 8-2 shows two possible ways in which cutting transaction costs can create value.[31] In Figure 8-2a assume that without transaction costs the buyer's valuation would be $16, and the seller's production cost is $5. Transaction costs are also $5, and $2 is borne by the seller and $3 by the buyer. The upper horizontal line in Figure 8-2a shows $6 of value that remains to be shared. A seller who cuts his transaction costs by $1 creates an additional $1 of value that he might choose to pocket or share with buyers depending on the situation. (Possibly a reduction in the price of the good will attract a large number of new buyers.) The buyer might also cut her transaction costs by $1, but it is hard to envision how or why she might share the savings. If she saves gasoline by driving a hybrid car to the seller's place of business the seller has no obvious way to capture any of those benefits. If both buyer and seller cut their transaction costs by $1, the economic value they can share will be $8.

Reducing the Other Party's Transaction Costs The seller can also create economic value by reducing the buyer's transaction costs, as long as doing so does not increase his own costs by more. He might open a store that is more convenient for the buyer and charge higher prices, but not so high that the buyer is better off driving to a cheaper outlet. Figure 8-2b again shows $6 of value net of transaction costs. If the seller spends

FIGURE 8-2
Creation of Economic Value by Reducing Transaction Costs

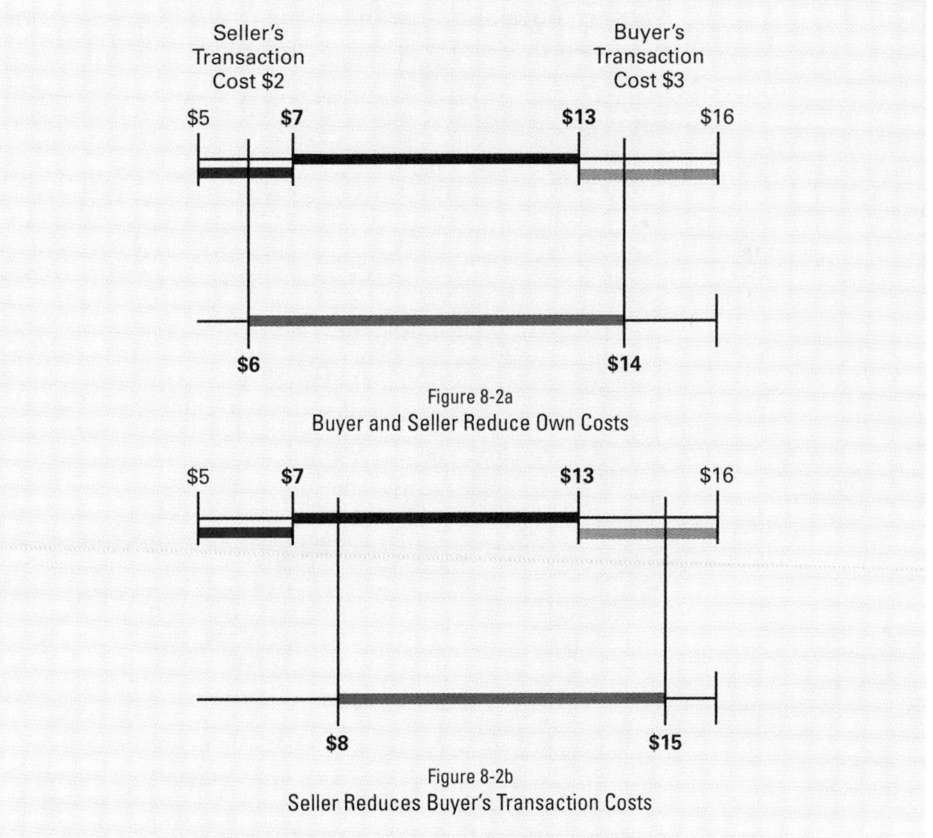

[31]In Chapter 2 we treated transaction costs as a reduction of the gains from exchange relative to the situation with no transaction costs, and we were uninterested in exactly who had to bear them. Here the identity of the bearer can matter, and the diagrams are slightly different.

$1 to cut the buyer's transaction cost by $2, additional value is created. The range of trading prices also changes, because the seller will not accept less than $8 while the buyer will pay up to $15. An outsider could also act to reduce the buyer's and seller's transaction costs. That party might be able to extract a profit from the buyer and/or seller but leave them both better off than if they had done the deal by themselves.

Q. Construct a graph like those in Figure 8-2 to show that a broker who can lower total transaction costs makes both the trading parties and herself better off.

One Seller, Many Buyers

If you are a seller you can compete by distinguishing yourself in hopes of attracting buyers who will pay a premium for whatever makes you distinctive—location, product design, service, and so on. Becoming distinctive means you are acquiring market power. You face a down-sloping demand curve for your good or service, but one that is more elastic the greater the ability of your buyers to substitute away from it. Assume for now that you must charge everyone the same price and are not yet considering any competitors' reactions.

Raising Buyers' Valuations *Raising valuation by increasing variable cost.* Just as in the two-person case, you can incur costs to increase buyers' valuations. You might use

FIGURE 8-3
Increasing Valuation

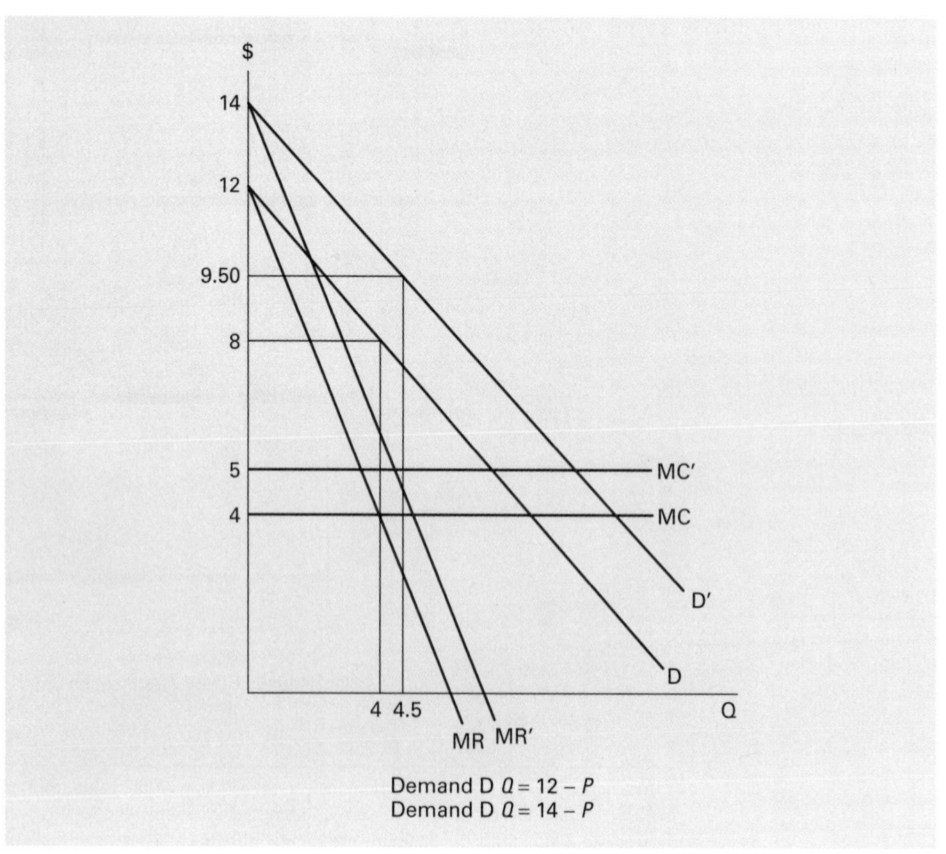

costlier inputs to improve your product's durability or the quality of the service you produce, for example. Figure 8-3 shows that your success will depend on the relationship between changes in your cost and changes in your buyers' valuations. Initially, demand is D and marginal cost is MC, constant at \$4. You produce 4 units per year that sell for \$8 each, for a profit of \$16. Assume that increasing your marginal cost by \$1 (i.e., to MC′) shifts the demand curve upward by \$2 for every unit to D′. Marginal revenue shifts to MR′, and you now maximize profit by selling 4.5 units per year for \$9.50 each. Profit is now \$20.25, so the strategy works.

Q. Show that MR′, is parallel to MR.

Raising valuation by incurring fixed costs. Figure 8-4 starts from the demand and cost curves of Figure 8-3, but now we assume that you can raise consumers' valuations of your product by making an investment that increases fixed costs while leaving marginal cost unchanged. You might, for example, build a new plant that produces fewer defective units of output from the same variable inputs as before. Assume that the new plant lasts forever and that the higher quality of its output raises the demand curve by \$2. You now maximize profit by raising output from 4 to 5 units per year and selling them for \$9 each. To see whether the plant is worth building, you must balance the additional revenue attributable to the new plant over the future against its cost. To do so requires calculation of the present values of future payment streams, which are discussed in Chapter 16. In common sense terms, however, you will generally not be willing to pay more per year to buy or rent the plant than the \$9 difference between your post-investment profit (\$25) and your original profit (\$16).

FIGURE 8-4
Investment to Increase Valuation

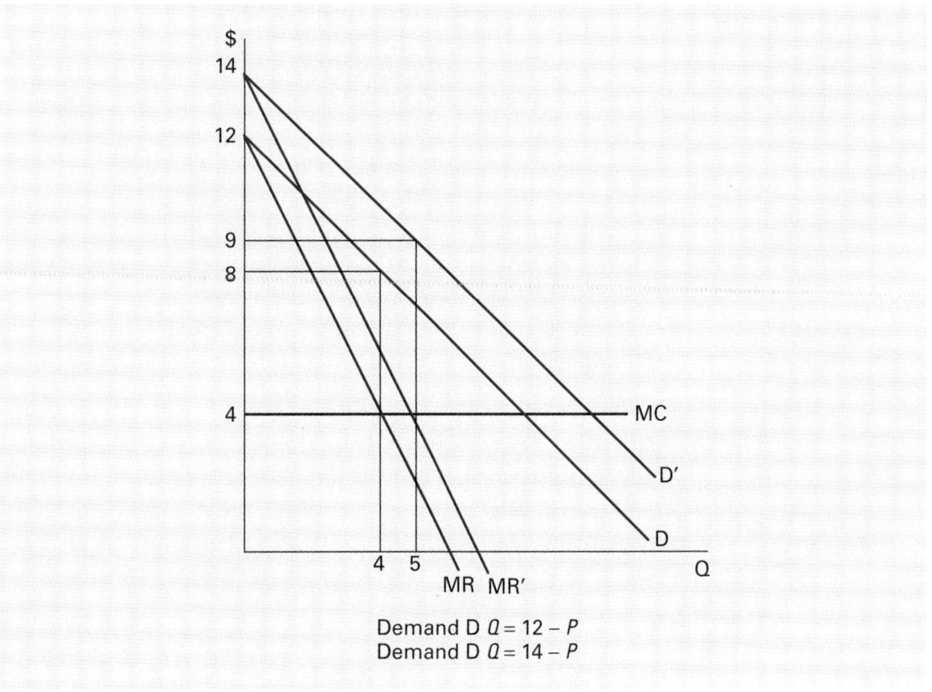

FIGURE 8-5
Lowering Production Cost

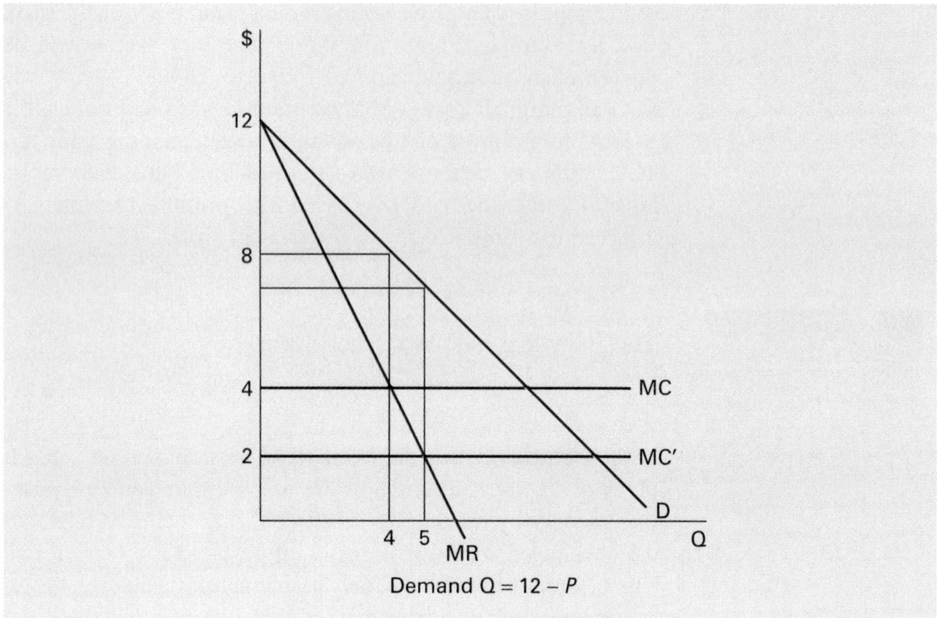

Lowering Production Costs Starting over, assume that you devise a way to cut marginal cost from $4 (MC) to $2 (MC′) while leaving buyers' valuations unchanged, as shown in Figure 8-5. You increase output to 5 units and cut price to $7. Before considering fixed costs, your annual profit rises from $16 to $25, so you would again pay up to $9 per year to invest in a plant that can produce at a marginal cost of $2.

Risk management. Say you manage an airline whose marginal costs are largely fuel-related, but you can hedge its price risk with futures, options, or other derivatives, as described in Chapter 3. If you think fuel prices are unlikely to rise you do not buy the derivatives and take your chances in the spot market. Airlines have different expectations and choose different hedging policies. Before a late 2004 run-up in oil prices, Southwest Airlines had hedged approximately half of its fuel purchases while other carriers hedged less or none at all. Southwest was one of only two major airlines to report a profit during that period. Of course, had fuel prices stayed low, the costs of Southwest's hedges would have weighed on its earnings and competitors who did not hedge would have won their gambles.[32] Between July 2008 and January 2009, world oil prices fell from $147 a barrel to below $40. As they did, Southwest paid above-market prices for fuel that its less-hedged competitors got at market prices. Southwest took a loss of $117 million in the last quarter of 2008.[33]

Reducing Transaction Costs *Per-unit transaction costs.* The seller in Figure 8-6 incurs transaction costs on each unit sold. Marginal production costs per unit are $4, and transaction costs are $1, so the seller's full marginal costs are $5, shown as MC′. Buyers incur their own transaction costs of $2 per unit, the vertical difference between D and

[32] "Southwest Airlines Net Income Soars," *Los Angeles Times*, April 15, 2005.

[33] "Southwest Soars Despite Fuel Costs," *Forbes*, January 22, 2009.

FIGURE 8-6
Seller and Buyer Transaction Costs

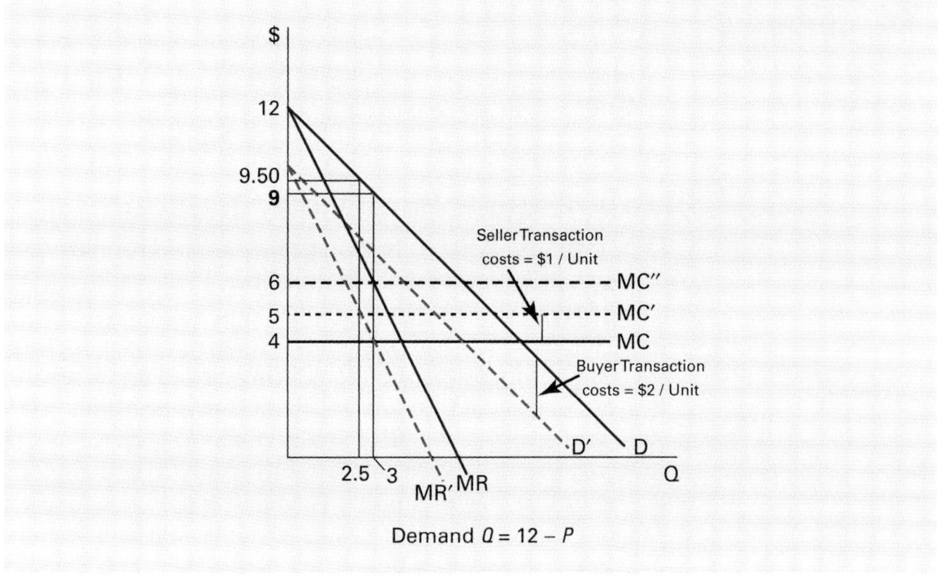

D′. D shows buyers' valuations, but a buyer who faces $2 in transaction costs will pay a seller at most the corresponding amount on D′. Initially, marginal cost (MC′) equals marginal revenue MR′ (from D′) at 2.5 units. Buyers spend $9.50 per unit, of which the seller receives $7.50 and the $2 transaction cost goes elsewhere. Neglecting any fixed costs, the seller's profit after accounting for its transaction costs is $6.25. Now assume that the seller can spend $1 per unit to reduce buyer transaction costs to zero. He now faces D and MR, while marginal costs have shifted up to MC″. He produces 3 units that will sell for $9 each, yielding a profit of $9. If the seller can cheaply reduce buyers' transaction costs, output and profit increase, as do benefits to buyers.

Q. Check all of the calculations in the text accompanyng Figure 8-6.

Investments that lower transaction costs on all units. A seller might also make a one-time investment that cuts transaction costs on all units. The investment might be tangible, like a new store located near many buyers, or intangible, like a brand name that signals quality. Both investments depreciate—buyers may lose their memories of a brand that does not advertise, and potential customers will remain uninformed about it.[34] We can analyze investments that reduce transaction costs in the same way we analyzed those that reduce production costs in Figure 8-5. Notice that a seller's investment to reduce transaction costs (for example, informative advertising) can raise the price to customers and still leave them better off by lowering their transaction costs in acquiring information.

[34] Intangibles are discussed in more detail later in this chapter.

Q. Produce a graphic example in which the price to consumers rises but they are still better off thanks to lower transaction costs.

Many Buyers and Many Sellers

Two Types of Sellers Next, we examine markets that approach perfect competition, with each seller having only the smallest ability to affect price. Figure 8-7 begins with 1,000 identical firms in long-run equilibrium at a market price of $16, where each produces 10 units and earns zero economic profit. These pre-existing firms' cost curves appear on the leftmost panel.[35] If all firms (including those not yet opened) are identical, long-run supply, LRS, is horizontal and equals demand at an output of 10,000. Now assume that a single innovative producer cuts its average and marginal costs to AC′ and MC′, respectively, shown in the center panel.[36] That firm can still sell all it wants at $16 and will choose to produce 12 units. Next, others adopt the innovation and operate along MC′ and AC′. If there are 200 adopters their short-run supply curve is SRS'_{200}. If non-adopters that are taking losses close quickly, price stays at $16, and higher-cost sellers produce the rest of the market output. When 400 firms have adopted the innovation, short run supply is SRS'_{400}. Eventually price falls below $16, but as long as it is above $7 users of the innovation profit and nonusers do not. In its new long-run equilibrium, 14,000 units trade at $7. New firms with costs MC′ and AC′ produce the extra 4,000 units, and long-run supply shifts downward to LRS′.

Q. If the sellers who are taking losses after the first 200 innovators start production cannot leave quickly, price may fall below $16. Why?

FIGURE 8-7
Adoption of a Cost-Reducing Innovation in a Competitive Market

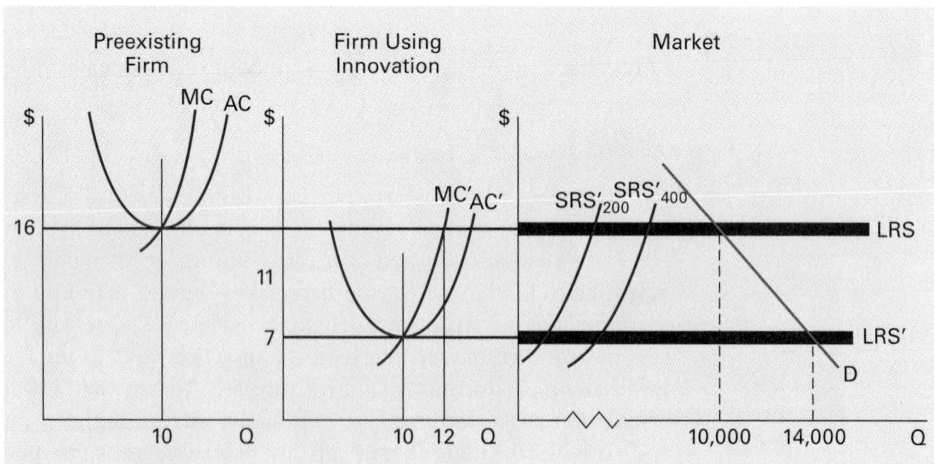

[35]Because changes in firm sizes are not of interest here, we are assuming that there is only one possible size, in which case the long-run and short-run cost curves coincide.

[36]The graphic disregards the costs (if any) of implementing the new method of production.

Four points emerge from this model. First, as the innovation spreads among producers the earlier adopters will see longer-lived streams of profit before the market reaches its new long-run equilibrium. These are returns above opportunity cost that the innovator and its early imitators compete for. Second, the number of firms that survive after the innovation depends on the direction in which the innovation shifts the minimum point of average costs. Third, as the percentage of sellers that use the innovation increases, those who are slower to innovate will take losses if they cannot shut down temporarily or leave the market quickly. Profit is both a carrot that rewards early adopters and a stick that punishes late ones. Fourth, any newcomer to the market will only survive if it uses the innovation.

Many Sellers, Upward-Sloping Supply Curves *Reducing transaction costs.* In the market of Figure 8-8 buyers face transaction costs of $2 per unit and sellers face transaction costs of $3 per unit. Demand D′ is $2 below D, and D′ shows the most buyers will pay for a unit of the good net of their transaction costs. The supply curve inclusive of sellers' transaction costs is S′, which is $3 above S. Equilibrium is at 75 units. Buyers spend $12 for each unit, $2 of which goes for transaction cost, and $10 goes to whichever producer sold it. Further, $3 of any producer's income from selling a unit goes to transaction costs. Now assume that something happens to (costlessly) reduce transaction costs to zero for everyone. Equilibrium now occurs at $9, with 110 units traded. What happens to market participants depends on their original transaction costs and the slopes of market supply and demand. Here, buyers whose transaction costs were formerly $2 now spend $3 less on each unit, and sellers whose transaction costs were $3 receive $2 more than before.

An outsider reduces transaction costs. An outsider who devises a way to cut transaction costs will produce benefits for buyers and sellers. In Figure 8-9, we assume that sellers have no transaction costs, while any buyer pays the market price of the good plus $18 in travel costs.[37] If transaction costs were zero, demand would be D_1, which intersects the supply curve S at $19 and 31 units. With transaction costs of $18 per unit, the net demand facing sellers is D_2, which is $18 below D_1. The market clears at 19 units, and

FIGURE 8-8
Reducing Buyers' and Sellers', Transaction Costs

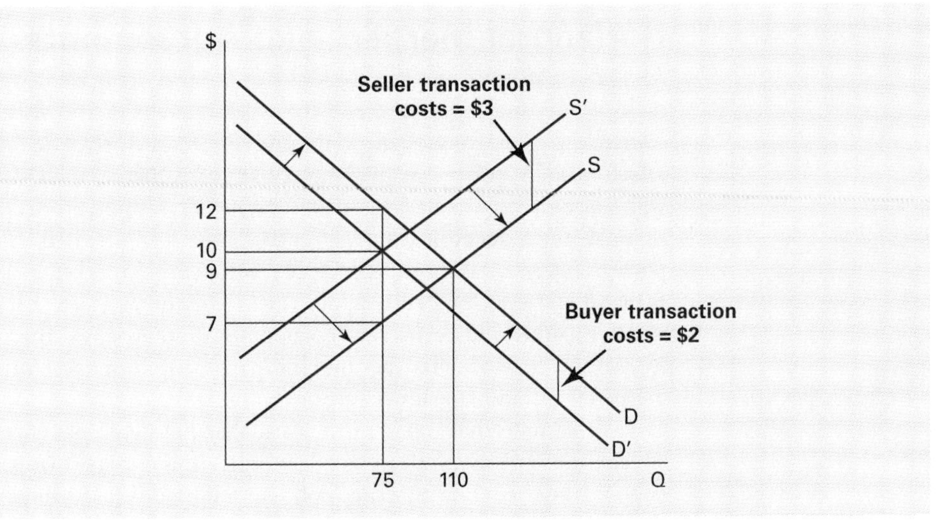

[37]We are assuming that no seller or group of sellers can build a store closer to customers, but the outsider can.

FIGURE 8-9
Buyers' Transaction Costs Reduced by Outsider

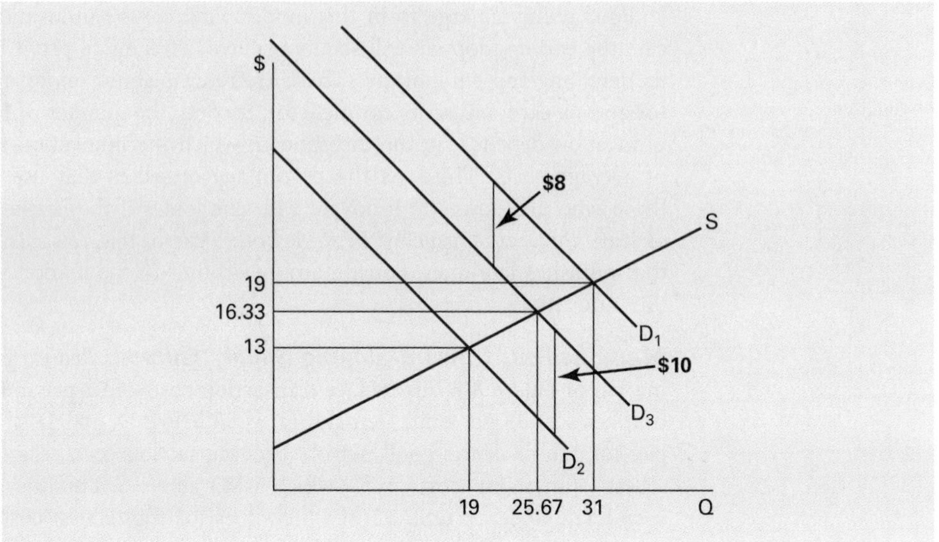

sellers receive $13 for each. Now an outsider tells buyers that for $8 per unit she will go to market for them and eliminate their former $18 transaction costs. Sellers now perceive demand curve D_3, $8 below D_1 and $10 above D_2. Sellers get $16.33 for each of the 25.67 units transacted. Both sides of the market benefit from lower transaction costs.

Q. Show that the coming of the outsider increases the benefits captured by both buyers (consumer surplus) and sellers (producer surplus).

MERGERS AND AGREEMENTS

Horizontal Mergers and Agreements

Mergers Mergers and acquisitions can be important elements of strategy. A *horizontal* merger puts the assets of two firms that operate in the same market under the same ownership. The consequences depend on market structure and on how the merger affects costs. If two perfectly competitive firms merge, their successor (the merged firm) will still be a price-taker. Because this merger cannot produce market power, it is only rational if it reduces post-merger costs. Large firms created by mergers can have market power. Figure 8-10 shows a perfectly competitive market in long-run equilibrium with demand (D) and long-run supply (LRS) horizontal at $8. Each of the 1,000 firms produces 12 units and earns zero economic profit. A single merger is like a cost-reducing innovation that benefits the merging parties while market price remains $8. Producers are better off and consumers are no worse off.

Now assume that other firms learn that merging cuts costs, and a wave of mergers sweeps the industry. With enough mergers the competitive market will become an oligopoly whose equilibrium can look like monopoly (i.e., sellers collude perfectly) or perfect competition (i.e., the Bertrand model) or anything between these extremes, as was shown in Chapter 6. The fall in output from 16,000 to 12,000 in Figure 8-10 is a mixed blessing. Because the mergers cut costs by $3, the 12,000 units cost $36,000 less. The

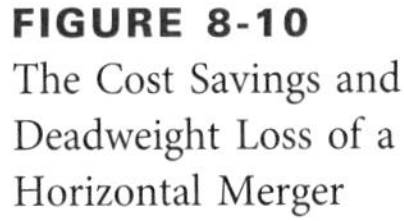

FIGURE 8-10
The Cost Savings and Deadweight Loss of a Horizontal Merger

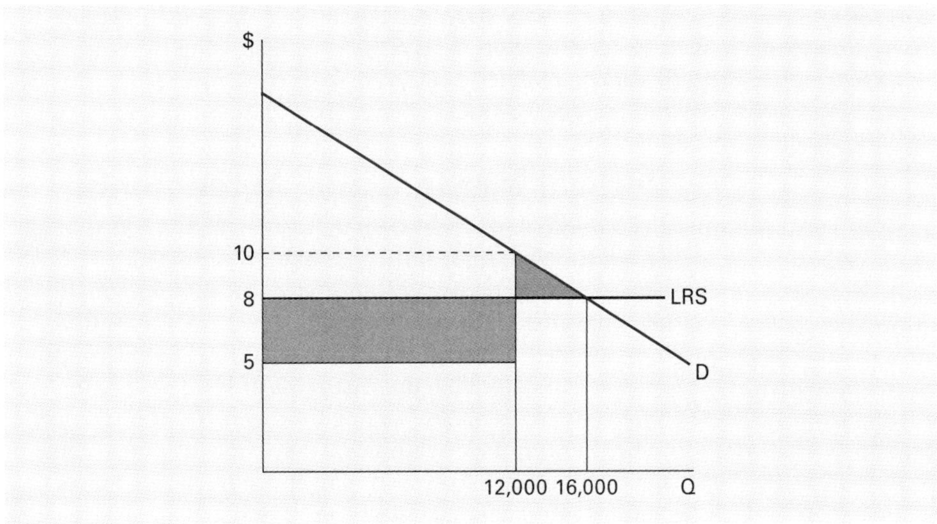

reduction in output, however, creates a deadweight loss of $4,000, the area of the pink triangle.[38] The net benefit of the mergers is the algebraic sum of cost savings and deadweight loss, which is positive in Figure 8-10 but could be negative under different assumptions about the market.[39]

Agreements U.S. antitrust law says that a "naked" agreement whose only goal is to fix prices is *per se* illegal—its very existence is unlawful. Other agreements among competitors can be both legal and economically desirable. For example, members of the Recording Industry Association of America (RIAA) long ago agreed on common technical specifications for music CDs.[40] Such a standard allows CDs from any RIAA member (or nonmember who uses the format) to work on many different players and computers. It facilitates entry into the market by new recording companies that intend to compete with existing firms. It also enhances competition in the market for CD players by lowering the cost to users of transitioning between them. Agreement on a format that makes unauthorized copying difficult can also foster competition, because artists have greater certainty their works will not be pirated.[41] Antitrust law treats agreements like these under a *rule of reason* standard that balances their favorable and unfavorable effects on competition.

In practice, the law usually cares only about agreements that could affect equilibrium in a relevant market, as discussed in Chapter 5. Many forms of business association restrict competition among their members without affecting the market. A group of doctors who form a partnership, for instance, may agree to charge identical prices for certain services rather than compete among themselves by cutting prices, or they may agree that

[38]Figure 8-10 originated in Oliver E. Williamson, "Economies as an Antitrust Defense: The Welfare Tradeoffs," *American Economic Review* 58 (March 1968): 18–36. The mergers may also favorably affect incentives to innovate, as discussed in Chapter 6, but this effect (if it exists) only unfolds over time and is not shown in Figure 8-10.

[39]This trade-off between cost savings and deadweight loss is a foundation of the U.S. government's standards for approving large mergers. See U.S. Department of Justice and Federal Trade Commission, *1992 Horizontal Merger Guidelines, with 1997 Additions*, at http://www.ftc.gov/bc/docs/horizmer.htm.

[40]For more information, see the RIAA Web site at http://www.riaa.com/whatwedo.php?content_selector=technical_standards.

[41]Other CD formats without copy protection are available to artists and recording companies that believe their long-term interests lie in allowing copying to disseminate their works more widely.

a doctor cannot have patients outside the group. Because the agreement covers only a handful of doctors, it can improve their competitiveness against other medical groups. A common pricing policy can lower consumer search costs, and an exclusivity restriction can prevent individual doctors from "free riding" on the reputation of the group.

Vertical Mergers and Agreements

Vertical Relationships An industry's output is often produced in stages. For example, oil is first extracted from the ground, then refined, and finally the refined products are retailed. A firm is *vertically integrated* if it subsumes multiple stages. The degree of integration matters because costs and revenues can vary with the number of stages in which a firm operates. A manufacturer that wholesales to independent retailers may (or may not) be more profitable than one that owns its retail outlets. Integration can produce savings if it improves coordination among the stages. Yet it might also raise costs if there are difficulties in managing such dissimilar activities as raw material production, manufacturing, and distribution. Changes in market conditions for inputs or outputs might warrant expansion into additional stages or divestiture of some facilities. When a manufacturer builds its own retail outlets, its scope changes by internal expansion. Scope can also change if the manufacturer merges with a firm that operates at another stage. Horizontal and vertical mergers differ in one important way. A horizontal merger can bring concerns about the merged firm's market power, but only rarely do vertical mergers raise such concerns. In most cases a firm will only merge vertically to improve its competitiveness.[42]

Vertical Mergers Figure 8-11 examines a hypothetical merger between two stages of the jewelry market. The DeBeers company (originator of the slogan "a diamond is forever") is a near-monopolist in raw diamonds. Currently, it sells diamonds to jewelry retailers, but might it make more by extending itself into retailing? To see the conditions for a profitable vertical merger, assume that line D in the figure is the public's demand for diamond rings. Line A is marginal cost of diamond mining for DeBeers, constant at \$2.[43] A retailer cuts the diamond, mounts it in a gold ring (one diamond per ring), and sells it. Assume that retailing is perfectly competitive and that rings are made and marketed at a marginal cost of \$4 (horizontal line B).

As a diamond monopolist, DeBeers profits more, the lower the costs of its retailers. Assume that if DeBeers does its own retailing, its marginal cost would be \$8 per ring (line D), twice that of existing stores. Its full marginal cost of producing a diamond and retailing a ring is \$10 (line E), which equals marginal revenue at seven rings. DeBeers will price them at \$17 each, which (disregarding fixed costs) yields a profit of $7 \times (17 - 10) = \$49.00$. If instead DeBeers sells its diamonds at wholesale it must allow retailers to recover the \$4 cost of making and selling each ring. The full marginal cost (DeBeers's plus the retailer's) of getting a ring to a buyer through an independent retailer is \$6. Now DeBeers maximizes profit by producing nine diamonds and wholesaling them at \$11 each. Retailers cover their \$4 costs by selling rings at \$15. DeBeers's profits are $9 \times (11 - 2) = \$81.00$, higher than if it retails the rings. DeBeers will only

---

[42]See Robert Pitofsky, "Vertical Restraints and Vertical Aspects of Mergers: A U.S. Perspective," October 16, 1997, at the Federal Trade Commission (FTC) Web site, http://www.ftc.gov/speeches/pitofsky/fordham7.htm. At the time, Pitofsky was chairman of the FTC. For theoretical examples of harmful vertical mergers, see Michael Riordan, "Anticompetitive Vertical Integration by a Dominant Firm," *American Economic Review* 88 (December 1998): 1232–1248.

[43]A fuller analysis would take note of the fact that diamonds are very durable and DeBeers's choices this year might affect its future profits because the public now holds more diamonds. "A diamond is forever" also means that everyone who owns a diamond is a potential competitor for the company.

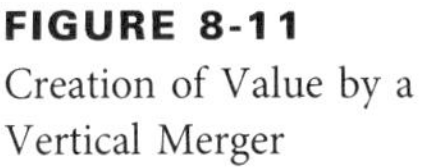

FIGURE 8-11
Creation of Value by a Vertical Merger

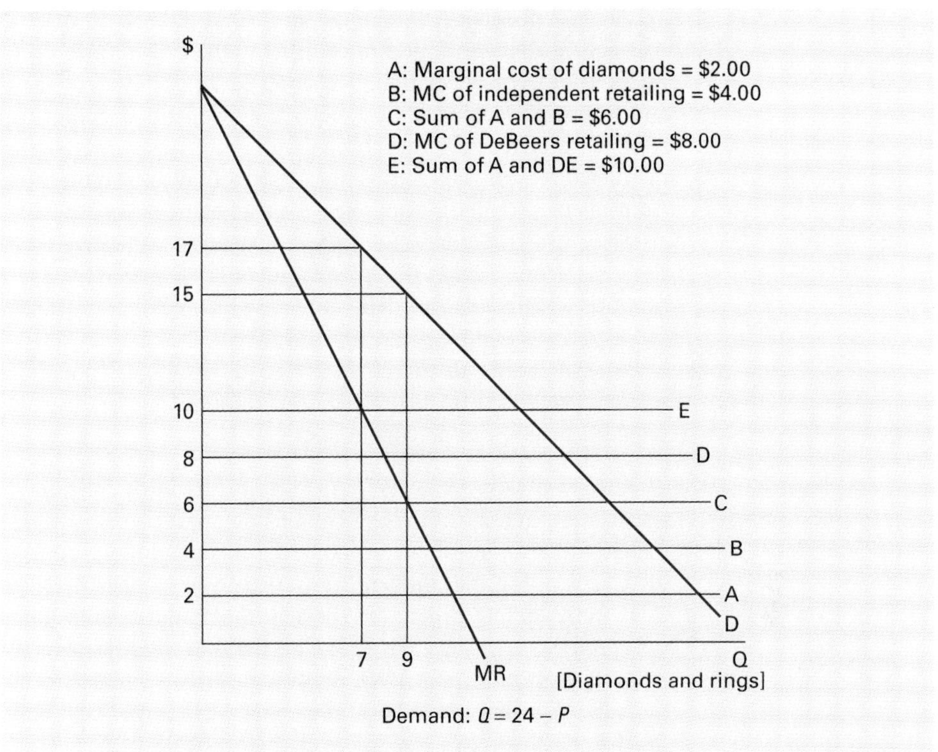

extend itself vertically if it can retail rings at lower cost than jewelry stores, which itself creates more economic value.

Q. Check all of the calculations in the previous paragraph.

Vertical Agreements *Interactions between stages of production.* Two firms in different stages of a vertical chain might reach an agreement that makes them a better competitor when they act as a team. An agreement will be preferable to a merger if a single management cannot monitor both stages as well as separate managements can. It is also possible that success requires motivating workers at one stage (e.g., retailing) to make sales efforts if the other stage (e.g., manufacturing) is to successfully compete. Independent retail store managers searching for profit might have better incentives than salaried employees of an integrated firm.

Vertical agreements in apparel and textiles. Retail sellers of wearing apparel face buyers with unpredictable desires for some styles but not others. There are high carrying costs for items that sell slowly and high costs of lost revenue and goodwill if the sellers run out of desirable items. Before information technology (IT) became cheap, retailers sent manufacturers paper orders with long lead times. Slow communication made it hard for stores to replenish inventories and hard for manufacturers to change output as fashions evolved. New technologies and new vertical agreements now allow manufacturers to reduce their textile inventories and retailers to keep smaller inventories on hand, while both respond more quickly to changing fashion. With these changes have come the manufacture and marketing of a larger variety of styles.[44]

[44]Frederick H. Abernathy et al., "The Information-Integrated Channel: A Study of the U.S. Apparel Industry," *Brookings Papers on Economic Activity, Microeconomics* 95 (1995): 175–246.

The agreements allow manufacturers and retailers to share the costs of IT investments that benefit them both and to coordinate their operation of the new systems to get accurate and timely information. The most basic of these are bar-code systems for garments and shipping containers. Cost-sharing agreements on point-of-sale (POS) scanners allow retailers to better plan their orders and manufacturers to better plan their production. A manufacturer can better schedule production and anticipate styles if it has POS data from all the retailers it supplies. The agreements between retailers and manufacturers also improve coordination with textile makers, who have their own inventory and lead-time problems. Textile makers in their turn can make more timely arrangements with producers of threads and dyes. Others who benefit from these agreements include sewing facilities that assemble garments and suppliers of specialties like zippers and buttons. The various businesses in the chain are so different that operating under these agreements appears preferable to full vertical integration. Integration is certainly possible, but integrated firms are rare in this industry.

"Restrictive" Agreements That Create Economic Value Many vertical agreements greatly restrict the future choices of both parties. A franchise contract between a carmaker and a dealer often prohibits the manufacturer from opening another outlet close by, that is, it specifies an *exclusive territory*. Fast-food franchises often require the owner of an outlet to buy all its food through the parent organization, and the parent organization promises to always have food on hand to fulfill its side of the *requirements contract*. A home electronics manufacturer might allow a retailer to handle its products only on the condition that it sell no other brands; in return, the manufacturer promises that no nearby stores will carry its line. The two have an *exclusive dealing* arrangement.

All of these contracts contain *vertical restrictions* that limit the parties' choices. A franchise agreement specifies the obligations of the two parties in accordance with their individual skills. For example, the parent organization can use its familiarity with the national market to design and finance more effective advertising, and it can use bargaining power over large volumes to negotiate low prices for supplies used in the outlets. On the other side a franchisee whose personal income rises with his outlet's might make more sales effort than a salaried employee of the parent. The owner may also have better information about local opportunities than the parent. If both parties keep the agreement their combined efforts will help them compete against other vertical chains in their market.

Vertical restrictions blur the distinctions between competition and monopoly. Automobile dealers who make sales efforts (e.g., offering test drives, financing), must be rewarded for those efforts. A nearby dealer that skimped on marketing could undercut a full-service dealer's prices. Free riding that discourages sales efforts can act to the detriment of the entire manufacturer-dealer organization. Paradoxically, a dealer may make greater efforts if it is a localized monopoly, because it is more likely to make the subsequent sales than if other dealers are nearby. Free riding also explains fast-food requirements contracts. If the parent cannot closely monitor the franchise owner she might try purchasing cheaper, lower-quality supplies. Customers who disliked her food might choose to shun all outlets that carry the name rather than just hers.

Vertical innovations like franchising spread widely during the last half of the twentieth century. Economists do not fully understand why, or why vertical integration boomed in some markets but not others. Insurance agents were first franchised in the nineteenth century, and car dealers and service stations in the early twentieth century. Often a parent franchises some of its outlets and hires employees to run others. The mix varies widely. Of McDonald's outlets in the United States, 85 percent are franchised, and only 15 percent are company owned.[45] By contrast, Starbucks Coffee has

[45]"U.S. Franchising," McDonald's Web site, http://www.mcdonalds.com/corp/franchise/franchisinghome.html.

no individual franchises. Each outlet is owned by the parent and staffed by employees, with the exception of those (e.g., in airports) that require ownership by a third party.[46]

Sustaining and Extending Competitive Advantage

Barriers to Entry—Size and Commitment

Building barriers to entry that protect profits against existing and future competitors can be an important element of strategy. A barrier challenges competitors but does not necessarily harm consumers. Economies of scale that require heavy investment by a new competitor may delay its entry. If lower costs only come with size, the quick entry of inefficiently small producers means high costs for them and fewer benefits for consumers. Intangibles like trademarks are barriers to unbranded competitors, but they can also assure consumers about quality. Large firms and firms with valuable trademarks may have market power that smaller firms without trademarks do not. Economists continue to debate how barriers affect competition and their importance in the economy.[47] Rather than join the debate, here we just examine ways to delay the entry of competitors and extend profits over time.

Size and specificity as barriers. Any newcomer to an industry is unlikely to succeed if it has higher costs than existing firms. In some industries firms must be large to achieve low costs, but size alone may not suffice. The firm may also need to invest in *specific assets* that cannot easily be redeployed to other uses or locations. For example, a power plant is only useful for producing electricity, and once in place it is costly to move elsewhere. Investment in specialized plants may be more costly than general-purpose facilities because the costs of the former are harder to recover if things go badly. Scale and specificity, however, may also allow such substantial cost reductions that a firm can protect its profits against competitors for a long time.

New competitors do not materialize from thin air, particularly where economies of scale are important. Except in very new markets, inexperienced competitors seldom attempt entry. Most entrants into manufacturing markets have experience in related goods or goods produced with similar technologies.[48] If an entrant must make large and risky investments, the capital markets will factor that risk into their terms of borrowing. The inability to finance a risky investment on favorable terms is not necessarily evidence of capital market imperfections.[49]

How barriers fell in the automobile market. Incumbents may also have weaknesses that newcomers can use to their advantage. The decline of the "Big Three" U.S. automakers provides several examples. General Motors, Ford, and Chrysler Corporation made almost all U.S. auto sales from the 1930s through the 1960s. The first successful

---

[46]"Frequently Asked Questions," Starbucks Web site, http://www.starbucks.com/customer/faq_qanda.asp?name=invest.

[47]For contrasting views, see William G. Shepherd, *The Economics of Industrial Organization* (Englewood Cliffs, NJ: Prentice-Hall, 1979); C.C. von Weizsacker, "A Welfare Analysis of Barriers to Entry," *Bell Journal of Economics* 11 (Autumn 1980): 399–420; and Harold Demsetz, "Barriers to Entry," *American Economic Review* 72 (March 1982): 47–57.

[48]Timothy Dunne, Mark Roberts, and Larry Samuelson, "Patterns of Firm Entry and Exit in U.S. Manufacturing Industries," *Rand Journal of Economics* 19 (Winter 1988): 495–515.

[49]For different perspectives on capital market imperfections see George J. Stigler, "Imperfections in the Capital Market," *Journal of Political Economy* 75 (June 1967): 287–292; and Joseph E. Stiglitz and Andrew Weiss, "Credit Rationing in Markets with Imperfect Information," *American Economic Review* 71 (June 1981): 393–410.

entrant was Volkswagen in the 1960s, but its Beetle did not directly compete with the Big Three. Volkswagen built its own dealer network and achieved economies of scale by exporting from efficient new German plants, while many U.S. cars were assembled in far older facilities. Instead of investing in dealerships, the first Japanese exporters made arrangements with existing U.S. dealers to sell cars that did not compete with the dealers' brands. As Japanese sales grew, manufacturers built their own dealer networks and extended their lines to include trucks and luxury models.

Strategic commitments: competitive or not? Economies of scale may allow first-mover strategies, like Wal-Mart's early construction of large new stores mentioned earlier. Theory says that if Wal-Mart builds a large low-cost store ahead of demand it conveys an implied threat: If another store opens Wal-Mart can charge prices that cover its operating costs but leave the newcomer with losses. The threat is credible because if some of Wal-Mart's investment is sunk a rational newcomer will not enter.[50] Despite the appealing logic, evidence is lacking that preemption is important or that it works as predicted. As noted earlier, Wal-Marts with few competitors charge the same prices as those with more.

Intangible Assets: Trademarks and Advertising

A seller wants to inform customers about more than price—consistent quality, for instance, may engender customer loyalty. Building contractors obtain surety bonds that pay the customer if their work is delayed or defective. The cost of a bond is small relative to that of a large building, but bonds would be too costly for a mass-market producer of inexpensive items who wanted to assure customers of quality. A firm that secretly intends to quit business might profit by degrading quality shortly before it closes, because the losses from dissatisfied customers over its remaining life span will have a low present value.[51]

Brands and trademarks. A producer can use a brand name or trademark to assure buyers it will produce the quality they expect.[52] The brand name may be intangible (literally, it cannot be touched), but it is a durable asset whose value increases as consumers associate it with quality. The name's owner, however, must maintain quality to obtain the higher future sales that make the investment in advertising profitable. New competitors can nullify an incumbent's brand-name advantage by investing in their own reputations. Unlike its usual definition, "quality" here means dependability and not necessarily excellence. "InterContinental" tells travelers that a hotel is dependably expensive and luxurious. "Motel 6" means dependably inexpensive and basic, but attractive to travelers whose alternative is unfamiliar and unbranded.

Influencing the Public and Government

Public Relations Public recognition and approval of a firm's practices can also be a competitive tool. In 2005, two hurricanes destroyed much of the New Orleans and Beaumont–Port Arthur areas. While the relief efforts of local and national governments faltered, companies like Wal-Mart, Home Depot, and Lowe's had stockpiled and shipped

[50]For contrasting views on preemptive investments, see Avinash Dixit, "The Role of Investment in Entry Deterrence," *Economic Journal* 90 (March 1980): 95–106; Frank H. Easterbrook, "Predatory Strategies and Counterstrategies," *University of Chicago Law* Review 48 (1981): 263–344; and A. Michael Spence, "Investment Strategy and Growth in a New Market," *Bell Journal of Economics* 10 (Spring 1979): 1–19.

[51]If you are not already familiar with them, present, values are discussed in detail in Chapter 16.

[52]Benjamin Klein and Keith Leffler, "The Role of Market Forces in Assuring Contractual Performance," *Journal of Political Economy* 89 (September 1981): 615–641.

necessities to the area before the storms hit, and the firms bypassed profits by keeping prices at pre-disaster levels.[53] Forgone revenue raised the value of their names as favorable media coverage gave customers reason to maintain their loyalty after the disasters. Actions can be both competitive and charitable.

Similarly, energy and auto producers advertise their environmental concerns. Campaigns for Toyota's and Honda's hybrid cars stress their ecological impact rather than their performance. This strategy might better maintain their first-mover advantages (if any) as U.S.-based manufacturers introduce similar vehicles. Until recently BP's advertising frequently supported policies to address global warming, while not mentioning the company's recent acquisitions of Amoco and ARCO, U.S. producers with large natural gas reserves. Gas has a lower warming impact than other fuels and will become more profitable if carbon dioxide regulation becomes tighter. BP's strategy has changed with energy markets. As disappointing financial results accumulated and climate change lost some of its emotional appeal in 2008, BP changed its CEO, dropped some environmental themes, and announced a re-commitment to its oil and gas business.[54] Altria, the maker of Marlboro cigarettes, risks large losses in cancer-related lawsuits. Its Web site provides links to help people quit smoking and documents its efforts to prevent young people from starting.[55]

Influencing Government Government can also help a business to advantage itself or disadvantage competitors. A business seeking favors from the government is exercising its constitutional rights, which need not entail corruption. Among possible strategies, a firm might seek legislation that makes competition illegal, as cable TV operators have done in many cities. Cable, however, has failed to suppress satellite TV, which is beyond local control.[56] Government can also make competition costly for foreigners by imposing quotas or tariffs in return for support from the domestic industry. More subtly, a firm can favor laws that raise its costs but raise competitors' costs by more. Health, safety, and environmental laws can require the installation of equipment that raises the average costs of large producers by less than small ones.[57] Railroads losing business to truckers, for example, have sought safety laws that require shorter work shifts for truck drivers, and owners of mechanized mines have supported legislation that would harm labor-intensive competitors by requiring union-scale wages in all mines.[58]

Other portals can provide strategic access to government. Regulatory agencies like state public utility commissions and the Federal Communications Commission (FCC) set rates that telecommunications providers can charge, and they sometimes have powers to exclude competitors from markets. AT&T's legal strategies suppressed long-distance phone competition long after it became possible.[59] The three original over-the-air networks (ABC, CBS, and NBC) obtained numerous FCC rulings that limited competition,

---

[53]"The Only Life Line Was the Wal-Mart," *Fortune*, September 29, 2005. Home Depot employs a full-time weather expert to anticipate and react to situations like these. "How Home Depot's Hurricane Honcho Handled Katrina," *Fortune*, September 23, 2005.

[54]"Back to Petroleum," *Financial Times*, July 8, 2009.

[55]See "Helping Reduce Underage Tobacco Use," Philip Morris USA Web site, http://www.pmusa.com/en/our_initiatives/ysp.asp.

[56]Cable systems require governmental grants of access to rights-of-way, but satellite dishes do not, so cities can only prohibit other cable operators from entering.

[57]See B. Peter Pashigian, "The Effect of Environmental Regulation on Optimal Plant Size and Factor Shares," *Journal of Law and Economics* 27 (April 1984): 1–28.

[58]See Oliver E. Williamson, "Wage Rates as a Barrier to Entry: The Pennington Case in Perspective," *Quarterly Journal of Economics* 82 (February 1968): 85–116.

[59]David S. Evans and Robert Bornholz, *Breaking Up Bell* (New York: Elsevier Science, 1983).

first from over-the-air UHF channels (channels 14 through 99) and later from cable systems. Cable TV systems were operating as early as the 1960s, but the market only opened in the 1980s when cable operators were authorized to compete in cities already served over the air.[60] Competition also happens in court. Any business can seek a redress of harms, but lawsuits can also be competitive strategies. One can attack a poorly funded competitor by filing questionable claims that are costly to defend. Sham litigation violates antitrust law but is not always easy to identify.[61]

Choosing a Competitive Strategy

Resources and Strategies

Economic models can help us to classify and analyze strategies, but we have not yet asked how a business might choose among them. The choice is situation dependent. We often see successful competitors with different strategies, as well as competitors with similar strategies, not all of whom survive. Strategy is resource-based and market-based. Two businesses in the same market may have different resources at their disposal that lead to different choices. Strategic choice requires a change in how we think about markets and firms. Our earlier models often assumed that competing firms were identical, or that if not we (and the firms) could easily spot their important differences. Now we will see firms discovering their resources and basing competitive strategies on them. We have seen that strategy is about more than price—it can range from product design to mergers to political activity.

What Are Resources? Strategy is shaped by both resources and markets. Resources include familiar inputs, like fuel and workers, as well as less obvious ones, such as intangible assets, internal organization, and relationships with outsiders. The originator of the resource-based model, Birger Wernerfelt of MIT, writes:

> By a resource is meant anything which could be thought of as a strength or weakness of a given firm. More formally, a firm's resources at a given time could be defined as those (tangible and intangible) assets which are tied semipermanently to the firm. Examples of resources are: brand names, in-house knowledge of technology, employment of skilled personnel, trade contacts, machinery, efficient procedures, capital, etc.[62]

A resource is not necessarily identifiable as a particular input. A firm that has patented its production equipment can both produce with it and license the patent to others. Some countries have legal systems that confer advantages relative to other countries on all firms in the country that produce certain goods.[63] The right location can also be a resource. Thanks largely to FedEx and UPS, the seemingly isolated airport in Anchorage, Alaska lands more cargo than any other in the United States.[64] From Anchorage

---

[60]Thomas W. Hazlett, "The Rationality of U.S. Regulation of the Broadcast Spectrum," *Journal of Law and Economics* 33 (April 1990): 133–175.

[61]See the Supreme Court's decision in *Otter Tail Power Company v. U.S.*, 410 U.S. 366 (1973).

[62]Birger Wernerfelt, "A Resource-based View of the Firm," *Strategic Management Journal* 5 (April 1984): 171–180.

[63]Nathan Nunn, "Relationship Specificity, Incomplete Contracts and the Pattern of Trade" *Quarterly Journal of Economics* 122 (May 2007): 169–200. Nunn shows that nations with more predictable systems of contract law manufacture more goods of the types that might give rise to contract disputes. Contracts are discussed in more detail in Chapters 10 and 11.

[64]See Anchorage Airport Statistics at http://www.dot.state.ak.us/anc/business/airServiceDevelopment/statistics/index.shtml. Worldwide, only Hong Kong handles more freight. The second-largest U.S. volume lands at FedEx's Memphis hub, where overnight packages change planes.

their planes can reach 80 percent of the industrialized world in ten hours or less (and no blizzard has ever closed the airport).[65]

Resources like workers, machinery, and control of a patent often trade on markets, but others are difficult or impossible to exchange.[66] Strategies available to a firm with a good reputation (the resource) may be unavailable to a firm with a poor one—for instance, important commitments can be made with a handshake instead of a contract that requires weeks to agree on. A firm with a reputation for customer care may be able to make better long-term arrangements with suppliers because they know the firm can depend on repeat business from its customers. Reputation is an intangible asset that requires continual investment to maintain. Similarly, a firm's culture may be a resource that cannot be marketed. A firm that is open to innovation will be able to choose and execute competitive strategies that a firm with rigid procedures cannot, and vice versa.

Q. In what lines of business might a firm with rigid procedures be a more successful competitor than one whose employees have wider ranges of discretion in decision making?

Innovation Pro and Con Strategy need not entail innovation or entry into new markets—some firms have resources better suited to perfecting an established product. Success as an innovator may require research facilities and a culture that respects scientists and engineers, but less obvious resources may also matter—close relations between salespeople and customers, for example, can encourage customers to suggest new products or improvements. Properly carried out, imitation can be as profitable as innovation and sometimes less risky. Ampex invented the VCR and Xerox invented the first office computer, but neither firm found commercial success in those areas. Success is surprisingly short-lived. The late economist Edwin Mansfield of the University of Pennsylvania estimated that 60 percent of successful innovations were imitated within four years, and the imitator's average development cost was only 35 percent of the innovator's.[67]

Competence and Sustainability

Identification of Resources and Feasible Strategies *A firm and its competitors.* Competition starts with ideas, and a firm's resources influence what its managers can imagine and what they can execute. A firm's strategy choice starts by identifying its resources and the resources of its competitors, paying attention to those resources competitors have that it does not itself, and vice versa. Knowing our resources helps determine the limits to our choices, and knowing our competitors' resources might help us to estimate the likelihood of success and suggest ways to minimize the impacts of our

---

[65]"Why FedEx is Flying High," *Fortune*, November 1, 2004.

[66]For a general treatment of intangible and organizational resources, see Hiroyuki Itami and Thomas Roehl, *Mobilizing Invisible Assets* (Cambridge, MA: Harvard University Press, 1987).

[67]Edwin Mansfield, Mark Schwartz, and Samuel Wagner, "Imitation Costs and Patents: An Empirical Study," *Economic Journal* 91 (December 1981): 907–918. Another study of 129 lines of business showed that in more than half a major patented innovation could be imitated or improved upon within three years. Richard C. Levin et al., "Appropriating the Returns from Industrial Research and Development," *Brookings Papers on Economic Activity* Special Issue, no. 3 (1987): 783–820.

inadequacies.[68] As noted earlier, identifying resources and feasible strategies based on them may be difficult. If our resources include a more loyal customer base than our competitors have, how can it be part of a strategy that is unavailable to them? A faithful base may be more willing to take the effort to suggest improved products, but other resources can matter as well: What if our culture is less receptive to new ideas than those of competitors? A firm's resources interact with one another and condition its strategic choices because they must be monitored and coordinated. Identifying complements to a resource can be as important as identifying the resource itself. A competent sales force, for instance, will not help us compete if the development team brings forth outmoded products. Finally, the choice of strategy can indicate resources that the firm should divest or cease trying to develop.

Interactions and constraints. Discussions of strategy must go beyond simple models that treat constraints as unalterable by the decision makers. In practice a strategy's success may depend on ingenuity in loosening some constraints or devising alternative plans of attack that render them less relevant. Some constraints are more easily adjusted than others. For example, a firm that is willing to bear the cost can easily erase scarcities of some material resources (including certain types of workers) by buying more of them. Other resources, like reputation, may be impossible to alter quickly and will require investments whose payoffs only come with time.

Durable strategies. The best choice depends on our resources and those of our competitors. We will often wish to use or acquire resources that make our strategy more resistant to their attacks.[69] These are most likely to be resources competitors cannot easily purchase or develop in-house. Some resources may be intrinsically impossible to duplicate (e.g., a unique location) and competitors must settle for substitutes, even in the long term. If a firm's critical resource cannot be duplicated (e.g., a unique person) or if management deploys it more skillfully, it might be the source of competitive advantages that continue even after rivals have acquired substitutes for it.[70] Economics, however, shows that highly productive resources acquired at bargain prices will not long remain bargains. Competitors will bid for whatever resource is behind our firm's profit—and possibly for ownership of the firm itself. As resources are revalued profits become costs. There is no finish line to the quest for competitive strategies. Rather, there must be a constant search for resources whose potential the market does not yet recognize.

The Search for Strategies *A continuing quest for tactical advantage.* Models of competition carry some important lessons for strategy choice. We can discuss in general terms the search for resources that may be sources of competitive advantage, and some management advisers recommend that their clients regularly undertake a strategic audit that enumerates and evaluates them. The optimal strategy depends on those resources, but few general principles are available to guide the choice. Sometimes we cannot even say in retrospect whether a strategy, once implemented, was successful. Competitive imitation and subsequent innovations can make profits vanish quickly, and unforeseen events may make a good strategy fail or a poor one succeed. The idea remains that no strategy that competitors can easily duplicate will produce long-term profit. The search for strategy must be a continuing one.

---

[68]For a fuller exposition of the resource-based theory of the firm and a contrast with other theories see Kathleen Conner and C.K. Prahalad, "A Resource-Based Theory of the Firm: Knowledge versus Opportunism," *Management Science* 7 (September 1996): 477–501.

[69]The quest for durability is key to an extensive literature on strategic management. See Michael Porter, *Competitive Strategy* (New York: Free Press, 1980).

[70]This is the standard for long-term advantage set in Jay B. Barney, "Firm Resources and Sustained Competitive Advantage," *Journal of Management* 17 (April 1991): 99–120.

Strategy or tactics? Despite the superficial appeal of having a grand strategy to guide a business, management may have good reasons not to adopt one. The longer your firm behaves predictably, the more likely competitors will learn the weaknesses of your strategy (and they all have some). Battlefield terminology is overused in management, but here it provides insight. Instead of a global strategy to cope with every possible situation, like the United States and Soviet Union both had during the Cold War, managers should often think in terms of tactics.[71] During a battle, field commanders look for unexpected opportunities to advance their own troops or exploit unexpected enemy weaknesses. Tactical moves are responses to idiosyncratic, short-lived developments. If your competitors are flexible and unpredictable you might do better by deemphasizing global strategy and seeking to seize more immediate opportunities.

New types of resources. Our current discussion of resources and strategies has been quite general. Earlier in this chapter we used the microeconomics of firms and markets to describe some strategies. Now we have begun viewing these choices as alternative resource deployments, using an expanded concept of resources that includes a firm's organization, culture, and relationships with outsiders. If competition is resource based, we will require a better understanding of the types, potential, and limitations of these and other intangible resources. To do so, we must proceed beyond transactions in markets. In the upcoming chapters we examine relationships that are based on contracts with enforceable commitments. Complex contracts can sometimes allocate our competitive resources more effectively than the relatively simple transactions we have thus far seen in markets.

Chapter Summary

- Competition in actual markets attempts to make a firm distinguishable from its competitors in order to increase its profitability.
- Competition is a risky search for market power that will produce economic profits, but the entry of imitators and other innovators will drive those profits downward.
- Selection bias often taints popular discussions of competitive strategy. Looking only at companies that used a certain strategy and succeeded tells nothing about those who used the strategy and failed. It is also difficult to show that the strategy was the true source of success.
- Competitive strategies are attempts to create economic value in the difference between buyer valuations and seller costs. A competitor can attempt to raise buyer's valuations of its product, reduce production costs, or reduce transaction costs.
- Transaction costs can be lowered by buyers, sellers, or outside parties like intermediaries. Strategies that lower transaction costs can entail fixed investments or per-unit changes.
- We can analyze strategies for a single firm with market power, and we can analyze their effects in competitive markets as many participants adopt them.
- Strategies can also take the form of transactions in corporate control, in which two firms merge or one acquires another.

[71]Grand strategies may have made sense in the Cold War because the underlying geography and military balance changed very slowly from the 1950s through the 1908s. Most importantly, no important competitor nations arose to alter the strategic balance between the two superpowers.

- Mergers between firms in the same industry (i.e., horizontal mergers) can take place for competitive reasons or purely to exercise market power. Mergers between firms in a production chain (i.e., vertical mergers) are generally made to reduce costs and are seldom cause for concern about market power.
- Vertical agreements, such as franchises, restrict the behavior of the parties to them, but by doing so they can make them better competitors.
- A successful firm may wish to create barriers to entry that protect its profits from erosion by the entry of competitors. Barriers, however, also have pro-consumer aspects, such as the informational value of a product's brand name.
- A firm can also compete by attempting to favorably influence public opinion or attempting to influence the government to make policies that advantage it against competitors.
- When thinking about competition, it is helpful to view a firm as a collection of resources that can be deployed against rivals. These resources include important intangibles like its culture and its customer relationships.

Questions and Problems

1. Most supermarkets today are staffed by employees of a chain like Kroger. Piggly Wiggly and IGA, however, operate under franchise agreements with independent owners. Why are franchised supermarkets rare relative to stores owned by chains? Why do you expect franchised stores to be more common in small cities (where most Piggly Wigglys and IGAs are located) than in large ones?
2. Like supermarkets, full-service department stores like Macy's are generally in decline. What factors might these types of stores have in common behind their declines? How would you determine which were important and which were not?
3. Go to the library or the Internet and discover some other reason for Wal-Mart's success not mentioned in the chapter. How would you test whether or not that reason is actually responsible?
4. Compile a list of strategies that have been identified as sources of McDonald's success. Then see which of its successful (and unsuccessful) competitors have also used these strategies.
5. Find a successful Internet retailer and enumerate some ways its existence lowers transaction costs.
6. Yahoo.com is called a "sticky" Web site because people frequently use it as a home page or to track news of interest, personal investments, and so on. Has Yahoo.com created a barrier to entry? In what ways is this barrier desirable? Undesirable?
7. Looking at a single seller and a single buyer, we said that "[b]ecause any price below $11 brings the buyer greater benefits than the old $9 transaction did, both parties benefit from a price between $10 and $11." Explain this fully.
8. The city governments of Anaheim and Los Angeles are each constructing packages to attract a National Football League team to locate in one of them. The packages include construction of a stadium from taxpayer funds and preferential tax treatment for the team. We have usually argued that competition benefits consumers. Does that necessarily hold here? Explain.
   For what sorts of activities do you prefer a monopoly government? Competitive governments? Why? [Hint: The cities in a geographic region can sometimes be usefully viewed as examples of the latter.]

9. PepsiCo produces both a cola and a major brand of potato chips. Coca-Cola produces only drinks. When might it make sense for PepsiCo to divest its potato chip operations? For Coca-Cola to begin manufacturing snacks? Be sure to examine both cost and demand factors.

10. [Requires calculus] In Figure 8-3 the demand facing your firm is $Q = 12 - P$, and total cost is $C = 4Q$. Q is your annual output, and P is its price. Show that your profit-maximizing output is 4 units, priced at $8 each, and that your economic profit is $16.

   a. Now assume that raising marginal cost to $5 raises the demand curve by $2 at all outputs. Show that you now maximize profits by producing 4.5 units, which you sell at $9.50 each. What is the largest increase in marginal cost you will tolerate to shift the demand curve upward by $2? Explain in commonsense terms why it is less than $2.

   b. Start again from the original demand and marginal cost, and assume that you can invest in advertising to inform buyers about a new use for your product. With probability 0.5 it raises the demand curve by $4 at all outputs, and with probability 0.5 it has no effect. Before considering the campaign's cost, by how much per year does expected profit increase if you undertake it?

11. [Requires calculus] Referring to Figure 8-5, show that if you cut marginal cost from $4.00 to $2.00 you will raise output from 4 to 5 units and cut price from $8.00 to $7.00. Then show that you will pay up to $9.00 per year to invest in a lower-cost plant that lasts forever.

   a. Earlier you showed that if the original demand shifts upward by $2, and marginal cost remains $4, optimal output is 5 units and price is $9. Can you show algebraically that an upward demand shift of X dollars changes profit by the same amount as a downward marginal cost shift of X, assuming linear demand and constant marginal cost?

   b. Why do you expect that if marginal cost is upward-sloping your previous result will no longer hold? Or will it? Explain.

   c. If you face a relatively elastic demand, are your gains from a cost-reduction strategy greater or smaller than if demand is relatively inelastic? Explain in commonsense terms.

12. Southwest Airlines hedged half of its fuel supplies last year. Why not choose to fully insure by hedging 100 percent of them? Jet Blue hedged almost none of them. Was Jet Blue's management necessarily incompetent?

13. [Requires calculus] Again our seller starts with demand $Q = 12 - P$ and marginal production costs of $4 per unit. The seller's transaction cost is $1 per unit, and buyers' are $2 per unit.

   a. Show that profit-maximizing output is 2.5 units per year and that buyers incur costs of $9.50 per unit, of which the seller receives $7.50. Then show that profit is $6.25.

   b. Now assume that the seller can reduce the buyers' transaction costs to zero by incurring an added marginal cost of $1 per unit. Show that the new profit-maximizing output is 3 units, price is $9, and profit is $9.

   c. Calculate the annual consumer and producer benefits before and after.

14. In a perfectly competitive market, demand is $Q_D = 32 - 1.5P$ and supply is $Q_S = -20 + 2.5P$. Find equilibrium price and quantity and producer and consumer benefits. Say an innovation then lowers every seller's marginal costs by $5 at all outputs. Find the new price, quantity, and producer and consumer surpluses.

15. Again, demand is $Q_D = 32 - 1.5P$ and supply is $Q_S = -20 + 2.5P$. Now, however, buyers and sellers have transaction costs of \$2 and \$3 per unit, respectively. Compare the equilibrium values with those you calculated for Problem 14.

16. For Figure 8-9, demand with zero transaction costs is $Q^1{}_D = 50 - P$ and supply is $Q_S = -7 + 2P$.

a. Verify all of the prices and quantities calculated in the discussion.

b. Now assume that intermediaries come from a competitive market with an equilibrium price of \$8 per unit for their services, that is, any buyer or seller who wants an intermediary's services must pay \$8 for them. What is the maximum per unit that sellers are willing to pay intermediaries if hiring them saves buyers \$8 in transaction costs?

c. Does your answer to Question 16a change if buyers pay \$8 per unit to the intermediary but sellers offer to rebate part of that expense to buyers?

17. [Required calculus] If the mergers in Figure 8-10 created a monopoly rather than the situation shown in that figure, what would its output and price be?

18. Assume that the demand for diamond rings is $Q = 24 - P$, and each ring contains one diamond. The marginal cost for DeBeers of mining a diamond is \$2, and an independent retailer's marginal cost of retailing is \$4. If DeBeers did its own retailing, its costs would be \$8 per ring (plus \$2 for the diamond). Neglect any fixed costs.

a. [Required calculus] Show that If DeBeers deals with independent retailers it sells them nine diamonds at \$11 each, for a profit of \$81. Then show that if the company does its own retailing it sells five rings at \$19 each, for a profit of \$45.

b. How will your analysis of this problem change if DeBeers must deal with a monopoly retailer? Is it more or less likely that DeBeers will wish to go into retailing?

c. DeBeers actually operates 39 retail shops, all at very affluent locations like Fifth Avenue in New York and Boulevard Haussmann in Paris. Why might it market its own diamonds and jewelry in these neighborhoods but not others?[72]

---

[72]See the Web page for the Paris DeBeers store at http://www.debeers.com/Europe/Paris-Galeries-Lafayette/stry/parisgalerieslafayette.

Part Three

Contracts

Chapter 9

Beyond Markets: Property and Contracts

INTRODUCTION

Surf City's Lost Oil

Huntington Beach, California, officially calls itself Surf City USA.[1] Surfboards first turned up in the 1920s, though they only became popular in the 1960s. In the 1920s Huntington Beach was called "Oil City." As production began, oil workers rushed to buy beachfront cottages on 25-foot lots. A few years later they obtained permission to drill wells in their backyards, and soon the area looked like Figure 9-1. By the mid-1930s, the boom was over. Extracting so much oil so quickly had reduced underground pressure to the point that it could no longer drive oil to the surface. The uncoordinated activities of several hundred well owners left about 70 percent of the oil unrecovered. At

FIGURE 9-1
Huntington Beach, California 1928

Bettmann/Corbis

[1]See the Huntington Beach City Guide at http://www.orangecounty.net/cities/HuntingtonBeach.html; and Barbara Milkovich, "A Brief History of Huntington Beach," 1986, http://www.hbsurfcity.com/history/history1.htm.

today's high prices it has become profitable to use modern enhanced-recovery technologies and production has resumed.[2] Today's wells are fewer, deeper, and more productive than before, but the uncoordinated drilling of the 1920s left some of the oil permanently unrecoverable.

At first glance, the 1920 oil rush looks like the entry of new producers as a competitive market moves toward long-run equilibrium. After comparing their expected revenues and costs, many homeowners found it profitable to sink their own wells, but this time something went wrong. When people looked out for their own interests, without considering their neighbors' choices, they extracted less oil as a group than they might have and received less revenue. By coordinating their drilling and production the well owners and consumers would have seen more oil brought to the surface.

Coordination, however, would have required hundreds of property owners to reach agreement on where and when to drill and how to share costs and revenues. Reaching consensus would have been difficult even if they had known the underground geology of the oil deposits, which could not be determined using then-available methods.[3] The large number of people was an obstacle because any subset of them could have held out for special treatment as a condition of agreement. Even if the neighbors had reached agreement and everyone said they would abide by it, enforcement would have been necessary. If everyone else extracted oil by the rules one well owner could gain at their expense by extracting more oil than the agreement allowed. If enough people figured out that they could individually profit by operating when no one was watching the agreement would collapse. In today's oil industry, however, agreements like this exist and can be enforced. Chapter 9 introduces the concepts of forming and enforcing agreements.

As the oil industry developed many localities had experiences like Huntington Beach. Our purpose here is to understand how such agreements come about and how disagreements might be avoided. We proceed as follows:

- Buyers and sellers in our previous market models had no particular loyalty to each other, and their relationships ended when one encountered a cheaper seller or a buyer willing to pay more. In reality, both parties can often benefit from longer-lasting relationships.
- Long-term gains result when the parties make investments and commitments that create more economic value than they could realize in isolated transactions.
- Investments that are *specific* to a relationship (i.e., of lower value elsewhere) are risky because a party may act opportunistically to further his own interests and lower the value of the other party's investment. Avoiding this can require an enforceable contract that specifies each party's future rights and obligations in detail.
- Extending the model of two-person exchange will show how transactions governed by contracts can create more value than those that are not. Contracting, however, may have transaction costs so high that the parties cannot reach agreement.
- A contract contains provisions that define the parties' property rights, and it is often helpful to think of them as exchanging packages of rights rather than goods or services.

---

[2] "Well, Well: Oil Rigs Return," *Los Angeles Times*, (Orange County Edition), November 28, 2005.

[3] Unlike the 1920s, contracting is easier today because we can obtain fairly accurate information about the size and geology of an oil deposit thanks to seismic techniques, improved downhole (i.e., drill bit) data gathering, and three-dimensional maps made by supercomputers.

- If property rights are not defined efficiently (or possibly not at all), transaction costs and uncertainty over these rights will reduce the potential economic value two parties can create.
- Economically efficient definitions of property in different goods depend on their values and physical characteristics, as well as on the transaction costs of reaching and enforcing agreement. Several case studies will show how property rights in goods evolve as they become more valuable and legal changes allow new types of contracts for them.

MARKETS AND PROPERTY RIGHTS

Interchangeability

Perfect Competition In perfectly competitive markets all sellers produce an identical good or service. Any buyer has abundant alternatives if her current trading partner tries raising price and other sellers do not. Adding in the model's assumptions of identical products and near-costless information generates a strong conclusion: the products of different sellers are indistinguishable to buyers, and so are the sellers themselves. Even if you have long dealt with a certain seller, you can shift to another and get the same product at the same price. Some commodity markets even pool the output of many producers. You cannot determine who grew the particular kernels of corn you purchased, for example, but you also have no reason to care about that.[4]

A seller in a perfectly competitive market makes no special arrangements to deal with any particular customer. No investments are dedicated to that relationship that will lose value if it ends. A seller who has built a specialized warehouse in your neighborhood will take a loss if you are the only customer she is capable of serving and you choose to leave. A seller who is uncertain about your staying a customer might choose not to build the warehouse. If she does not build it the transaction costs of your exchange will be higher, and the benefits the two of you can reap will be lower.

Contracts as Promises and a Market for Contracts A *contract* is an enforceable set of promises to take certain actions over the future. A buyer might promise to pay a prearranged price for delivery of 100 units of some good next Friday, but she might also want more or fewer depending on events that will take place between the agreement date and next Friday. The seller must incur costs to arrange a flexible supply sufficient to meet the buyer's desires in the event she wants more. If the seller decides to sell part of his inventory before Friday to an outsider who is offering a very high price, he risks being unable to fulfill the agreement and may have to compensate the buyer for some or all of her lost benefits. A contract like this with a flexible "take" will likewise probably require the buyer to compensate the seller if she abandons him for someone offering a lower price. Seemingly restrictive provisions like these exist because at the time of agreement both parties perceive that the benefits of the contract taken as a whole exceed the gains from having free access to other potential trading partners (often called *counterparties*). The seller's creditors might finance his inventory on better terms if they are sure that a buyer exists, and the buyer avoids the costs of last-minute shopping (including higher prices) in the event she unexpectedly wants more of the good.

[4] In the most extreme such case, natural gas is sold by its heat content (millions of British thermal units) rather than its volume or weight.

If the buyer wants to pay a month after taking delivery and no sooner, the seller will probably also take precautions both inside and outside of the contract. He will probably check her credit records, and the contract will likely charge her for the lost interest that could have been earned on an earlier payment.[5] Each party may also informally ask acquaintances about experiences that might better help them understand the other's character. Before they form a contract both the buyer and seller will solicit offers from other counterparties and engage in preliminary negotiations. It is helpful to view these pre-contract activities as actions in a market where people search for information about counterparties and their terms before settling on the ones that best suit their situations. (Remember that we originally defined a market as a place where people compare their evaluations of goods.) The movement from markets to contracts is an important one. Contracts will be more costly to arrange and enforce than spot market transactions, but they can also bring benefits that are unobtainable in spot markets.

Specificity and Property

The parties to a contract transact something quite unlike the interchangeable units of a spot market commodity. A term like "1,000 bushels of corn at $2.04 per bushel delivered and paid for today" sounds as if it came from a supply-and-demand diagram, and it is what most people mean by the purchase or sale of 1,000 units.[6] But how can we summarize a contract that gives the buyer an option to refuse delivery of part of a shipment or one that allows the seller to pass part of a good's price risk on to the buyer? The buyer must give up something of value if the seller is to take on the risk that the buyer will refuse delivery, and the seller must compensate the buyer for bearing the price risk. What is given up may take the form of cash or concessions in contract terms (i.e., "quid pro quos") that the parties agree on. Even after we see the quantity exchanged and the amount paid, the per-unit price we calculate may not be useful. It will reflect both the characteristics of the market for the good and the contract terms under which it has been transacted. That contract is a package of rights and obligations that some may view as a poor alternative to other arrangements under which they can trade the good.

We often say that a contract specifies a set of *property rights* connected with the exchange of some good or service. These are rights to use something in a defined manner, and they often include the right to sell or otherwise transfer it. Property rights are often open-ended and do not exhaustively specify the owner's alternatives. For instance, a hammer can be used to build anything its owner might like, but it cannot be used to interfere with a neighbor's rights to an unbroken window. Different packages of rights can exist for the same good. You have an unquestioned right to repaint the interior of a home that you own, but doing the same in a rented house depends on your contract with the landlord. In some communities a homeowner has an unconditional choice of exterior color. In others, at the time of purchase buyers agree to restrictions on their choices to maintain a neighborhood with a uniform appearance that may make all homes in it more valuable. Obligations are the backside of rights. Your right to payment from me depends on your meeting the delivery obligations of our contract.

---

[5]Instead of interest charges we often see discounts. Sales agreements include provisions such as "2 10 net 30," meaning that the buyer can take a two percent discount if she pays within ten days but must in any case pay the full (net) amount in 30 days.

[6]In reality, organized commodity markets have numerous rules governing transactions, and subjects range from certification of product quality to extension of credit. For an example, go to the New York Mercantile Exchange Web site, and see the details of its natural gas futures contract at http://www.nymex.com/NG_spec.aspx.

THE BENEFITS AND COSTS OF CONTRACTS

Bees and LoJacks

Bees: Low-Cost Contracting The United States has about 200,000 beekeepers, many part-time.[7] Some travel with their beehives and arrange with farmers to park in their vicinity for several days. The bees gather nectar from flowers and turn it into honey, in the process transferring pollen between flowers. Pollination of fruit trees and crops like alfalfa increases their yields. The longer the bees stay, the fewer the flowers still unvisited and the smaller the daily yields of honey. To see how a contract creates value, begin with a beekeeper who wants to maximize his profits from honey production and disregards his bees' effects on farm crops. Table 9-1 shows the beekeeper's total revenue for different stays and the marginal revenue from each additional day. If his opportunity cost of locating elsewhere is $11 per day, he will remain four days and profit by $16.

Next we meet the farmer, whose apple crop increases with each day the bees are around, but at a diminishing rate. When the beekeeper maximizes his profits with a four-day stay, the farmer's crop increases in value by $34. The beekeeper will not stay a fifth day because his marginal honey revenue of $10 does not cover his $11 marginal cost. But a fifth day of pollination yields an additional $6 of apples for the farmer. If the farmer offers the beekeeper half that amount she still gains $3, and the beekeeper's total income of $10 from honey and $3 from the farmer exceeds his opportunity cost. The rightmost column of Table 9-1 shows the total value of honey and apples for the various durations of the beekeeper's stay. If he remains for a sixth day the farmer can pay him $4 (anything between $3 and $5) from her increased output and leave both of

TABLE 9-1 THE BEEKEEPER AND THE FARMER

DAYS	TOTAL HONEY VALUE	MARGINAL HONEY VALUE	BEES' OPPORTUNITY COST	TOTAL BEES COST	PROFIT FROM HONEY	TOTAL VALUE OF APPLES	MARGINAL VALUE OF APPLES	TOTAL HONEY PROFIT + APPLE VALUE
1	$18	$18	$11	$11	$7	$10	$10	$17
2	34	16	11	22	12	19	9	21
3	48	14	11	33	15	27	8	42
4	60	12	11	44	16	34	7	50
5	70	10	11	55	15	40	6	55
6	78	8	11	66	12	45	5	57
7	84	6	11	77	7	49	4	56
8	88	4	11	88	0	52	3	52
9	90	2	11	99	−9	54	2	45

[7]For more facts and economic analyses of the bee business, see Steven N. S. Cheung, "The Fable of the Bees," *Journal of Law and Economics* 16 (April 1973): 11–33; and David B. Johnson, "Meade, Bees, and Externalities," *Journal of Law and Economics* 16 (April 1973): 35–52. Beekeeping is notorious as an example of economists too interested in their logic to examine the world around them. In a famous article English economist James Meade used a beekeeper–farmer example to show that if the beekeeper acts without considering the farmer the outcome will be inefficient for reasons discussed in the text. Instead of examining how beekeepers and farmers actually conduct their businesses, Meade chose to simply assert that governmental intervention (perhaps in the form of a subsidy for beekeepers) might be necessary to eliminate inefficiency. See J. E. Meade, "External Economies and Diseconomies in a Competitive Situation," *Economic Journal* 62 (March 1952): 54–67.

them better off. After six days the beekeeper will leave, because the sum of their extra revenues for a seventh day ($6.00 + $4.00) is less than his opportunity cost.

How the beekeeper and farmer arrive at an agreement is not of immediate interest. Instead of negotiating every morning, at the outset they could sign an agreement for two additional days.[8] Because services and payments take place over a span of time, the agreement is not self-enforcing. If the farmer pays at dawn the beekeeper can abscond with the money to earn his opportunity cost elsewhere. Paying at sunset might allow the farmer to escape the bill by going into hiding or trying to compel the beekeeper to settle for less. Either way a court would find that someone breached (i.e., broke) the contract by failure to perform and order a remedy. That remedy might take the form of a payment by the farmer or an order that the beekeeper release the bees for another day. Chapter 10 considers remedies in more detail. Still later we will consider a merger that puts the bees and the trees under a single owner and a common management.

Q. How would the example change if the apple farmer had opportunity costs?

LoJack: Some Agreements Are Too Costly LoJack Corporation has developed a highly effective system for retrieving stolen vehicles.[9] Police recover about 95 percent of LoJack-equipped cars intact but only 60 percent of unequipped cars. The company charges about $700 to hide a radio transmitter somewhere (unknown to the owner) in the vehicle, followed by a monthly fee. When a car is reported stolen the police remotely activate its transmitter and track it. Although only a small percentage of cars actually have LoJack, one installation confers a benefit on other owners. Police who spot a LoJack-equipped car can follow it to a shop where criminals tear down stolen cars for their parts. A single LoJack can recover more than one car and put a dismantling operation out of business.

Ian Ayres of Yale Law School and economist Steven Levitt of the University of Chicago ran the numbers and concluded that equipping three additional cars with LoJacks (which last for the life of a car) will deter one auto theft a year in a city, most likely of an unequipped car.[10] From the community's standpoint the net benefits are positive. Ayres and Levitt found that annualized installation and service charges on a LoJack averaged about $97 per year, and the loss per stolen car (averaged over those recovered and not recovered) is approximately $4,000. All of the cars in a city share the benefits of an additional LoJack, and those benefits are more than ten times the cost of installing and maintaining it. A car owner looks at her own costs and benefits when considering LoJack, but the full effect of her choice is like the effect of another day of bees on crop yields.[11] Non-installers capture some of these benefits—lower theft risk means lower insurance rates and smaller police budgets for all.

---

[8]In reality, beekeepers and farmers often sign "standard-form" contracts with local farmers' associations. These contracts (like insurance policies or apartment leases) allow the parties to specify the services and payments without having to devise large amounts of boilerplate text necessary to meet legal requirements.

[9]See the LoJack Web site at http://www.lojack.com/. The company has since extended its system to computers and cargo shipments.

[10]Ian Ayres and Steven D. Levitt, "Measuring Positive Externalities from Unobservable Victim Precaution: An Empirical Analysis of LoJack," *Quarterly Journal of Economics* 113 (February 1998): 43–77.

[11]LoJacks are more frequently installed on expensive cars, and some insurers give discounts to LoJack users. The most frequently stolen models, however, are mid-range models of popular brands like the Honda Accord and Toyota Camry whose parts are easy to sell.

Q. Use the numbers to show that the benefits are more than ten times the cost of installing and maintaining a LoJack. Be sure to explain what "annualized" means.

Introducing Government Being just two people with a simple problem to resolve, the beekeeper and farmer probably reached agreement with ease. Now imagine the problems of forming an agreement that must cover a large number of farmers, some with few flowers and some with many. Bargaining with many farmers carries another complication beyond the sheer number of parties: each has an incentive to understate the value she places on having the bees around, while hoping that her neighbors will voluntarily contribute enough to induce the beekeeper to stay. Because the bees visit plants at random, both payers and nonpayers will enjoy larger crops, so each farmer will wish to be a *free rider* (the economist's standard term) and try to avoid paying for benefits received.

If the entire population consists of only you and me, and a single LoJack makes both of us theft proof, we can easily agree on whose car gets it and how to share the costs. But even if a million residents of a large city could somehow negotiate, many who would actually benefit will claim that they do not value the protection while secretly hoping others will pay. Government might cut the negotiation cost by requiring LoJacks on cars (like smog controls), but no government has done so. Farmers avoid the free-rider problem because their local associations, rather than individual farmers, usually contract with beekeepers.[12] Association members pay dues that provide them with services like those of beekeepers, weather forecasters, and market analysts. Even if association membership is voluntary, social pressure from longtime neighbors may suffice to ensure that everyone pays.

Q. The Federal Government does require auto makers to take certain steps intended to discourage theft. Before looking at the URL in the footnote, try to guess what some of these measures might be, and why most of them do not apply to all new cars.[13]

The farmers' association is like a government with a limited jurisdiction and no explicit powers to tax and regulate.[14] It is both a forum where farmers decide what their dues will purchase and an organization that informally coerces payments from them. Sometimes only a real government can do the job, as happens with air pollution from automobiles. Each member of the community benefits privately from his car, but each also pollutes in the process and endangers the health of others. Government reduces the transaction costs because it can force changes in car design, can impose taxes on drivers, and has the power to punish those who fail to comply. A majority of citizens have

---

[12]Johnson, "Meade, Bees, and Externalities," 46.

[13]The URL to search is that of the National Highway Traffic Safety Administration, at http://www.nhtsa.dot.gov/portal/site/nhtsa/menuitem.2afa3cb5b16547a1ba7d9d1046108a0c/.

[14]Some farmers' associations do have quasi-governmental status. Pesticides kill 11 percent of California's bee population in an average year, leading to millions of dollars in losses due to under-pollinated crops. To cope with this region-wide difficulty, state law allows the formation of bee protection districts that enforce regulations on the timing and coverage of pesticide treatments. See John W. Siebert, "Beekeeping, Pollination and Externalities in California Agriculture," *American Journal of Agricultural Economics* 62 (May 1980): 165–71.

indirectly chosen to buy cleaner air by electing politicians who will enact regulations and taxes like these.[15]

Q. What would determine the efficient size of a farmers' association? In other words, what size would maximize the association's net benefits per member? Hint: Imagine you and some neighbors are thinking of purchasing land that will provide you with a golf course that only group members can use. A bigger group spreads the costs more widely, but it also means the golf course will be more crowded. Explain the analogy to the story of the farmers' association and the beekeeper.[16]

Efficient Allocations and Coasian Reasoning

External Costs and Benefits Every voluntary transaction creates economic value for the buyer and seller. A self-interested beekeeper trying to maximize his wealth would want to reach agreement with the farmer, who has a similar interest in her own wealth. The bees produce an *external benefit* or *beneficial externality* in the form of a more valuable apple crop. An externality occurs when one person's action affects another's wealth, whether positively or negatively.[17] Extending the beekeeper's stay benefits both parties, and it will happen if the costs of agreement are low enough. We can get a fuller understanding of externalities and transaction costs by bringing another person into the model. He is a writer who suffers from an allergy that the presence of bees makes worse. The allergy cuts his daily writing output and income, which reflects the value readers place on his work. Assume that the allergy's effects worsen disproportionately with exposure, i.e., his marginal loss from the third day of bees exceeds that from the second day.

The activities of the beekeeper and the farmer impose an *external cost* on the writer. If they disregard the writer's losses, they will keep the bees for six days and get $57 in benefits net of the beekeeper's cost. This $57, however, is an overstatement of the actual benefits from honey and apples because it fails to net out the value of the writer's lost output. From Table 9-2, six days of bees cuts the writer's revenue by $36 and leaves the group with only $21 of benefits. If the bees stay for five days rather than six, Table 9-1 shows that the farmer and beekeeper lose $2 in benefits, here also called profits, but Table 9-2 shows that the writer gains $11. The net effect is a rise in total benefits to $30. Likewise, a fifth day without bees raises total benefits to $34. Cutting down from four days to three, however, drops the group's benefits to $33. The total benefits to all three parties are maximized if the beekeeper stays four days.

We have thus far said nothing about the underlying laws that define the rights of these three people. You might expect that how long the bees stay (if they stay at all) depends on what the law says. If the law lets the beekeeper and farmer disregard the writer, you might expect the bees to stay the six days that maximize the benefits of that pair. If instead the law grants the writer unconditional freedom from bees, you might expect that the

[15] The text assumes that the political process will in fact provide the pollution standards a representative voter prefers. This reasoning has numerous problems, as will be seen when we discuss workplace teams in Chapter 12 and voting in Chapter 17. For more on the economic analysis of political behavior, start with James Buchanan and Gordon Tullock, *The Calculus of Consent: Logical Foundations of Constitutional Democracy* (Ann Arbor: University of Michigan Press, 1965) and Dennis C. Mueller, *Public Choice III* (New York: Cambridge University Press, 2003).

[16] See James Buchanan, "An Economic Theory of Clubs," *Economica N.S.* 32 (February 1965): 1–14.

[17] This is the original definition, found in A.C. Pigou, *The Economics of Welfare* (London: Macmillan 1920), 166–68.

TABLE 9-2 THE BEEKEEPER, THE FARMER, AND THE WRITER

DAY	MARGINAL PROFIT IN HONEY	TOTAL PROFIT IN HONEY	MARGINAL PROFIT IN APPLES	TOTAL PROFIT IN APPLES	PROFIT FROM HONEY + APPLES	MARGINAL LOSS TO WRITER	TOTAL LOSS TO WRITER	HONEY + APPLE PROFITS LESS WRITER'S LOSS
1	$7	$7	$10	$10	$17	$1	$1	$16
2	5	12	9	19	31	3	4	27
3	3	15	8	27	42	5	9	33
4	1	16	7	34	50	7	16	34
5	−1	15	6	40	55	9	25	30
6	−3	12	5	45	57	11	36	21
7	−5	7	4	49	56	13	49	7
8	−7	0	3	52	52	15	64	−12
9	−9	−2	2	54	52	17	81	−36

beekeeper will not operate at all. Either way, you probably expect that the law's details will influence the outputs of honey, apples, and writing that are produced. Arriving at this conclusion, however, depends on what you assume about the three parties' costs of negotiating.

Negotiation On Table 9-2, marginal profit in honey and marginal profit in apples are benefits to the beekeeper and farmer from an additional day of bees. The writer's loss increases with the time the bees stay, and his marginal loss is increasing. Adding these three marginals algebraically shows the net effect of another day of bees on total benefits; for example, the marginal effect of the first day is a $16 increase. Let's consider two possible legal rules:

1. The farmer and beekeeper can do as they wish without considering the writer.
2. The writer has a right to live without bees regardless of the effects on the beekeeper and farmer.

Finally, assume that negotiation among the parties is costless. Under the first rule, if the farmer and beekeeper disregard the writer's existence they will release the bees for six days. But now allow the writer to intervene before they start, for example with an offer of $7 they may divide as they wish if they limit the bees to five days. Because a bee-free sixth day is worth $11 to the writer, he gains $4. As for division of the $7, because the farmer forgoes $5 of extra income, a $6 payment makes her better off. The beekeeper gets the remaining $1, but in reality he gains $4 because eliminating the sixth day removes a $3 loss. The same reasoning holds for reducing five days of bees to four. The writer could offer $7 of his $9 gain for that day, $6.50 of which compensates the farmer's $6 loss, and the remaining $0.50 gains the beekeeper a total of $1.50 because he no longer loses $1 from staying a fifth day. You should check that the writer cannot offer the pair enough to induce the beekeeper to stay for only three rather than four days.

Now look at the effects of the second law, which gives the writer a bee-free environment. Starting from zero days of bees, the beekeeper and/or the farmer can offer the writer some amount between $1 and $17 to obtain his permission for a day of bees. Likewise, for a second day the pair will offer up to $14, and the writer will accept any amount over $3. The same reasoning holds for the third and fourth days of bees. The most they will offer for the fourth day is $9, and the least the writer will accept is $7. Again, you can check that there is no payment the pair can offer that will make the writer accept a fifth day of bees.

Q. Show that the following statements regarding the two legal rules are true: (1) the writer cannot offer the farmer and beekeeper enough to induce the beekeeper to stay for only three rather than four days; and (2) there is no payment the pair can offer that will make the writer accept a fifth day of bees.

Q. What if the beekeeper is required to disregard his effects on the farmer (i.e., she cannot participate in any negotiations) but is responsible for any harm the writer suffers. How (if at all) does the solution change?

Coasian Reasoning Our original expectations about the importance of the legal rule have turned out to be wrong. No matter who has the initial rights, if negotiation is costless the three will arrive at the same efficient outcome that maximizes their net benefits as a group—four days of bees. The example contains the fundamentals of what economists call "Coasian" reasoning, named for 1984 Nobel laureate Ronald H. Coase (rhymes with toast) of the University of Chicago Law School. His 1962 publication of these ideas upset the foundations of economic and legal reasoning.[18] Until Coase showed the importance of transaction costs by asking what would happen if they did not exist, most scholars and lawyers believed legal details mattered—the outputs of honey, apples, and writing depended on who had which rights. But if there are no costs of negotiating, the three can exchange these rights to reach an economically efficient outcome. It does not matter whether the law allows the beekeeper and farmer to disregard the writer who can pay them not to release bees, or whether it gives the writer a right to freedom from bees that he can sell to the two of them.

Coasian reasoning also provides a new perspective on the concepts of benefit and harm. People often think of the beekeeper as a wrongdoer whose arrival harms the writer, so they propose measures to prohibit or limit bee releases. Efficiency, however, is not a matter of who was there first. Coasian reasoning allows us to see a symmetry—why not think of the writer as harming the beekeeper and farmer because he keeps them from creating economic value for themselves as well as honey and apple consumers? If negotiation costs are low enough, the law's function is to be a starting point for negotiations toward an efficient outcome.

Coasian reasoning is only about efficiency and does not directly consider how costs and benefits are distributed among the parties. If the law gives the beekeeper and farmer a right to release bees, they get income from their own businesses and payments from writer, who earns less than if he had the initial right to freedom from bees. If the writer has a right to a bee-free environment, part of the beekeeper's and farmer's gains are paid out to him. If the distribution of income after bargaining is politically unsatisfactory, other laws may be enacted or enforced to tax the gains and redistribute them. Of course, in a complex society where external costs and benefits are pervasive, everyone will be a beneficiary of some laws and a loser from others.

High Transaction Costs When negotiation has costs the law can affect outcomes. Assume that three-person situations like this one occur frequently and that usually (unlike the previous example) the efficient solution gives the writer a totally bee-free world; that is, consumers value written material very highly relative to crops and honey. If

[18] R.H. Coase, "The Problem of Social Cost," *Journal of Law and Economics* 3 (October 1960): 1–44.

negotiation is very costly, and the law gives the beekeeper and farmer the right to use bees, valuable written works will go unproduced while less valuable apples and honey are produced. The writings are lost because the cost of negotiations to reverse the law's assignment of rights is too high. If, alternatively, the law gave the writer freedom from bees, the status quo without bees would be closer to the efficient solution, that is, there would be relatively more writing and relatively less apples and honey.

Coasian reasoning has one very important consequence for the analysis of contracts. If the costs of negotiating and enforcing contracts are low relative to the benefits, buyers and sellers will have incentives to make economically efficient arrangements that increase value, and they will avoid making contracts that destroy it. Value-creating contracts, however, require underlying laws that clearly define the rights and obligations of the parties. Without clear definitions they will be less able to predict the consequences of the commitments they are making. Where transactions are costly, some legal assignments of rights will be more efficient than others. The Huntington Beach oil wells exemplified inefficient assignment with high transaction costs.

Defining Rights and Contracting Over Them

Property: A Sequence of Cases

The Meteor Shower To make agreements that create value, the parties' underlying rights must be clearly defined in the law. If they are undefined or unclear, the promises they make to each other in a contract may be impossible to carry out or enforce. Assume that a meteor shower has left your land (and no one else's) covered with diamond-hard stones that you think would make superior industrial abrasives. They will, however, only be marketable if cleaned and cut in special ways. Cleaning and cutting requires a highly specialized plant that you cannot cheaply dismantle or convert to another use. Rights to the stones that are well-defined and enforceable will give you greater certainty of realizing their market value after cutting. (Of course, prospective buyers may still not want them.) You are more likely to build the plant if the law ensures your rights than if it does not.

But what if there is no law, or what if the existing law is unclear? You know you can cut trees on your land and sell the lumber, but there are no laws or precedential court decisions on stones that fall from the sky. Your rights may be insecure because the law treats the stones like fish in the open ocean or oil under Huntington Beach in 1920, the property of whomever takes them first. Or perhaps the law gives your neighbors rights to enter your land to take stones (but not to take your furniture), and the cost of fencing off your land is very high. Maybe the stones are something fundamentally novel, like the rights to use radio frequencies that only became valuable after the invention of broadcasting. In all these situations you are less likely to build the specialized plant than if you have certainty about what you can do with the stones. With an enforceable right to cut and sell the stones, you still bear risks—your guess about customers' willingness to pay for them could be wrong. A well-defined right, however, eliminates the risk of losing the value of your investment in the specialized plant, which could happen if a court later ruled that the stones were not yours to cut and sell.

The Chickens Imagine a farmer who raises chickens for market in facilities that she owns. The law gives her what are known as possessory property rights in both the chickens and the facilities.[19] She may do what she wants with them, subject to not interfering

[19]A possessory right is a right to engage in a particular act or a right to prevent others from engaging in it. See Steven Shavell, *Foundations of the Economic Analysis of Law* (Cambridge, MA: Harvard University Press, 2004), 9.

with the same rights of others. She cannot allow the chickens to run away and eat feed from a neighbor's barn, and she cannot knowingly take one with a contagious disease to market. She may choose to have a particular chicken for dinner, to sell it, to lease it for a year to someone who likes fresh eggs, or to keep it and do what she pleases with the eggs. Well-defined property rights increase the value of any transaction she might make with a chicken buyer. If the buyer's rights were for some reason insecure, he would only be willing to pay less for it. Here there will be no discount for insecurity because the law ensures that a sale gives the buyer the same rights in the chicken as the farmer gave up. If they later have a dispute over it, they (or their attorneys) can rely on a large body of law to help them predict a court's decision and possibly save them the cost of litigation. If fences are in place there will be little difficulty identifying this farmer's chickens and distinguishing them from chickens owned by neighbors.[20] Easy identification means the farmer can use the chickens as collateral on a loan, contract with another farmer to raise them, or will them to her heirs.

Wealth means a person has more choices, and more inclusive property rights are sources of wealth. Such property rights give the farmer more options and greater incentives to avoid inefficient choices. Overspending on the chickens' feed or neglecting their health leaves the farmer poorer. Her possessory rights facilitate investment in specialized buildings that will cut production cost. A dependable legal system allows her (and her bankers) to better predict future flows of income and loan repayments from constructing a specialized a new building. Some other rights may be less secure and could affect her wealth. In earlier times, for example, farmers generally disposed of chicken waste as they saw fit, but today's environmental regulations require more costly treatments, and future regulations are uncertain.[21] The regulations limit her choices, but chicken-caused pollution infringes on rights of others to enjoy their landholdings or sell them at prices they had expected.

The Wild Bird Suppose you and I are neighboring landowners. A wild pheasant has chosen to nest in one of your trees. The bird flies over my property while I am hunting, and I succeed in downing it. The legal rule of "first possession" makes me its owner, which makes sense from the standpoint of economic efficiency.[22] First, the bird has a low value relative to the transaction cost of finding its nest. Second, a choice to let me rather than you have it (or vice versa) will have no impact on other economic activity. Nothing either of us does will noticeably affect the pheasant population, almost all of which breeds in the wild. (Hunting seasons are limited to ensure against extinction.) Third, assume that the law instead makes me give up the bird if you can prove it is yours. You would bear high costs (maybe photographic surveys and DNA checks) identifying and tracking the birds nesting on your land. After you and I incur the costs of going before a judge (who might still make a mistake), all you will get for your effort is a dead bird of low value, and probably a tough one at that. The rule of first possession (which probably also applies to the meteor stone example) is economically efficient—there is no reason for the law to prefer either of us, and the cost of locating the bird's nest is high while the benefits are nearly zero.

The Cave On your property you discover the mouth of a previously unknown cave that extends under land owned by others. To keep the story simple assume that somehow you know in advance that it contains a single large diamond that anyone who explores for a few hours will surely find. Now we have an object more valuable than the

---

[20]The law might require the farmer to put up a fence to reduce transaction costs like those of identifying ownership. This was the same job performed by cattle branding in unfenced open-range areas.

[21]"An Unsavory Byproduct: Runoff and Pollution," *Washington Post*, August 1, 1999.

[22]Dean Lueck, "The Rule of First Possession and the Design of the Law," *Journal of Law and Economics* 28 (October 1995): 393–436.

wild bird, along with a new type of transaction cost. The law might award the diamond to the owner of the land above it, to the person who owns the opening of the cave, or to whomever is the first to find it. In practice, the law awards both the diamond and the cave to the person whose land it opens onto. Economic efficiency requires that someone find the diamond, which is far more valuable above ground than below it. There is, however, no reason to care about exactly who that person is—any discoverer can quickly capture much of its value by selling it.

An efficient assignment of rights brings the diamond to the surface at minimum cost. Giving ownership to the person who owns the cave's opening is a clear rule that minimizes transaction costs. Before global positioning systems, awarding the diamond to the landowner above it would have invited costly and meaningless litigation. There would still be only one diamond, but all of the contenders would use up scarce resources trying to prove their claims. (Imagine the complications for a mine where different amounts of coal lie under every surface owner's land.) Duplicative investments could further waste valuable resources. If several surface owners have rights to anything below their land they might individually excavate mine shafts that are a waste of resources because their only purpose is to get the diamond before someone else does.

Contracts and Government

The Oil Pool Looking at the previous examples helps us see why growth of the oil and natural gas industries early in the twentieth century created a novel legal problem. Oil is in various ways similar to chickens, wild birds, and the diamond in the cave. Oil at the surface can be traded like a chicken or other commodity. Originally, courts put underground oil under a right of first possession like the wild bird, which led to races among landowners to extract it before their neighbors. Like the diamond the oil is hidden and must be found, but an underground pool has no opening like a cave or similar characteristic that might serve to identify an owner. In addition, the boundaries of an underground pool may remain unknown well after its discovery.

Another property of underground oil greatly complicated the definition of rights to it. Figure 9-2 shows a common oil-bearing formation.[23] Oil is usually trapped in porous rock and seldom exists as a liquid deposit. In Figure 9-2, the rock containing oil lies above rock containing water, and the oil is capped by an impermeable salt dome. Between the oil and the dome is a pocket of high-pressure natural gas. The well's yield depends on proper use of the gas, and on how oil flows through the rock to fill space left vacant by oil that has been extracted. Extraction lowers the pressure, driving the oil upward, and thickens the remaining oil, making it less mobile. The bottom half of Figure 9-2 shows a deposit from which some oil has been extracted. Too many wells located in the wrong places can leave as much as 70 percent of the oil behind. Unextracted oil brings no revenue to producers and no benefits to consumers.

Q. To further complicate matters, underground oil is capable of migration. If some has been extracted from one spot, unextracted oil from elsewhere will flow toward that spot. How does this affect people's incentives to extract oil as quickly as possible? Explain why the answer is not necessarily that it will further strengthen those incentives.

[23]The figure is from Bill D. Berger and Kenneth E. Anderson, *Modern Petroleum: A Basic Primer of the Industry*, 3rd ed. (Tulsa, OK: PennWell Books, 1992), 43.

FIGURE 9-2
Extraction of Oil

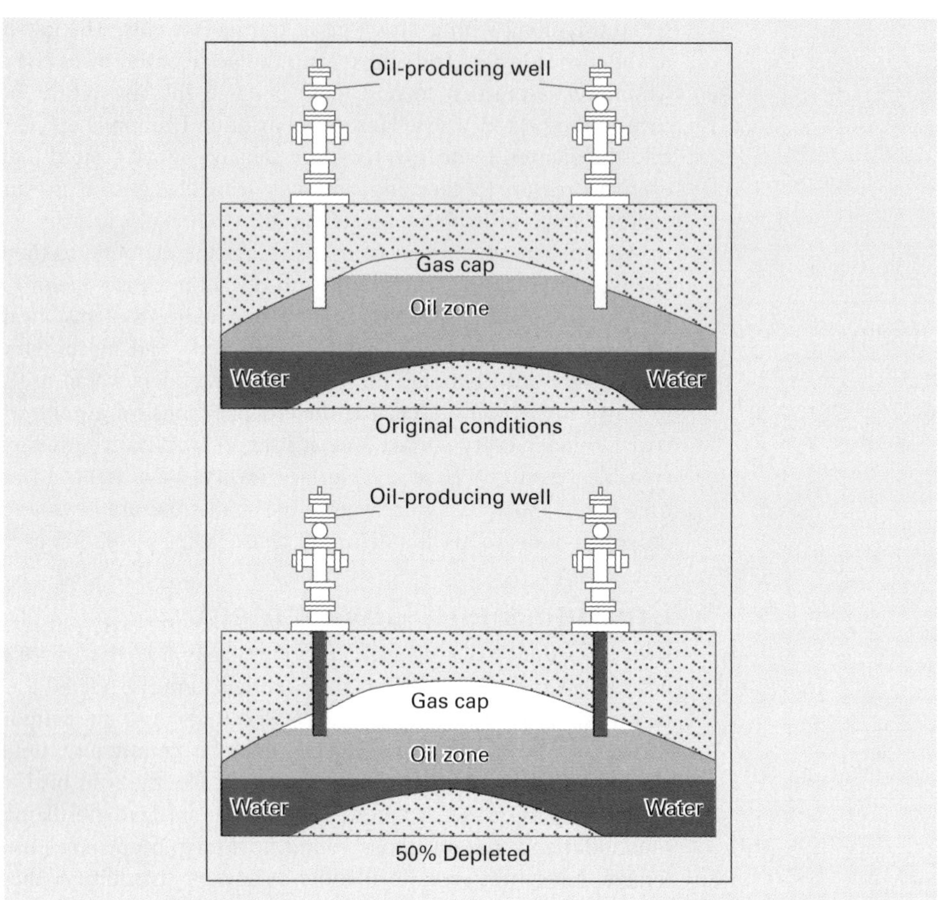

A Contract to Coordinate Production Table 9-3 shows a simple version of the Huntington Beach problem. Jones and Smith are the only two landowners above an oil deposit. Assume that they know the exact amount of oil in the pool and its market price.[24] Each can put one well or two on her land. With one well apiece they will extract all of the oil and each will earn $15. If each puts two wells on her property, profits fall to $10 each. The decline comes because less oil is produced and each must pay for a second well. In the northeast corner, Smith sinks two wells and Jones sinks one. Smith makes $20, more than if she stays with one well, and Jones makes only $5. Note that less oil is produced than when each has only one well. If only one person has two wells, that person is better off than she would have been if each owned one well, but the owner of the single well is worse off than she would have been if she also had two. The structure is the same as the price-fixing agreement in Chapter 6, and it gives rise to the same enforcement problem. An important difference here is that an agreement will increase total oil recovered. By contrast the price-fixers wish to coordinate a permanent reduction in output.

Jones and Smith can end up in the northwest corner of Table 9-3 rather than the southwest corner if they sign a *unitization* contract. That agreement will specify how many wells each can own, where the wells can be located, when the wells can be operated, and other practices they must follow. The contract will also specify the shares of

[24]For this example, also disregard any discounting of future income.

TABLE 9-3 COOPERATION AND CONFLICT IN THE OIL FIELD

		Smith	
		One Well	Two Wells
Jones	One Well	\$15, \$15	\$5, \$20
	Two Wells	\$20, \$5	\$10, \$10

income each is to receive and the costs for which each is responsible. Some unitization contracts require landowners to turn operations over to a third party. Doing so cuts their costs of administering the agreement and makes it harder for one of them to secretly increase output.

But why will Jones and Smith reach agreement? Each understands that failure to agree puts them both in the southeast corner, worse off than with an agreement. This unpleasant prospect might induce them to agree, particularly if they are neighbors who must interact every day. Further, there are only two of them, and their positions are symmetric. The picture is not so simple if 100 landowners have different acreages and some are above richer locations that can produce more oil quickly. The number of landowners alone makes negotiation difficult, and any further dissimilarities make it even harder. Sometimes an agreement will be so beneficial to large owners that they will settle for allowing a few small holdouts to stay outside the agreement.

The governments of oil-producing states have interests (tax revenue, for one) in maximizing the total output from an underground pool. Some of them have laws which specify that if the landowners cannot agree on unitization the state government will step in and require them to sign a contract it has designed. It will be a standard-form agreement (like a typical apartment lease), with blanks for them to fill in. Government reduces transaction costs because it can force the parties to sign this backstop contract. With the backstop as their only alternative, the landowners may have stronger incentives to reach an agreement of their own that better accounts for their individual situations. Legal definitions of "agreement" differ from state to state. In Oklahoma, for instance, favorable votes by 63 percent of leaseholders (or holders of drilling rights) can force all of them into an agreement, but Texas requires unanimity. Land in Wyoming is largely owned by the federal government, which will not even allow exploration before a unitization agreement has been signed by all parties. Not surprisingly, in 1975 82 percent of Wyoming's output came from unitized fields, but only 38 percent of Oklahoma's and 20 percent of Texas's.[25]

PROPERTY, CONTRACTS, AND MARKETS

The Origination and Adaptation of Property Rights

Fish The ability to construct value-increasing contracts depends on the definition and enforceability of property rights. As the oil example shows, establishing property rights in a resource is far from costless, but as the resource grows in value the benefits of contracting can become greater than those costs. Peoples' abilities to make mutually beneficial transactions depend on their legal and technological environments. In this section we will see new property rights being defined for valuable resources as a result of changes in laws and technology. Overfishing has long been a classroom example of

[25]Gary Liebcap and Steven Wiggins, "The Influence of Private Contractual Failure on Regulation: The Case of Oil Field Unitization," *Journal of Political Economy* 93 (August 1985): 690–714.

unclear property rights that are difficult or impossible to enforce. Overfishing is said to occur because no one can tag the fish to identify himself as their owner and enforce his rights against thieves. Because enforcement of rights is impossible, no one has incentives to leave some fish behind to breed for the future.[26]

Like the exaggerated fish stories anglers tell, this example is fast becoming a fish story. When fish were abundant relative to demand they posed no economic problem. Their value was low, but the small volume of fishing was no threat to their populations. As demand for fish grew over the twentieth century, catches became larger and fewer fish were left to breed. Both suppliers and consumers of fish could benefit from the establishment of property rights that would allow higher sustainable catch levels.[27] Today, law and technology are defining new property rights in fish.

- *New laws:* Governments around the world have expanded their offshore jurisdictions to as far as 200 miles from land. More than 80 percent of marketable fish are in these areas. Governments now issue licenses that limit catches and fishing seasons. An increasing number of countries allow holders of fishing rights to resell them to others, which has the same effect as trading fish. Quotas have enforced lower catches in coastal areas, where some fish populations are again reaching sustainable levels.[28]

- *Farming develops*: Some fish and shellfish that need not migrate or do not move at all are now "farmed" in the ocean and inland.[29] Some states offer tradable rights in portions of the sea floor near the shore for stationary species like oysters.[30]

- *Regulatory changes*: Governments also set detailed rules that increase the likelihood of reaching sustainable fish populations. For example, nets must have holes large enough for young fish to avoid capture, and there are limits on the sizes of crab and lobster traps.[31]

- *Oceangoing cages*: Giant cages that can contain and protect large numbers of fish are on the horizon. They can be mobile (one proposed design will take the Gulf Stream from Florida to Europe) and contain robotic feeding devices. Sonic systems under development can create the equivalent of walls that fish are reluctant to cross.[32]

---

[26]The earliest economic research on fishing rights is in H. Scott Gordon, "The Economic Theory of a Common-Property Resource: The Fishery," *Journal of Political Economy* 62 (April 1954): 124–42.

[27]The story of the fish is just one of many about property rights in wildlife. In the 1600s and 1700s, European colonization of North America raised the value of some fur-bearing animals that could formerly be trapped without limit. As that value grew, Indian tribes began to establish territorial hunting and trapping rights. Because holders of these rights could exclude nonholders from their territories, they could enjoy the longer income stream that came from limiting hunting to sustain the animal population. See Harold Demsetz, "Toward a Theory of Property Rights," *American Economic Review* 57 (May 1967): 347–59.

[28]Gardner M. Brown, "Renewable Natural Resource Management and Use Without Markets," *Journal of Economic Literature* 38 (December 2000): 875–914.

[29]Robert L. Stokes, "The Economics of Salmon Ranching," *Land Economics* 58 (November 1982): 464–77. Frederick W. Bell, "Competition from Fish Farming in Influencing Rent Dissipation: The Crawfish Fishery," *American Journal of Agricultural Economics* 68 (February 1986): 95–101.

[30]Richard Agnello and Lawrence Donnelley, "Property Rights and Efficiency in the Oyster Industry," *Journal of Law and Economics* 18 (October 1975): 521–33; Emmanuel Ajuzie and Marilyn Altobello, "Property Rights and Pollution: Their Implications for Long Island Sound and the Oyster Industry," *Review of Agricultural Economics* 19 (Autumn 1997): 242–51.

[31]William Furlong, "The Deterrent Effect of Regulatory Enforcement in the Fishery," *Land Economics* 67 (February 1991): 116–29; Ralph E. Thompson, "Entry Restrictions in the Fishery: A Survey of the Evidence," *Land Economics* 66 (November 1990): 359–78.

[32]Charles Mann, "The Bluewater Revolution," *Wired*, May 2004, 183–87.

- *Identifiable ownership*: New breeds of fish are under development that can be tagged to prevent and detect thefts. Possible tags include genetic markers, inner-ear markers (like a human fingerprint), and scale markers that will allow optical detection of trace elements in the waters where a fish was born.[33]

Scarce Property in Outer Space Space may be the final frontier, but parts of it are already crowded. A narrow band 25,000 miles above the equator is the only possible orbit for geostationary satellites that are always over the same spot and have become vital for telecommunications and security.[34] (A possible future use is tracking fish in the oceans.) Initially, slots for satellites and their radio frequencies were allocated first-come, first-served (a variant of the rule of capture). Today there are several hundred geostationary satellites, and radio interference is a common problem. To cope with that problem a market in extraterrestrial rights is emerging. Nations and businesses are trading frequency assignments and rights to use each others' satellites to minimize interference and put existing equipment to more valuable uses.[35] Governments are working to replace the inefficient first-come, first-served system with auctions that will allocate equipment and radio frequencies to high bidders. This a natural extension of the Federal Communications Commission's highly successful ($22 billion in revenue) recent auctions of terrestrial frequencies.[36] The growing value of extraterrestrial resources has spurred innovations that use them more efficiently. These include technologies that carry signals at previously unusable frequencies and that allow existing capacity to carry more messages. Also under development are transmitters and receivers that can better discriminate among signals.[37]

The Effects of Property Rights Changes on Markets

A New Type of Ownership The development of new property rights can lower the costs of existing transactions, increase their potential benefits and allow contracts that were not previously legal or feasible. This section is a case study of how a new type of market grew after rights to provide air transport were redefined. The Federal Aviation Administration (FAA) regulates aircraft owners who wish to carry paying passengers.[38] Their planes must meet design standards (e.g., emergency exits are required) and be maintained according to strict timetables. Owners must use properly trained crews, operate under filed flight schedules, and be adequately insured. A business whose executives travel a lot can avoid some of these costs by purchasing or leasing its own plane, which also gives it the convenience of making its own flight plans. Businesses with lower

[33]Michael DeAlessi, "Technology, Marine Conservation, and Fisheries Management," in *The Half-Life of Policy Rationales: How New Technology Affects Old Policy Issues*, ed. Fred Foldvary and Daniel Klein (New York: New York University Press, 2003), 21–37.

[34]Clas Wihlborg and Per Magnus Wijkman, "Outer Space Resources in Efficient and Equitable Use: New Frontiers for Old Principles," *Journal of Law and Economics* 24 (April 1981): 23–43.

[35]Harvey J. Levin, "Trading Orbit Spectrum Assignments in the Space Satellite Industry," *American Economic Review* 81 (May 1991): 42–45.

[36]Molly K. Macauley, "Regulation on the Final Frontier," *Regulation* 26 (Summer 2003): 36–41; Paul Milgrom, "Putting Auction Theory to Work: The Simultaneous Ascending Auction," *Journal of Political Economy* 108 (April 2000): 245–72.

[37]Molly K. Macauley, "Out of Space? Regulation and Technical Change in Communication Satellites," *American Economic Review* 76 (May 1986): 280–84.

[38]All facts and figures for this example are from Eileen Gleimer, "When Less Can Be More: Fractional Ownership of Aircraft—The Wings of the Future," *Journal of Air Law and Commerce* 64 (Fall 1999): 979–1032.

executive travel demands can use scheduled airlines, and if necessary, they can use expensive charters and air taxis that operate under the rules similar to airlines.

Between jet owners and airline users lies a growing pool of businesses and individuals whose travel requirements are not served well by either. They value setting their own itineraries and schedules but do not find these benefits worth the cost of ownership. Their options changed after the FAA changed its regulations in response to a proposal for a new type of service. In 1986, Richard Santulli was CEO of Executive Jet Aviation, which sold charters and leased airplanes. He was considering a jet for his staff but concluded that it would get too little use to justify a purchase or a long lease. Co-ownership was possible but often led to scheduling conflicts. It also left the owners responsible for hiring a crew and servicing the plane. Santulli proposed NetJets, the first time-share program for aircraft. It was the same sort of logic that had earlier produced time-sharing for condominiums in vacation areas.

NetJets would sell shares in each of its planes, and holders would pay only for the fractions of time when they expected to use the plane.[39] If a scheduling conflict made a particular plane unavailable to one of its owners, NetJets would require the owners of some unused plane to allow its use by that person. NetJets cut transaction costs by being responsible for crews, maintenance, and compliance with federal regulations. Owners who wished to sell their shares, change the sizes of those shares, or switch to another type of plane could do so. (NetJets offers 14 different ones.) The NetJets business model would have been in violation of 1986 FAA rules, which did not allow owners to assign staffing and maintenance to others and did not allow the exchange of rights to use planes owned by others without government clearance. NetJets obtained exemptions from the regulations after showing that its proposal did not sacrifice safety or reduce its liability for accidents. (Its safety performance is equal or superior to that of scheduled airlines.) The exemption allowed NetJets to offer a new property right, through a contract that would not have been legal before the FAA's decision.

The record shows that allowing NetJets to operate created substantial economic value: By 1997 it had 95 planes and 700 owners. Competing time-share operators entered the market; some succeeded and others failed. By the mid-1990s, NetJets had obtained permission from other governments to operate in Europe and the Middle East. In 1999, it had 300 time-shared aircraft with 1,500 owners. In 2003, NetJets flew more than 250,000 flights in more than 140 countries. As businesses relocate into rural areas (think Wal-Mart of Bentonville, Arkansas), the value of time-shares to reach inconvenient locations with poor airline service is growing. Time-shares were not just a substitute for solely owned planes—between 70 and 80 percent of time-share owners are new to business aviation. Fractional ownership now accounts for about 20 percent of all new business-jet purchases worldwide.

Analyzing the Creation of Value The introduction of time-sharing resembles some competitive strategies described in Chapter 8. Figure 9-3 shows what happens if the market for executive travel is perfectly competitive. Market supply before time-shares is shown by S, and demand by D. Equilibrium is at $10 (per minute) and 10,000 hours of flight. The availability of time-sharing affects supply and demand. Transaction costs have fallen and so has cost per mile. NetJets cuts its owners' costs of negotiating for individual trips, and the interchangeability of planes means less costly "deadheading"—that is, empty flights made only to reposition a plane. If this raises consumers valuations of each unit by $6 and lowers marginal cost by $2, the market will reach equilibrium at

[39]For details on NetJets and available sharing arrangements, see the NetJets Web site, http://www.netjets.com. The company was purchased in 1998 by Warren Buffett's Berkshire Hathaway Corporation.

FIGURE 9-3
Time-share

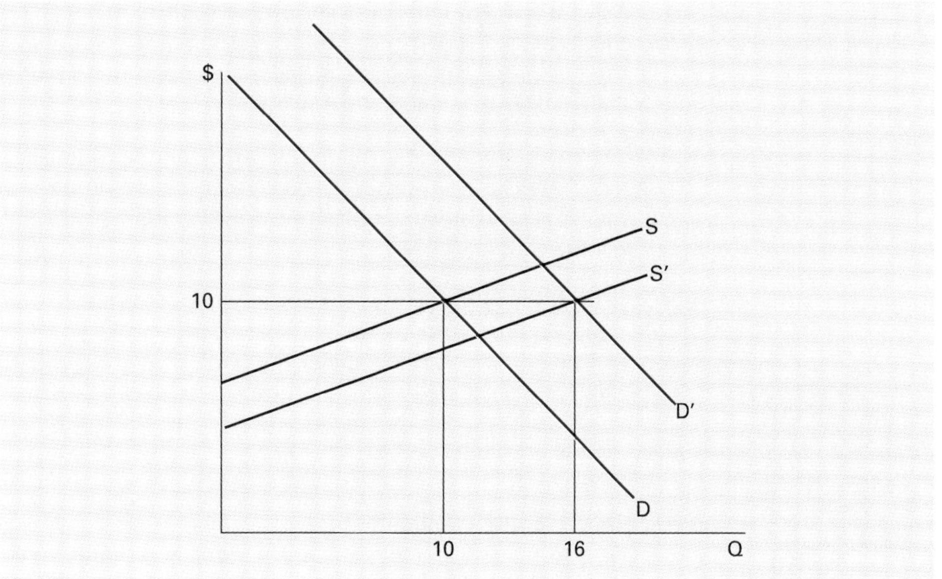

$10 (a coincidence) and 16 units. NetJets' customers benefit by the offer of reduced transaction sizes but could not benefit by owning their own planes. This may explain why so large a fraction of time-share owners had no former connection with business aviation.

The NetJets case study summarizes some of this chapter's lessons. It shows how a market's ability to create value will depend on the types of contracts allowed in it. Of course, we could instead have assumed, contrary to fact, that a contract like that of NetJets had always been possible but no one had yet gotten the idea for it. Whether or not NetJets required the government's permission, its contract is an innovation quite like a technology breakthrough. Like new technology, an efficient new contract cuts sellers' costs and/or raises buyers' benefits, net of the costs of creating and enforcing it. When unitization was impossible, the benefits of oil and gas transactions were smaller, and wasted oil made buyers and sellers worse off. The coming of the automotive age required innovations in cars and fuel—and contracting. Without the availability of low-cost insurance contracts the risks of liability for a traffic accidents would have been so great that few people would have been willing to bear them.

Chapter Summary

- A contract is an enforceable set of promises to take certain actions over the future.
- The detailed provisions of a contract specify a set of property rights connected with a transaction. A property right gives a person the ability to use something in a defined manner, including the right to sell or transfer it.
- If a contract can be formed at a low enough cost, it can create benefits for the parties that they cannot achieve through simpler transactions. The benefits arise because a contract gives the parties confidence that they will earn returns on investments specific to their relationship.

- When there are numerous parties the costs of negotiating and enforcing a contract that benefits the group can be so high that they will not make one. Government represents a way of lowering these transaction costs because it can enforce laws and collect taxes, but political factors may result in inefficient policies.
- External costs and benefits occur when one person's activity affects the economic value another can capture, whether positively or negatively. If negotiations have low enough cost, the parties can achieve an efficient solution that maximizes their net benefits.
- If the costs of negotiation are low, Coasian reasoning shows that in situations of external costs or benefits the parties will negotiate to an efficient outcome, regardless of who has which rights under the law. What matters is that the law clearly specify those rights.
- If property rights in some resource are not defined or not enforceable, people will be less willing to make investments that increase the value the resource might create.
- The efficient definition of property rights in some good will depend on its value relative to the cost of enforcing those rights and the technologies that are available for their enforcement.
- Many contracts can be modeled using the prisoners' dilemma game previously used to analyze cartels. The value a contract creates can only be maximized if a party that breaches it can be sanctioned.
- As resources become more valuable, the benefits of establishing property rights in them become greater, and people will be willing to incur higher costs to define and enforce those rights.
- Changes in the legal environment may allow new property rights that can increase the potential economic value created by contracts.

Questions and Problems

1. Some crops have flowers that are rich in nectar, but pollination by bees has only a small effect on their yields. Construct an example to show that in this case the beekeeper will probably pay for the right to locate his bees near farmers. How might your answer change if beekeepers are competitive and there is only one farmer?
2. What sorts of provisions might a contract include to handle days when it rains and the bees cannot be released? What if the beekeeper has a contract with farmers in another area and cannot stay an extra day without being in breach of that contract?
3. In footnote 7 we suggested that if transaction costs are too high, a government subsidy to beekeepers might produce an efficient solution to the external benefit problem. Explain why.
4. Grade-school education is said to yield a beneficial externality because all of us benefit from interacting with people who know basic reading and writing. Assuming that this is true, make a case for providing education from taxes. Then make a case against it. Can you think of any comparable beneficial externalities from college education? If they exist, is there necessarily a case for public funding of colleges?

5. In the earlier beekeeper, farmer, and writer example, show that it is impossible to find a payment by the writer that induces the beekeeper and farmer to arrange for the beekeeper to stay for only three days.
6. What are the highest and lowest payments from the writer that the beekeeper–farmer team will accept for the sixth day? Assuming that the farmer can dispose of $7 from the writer as she wishes, what range of payments will the beekeeper accept? Assuming that the beekeeper gets that amount, what range of payments will the farmer accept? (Remember that negative payments are also possible.) Answer the same questions for the fifth day.
7. In the famous case of *Sturges v. Bridgman*, Bridgman, a candy maker, had an established business, and Sturges, a dentist, moved into the office next door.[40] Bridgman's sugar-crushing machines set up such strong vibrations that Sturges was unable to use his drill safely when the machines were operating. Is it efficient for a court to order Bridgman to cease doing business because of the harm to Sturges? Explain why or why not.
   a. The following table below shows the marginal benefits to Bridgman for each additional hour of candy making in a 12-hour day and the corresponding marginal losses to Sturges. If negotiation is costless, how many hours of the day will Bridgman be making candy? Will this still be the case if the court had instead ruled that Bridgman could operate his equipment without regard to its effect on Sturges? Explain.

HOURS OF CANDY MAKING	INCOME GAINED BY BRIDGMAN IN AN HOUR	INCOME LOST BY STURGES IN AN HOUR
1	$35	$4
2	30	5
3	26	7
4	23	9
5	20	11
6	17	14
7	15	17
8	13	21
9	11	25
10	9	30
11	8	36
12	7	42

8. In October 2001, Barry Bonds of the San Francisco Giants hit his record-setting 700th home run. After fan Alex Popov caught the ball, another fan, Patrick Hayashi, bumped him and grabbed the ball when he dropped it. The ball ultimately sold for $450,000 and Popov and Hayashi went to court, where they were ordered to split the money. If you were interested in efficiency, how would you decide the case? Why, if at all, would your exact decision matter?[41]

[40]See Coase, "The Problem of Social Cost," 8–10.

[41]"Man Who Caught Bonds' 700th Homer Sued," *San Francisco Chronicle*, September 28, 2004.

9. In the example of the diamond in the cave, what would be efficient law if any one explorer had only a very small probability of finding the diamond? How would your answer change if the costs of exploration were very low?
10. In the case of the diamond, duplicative mineshafts were a waste of economic resources, and the law makes them unprofitable. Instead of a diamond, what if a number of independent inventors are racing to be the first to obtain a valuable patent and the monopoly it grants. Does the patent system encourage duplicative efforts solely for the chance to be first? Why might you want the patent system to do this?
11. Will it be inefficient if the owner of the cave's opening chooses to take bids and award the rights to enter the cave and find the diamond to the highest bidder? Why or why not?
12. State A requires a unitization contract before oil production begins from a field, while State B requires a contract only after production has begun. Do you expect that State A or State B will have a larger fraction of contracts imposed by government? Explain.
13. Some fields have large enough quantities of both oil and natural gas that coordination must be achieved for the production of both, rather than oil alone as in our examples. Will fields with both oil and gas have greater difficulties in unitization than fields with oil or gas alone? Explain. (Hint: Look closely at Figure 9-2.)
14. We said earlier that the invention of liability insurance was a precondition for the creation of value that resulted from driving. But because liability insurance also encourages drivers to take additional risks, why wouldn't the world be a better place without it?
15. Explain why the fish left behind are a type of investment. Some opponents of property rights in fish have argued against ownership because the fish already belong to "everyone." Try to define what (if anything) is meant by everyone being an owner, and how "everyone's" property rights might be defined and enforced.
16. In Figure 9-3, supply before NetJets is $Q_S = -20 + 3P$ and demand is $Q_D = 20 - P$.

    a. Show that equilibrium is at $10 and 10 units. Assume that time-sharing cuts marginal costs by $2 and raises demand by $6 at all outputs. Show that the new equilibrium is at $10 and 16 units. Then calculate producer and consumer surplus before and after NetJets introduces its contract.
    b. [Requires calculus] Now assume that NetJets is a monopoly. Before it introduced its contract the marginal cost was $MC = 6.67 + Q/3$ (fixed costs are absent) and demand was $Q_D = 20 - P$. Calculate its profit-maximizing output and price. Then show the new equilibrium after the contract shifts marginal cost downward by $2 and demand upward by $6. Why does price increase here but not in the competitive market?
    c. [Requires calculus] Try analyzing this situation when NetJets and Brand X both offer time-shares and behave as Cournot-Nash duopolists. Market demand is again $Q_D = 20 - P$, and marginal costs of both sellers are constant at $8. Compare this solution (and consumer and producer benefits) with the outcome when demand shifts upward by 8.00 and marginal cost falls to $6.

Chapter 10

The Economics of Contracts

INTRODUCTION

A Tale of Two Tank Farms

In Figure 10-1 both photos show storage tanks that can hold crude oil, petrochemicals, or refined products like gasoline. The tanks in Figure 10-1a surround BP

William Boyce/Corbis

frans lemmens / Alamy

FIGURE 10-1
(a) Carson, California: BP ARCO Refinery
(b) Bayonne, New Jersey: Waterfront Storage Facilities

ARCO Corporation's refinery in Carson, California, near Los Angeles. The refinery is the only such facility in its area, and BP ARCO owns all of the tanks. Figure 10-1b is an aerial photo of the industrial waterfront in Bayonne, New Jersey, with tanks as far as the eye can see. Some are owned by Bayonne's many refiners and petrochemical producers, and some are the property of specialists like PD Oil and Chemical Storage, Inc. PD leases tank capacity to the oil and chemical processors. Most of them also have their own storage facilities, but rather than be completely self-sufficient they choose to contract with PD when they have special requirements or are using their own tanks to capacity. The availability of facilities like PD's lowers the costs of oil and chemical plant owners, who do not have to build large amounts of storage that they will seldom fill. The area around BP ARCO's refinery contains no standalone storage operators like PD whose facilities might be available for lease. But even if an independent storage company like PD existed near BP ARCO, that company might still prefer to incur the costs of building enough tank capacity to meet all of its demands. In this chapter we will see why contracts that lower a refiner's cost are feasible in Bayonne but not in Carson.

Any mutually agreed-upon exchange creates economic value. The benefits of any transaction, however, can be increased if its terms are better tailored to the parties' particular situations. Our basic transaction and market models were purposely simple—a standardized good changed hands at the same time payment was made. Now we look in more detail at the arrangement and enforcement of more complex agreements to see the benefits and difficulties they can create.

- Maximizing the benefits of a transaction often requires specific investments, such as specialized facilities that will lose value if the parties fail to fulfill the commitments they have made in a contract.
- Many contracts are not self-enforcing. One party can make itself better off by breaching the contract (i.e., not performing as specified), and the other can become worse off than if no contract had existed. This means contracts must contain enforceable provisions that require the breaching party to make good the other's loss.
- Breach of a contract often entails acts by one party that degrade the value of contract-specific investments made by the other.
- In some cases where monetary damages are difficult to estimate or enforce, a court will require "specific performance" of the breaching party's obligations under the contract.
- Many contracts involve principal/agent relationships, in which the principal faces high costs of determining whether the agent is actually making efforts that the principal expects. Methods of payment can lessen the principal's difficulties, and these methods vary with the particulars of the situation.
- Many contracts do not fully specify what the parties are to do in all possible situations. Incompleteness may reflect the costs of writing a more complete contract but sometimes can serve to discourage opportunistic behavior by one or both parties.
- It can be economically efficient to include provisions in a contract that terminate it or open up parts of it for renegotiation if certain events take place that are beyond the parties' control.

SPECIFIC INVESTMENTS AND OPPORTUNISM

What a Contract Does or Doesn't Allow

The Missing $6 Million One day in September 2004, Delta Airlines Flight 118 was about to leave New York on its 18-hour journey to Mumbai, India. The pilot's preflight announcements included an odd one: He thanked the cabin crew for driving to a supermarket to buy muffins. A few hours earlier food supplier Gate Gourmet had halted all deliveries to Delta. The companies, of course, had a contract, but several months earlier Delta had refused to pay Gate Gourmet $6 million, claiming it was an overcharge under the contract's terms. Unable to resolve the dispute and concerned about Delta's worsening financial condition in a declining market for air travel, Gate Gourmet ceased food deliveries. A few days later a court ordered Gate Gourmet to resume service to Delta, but several days of foodless flights had harmed Delta's reputation with the regular passengers who accounted for much of its revenue.[1]

Delta and Gate Gourmet eventually reached a confidential settlement regarding the $6 million and continued to do business with each other. As often happens in such disputes, some important facts are not publicly available. So let's consider some ways the dispute might have actually arisen. First, Delta was financially stressed and may have chosen to claim that a payment it properly owed Gate Gourmet was in fact an overcharge. The choice was not costless for Delta, which incurred expenses, delays, and the risk of a bad outcome in court. There might also have been benefits, however, even if Delta lost in court—if its finances improved, it might obtain the money on more attractive terms. As a second possibility, Gate Gourmet might have known that its billing was questionable but nevertheless took the chance that Delta would pay routinely or quickly settle over part of it rather than risk interruption. As a third possibility (and we can envision lots of others), the contract may have been silent about the $6 million, which (let us assume) arose in a situation that neither party had expected when they negotiated their contract. Now that the situation had materialized, they would either negotiate a settlement or go to court if they could not reach one.

Q. Why would the two parties agree to keep the terms of their settlement confidential? It is easy to envision situations where one party would want to publicize the terms. For example, if the settlement relieved Delta of all or most of the alleged $6 million obligation, its management would probably want to tell shareholders the good news. Why would they agree as a condition of settlement that the details not be made public?

Now look at three possible explanations of Gate Gourmet's decision to cease deliveries. First, it may have believed in good faith that the contract allowed it to halt all deliveries if Delta refused to pay any part of its bills, even if Delta was up to date on the portion that was not in dispute. Second, Gate Gourmet might have known that the contract did not allow it to curtail deliveries but believed Delta was so close to bankruptcy (it was) that it would soon cease paying for all of its food. If Gate Gourmet continued

[1] "Delta Gets Court Order Requiring Gate Gourmet to Resume Catering," *Wall Street Journal*, September 23, 2004; "Food Fight: Caterer Stews Over Delta," *Wall Street Journal*, September 29, 2004.

serving and Delta went into bankruptcy, its debt might be paid off at less than face value.[2] In a third possibility, during the months since they signed the contract, certain changes in the food or air travel markets might have left Gate Gourmet with lower profits than it had originally expected.[3] The refusal to continue service could have been an attempt to coerce Delta into renegotiating some of its terms.

Q. Gate Gourmet is currently the world's largest airline food supplier, with facilities on every continent. Looking at the three possible explanations for Gate Gourmet stopping food service, how would learning this fact change your beliefs about which explanations are more likely or less likely?

Opportunism An outsider cannot definitively determine why Delta refused to pay or Gate Gourmet stopped delivering. They may have reasonably differed over exactly what the contract required. The contract language may have been unclear or might not have addressed some particular situation they found themselves in. It is also possible that Delta or Gate Gourmet was trying to profit from actions it knew the contract might not allow, hoping the other party would drop the dispute or pay up. Such actions are examples of *opportunistic* behavior or *opportunism*, competing not just according to pre-established rules but also by breaking or bending those rules.

Up to now in our study of economics we have only seen sellers who competed for the business of buyers on the basis of price, product design, or other aspects of their transactions. Without spelling it out, we assumed that people lived up to whatever agreements they had made, paying or delivering in accordance with agreed-upon terms. Opportunism adds the possibility that a party can gain by disregarding or breaking the rules. If people never behave opportunistically, a trader's word is as good as his bond. People can concentrate on maximizing the value their transaction creates and bargaining to mutually beneficial outcomes where the contract is incomplete or unclear.[4] Opportunism then entails transaction costs the parties will wish to minimize, and they will attempt to do that by their choices of contract provisions.

Either Delta or Gate Gourmet might opportunistically stage a "holdup" to extract wealth from the other.[5] Delta may believe Gate Gourmet will tolerate a single delayed or omitted payment rather than lose a large stream of future income by terminating the relationship. Gate Gourmet has contracts of its own for facilities and ingredients that it made it made in order to serve Delta, which it will only be able to modify or terminate at substantial cost. With no way to avoid the loss on its specialized facilities and commitments, Gate Gourmet will continue to serve Delta as long as it receives enough to cover its operating costs. By the same token, Gate Gourmet might threaten to cut Delta off (or actually do so for a short time), because it knows the airline cannot quickly contract with another supplier that offers comparable service. Both face high transaction costs of finding new trading partners.

---

[2]Delta in fact went into bankruptcy and reorganization a year later, in September 2005. In 2007, Delta merged with Northwest Airlines, which had also gone into bankruptcy.

[3]Gate Gourmet's revenue fell by 34 percent between 2000 and 2004, in part a consequence of the airline industry's trend to economize on food service. See "Airline Caterers Find Cuts Hard to Digest," *Los Angeles Times*, January 15, 2006.

[4]Oliver E. Williamson, *Economic Organization: Firms, Markets and Policy Control* (New York: New York University Press, 1986), 181, 201.

[5]"Holdup" is a colorful but common economic term for this behavior.

Q. In light of the reasoning about games from Chapter 6, will Delta find Gate Gourmet's threat to cut off service credible? Explain. If it does not, what is the point of Gate Gourmet's even making this threat?

Specific Assets and Opportunism

The Importance of Specific Assets The food preparation facilities Gate Gourmet uses to serve Delta are examples of *specific assets*, those that create more economic value when making meals for Delta than in any alternative use. If Gate Gourmet and Delta's relationship unexpectedly ends, part of these facilities' value will be lost. It may be costly to redeploy them, and they may end up in less valuable uses. Gate Gourmet's equipment will stand idle while it looks for a new customer. Even after it gets the customer the facilities may be poorly adapted to the new relationship—for example, they might not be suitable for preparing that airline's national cuisine, the sizes of servings desired, or the food at the appropriate time of day. Some facilities (e.g., general-purpose ovens) may be transferrable to non-airline uses, and some (e.g., serving trays with the airline's logo) may not. Even if Gate Gourmet finds another airline caterer to buy the specialized equipment, there will be costs of relocating it.

Many aspects of specificity can raise the cost of redeployment and the risks of opportunism:

- *Task specificity*: Specialized equipment is often necessary for low-cost production. Auto manufacturers use one-of-a-kind tools to attach a transmission to an engine; specifically designed for the limited space and tight tolerances required. One manufacturer's machine may only work for another make of car after costly modification.
- *Locational specificity*: Once built, facilities like electrical generators are immovable. In addition, reliability can require that a generator be located in a particular place. Such a facility is also task-specific—its only possible output is high-voltage electricity.
- *Dedicated specificity*: Gate Gourmet's capital probably included equipment that it only bought in the expectation that Delta would remain a customer for a long time. Even if some of the equipment can be used elsewhere, a sudden stop in Delta's business leaves Gate Gourmet with the costly job of finding another buyer.
- *Human specificity*: Workers can also have degrees of specificity. An employer's investment in company-specific skills can make a worker more productive, but that worker also has leverage during a salary review because if she leaves the employer incurs the cost of training a replacement.

Why Limit Your Options? Having a choice of many trading partners at all times is not always as desirable as may first appear. More value might be created if a buyer agrees to limits on his ability to deal with different producers or if a seller agrees not to deal with customers other than this particular buyer. For example, the buyer might promise to take delivery of a specified amount of some good in every week of the next year, with delivery and payment dates specified in advance. The agreement can give the seller the benefits of steady operation, avoiding the costs of shutting down and restarting production unpredictably. Fixing a payment schedule might allow her to borrow on better terms than if sales were less predictable. If the contract fixes her production schedule, her suppliers may be able to operate at lower costs because their production and shipments are also more predictable. The buyer can benefit because a contract that ensures deliveries at predictable prices allows him to make more competitive price and delivery commitments to his own customers.

Vertical Integration

The Refineries Revisited An oil refinery is an ideal example of a highly specific asset. A refinery is a custom-constructed complex of very costly equipment, much of which is useless for any purpose other than processing crude oil. A refinery cannot somehow be converted to the manufacture of other goods; modifying it to produce, for example, oil-based petrochemicals will be costly, and it is virtually impossible to relocate. For this example, one more aspect of specificity is important: refining oil requires a continuous flow of feedstocks and coordination of many distinct operations. A quick or unexpected shutdown of the refinery can damage costly equipment, and even a startup that follows a nonemergency shutdown can cost millions.[6] To operate continuously, the refiner must have access to storage at all times for its working inventories of crude oil and refined products.

Storage tanks at a particular location also have a degree of specificity, and different locations have differing degrees of specificity. To understand why this matters let's start with an unreal story. Assume that Jones has built a refinery but for unknown reasons has no storage facilities of his own. Seeing Jones as a potential user, Smith builds some storage tanks next door. Assume that Jones is the only customer who can give Smith enough business to make her investment profitable, and also assume that Smith is the only possible supplier of storage to Jones. Like Jones's refinery, Smith's tanks are costly to salvage or move if she gets too little business. At the outset, Jones and Smith devise a contract specifying the price Jones will pay for storage along with other provisions that will govern his access to and use of the tanks.

If their contract is unclear, Smith will soon realize that she can greatly complicate Jones's life. Assume that she discovers a clause she thinks might allow her to charge more than the originally agreed-on price. She mentions her discovery to Jones and strongly suggests that he pay it, because failure to do so will (in her opinion) be a breach that entitles her to claim financial damages. In an alternative story, Smith might reread the contract with her lawyers and claim that it allows her to restrict Jones's rights to access her tanks in ways that will raise Jones's operating costs. If Jones agrees to pay a bit more, however, she promises not to interpret the terms in this way. Of course Jones retains the option of taking her to court. Doing so, however, is costly, and Jones risks a decision that will validate Smith's claim. The opportunism in this example can go either way because Jones and Smith are in symmetric positions, each in control of a resource essential for the other's survival.

Q. What if Smith tries to raise the price that Jones is charged, and Jones responds with a threat that he will build his own tanks and use less of Smith's capacity unless Smith agrees to a lower charge for storage. When will Smith find this threat credible?

---

[6]Recall the experience on the Gulf Coast after the hurricanes of 2005. See "Refineries Are Packing It In," *Houston Chronicle*, September 21, 2005.

Why Vertical Integration? Now we can explain why a stand-alone tank farm is feasible in Bayonne while the refinery in Carson owns all of its tanks. An extensive system of railroads and pipes on the New Jersey waterfront gives over 50 nearby refiners and petrochemical producers the option to store with PD. That company can survive as a standalone specialist in storage because it need not do business in the future with a customer who tries to act opportunistically—there are many others in the area who might use its tanks. Likewise, PD cannot act opportunistically toward a particular customer, because there are other storage facilities in the area (and refiners sometimes exchange storage among themselves).[7] If BP ARCO's only alternative to self-storage is an independent operator next door (who has no other potential customers), the two parties are like Smith and Jones. BP ARCO can eliminate these problems by building its own storage facility and becoming vertically integrated, as discussed in Chapter 8.

For a refiner, vertical integration into storage is an obvious solution, and we see it quite generally in that industry. Storage facilities are a relatively small part of a refinery's assets, and its local management may be able to cut costs by coordinating refining and storage operations. Delta's situation is somewhat different. Vertically integrating into food service is certainly possible, but to become its own supplier Delta must manage some activities that are quite unlike those of operating an airline. A partial list would include operating kitchens near a large number of airports; arranging for dependable deliveries of food and drink to them; finding and training a workforce with skills quite different from most airline employees; and complying with complex health, safety, alcohol, and environmental laws. Delta must further perform these tasks in a number of countries, where the availability of ingredients and the legal environment differ greatly.[8] An airline that vertically integrates into food service has in effect entered a completely different line of business.

Nowadays, no major U.S. airline operates its own food service. Today, a competitive airline must concentrate on cost reduction, attractive flight schedules, and aspects of service quality like on-time arrivals. Through the 1950s, airlines were a minor industry, protected from almost all competition by government regulation. Each either served food prepared by employees or obtained meals from other airlines. Specialized operators like Gate Gourmet only came with the market growth of the 1970s, when the airline industry became large enough to support a separate industry of food providers who could supply them at lower cost than they could supply themselves. As the market grew, airlines deintegrated out of food preparation and began contracting for the service. The experience of Delta and Gate Gourmet, however, is a reminder that contracting is not without problems of its own.

What Happened to Coase?

This chapter's analysis of contracts looks quite different from what we encountered only one chapter ago. There we described the how economist/lawyer Ronald Coase showed that if transactions and negotiations were costless, people would arrive at agreements that maximized the economic value they created. The farmer and beekeeper of Chapter 9 lived in an unreal world where they could costlessly set up and enforce complex agreements that maximized their joint benefits. We introduced Coasian reasoning with zero transaction costs for one of the same reasons that we earlier introduced the model of perfectly competitive markets. Each gave us a standard for efficient resource allocation

[7]They can also exchange products to the same effect. Refiner A's crude oil storage tanks are full, but it can sell an incoming shipment to B, whose tanks have capacity. Later, B might divert one of his shipments to A as part of a reciprocal deal.

[8]Gate Gourmet, for example, operates kitchens in 30 countries. See its location lists at http://gategourmet.gategroupmember.com/index.php/global-locations.

to compare against markets and agreements that were not so perfect. The discussion of specific assets and opportunism introduced only the first of many obstacles that stand in the way of perfectly efficient contracts in real life.

Coasian reasoning also puts the example of the refiner and the storage operator into perspective. The risks of opportunistic behavior illustrated by that example will vanish if their agreement is complete and not subject to uncertain or ambiguous interpretations. Any real contract between a refiner and tank owner would permit deviations from the contract price only in precisely defined situations. Behind every contract stands a body of commercial law that has developed over centuries and that tells the parties how a court is likely to rule if a dispute arises. If the parties can both anticipate a court's decision with some degree of certainty (and they expect the same decision), both will have less room for opportunism. If opportunistic behavior is more likely to be detected and punished, less of it will occur. Talk about a litigation explosion is commonplace today, but at least 95 percent of all contract disputes are settled by negotiation rather than in court.[9] The reason for that may come as a surprise. As we will see in Chapter 17, failure to negotiate an agreeable outcome throws the matter into the hands of judges and jurors who cannot possibly know as much as the parties themselves about actual business practices and about their options for settlement.

DAMAGES FOR BREACH OF CONTRACT

Liquidated Damages and Penalties

Two parties who enter into an efficient contract can create more economic value than they can without a contract. Often, however, the gain to one of the parties from acting opportunistically (assuming that the other adheres to the contract) can exceed that party's share of the wealth that would have been created if they had both honored their agreement.[10] If they do not care about their reputations (perhaps they will never interact with each other again), they must somehow be induced to keep to the terms of the contract. As we saw earlier, contracts often require the parties to invest in specific resources. Breach by one of them leaves these investments worth less than if both had kept to the agreement. The parties themselves have an interest in enforcing performance of their contract, and so does the larger society. Breach of the contract reduces the value of the wealth that could have been created by the parties' investments.

The legal remedy for a breach is often *liquidated damages.* Assume that Jones breaches a contract with Smith that would have created substantial economic value had they both performed as agreed upon. If a court determines that there was a breach, their contract may specify that Jones pay Smith a particular form of them called *expectation damages.* These are an amount that leaves Smith as well off as if Jones had not breached. Smith will be paid the amount she expected to gain at the time they made the contract, net of any amount she actually did receive after the breach. The oilfield unitization contract of Table 9-3 is reproduced as Table 10-1. Recalling the situation, if Jones and Smith limit themselves to one well each, they can each earn $15 net of the costs of sinking the wells and other expenses. If they each have two wells, each makes $10. Disregarding the costs of a well, higher total profit means a larger yield of oil from the pool, that is, when Jones sinks two wells and Smith sinks one, the $25 worth of oil they recover is smaller than if each has only one well.

---

[9]Samuel R. Gross and Kent D. Syverud, "Getting to No: A Study of Settlement Negotiations and the Selection of Cases for Trial," *Michigan Law Review* 90 (November 1991): 319–93.

[10]For a much fuller discussion of damages from economic and legal standpoints see Richard A. Posner, *Economic Analysis of Law*, 2nd ed. (Boston: Little, Brown, 1977), Chapter 4.

TABLE 10-1 UNITIZATION (ONE WELL) AND BREACH OF A UNITIZATION CONTRACT (TWO WELLS)

		Smith	
		One Well	Two Wells
Jones	One Well	\$15, \$15	\$5, \$20
	Two Wells	\$20, \$5	\$10, \$10

Under expectation damages, Jones's breach entitles Smith to a \$10 payment from him. It is the difference between what Smith actually received (\$5) and the amount she would have gotten had each of them sunk only one well (\$15). If the cost of going to court is low, \$10 is the economically efficient amount of damages. After paying damages Jones is left with only \$10 of the \$20 he got from breaching, less than if he had kept to the agreement and made \$15. As for Smith, the \$10 leaves her as well off as if Jones had not breached the contract. As long as Jones extracts between \$15 and \$25 worth of oil when he breaches, the expectation damages will deter him from doing so.

Can Breach Be Desirable?

We often speak of "sanctity of contracts" or assert that "a deal is a deal," but in certain situations breaching an agreement can be economically efficient, because it creates more value for the two parties than they can get if they both abide by the contract. In Table 10-2, assume that Jones is the producer of a certain good and Smith is the purchaser. The table contains only two entries because for now we assume that Smith has no reason to breach regardless of what Jones does.[11] If both of them perform as specified by the contract, each benefits by \$15. Now assume that another purchaser approaches Jones and offers to pay \$35 for immediate delivery of the goods Jones intended to sell to Smith. Now more economic value is created if Jones breaks the agreement than if he performs under it. When Jones pays Smith \$10 in expectation damages he leaves Smith as well off as under the contract. Jones is left with \$25 and is wealthier than if he had not breached the contract, Smith is no worse off than if Jones had delivered her the goods, and the outside purchaser has paid less for the goods than his valuation.

Q. How do we know that the outside purchaser has paid less than his valuation?

TABLE 10-2 EFFICIENT BREACH OF A CONTRACT

		Smith
		No breach
Jones	No Breach	\$15, \$15
	Breach	\$35, \$5

[11]Things become more complex if Smith is not helpless in the face of breach by Jones. Instead of being left with only \$5, Smith might be able to go to market and recover part of her loss by striking a deal with someone else that leaves her with \$10 of value. The law often requires such efforts by Smith to *mitigate* her losses. If Smith does not mitigate, the court might award her only \$5 of damages, the difference between the value created with mitigation (\$10) and the value created if Jones had not breached (\$15).

To maximize value the contract must set damages properly. If damages are too low, inefficient breaches will be profitable, and if damages are too high, efficient breaches will not occur. In Table 10-1 assume that the contract specifies that the breaching party need only pay $3 in liquidated damages and that Smith sinks only one well regardless of what Jones does. If Jones breaches the contract, he is left with $17 after paying the damages and thus profits from his action. But in this example economic value is maximized only if both parties keep to the contract's terms: $3 is too little to deter breach. but economic value is maximized only if both keep to the contract's terms. Damages can also be too large. In Table 10-2, a requirement that the breaching party pay $40 would leave Jones abiding by the agreement when efficiency requires that he breach it. Further, the prospect of $40 in damages may encourage Smith to attempt to induce breach by Jones, itself a violation of contract law. The possibilities of inefficient breach and inducement to breach both underlie the general legal prohibition against penalty provisions that require payment greater than actual damages.[12]

Q. Does economic efficiency require Jones to pay the expectation damages to Smith, or will it be equally efficient to require that he pay it to a charity (or any other person unconnected with Smith)? Is your answer the same if many other parties may be interested in making contracts like this one over the future?

Q. Construct an example about the two oil drillers in which breach is efficient along with the numbers, try to construct a plausible background story to go with them.

Specific Performance

In some contract disputes a court will require the breaching party to take a particular action rather than pay damages. Assume that you are assembling a group of lots on which you intend to build a shopping mall. You want to keep their owners unaware of your intentions, because the value of each acre will jump after you acquire all of the lots. Assume that the last of the owners has contracted to sell you her land for $1 million, but just before conveying the title she learns about the mall and refuses to deal with you. In this case a court will probably order *specific performance*, in which the owner must accept the originally agreed-on price for her property and turn it over to you. Specific performance makes economic sense when lost economic value is hard to calculate. What will be your loss if the holdout forces you to build an irregularly shaped mall, or if you must abandon the project and resell previously acquired lots at unpredictable prices? Uniqueness can also rationalize a requirement of specific performance in other contexts. A well-known actor who has breached his contract to star in a movie may be ordered to perform even if other actors are available for the part.

Issues of specific performance also arise in situations that involve promises, even if the promises are unwritten. The changing social significance of promises to marry, for

[12]So-called *punitive damages* that are intended to teach a lesson to a defendant engaging in egregious behavior are an exception to this rule. They are, however, seldom imposed in contract litigation and are more likely in tort cases.

instance, can explain fluctuations in the use of engagement rings.[13] Before the 1930s, only a small fraction of marriage proposals were accompanied by diamond rings, but during that decade they began to appear in greater numbers. A change in the legal enforceability of promises to marry can explain the change. Before the 1930s, a woman whose fiancé had broken off an engagement could sue him for breach of promise. Break-ups often occurred after the woman discovered the man consorting with another woman, or after she had engaged in premarital sex with him in the mistaken expectation that they would soon be married. In the 1930s, new laws prohibited these lawsuits in many state courts. Legal action was now impossible, but older social standards remained in effect—the reputations of women who had had the experience were diminished, along with their future marriage prospects.

A diamond engagement ring provided an almost-ideal alternative to legal actions that were no longer available.[14] The man who gave one was in effect putting up a surety bond, like those contractors use to guarantee compensation to a customer whose project was not completed to specifications. If the marriage did not take place the woman could keep the ring, but if it did take place the diamond retained its value and became part of the new household's wealth. The proportion of marriages bound by engagement rings reached its high in the 1960s, just before the sexual revolution of the 1970s. At that time influential parts of society came to view premarital experiences as irrelevant, or possibly even desirable. A woman abandoned by a man who had promised marriage now suffered a smaller loss in reputation than before, and sales of engagement rings began a decline that has continued to this day. Specific performance (i.e., marriage) became less important as the value of women's lost reputations fell with changing social standards.

Q. Why do counselors (and jewelers) often recommend that the man buy a ring worth, say, twice his monthly salary? If the woman's reputation is at issue, why not determine the price range of the ring by looking at her earnings?

Principals and Agents

Observability and Opportunism

Remittances by foreigners working in the United States to their home countries are a little-noticed form of foreign aid, far larger in total than the U.S. government's official aid budget. In 2008, remittances to Mexico alone were $25 billion, and worldwide remittances from workers to their home countries totaled an estimated $283 billion.[15] Often the senders want the members of their households to spend the funds in particular ways, while the recipients prefer to spend them otherwise. Many senders want their relatives to purchase materials to build homes that the senders plan on occupying when they return from the United States.

---

[13]Margaret F. Brinig, "Rings and Promises," *Journal of Law, Economics and Organization* 6 (Spring 1990): 203–15.

[14]Brinig shows that other explanations for the changing use of engagement rings do not predict the facts as well as one based on legal change. In particular, she shows that the DeBeers "diamond is forever" campaign, begun in the 1930s, cannot explain much of the rise in diamond sales during that decade.

[15]"Mexicans Working Abroad Sent Less Money Home in '08," *Los Angeles Times*, January 28, 2009.

A sender faces a *principal/agent problem*. The sender is the principal, who wishes to see the house built according to his specifications. That person, however, is in the United States and cannot easily monitor the relatives' expenses and efforts. The relatives are the sender's agents and are expected to construct the house. The sender cannot determine in a timely way whether the relatives bought the proper materials or chose lower quality and spent the difference on themselves. She also cannot easily verify relatives' claims that an emergency prevented them from spending the money on building materials. The sender would greatly value the services of someone who could monitor the relatives more closely or better yet, make sure that they were buying the right materials.

Mexico's Cemex (Cementos Mexicanos) is North America's largest cement supplier and the world's third largest. It owns plants on five continents and is scaling up operations in California and the southwestern United States. Cemex learned from surveys that Mexican workers in the United States saw opportunistic relatives as a major problem, along with high service charges for remittances they were sending.[16] Cemex responded by setting up Construmex, a service that provides house plans, construction advice, and cheap transfers of funds. When Construmex receives the funds it pays suppliers like Cemex subsidiary Construrama or Home Depot Mexico to deliver the materials to the construction site.

Cemex and Construmex help migrants resolve part of their principal/agent problem. First, they lower the cost of monitoring what the relatives are doing by taking away their option to spend the money elsewhere. They guarantee that the quality and price of materials are what the migrant expects and provide assurance that they are the right materials for the house the migrant is building. If the relatives attempt to act opportunistically (perhaps by reselling the materials) the migrant can easily see that a delivery will have to be repeated. When Construmex supplies plans and construction advice, it acts as an agent interested in maintaining its long-term reputation for quality and reduces the likelihood that the relatives will perform some tasks poorly or spend insufficient amounts on them. Cemex and Construmex lower a host of transaction costs ranging from converting dollars into pesos to minimizing errors due to communication difficulties between the migrant and the relatives. By doing so Cemex and Construmex make it more likely that the house will be built within the migrant's intended budget and that it will be well constructed.

Payment Arrangements

Inducing Effort Assume that you have been injured while using a product you recently purchased. Perhaps a bottle unexpectedly exploded or a gadget released a toxic chemical when you inadvertently dropped it. You contact an attorney who believes you are likely to win if you sue the manufacturer. You are the principal and the attorney is your agent. You have hired her because you do not have the expertise (or perhaps your opportunity cost is too high) to pursue this claim on your own. You have the same monitoring problem as the migrant. You cannot personally observe her during the hours she claims to be working on your behalf. Even if you could watch you could not evaluate the quality of the motions she files or her negotiations with the defendant's attorneys. The attorney, of course, understands this, too. Knowing that you cannot evaluate the diligence of her efforts or the quality of her work, she might act opportunistically. If paid

[16]All facts in this section are from "Migrants' Dollars Cross Border, Brick by Brick," *Los Angeles Times*, June 1, 2003.

by the hour, she might overcharge you because you cannot verify her claimed work time and you do not know many hours a given task typically requires.

Alongside monitoring problems, this principal/agent relationship contains a second source of uncertainty. If your case goes to trial you might win a large judgment or you might get nothing. Even after the results are in you will still be uncertain about the lawyer's quality. What happens at the trial depends on the lawyer's efforts and on random events. You may have won because the judge made a technical ruling in your favor on some point of law that another judge might have seen differently. An objective expert might say you had a high-quality lawyer, but you might still have lost. Perhaps the defendant had an even better attorney or the technical ruling could have been different. Your lawyer could also have been lazy or incompetent, but the jury found you so sympathetic that it disregarded the weakness of her case and awarded you a substantial amount.

Payment, Performance and Information *Contingency fees for the plaintiff's attorney*: A plaintiff's attorney in a case like yours will probably not be paid by the hour. Instead, she will get a fraction of what you win or settle for, usually 30 or 35 percent. (You must generally pay other expenses from your share.) This is called a *contingency* or a *contingent fee* arrangement. If your lawyer wins nothing, you owe nothing. A contingency arrangement partially aligns your interests and your attorney's in maximizing the amount recovered.[17] To see why the incentives are partially matched, consider two possibilities. First, assume that the attorney can instantly see that your case is worthless. It will either be thrown out of court or settled for a tiny amount. Someone paid on contingency will either refuse your case or make only efforts likely to lead to a small settlement. Second, assume that the lawyer has worked 100 hours on your case and expects that one more hour will bring in an extra $1,000 (here we disregard uncertainty). As long as her opportunity cost is below $350 (at a 35 percent contingency rate), both of you benefit if she works that hour. It is not in her interest to loaf, which would reduce both of your incomes. A contingency arrangement, however, does not perfectly align your interests and your lawyer's. If her opportunity cost is $350 and an extra hour would increase your side's winnings by $500, she will not work because her 35 percent share of the $500 is only $175. She would work if her share for this hour were, say, 80 percent, which would still give you an extra $100. In Chapter 15 we explain why arrangements with sliding percentages are rare.

To see the importance of incentives let's look at a payment scheme that fails. Assume that (for unknown reasons) you and the attorney agree to a fixed dollar payment at the outset and no more in the future regardless of how the case develops. An arrangement like this (known in medicine as *capitation*, where it is frequently seen) fails on two counts. First, the attorney will happily accept a worthless case, work very little on it, and pocket the fee. Second, many potentially valuable cases will require extra effort by the attorney. Even if an extra hour of work on his part will yield you a large sum, he will choose not to work because he receives zero in return for his effort.

Hourly billing for the defendant's attorney: The principal/agent model also helps explain why the defendant's lawyer will most likely bill by the hour, plus expenses. Alternatively, that lawyer might be an employee of the defendant who gets the same salary whatever the outcome of your case. The difference between the plaintiff's and defendant's payment methods reflects differences in the cost of monitoring. The product's manufacturer may

[17]Contingency is also sometimes viewed as desirable because it allows low-income plaintiffs access to courts. There is, however, no reason why an attorney who believes he has a good case cannot work for delayed payment, take his hourly fees from the winnings, and shoulder the loss if one occurs.

already have defended a number of similar cases, perhaps so many that its executives know the probability distribution of outcomes. The defendant knows plaintiffs will abandon a certain percentage of cases or settle them for small amounts, while others manage to settle for more. If enough cases go to trial, the defendant can estimate the probabilities of winning the case and of losing various possible amounts. A defendant who knows this much about the probabilities of different outcomes may also know the characteristics of a case that make it more likely to win or lose. This information allows more accurate comparisons between attorneys than the raw data in their records would indicate.

Experience with a number of cases also helps the defendant's executives to estimate their attorney's likely preparation time and to anticipate events that might happen as the lawsuit progresses. The defendant may also be able to identify cases that will require more or fewer hours than average. The corporation probably has an officer in charge of legal matters (the general counsel), and may have in-house lawyers who can monitor and evaluate attorneys who practice law outside of the firm. The defendant's principal/agent problem is less acute than the plaintiff's because its executives understand how lawyers go about their work and how random factors can affect individual cases. They can compare the bills of different attorneys and request explanations of abnormally high or low amounts, but where extra effort is warranted the attorney can be certain of pay for the hours. The defendant has the alternative of dismissing poor performers and going to the market to find better ones for future cases.

The Generality of Principal/Agent Relationships

The examples in this section are a very small sample of the wide range of principal/agent relationships. They exist in almost any business situation. For example, the principal/agent relationship between a corporation's shareholders and its board of directors is particularly important for the analysis of managerial decisions. Dispersed shareholders with small individual holdings lack strong incentives to monitor management, and other shareholders can benefit by free riding on the efforts of those who choose to monitor. Shareholders may lack important knowledge (e.g., of competitive strategies that are confidential), and they can only replace poor management in certain situations. The model of principal and agent can also provide insight into situations that do not take place in markets. Lower-level employees act as agents performing tasks for higher-level employees who cannot monitor them perfectly, and employees as a group are agents of the firm's owners (i.e., shareholders). Within a business a supervisor must elicit effort from subordinates who cannot be fully monitored and are not directly paid for performance. Beyond the business world, voters play the role of principals and elected officials act as their agents, giving rise to monitoring difficulties and risks of opportunism on the part of officials.

Incomplete Contracts

Incompleteness: The WTC's Insurance Policy

On September 11, 2001, terrorists hijacked four airliners in a coordinated attack plan. One crashed in Pennsylvania, one inflicted damage on the Pentagon, and two hit New York's World Trade Center (WTC). Each of the building's towers was hit by a separate plane in a space of minutes, with great loss of life and total destruction of the WTC. The WTC's developer, Silverstein Properties, Inc., of course carried insurance, issued by a consortium of companies led by Swiss Reinsurance Co. Like all insurance contracts, it listed events that would trigger a payout and the maximum amounts payable if they happened. All parties also agreed on procedures they would follow in the event of a dispute.

If there was a dispute a large body of legal precedents could surely provide very precise definitions of the contract's terms.

No one disputed that the policy covered an air crash, or that it would pay a maximum of $3.5 billion "per occurrence."[18] A term like "occurrence" is common in insurance policies, and its exact meaning has been refined by centuries of industry practice and litigation. No previous case, however, clearly applied to the facts of the WTC. If the court accepted Silverstein's claim of two occurrences, he would receive an extra $3.5 billion. Everyday language was of little help. Two airplanes hit the same building at different times, but did this mean two occurrences? Both planes were dispatched as part of a plot intending both of them to strike the building, but did this mean one occurrence? On April 29, 2004, a jury determined that 12 of 15 insurers in the Swiss Reinsurance group had issued a policy whose language implied only one occurrence.[19] Another group of insurers who used a slightly different policy format went to a separate trial, and on December 6, a jury found them liable for two occurrences. On October 17, 2006 an appeals court confirmed the jury's decision for a total payout of $4.6 billion to be allocated between the two insurer consortia.[20]

Why Keep a Contract Incomplete?

An insurance policy is a contract that specifies actions to be taken if various situations (i.e., "states of the world") come to prevail. A contract might not describe the relevant situation in enough detail for the parties to agree that it occurred, or not all parties might be able to verify its occurrence. A singer's contract to entertain at an outdoor gathering, for example, may promise him some amount for performing in good weather and a smaller payment if it rains and the show cannot go on. But what constitutes rain? More than a certain amount before or during the show? What if there is no nearby weather station to measure it? The parties might let an impartial umpire determine whether the critical amount has fallen (as in baseball), but this requires agreement on who will make the call. One side probably does not want the other to be the sole judge of whether it has rained enough to cancel the performance.

The cost of negotiating sets limits on the completeness of an actual agreement. Even for the WTC insurance policy there are events (like those that actually happened) that appear so unlikely while negotiations are taking place that the parties will leave them out of the contract. The basic rule will be one of marginal choice: resolve an unclear condition only if expected marginal benefit to the parties exceeds expected marginal cost. A contract can be greatly simplified if the parties agree on default terms. Contracts often stipulate that the Uniform Commercial Code (UCC) applies to any terms in a contract that are not explicitly mentioned in it.[21] In some industries, trade associations have devised standard contracts whose provisions take into account the characteristics of the traded good and their industry's generally accepted practices. Buyers and sellers of high-voltage electricity, for instance, often fill

---

[18]The text treats the dispute as one involving the meaning of a particular word. The most important issue before the court was one regarding which of two policy formats the insurers were actually working with, an issue that would be determined in part by how the court would treat e-mail. Upon deciding that question, the exact meaning of "occurrence" would have been easier to discern. See "Jottings May Cut Insurers' Payouts on Twin Towers," *Wall Street Journal*, February 4, 2004.

[19]"Jury Rules Most WTC Insurers had Single-Attack Coverage," *Dow-Jones Newswires*, April 29, 2004.

[20]"Jury Decides Terrorist Attacks on WTC Were Two Events," *Dow-Jones Newswires*, December 6, 2004; "Appeals Court Upholds Verdicts in Mammoth WTC Insurance Cases," *Associated Press Newswires*, Oct. 18, 2006.

[21]The UCC is an attempt to form a nationally uniform law for business transactions and is particularly valuable in cases where state laws are not in agreement. You can download it at http://www.law.cornell.edu/ucc/ucc.table.html.

in the blanks of a master contract formulated by the Edison Electric Institute (EEI), a trade association of utilities.[22] If the parties decide to make their own contract, they can reduce their transaction costs by stipulating that the EEI master contract covers all items not explicitly discussed in their agreement.

Incompleteness and Opportunism

A contract can be so complete that it can encourage the parties to act opportunistically. Reaching agreement on what the contract will *not* specify can reduce those incentives and increase the economic value it creates. Assume that you have agreed to supply me with fuel for my manufacturing plant, and that deliverability can pose a problem because my desired daily burn varies widely. It may, for example, depend on my production level, which I cannot predict more than a few days ahead. I can avoid costly shutdowns and startups by arranging for you to supply all of my daily requirements between some maximum and minimum limits. Fulfilling your part of the deal requires that you make costly arrangements for storage and plan your own purchases from producers in advance. Because you have made some investments specific to this contract, we might agree that I must buy all of my fuel requirements from you. But what will you charge me for it? Fixing the price per unit in advance for the duration of the contract invites opportunism because the market offers alternatives. If market price rises above the contract price, you will want to evade your obligations and profit by selling my shipment elsewhere. If it falls below the contract price, I will want to purchase in the market and reject your shipment.

The risk of opportunism falls if the contract price changes with the fuel's market price. If it rises with market price your gain from breaching our agreement is less, and vice versa for me if market price falls. Contract prices for widely traded items often carry provisions called *adjustment clauses* or *escalators* that change their prices as market prices change.[23] An adjustment clause must state when the price will change and by what formula the new price will be calculated. Energy commodities are often repriced monthly because more frequent changes would add to uncertainty and provide no clear benefits. The contract must also specify the data to be used in calculating the adjustment. For widely traded commodities, averages from industry newssheets are a common choice, as are figures derived from commodity exchange prices.[24]

Q. Often we see formulas in adjustment clauses that include "lagged" terms. For example the contract's April price will equal 50 percent of the market's March price and 50 percent of its February price. Why might both parties to a contract find this superior to using 100 percent of the March price?

Termination and Reopening

Assume that the market price of our fuel is almost always between $7 and $11 and that the few times it has crossed those boundaries have been short-lived situations. We

---

[22]You can view the contract at http://www.eei.org/ourissues/ElectricityGeneration/Documents/contract0004.pdf.

[23]Whether we call a contract with an adjustment clause incomplete may be a definitional matter. It is incomplete because we do not know the prices that will emerge in the future, but it is complete (in this respect) because whatever the market price a formula will tell us how to calculate the adjustment.

[24]For an example, see Section 2.6 of the North American Standards Board's base contract for gas deliveries, which lists acceptable newssheets like *Gas Daily*.

cannot, however, be sure that it will always stay in that range or that movements beyond it will be short-lived. If the world's supply of the fuel comes from a politically unstable country, a revolution there could raise its price to $20 for a long time. If that happens both you and I will be in unknown territory. $20 is so high a price that continuing to make my product may bring me losses relative to competitors who burn other fuels, and I will either close down production or incur the cost of equipment that burns some other fuel. Likewise, at that price you will see yourself losing sales and building up inventories or financial commitments, and you may wish to reconsider whether to stay in business. We might both agree to scrap our relationship because after the price change our transaction no longer creates economic value. Our contract can anticipate this by automatically terminating when the price has stayed above or below some extreme value for a long enough time. We can of course agree to continue operating under the contract or change some of its terms while keeping the rest of it in force. Alternatively, our contract may have a *reopener* provision that requires us to renegotiate certain portions of it after a drastic change in market price. (If we cannot reach agreement it may terminate.) In situations like this an incomplete contract is a boundedly rational choice. The cost of deciding in advance what will happen to our relationship if the fuel price rises to a previously unheard of level is not worth incurring if we both think the event is so unlikely. If price does rise, the contract acknowledges in advance that one or both of us may no longer wish to operate under it.

Events outside of markets can also trigger termination or reopen a contract, as sometimes occurs in regulated industries. The Federal Energy Regulatory Commission's (FERC) rules allow natural gas producers and large consumers to acquire rights to ship gas in interstate pipelines and to repackage them in ways they can agree upon. A holder can sell its rights, lease them to others, or change their characteristics, for example, from guaranteed deliveries to interruptible service. The rules are very complex, and unexpected changes can alter the value of shipping rights in unexpected ways. A new rule might harm one party to a shipping contract while the other benefits. To avoid these unexpected changes most gas transport contracts contain "FERC-out" clauses stating that certain changes in FERC's rules will require the parties to renegotiate parts of their agreement.

Chapter Summary

- Specific investments associated with a contract are costly to redeploy to uses other than the relationship governed by the contract. An investment may be specific to a particular task, location, or relationship.
- Opportunistic behavior consists of attempts by one party to a transaction to improve her outcome by bending or breaking the rules the parties have agreed upon.
- Contracts facilitate the creation of economic value in situations where the parties must invest in specific assets that are subject to risks of opportunism. If opportunism is not controlled, fewer specific investments will be made.
- By precisely outlining the parties' rights and obligations, contracts can control opportunistic behavior and increase the economic value created by their relationship.
- In situations where contracts are too costly to form or enforce, vertical integration that puts all of the relevant assets under the same control can be an efficient mode of governance.

- If efficiency is to prevail, a party that breaches a contract must generally be sanctioned, either by payment of liquidated damages or a requirement of specific performance. If they are set at the right level and imposed with certainty, expectation damages can deter breach.
- Contracts that govern a principal/agent relationship must contain payment provisions that induce the agent to make efforts that the principal wants made in his behalf, given that he cannot monitor the agent and that random events can affect the results the agent produces.
- The efficient payment scheme in a principal/agent relationship will depend on the principal's monitoring ability and the importance of random events. Thus, the plaintiff in our example hired a lawyer on contingency while the defendant paid by the hour.
- A contract may remain incomplete because the expected benefits of greater completeness do not cover the costs of drafting it. In some situations an incomplete contract can discourage opportunistic behavior. Incompleteness may also be helpful if at the time the parties draft the agreement they do not know how they can best react to certain contingencies.
- Incompleteness can take the form of automatic price adjustment clauses and provisions requiring termination or renegotiation in the event that certain events occur.

Questions and Problems

1. Franchise arrangements involve a number of highly specific investments on the parts of both the parent company (e.g., McDonald's or Hilton Hotels) and the franchisee (the owner of a particular McDonald's or Hilton). Identify some of these investments. Then explain how each of the parties might act opportunistically to gain from the other's specific investments. Does it surprise you that franchise contracts are usually very long and complex, and that they are the subject of much litigation?
2. Why might a parent company like McDonalds or Hilton choose to franchise its local outlets rather than own them and staff them with employees? In many smaller cities all McDonald's outlets are owned by the same franchisee. Why is (or isn't) this fact consistent with our discussion of specific investments?
3. Some large power plants are mine-mouth facilities, located at the opening of the coal mine that will supply their fuel. In areas with few coal mines, both the power plant and the mine are likely to be under the same ownership, but in areas with numerous mines they are more likely to be owned by different parties. Why the difference? If they are owned by different parties, what sorts of provisions might you expect to see in the contract between them?[25]
4. Only a small number of employment arrangements are governed by (relatively) complete contracts. One such area is professional sports, where a player's contract requires, among other things, that he show up for games, be available for interviews, obey certain rules when endorsing products, and so on. Most other workers are employed under extremely incomplete contracts, if they even have

[25]See Paul Joskow, "Contract Duration and Relationship-Specific Investments: Empirical Evidence from Coal Markets," *American Economic Review* 77 (March 1987): 168–85.

anything at all in writing. Why would both employers and employees often choose to operate under an incomplete contract rather than a more complete one?

5. Most surgeons charge for operations by capitation, that is, a flat dollar amount for a specific procedure, such as setting a broken bone. Most psychiatrists charge an hourly rate for psychotherapy. Why the difference?
6. We The People is a national chain that offers paralegal services such as filing forms in court for property transfers, wills, and simple bankruptcies.[26] It charges flat fees for such services. Why might it choose not to bill by the hour? We The People is receiving unwanted attention for allegedly incompetent and incomplete work on bankruptcy applications, but it receives virtually no such complaints regarding wills.[27] What might this have to do with its methods of charging customers?
7. Jones and Smith have a contract that will produce $100 in benefits for each of them if they both carry out their duties under it. If Jones breaches the contract, he will create $140 in benefits for himself, and Smith will only get $40. What are the expectation damages a court should order Jones to pay? Explain. What if Jones's breach gives him benefits of $170, while Smith again gets $40? In this case, why would an economist recommend that Jones breach the agreement? Does your answer change if a court for some reason lets Jones keep all of his gains, leaving Smith with just $40? Why or why not?
8. In the United Kingdom and several other countries, the loser of the case pays the winner's legal fees. Do you expect to see plaintiffs' attorneys operating under contingency arrangements in these countries? Why or why not?
9. If your instructor is an agent, who is (are) the principal(s)? Do not say "the university," because there is no such identifiable individual. If you think it is the students, explain why. If not the students, who? Do you have any evidence that agents like your instructor sometimes act opportunistically, in ways the principals do not want to them to?
10. You are on the board of directors of a nonprofit art museum supported by donations from wealthy members of the community, and are responsible for acquiring new works and staging exhibitions for the public. You are clearly an agent, but who is (are) the principal(s)?
11. Every so often, a disgruntled college graduate sues her school on grounds that her tuition payments did not land her the good job she was expecting when she started there. Courts invariably throw out cases like hers. They are, however, willing to entertain suits against trade schools (those that teach skills such as welding and computer repair) by graduates who make the same claims about inability to qualify for jobs that use the skills they learned in them. Why the difference?
12. You and I have signed a contract. You hired an incompetent lawyer (but one who was officially certified to practice law) to negotiate your side of it. I engage in some action that triggers a contract provision that imposes a financial burden on you and benefits me. Had your lawyer been competent she would not have allowed that provision into the contract. Was I acting opportunistically under our definition? Is it economically efficient if the law allows you to avoid paying me (it usually does not) because you claim your lawyer was incompetent

---

[26]See the We The People Web site at http://www.wethepeopleusa.com/default.asp.

[27]"Challenges Beset Low-Cost Paralegal Aid," *Washington Post*, May 30, 2004.

Chapter 11

Information and Risk in Contracts

INTRODUCTION

A Sight to See, but Buyers Can't Peek

The hand holding the tweezers in the photo is examining and sorting a pile of uncut diamonds that are probably worth a million dollars now and will be several times that figure after they are cut and mounted in jewelry. The work is taking place at the Diamond Trading Company (DTC) of London, a unit of the DeBeers Group, which markets most of the world's supply of raw diamonds.[1] After checking that the measurements and other specifications of the stones are all met, the person with the tweezers will put them into a small yellow box, seal it and put it in a safe place to wait for a buyer. The buyers turn up every five weeks for an event known as a "sight."[2] They are a very select group

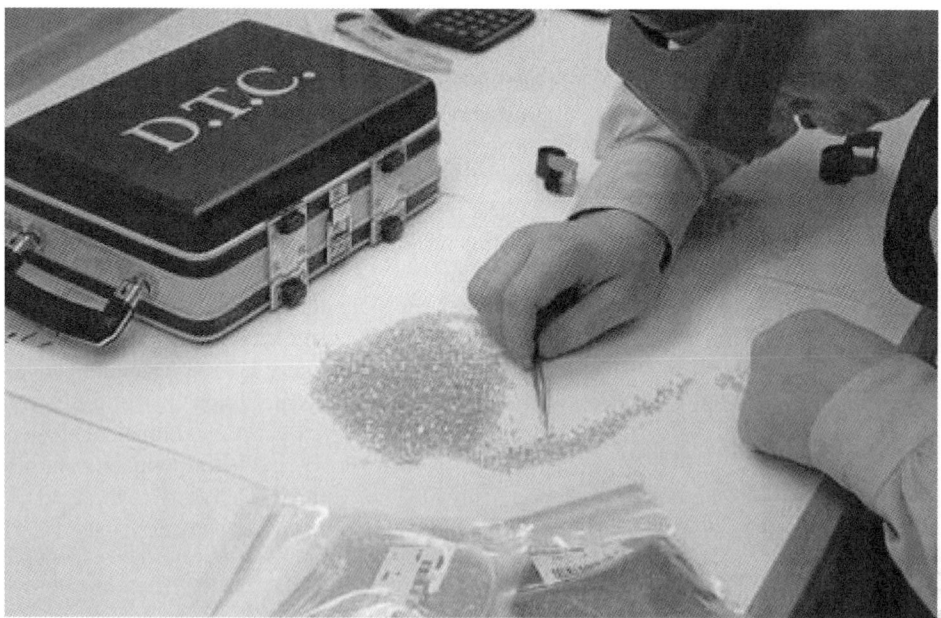

Karin Duthie/Alamy

[1]DTC's Web site is at http://www.debeersgroup.com/en/Sales-and-distribution/Diamond-Trading-Company/.

[2]More facts about DTC and sights can be found in Matthew Hart, *Diamond* (New York: Penguin Plume Books, 2001), 122–134.

of approximately 100 wholesalers called sightholders. Earlier each of them gave DTC the specifications (weight, color, shape, etc.) of the diamonds it sought, DTC responded with a price and a deal was made, usually without any haggling. The deal requires payment in full from each buyer upon delivery. Sightholders who arrive at at DTC's headquarters first hand over their payments (often electronically). Only later are they given the boxes they have ordered and escorted into rooms where they can examine the stones. DTC has so reliable a reputation for delivering diamonds with the agreed-upon specifications that a buyer need not examine individual stones. The buyer can refuse the box and DTC will refund the money, but at a high cost - The company will not invite him to future sights and he will be forced into less organized markets to deal with sellers whose reputations are more questionable.

In this chapter we examine how contracts can reduce the costs of information to the parties and thereby increase the economic value they create. Contract provisions that reallocate risk between the parties are often closely related to those that reduce information costs. Information is, however, a two-edged sword. The abilities of two parties to construct a contract may be limited if one or both of them has relevant knowledge that he cannot or will not convey to the other, a situation called *asymmetric information*. Economists do not yet have a general model of how asymmetric information affects the behavior of individuals and the equilibria of markets. Lacking a general theory, the best that can be done is to provide examples that may shed light on some common business practices. This chapter covers the following:

- How contracts allow people to trade risks by choosing the terms to include, and how certain types of transaction costs can limit the potential benefits.
- How the damages provisions of a contract can shift risks to the benefit of both parties, particularly in cases involving insurance.
- How asymmetric information can increase the costs of making a contract, perhaps to the point that one cannot be written at all.
- How people can reduce contracting problems caused by asymmetric information, one simple way being to build reputations for trustworthiness.
- How asymmetric information can cause adverse selection and moral hazard, which may make some types of insurance contracts impossible or prohibitively expensive.
- How menus of insurance policies can be structured to reduce the problems of adverse selection, and how restrictions on allowable claims, co-payments and deductibles within a policy can reduce moral hazard.
- How economic value is created if a seller can signal that the transaction offered a buyer has some attributes that the buyer finds valuable but cannot measure directly. The value of those benefits, however, must be weighed against the cost of giving the signal.
- How markets in which buyers cannot accurately judge the value of some good may exhibit a winner's curse, where the person who wins the bidding may end up disappointed because his available information resulted in an overoptimistic bid.
- How practices like DTC's blind sights can save resources that would be wasted if buyers duplicated the seller's activities on inspecting the product.

- Why the law requires disclosure of certain information in contracts but allows other information to remain private.

CONTRACTS AND THE ALLOCATION OF RISK

Trading Risks by Insuring

In a friendly game of cards you bet \$10 in hopes of winning \$12. Having studied the game in some detail, you happen to know that this is a smart bet—with probability 0.5 you will lose \$10, and with the same probability you will win \$12. Your expected payoff is $-0.5 \times 10.00 + 0.5 \times 12.00 = \$1.00$. Over a large number of \$10 bets your average win on each will approach \$1.[3] The stakes are so small relative to your wealth that you can endure a run of bad outcomes and still be confident that continuing to play will make you richer. But small-stakes reasoning doesn't scale upward. You will be less enthusiastic about betting the same odds that \$100,000 will turn into \$120,000. Your expected win is \$10,000, but assume that you are not wealthy enough to repeat the bet in the event that you lose on your first try. Losing \$100,000 means losing your house, which happens on half of the bets. Turning \$100,000 into \$120,000 is nice, but the lavish vacations you would now be able to take add less to your well-being than the loss of your house would subtract from it.

The difference is that your well-being is not measured by your wealth. Instead, assume for now that there is a numerical measure of your well-being, called your *utility*, that increases with your wealth but at a diminishing rate.[4] Figure 11-1 graphs one possible relationship of this type. Such a relationship is graphed. Assume that your current wealth is \$100,000, and you are considering a gamble in which you will win \$100,000 (i.e., your wealth will be \$200,000) with probability 0.5 and lose \$100,000 with the same probability, leaving you with zero wealth. The expected value of your wealth after the gamble will be \$100,000, but this is a gamble you do not want to take. Your expected utility will be $0.5 \times 0 + 0.5 \times 5.2 = 2.6$ units. Your expected wealth after the bet will still

FIGURE 11-1
Utility and Wealth for a Risk-Averse Person

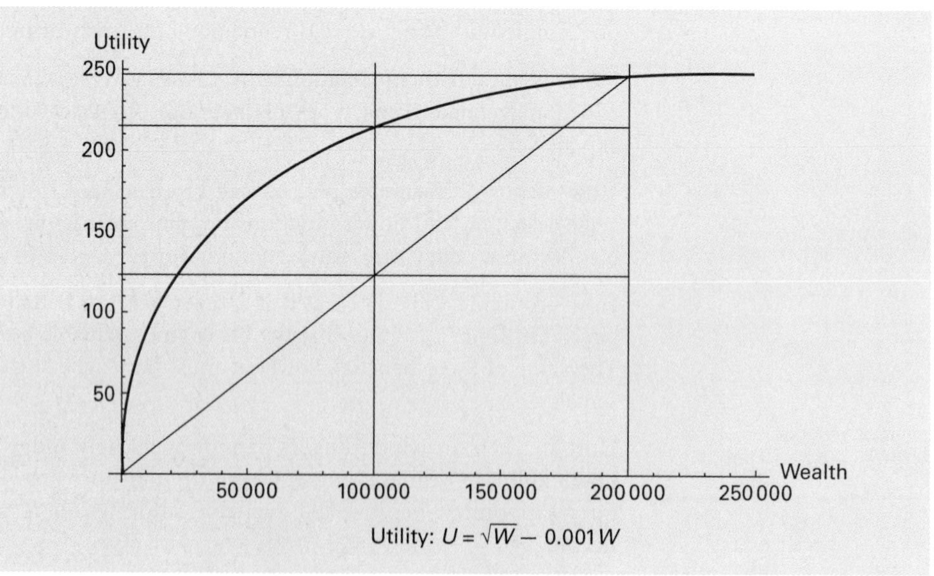

[3]Disregard the question of why your opponents repeatedly make bets that have negative expected payoffs for them.

[4]If utility U is a function of your wealth, $F(W)$, we are assuming $F'(W) > 0$ and $F''(W) < 0$.

be \$100,000, but your expected utility will fall. In Figure 11-1, your utility of \$200,000 is 247.2 units, and your utility of \$0 is zero, so your expected utility is $(0.5 \times 247.2) + (0.5 \times 0) = 123.6$ units. Not taking the gamble and hanging on to your \$100,000 leaves you with utility of 216.2 units for certain. You are not just unlikely to make this bet—You would pay someone to take the gamble off your hands. In the language of economics you are *risk averse*. If you are indifferent between taking and not taking a gamble with a zero expected return you are called *risk neutral*.

Q. The relationship between utility and wealth in this example is given in Figure 11-1. Check the figures in the above paragraph. What is the maximum you will pay for insurance if you must take the gamble? That amount is the maximum payment you will make to an outsider who will take the gamble off your hands. In other words, what premium would make you indifferent between taking the bet and not taking it?

Q. Show that if you are risk neutral for all possible levels of wealth, your utility of wealth will be a straight line that passes through the origin.

You can free yourself from the gamble by purchasing insurance or incurring the cost of taking your own precautions. You will sacrifice some relatively small amount of money with certainty to avoid a massive loss from a random disaster like a house fire or major medical bills. Insurance is a contract that reallocates risk between the insurer and the insured. This exchange of risks benefits both sides of the contract if they have different degrees of aversion or different abilities to bear risk. Your insurance premium is the price you pay to sell the risk to the insurer, which must cover its payout if the disaster happens. Your ability to bear risks increases with your abilities to diversify your asset holdings. A home is a large part of many peoples' wealth, and few people have other holdings that are large and diverse enough to make living without fire insurance a sensible risk to take. (In any case, mortgage lenders protect their interests by requiring insurance.) An insurer's position is quite different. It writes policies on thousands of homes whose probabilities of fire are independent. If the company holds enough funds in reserve to pay claims, the algebra of probability (i.e., the "law of large numbers") shows that its funds are unlikely to be exhausted in payouts.[5] Size affects risk-bearing ability. A person who loses a \$400,000 home to fire may be financially ruined, whereas the same loss leaves the wealth of the insurance company's shareholders as a group virtually unaffected.

Transaction costs affect both exchanges of ordinary goods and the range of risks that people can reallocate among themselves. It is more costly to write a more detailed contract, whether for goods or risks. A standard-form contract like an insurance policy may be difficult to tailor to the particular situations of some people, who will either require costly special provisions or be forced to do without beneficial coverage. The parties to a risk-shifting contract like insurance will sometimes have no accurate way to estimate the probability of a loss or its expected value. (Think of accidents at nuclear power plants.) An insurer whose estimates are inaccurately low may face insolvency if policyholders make an unexpectedly large volume of claims. Market conditions may also affect risk—the value of a farm crop lost to a storm depends on its price.

[5]The insurer can further cover risks of insolvency by reinsuring, i.e., buying its own insurance against excessive payouts on claims. This was the function of the reinsurers in the World Trade Center case of the previous chapter.

Damage Provisions to Reallocate Risk

Many contracts besides insurance reallocate risk between the parties. For example, the liquidated damages provisions discussed in Chapter 10 are remedies for breach of contract, but they can also be set at levels that shift risk. Assume that I have promised you 1,000 bolts at $10 apiece, payable on delivery. My costs are $9 per unit. For every undelivered bolt the contract requires that I pay up to $5 in liquidated damages, depending on particulars like the price at which someone else would supply them to you. After I commit to delivery at $10, an input rises in price, and my costs become $25, enough to bankrupt me if I only get $10 per bolt.[6] Assume that I do, however, have enough in the bank to pay you $5 per undelivered unit and that you so want to work with me in the future that you will accept $5 and treat your unrecovered loss as payment for my continued survival.

But why would we have chosen to cap damages at $5 per bolt? If their market price rose to $25, the principle of expectation damages would have me paying $15. This is the difference between what you must pay someone else ($25) and what you would pay under our agreement ($10). My damage payment per bolt covers only $5 of your cost, and you must pay $20 out of your own funds. This allocation of risks is not efficient (it encourages me to breach whenever my costs increase by more than $5), but it may be the best way of ensuring that our relationship continues. Allocating the first $5 of risk to me and the rest to you can make sense if my choices for risk management are more limited than yours.

I breached this contract because it did not allow me to pass on an increase in costs that affected the entire market. As discussed in Chapter 10, an escalation or adjustment provision could have deterred opportunistic behavior while automatically reallocating risk as the input price changed. At one extreme the formula could allow 100 percent passthrough and leave you with all the risk, but this gives me no reason to shop carefully for the input. One possible compromise is to agree that if the input price goes above some amount I will only receive some fraction of my actual expense over that amount. This reallocates risk while maintaining my incentive to shop carefully for the input.

Q. Devise another set of compromise terms that discourages both of us from breaching the contract and gives us incentives to operate efficiently.

Market Transactions to Reallocate Risk

A contract can reallocate risk, and market transactions may allow additional changes in the parties' risk positions. Assume that I am to provide you with a fuel supply, possibly at prices that adjust with its market price. My costs will be more predictable if I hold derivatives. If the contract allows you to take less than the full supply, buying a "put" option will allow me to resell the excess at a predictable (but not necessarily profitable) price.[7] Insurers can arrange reinsurance to cut the risk of unexpectedly large claims, and a group of insurers can form a single-purpose consortium to stand behind a policy they have jointly written. Vigilance can also counter the possibility that someone with insurance will take more risks because she knows she is protected against disaster, a phenomenon known as "moral hazard" that we discuss later in the chapter. Industrial fire

[6]The text does not consider the possibility of our renegotiating the contract after the increase in the input price becomes known.

[7]If you are not yet familiar with options, a "put" gives you the right (but not the obligation) to sell the underlying good at a predetermined price, and a "call" gives you the right to buy it at such a price. In Chapter 16 we discuss options in more detail.

insurance policies, for example, often specify that the insurer has a right to inspect the insured property for hazards and can cancel the policy if it finds them.

If alternative arrangements are feasible, a business may choose not to "sell" certain risks to an insurer. The market for insurance on a unique good may be so thin that no policy is available at a price its owner finds acceptable. A business cannot insure against accumulating too many bad debts, for instance, because recovery depends in part on collection effort. A firm can cut the risks from nondelivery of a vital input by purchasing business interruption insurance, but it can also do so by diversifying its supply sources. If the input is easily storable it might instead choose to keep a larger inventory on hand. Rather than deal with outside insurers, for example, some large companies hire their own medical staffs and operate their own facilities for patients.

Self-insurance can be attractive if it is possible to monitor risks and reduce potential losses by managing them well. Workers' Compensation laws require employers to pay premiums to private insurers for employee injuries or to self-insure by making their own arrangements. As an example of the latter, experience may give a chemical producer superior information about injuries due to exposure, how to treat them economically, and how to prevent them from happening. That firm may prefer to incur the costs of setting up and operating its own program, while a smaller firm or one with more diverse workplace hazards will prefer an outside insurer. A small firm that self-insures might also face a greater risk of large losses (relative to its size) from a small number of unexpectedly large claims.

Q. Using a supply-and-demand diagram for labor, show conditions under which (1) employers will incur the full cost of workers' compensation as lowered profits, and (2) employees will incur that cost as lower wages.

ASYMMETRIC INFORMATION AND THE LEMON PROBLEM

Asymmetric Information

If one party to an agreement holds information that the other does not, the difference can affect both of their incentives and behaviors. In this situation of *asymmetric information*, the economic value their relationship could potentially create may be diminished if the uninformed party cannot easily learn or verify important information, or if the informed party cannot credibly convey it. The following actually happened to an acquaintance of mine:

> Jones had recently joined an auto dealer's sales force and was paid on commission. One day he told the sales manager that friends and relatives had learned about his new job. "What do I do," he asked, "when one of them wants me to give them a good deal?" "Easy," responded the sales manager, "those are the ones you make the best money from. They trust you so much that they won't shop anywhere else."

This example contains several instances of asymmetric information. Let's assume that Jones's relatives strongly believe he will offer them a better deal than a salesperson they do not know. If the sales manager is right they hold the belief so strongly that they will never test its correctness by seeing another dealer. Jones knows he will get a bigger commission if he does not reveal his near-certain belief that they foolishly trust him to give them the best possible deal. It pays him to withhold information that his relatives would benefit from knowing. If he believed they were likely to see another dealer, he would probably quote them a more competitive price.

Asymmetric information differs from incomplete information. Neither you nor I know for certain what the market price of some good will be a year from today when you want me to deliver it to you.[8] Using my available information I expect \$6, but your information says it will be \$10. Even if we both have identical information we might differ about its effects on price. We agree on \$8, and both of us are happy with the deal we made. You will get the item for \$2 less than the price you expect, and I will be able to resell it to you for \$2 more than I expect to pay at wholesale. If market price is \$10 on delivery day, however, you will be happy and I will be regretful. You will have profited indeed, but not from asymmetric information. I have no information that I could have withheld or misrepresented to my advantage, and the same holds for you. Each of us had to use information we knew was not perfectly accurate.

Conveying Information Credibly: The Logic of Lemons

Looking at Table 11-1, assume that you have just bought a new \$20,000 car. It runs well and you intend to keep it for several years. A month later your employer reassigns you to a distant country for the next two years. Unable to bring the car, you have two options: sell it for the best available offer or store it for the two years. The car has been driven so little that a buyer who knew its true condition would pay up to \$18,000, and you would sell for any amount above \$15,000. If you store it, upon returning you will have a less stylish car and possibly one of lower quality (a family of mice may move in while you are gone). Driving it after you come home is worth only \$15,000 to you.

The used car market in this example fails to satisfy the perfectly competitive model's assumptions about information.[9] In the latter, people can easily inform themselves about the seller's asking price and the quality of the car. Here, however, you cannot credibly say that the car is good because a potential buyer has no reason to trust you. That person has no way to verify your story about an overseas transfer and is, in fact, aware that many near-new cars being sold as used are in fact defective, or "lemons." Your potential buyers are not mechanics who can check the car's true condition or use a short test drive to see if you are trying to conceal any problems. Assume that each possible buyer knows the probability the car is good is 0.5, the same as the probability it is a lemon. If the car is a lemon, the buyer must pay \$8,000 to repair it. A risk-neutral buyer should offer no more than $0.5 \times 18{,}000 + 0.5 \times 10{,}000 = \$14{,}000$.

Q. Would a risk-averse buyer in the same situation be willing to offer more or less than \$14,000? Explain.

TABLE 11-1 THE LEMON PROBLEM

Purchase price of new car	\$20,000
Market value to an accurately informed buyer	18,000
Car's value to you if stored	15,000
Maximum an uninformed buyer will pay	14,000

[8] For this example disregard the possibility that we could simply agree that you will pay the market price prevailing at the time of delivery.

[9] You are probably also not a price-taker, a fact that we neglect here.

Asymmetric information stands in the way of a sales contract between you and a potential buyer. You cannot dissuade any buyer from the mistaken belief that the car is likely a lemon. Your friends may know you are an honest person, but strangers will assume that you are lying. If no one offers more than $15,000 you will store the car. Asymmetric information has left both you and some potential buyer worse off. A buyer who knew the car's true condition would pay up to $18,000, but one who is uncertain about the condition will pay at most $14,000. You are left with a stored car worth $15,000 to you, and some buyer goes without a good car.[10]

Reducing the Scope of the Lemon Problem

The lemon story is intriguingly clever, but it might also be just another "$100 bills left lying on the sidewalk" problem from Chapter 1. Specifically, someone who devises a way to find out a car's true condition can capture some of the benefits of a transaction that will now take place. That person might operate a diagnostic lane that itemizes a car's defects. You may, of course, have greater confidence in a lane owner who does not also do repairs. Some institutions certify the quality of inspection lanes. The American Automobile Association (supported by member dues), for example, maintains a list of accredited test facilities that promise to inspect a specified list of potential problems and provide a standardized report for a pre-set price.[11]

Credibility comes in different forms, and people's confidence will depend on the source of their information. In front of the American Express office in Amsterdam (where many tourists congregate), I once saw a person on the sidewalk with a metal tool box. Pasted on it was a sign that read "Trained mechanic from Milwaukee will check any used car for $50." Owners of bad used cars might find tourists particularly attractive. Many of them will not see Amsterdam again or be willing to bear the costs of going to court against a seller who speaks a different language and operates under a different legal system. A quality mechanic can facilitate transactions in good cars and discourage transactions in bad ones. Quite possibly the mechanic attempts to convey his trustworthiness by claiming to come from Milwaukee rather than, say, Las Vegas.

The lemon story neglected another solution to the asymmetric information problem—the seller might offer a warranty that covers the cost of certain repairs. In reality, all automakers offer warranties with options to extend them for an extra charge. If the warranty changes hands when the car does (as usually occurs) the new buyer's repair costs will be minimal. Without telling you at the time, our story simply assumed that there was no warranty or other method by which the seller could commit to pay for repairs.

Experience and reputation can also weaken the effects of asymmetric information. Our lemon story was about a once-in-a-lifetime transaction by two people who will never deal with each other again. A buyer will more likely believe a seller with a reputation for honest dealing. The durability of a dealership might matter because it possibly signifies that some customers have made repeat purchases there. Acquiring a good

---

[10]We might take this logic further into the long run. Fewer cars that are actually good will come to market because their owners learn that the best that can be done under asymmetric information is to keep them in storage. Those who own cars they know are lemons, however, may still want to sell them. As buyers learn that more cars on the market are lemons they further reduce their bids, leading to a further exodus of good cars. If bad cars become a large enough part of the market it goes to an odd equilibrium: buyers expect low-quality cars and sellers fulfill buyers' expectations by putting lemons on the market where they will sell for very low prices. For more on the model of vanishing markets see George Akerlof, "The Market for 'Lemons': Quality, Uncertainty and the Market Mechanism," *Quarterly Journal of Economics* 84 (August 1970): 488–500.

[11]See, for example, the Automobile Club of Southern California's Web site at, http://www.aaa-calif.com/auto/maintain/vip.aspx. Members get a rebate on the price of the inspection.

reputation takes time, and so does outgrowing a bad one. The desire to maintain a reputation may explain why a new car dealer is likely to resell only high-quality trade-ins on its own lot. A satisfied used car buyer may become a satisfied new car buyer, and a dissatisfied one will often tell her friends about the experience. Lower-quality cars go to wholesale auctions, where they are mostly purchased by used car dealers.

Economists have tried testing the lemons model with a variety of data. Evidence of a lemons effect appears in a study of stamp auctions for collectors by Sanjeev Diwan of the University of California, Irvine and Vernon Hsu of George Mason University.[12] They first found prices from Internet auctions held by Michael Rogers, Inc., a firm known for its accuracy in describing the condition of stamps it is offering. They then looked at eBay auctions for the same stamps, restricting themselves to those described as being of the same quality as stamps offered by Rogers. They reasoned that if the lemons model is true, buyers who are uncertain about quality (they cannot inspect the stamps) will pay less on eBay than they would pay Rogers for a stamp claimed to be in the same condition. They found that prices on eBay averaged 10 to 15 percent lower than what Rogers received. Diwan and Hsu also found that reputation can undo the effects of asymmetric information. For example, eBay tracks complaints about sellers and allows bidders to see them. Although eBay sellers receive less than Rogers on average, those with better reputations (measured by the ratio of complaints to transactions) receive prices closer to Rogers's.

For evidence against the lemons model, Christopher Adams and his colleagues at the Federal Trade Commission examined all 8,000 used Corvettes sold on eBay between 2001 and 2003.[13] The lemons model suggests that owners will have superior information about the quality of their cars and incentives to conceal it, to which buyers will respond by lowering their bids. Comparing new and used Corvettes under one year old, they found that the median winning bid on used Corvettes actually exceeded that on new ones. The lemons model also suggests that last-minute bids (which may come from those who are better informed about a car's quality) are more likely for used than for new cars, but in reality there was no difference in their frequencies. In a similar study, Eric Bond of Vanderbilt University studied the repair histories of a large sample of pickup trucks over three years old.[14] He found no significant difference between repair bills for trucks still held by their original owners and similar trucks that had been purchased as used, and he concluded that the lemons effect was absent.

Adverse Selection

Choosing Insurance Policies

In the lemons model, a seller could not convince any buyer that his claims about a car's quality were true. In the related model of *adverse selection*, the seller cannot obtain reliable information from a number of buyers. Incentives to withhold or falsify facts can affect market equilibrium. As an example, assume that health insurers are unable to determine a person's underlying healthiness before writing a policy. Assume there are two types of policy. Comprehensive ones cover a wide range of treatments and have high limits on hospitalization costs. By contrast, a health maintenance organization (HMO)

[12]Sanjeev Diwan and Vernon Hsu, "Adverse Selection in Electronic Markets: Evidence from Online Stamp Auctions," *Journal of Industrial Economics* 52 (December 2004): 497–16.

[13]Christopher Adams, Laura Hosken, and Peter Newberry, "'Vettes and Lemons on eBay" (February 2, 2006), Working Papers Series, available at Social Science Research Network Web site, http://ssrn.com/abstract880780.

[14]Eric W. Bond, "A Direct Test of the 'Lemons' Model: The Market for Used Pickup Trucks," *American Economic Review* 72 (September 1982): 836–40.

policy reimburses fewer treatments and has inferior cost coverage. Not surprisingly, the comprehensive plan must charge more than the HMO to survive. If enrollees in both plans are random samples of the population, each policy's premium can be set so that it breaks even. An insurer that does not know a person's riskiness will set rates as if its customers are typical of the population. Adverse selection means the population does not choose at random between the plans. A motorcycle racer who is likely to have an accident that will generate large medical bills will probably prefer fuller coverage than a stamp collector, other things equal. The motorcycle racer will choose the comprehensive plan, and the stamp collector will choose the HMO.

In Table 11-2 we assume a population with 1,000 low-risk members and 200 high-risk ones. A low-risk person submits $100 in claims each year, and a high-risk person $1,000. If a single plan applies to everyone, the insurer breaks even by setting a premium of $250, equal to the expected payout per policy. Compare this with what happens when people can choose different plans. Assume that a low-risk HMO plan member will submit $100 in claims a year, and one under the comprehensive plan will submit $200. A high-risk person who chooses the HMO will submit $1,000 in claims per year and one who chooses the comprehensive plan will submit $2,000. If everybody chooses the HMO plan it breaks even at a $250, and the comprehensive plan does the same at $500. Start with half the population enrolled in each plan, with the same ratio of high to low risks in each half. This situation is unsustainable. A low-risk person in the HMO can expect net benefits of −$150, that is, $100 in claims less a $250 premium. Migration to the comprehensive plan would make her even worse off with −$300 in net benefits. A low-risk person in the HMO makes the best of a bad thing by staying in it, and if she is in the comprehensive group she will move to the HMO. By the same reasoning, high-risk persons will migrate toward the comprehensive plan.

Q. Show that an insurer who covers everyone in an HMO plan breaks even by charging $250 per year, and the corresponding figure for a comprehensive plan is $500.

TABLE 11-2 ADVERSE SELECTION

	TYPE OF RISK	
	HIGH	LOW
Numbers in population	1,000	200
Expected value of claims per policyholder	$100	$1,000
Premium under single plan	$250	$250

	HIGH	LOW	PREMIUM PER PERSON IF HALF TAKE EACH PLAN
Expected claims per HMO policy	$100	$1,000	$250
Per comprehensive policy	$200	$2,000	$500
Net benefits of HMO policy	−$150	$750	
Net benefits of comprehensive policy	−300	$1,500	

If people move between the plans in both directions the insurer no longer breaks even charging a $500 premium on the comprehensive policy. If that policy must stand on its own the premium must increase. As higher-risk policyholders leave the HMO, the premium at which it breaks even will fall. If it takes time for people to move between the plans, we might witness a "death spiral" (a colorful industry term). Too many high-risk persons will migrate to the comprehensive plan, and the premiums will become prohibitively high.[15] The problem is greatly diminished if insurers can learn about peoples' true riskiness and adjust rates to levels at which the different policies break even. Unfortunately, no pair of premium rates will likely put all of the low-risk persons into one type of policy and high-risk persons into the other.[16] Table 11-2 also suggests a more extreme way to eliminate adverse selection: requiring everyone (e.g., all of a corporation's employees) to purchase the same coverage will end migration by ending choice. An important feature of many such plans is that they do not require medical examinations.[17] People who are low risks will, of course, be unhappy about losing the option of paying lower premiums on policies that better reflect their lower likely future claims.

Adverse selection is generally not a problem for automobile insurers, because they can easily obtain information to set premiums that more accurately predict expected losses. A Rolls-Royce owner will pay more for collision insurance than a Ford owner because a new fender for the Rolls costs more. If you own a Rolls and tell the insurer that you drive a Ford it can terminate your policy or refuse payment on a fraudulent claim. An insurer can easily obtain information about you—age, gender, miles driven, and traffic record—that affects the likelihood of an accident. The probability that your car will be stolen or involved in an accident with an uninsured driver depends in part on where you live. If your insurer knows all of these facts you will not be able to buy an underpriced policy like the motorcycle racer's health insurance plan.

Q. Do you expect adverse selection to be a serious problem for medical malpractice insurers? Give reasons pro and con.

Some Evidence

Adverse selection is possible, but is it likely?[18] Our model assumed that people knew more about their riskiness than insurers could possibly discover, but the evidence on

[15]A history of Harvard University's experience with choice among health insurance plans is consistent with this model of a death spiral that causes one of the plans to vanish. See David M. Cutler and Richard J. Zeckhauser, "Adverse Selection in Health Insurance," in *Frontiers of Health Policy Research* 1 (June, 1998), 1–44. Another study explains differences between higher medical bills in the 1950s for persons insured by Blue Cross (which was not allowed to give a new policyholder a physical examination) and lower bills for those under private insurers (who were allowed to do so) as evidence for adverse selection into Blue Cross. Adverse selection became a smaller problem after the law allowed Blue Cross to screen applicants more carefully and adjust their rates accordingly. See Melissa Thomasson, "Early Evidence of an Adverse Selection Death Spiral? The Case of Blue Cross and Blue Shield," *Explorations in Economic History* 41 (2004): 313–28.

[16]Michael Rothschild and Joseph Stiglitz, "Equilibrium in Competitive Insurance Markets: An Essay on the Economics of Imperfect Information," *Quarterly Journal of Economics* 90 (November 1976): 629–49.

[17]Yoram Barzel, "Some Fallacies in the Interpretation of Information Costs," *Journal of Law and Economics* 20 (October 1977): 291–307.

[18]For a survey that questions the relevance of adverse selection but also cites some evidence for it, see Peter Siegelman, "Adverse Selection in Insurance Markets: An Exaggerated Threat," *Yale Law Journal* 113 (April 2004): 1233–80.

people's abilities to self-diagnose is mixed. Some research shows that people can predict their expected life spans with some accuracy. Others have found that insurers are more accurate than policyholders at estimating expected life spans, even after accounting for important influences like smoking, education, and income.[19] Even if people have personal information that insurers do not, insurers may still be able to use publicly available information (e.g., mortality tables) to accurately predict life spans.

Adverse selection only occurs if high-risk persons insure themselves more heavily than low-risk persons. There is little evidence that this occurs and much evidence that it does not. For example, drivers who are more likely to have accidents typically purchase lower coverage.[20] In jurisdictions where auto insurance is required by law, the highest-risk persons are less likely than the average person to buy any insurance at all. Observations like these have led some economists to propose theories of *propitious* or *advantageous selection*.[21] People with differing attitudes toward risk choose different lifestyles and different insurance coverage. Those who are highly risk-averse are less likely to engage in high-risk activities, and if they do they are more likely to take precautions. Even though they are lower risks they are more likely to insure. As one example, consider the insurance credit card issuers offer to cover financial obligations incurred by the owner of a lost card: 4.8 percent of credit cards in the United Kingdom are reported stolen each year, but only 2.7 percent of insured cards.[22] People who arrange their finances in low-risk ways (e.g., minimizing unsecured debt such as credit card balances) are less likely to smoke or do hazardous work and are more likely to buy insurance than people with riskier finances.

Moral Hazard

Insurance and the Cost of Accidents

A risk-averse person raises his expected utility by purchasing insurance, but utility depends on more than wealth. Your desired working hours depend on how you value income relative to leisure. Building owners weigh the risk of fire against the costs of checking extinguishers every day and treating flammable materials with extreme care. If you take lower levels of care and no fire occurs, you have successfully economized. If a fire occurs your insurance lets you recover all or part of your loss.[23] If being insured induces enough policyholders to take fewer precautions, their paid-in premiums will not suffice to cover the larger number of claims. The insurer, however, has defenses—a fire insurer may have rights to send inspectors to your business without notice and to terminate your policy if they find carelessness.

An insured person's incentive to behave in ways that raise the probability of a claim is known as *moral hazard*. Here "moral" is not a normative concept—comprehensive health insurance can encourage more frequent visits to the doctor that many people

[19]Compare Daniel Hamermesh, "Expectations, Life Expectancy, and Economic Behavior," *Quarterly Journal of Economics* 100 (May 1985): 389–408 (accurate predictions) with Jon Cawley and Tomas Philipson, "An Empirical Examination of Information Barriers to Trade in Insurance," *American Economic Review* 89 (September 1999): 827–46 at 841 (inaccurate predictions).

[20]Pierre-Andre Chiappori and Bernard Salanie, "Testing for Asymmetrical Information in Insurance Markets," *Journal of Political Economy* 108 (February 2000): 56–78.

[21]David Hemenway, "Propitious Selection," *Quarterly Journal of Economics* 105 (November 1990): 1063–69.

[22]David de Meza and David C. Webb, "Advantageous Selection in Insurance Markets," *Rand Journal of Economics* 32 (Summer 2001): 249–62.

[23]Failing to check your fire extinguishers must be distinguished from purposeful frauds like burning a factory to collect the insurance and then taking your chances with the justice system.

would view as prudent. Policyholders with full coverage for all medical services bear only the opportunity costs of time spent obtaining them. If a doctor suggests a costly test to detect a rare condition, you might choose not to spend your own funds but will submit to it if your insurer is paying.[24] Taking moral hazard a step further, giving the test might increase the doctor's income. Insurers understand this principal/agent problem and may require the doctor to submit information about you before they approve reimbursement for it. (They can also perform audits and order refunds.) Insurance can also affect the patient's choice to seek care. A runny nose that will soon go away might still be worth a doctor visit if insurance allows you to recover its cost. Insurers also reduce moral hazard by limiting coverage of open-ended (and for some, enjoyable) treatments like psychotherapy. Fully elective treatments like nose jobs are seldom covered. The progress of medicine is leading to a near-limitless range of treatments for many ailments, and insured people with low opportunity costs are likely to take more of them. The cost of Medicare for the elderly consistently outruns projections, and there is little evidence that additional treatment by specialists prolongs life or improves its quality.[25]

Q. Many health insurance policies cover cosmetic plastic surgery for accident victims but not for other types of patients. Why the difference?

Controlling Moral Hazard

Insurance and other contracts often contain provisions designed to reduce the attractiveness of morally hazardous behavior. To avoid defeating the purpose of insurance, these provisions attempt to raise the costs of making claims that the policyholder can control, while still allowing recovery for major uncontrollable incidents.

- *Co-payment or coinsurance* provisions stipulate that the policy will pay only some percentage of a claimed loss. Incomplete recovery leaves the policyholder to bear part of an accident's cost. Co-payment provisions usually include a ceiling above which the insurer pays claims in full. If policyholders can control small claims but not large ones an upper limit on co-payment may be economically efficient.
- *Deductibles* are fixed amounts for which the policyholder is responsible. Automobile insurance often excludes several hundred (or thousand) dollars of collision damage but pays amounts above that. A deductible may be efficient if the insured person can affect the likelihood of minor accidents like those that happen in parking lots. (It also reduces the insurer's costs of processing many small claims.) The policyholder has less control over major accidents that come as random surprises on the road, and the policy will allow her to recover all of her loss above the deductible.
- *Non-price exceptions,* like those for prior authorization of medical procedures, appear in other contexts. Auto insurance sometimes limits or prohibits a drunk

[24]Have you ever asked your doctor the price of a recommended procedure that was fully covered by insurance?

[25]"Research Suggests More Health Care May Not Be Better," *New York Times,* July 21, 2002. By one estimate, at least one of every three Medicare dollars is wasted on unnecessary or inappropriate care. See "Bad Practices Net Hospitals More Money," *Washington Post,* July 24, 2005. For at least some of the elderly, medical care appears to be more like a consumption good than an investment in health. See "Patients in Florida Lining Up for All That Medicare Covers," *New York Times,* September 23, 2003.

policyholder's recovery from an accident even if he was not at fault. An insurer may also require a policyholder with a collision claim to submit more than one estimate of the repair costs.

Q. Food is a necessity of life, just like medical care. Thus why isn't there "lunch insurance" like there is health insurance?

SIGNALS

Inferring Unobservable Characteristics

As graduation approaches you will surely get advice about job interviews. Besides the usual reminders to be on time and not wear a baseball cap, the counselor may suggest that you learn about the firm interviewing you. At first this looks like a smart way to make a good impression. You can make small talk about why you want to work with the company's products or how its earnings last quarter surpassed Wall Street's expectations. On second thought, however, it looks like wasted time for both you and the interviewer. Your visit to the library or search on the Internet had opportunity costs. The two of you have just a half hour to exchange information that will help the company decide whether to make an offer and help you decide whether to accept it. Five minutes of small talk means five fewer minutes to exchange information that may be important for both of you, and if you accept an offer you will soon learn the information that matters for your job.

But what if you looked at the costs and benefits and decided not to study the company? Your failure to make small talk may provide information that the interviewer could not otherwise have discovered. The personal traits that are actually important for the job may have little relation to objective data like grades. Some straight-A students lack social skills or owe their grades to memorization. Instead of book smarts, the employer might want employees who can take the initiative, or who can quickly find valuable information and digest it into a few minutes of conversation. The conversation might also provide evidence on the candidate's social skills: Does she talk about the company's global expansion or the recent scandal on its board of directors?

The point of small talk is not its subject matter but rather the fact that it takes place at all. Assume that a person who is a self-starter and a good researcher can find information on the employer's company and organize it for conversation in two hours, while a person with less initiative or investigative ability needs an entire day. If a day is too much time to lose (but two hours is acceptable), the second person will choose not to check out the company. Economists call the small talk a *signal.* A conversation about the company may indicate that a candidate has traits the employer wants but cannot observe directly, and failure to make small talk may provide information that the traits are missing. The signal can help the interviewer sort candidates more accurately.

Table 11-3 shows a hypothetical population of 100 interviewees, each of whom could have researched the company beforehand. Assume that several years after their interviews, psychologists devise a test to conclusively tell whether a person has the trait of interest. They somehow find all of the interviewees and learn whether they were hired or rejected. (No one turned down an offer.) The results show 25 persons with the trait, of whom 21 studied the company before interviewing. Of the 75 who lack the trait, 64 failed to do the research. This signal is not perfect, however; 11 undesirable interviewees

TABLE 11-3 SIGNALING

		DESIRED TRAIT PRESENT?	
		YES	NO
Learned about Company	Yes	21	11
	No	4	64

made small talk and 4 interviewees who had the ability chose not to study the company. There is, however, a clear association between presence or absence of the small talk signal and presence or absence of the employer's desired characteristics.

Warranties and Education as Signals

The buyer of the suspected lemon car could not be sure that the seller's claims about its quality were credible. The seller, however, might have the option of offering a warranty. The expected repair bills on a high-quality car may be low enough to cover the cost of writing and honoring a warranty, while those on a low-quality car are not. The presence or absence of a warranty then signals the car's quality, which we assume a buyer cannot directly observe. Only the seller of a high-quality car will feel secure in offering a warranty. Evidence suggests that manufacturers signal in this way. Because higher quality costs more to produce, our model predicts that warranties on more expensive varieties of a product will be more complete, as is indeed the case for cars and trucks.[26]

Our model also points to the possibility that signaling is inefficient. In our interview example, the time spent by interviewees in their research allows those who have the trait to separate themselves from those who do not. Using fairly extreme assumptions, Stanford University's Nobel Laureate Kenneth Arrow showed theoretically that higher education might be wasteful if all it does is sort people by their traits without improving their productivity. It is a filter that lets through only those persons with unmeasurable traits (e.g., persistence) that employers find desirable.[27] The signal works if those with the traits have lower opportunity costs of completing college (perhaps they need less study time) than those without them. This reasoning, however, simply assumes that better matching of workers and positions does not increase the value of output that they create. The model of signals is at odds with the view that education is an investment in human capital that improves productivity, and the costs incurred by employers in finding the right persons to fill particular job slots.

The evidence on higher education as a signal is mixed at best. If college attendance does not raise productivity and higher wages only come because the student has earned an otherwise meaningless diploma, we should expect that dropouts earn no more than high school graduates. The opposite is true—earnings of dropouts are between those of high school and college graduates.[28] If the diploma is a signal, the theory predicts that it will probably be more important in the early years of employment. As time passes, employers will learn about employees' productivity, and wages of high school and college graduates should converge. In reality, more workplace experience raises the difference

[26]Joshua Weiner, "Are Warranties Accurate Signals of Product Reliability?" *Journal of Consumer Research* 12, no. 2 (1985): 245–50. For a survey of theory and evidence on signals, see John G. Riley, "Silver Signals: Twenty-Five Years of Screening and Signaling," *Journal of Economic Literature* 39 (June 2001): 432–78.

[27]Kenneth Arrow, "Higher Education as a Filter," *Journal of Public Economics* 2 (July 1973): 193–216.

[28]George Pscaharopoulos and Richard Layard, "The Screening Hypothesis and the Returns to Education," *Journal of Political Economy* 82 (September 1974): 982–98.

between them.[29] Perhaps most importantly, if college is just an expensive way to identify people's traits then $100 bills have been left on the sidewalk—surely someone can devise a less costly filter and sell it to employers or prospective employees.[30]

The Winner's Curse

A painting contractor once complained to his economist son about bidding for jobs. "On most of the ones I win my bid is too low—I make less than I expected and sometimes take an outright loss." The same effect occurs when the U.S. government opens new underwater tracts (rectangles with 5 mile long edges) for oil and gas exploration. Whoever is willing to pay the highest cash up front (or sometimes royalty percentage) wins the right to explore a tract. Of 1,223 leases in the Gulf of Mexico awarded between 1954 and 1969, 62 percent were dry, and another 16 percent were unprofitable, although some production occurred. Only the remaining 22 percent were profitable.[31]

The painter and the oil bidders both face the *winner's curse.*[32] A short visit gives the painter very little time to measure and estimate the cost of painting the complex interior of a house. All estimates have some degree of error. The winning bid probably comes from the contractor whose estimate has the largest downward error, which probably earns her less than she expected from the job. Likewise, expert geologists will produce differing estimates of the amount of oil under a tract. Whoever employs the geologist whose estimate is highest will bid the most, but that bid is probably overoptimistic. The winner has been cursed. Even if a bidder understands the curse and lowers its bid, the possibility that someone else might win limits that bidder's options.

Some contracts allow renegotiation if a winner's curse has occurred. To start, assume that a painter has no labor costs and his only expense is paint. If an area remains unpainted because the contract amount was not large enough to cover the space, the agreement may allow the parties to negotiate a new limit. Opportunism is unlikely, because each gallon covers roughly the same square footage. By contrast, we will probably not see a reopener if labor costs go past a certain level. An industrious contractor and crew can finish in fewer hours than a lazy one, and the customer cannot easily monitor effort. Because an experienced painter is better suited than the customer to monitor the workers, the contract will leave the risk of underestimated labor costs with the contractor rather than the customer.

Opportunities to renegotiate may benefit a well-informed principal working with a well-informed agent. Only a handful of specialized suppliers can possibly bid for a contract to produce a new fighter plane that meets specifications set by the U.S. Department of Defense (DOD). Each supplier with an acceptable design must build a working prototype, and the winner will be determined by its cost (estimated from the prototype) and performance. The winner then produces planes on a "cost plus" basis. If it experiences an unforeseen difficulty in production or an unexpected change in costs, its contract with DOD may allow renegotiation. Unlike the person who hires the painters, DOD can use internal experts and consultants to evaluate the credibility of the contractor's

---

[29]John G. Riley, "Testing the Educational Screening Hypothesis," *Journal of Political Economy* 87 (supplement, October 1979): S227–52.

[30]Barzel, "Some Fallacies in the Interpretation of Information Costs," 299–300.

[31]Walter Mead, Asbjorn Moseidjord, and Philip Sorensen, "The Rate of Return Earned by Lessees Under Cash Bonus Bidding of OCS Oil and Gas Leases," *The Energy Journal* 4, no. 1 (1983): 37–52.

[32]Richard H. Thaler, "Anomalies: The Winner's Curse," *Journal of Economic Perspectives* 2 (Winter 1988): 191–202.

claims. Because the principal understands and can monitor the agent's actions, renegotiation may be a superior way to cope with unforeseen events. Renegotiation is particularly attractive because the market for major weapons is thin—both DOD and the contractor understand that they will surely be together on future projects and must maintain their reputations.

Q. A compilation of data from 2,000 wars from ancient to modern times shows that the country that starts a war is significantly more likely to lose it than the country that must defend.[33] What might this have to do with the winner's curse?

Deterring Excessive Search for Information

Duplicative Information and the DeBeers Puzzle

A contract will often require one or both parties to uncover information. You might, for example, hire a private investigator to find a missing person. You could value that information so highly that you hire an independent second detective. They may partially duplicate each other's efforts, but adding the second detective increases the probability that at least one of them will find the person. You believe the expected value of extra information from the second (and the probability that the first will fail) makes it worth the cost of employing her. You choose, however, not to hire a third detective—the increase in the likelihood of success is outweighed by his cost.

But say you and Jones are both searching for this person and for some reason you cannot coordinate your activities and share costs. Jones will hire one or two additional detectives, whose activities will for the most part duplicate those of the detectives you have already hired. Relative to the benefits, the resources the two of you have invested in the search will be excessive—more economic value could be created if, for example, you and Jones had made an agreement to share information and the people Jones might have hired were working at other jobs. We previously encountered this problem when we examined ownership of a newly discovered cave. There we learned that the law gives it to whomever owns the land that contains the cave's mouth, and that person will often have exclusive rights to extract and sell minerals discovered in it. Certainty of rights in the minerals gives the owner an incentive to explore the cave, and the law prohibits others from expending resources on duplicative excavations that will find no additional minerals.

This reasoning explains why DTC's contracts do not allow buyers to inspect diamonds in advance.[34] Prohibiting inspection brings additional benefits to both sides of the deal. DTC chooses a customer's diamonds and guarantees that they will meet the customer's specifications. Every diamond in the box may be as specified, but experts can still distinguish stones that will be worth more when cut from stones that will be worth less. Now assume that instead of using closed boxes, DTC empties all of the customers' orders for a given specification into a single large pile. Each buyer's agents search for the diamonds that promise the largest profit after cutting. (Assume that they take turns to grab one stone apiece.) The very best diamonds will go first, followed by the

[33]See Quincy Wright, *A Study of War* (Chicago: University of Chicago Press, 1965).

[34]For a fuller analysis of DTC's practices, see Roy Kenney and Benjamin Klein, "The Economics of Block Booking," *Journal of Law and Economics* 26 (October 1983): 502–516. At the time of their writing, DTC was known as CSO.

best of the remainder. When the entire pile is gone, each buyer will end up with a random sample of diamonds. Each hired someone to pick the best diamonds, but all of them took home boxes containing the same average quality.

If DTC puts a random sample of the diamonds into the buyers' boxes, each gets the same expected outcome as if it had sorted through them. Customers who are not allowed to select their own stones will be willing to pay DTC more because they save on search costs. The economic value thus created is potentially available to both DTC and its customers. For this to work, however, customers must thoroughly trust DTC. That trust has been built during their long relationships with DTC. If DTC could not always be trusted, buyers would pay less for a blind sight than one they could inspect in advance.[35]

Q. My local supermarket offers two ways to buy five pounds of onions. Customers can select their own and pay by the pound at checkout, or they can purchase approximately five pounds in a brown paper bag at a fixed price (they cannot peek into the bag) that translates into a lower price per pound. What kinds of customers are more likely to purchase the bag? What does this have to do with the DTC example?

Q. Grocery stores generally price some types of produce, like tomatoes and apples, by the pound, and others, like lemons, cucumbers, and lettuce, by the unit. Why the difference? At some times of year bell peppers sell by the unit and at others by the pound. Why? What determines whether grocers will sell a given vegetable by the pound or by the unit?

Disclosure in Contracts

A contract can contain information that is valuable to both the signing parties and outsiders. Sometimes the law requires that certain facts be disclosed in it. Disclosure is economically desirable where a failure to disclose would reduce the economic value the agreement can produce. If you put a house on the market you must generally inform potential buyers that it has structural defects or is infested by termites. A buyer with this information is in a better position to determine its suitability than one without it. Information about the termites is of little interest to someone who intends to completely remodel the house and of great interest to someone who does not.

Successful concealment of defects may get the seller a higher price, but high or low prices by themselves are not the important problem. Rather, if I do not know these facts I might buy the building when in reality it is unsuitable for my plans. Assume that I want a building to house a billion-dollar supercomputer, but the undisclosed defect makes it likely to collapse and destroy the computer. Your only reason for withholding the information was to extract a higher price from me, but the mistaken placement of a supercomputer in the building destroys economic value. Usually it is costlier for the buyer to find the flaws on her own than it is for the seller to disclose their existence in advance.

The creation of economic value may also require that information be protected. Assume that I want to buy your land because my long experience in geology leads me to

[35]Barzel, "Some Fallacies in the Interpretation of Information Costs," 304.

believe there is oil beneath it. Because farming is the best use you are aware of for the land, you base your asking price on the income a successful farmer could earn by tilling it. If the law required me to disclose my suspicions about oil you might ask for more, invite other bidders, or take the land off the market and do your own prospecting. If I am right about the oil, my investigation will have brought the world previously undiscovered wealth. It is likely that I have borne the costs of investigating other properties, only to conclude each time that they contained no oil. Buyers who must disclose their plans will have fewer incentives to search for information that will create economic value. As we will see in Chapter 12, corporate acquisitions, mergers, and takeovers are often sources of economic value. Competent new managers may be able to use a firm's assets and workforce more efficiently to create higher shareholder returns. Your decision to acquire or take over a firm is costly and risky. Nonpublic information about its status and prospects may be particularly valuable in deciding whether to go forward. That information may be costly to obtain and hard to interpret. If others can use the information after you uncover it, you will be less likely to incur the costs of discovering undervalued corporations and attempting to change their managements.

People contemplating takeovers or acquisitions could generally keep their information private before 1968, when the Williams Act became federal law. It required anyone who had acquired 10 percent of a corporation's stock (later amended to 5 percent) to publicly disclose the fact. Ownership on that scale can indicate a takeover in the making, most likely a tender offer to buy stock that will give you a controlling interest if successful. Requiring early disclosure informs others about a new opportunity, and these newly informed parties do not incur the costs of determining that the firm is a good target. The Williams Act substantially reduced takeover activity and increased competitive bidding for target firms. Before its passage the average cash tender premium in takeovers was 37 percent; afterward, it rose to 53 percent.[36]

Chapter Summary

- Contracts often contain provisions that allocate risks among the parties. Risk allocation can be viewed as a type of exchange between parties that have differing attitudes toward risk and differing abilities to control it.
- Contracts such as insurance may be used to reallocate risk, but there are situations where self-insurance is superior to a contract with an insurer.
- Asymmetric information can prevent people from reaching mutually beneficial agreements that they would reach if all of them had the same information.
- Markets can provide remedies for problems of asymmetric information in forms that range from warranties to information-producing services to seller reputations.
- Adverse selection can be a problem in insurance markets, because individuals may want to conceal their true riskiness when choosing coverage.
- Moral hazard is a problem of asymmetric information. A person who is insured and cannot easily be monitored by an insurer will have incentives to take fewer precautions than if uninsured.

[36]Gregg A Jarrell and Michael Bradley, "The Economic Effects of Federal and State Regulations of Cash Tender Offers," *Journal of Law and Economics* 23 (October 1980): 371–407.

- Asymmetric information can also give rise to signaling behavior, particularly in employment. There, people who have a desirable underlying trait and a lower cost of signaling that they have an attribute the employer desires will identify themselves to the employer by giving the signal.
- Asymmetric information may give rise to a winner's curse, in which the person who is awarded some right will have overpaid for it because he chose how much to bid on the basis of evidence that led to excessive optimism.
- A requirement that a party to a contract disclose certain information can increase the likelihood that economic value will be created. Not requiring disclosure can be efficient if doing so would allow others to free ride on the efforts of the person who discovered that information, but nondisclosure of other information is efficient in situations where a party to the contract incurs costs in discovering information that others will be able to free ride on.

Questions and Problems

1. Why does the assumption of independence of risks matter in the examples of insurance? What would happen to premiums if the probabilities of houses burning were positively correlated? Can you think of a situation where they might be negatively correlated?
2. Assume that your utility of wealth is given by $U(W) = W - 0.1W^2$, if $W < \$1,000$. Again, you start with wealth of \$100 and are considering a gamble that has a 0.5 probability of yielding you zero and a 0.5 probability of \$200. Show that you will not take this gamble, and calculate the maximum you would pay to avoid having to take it.
3. Some companies offer programs that give employees a financial reward if they successfully quit smoking. Is a company more likely to offer this if it self-insures or if it contracts its health care to an outside organization? Why? Is this plan more likely to be offered by an electric utility company or a high-tech internet company? Why?
4. A business that engages in substantial trading of commodities, currencies, and financial instruments must trust its traders to act with some prudence and with knowledge that the company's overall financial performance may depend on their activities. Lloyds of London recently announced that it would write "rogue trader" insurance policies that make good the losses of a trader's employer if, for example, she violates established limits and rules on trading. Enumerate some elements of moral hazard and adverse selection that might pose obstacles to Lloyds successfully marketing such a policy.
5. Chapter 8 explained that thousands of new grocery products are developed every year. Often the grocer will give the developer of a new product the chance to sell it through the grocer's stores, but only if the developer agrees to purchase the grocer's inventory of items its product is replacing, or to engage in a coordinated advertising campaign with the grocer.
   a. Use the economics of asymmetric information to explain why practices like these might exist.
   b. Is the grocer more likely to make this request if the new product comes from Campbell Soup or General Mills, rather than an independent inventor?
6. Currently, the law prevents courts or police from releasing information about the criminal records of people under 18 years old. Members of certain minorities are

more likely than other persons to have had problems with the law. Use the theory of signals to construct (a) an argument that the authorities should be allowed to release data on a person to any employer considering a young person for a job, and (b) an argument that there should be a blanket prohibition on releasing it, as there is now. Identify the gainers and losers from each policy.

7. I own a business that burns a million dollars a year of some fuel, and I cannot easily pass on increases in its price to my customers. Therefore, I trade futures and options to protect myself against increases.
   a. When I trade futures and options am I purchasing a form of insurance or am I just speculating? How would you distinguish between insuring yourself and speculating?
   b. Might it be reasonable to say that I am insuring because my risks involve delivery of a real commodity, while a speculator is simply gambling?
   c. If, say, I buy a call option to protect myself against a price increase, is the person who writes it a speculator or a seller of insurance? (A call gives me the right to purchase the commodity at a predetermined "strike" price.)

8. Do you expect that the winner's curse will be a bigger problem for a painter bidding to do the interior or the exterior of a house? The exterior of a house or a car? Explain.

9. Car warranties help eliminate a lemons problem but can also create moral hazard. Can society put an end to the lemons problems by requiring that all sellers offer warranties?

10. Married people occasionally report that they are less happy with their spouses than they expected to be before marriage. What might this have to do with the winner's curse?

11. Many auto insurance policies have "uninsured motorist" provisions that pay the insured if his car is involved in a hit-and-run accident or one in which the other party does not carry insurance. Here moral hazard is reversed and threatens the insured person. Explain why, and give the argument in terms of a principal/agent model.

12. Even without adverse selection, few insurers are willing to write policies that offer 100 percent coverage of losses. There are, however, some policies that do this. What sorts of losses do you think they cover? Why these losses and not others?

13. Why can you not buy insurance against failing this course? Against getting divorced?

14. Small firms can discover the abilities of their workers more quickly than large ones because they can observe the workers more closely at a variety of tasks. Does it then make sense for people with high abilities to go to small firms? Give some reasons why and some reasons why not.

Part Four

Organizations

Chapter 12

Organizations in Concept and Practice

INTRODUCTION

Tote That Barge

There have always been lots of unpleasant jobs. Quite possibly one of the worst appears in Russian artist Ilya Repin's nineteenth-century painting "Barge Haulers on the Volga."[1] But are you sure all of the people in the picture are actually working and none are just acting like they are working? If some of them are faking effort the group will haul fewer barges, and its members will earn less than if they are all working. Disregarding any possible team spirit (unlikely if this is your lifetime career), each understands that if he alone is shirking, the effect on team output (barge hauls) will be small. Self-policing is a distraction from effort and unlikely to work well. If Ivan complains that Boris is just going through the motions, Boris can with equal credibility deny the allegation or accuse someone else. If each worker understands that he can sometimes loaf and not be caught the team will fall short of its potential income.

[1]Convicts pulling a boat along the Volga River, Russia, 1873 (colour litho), Repin, Ilya Efimovich (1844-1930)/Bibliotheque des Arts Decoratifs, Paris, France/Archives Charmet/The Bridgeman Art Library

To resolve problems like this one we introduce the concept of *organizations* or *hierarchies,* in which some individuals have authority to issue orders that others are expected to obey and face penalties if they do not. The organization's members are paid, but generally not for performing particular actions. Pay is often agreed upon before work starts, and a worker may not have rights to negotiate additional payments for particular tasks. In this chapter we will delineate the situations in which hierarchies with command structures can create more economic value than markets or contracts, and explain why.

The barge haulers' elementary organization will be the foundation for more complex ones with specialized workers and intricate authority relationships. This chapter addresses the following:

- How teams can be more productive than individuals acting alone, and how supervision can improve the well-being of all of a team's members.
- Why the division of labor allows a team whose members have different specializations to produce more efficiently than a team whose members are unspecialized.
- Why specialized capital improves productivity, but coordination of investments is necessary if a team is to produce efficiently.
- How authority in the form of a boss can facilitate coordination of operations and investments by reducing the transaction costs of working as a group.
- How workers can gain if responsibility for investments is taken away from them and put in the hands of outsiders who provide the funds, bear the risks, and serve as residual claimants who keep the firm's profits or take its losses.
- Why a sole proprietorship is an economically efficient organizational form for only the smallest businesses.
- Why only a few types of businesses can benefit from being organized as partnerships with more than one decision maker.
- What are the basic characteristics of a corporate organization with publicly traded stock, and the principal/agent problems between shareholders and management that can arise in it.
- How a market for corporate control helps resolve the principal/agent problem by placing assets under managements that are more capable of using them to create value.
- The economic and organizational effects of transactions in corporate control, including acquisitions, mergers, divestitures, and takeovers.

Teams and Rewards

Team Production

In Chapter 2, Jones and Smith each chose a product to produce and both benefited from exchanging them. Because they produced different goods and each acted alone, there were no gains from such forms of coordination as working in the same place or at the same time. More often, however, people are members of a producing group. We call a group a *team* if three assumptions are satisfied.[2] First, several resources must be

[2]Armen A. Alchian and Harold Demsetz, "Production, Information Costs, and Economic Organization," *American Economic Review* 62 (December 1972): 777–795.

combined to produce output. They might be labor services of different individuals who can choose their own levels of effort. Second, total output cannot be separated into individual outputs. Team members are strongly complementary in production—ten haulers can pull the barge 1,000 feet in an hour, but one hauler acting alone cannot move it at all and five acting together can only pull it a few feet. Third, the resources are owned by different persons who will need to agree beforehand on organizational relationships that define their responsibilities toward one another.

Free Riding and Monitoring Team Effort

Assume for now that the barge haulers are paid equal shares of the revenue they earn from making trips between points A and B. Revenue per trip is determined in a competitive market, and they cannot influence price. A team member cannot monitor the efforts of other members without so distracting himself that his own productivity falls. If one accuses another of acting like he is working rather than actually working the claim will be hard to prove, and it will invite counterclaims. You probably have enough experience with professors to know that a competent loafer can convince most observers that she is really putting forth effort. As a group the barge haulers benefit so greatly from having a boss that they will pay to hire one.[3]

Barge haulers in China once did exactly this, according to Steven N. S. Cheung, a former professor at the University of Hong Kong.

> My own favorite example [of this type of cooperation] is riverboat pulling in China before the communist regime, when a large group of workers marched along the shore towing a good-sized wooden boat. The unique interest of this example is that the collaborators actually agreed to the hiring of a monitor to whip them.[4]

This example was purposely selected to shake up your thinking about relationships within organizations. The haulers produce so much more with supervision than without it that they sacrifice some of their income to hire a boss to monitor their efforts and punish those caught loafing. Treating the laborers as employers helps explain why we view a business as a set of contract relationships (some unwritten) that create benefits for the parties. In most of our experiences a boss offers employment to a worker, and we still must figure out why we seldom see workers hiring supervisors. An answer will emerge as we examine more complex organizations.

Q. Must the boss receive higher pay than the workers? Give an example of a workplace situation where this does not happen and provide an explanation for it.

Q. Are the members of a football team part of a team as it is defined here?

---

[3]The text says "as a group" because as individuals, they will have incentives to avoid paying and be free riders. As long as enough of them chip in to pay the boss, those who do not pay will also benefit unless they can be excluded from the crew.

[4]Steven N. S. Cheung, "The Contractual Nature of the Firm," *Journal of Law and Economics* 26 (April 1983): 1–21. Those who think economics professors lead unexciting lives should note that Cheung's whereabouts are currently unknown. A U.S. citizen, he became wealthy from parking lots in Hong Kong while teaching there. He was indicted in 2003 for evading several million dollars in U.S. taxes, did not appear for arraignment, and is thought to be living in China. Unlike the special zone of Hong Kong, China itself has no extradition treaty with the United States.

The Division of Labor

Setting the Stage

The barge haulers pointed up the importance of team production and the efficiency of forming an organization consisting of the workers and a boss. The example, however, used special assumptions to make its point, so to understand the structure of today's business organizations we must add some realism. In particular, the following assumptions need to change:

- *No specialization*: No hauler had a specialty that distinguished him from the others and required him to be supervised in a different way.
- *No outsiders concerned with performance*: It did not matter to barge owners or others whether the team worked slowly or quickly. A slow-hauling team would not lose customers to faster ones.
- *No investments*: Workers needed no other equipment to haul barges. We implicitly assumed no capital goods, such as mules or tractors, that might improve team productivity.
- *No risks*: A team faced no risks beyond its control. Barges were always waiting to be hauled, and there were no hazards like bad weather, accidents, or recession.
- *A trusted boss*: The haulers assumed that their boss would work hard for them but could not monitor that person's effort, examine his reputation, or compare him to other bosses. The boss' earnings were not linked to team performance.

We begin with one of the most famous stories in all of economics.

The Costs and Benefits of Specialization

A Quick Course in Pin Making Adam Smith's 1776 book *The Wealth of Nations* taught us about markets in Chapter 3. Now he comes back for a return engagement in organizational economics. Smith called the specialization of workers and their assignment to different tasks the *division of labor.* He saw it as a major cause of rising incomes at the dawn of the industrial age. In a famous passage he tells of his visit to a pin factory:

> … a workman not educated to [pin making] … could scarce, perhaps, with his utmost industry, make one pin in a day, and certainly could not make twenty. But [pin making] is divided into a number of branches, of which the greater part are likewise peculiar trades. One man draws out the wire, another straights it, a third cuts it, a fourth points it, a fifth grinds it at the top for receiving the head; to make the head requires two or three distinct operations; to put it on, is a peculiar business, to whiten the pins is another; it is even a trade by itself to put them into the paper; and the important business of making a pin is, in this manner, divided into about eighteen distinct operations.… I have seen a small manufactory of this kind where ten men only were employed, and where some of them consequently performed two or three distinct operations. But … they could, when they exerted themselves, make among them about twelve pounds of pins in a day. There are in a pound upwards of four thousand pins of a middling size. Those ten persons, therefore, could make among them upwards of forty-eight thousand pins in a day. Each person, therefore, making a tenth part of forty-eight thousand pins, might be considered as making four thousand eight hundred pins in a day. But if they had all wrought separately and

> independently, and without any of them having been educated to this peculiar business, they certainly could not each of them have made twenty, perhaps not one pin in a day; that is, certainly, not the two hundred and fortieth, perhaps not the four thousand eight hundredth part of what they are at present capable of performing, in consequence of a proper division and combination of their different operations.[5]

The Costs of Being a Generalist A single worker can perform all the steps in pin making. He could be in business with no more than a wire cutter, a file to sharpen the points, a device to put heads on the pins, and paper to stick them onto for packaging. He might buy the wire on Monday, spend the week turning it into pins, and sell the pins on Saturday.[6] His rudimentary tools and forced multitasking leave him with only a few marketable pins per week. Not all of his time is spent making pins either. He has to buy the wire, sell the pins, set up his equipment, and move partially finished pins from step to step. Performing all of the steps means he loses the productivity that comes with immersion in just one task. Financial limitations leave advanced tools out of his reach, but even if he owned one advanced machine (say, for attaching heads) it would be underutilized unless his other equipment had the same capacities.

First Step Toward Specialization: A Purchasing and Marketing Cooperative Begin with several independent persons, each a self-contained pin factory. One Monday Jones offers to take money supplied by the others to market and buy a week's supply of wire for all of them, with compensation for his time. Each pin maker gets more working time if they split the cost of Jones's time. They might do even better by hiring a specialist buyer who understands the wire market and knows how to strike deals. They could also save by contracting with a marketer or wholesaler to purchase their output. Contracts like those with the buyer or marketer are easy to write, and there are enough potential partners that risks of opportunism will be low. The pin makers can control their own opportunistic urges by threatening to exclude those of their group who do not pay their shares of the costs. The pin makers' arrangements with their suppliers are like those between farmers and cooperatives such as Ocean Spray Cranberries or Sunkist Oranges, where farmers oversee their own operations and pay outsiders to sell the crops for them.

Next Step: Independent Workers with Specialized Capital Having seen the benefits of hiring specialists to purchase wire and market their output, the pin makers might try to get the benefits of specialization by agreeing that each will work exclusively on some particular step of the process. They agree that each person will sell his old equipment (and borrow if necessary) to buy or lease a machine specialized for his particular task. They will also cut the cost of transferring partially finished pins between themselves by sharing the rent on a building they will occupy. To avoid some contracting costs, each will work on a cash basis. After A pays for the wire he cuts it and sells the pieces to B, who points them and resells to C, who attaches the heads. C sells the finished pins to D, who packages and sells them.

The workers have saved the costs of contracting but now they risk opportunism on all sides. B and C, for example, each own highly specific assets. When B sells headless pins to C he is a monopoly seller negotiating with a monopoly buyer (a "monopsonist"). There is no market where C can buy partially finished pins if he cannot reach

---

[5]Adam Smith, *The Wealth of Nations (1776)* (New York: Modern Library, 1937), 4–5.

[6]In Smith's time the workers would have almost certainly all been men, so this example uses only one gender.

agreement with B, or in which B can sell them if C holds out for a low price. The effects extend to everyone in the chain. The most C will pay B depends on what C expects to receive from D, and B will not survive for long if C's payment to him does not cover B's obligations to A.

Q. Let's say that C's job contains two distinct tasks—making the pinhead and attaching it. When will it be efficient to split C's work between two specialized persons, each with specialized equipment? Remembering that the outcome will affect the financial well-being of every worker, who should make the decision? Evaluate the strengths and weaknesses of alternative solutions to both questions.

Investment and Risk *Coordination of individual investments.* Even if the pin-making specialists resolve the problems of buying and selling unfinished pins among themselves, they must agree on how much to produce over the day, month, or year. If their plans differ, their investments will be mismatched. Some will own machines that are too small, and others will have chronically unused capacity. Mismatches are inefficient because they mean the group could have produced its desired output with a smaller total investment in equipment.

Difficulties in diversification. Risk-averse people cut their risks by diversifying their wealth into different forms. In general they will wish to avoid holding assets whose returns have a high positive correlation (i.e., if one earns an abnormally high [or low] return, the other is also likely to do so). A pin maker who owns his machine bears risks that he can avoid if someone else owns it. The machine's market value will be higher as the price of pins and the owner's income from pin production increase. If the price of pins drops the machine owner loses current income and takes a capital loss on the machine. Not owning the machine leaves the worker with funds to invest in assets whose value is not likely to vary in the same direction as his income. Insurance protects against fire or theft, but losses from decreased sales cannot be directly insured and may be difficult to hedge.

Income risk. In the normal course of business, a worker's income depends on the state of the pin market. If offered attractive enough terms, a risk avoider would trade an unstable income stream for a steadier one. He can of course make deposits and withdrawals from a savings account, but financial instruments (i.e., "swaps") that trade his income for a steady payment may not exist. If they do, moral hazard will make them expensive because they reduce the cost, for example, of calling in sick on a work day.

Strategic decisions. Our diversely specialized pin workers may have difficulty responding as a group to market opportunities. Assume that they learn about a new gadget, the safety pin. Some of them think it will replace the straight pin in applications like baby care and view it as a serious threat to their livelihoods. Others in the group see safety pins as a short-lived fad. Even if they agree about the threat some will be more enthusiastic than others about acquiring capabilities to produce safety pins. Their individual costs and benefits from a changeover will differ, as will their losses if it turns out to have been a mistake. Pin-pointer B's machine easily adapts to safety pins and can just as easily return to making straight ones, but pinhead applier C's machine is not needed to produce headless safety pins. C might sell his pinhead machine (possibly at a loss) and buy one that bends wire into a safety pin, but his changeover will cost more than B's. Whether or not the group continues making straight pins, it is ill-suited to foresee, adopt, and capture the benefits of new technologies and products.

Q. Assume that conditions in the pin market deteriorate so that the group as a whole takes losses. As individuals they can declare bankruptcy or leave the group. What are the advantages and disadvantages of legal provisions that allow the entire group to declare bankruptcy?

SUPERVISION AND THE RESIDUAL CLAIMANT

Hierarchy and the Division of Labor

The organization of our specialists makes their competitive success against differently organized pin makers unlikely. Our group benefits from the division of labor, but not as much as it might. Many of their difficulties have a common source: they were attempting to make transactions resembling those that took place in markets, but markets did not exist or were costly to use. Traders of partially finished pins risked opportunism because they could only deal with each other rather than being able to choose from numerous potential counterparties in a market. They faced high transaction costs that left them less time to productively exercise their pin-making skills.

The alternative to independent specialization by individual workers is a *hierarchy,* which we will sometimes call an organization. A hierarchy requires workers to comply with orders from a boss, who need not consult them when making decisions, and to be paid for their cooperation.[7] A given hierarchy may contain multiple levels, each containing persons who simultaneously carry out the orders of superiors and issue orders to subordinates. Assume that an outsider familiar with pins offers to buy the specialists' equipment for cash, after which they will operate it as before. Instead of reselling partially finished pins to each other the workers will just pass them along. The boss promises steady wages that beat income from self-employment and sweetens the deal by making the wages independent of small fluctuations in group output or price, at least for the near term. The workers may, of course, choose not to take the offer, but those who accept must agree that the boss may reassign them as she wishes and fire them if she chooses. She alone chooses who will replace a fired worker or fill some vacancy. Her income is the difference between the group's revenue and its bills for wages and supplies. If that figure is negative she is responsible for obtaining the funds, from outside the business if necessary. If this new organization improves productivity and profit both she and the workers share the gains.

Q. In some workplaces employees can recommend to the boss which person should be promoted to a supervisory position. (The boss, of course, need not heed this advice.) In other workplaces this practice is rare. Distinguish between the types of business where one would expect to see employees nominating people for promotion and those in which one would not. (Hint: compare how professors and assembly-line workers are suggested and screened for promotion.)

[7]Oliver Williamson, "Markets and Hierarchies: Some Elementary Considerations," *American Economic Review* 63 (May 1973): 316–25.

Supervision and Investment

Who Buys the Capital Goods? The boss in the pin-making example had good reason to purchase the workers' capital goods, because continued ownership of a machine by the person who operates it is almost an open invitation to behave opportunistically. Workers will probably also prefer that the boss own the equipment, because then they will no longer risk losses in its value due to market events they cannot control, and they will be better able to diversify their asset holdings. Centralizing responsibility for the capital goods makes one person responsible for all investment decisions, eliminating the need for the group to agree on its individual members' responsibilities and fund its own investments. Individual workers' abilities to borrow will not by themselves constrain the choices of capital goods that the firm might work with. Finally, ending the workers' role as equipment owners resolves the problem of continuity. If one of them quits, retires, or is fired the capital remains for successors to operate.

The Residual Claimant Adding responsibility for investment and other financial decisions (e.g., owning or leasing equipment and choosing which risks to insure) to the boss's supervisory activities turns her into a *residual claimant.* After taking in revenue and satisfying all payment obligations, the residual claimant gets to keep the difference. If we somewhat unrealistically envision paying off all of the firm's costs, collecting all revenues payable by outsiders, and dissolving the firm, the residual claimant gets whatever is left, including possibly the obligation to make good some losses.[8] The person who is both boss and residual claimant has incentives to make value-maximizing operating and investment decisions. She can make those decisions unilaterally, to the extent allowed by other agreements with workers, lenders, customers, and others (e.g., tax agencies). Except in rare cases (e.g., allegations of illegality), people unhappy with her choices cannot appeal to some higher authority.

A residual claimant with supervisory powers also resolves the difficulties independent workers had in arriving at choices that affected the entire group. Those problems arose because the workers had different investment responsibilities for their equipment, different attitudes toward risk, and differing beliefs about a new strategy's probability of success. Now the boss/residual claimant decides (possibly with advice from others) whether to begin producing safety pins. Having made the decision she may hire or terminate workers, change their assignments, and replace existing capital goods with equipment better suited for safety pin manufacture. She is the logical person to make this decision because as residual claimant she has the greatest incentive to make a correct choice.

Q. If a majority vote of the workers decides whether to switch to safety pins, why might the choice not be one that maximizes the economic value created in the firm? Does your answer necessarily change if a unanimous vote is required? Explain.

Separating Ownership and Management

Only in the tiniest businesses do we encounter someone who is simultaneously a hands-on boss, a provider of capital, and a residual claimant. A doctor in solo practice or the owner of a small store may take on all these duties because it is too costly to hire specialists. For more sizable organizations, however, the principles of division of labor and

[8]Limited liability and incorporation will be examined later.

efficient risk bearing also apply to ownership, investment, and management. In the next section we will examine corporate structures in which shareholders are residual claimants. Here we examine separation of the management function from those of finance and residual claimancy.

Different skills and opportunity costs: Limits on a manager's knowledge and capabilities may make her a poor candidate for residual claimant. Training in management entails psychological and organizational skills, while training in finance requires very different specialized knowledge. If a single person handles both functions, more time spent supervising operations means less time to spend exploring the organization's financial choices.

Risk and diversification: Residual claimants who have interests in more than one firm are diversified in ways that managers who depend on a single employer for most of their incomes cannot be. If so, risk-averse managers may make safer choices for the business than its residual claimant(s) would prefer.[9] In Chapter 15 we will learn how to dampen this potential conflict by rewarding top managers with a mix of a fixed salary and pay that depends on the firm's performance.

Ownership and control: Residual claimants ultimately choose a firm's managers. Later we will see that that the residual claimants often prefer to be passive and allow managers to make executive decisions in all but exceptional situations. A diversified residual claimant generally has less understanding of the firm than a manager and has little knowledge that is likely to improve the quality of the manager's choices. The separation of corporate ownership (shareholders are residual claimants) and control (management) removes most executive decisions from shareholder scrutiny, but this may be an efficient division of labor between persons with differing skills, goals, and wealth. We will return to corporations after an introduction to the legal forms of business organization.

THE ORGANIZATION'S LEGAL FORM

The Sole Proprietorship

The Proprietor's Problems You intend to open a manicure salon, renting the location and owning or leasing the equipment. Because you are the residual claimant, any profit or loss is yours to enjoy or suffer. Assume that the startup money comes from your personal savings. The salon succeeds and you want to open at another location. If you wait until you have saved enough you forgo valuable opportunities over the interim. A loan might help, but your bank is concerned about risk. Your credit record or your business prospects may deter the bank from lending you all the funds you want, and it might require you to secure the loan by the assets you are financing or the signature of a creditworthy relative. There are many other lenders, but their terms will probably be less attractive if they know (and you must inform them) that the bank already has first claim on your assets.

If things go badly the business might not generate enough cash flow to meet your expenses and repay your creditors. Assume that an irate customer sues you, claiming that unsanitary equipment gave her an infection.[10] You lose and the court orders you to pay more than the value of the salon's assets. Because you are a *sole proprietor* with *unlimited*

[9]Some research findings say otherwise. A 2005 study found that many CEOs of large corporations are so overconfident that they voluntarily buy more of their firm's stock as their tenures increase. See Ulrike Malmendier and Geoffrey Tate, "CEO Overconfidence and Corporate Investment," *Journal of Finance* 60 (December 2005): 2661–2700.

[10]In reality, you will probably have insurance to cover a loss like this one.

liability, you can be forced to pay the remainder from other resources, such as your house. The fact that the business is inseparable from your other wealth will be factored into the terms of any loans you receive.

The Creditors' Problems Your creditors will limit your loans for another reason: unless the agreements give them special rights, which are unlikely on a small transaction, they can only influence your operating decisions by persuasion. They usually cannot force you to fire employees they believe are incompetent or to use a particular brand of supplies. Uncertainty and lack of control imply that you will be borrowing on less favorable terms than if the lender can compare your operation with others or have a say in your management. Your contract with a lender entails a preset schedule of fixed interest payments and repayment of the principal. Offering the lender a share of your profits makes for a much more complex contract because it cannot easily check whether you are treating expenses made for your own benefit (e.g., a lavish office or midwinter trips to Miami Beach) as costs of the business.

Each creditor also faces a *liquidity* problem. Without special arrangements it will not be able to call in its loan or sell it to someone else if it wants to use the funds elsewhere or thinks you are misspending them. A creditor's inability to cash out means you will pay a higher interest rate, but if your creditors have the right to repayment on short notice you may be forced to borrow on unattractive terms to make up the shortfall. Finally, the business may be almost inseparable from you. If you die or retire its management may pass to people who are less competent or who have priorities or conflicts that lower its value. It may be costly to protect creditors in advance of your decision to transfer or abandon the business.

Partnerships

Lenders are unlikely to know as much about your business and its prospects as you do, which might make them unwilling to fund you on reasonable terms. If you can, however, find a person who understands it and has funds to invest, the two of you could become joint decision makers in a *partnership*. You can agree (formally or informally) on your responsibilities and how to share the work and finances. Unless you have made other legal arrangements you will both have unlimited liability, responsible up to the limits of your assets for the partnership's debts. Agreements to cut these risks include *limited partnerships*, in which decisions are made by general partners whose liability is unlimited unless other arrangements have been made. The limited partners have no decision-making powers but can lose no more than what they have invested.

Disagreement between you and your partner can complicate the relationship and possibly lead to its dissolution. Your agreement will contain provisions that apply to departure of a partner and outline that person's rights (if any) to recover her investment. Termination may entail liquidation of the organization's assets, or may require one partner to buy out the other's interest. Adding a new partner requires approval by the existing partners and revised agreements for sharing revenues and costs.

Partnerships whose members have specialized functions can face difficult problems operating and reaching decisions. Assume that Jones has invented a product, Smith understands how to produce it, and Murphy knows how to sell it. Agreement may be difficult because each has knowledge the others do not. If a distant market looks promising, Smith may want to build a plant there while Murphy wants just a sales office that will be supplied from a distance. Jones must concur with one of them, but he originally partnered with Smith and Murphy because he knew little about production and sales. If the partners can clearly delineate their individual competencies, they may choose to leave certain decisions in the hands of the person with the most expertise, with only token review by the others. Many high-end restaurants, for example, are partnerships between a financier and a famous chef that leave all food-related decisions in the chef's hands.[11]

Problems of liability, membership, and decision making lead us to expect that a partnership will be an efficient organizational form only in some special situations. The areas where partnerships are common include single-purpose ventures where the scope for disagreement is likely to be small and long-term plans need not be made, for example, the purchase and remodeling of a building that the partners intend to resell. Professional group practices in medicine, law, and accounting, are another example.[12] Partners in such groups will have similar backgrounds and skills, and each of their incomes will largely be determined by individual effort. It is thus relatively easy to evaluate potential new partners, to change existing agreements that treat partners symmetrically, and to evaluate an individual partner's performance.

The Corporate Form

A proprietorship with unlimited liability suits only the smallest businesses, and partnerships work well in only a few types of organizations. Most large enterprises are corporations, defined as "legal and contractual mechanism[s] for creating and operating a business for profit, using capital from investors that will be managed on their behalf by directors and officers."[13] Separation of ownership and management distinguishes corporations from proprietorships and partnerships. A corporation's shareholders are its residual claimants. Because they do not actively manage their firm, a sale of stock from one of their holdings cannot affect the others.

The owner of each share of a corporation's stock (also called common stock) may generally cast one vote for its board of directors.[14] Unless its charter (issued by the state government under which it incorporated) says otherwise, all shares carry equal voting rights.[15] If its directors announce a dividend, all share equally. Shareholders delegate management responsibilities to the directors and persons acting on their behalf. Some have viewed this separation of ownership and control as a basic flaw of corporate organization.[16] They reason that shareholders' low ability to actively monitor the corporation's management allows managers to make decisions that are more aligned with their personal interests than with those of shareholders. As noted earlier and discussed in more depth later, this separation may instead be an economically efficient division of responsibilities.[17]

---

[11]Disagreements among partners that own professional sports teams are apparently quite common and unpleasant. See "Bad Sports," *Wall Street Journal*, May 5, 2006.

[12]Suppliers of services like these may form specialized professional corporations that limit each partner's liability.

[13]Robert Hessen, "Corporations," in *The Concise Encyclopedia of Economics* (2004), http://www.econlib.org/library/Enc/Corporations.html.

[14]We do not consider many other possible financial devices, including preferred stock and multiple classes of shares.

[15]A corporation's founders have leeway to write special provisions into their charters as they believe necessary. For example, normally all shareholders have limited liability, but the founders may believe they will be unable to obtain financing on reasonable terms unless, say, one of them agrees to unlimited liability for herself. Incorporations can take place in any state regardless of where the company is headquartered. More than half of the companies on the New York Stock Exchange are incorporated (i.e., domiciled) in Delaware, in part because of its consistent and predictable incorporation laws.

[16]Adolf Berle and Gardiner Means, *The Modern Corporation and Private Property* (New York: Macmillan, 1932).

[17]Eugene Fama and Michael Jensen, "Separation of Ownership and Control," *Journal of Law and Economics* 26 (June 1983): 301–25.

Shareholders generally enjoy limited liability and can lose no more than what they paid for their shares. The shares of many large corporations are publicly traded, but smaller businesses can become nontraded Subchapter S corporations. Limited liability has less importance for them because creditors can require pledges of payment that include claims on resources the owner holds outside the corporation. Historians have debated whether limited liability is necessary to generate large amounts of capital. Many nineteenth-century ventures, including major railroads and Andrew Carnegie's steel empire, were partnerships with many limited partners and a few decision makers who had unlimited liability.[18]

Firms obtain capital from an initial public offering (IPO) of stock and later issues of additional shares. They may also borrow for shorter terms and issue long-term debt in the form of bonds. The shares are subsequently traded on markets like those of the New York Stock Exchange (NYSE) or the National Association of Securities Dealers Automated Quote system (NASDAQ). As with other assets, an investor may be "long" (i.e., holding the stock) or "short" (i.e., committed to delivering it). Because the public holds millions of shares in a typical large corporation, the market for its stock will usually be quite liquid—all but the largest trades take place without noticeably affecting the stock price. If a shareholder dies her shares pass to her heirs with no impact on the company. U.S. corporations must pay federal (and sometimes also state) income taxes before any dividends may be declared, and dividends and capital gains received by shareholders are subject to personal income taxes.

Shares are claims to future dividends and capital gains that are uncertain at the time of purchase. New information about a firm's future profitability will be incorporated into its stock price, as we also saw in the Chapter 3 discussion of futures markets.[19] The U.S. Securities and Exchange Commission (SEC) requires corporations to disclose financial data and provide other information about major developments. Corporate accounting scandals led to the 2002 enactment of the Sarbanes-Oxley Act (also called "Sarbox" or "SOX"), which requires extensive verification of reported data and statements signed by corporate officers attesting to its accuracy.[20] The analysis and comparison of financial data are difficult, but close study might help experts identify poorly managed corporations that create less than their potential value for shareholders. We turn next to relations between shareholders and management.

Shareholders and Managers as Principals and Agents

Identifying Mis-valued Firms Individuals trade shares based on expected returns and riskiness. Two people with different attitudes toward risk will hold different portfolios,

---

[18]According to Hessen, "Corporations," problems of asymmetric information rendered external financing by stock issues very difficult before the twentieth century. Accounting was unstandardized, the content of prospectuses was unregulated, and there were no standards for public disclosure that might help investors compare the possible worth of investing in one corporation rather than another.

[19]The possible existence of "bubbles" is a question of debate among economists. In a bubble, the price of some stock or other tradable asset rises because investors expect that other investors will continue to bid it up, instead of rising because they view its future prospects more favorably. The frequently cited tulip mania that overtook Holland in the eighteenth century in fact may *not* have been such a bubble. See Peter Garber, "Famous First Bubbles," *Journal of Economic Perspectives* 4 (Spring 1990): 35–54. The "dot-com" boom in Internet-related stocks between 1998 and 2000 (and their subsequent decline) is sometimes also cited as a bubble.

[20]Some scholars believe Sarbanes-Oxley may actually stand in the way of efficient governance and impede the flow of information useful to investors. See Roberta Romano, "The Sarbanes-Oxley Act and the Making of Quack Corporate Governance," *Yale Law Journal* 114 (May 2005): 1521–1611. One response to the law has been a growth in foreign incorporations of companies that will generate most of their income in the United States.

which might also include short positions. Even if we have the same attitudes toward risk we will choose our holdings on the basis of available information that we individually believe is correct. The particular information to be used is a matter of choice. I may think that work experience qualifies me as an expert on the industry that employs me, and you may trust your accountant sister-in-law's recommendation to buy an otherwise unknown company. Others believe they can predict the future by charting a stock's past prices. If the market is informationally efficient (as described in Chapter 3) a stock's price today will be the best predictor of its future performance, because it incorporates all of the information currently known about its prospects. You may, however, believe you can uncover information unknown to others that will affect its future prospects. If you find such information you can profit by purchasing the stock (if you are optimistic) or selling it short (if you are pessimistic).[21]

If your stakes are small, so are your likely gains from discovering information you think the market has disregarded. Even after obtaining such information, it is prudent to remain diversified. Your search may lead to nothing of value, your belief in the significance of your discovery can be wrong, or others may have found the information earlier and the share price already accounts for it. Seeing these obstacles you might prefer to follow the recommendations of a specialist with better investigative resources and more to gain from discovering the information. That person might, for example, represent an *institutional investor* like a large mutual fund or a pension fund whose decisions you can track.[22]

The Principal/Agent Problem Shareholders are principals and directors are their agents. Shareholders want decisions from the board of directors that maximize the value of their shares. As in other principal/agent situations, shareholders entrust others to perform tasks that they cannot easily monitor. Monitoring is costly, and evaluating the quality of the board's work is difficult because the best decisions in many business situations are seldom obvious, even in retrospect.[23] As in other applications of principal/agent theory, random events can further compound the monitoring problem. An otherwise sound strategy for expansion can fail, for example, because of an unpredictable recession. (Or perhaps the directors were too optimistic and failed to use information about the recession's likelihood.) On the other hand, random events can make a poor strategy look good. As we noted in Chapter 8, acquiring a company in an unrelated industry (a "conglomerate" acquisition) is normally a questionable use of funds, but the market for the acquired firm's product might unexpectedly thrive.

New information about the quality of a firm's management has attributes of a public good that others can use in the same way as the discoverer of that information. Installing a new board of directors can benefit all shareholders in proportion to their holdings, including those who did not make efforts to discover the old board's low quality or bear the costs and risks of replacing it. A small investor earns only small personal returns from discovering such incompetence and faces high costs of organizing a large enough bloc of shareholders to take action. If organizing shareholders is costly, the directors

---

[21]There are numerous other ways to capture changes in the stock's price, for example, by trading put and call options on it.

[22]This discussion neglects the research described in Chapter 1 showing that mutual funds generally underperform market averages.

[23]This is why it is hard to win lawsuits to remove or penalize executives for incorrect decisions. Under the "business judgment rule," a court must presume that a decision was made in the shareholders' interests unless there is strong evidence to the contrary.

will feel more secure if they make opportunistic choices to advance their personal interests instead of maximizing shareholder value.[24]

Such choices can take several forms. First, executives might use corporate funds in ways that appear legitimate but primarily benefit themselves. For example, they can buy a jet when commercial airline service is adequate or employ unnecessarily large and servile staffs. Second, they can use corporate funds to acquire social status, underwriting the costs of cultural activities or investing corporate funds to show that they share the political views of influential persons.[25] (Of course, corporate funds may also go to political candidates who espouse policies that will increase the value of the company's shares.) Third, free cash flows may be used for investments that do not maximize shareholder value. Free cash allows the directors to undertake acquisitions and expansions without going to the capital markets, which might view them unfavorably. Consultants who advise managers on strategy seldom recommend shrinking the business or narrowing its range of activities. Larger clients give them more consulting opportunities, and the managers of larger firms often enjoy higher incomes and social status. When a consultant recommends a merger or acquisition, shareholders have no easy way to obtain a second opinion on it.

Changing the Control of Corporate Assets

If you have massive resources, analytical skill, and a willingness to take large risks you might try gaining control of a company whose management you believe is responsible for its low market value. Finding that company and correctly attributing its performance to management is seldom easy, however. Even if your research shows that a certain company performs more poorly than comparable firms, the difference might be due to chance. You will have to evaluate the company, its environment, and its directors' decisions in detail before you can decide whether the directors are truly incompetent or competent but unlucky. Going forward you must also have a strategy in mind to increase shareholder value and a slate of directors to put it into action. You may, for example, have determined that earlier management teams acquired poorly performing firms and attempted to expand operations whose actual prospects were poor. If so, divesting the acquisitions and paring down the expansion plans might increase shareholder wealth. (Whoever buys the divested assets will pay shareholders for them.) There is, of course, no guarantee that your analysis was correct or that your plans will succeed. A takeover like this is a costly and risky way to resolve principal/agent problems, and there may be easier ways to get the job done. We next examine a series of alternative methods.

The Influence of Large Shareholders

Large shareholders (often called *block* holders) can sometimes influence a corporation's decisions without making efforts to replace its management. As one example, the California Public Employees Retirement System (CalPERS) annually issues a "focus list" of a few of the 1,800 companies whose shares it holds. CalPERS singles out those it believes are poorly managed or whose bylaws impede shareholders who want to unseat directors or allow other policies that CalPERS believes are not in their shareholders'

[24]For a more detailed model of the principal/agent problem between shareholders and management, see Michael Jensen and William Meckling, "Theory of the Firm: Managerial Behavior, Agency Costs and Ownership Structure," *Journal of Financial Economics* 3 (1976): 305–60.

[25]See, for example, Enron Corporation's sponsorship of works by architect Frank Gehry at New York's Guggenheim Museum and the associated book, J. Fiona Ragheb, ed., *Frank Gehry, Architect* (New York: Abrams, 2001).

interest. Some managements on its 2006 list, for example, are protected by supermajority requirements that mandate a 70 percent vote of all shareholders to change the bylaws rather than a simple majority of those actually voting.[26] CalPERS seldom threatens to sell stocks of focus-list firms, but the publicity alone often leads to changes. Brad Barber of the University of California, Davis found that stocks on the focus list outperform market averages after leaving the list. Between 1992 and 2005, these changes increased the value of CalPERS' portfolio by $3.1 billion.[27] Because CalPERS owns only small percentages of the listed companies, other shareholders enjoyed a free ride on CalPERS' efforts.

Proxies: Voting in New Directors

A large shareholder or group can solicit votes for a slate of directors that it has proposed as an alternative to candidates endorsed by the current board, which may include the board members themselves. Shareholders who favor the alternative are said to give their "proxies" (i.e., votes) to those proposing the new directors. The larger the percentage of stock owned by small holders, the costlier it is to wage a *proxy fight*. Soliciting proxies, however, is sometimes the only way to oust a board that has so protected itself that acquisition or takeover by outsiders is unlikely to occur. Regulatory and accounting requirements make proxy fights so costly that they are seldom seen. Like the influence of large shareholders, an unsuccessful but close proxy fight (or sometimes just the threat of one) may lead to a change in policy.[28]

Mergers and Acquisitions

A *merger* puts the assets of two corporations under a common management. As discussed in Chapter 8, mergers can be competitive strategies, or they can be attempts to create firms large enough to exercise market power. The U.S. Department of Justice or the Federal Trade Commission (FTC) must approve all mergers between large companies for their possible effects on competition.[29] In fiscal 2008 only 37 of 1,454 applications were challenged.[30] If most mergers in fact promote competition, then the performance of the market for corporate control will in part determine the performance of markets for consumer and producer goods. With some possible exceptions (discussed later), the market for corporate control will be more competitive if a company's management is not allowed to devise rules or engage in practices that increase the difficulty of acquiring control of its company.

[26]"CalPERS Takes Aim at 6 Underperformers," *Los Angeles Times*, April 20, 2006.

[27]Brad Barber, "Monitoring the Monitor: Evaluating CalPERS' Shareholder Activism," *Journal of Investing* 16 (Winter 2007): 66–80.

[28]As an example, El Paso Corporation, a large gas pipeline operator and energy supplier, faced a proxy fight in 2003. Its organizers accused existing directors of standing aside while the company violated the law to raise gas prices during California's 2001 energy crisis and then having to pay a $2 billion settlement. They also claimed that the board had purchased energy assets inappropriate for El Paso's core mission, that it had too few members with energy experience, and that the members had so protected their positions that a proxy battle was the only way to replace them. The organizers narrowly lost. Most of El Paso's directors kept their positions, but they soon sold some poorly performing assets, put more people with industry experience on the board, and changed some of rules they had devised to entrench themselves.

[29]As of 2009, at least one party to the merger must have assets of more than $130 million, and the other must have assets of more than $13 million. See Federal Trade Commission (FTC), *Introductory Guide I: What is the Premerger Notification Program?*, March 2009 2–3. http://www.ftc.gov/bc/hsr/introguides/guide1.pdf.

[30]FTC and U.S. Department of Justice, *Hart-Scott-Rodino Annual Report, 2008*, 1. http://www.ftc.gov/os/2009/07/hsrreport.pdf.

Two management groups will often agree on a merger that replaces their firms with a single new one, subject to approval by shareholders. The most important agreements will be on the successor company's governance (e.g., which of the predecessors' directors and officers will remain) and on how shares of the new corporation will be distributed among existing holders. One company may also acquire the other by purchasing a controlling interest in it, or shareholders of the acquired company may be given an agreed-upon number of shares in the acquiring company. Directors of the acquired company will not oppose a friendly transaction, often because their compensation packages reward them for getting out of the way or because they will continue as decision makers after being acquired. A transaction may also be unfriendly and opposed by the directors of the target.[31]

Leveraged Buyouts

Tender Offers and LBOs An outside organization may also try to gain control of a corporation through a takeover, which is often implemented by purchasing sufficient stock from existing shareholders. In a *cash tender* offer the outsider announces its intent to purchase up to a certain number of the target's shares at a premium over their market price. Having obtained enough shares to gain control, the outsider will replace the directors with ones who will carry out its desired policies. In a *leveraged buyout* (LBO) the outsider buys the shares with debt collateralized by its other assets—and sometimes also by the target's assets. The taken-over firm is more highly "leveraged," that is, it has a higher ratio of debt to equity. Because required interest payments are now higher, so is the risk of default on the debt. Bonds that have financed LBOs are pejoratively known as *junk bonds*, but their higher yields are no more than reflections of their higher default probabilities.[32]

LBOs are generally undertaken by specialist organizations that do not intend to take over the target's day-to-day management.[33] The LBO organization installs directors whose function is to reshape the target to improve shareholder value and then step aside. For example, the LBO organization may have determined that the target's stock performs poorly because its management has refused to divest an unprofitable division. Perhaps those managers do not want to admit their mistake, or possibly they believe they are better judges of the division's prospects than investors who do not have their detailed knowledge. The new directors can attempt to create additional value by divesting that acquisition. It might be sold for cash or set up as a new corporation managed by specialists. After the restructuring, directors from the LBO will cede their authority to new ones they believe are better suited to manage the company's normal activities. The financial restructuring of the LBO, however, will leave the firm with smaller free cash flows, which will stand in the way of its making acquisitions that the capital markets have not screened.

The Target Management's Defenses A target that is unwilling to cede control to an outsider has two basic defenses. First, before any threat materializes it can write bylaws

---

[31]There is no clear way to distinguish between friendly and hostile acquisitions using financial or stock market data. One author suggests defining hostile takeovers as taking place if the target's directors publicize their opposition, possibly as part of a bargaining strategy. See G. William Schwert, "Hostility in Takeovers: In the Eyes of the Beholder?" *Journal of Finance* 55 (December 2000): 2599–2640.

[32]For more on high-yield bonds and their consequences, see Edward Altman, "Revisiting the High-Yield Bond Market," *Financial Management* 21 (Summer 1992): 78–92.

[33]For more on the forms and activities of LBO organizations, see Michael Jensen, "Eclipse of the Public Corporation," *Harvard Business Review*, Sept–Oct, 1989.

that will raise the outsider's cost of obtaining a controlling interest in the firm. For example, the bylaws might set staggered terms for members of the board of directors, which imply that an outsider will have to wait a year or more before it has a majority of board members. Corporations with staggered boards tend to have lower market values than similar firms without them.[34] Other defenses in the charter or bylaws can include "shareholder rights" plan, which exemplify, a more general class of provisions popularly known as *poison pills*. A typical plan is triggered automatically when an outsider acquires some fraction (usually 20 percent or more) of the target's stock. One such pill is called a "flip-in." When triggered, all holders other than the outsider gain the right to purchase additional shares at a discount. Because the outsider's shares fall in value and carry less voting power, the provision may discourage that person in advance from even attempting a takeover. Another poison pill triggers early repayment of large amounts of debt when a potential acquirer's holdings cross the threshold, which may require divestiture of some assets to obtain the necessary funds. There are numerous other poison pills.

Second, management can attempt to ensure that even a successful acquirer gets control of a less valuable firm. A threatened board can, for example, try a "crown jewels" defense—selling to a third party those assets that the outsider values most highly. It can also barricade itself behind legally binding promises to customers or suppliers. In 2003, software producer PeopleSoft responded to Oracle Corporation's attempted acquisition by guaranteeing customers that if it were to be acquired (and other conditions were met) it would pay them $1.5 billion in rebates on their user licenses. On at least one occasion a target's management has responded by attempting to obtain a controlling interest in a potential acquirer.[35]

Should the Target's Management Fight? An organization attempting a takeover must believe so strongly that the target is poorly managed that it is willing to bear the costs and risks of installing its own directors. Sometimes a target's directors tell shareholders that its stock is actually worth more than the tender price, but statements like this are seldom convincing. If markets quickly build information into prices, today's share value will be the best available estimate of a stock's discounted future returns. Some management groups go further by claiming that the very existence of a takeover attempt means the stock is worth more than the tender price, and they should therefore have time to see if they can attract higher bids. Shareholders may benefit from a higher offer, but so might management if it can find a "white knight" bidder who will continue to employ some of them or offer them large amounts to depart. To discourage delay and defense, executive pay packages often contain liberal severance amounts and "golden parachutes" payable upon departure.

The target's shareholders can benefit when management solicits higher bids, but if solicitations are common they may adversely affect the overall volume of takeover activity. The initial bidder will have incurred substantial costs (including those of investigating and rejecting other potential targets) to determine that restructuring the firm could make it more valuable. Directors searching for a white knight are allowing others to free ride on the initial bidder's information and potentially increasing the initial bidder's costs of gaining control. Over the long term such searches may discourage efforts by outsiders to find underpriced companies and raise the costs of takeovers that do occur. If it

---

[34]Lucien Bebchuk and Alma Cohen, "The Costs of Entrenched Boards," *Journal of Financial Economics* 78 (2005): 409–33.

[35]In 1982, Bendix Corporation attempted a takeover of Martin Marietta Corporation, which responded with its own purchases of Bendix stock. Bendix subsequently found another acquirer more congenial to its directors. The episode introduced the Pac-Man defense, named after the 1980s video game character who turned on his pursuers and ate them.

is hard (or illegal) for the initial bidder to maintain secrecy, corporate assets will create less shareholder value. The Williams Act of 1968 required any bidder acquiring more than 10 percent of a company's stock to disclose its identity, file a report with the Securities and Exchange Commission, and keep its tender offer open for at least ten days. Researchers have found that the Williams Act was responsible for a long-term decrease in tender offers and a 20 percent increase in tender premiums. Some state governments also enacted versions of the Williams Act, producing a further 20 percent increase in takeover premiums in their jurisdictions.[36]

The Effects of Transactions in Corporate Control The bulk of the evidence on transactions in corporate control is that they increase the combined values of the acquired and acquiring firms. The increase generally stems from gains in economic efficiency rather than increased market power.[37] Mergers and takeovers do not appear to be randomly chosen raids. Rather, they cluster in different industries at different times and take place when growth and reorganization are most important as competitive tools.[38] Sanjai Bhagat of the University of Colorado and his coauthors found two benefits stemming from hostile takeovers that took place in the 1980s. First was the "de-conglomeration" of firms whose former managements had expanded into industries beyond their competence.[39] Second was the release of redundant middle managers that had accreted at headquarters. By contrast, employment of production workers was more likely to increase in firms that were taken over.[40] There is no evidence that changes in corporate control (or fear of such changes) sacrifice long-term efficiency for short-term investor gains. For example, the number of employees in research and development at firms that were taken over has grown at the same rates as those in firms that were not targets.[41]

Chapter Summary

- In team production all members must combine their efforts, but it is hard to monitor the effort and productivity of any one member. Incentives to shirk may be so strong that all members can benefit if a boss monitors their efforts and apportions their rewards.
- The principle of the division of labor explains how productivity of a group can increase as its members become specialized. To be successful, the group's members must coordinate their activities and their investments in capital goods.

---

[36]Gregg Jarrell and Michael Bradley, "The Economic Effects of Federal and State Regulations of Cash Tender Offers," *Journal of Law and Economics* 23 (October 1980): 371–407.

[37]Michael Jensen, "Takeovers: Their Causes and Consequences," *Journal of Economic Perspectives* 2 (Spring 1988): 21–48.

[38]For example, airlines, pipelines, broadcasting, and electric utilities saw considerable merger activity in the years after deregulation. Regulation had restricted the sizes of firms in these industries and the scopes of the activities they were allowed to engage in. Survival in the more competitive post-deregulation markets required some of them to grow larger to capture economies of scale or to change the scopes of their businesses. See Gregor Andrade, Mark Mitchell, and Erik Stafford, "New Evidence and Perspectives on Mergers," *Journal of Economic Perspectives* 21 (Spring 2001): 103–120.

[39]Sanjai Bhagat et al., "Hostile Takeovers in the 1980s: The Return to Corporate Specialization," *Brookings Papers on Economic Activity: Microeconomics* (1990): 1–84.

[40]Frank Lichtenberg and Donald Siegel, "The Effect of Ownership Changes on the Employment and Wages of Central Office and other Personnel," *Journal of Law and Economics* 33 (October 1990): 383–408.

[41]Lichtenberg and Siegel, "The Effect of Ownership Changes," 399.

- Specialists who buy and sell outputs in process from each other incur transaction costs and risk opportunism because they have few or no alternative trading partners.
- Specialized capital goods improve a worker's productivity, but efficient team production requires coordination of its members' investments. Workers who own their capital forgo the benefits of diversification and will have difficulty adapting to competitive developments as a group.
- The specialists' problems with transaction costs, opportunism, investment coordination, and risk aversion can all be reduced if they agree that someone else will supervise them, pay them, and invest in the capital goods.
- Further gains are possible if supervisory duties are separated from decisions on investment, particularly if the person who makes investment choices is the residual claimant, that is, the ultimate bearer of the firm's gains and losses.
- Difficulties in finance and outsiders' monitoring of management decisions ensure that most proprietorships with unlimited liability are very small businesses. High costs of decision making in partnerships confine them to a small number of business areas.
- A corporation puts capital supplied by investors with limited liability under the control of the directors they elect. Because shareholders are principals, and directors are their agents, shareholders face problems in monitoring and evaluating performance.
- The prices of publicly traded stock shares reflect the market's expectations of future shareholder returns. Prices and other data can reduce principal/agent problems between shareholders and management by helping analysts identify poorly managed companies.
- The market for corporate control arranges changes in the management of corporate assets. Techniques for a changeover include proxy solicitations, mergers and acquisitions, and takeovers or buyouts.
- The management of a firm threatened by acquisition or takeover has ways to resist the attempt. Except in rare situations, resistance impedes transactions in the market for corporate control and leaves resources to create less shareholder value.

Questions and Problems

1. In the example of the pin makers who each owned specialized equipment, sales of half-finished pins between them are costly transactions. As noted in the text, each of them has market power as both buyer and seller, and as a group they are known as "successive monopolists." Wire cutter A will maximize his profit by charging point filer B a price above his costs, which will lower the amount B wishes to buy. Point filer B will take a further markup when reselling to C, who will in turn sell to D at a price that is further marked up. When each worker exercises his market power in this way the group will produce so few pins that each makes a smaller profit than if they sell and resell partially finished pins to each other at cost.

   Show that their total profits from acting individually are less than their profits when each worker pays his predecessor on the line that person's marginal cost of pins.

2. If workers contribute to their group's investments and decide on these investments, workers at different stages of their careers may want different types of capital, for example a durable building versus a temporary one.
   a. How might the age distribution of the workers make the building they choose to build too temporary or too durable? How can a building be too durable?
   b. There are also young and old shareholders. Why isn't the choice of the building's durability also a problem if they or an elected management makes the decision on it?
3. Unlike the pin makers after the boss arrives, employees in some businesses do provide their own capital goods.
   a. In some cities taxi drivers must buy their own cars or lease them from an approved agency rather than operate cars from a fleet owned by the company they work for. What are the characteristics of cabs and drivers (and possibly cities) that would lead to this relatively unusual outcome? Why might taxi companies in other cities own their cars?
   b. Haircutters at salons often own their own scissors and blow dryers. Is your explanation for this phenomenon the same as your explanation of why taxicabs might be owned by their drivers?
   c. Which types of construction workers (e.g., carpenters, electricians, bricklayers) do you expect will own their own tools and which will not?
4. In some ways monitoring is easier in a partnership than a corporation, where shareholders monitor directors. In what ways is monitoring easier? In what ways is it not?
5. Thinking about famous corporate scandals like Enron and WorldCom, some analysts have suggested that these are the tip of the iceberg and that there are many other large corporations whose problems have not yet been made public. Give two reasons for taking this argument seriously, and two reasons for not taking it seriously.
6. Corporate directors are either insiders who hold (or have held) important positions within the company or outsiders who have achieved distinction elsewhere.
   a. Why do you as a shareholder probably prefer that the board of your company not consist entirely of insiders or outsiders?
   b. There are different kinds of outsiders. What types of companies are more likely to have boards on which outsiders with experience in other industries are more heavily represented? What sorts of companies will have outsiders such as community leaders who have little business experience? Board members without business experience will probably not make management decisions as well as board members with experience, so why would you as a shareholder want them on the board?
   c. Do you expect that a regulated electric utility company that serves all customers in a certain area will be more or less likely to have community leaders on its board of directors than a company that produces high-tech gadgets for a highly competitive market? Why?
7. In some industries, merger agreements stipulate that a high-ranking executive of one company will be president or chairman of the board of the merged company for a certain period of time, say four years, after which a high-ranking executive from the other will get the job for the same term. Is this sort of behavior evidence of a principal/agent problem between executives and shareholders? Why or why not?
8. Why might you expect that disagreements among partners who own a professional sports team will be particularly difficult to resolve? Look up the frequency of

ownership partnerships in a sport of your choice. If the partnership teams experience, on average, financial performance that is no better or worse than enjoyed by solely owned or corporate-owned teams, how would you explain this? (Hint: think about the organizational characteristics of sports leagues, which we discuss in Chapter 13.)

9. Jones has organized a proxy fight to take control of XYZ corporation. He purchases several million shares on the market (which he can vote) and simultaneously sells them short. Thus, disregarding the cost of arranging the deal (and its possible price effects), Jones is perfectly hedged. Every dollar rise (fall) in the stock price produces roughly a dollar fall (rise) in the value of his short position. Jones votes his shares and the board is changed. As a business strategy, should this behavior be legal? What if he pays to unwind his short position and continues to hold the shares he bought?

10. Regarding separation of ownership and control, A major change in most corporate policies requires that a majority of stock shares that are voted favor it. Would you prefer that approval by a smaller (or possibly larger) fraction of the shares be sufficient to change the policy? Why or why not? (We discuss majority voting in more detail in Chapter 17.)

11. A friend convinces you that she has a great idea for a business, and the two of you incorporate. You supply her with funds and let her make all of the executive decisions. Under the agreement you hold 30 percent of the firm's stock and your friend holds 70 percent. Why should you ever put yourself into a position where your friend's decision will carry the day, whether you agree with her or not? What does this tell you about problems that allegedly stem from separation of ownership and control?

12. When discussing the pin makers we brought up marketing cooperatives like Sunkist Oranges. Unlike the pin makers, orange growers control Sunkist's policies by their votes (weighted by their shipment volumes), for example, on advertising budgets and decisions to sell in new territories. What differences between pin makers and orange growers might make majority voting a feasible way to run one organization but not the other?

13. It has been said that the market for corporate control is unimportant to the economy because people in it make only "paper profits." Try defining paper profits and distinguishing them from real ones, which you should also define.

14. There is a growing interest in strategies that separate the financial rights (to dividend income) associated with a share of stock from its voting rights (for the corporation's directors).[42] For example, if I borrow shares from you for a short sale I can vote them, but you retain rights to the dividends. Conversely, you might continue to own and vote the shares, but we can arrange a swap that gives me the right to its future dividends in exchange for some payment today. How might the growth of transactions that separate income from voting rights affect the efficiency of the market for corporate control? Give an example of improved efficiency and one of decreased efficiency.

---

[42]Henry Hu and Bernard Black, "Hedge Funds, Insiders, and the Decoupling of Economic and Voting Ownership: Empty Voting and Hidden (Morphable) Ownership," *Journal of Corporate Finance* 13 (Feb. 2007): 343–367.

Chapter 13

Organizational Designs

Introduction

The Animal Refiner

In 1936 Arkansas farmer John Tyson heard that chickens were selling for high prices in Chicago. He loaded his truck, borrowed money for the trip and discovered that the rumors were right. Tyson got $235 for the chickens, repaid his borrowings and made a small profit. Within a few years he was shipping chickens to cities around the midwest and south. He contracted with farmers to raise chickens for him and expanded vertically into feed production.[1] Tyson managed some risks then like he would manage them today—he insured his trucks against accidents and his buildings against fire. Unlike today, however, he had few ways to cope with price risk. Before the coming of futures contracts on chickens he could only guess at the price a newborn chick would bring when it was ready for market. Tyson made his own feed but was unable to lock-in the prices of its ingredients. The New York Mercantile Exchange would begin trading natural gas futures

FIGURE 13-1
The Risks Confronting Tyson

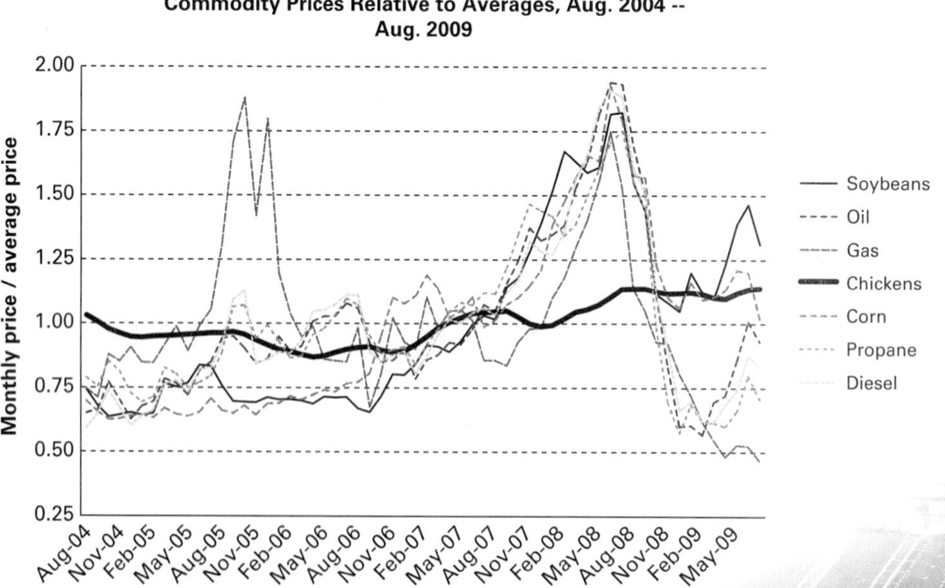

[1]Tyson Foods, Inc. Fiscal 2008 Fact Book pp. 24–25. http://media.corporate-ir.net/media_files/irol/65/65476/FY08_Fact_Book_FINAL.pdf.

in 1990, but in the 1930s Tyson could do no more than guess the costs of keeping thousands of temperaturesensitive chickens warm. Every new flock was a new gamble.

Today Tyson Foods, Inc. is the world's largest processor and marketer of chicken, beef and pork.[2] The company faces the same risks that John Tyson did and many new ones. Figure 13-0 shows that the six commodities that account for most of Tyson's costs have some of the most volatile prices in the economy.[3] The mass of thin lines, one for each commodity, shows that at some time during the past five years every one of them has at sold for nearly double its average price during those years, and at some time for just over half of that price. Th ey do not all move together, and they all change quickly. In July 2008 all of them peaked, but by July 2009 natural gas was at a record low while corn was well above its average and rising.[4] Through all of these changes, the wholesale price of chicken was remarkably stable. Tyson cannot count on automatically increasing its revenue as its costs change.

Risk management today is so complex and so important for Tyson's competitive success that the company has changed its structure to better oversee those risks. It followed the lead taken by multinational banks and integrated energy companies over the past ten years. Tyson hired Jean Beach, a former trader for Enron Corporation, and gave her an unforgettable job title: "Senior Vice President, Commodity Trading and Risk Management, Price Optimization and Meat Procurement." Other employers would call her their Chief Risk Officer.[5] Beach oversees what we will later call a "self-contained unit" within Tyson, managing risks in feed, fuels, live animals and dressed ones the same way an integrated energy company manages those of crude oil, natural gas, pipelines and gasoline. She calls Tyson a "refiner of animals," but riskier than an oil refiner because "a lot less product comes out of a barrel of crude [oil] than comes out of a chicken."

Beach manages billions of dollars worth of risk. Trading futures, options, and other derivatives on its raw materials and outputs is only the start. The details of Tyson's procurement policy affect its risk position—how many chickens the company will raise, how many will be bought under contracts with farmers, and how many will be purchased for cash in markets. Government policies that require blending corn-based ethanol into gasoline have driven the price of chicken feed to unprecedented levels, and the possibilities of substituting soybeans for corn are shrinking as a wave of soy-based biofuels comes to market. Tyson hedges by taking positions in both corn and gasoline. Beyond risks like these are many common ones—delayed deliveries, disasters that put plants out of operation, unpredictable interest and exchange rates, recessions that delay customer payments, and the possibility that vegetarianism might become more than a fringe dining habit.

Before it formed Beach's self-contained unit, Tyson assigned responsibility for risk management to employees familiar with different commodities: feed purchasers handled corn, fuel purchasers worked with gasoline, and marketers handled dressed chickens and beef. But risks like the newer ones between corn and gasoline show that the company can no longer count on uncoordinated departmental decisions to manage them effectively. In addition, financial innovations have put important aspects of risk

---

[2]Tyson Foods, Inc. Fiscal 2008 Fact Book, unnumbered page. http://media.corporate-ir.net/media_files/irol/65/65476/FY08_Fact_Book_FINAL.pdf.

[3]For more information about positions like this, see the Web site of the Committee of Chief Risk Officers, http://www.ccro.org/.

[4]"Volatility and the Protein Refinery," *New Power Executive,* November 10, 2006.

[5]The photo is from "Tyson Foods Refines a Recipe by Energy Firms," *Wall Street Journal*, December 1, 2006.

management beyond the competence of nonspecialists. Tyson responded by restructuring its organization to include Beach's position and reallocate responsibilities to put her in charge of risks that were formerly managed by individual departments. This chapter is about business organizations, why they take the shapes they do, and how they change with their environments.

- A firm's organization is an intangible productive resource, and different structures can advantage or disadvantage it competitively.
- There are important trade-offs between centralized and decentralized decision making that depend on the type of information that is important for the firm and the skills of different persons making the decisions.
- Links between members of an organization must efficiently send information to the best decision maker(s) and accurately transmit orders based on those decisions.
- Departments (or individuals) within an organization often play dual roles—they are principals that must elicit effort from subordinates and agents who carry out the requests of those above them. These two facts make the design of incentives both difficult and important.
- Organizations can divide tasks according to a functional or U-form design that gives all responsibility for a certain task to a single department. They may also be divisionalized into an M-form with units for individual products or activities in different geographic areas.
- The sizes and types of markets a firm operates in will be important in determining whether a U-form or M-form is the economically efficient organization, as will the types of information and responses to it that are important for the organization's success.
- It is also possible to combine product-based M-form organizations with geographically based ones to construct a matrix-form organization. The matrix form can facilitate some important information flows, but it can also leave gaps and conflicts in authority.
- Another type of organization resembles the matrix form, but includes self-contained units whose authority bridges individual divisions. Such units can be particularly valuable in activities like risk management, where decentralization of decisions is unlikely to produce efficient policies, and where costly specialized information is required to determine strategy.
- Organization charts only portray formal authority relationships as they were designed to function, but the actual pattern of relationships used in making a firm's decisions may reflect informal authority that does not appear on the chart.

Organizational Activities, Centralization, and Decentralization

It Takes More than a Mousetrap

The first industrial revolution occurred in the eighteenth and early nineteenth centuries as steam power reshaped manufacturing, first in Europe and later in the United States. Steam alone, however, did not greatly change the sizes of most businesses that adopted it. What scholars have called "the second industrial revolution" came later in the nineteenth century. Commercialization of railroads, telegraphy, and steamships, and new processes for producing chemicals and metals, were often most efficient at scales that dwarfed those of earlier businesses. These capital-intensive firms had to produce continuously, which required the real-time coordination of numerous activities. Chemical and metals manufacturers in the United States and Germany were the first to organize themselves in ways that took full advantage of the new technologies.

Contrary to the proverb, if you want to bring the world to your door you need to do more than invent a better mousetrap. Coal-based dyes were invented in England, and the English textile industry was the world's largest user of them. Nevertheless, British manufacturers lost their market to large low-cost German suppliers who continually expanded their offerings and better coordinated manufacturing with distribution. Important electrical technologies were invented in England, but by the early 1900s Britain had lost its advantage to General Electric and Westinghouse in the United States and Siemens and AEG in Germany. The late Harvard business historian Alfred Chandler linked Britain's competitive difficulties with the structures of its firms—they were smaller and incapable of the organizational learning that grew with size and experience. That learning took larger companies in new directions that smaller ones could not follow and helped them dominate new markets. German chemical producers moved into pharmaceuticals (Bayer's aspirin) and American firms began making household products (DuPont's cellophane).[6]

Any multi-person activity requires the assignment of responsibilities and the definition of relationships, whether it be a club, a political group, a church, a business, or a government agency. In this chapter such activity is confined to profit-seeking firms that operate in markets. When we introduced business firms in Chapter 4, we left important aspects of decision making for later. We explained how to allocate resources to minimize costs or maximize profits, but did not specify who made the decision or why it was in that person's hands. We simply assumed that someone would make the choice, order others to carry it out, and that those receiving the orders would obey without complaining or making mistakes. This chapter asks who in an organization would best be given authority to make different decisions, and why. Doing so requires understanding how information originates within a firm, how it is transferred, and who can put it to the most effective use. The firm does not just process material, financial, and human inputs. It also processes information, and its ability to do this well depends on its organizational design.

Centralization

What to Centralize One of the most important aspects of an organization is its ability to convey information from those who have it to those who are the most competent at using it to make decisions. Some decisions will best be centralized, that is, one person (department) uses information from different sources to set a policy that may affect those who provided the information.

Decisions are better made centrally under the following conditions:

1. They require information from more than one source. Some good sources will be internal. If the boss in Chapter 12's pin factory must decide which machines to replace, their operators will know the most about breakdown rates and the effect of breakdowns on production. Other sources will be external. When deciding whether to go into safety pins, for example, the boss might hire a marketing consultant.

[6]Alfred D. Chandler, "Organizational Characteristics and the Economic History of the Industrial Enterprise," *Journal of Economic Perspectives* 6 (Summer 1992): 79–100.

2. They require decision-making skills (e.g., knowledge of forecasting techniques) that those who produced the information do not have. The pin factory boss's decision about a changeover to safety pins must consider the available budget, the cost of retooling, worker attitudes, and market conditions for safety and straight pins. In a more complex organization than the pin factory the person with the best decision-making ability (perhaps someone with experience in similar decisions) is likely to be higher in the hierarchy.
3. The decision maker's incentives are aligned with those of the principals, in this case the firm's shareholders. Some firms delegate important decisions like safety pins to committees (including boards of directors) whose members have expertise in the different aspects of that decision. Members may include executives with substantial shareholdings and outsiders who were appointed because of their extensive business experience. Personal attitudes and relationships among the members of such groups, however, may lead to compromises that are not in the interests of the shareholders.[7]

Transmitting Information and Commands It seems obvious that better information makes for better performance, but what is meant by good information is far less obvious. A perfectly accurate forecast only occurs by coincidence, and even the likely direction of its error may be hard to determine in advance. The information to be gathered depends on the model that underlies a decision and on the expected costs and benefits of acquiring the information. We learned in Chapter 1 that a model is necessary to organize the decision maker's thinking and guide her to relevant data. Exactly who has that data and how it gets to the decision maker are both critical questions in organizational design.

To achieve a desired outcome, decisions generate orders that subordinates must follow. Orders both transfer information and bind their recipients to take certain actions. Any order should go to the person or persons most likely to execute them as intended. The right recipient may either command the resources (e.g., staff, machinery) best suited for the job or be in a superior position to monitor the compliance of others. Orders can lose accuracy as they are transmitted, and recipients of an order may not carry it out as intended, which might be due to incompetence, opportunism, or impossibility. To find out exactly what happened and cope with mistakes, an organization must contain pathways for informing decision makers about the results of their orders and for assigning responsibility for good or bad performance.

Q. Other things equal, if Jones can almost always carry out Smith's orders to the letter but Smith can only carry out Jones's orders correctly a smaller percentage of the time, does it necessarily mean Smith should supervise Jones? Give two counterexamples.

Decentralization

Management The second industrial revolution marked the emergence of management as a defined occupation. In 1900, the U.S. Census counted 3.4 million workers in management or management support, or 11.6 percent of a labor force of 29.0 million. By 1980, that figure had grown to 45.6 million, or 43.8 percent of a labor force of 104.1

[7]See, for example, the discussions of smart crowds in Chapter 1 and committees in Chapter 17.

million.[8] Relatively few of these workers are exclusively managers, however; a supervising hospital nurse, for example, also treats patients, and a lead programmer may write some of the code for which his group is responsible.

As organizations grow in size they usually also grow in complexity. Greater size and complexity mean a higher proportion of their members' activities must be devoted to management. In any organization larger than a sole proprietorship it is impossible for one person to hold all of the information that matters for all types of decisions. In a complex organization a manager will both serve as an information conduit and have final responsibility for certain activities. Size alone requires people lower in the organization to be responsible for some of those decisions. Organizational design is the study of who can best decide what, and the best design depends on the organization's purpose—what it produces and what markets it operates in.

Q. Chapter 2 described the benefits of specialization and rules for efficiently assigning persons to different tasks. This section, however, gave examples of people who are assigned a particular task and who must also engage in some supervisory activities. Under what conditions is it efficient for a manager to split a subordinate's assignment between management and specialization in a particular task?

Principals and Agents Everywhere Many members of an organization are simultaneously principals attempting to obtain performance from subordinates and agents expected to perform for their supervisors. Each generates information for the use of others, and each must use information from others in making decisions. Because knowledge is specialized and time is limited, a principal cannot perfectly monitor an agent. In addition, random factors may make it impossible for the principal to determine whether an agent's poor performance is due to lack of effort or bad luck. Everyone in an organization produces information that others in the organization would find costly to obtain or verify. A person who is the only source of important information for her superiors might choose to act opportunistically, selectively disclosing facts in hopes of eliciting decisions that favor her.

Contracts determine methods of payment that a principal can use to elicit effort from an agent. In Chapter 10, for example, the plaintiff's lawyer was paid a percentage of his winnings, while the defendant's billed by the hour. There are important similarities between incentives in contracts and those in organizations, and important differences as well. To reach the best decision for her principal Jones may require full and accurate information from Smith, but in most organizations Jones does not directly determine Smith's pay or the method of compensating him. The performances of Jones's superiors are also indirectly affected by the quality of Smith's disclosures. As an alternative to pay arrangements the organization itself can be designed to make it easier to detect opportunism and reduce errors in transmitting information. Both distortions and errors (sometimes called "garbling") depend on how information moves from the source to

[8]Roy Radner, "Hierarchy: The Economics of Managing," *Journal of Economic Literature* 30 (September 1992): 1382–1415 at 1387. The figures are calculated from the U.S. Census of Population, but the source does not provide details that would allow figures to be calculated for today's economy. As of January 2009, U.S. Bureau of Labor Statistics counted approximately 154 million people in the labor force. See http://www.bls.gov/news.release/empsit.nr0.htm.

the user. The best path may not be the shortest—additional steps might allow others to check the information for accuracy or consistency with other facts. Organization charts will help us to better understand these paths.

Organizational Linkages

A "Tree" without Roots or Branches

Before you read ahead try to figure out what sort of business might have an organization chart like the one in Figure 13-2. It consists of a single row of Xs that represent individuals. No important authority relationships are shown above or below them. More strangely, the individuals have few responsibilities toward each other, a weak linkage usually shown by dotted rather than solid lines. To better understand the logic of some common relationships we start with an organization in which relationships are unimportant.

One possibility is that Figure 13-2 describes a group medical (or possibly a law or accounting) practice. Partnership in the group reduces some important costs. The doctors share the expenses of a waiting room and a lab they can all use and are jointly responsible for paying receptionists and nurses. A more detailed chart than Figure 13-1 might show an administrator (quite possibly one of the doctors) overseeing the doctors' responsibilities to the organization, including their shares of those costs. Below the doctors would be clerical and professional (nurses, X-ray technicians) support staff used by all of them. The organization is simple because team production is unimportant. Each doctor's income depends largely on the number of patients she attracts, and a lack of effort by one partner will seldom affect another's revenue prospects. Unlike the barge haulers, it is easy to see the income each doctor generates. If there is no sharing of income a doctor who loafs will suffer directly while doctors who continue to put forth effort will continue to earn. This group's structure facilitates monitoring. A doctor sued for malpractice will pay higher insurance premiums and cannot shift those sts onto the others. If matters are serious enough to consider expulsion from the partnership, specialists with the same credentials are likely to be good judges of whether she is incompetent or just unlucky.

Q. In a group legal partnership senior lawyers usually decide on annual bonuses for those who attract high-revenue clients to the firm or win cases that reflect favorably on its public reputation. In corporate hierarchies bonuses are seldom set by people with the same skills as the recipients. Why is there a difference?

A Simple Hierarchy

Limits on the abilities of individuals to process information suggest a basic principle: *Put the decision where the information is.* If a person at a low level of the organization has all of the information that is relevant to a decision, assigning responsibility for that decision to person at a higher level will not improve the quality of the decision that gets made. (Remember we said *all* of the information.) Irrelevant or excessive information can even degrade the expected quality of a decision as it overwhelms the decision maker's mental

FIGURE 13-2
What Sort of Organization Is This?

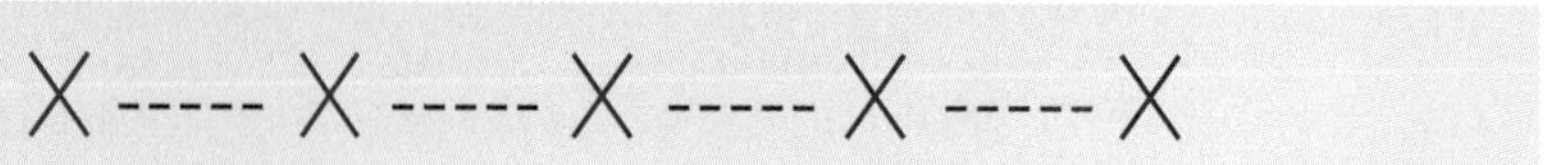

abilities and increases the risk of misunderstandings or errors. In a hierarchy the necessary information may originate in a number of places. Deciding on next month's production run requires historical information and forecasts from the sales department, cost data from accountants, inventory data from the warehouse, and other data from outside (an ice cream producer might want a weather forecast). The decision maker should receive only that information whose marginal benefits are likely to exceed its marginal costs, including those of inaccurate transmission.

Decentralizing decisions is efficient if people at lower levels have knowledge to which those at higher levels can add little. The right mix of centralization and decentralization in a firm can depend on what it produces and its market environment. The management of a firm that engages in many dissimilar activities (e.g., a conglomerate) will delegate decisions to lower-level specialists rather than risk overloading itself. Higher levels in such a firm are less likely to have (and be able to process) all of the knowledge that exists at lower levels. Faced with a certain problem, the executives of a firm that has long been specialized in a single activity might know more than people at lower levels about what worked and what did not when similar choices arose in the past. Compared with a more specialized firm, relatively more of the decisions in a vertically integrated business will probably be made at lower levels.

Q. Relate the preceding material on decision making in a conglomerate to the fact that a given division of such a firm is likely to be less profitable than a stand-alone firm that specializes in what that division produces.

At the top of the organization chart of Figure 13-3 is HQ (or headquarters), which presumably contains a principal. It could be the proprietor or an executive acting as the agent of the owners (shareholders) whose interests are assumed to coincide with theirs, at least for the time being. In a large organization HQ may itself be a hierarchy. Information generated in boxes A and B guides HQ's decisions, some of which affect the people in those boxes. Different ways of filling the boxes—such as turning them into departments or divisions—can affect information flows to HQ that in turn affect the firm's performance. Which department produces which information is itself a matter that may need to be decided. Perhaps information currently generated in Department A will be less costly or more accurate if HQ reassigns responsibility for it to Department B. The latter might have better forecasting software or contacts with suppliers and customers that A's people do not. Or, possibly, A and B can collaborate to produce better information for HQ than either can if it acts alone. If A and B both produce relatively inaccurate information, perhaps the people at HQ should take responsibility for producing it or outsourcing its production.

Information flows upward and downward along the lines that link HQ with A and B. The HQ makes decisions using information that flowed up from A and B and transfers

FIGURE 13-3
An Extremely Simple Organization

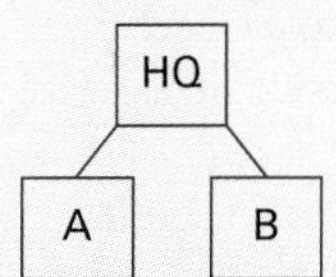

orders and information back down to them. There are two possible reasons to keep A and B separate rather than combine them. First, they might provide HQ with dissimilar information like financial data and sales statistics. The manager of a department that provides both must, for example, have expertise in both accounting (Division A's function) and marketing (Division B's function) and must be competent to supervise both activities. The principle of the division of labor extends to organizations. Second, separate paths to A and B allow HQ to avoid overloading each manager with irrelevant information and makes it more likely that orders will be sent to those best positioned to carry them out as HQ wishes.

U-FORM AND M-FORM ORGANIZATIONS

Functionalization and Divisionalization

There are two broad ways to categorize the activities that take place in A and B. The first is *functionalization*, where each box contains only specialists in some aspect of the firm's operations. Box A might be the purchasing department, responsible for buying all of the firm's inputs. Box B might be the sales department, which markets all the company's products and is in charge of both its sales force and its advertising campaigns. (A real company will certainly contain more than two boxes.) Each department will probably itself be a hierarchy, and each will contain subspecialists. In the purchasing department, for example, the person with the skills and experience to negotiate a fuel supply contract is probably not the same person who knows whether buying or leasing office furniture makes more sense.

The second way to fill the boxes is to divisionalize along product or geographic lines. As discussed later, each General Motors (GM) auto brand is a division whose internal management operates an organization resembling that of a stand-alone company. Every major oil refiner has a petrochemical unit separate from its gasoline division, with different facilities and different customers. Products can differ in numerous ways, so one division of Procter & Gamble sells railroad cars full of detergent to industrial customers and another sells it by the case to grocers. In a geographic divisionalization, Box A might contain all the company's North American activities, including production, input procurement, and sales, while Box B contains the corresponding activities for Europe. Geographic divisionalization is growing with globalization.

U-form Organizations

The Green Bay Packers A functionally organized firm is often called U-form, where "U" stands for unitary. In a U-form organization headquarters makes decisions using information submitted by various departments, and possibly itself as well. Figure 13-4a is the 1996 organization chart of a well-known U-form firm, the National Football League's Green Bay Packers.[9] Specialized functions such as public relations, ticketing, security, and building (stadium) supervision are each departments staffed by specialists who report to the president and chief executive officer (CEO). The departments are separable because there are few commonalities and interactions between, say, stadium maintenance and public relations. Each functional division lends itself to supervision by a specialist who is likely to have little expertise in most of the other functions. If in fact there is a mix-up in

[9]Figures 13-4a and 13-4b are from John G. Maurer et al., eds., *Organization Charts,* 2nd ed. (Detroit MI, Gale Research 1996), 86–87.

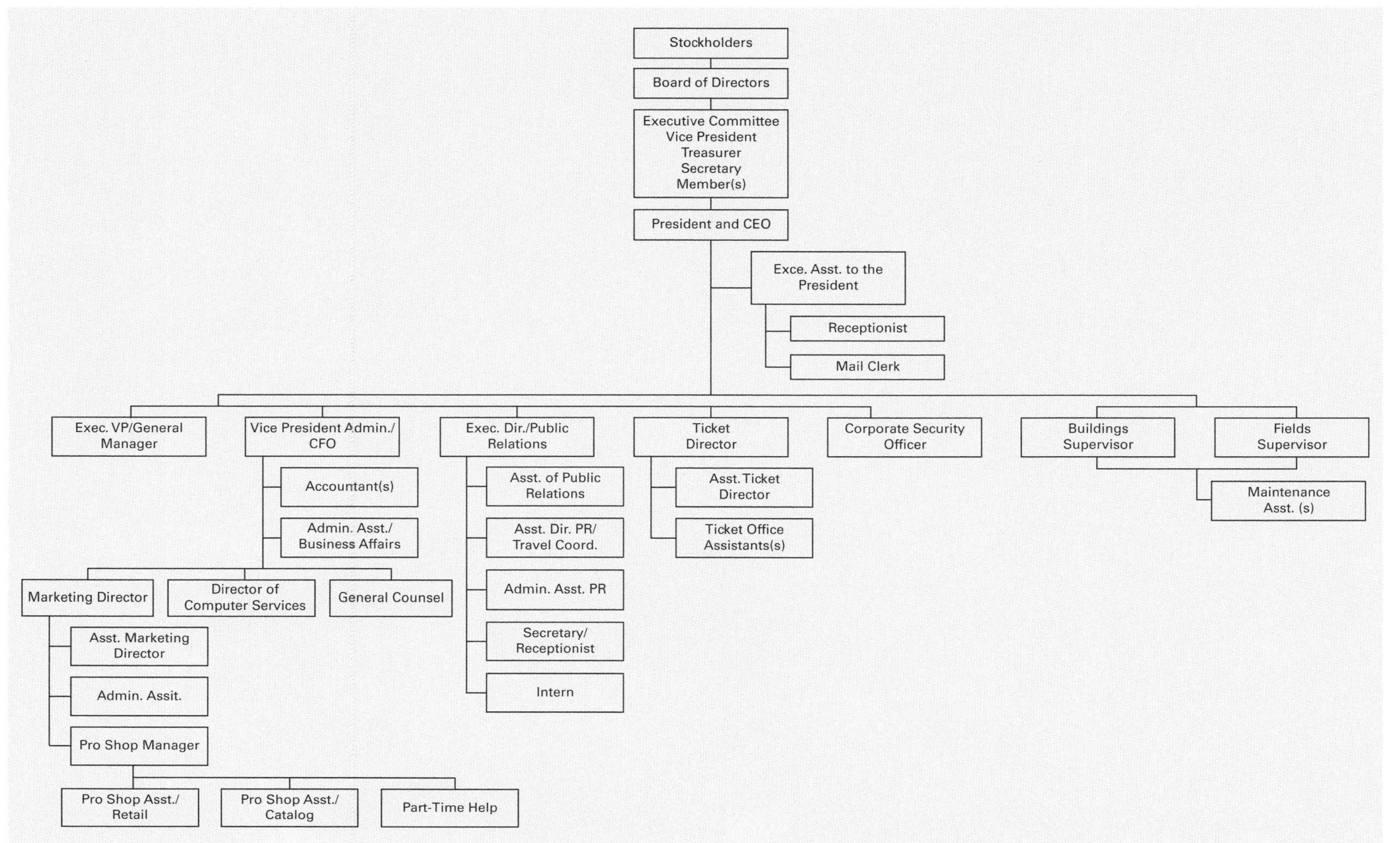

FIGURE 13-4a Green Bay Packers Organization Chart

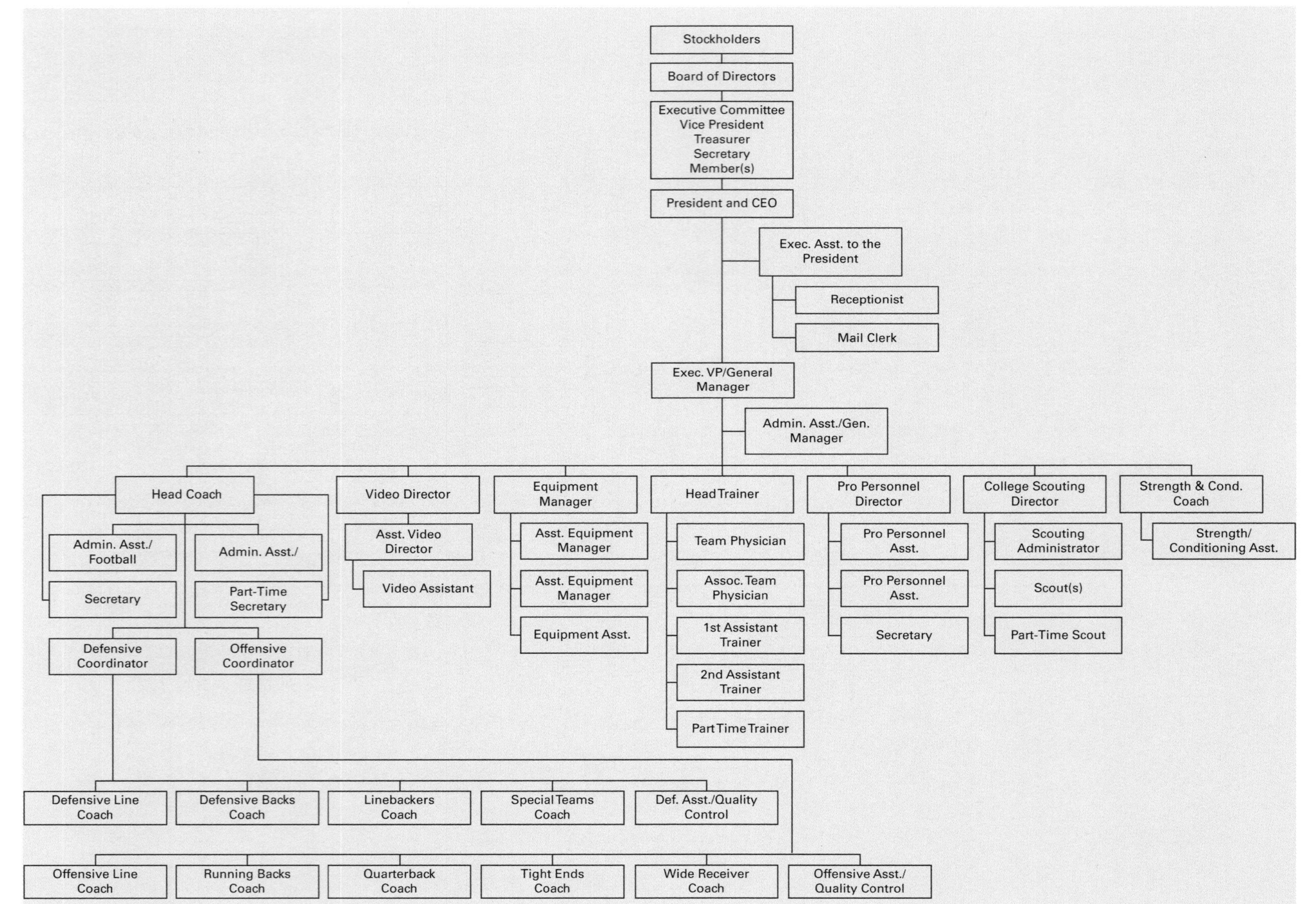

FIGURE 13-4b Green Bay Packers Operations

ticketing, headquarters can be confident in placing responsibility on the ticket director and not on the buildings supervisor or someone else in the organization. The team itself is under the executive vice president, who apears on the far left of the diagram. The executive vice president supervises a U-form organization within the firm (Figure 13-4b) with departments like coaching, equipment, pro personnel, and college scouting.

A U-form organization should serve the Packers well for several reasons:

- The firm produces a single product—football—in a single location.
- The operating environment changes little from year to year. The work of building a team and making games enjoyable for fans is much the same as always. Thus, the Packers' extensive experience will remain useful in the future. Problems of parking and crowd control, for example, are always there, and the chief financial officer can expect much the same pattern of revenues and expenses as five years ago.
- The Packers face hardly any direct competition from other teams for customers.[10] The NFL's purpose is to maximize the joint profits of its members as they compete against other sports and entertainment by staging exciting games among its teams.[11] New teams must be approved by existing teams, and the last football league to compete with the NFL was absorbed into that organization in the 1970s. A company that must adapt to unexpected competitive threats will probably put more decisions at lower levels. The European and U.S. branches of a multinational firm make decisions independently, and headquarters does not have their localized knowledge.

Southern California Edison A few businesses that are far larger than the Packers are also U-form. Southern California Edison's (SCE) 17,000 employees produce and deliver electricity to households and businesses in an area of 14 million.[12] Some of that power comes from its own generators, and the rest is purchased from other utilities or independent producers. Figure 13-5 shows how SCE is functionally organized into departments such as power procurement and transmission and distribution.[13] All the company's financial activities are combined in a single department, and corporate communications and legal affairs occupy their own boxes. The company's only business is electricity, and it has no direct competitors for service to most of its customers. Uniformity is a hallmark of SCE's business. All its finances are under the jurisdiction of the California Public Utilities Commission, which sets the prices it can charge all consumers in its area. To maintain reliability, the company must be sole controller of all power that flows over its grid at all times.[14] If production fails to match demand (whether above or below

---

[10]For instance, fans in Philadelphia are too far away, and most do not view a Packers game as a good substitute for an Eagles game.

[11]To understand the NFL as a cooperative organization, see what happened when the Los Angeles Rams moved to St. Louis in the early 1990s. Franklin M. Fisher et al., "Sports League Issues: The Relocation of the Los Angeles Rams to St. Louis," in *The Antitrust Revolution,* 4th ed., ed. John Kwoka Jr. and Lawrence White, 277–300 (New York: Oxford University Press, 2004).

[12]SCE is actually a unit of Edison International, a holding company whose other units are Edison Mission Energy and Edison Capital. Federal and state rules require SCE to separate its operations and financial affairs from those of Edison Mission and Edison Capital, which operate in competitive markets around the world. This separation allows SCE to view itself as a stand-alone business. See the Edison International Web site at http://www.edison.com/ourcompany/eix.asp.

[13]The organization chart is current as of November 2006 and can be found at http://www.sce.com/NR/rdonlyres/158D0876-A477-4A75-8BA3-07DE6C5FC81C/0/ParentCompanyOrgChart20061106.pdf.

[14]SCE still owns its transmission system, but since 1998 it has been operated by and coordinated with other transmission grids by the California Independent System Operator, which we discussed in Chapter 4. How and why this happened are not of immediate interest here. See the ISO Web site at www.caiso.com.

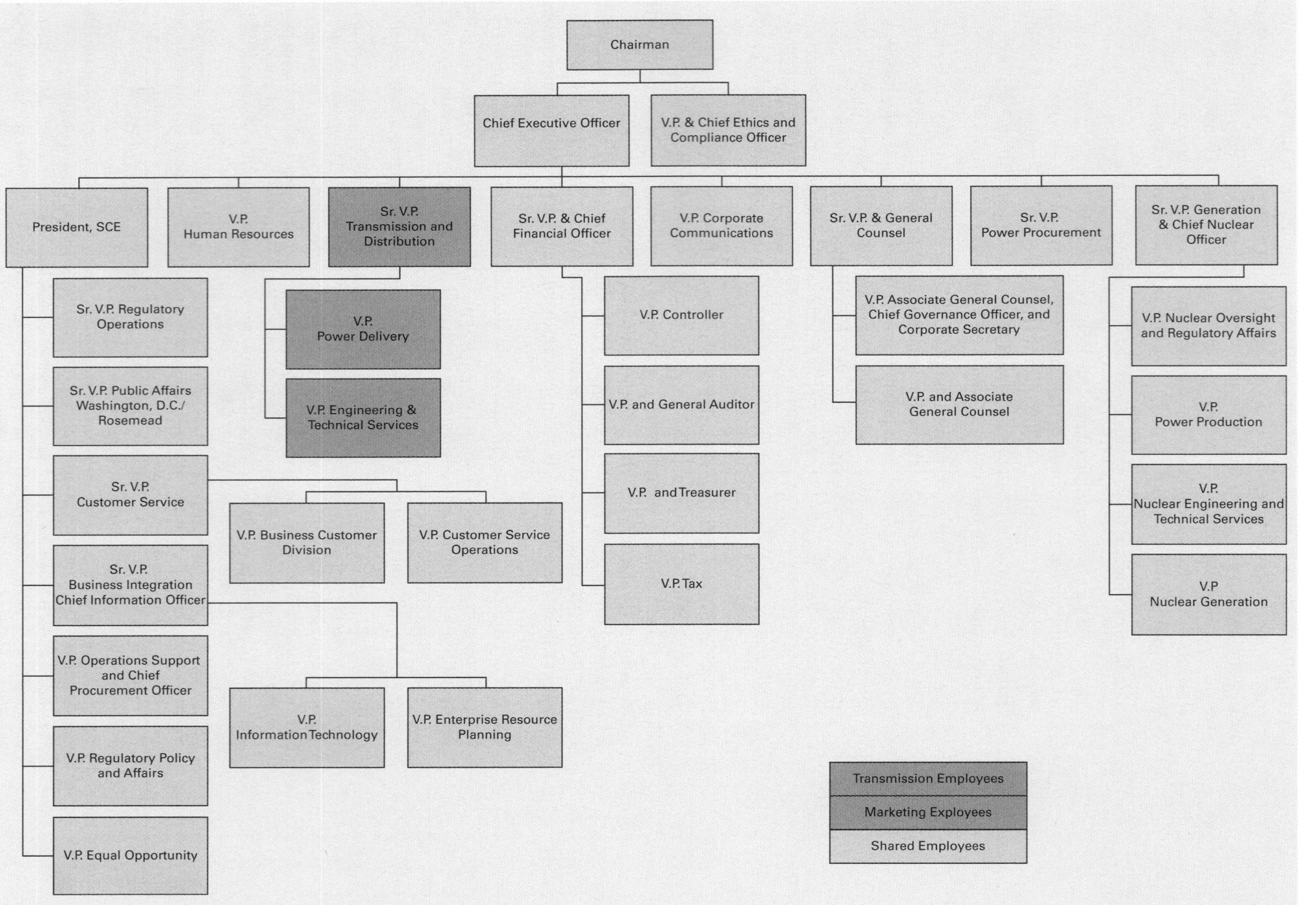
Chairman
Chief Executive Officer
V.P. & Chief Ethics and Compliance Officer
President, SCE
V.P. Human Resources
Sr. V.P. Transmission and Distribution
Sr. V.P. & Chief Financial Officer
V.P. Corporate Communications
Sr. V.P. & General Counsel
Sr. V.P. Power Procurement
Sr. V.P. Generation & Chief Nuclear Officer
Sr. V.P. Regulatory Operations
Sr. V.P. Public Affairs Washington, D.C./ Rosemead
Sr. V.P. Customer Service
Sr. V.P. Business Integration Chief Information Officer
V.P. Operations Support and Chief Procurement Officer
V.P. Regulatory Policy and Affairs
V.P. Equal Opportunity
V.P. Power Delivery
V.P. Engineering & Technical Services
V.P. Business Customer Division
V.P. Customer Service Operations
V.P. Information Technology
V.P. Enterprise Resource Planning
V.P. Controller
V.P. and General Auditor
V.P. and Treasurer
V.P. Tax
V.P. Associate General Counsel, Chief Governance Officer, and Corporate Secretary
V.P. and Associate General Counsel
V.P. Nuclear Oversight and Regulatory Affairs
V.P. Power Production
V.P. Nuclear Engineering and Technical Services
V.P Nuclear Generation
Transmission Employees
Marketing Exployees
Shared Employees

FIGURE 13-5 Southern California Edison

it) for as little as 1 second, the entire region will black out. Because SCE produces only one product, has no direct competitors, must charge regulated prices, and must control the power from production to delivery it is an ideal candidate for a U-form structure.

Q. Why might it be reasonable for SCE to locate both its power supply and corporate communications (public relations) departments on the same level of its organization chart? What might distinguish it from a company that puts corporate communications at a lower level than manufacturing?

Problems of U-form Organizations There are limits to the information a firm's headquarters can use effectively in making decisions. The management of a U-form firm like the Packers will probably be able to make a competent decision on where to invest available funds – the functional departments can provide it with much of the information it might need to determine whether to spend what is available on modernizing the stadium or buying a star player.[15] If a U-form firm makes several different products or sells the same product in different markets, information from functional departments will be less helpful to its management. A decision whether to build a new plant that produces Product A rather than Product B requires management to isolate important data from the functional departments that handle Product A and Product B to estimate which will produce the greater profit.

Whether a larger staff at headquarters improves top-level decision making depends on the types of information it must evaluate and the criteria for accepting or rejecting a proposed project. Multiple levels of decision making that use more information will not necessarily improve on fewer levels that use less.[16] Moving decisions downward into functional areas economizes on information but is hazardous because a functional department is by definition only expert at a subset of the firm's activities.

M-form Organizations

A divisionalized firm is often called M-form, where the "M" stands for multidivisional. M-form firms originated in the nineteenth century when manufacturers and metals producers reached unprecedented sizes after adopting new technologies, as described earlier in this chapter.[17] These firms often had plants in different locations and produced many products. If such a firm were U-form, its managerial decisions (e.g., whether to introduce a new product or open a plant in a new country) would be greatly complicated by difficulties in collecting and comparing information about products and geographic areas. An M-form organization reduces the problems of management acquiring information and making comparisons among products or activities within the company. Relative to the U-form, an M-form firm incentivizes managers in ways a U-form may not. In a U-form firm the head of a functional department may have incentives to inflate its costs for the personal benefits (higher salary) of managing a larger group, and

[15]In reality an NFL team operates under complex restrictions on the size of its player budget and rules that require it to share revenues with other teams. The text disregards these issues.

[16]Differently structured hierarchies that use different decision rules can reject too many worthwhile projects or accept too many poor ones. See Raaj Kumar Sah and Joseph E. Stiglitz, "The Architecture of Economic Systems: Hierarchies and Polyarchies," *American Economic Review* 76 (September 1986): 716–27.

[17]Alfred D. Chandler Jr., *Scale and Scope: The Dynamics of Industrial Capitalism* (Cambridge, MA: Harvard University Press, 1990).

FIGURE 13-6
An M-form Firm

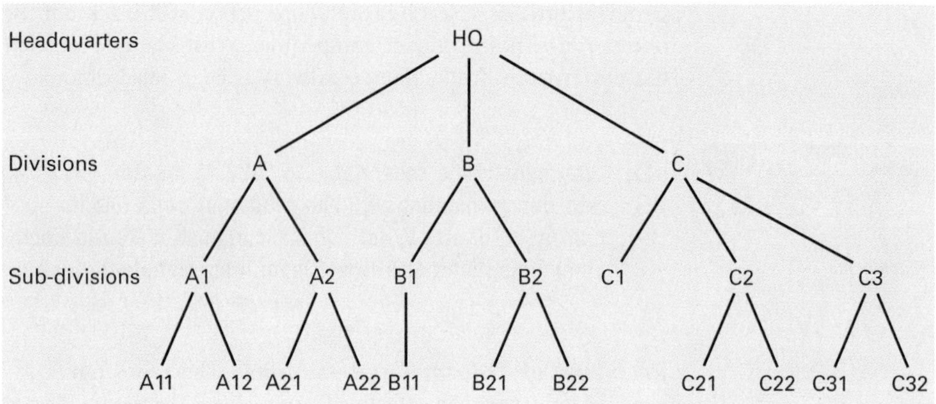

management will have difficulty evaluating whether increased size is actually necessary. In an M-form firm the interests of executives in product or geographic divisions can be better aligned with those of shareholders, because their performances will be judged by profitability, which is measurable, is comparable among divisions, and benefits shareholders.[18]

An M-form firm like the one shown in Figure 13-6 engages in activities A, B, and C. These might be different products it produces or units it operates in different locations. Product- or location-specific information is generated and largely used by a team whose members handle the various functional responsibilities associated with their product or location. Activities A, B, and C each resemble a stand-alone U-form firm. If management chose to divest C, it could possibly remain intact and viable as a U-form firm that now had its own management. The three divisions can have different substructures; for example, as shown, C has three subdivisions, and A and B have only two. These subdivisions can have functional subdivisions of their own, just as B1 has B11 and B12 (or they might not, like C1). The M-form keeps decisions at the divisional level that would be sent to headquarters in a U-form firm. Product-specific decisions at the lower level are made by those who are most likely to have the relevant information at hand and know how evaluate it. The headquarters of an M-form firm, however, must be able to identify, measure, and compare a division's performance (and its future prospects) with other divisions. Comparisons are complicated by the fact that much of the information used at headquarters comes from divisional managers, and there are few if any alternative sources. Headquarters must incentivize the divisional managers to provide accurate and adequate information, with awareness that the division's managers may have motivation to supply information that is more in own interests than those of shareholders.

Q. Why would we expect that divisional managers will not have the authority to split a division into two new ones or to merge two divisions into one? After all, the best information about the divisions is available at the divisional level, right?

[18]Paul Gooderham and Svein Ulset, "Beyond the M-Form: A Critical Test of the New Form," *International Journal of the Economics of Business* 9, no. 1 (2002): 121.

Product Divisions: Microsoft Microsoft Corporation is divisionalized into five business segments. The Client segment is responsible for the Windows operating systems and relations with personal computer (PC) manufacturers. Server and Tools handles the Windows Server Operating System. Platform Products and Services produces programming tools and server software. Online Services is in charge of the Microsoft Network (MSN), e-mail, and related services. The Business division produces application software, most importantly the Office suite. The Entertainment and Devices division produces the Xbox game console, Zune player, and operating systems for personal digital assistants.[19] These divisional separations reflect differences between the products and the markets they are sold in. Most of the world's PCs use Windows, which is sold primarily to computer manufacturers. Because the Windows code is language independent and almost the same worldwide, selling it requires the same skills in Europe as in South America. Additionally, Microsoft wants to learn quickly about bugs in the system and its vulnerability to security violations. Communicating directly with a single division rather than a local office probably improves Microsoft's ability to recognize and resolve these issues quickly. Office is a very different product, where Microsoft's concerns are more with retailers and individual users who purchase small amounts. Office is adaptable to almost any language, and its code requires few changes to cope with, for example, languages that read from right to left. The other products are based on non-PC platforms and sell to still other types of customers.

Geographic Divisions: Ingram Micro Ingram Micro is the world's largest ($35 billion sales in 2008) wholesale distributor of computer hardware and software, with staff in 34 countries and sales in 140.[20] Ingram links 1,300 suppliers and 160,000 retailers and other distributors. The company's four divisions cover North America, Europe and the Middle East, the Asia-Pacific region, and Latin America. Each has its own president who is also a corporate vice president. Instead of being centered on a single computer type or manufacturer, Ingram Micro handles many brands and types of computers and software. Marketing its products requires more attention to regional differences in demand and business conditions. Latin America's lower incomes make for different buyer preferences than prevail in more prosperous Europe, and the company must operate under European Union business regulations quite unlike those in Asian countries. Every business student nowadays learns that marketing in Asia requires very different relationships and different etiquette from North America. Geographic divisionalization, however, poses a problem for Ingram Micro's corporate management: How do they compare the performance of such dissimilar divisions? The next section addresses divisional comparisons in a case study.

From U-form to M-form: Ford and General Motors

The origins and early development of the U.S. automobile industry offer a comparison of the competitive advantages of U-form and M-form firms. Both GM and Ford Motor Company began as U-form organizations, and both became M-form when U-forms became unmanageable. They did so at different times and under differing circumstances, but the underlying logic of the change holds for both companies.

---

[19]Microsoft Web site, "Our Commitment to Our Customers," http://www.microsoft.com/about/company information/ourbusinesses/business.mspx.

[20]Ingram Micro's 2008 Annual Report is available at http://media.corporate-ir.net/media_files/irol/98/98566/Reports/IM_2008_AR.pdf.

U-form: Ford Henry Ford made history by turning the automobile into a mass-consumption good. Unlike other manufacturers whose production runs were small, Ford standardized his Model T and produced it in volumes that drastically lowered costs. Introduced in 1908, the Model T was built on assembly lines (themselves largely Ford's invention) with interchangeable parts and workers specialized to particular steps. A concern with dependable supplies and predictable quality led Ford to vertically integrate into production of raw materials. He operated his own steel mills and ensured his tire supply by opening his own rubber plantations in South America.[21]

Ford's production environment changed little over two decades. It produced the same Model T (and nothing but the Model T) from 1908 to 1926. Unlike a company in a constantly changing environment, information had a relatively long half-life at Ford. A low-level person in an assembly plant might encounter an operating problem that appeared unique, but Ford was unlikely to let him try his own hand at fixing it. The plant and the product had been unchanged for so long that people at higher levels were likely to have recollections or records that allowed them to check on similar incidents in the past and on solutions that did and did not work. Corporate memories within Ford's departments could improve the quality of its management, but only if past experience remained valid as time passed.

M-form: General Motors General Motors' William C. Durant had a quite different strategy. Believing buyers wanted choices that Ford would not offer, Durant (originally president of the independent Buick company) chose to make acquisitions in order to produce a wider variety of cars. GM offered options Ford would not, beginning with an electric starter in the 1912 Cadillac, which was so successful that GM made it standard equipment on low-end Chevrolets by 1920. (All Model Ts were hand-cranked.) By the 1920s, GM was producing nine different makes of cars and trucks, each in several body styles. Operated as a U-form, the company had become unmanageable. Headquarters could no longer make informed decisions about so many makes and models. It depended on reports from divisions whose financial performance could not be compared under the varied accounting systems GM had inherited from its acquisitions.

In 1923, Alfred P. Sloan became president of GM. Trained in accountancy, he first linked GM's poor corporate performance to overproduction of unpopular cars and underproduction of popular ones. He began requiring all dealers to submit comparable weekly data to headquarters, and headquarters could overrule divisional managers to order changes in production of particular models on short notice. The company's overall profits and market share rose, inventories decreased, and the fortunes of individual makes rose and fell.[22] After four years of trial and error Sloan's managers designed reporting procedures to compare divisional performance to meet the goal of better allocating capital by using the then-novel concept of return on investment.[23] Doing so allowed

---

[21]Greg Grandin, *Fordlandia: The Rise and Fall of Henry Ford's Jungle City* (New York: Metropolitan Books, 2009). Decisions at Ford were highly centralized, but that was still consistent with some degree of vertical integration. People actually working on the rubber plantations would still be best situated to make decisions about their day-to-day operation without further interference by higher management. Decisions such as whether to grow rubber trees or buy rubber on the market would be made by higher management, in part on the basis of information transmitted to them from the field.

[22]Seth Norton, "Information and Competitive Advantage: The Rise of General Motors," *Journal of Law and Economics* 40 (April 1997): 245–60.

[23]Alfred D. Chandler, Jr., *Giant Enterprise: Ford, General Motors and the Automobile Industry* (New York: Harcourt Brace, 1964): 112; and Robert S. Kaplan, "The Evolution of Management Accounting," *The Accounting Review* 59 (July 1984): 399.

better comparisons between division managements and gave rise to new types of incentive-based compensation. Comparability of reports also extended to estimates of the return on investment in divisions of the company that did not produce vehicles. GM used these comparisons to reshape itself. It abandoned auto brands like LaSalle (and more recently, Oldsmobile), remained a major manufacturer of locomotives, and divested itself of facilities for producing lead tetraethyl, the antiknock chemical used in premium-grade gasoline until the 1970s.[24]

The Competitive Consequences Over the 1920s General Motors cemented its lead over Ford, which continued producing only the Model T until 1926. Ford then compounded its mistake with its 1927 introduction of the equally standardized Model A, expecting that it would be in production as long as the Model T. Model A sales declined until 1932, when Ford introduced the option of a more powerful V-8 engine. Historian Chandler argues that Ford's U-form and its concentration on a single product generated information flows to management that favored the status quo, and that Ford's organization itself was an important reason for its failure to see and adapt to market changes GM had in large part caused.[25] Ford's attempts to broaden its line by acquiring luxury Lincoln in 1922 and introducing mid-range Mercury shortly afterward were not enough to match GM's variety. In the late 1940s, Ford attempted to divisionalize, but separation between the divisions was never as complete as at GM. Logistical problems and management's reluctance to abandon the old system left Ford with the mix of U-form and M-form activities shown in Figure 13-7.[26] Today, GM's management is concerned that the company cannot compete because it is over-divisionalized, and it is attempting to standardize its various brands around the world.[27] As one example, GM is currently trying to reduce the types of radios in its cars from 257 worldwide to 50.

Q. Looking at the radio example, summarize what GM's management should consider when deciding whether a given make of car should have a unique radio or a standardized one used by other GM lines.

[24]Oliver Williamson, "The Modern Corporation: Origins, Evolution, Attributes," *Journal of Economic Literature* 19 (December 1981): 1557.

[25]Chandler, *Giant Enterprise*, 98.

[26]The diagram is from David Hounshell, "Ford Automates: Technology and Organization in Theory and Practice," *Business and Economic History* 24 (Fall 1995): 59–71. Ford's organizational problems continue to this day. In 1998, the company moved Lincoln's and Mercury's divisional headquarters out of Dearborn, Michigan, to Irvine, California, believing it would help the brands compete against foreign luxury cars if they were closer to the customer demographic it wanted. By 2002, Ford had moved the divisions back to Michigan, claiming that Lincoln and Mercury did not really compete against high-end imports and should be folded back into Ford's North American division.

[27]Carol Loomis, "The Tragedy of General Motors," *Fortune*, February 20, 2006, 59–75; and "New Driver: Reversing 80 Years of History, GM Is Reining in Global Fiefs," *Wall Street Journal*, October 6, 2004. The text does not consider GM's current (2009) problems that resulted in bankruptcy and the U.S. Government becoming part-owner of the company. The company's insolvency has many sources, but few if any can be traced to the company's M-Form organization. Similarly, Ford's success in avoiding bankruptcy and federal ownership is better attributed to its financial acumen rather than its organization.

FIGURE 13-7
Ford's 1946 Mixed Organization

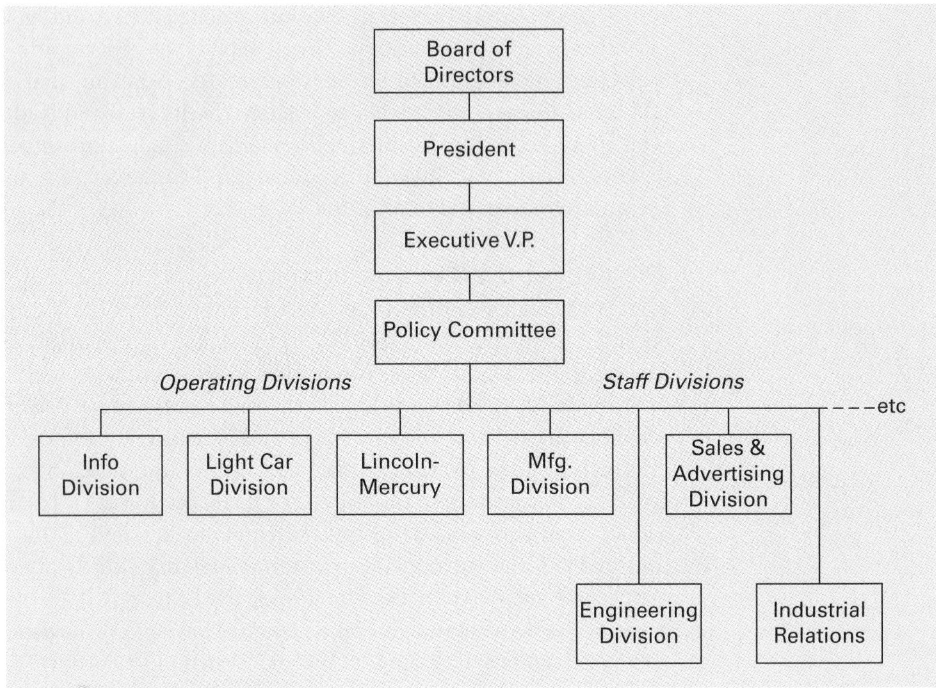

Matrix Organizations and Self-Contained Units

Matrix Organizations

Figure 13-8 is the 2008 organization chart of ABB Group, formerly known as ABB Asea Brown Boveri Ltd.[28] Headquartered in Zurich, Switzerland, ABB produces and sells five major product lines worldwide. The company produces transmissions and switchgear for electric utilities (the Power Products Division), sells engineering services for transmission systems (the Power Systems Division), produces lower-voltage transmissions and electronics for large power users (the Automation Products Division), designs control and energy management systems (the Process Automation Division), and makes robots for manufacturers (the Robotics Division). Revenue in 2008 was $34.9 billion, and earnings before interest and taxes were $4.6 billion.[29] A more detailed chart than Figure 13-8 would break each of these product classes into business area units containing subgroups of products. Figure 13-8 shows that the company has regional divisions for Europe (its largest), the Americas, Asia, and the Middle East/Africa. A more detailed chart would show country units that report to their regional parents. (The dotted line that boxes the product and geographic divisions indicates that they occupy the same positions in the hierarchy.) ABB is thus doubly divisionalized into superimposed M-form organizations.

[28]ABB Group Annual Report 2008, 61–62, http://search.abb.com/library/Download.aspx?DocumentID=9AKK104295D4448&LanguageCode=en&DocumentPartId=&Action=Launch&IncludeExternalPublicLimited=True. A fuller discussion of ABB's organization and its consequences appears in Christopher Bartlett and Sumantra Ghosal, "Beyond the M-Form: Toward a Managerial Theory of the Firm," *Strategic Management Journal* 11, no. 1 (1993): 23–46.

[29]ABB Group Annual Report 2008, 2.

FIGURE 13-8
Organization of ABB Group

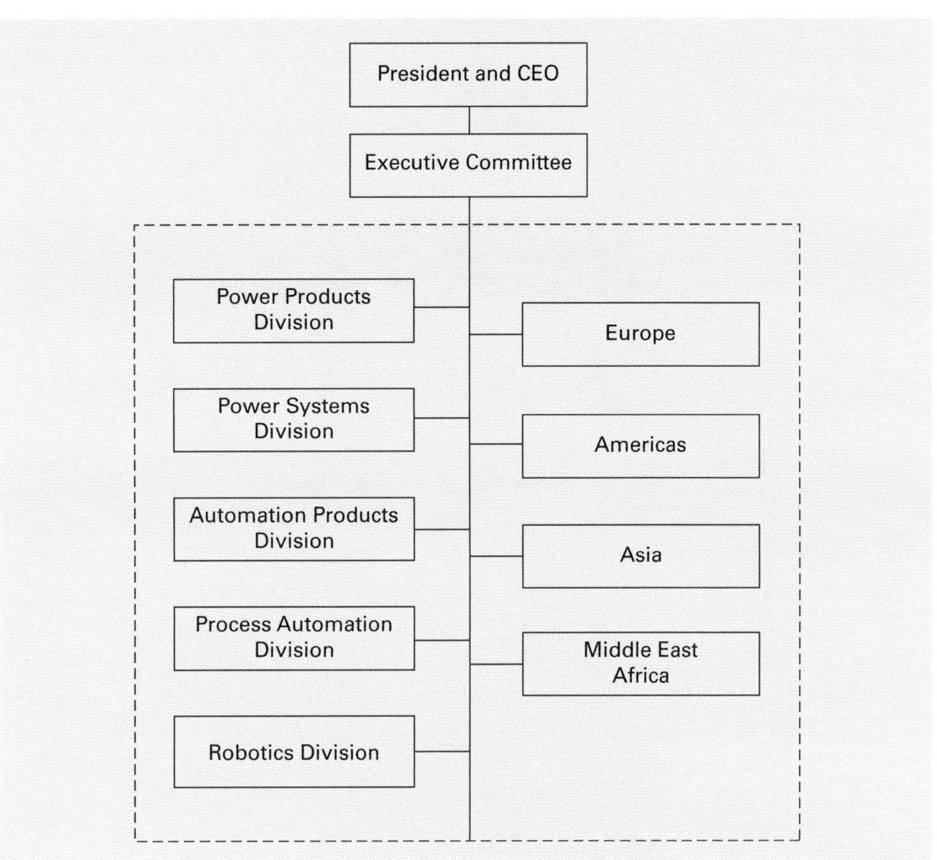

It is called a "matrix organization," or sometimes an "MX-form."[30] Not all of its activities are in the diagram—for example a single division coordinates all of the company's administrative activities and its financial services offerings such as credit to customers.

The matrix form has advantages and disadvantages and is more likely to be found in firms that produce diverse goods that are sold in diverse markets.[31] As an example of its potential benefits to ABB, many of its electrical equipment customers are utilities that are operated or regulated by governments. A country unit can use its accumulated experience to reduce the costs of dealing with government for all of ABB's products sold there. Likewise, all of ABB's product divisions can use a country unit to manage risks denominated in that country's currency. If several product divisions manufacture in a country there may be advantages in procuring inputs for them jointly. (For example most of ABB's divisions use copper wire, and copper is subject to great price risks that are cheaper to hedge as a unit.) ABB's MX-form also has potential advantages when broken down by product. If it produces and markets a certain good in several countries, the various plants may be able to share innovations or learn better operating practices from one another.[32]

---

[30]One way to picture the overlay is as data in a mathematical matrix, that is, the element in row 3 and column 4 would denote the business of producing product 3 in region 4.

[31]William G. Egelhoff, "Strategy and Structure in Multinational Corporations: A Revision of the Stopford and Wells Model," *Strategic Management Journal* 9 (January-February 1988): 1–14.

[32]See Robert M. Tomasko, *Rethinking the Corporation* (New York: Amacom, 1995); an excerpt from Chapter 8 is found at http://www.roberttomasko.com/Rethinking.Ch8.html.

On the downside, ABB's employees ultimately have two bosses—the country or regional manager and the business area manager—and their interests may be in conflict. A country manager may want to begin manufacturing a certain product there while a product manager favors continued transshipment to the country. A country manager might want to discourage information transfer from an efficient plant in her domain to an inefficient one elsewhere that will lower the local plant's relative performance. Matrix organization charts may treat country and business area managers as equals, but that word hides two aspects of reality. First, if they disagree and are truly equal, how does a decision get made? If they negotiate to a solution, it may resolve their conflicts but still not be in the best interests of shareholders. One of the two extreme positions might have been best. If the product division has formal authority over the geographic division or vice versa, its managers may attempt to expand that authority to include decisions that might best be made by the managers of the other. If disagreements are settled at higher levels, the settlement may disregard information held by those who handle the actual products and understand country operations.

Q. Assume that international trade restrictions between the Americas and Europe are under a new agreement that gives nations in both regions unrestricted abilities to ship goods across one another's borders. If you are CEO of ABB, will this development necessarily lead you to favor consolidation of the company's geographic divisions? Will you be more likely to favor consolidation if all countries in both regions adopt a common currency like Europe has done with the Euro?

Self-Contained Units

Why Redesign an Organization? Tyson redesigned itself to better adapt to the new importance and complexity of risk management in the markets for many of its inputs and outputs. Before then its individual divisions managed their own risks. The choice was reasonable because there were fewer available tools, there were fewer risks amenable to management, and one division's decisions would probably have little impact on the operations of the others. The financial revolution that began in the 1970s changed risk management from a relatively simple and standardized activity to an essential element of corporate strategy, and Tyson was one of the earliest firms to feel the impact of these changes, with its large exposures to so many risks. New financial models facilitated the design of new risk-sharing instruments, and cheap computing made possible markets for financial futures and securitized assets.[33]

The revolution had two consequences for a business like Tyson. First, risk management at the divisional level became inadequate. It took expensive specialists to master the new math and the new markets, and centralization of the activity became necessary as one division's choices became more likely to affect the risks faced by other divisions. Specialists like Jean Beach, however, could not do the entire job. They would have to interact with people in the divisions who were experts in operations. The company-specific knowledge of the latter employees could be a complement to the more general knowledge of the risk managers. Experienced employees might, for example, be able to devise production schedules that would improve the effectiveness of the risk managers'

[33]For a discussion of how these innovations developed and how their economic value increased, see Leo Melamed, "The Birth and Development of Financial Futures," at http://www.leomelamed.com/Speeches/96-china.htm. Melamed is the founding director of the Chicago Mercantile Exchange, the first successful trading venue for financial futures.

financial activities. An expert on some particular risk might not be fully aware of how it affected the risks faced by other divisions, as when Tyson must simultaneously hold positions in gasoline and corn. A multinational energy firm that produces oil, natural gas, electricity, and gasoline must account for their interrelationships. If prices are not predictable, large industrial customers who can switch between burning gas and fuel oil will cause problems in production planning and marketing. To manage risk in electricity production, the company must be able to predict and respond to differences between the market value of gas and the market value of electricity produced by burning it, known as spark spreads.

Self-Contained Units Managements once put risks into categories commonly called silos, covering operating risk, price risk, credit risk, and other risks that were handled in isolation from one another.[34] Now self-contained units (SCUs) of specialists responsible for all risk management, like Jean Beach's group at Tyson are becoming more common.[35] Figure 13-9 shows a firm before and after it reorganizes to include an SCU that takes over certain activities once performed entirely within divisions.[36] Figure 13-9a shows the subdivisions of each operating unit (A21, B2, and C22, boxed in gray) originally responsible for managing their units' risks. In Figure 13-9b the company has reorganized its risk management into an SCU that reports only to headquarters. It has final authority in that area, but doing its job requires contact with employees who have expertise in division-level risks. These contacts are shown by a dotted line, indicating that those employees remain subordinate to their divisional managers, interacting with the SCU only when it requires information or action from them.

GM provides other examples of SCUs. GM has long had a department reporting to headquarters whose purpose is to determine the basic shapes of all of its American cars. As long as the individual divisions stay with those shapes they are free to add stylistic details that identify their own brands. GM's styling SCU allows it to enforce a family resemblance among its cars that facilitates corporation-level marketing. The SCU also allows the company to standardize the very costly dies that turn sheet steel into bodies and fenders. Until recently, Chevrolet and Pontiac were designed around the same chassis and basic body shell while Buick and Cadillac shared larger ones.[37]

The benefits and drawbacks of a self-contained unit mirror those of the matrix organization. Ideally, people with different expertise will combine their knowledge to produce better policies than any subset of them could produce. There is, however, no guarantee that the relationship between the SCU and the operating employees will turn out this way. The SCU's staff of financial specialists might choose to de-emphasize information received from people whose backgrounds are in chicken farming. Employees in its operating divisions might in turn provide the SCU with biased or incomplete information. For example, say product division B employs workers who produce an important input into the production of B. B's managers may be concerned that the SCU will recommend that they cease producing the input and instead buy it on the market. If the pay and prestige of B's manager depends on the size of the division she heads, she might choose to submit self-serving information to the SCU in hopes of discouraging it from ordering her to outsource.

---

[34]Tom Aabo et al., "The Rise and Evolution of the Chief Risk Officer: Enterprise Risk Management at Hydro One," *Journal of Applied Corporate Finance* 17 (Summer 2005): 62–75.

[35]See "Morgan Stanley Roundtable on Enterprise Risk Management and Corporate Strategy," *Journal of Applied Corporate Finance* 17 (Summer 2005): 32–61.

[36]Tyson's organization chart does not appear to be publicly available.

[37]Alfred D. Chandler, Jr., *Giant Enterprise: Ford, General Motors and the Automobile Industry* (New York: Harcourt Brace & World, 1964): 154.

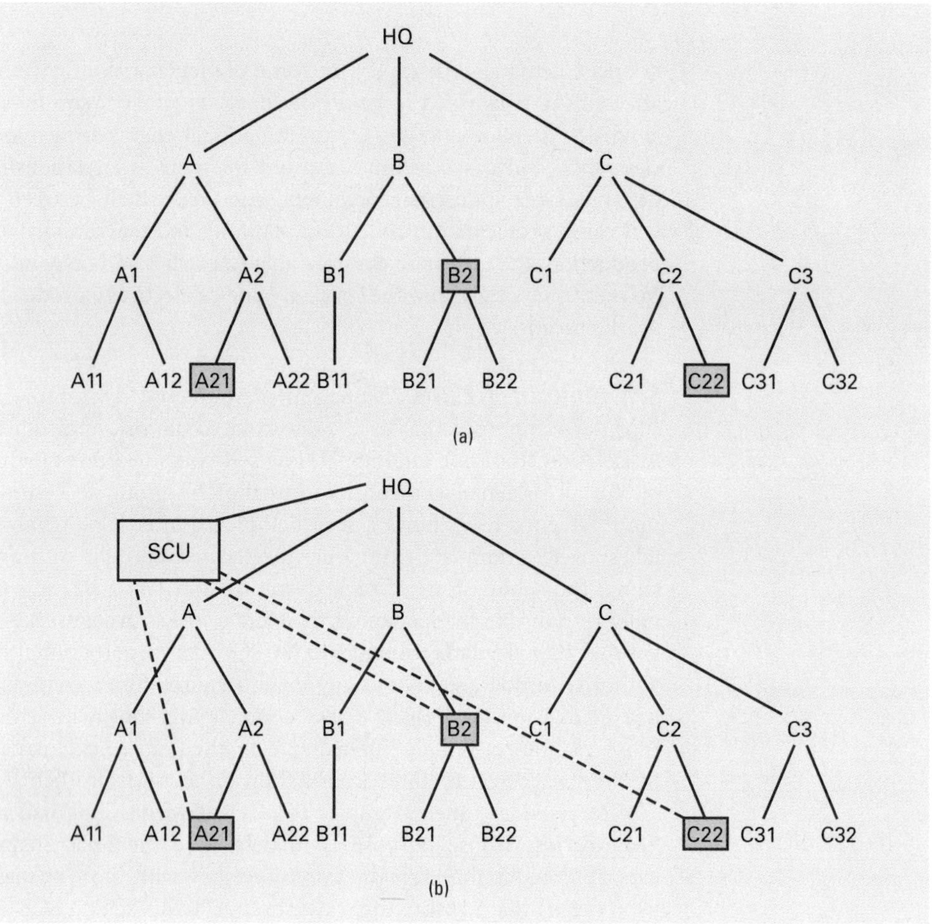

FIGURE 13-9
(a) Decentralized Decisions
(b) A Self-Contained Unit

Q. Why should Tyson's management be engaged in risk management activities at all when the firm's competitive competency is in raising and marketing chickens? Risk management is not a profit center but instead is an attempt to increase the likelihood of breaking even. The company's shareholders can and do protect themselves by diversifying, and their individual attitudes toward risk differ, so why should management be trading derivatives at all?

Formal and Informal Authority

Who Really Decides?

An expert once called an organizational diagram "an optimistic chart of expectations about relationships."[38] A graph of relationships may differ greatly in practice from their actual implementation. A line that links higher employees or divisions with lower ones

[38]Melville Dalton, *Men Who Manage: Fusions of Feeling and Theory in Administration* (New York: John Wiley & Sons, 1959): 18.

portrays *formal* authority. Their real relationships often play out in accordance with *informal* authority. Jones might stand above Smith on a chart, while in practice they treat each other as equals. Likewise, equality on the chart can mean inequality in practice. For example, given that SCE's core task is to obtain and distribute reliable, reasonably priced electricity, the vice president for power procurement probably carries more weight on its executive board than the vice president for corporate communications (public relations), despite the fact that their names appear on the same line. Financial markets and customers (as well as the state Public Utilities Commission, which sets its rates) will judge SCE by how well it succeeds at that task, so spending on procurement matters more than public relations. On the other hand, as the only power seller in most of its territory SCE is highly visible to the public, politicians, and the media. Because a poorly worded press release by a lower-level department or a bungled TV interview can have serious consequences, SCE centralizes all of its public contacts at the executive level.

A chart can also fail to reveal important relationships. A vice president's administrative assistant may not even appear on it, but the vice president may have given her authority to issue certain orders under the vice president's name without his active involvement. A person who has no official relationship with the vice president might know that the best way to get the vice president's attention is to approach him through the assistant. The viewer of a chart will often get no feel for the importance of informal alliances. The organization tree may show that only one executive's approval is necessary to greenlight a certain type of project, though in practice several approvals must concur. The project might affect departments run by the other executives, or their specialized information may be valuable to the executive with formal authority in reaching a decision.

Linkages between members of horizontally equal (or vertically unequal) departments may be at different levels. Two departments in a U-form organization may need to interact regularly, but their actual points of contact may be at different levels. Accounting and sales management departments must jointly determine how to respond to a change in an important customer's credit rating. Depending on the problem at hand, one department or the other might carry more informal weight in reaching that decision. The same reasoning applies to an M-form or MX-form organization. One of GM's automobile divisions might devise an innovative production method, but its details will only reach other divisions (at least initially) through informal rather than formal channels.

Informal Authority, Contingencies, and Competition

In Chapter 12 we compared transactional governance by organizations with governance by markets or contracts. Organizations will be preferred when contracts are costly and risks of opportunistic behavior are substantial. Problems encountered in contracts are mirrored in organizations. In both, negotiations over an unforeseen problem may take place outside the formal relationship outlined in the contract or chart. If there are concerns that one party may have breached a contract the parties will often prefer a negotiated resolution rather than a trip to court, even if the contract specifies court as an option. Similarly, situations might arise within an organization that are incompatible with existing authority relationships. In response, members of the organization may negotiate new relationships whose authority characteristics do not appear on the chart but are generally acknowledged to exist.

Whether they are linked as members of an organization or parties to a contract, Jones and Smith may find themselves in conflict in a situation where Jones's choice is the final one under a literal interpretation of the chart. Smith, however, might object so strongly that Jones will help negotiate a more agreeable solution for the sake of their long-term relationship. If subordinate Smith holds some highly specific information he may be able to renegotiate a solution with boss Jones that is better for both of them. Whether Jones and Smith are parties to a contract or members of an organization, they may disagree on whether Smith acted according to the terms of their contract or properly followed Jones's order. Like contracts, organization charts can be incomplete. Links on a chart show interactions that occur in the ordinary course of business, but situations arise in which no formal authority exists or in which there is general agreement that certain relationships exist in reality that do not exist on the chart. If a random selection of vice presidents and division heads die in a disaster, the surviving executives will have little choice but to forge a new organization and agree among themselves on new responsibilities.

The stories of GM and Ford show the potential importance of organizational form as a competitive tool. An inappropriate form can obstruct a firm that would otherwise be competitive. Many companies treat their organization charts as confidential documents that must not fall into the hands of competitors. Charts can provide information about strategies. If a firm's sales function is headed by a senior vice president who reports directly to the president, but engineering is under a lower-tier vice president, a competitor might infer that sales effort is more important to this company's competitive strategy than product design.[39] Competitors may be familiar with the individual executives named on an organization chart and be able to size up their informal authority on the basis of experience or other knowledge. The promotion of a person known to have strong informal authority to a position of great formal authority might well signal an important change in corporate policy.

Chapter Summary

- A firm's internal organization can be one of its resources. Well-designed authority relationships and communications channels can facilitate decisions that determine its competitive performance.
- The principle of locating decisions where the relevant information is located can help determine which decisions are best decentralized and which are best centralized. Centralized decisions require internal reporting procedures that send accurate information to decision makers in amounts that they can usefully process.
- An organization chart describes principal-agent relationships within the firm. Decision makers depend on subordinates to carry out their orders, but it is costly to monitor them and to detect whether undesirable outcomes are the result of opportunism or adverse random factors.
- A decision to centralize or decentralize a decision may depend on the firm's methods of production and on the markets that it operates in.
- U-form firms contain departments that perform functions like purchasing or legal services for the entire firm. Divisions of M-form firms perform all or most of the required functions for a particular product or geographic area.
- If information is durable and applies to all or most of a firm's activities (perhaps because products or markets change little with time), a U-form firm with centralized decisions may be better able to access knowledge that has accumulated over time and is still valuable. If information has a short lifespan and is specialized to

[39]This example appears in Maurer et al., xviii.

particular products or areas, an M-form firm that leaves more decisions to divisional managers is superior.

- Changes in markets or technology can induce a firm to reorganize in order to better respond to these changes. Corporate cultures and costs of reorganization can make that process difficult.
- If a firm produces a diverse range of products that sell in diverse geographic markets, a matrix form organization that treats each pair of product and geographic markets as a separate division may be superior. Problems in communication and the definition of managerial jurisdictions can reduce the benefits of the matrix form.
- A self-contained unit that bridges an M-form firm's divisions can make the firm more efficient by eliminating duplicative activities or better accounting for the interrelationships of decisions that would otherwise be made independently at lower levels.
- An organization chart shows channels of formal authority. It will not contain information about important informal relationships, and the formal relationships it portrays may have important elements of informality. Equals on the chart may be unequal in practice, informal departmental alliances may affect decision making, and lower-level persons or departments can importantly influence decisions made at higher levels.

Questions and Problems

1. Microsoft's divisions include PC operating systems, PC application software, and non-PC software like the programs that run its X-Box game console. All of this software was devised by Microsoft's employees or contractors and is kept as secure from outsiders as possible. Recently, "open source" software like Linux has threatened Microsoft's dominance in operating systems and applications. Open source software has publicly available codes, and anyone can attempt to improve its functionality or bring new applications as long as their work is available to the public without charge.

   Assume open source software becomes a more significant competitor to Microsoft's operating systems and application programs. How (if at all) would you reorganize Microsoft to better cope with Linux's threat to its existing operating systems and application software?

   There is no formal organization that produces Linux code, save for a central office that approves or disapproves of new code that might be incorporated into the system. Why does such an informal organization make sense for open-source software but not for Microsoft?
2. Why do you expect that a group medical practice in a large city will be made up of doctors who have the same specialty rather than a range of them?
3. Southern California Edison's prices, service quality, and investments in new facilities are pervasively regulated by governments under long-standing rules. Do you expect that a given decision will be made at a higher or lower level in a company like SCE than in one that is unregulated or that faces competitive threats? Explain. Is your answer consistent with the earlier discussion of its corporate communications?
4. Consumer service at SCE consists of handling outages, resolving bill disputes, extending service to new customers, and similar activities. Consumer service is a

major functional department of the company, but that department itself is organized in an M-form. The company's territory is split into five regions, each with its own vice president and its own workforce. Why would an arrangement like this make sense for consumer service but not for most other departments of a company like SCE?

5. A U-form firm's management is considering an important decision that will affect the entire company. Why don't they just set up a meeting attended by delegates from the various departments? Each delegate will bring specialized information, and they can negotiate among themselves to produce a recommendation that considers all of the information generated in the departments. Explain why we never see this practice.

   Is your above answer consistent with the observation that firms often retain business strategy consultants who meet with the various departments and then recommend a policy to management? Why the difference?

6. Even before the metals and manufacturing companies described earlier, U.S. railroads in the nineteenth century were M-form organizations based on geography. Why might a large railroad be better organized as M-form than U-form?

7. It has been claimed that M-Form firms are superior to U-form firms in their abilities to experiment, and this greater flexibility leads to more innovation in the long run. Give reasons why this statement might be true, and reasons why it might be false.[40]

8. A firm that maintains the same organizational structure for too long may become a competitive loser, but so might one that changes its structure too frequently. Explain.

9. A multinational corporation is currently organized as a matrix form based on products and geography. How might its organization change if governmental barriers to trade between countries become less stringent? What if it had started as a geographically-based M-form? A product-based M-form?

10. Early in our study of principal-agent relationships we used the example of shareholders as principals and management as their agent. Is it possible that Tyson's corporate management only engages in extensive risk management to make itself look good to shareholders by generating steadier income for them in the short term? In other words, if it did not have to bear the costs of risk management Tyson's long-term profits would be greater but shareholders would have difficulty discerning this fact. (Remember that risk management is not a profit center but an activity that is expected to do no more than break even.)[41]

    As a shareholder in some other company you probably have no objection to management insuring its buildings against fire, itself a basic form of risk management. Why is that practice unlikely to generate principal-agent problems?

11. Your university is probably an M-form organization. Its president administers schools, for example, a college of business and a college of liberal arts. The college of business Each of these in turn has a dean who is responsible for faculty

[40]Which is true in reality? One economist compared pairs of leading firms in 19 industries ranging from electrical equipment to meat packing. He found that in most of the industries the first firm to convert from U-form to M-form became more profitable. See David J. Teece, "Internal Organization and Economic Performance: An Empirical Analysis of the Profitability of Principal Firms," *Journal of Industrial Economics* 30 (December 1981): 173–99.

[41]For additional perspective on in-house versus shareholder risk management, see Kenneth A. Froot et al., "A Framework for Risk Management," *Harvard Business Review* 72 (November 1994): 91–102.

departments such as economics and finance. Why is an M-form more likely than a U-form to be an efficient way of organizing a university and to organize the schools within it?

In most universities faculty with specialized interests will often attempt to break off from existing departments and form ones devoted to their own specialties. Do you expect that this will produce an inefficiently large number of departments? Why do you expect that pressure by employees to form fragmented departments will be a smaller problem in for-profit corporations than in nonprofit or governmental universities?

Part Five

Applications and Extensions

Chapter 14

Vertical Relationships

Introduction

The Ore Carrier

U.S. Steel Corporation's *Roger Blough* (rhymes with "how") is a type of boat seen only on the Great Lakes. She (ships are still gendered female) is an iron ore carrier, 858 feet long, narrow-beamed, with a deck that rides close to the water when fully loaded. The deck's many hatches facilitate loading and unloading. In the picture the Roger Blough is at Presque Isle Bay outside Erie, Pennsylvania. She has just unloaded 40,000 tons of enriched iron ore (taconite) from U.S. Steel's mines in northern Minnesota. After crossing Lakes Superior, Huron and Erie, her cargo has been transferred to railroad cars. They will carry the taconite to the company's Mon Valley plant near Pittsburgh, where it will be transformed into steel.

FIGURE 14-1 The Roger Blough at Presque Isle Bay, Pennsylvania

Richard Pearson/Alamy

Why does U. S. Steel own the Roger Blough (named after a former executive), the ore mine and the processing facility?[1] Why would the company have its own fleet, when many boats can carry the ore for hire? And why own an iron mine and enrichment facility when ore and taconite are both available from others? The company's core business is the production and marketing of steel, so why invest scarce capital in ore carriers and mines, which also take some of management's attention away from steelmaking?

In this chapter we explore why U.S. Steel is *vertically integrated* into shipping and mining. We will examine how businesses determine the activities they will perform in-house and those for which they will rely on outsiders. A management's decision on the vertical scope of its business is as important as its decision on the good or service to produce. In fact, the scoping decision *is* about what to produce, the inputs it will self-provide and those outsiders will supply. Understanding these decisions will also further our understanding of more general changes that are taking place in the internal organizations of businesses in almost every industry. A decision on vertical scope is sometimes called a *make-or-buy* choice, but most decisions are more complex than the binary choice of producing an input or procuring it in a market. Between these extremes are a range of contracting possibilities that have their own costs and benefits, including some now-common relationships like franchising. Specifically we will learn:

- At the most general level, a firm's vertical scope is determined by the costs of transacting in markets versus the costs of transferring goods or services between parts of the organization. These include the costs of coordinating volume flows of goods-in-process and organizing coordinated responses to uncertainty.
- By putting activities under the same management, vertical integration can reduce risks of opportunistic behavior by persons who control specific assets. These risks are greater in thin markets, where few alternative assets or supplies are available.
- A firm's degree of vertical integration depends on the degrees to which it must cope with asset specificity and uncertainty, and it will change as these factors change.
- Vertical scopes of firms may also change as a result of mergers or internal expansion for reasons of market strategy.
- Rather than integrating, firms specialized in different parts of a vertical production chain are often linked by contracts. These include, franchise agreements that contain seemingly uncompetitive provisions whose actual purpose is to make the contracting parties more competitive as a team.
- The decision to outsource is in many ways the mirror image of vertical integration, and the principles of efficient integration also apply to efficient outsourcing.
- Broad trends toward de-integration and smaller firms are emerging in many industries. Those trends reflect changes in their operating environments that include growing markets, lower costs of information processing and transfers, and improved methods of risk management.

[1]See U.S. Steel 2005 SEC Form 10-K, 14-18, at http://www.uss.com/corp/investors/annual_reports/2005_AR.pdf.

THE VERTICAL DIMENSION

Goods (or Services) in Process

Figure 14-2 shows how about 50 percent of America's steel is currently produced.[2] Iron ore is mined, enriched, and transported to a blast furnace. Next to the furnace, super-heated coal is turned into coke, a type of charcoal that burns very hot and pure.[3] The ore, hot coke, and other materials like limestone are packed into the furnace and heated until the metal is liquefied as pig iron. While still liquid the pig iron goes to a second basic oxygen furnace and is mixed with chemicals that convert it into steel suited for some particular function—flexible sheets, ductile steel for wire making, rust-resistant stainless steel, hard (and brittle) carbon steel, and so on. The liquid metal is poured into castings or solidified into ingots that will come out of a rolling mill as sheets, I-beams, reinforcing bars for concrete, pipes, and other shapes.

Figure 14-2 summarizes the *vertical* steps in steelmaking. An earlier step is called *up-stream* and a later one *downstream.* A firm that controls several steps is *vertically integrated.* The alternative to integration is a contract or market relationship in which a downstream firm buys an upstream producer's output. A steel supplier might own its furnaces and mill but buy ore and shipping services on the market, or it might own its ore supplies and boats, like U.S. Steel. Downstream, a company might have a paid sales force or it might contract with distributors to sell the product to ultimate consumers.

Transaction Costs and Vertical Integration

Volumetric Interdependence Every steelmaker owns its blast furnace, basic oxygen furnace, and mill, adjacent to each other. These assets are highly specific to steelmaking and to their location, that is, there are very high costs of converting them to other uses or moving them to other locales. The production and milling of hot steel have a high *volumetric interdependence.* The blast furnace must produce just enough pig iron for steelmaking, and at just the right times. If coordination fails and the liquid solidifies, reheating is costly. If a company owned by Jones controls the blast furnace and one owned by Smith controls the mill, a mismatch is more likely than if one of them owns (or at least operates) both. Even if the two owners hire an outsider to coordinate their operations, they must make compatible decisions on maintenance, agree on new investments they will make in the facilities, and agree on how to adapt to unforeseen situations.

Adapting to Uncertainty If different people own the furnaces and mill they face risk-sharing problems like the pin producers of Chapter 12. A complete contract that handles all possible risks will be impossibly costly to write and enforce. Even if such a contract

---

[2]For animated diagrams of the flow chart, see the American Iron and Steel Institute Web site, "Steelmaking Flowlines," http://www.steel.org/AM/AMTemplate.cfm?Section=Steel_Flowlines1&TEMPLATE=/CM/HTMLDisplay.cfm&CONTENTID=12908. Details and photos of the individual steps are at "How Steel Is Made," http://www.steel.org/AM/Template.cfm?Section=How_Steel_is_Made&Template=/TaggedPage/TaggedPageDisplay.cfm&TPLID=36&ContentID=8213.

This production of Figure 14-2 chain was typical between about 1950 and 1980. Some descriptions are simplified to emphasize the causes and effects of vertical integration. For a comprehensive history of the industry before 1980, see William Hogan's five-volume work, *The Economic History of Iron and Steel in the United States* (Lexington Books, 1971).

[3]The coking process also captures gases from the coal that will heat the blast furnace. See Hardarshan S. Valia, "Coke Production for Blast Furnace Ironmaking," American Iron and Steel Institute Web site, http://www.steel.org/AM/Template.cfm?Section=Articles3&CONTENTID=12304&TEMPLATE=/CM/ContentDisplay.cfm.

FIGURE 14-2
The Process of Steelmaking

Iron Ore Mining & Enrichment

Coal Mining

Coke Production

Limestone etc.

Blast Furnace

Molten Pig Iron

Basic Oxygen Furnace

Molten Steel

Casting, Ingot Pouring

Hot Solid Steel

Mills

Sheets, Bars, Tubes, Structural Shapes, etc.

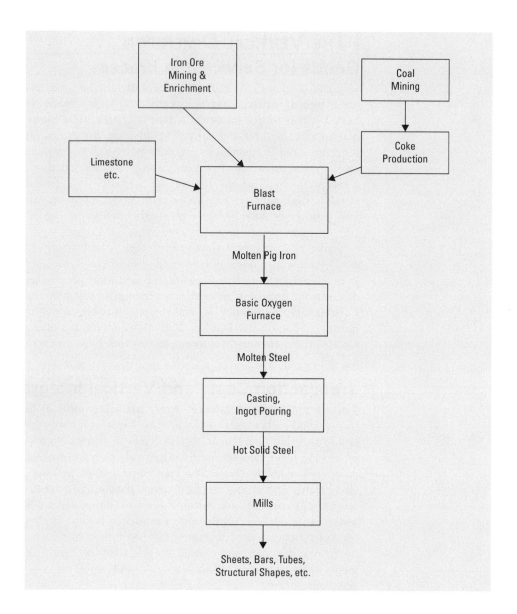

exists it must also motivate all parties to make efforts that increase the economic value they can create when acting as a team. Individual owners must also coordinate investments like capacity expansions in ways that create the most value for them as a group, but reaching a decision may be hard because they have different attitudes toward risk, different degrees of exposure, and different abilities to protect themselves against bad outcomes.

Q. Assume that there are laws that for some reason prevent the same entity from owning both a furnace and a steel mill. What kinds of contract terms might the two owners choose to minimize transaction costs and risks of opportunism?

Opportunism, Thin Markets, and Vertical Integration

Integrated Ore Mines and Shipping Transaction costs and coordination problems suffice to explain why the production and milling of hot metal are integrated. The risk of opportunism adds yet another reason. The furnace(s) and mill are all highly specific, both to steelmaking and to this particular location. Hot steel waits for no one, and if the assets have different owners each will have few if any readily available substitutes for services from the others. A resource owner threatened by opportunism has the alternative of investing in relatively less specific facilities, but here the substitution possibilities are quite limited. Even if substitute equipment exists, the resultant vertical chain is less productive because its components are less specific. Having employees of a single owner operate all the steps reduces any threat of opportunism because misbehaving employees can be fired.

Transaction costs, uncertainty, and risks of opportunism can also explain why U.S. Steel owns its mines, enrichment facilities, and ore carriers. First, blast furnace owners also face volumetric risk in iron ore and coke. A furnace that operates continuously wastes less fuel and lasts longer than one that is repeatedly heated and cooled, so efficient operation requires coordination between ore transport and furnace operations. Second, a scarcity of alternative producers who can supply U.S. Steel's desired volumes makes the ore market thin, with less predictable prices and heightened deliverability risk. Over 60 percent of U.S. taconite output comes from only six mines in Minnesota.[4] A few smaller ones sell ore in spot markets, but the owners of large mines have contracts giving them first claim on the output of small mines if they need it for their own customers. If price and deliverability problems materialize, U.S. Steel faces higher costs and becomes disadvantaged against competing steelmakers.[5] When ore supplies are scarce U.S. Steel will probably pay high prices if it must purchase from competitors. A thin market is also unlikely to allow the use of futures contracts or other hedging tools. Third, owning an enrichment facility allows U.S. Steel to ensure itself a supply of taconite with specifications best suited to its operations. It might also be easier to coordinate operations of the mine and enrichment plant than if they have different owners. Fourth, the costs of mining, loading, and shipping ore are lower if ships and docking facilities are customized. Other ships are available, but they will be costlier to load and unload at U.S. Steel's specialized facilities.

Q. U.S. Steel's mining, enrichment, and dock facilities were all custom engineered and built for the company. All else being equal, are necessary repairs on these facilities more likely to be performed by company employees or outside contractors? Why or why not?

Unintegrated Coal Mines Operation of the blast furnace requires that coke, iron ore, and limestone all be ready at the same time and at the right temperatures. But although U.S. Steel is integrated into iron mining, it currently does not own any of the mines that supply its coking coal.[6] Unlike iron ore, the company's coking requirements are a tiny

---

[4]The operation of an iron ore mine can be seen at "Iron Ore Processing for the Blast Furnace," American Iron and Steel Institute Web site, http://www.steel.org/AM/Template.cfm?Section=Articles3&TEMPLATE=/CM/ContentDisplay.cfm&CONTENTID=12309.

[5]Most steel operators have only limited storage facilities around their mills.

[6]The company divested its last coal properties in 2002.

percentage of the coal industry's output, and coal is easily transportable by rail. No coal producer can profit by acting opportunistically toward U.S. Steel because so many other mines produce coal that it can use. The company has delivery contracts with several mines, but if necessary it can enter the spot market to obtain or dispose of coal. Futures and options markets are available for coal, and the company can manage its risks with them as it cannot in the much thinner market for iron ore. Coal is a less specific resource than iron ore; it trades at competitive prices, and U.S. Steel can hedge any remaining risks without having to own mines.

Changes in Vertical Integration

How Steelmakers Became Integrated When the Minnesota ore deposits were first developed in the mid-nineteenth century, the steel industry consisted of many small firms that produced in small lots. Numerous small mines scattered around the country could supply these firms with ore. (Every state contains iron ore deposits.) The invention of the Bessemer converter in 1856 greatly increased the efficient scale of steel production and the cost savings from continuous and coordinated operations. Over the remainder of the nineteenth century, the industry consolidated into large, integrated firms, some of which eventually merged to become United States Steel, U.S. Steel's predecessor. Because these firms required dependable ore supplies at predictable prices, they integrated upstream into mining or formed investment partnerships to operate mines and transport ore.[7] Economies of scale drove firm sizes upward, and the Bessemer converter's operating characteristics motivated their integration into mining.

Q. Shortly after the Model T went into production in 1906, Ford Motor Company vertically integrated by opening rubber plantations in South America. It sold them off around 1925. Give two reasons why both the acquisition and the sell-off made competitive sense for Ford when they took place.

Why Steel Is De-integrating Today For the past 40 years, the percentage of America's steel produced in vertically integrated firms like U.S. Steel has declined. Once-familiar names like Bethlehem, Inland, and Armco have vanished, to be replaced by newcomers like Nucor, Chaparral, and Bayou Steel.[8] Commonly called mini-mills, they use relatively small electric furnaces instead of giant blast furnaces.[9] Fill an electric furnace with scrap steel, feed in high-voltage power, and in as little as two hours the scrap will be melted and ready for casting. Unlike blast furnaces, electric furnaces can be turned on and off almost at will. They often operate late at night when electricity rates are very low, because utilities cannot turn their generators off and restart them in time to meet the next day's load. Figure 14-3 shows the simplicity of electric furnace production. Like an integrated producer's, a mini-mill's volumetric interdependence explains the integration of its casting and milling activities. There are, however, few reasons for a mini-mill to own a

[7]Richard B. Mancke, "Iron Ore and Steel: A Case Study of the Economic Causes and Consequences of Vertical Integration," *Journal of Industrial Economics* 20 (July 1972): 220–29.

[8]See www.chaparralsteel.com/; www.nucor.com/; and www.bayousteel.com/.

[9]Donald Barnett and Robert Crandall, *Up from the Ashes: The Rise of the Steel Minimill in the United States* (Washington, DC: Brookings Institution, 1986).

FIGURE 14-3
Electric Furnace Steelmaking

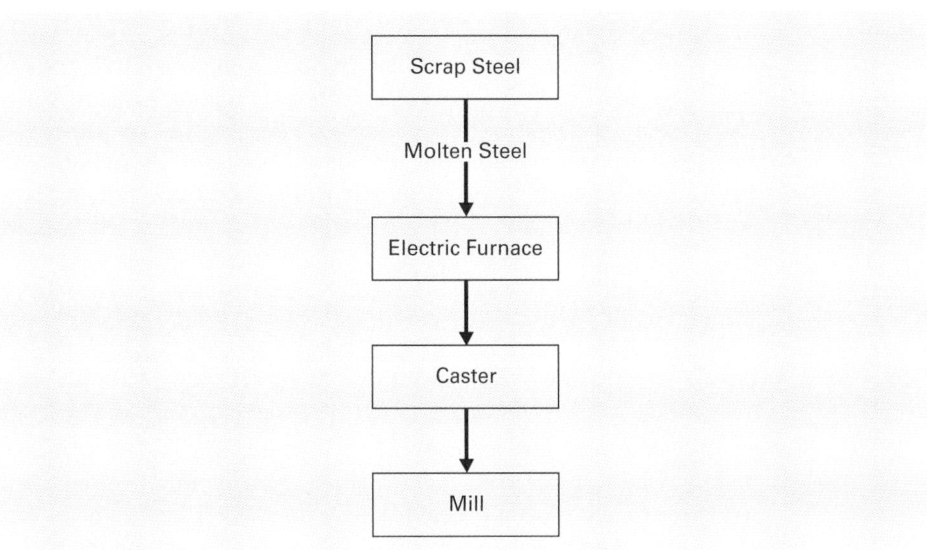

source of scrap steel, which trades in a worldwide market with many competing sellers.[10] It is more efficient for a mini-mill to use the market than to integrate upstream.

Demand-Driven Changes Looking at another industry, most meats and vegetables were once produced by independent farmers, who sold them in spot markets to independent packers or grocers. Economies of scale became pervasive over the twentieth century for some farm products. (Today there are 10 percent fewer pork farms than in 1970, but they produce more than twice the total output.) Large farmers can benefit from contracts that link them with larger purchasers, or by becoming part of vertically integrated organizations like Tyson Foods in Chapter 13. Firms like Tyson have lately taken on new responsibilities and are known in their industry as "integrators"; they are responsible for controlling the quality of chickens they or their subcontractors raise for packing or selling to other food processors.[11] Tyson ensures uniformity by hatching its own product or by contracting with producers whom it supplies with chicks, feed, and advice.[12] The contracts give farmers certainty about the prices they will receive while keeping in place their incentives to operate efficiently. Such relationships also allow also allows processors to quickly change their product mixes to meet changes in consumers' tastes.

Q. Tyson's contracts with chicken farmers pay them in the event that they beat the company's estimated cost of raising the chickens. They receive several times the actual savings they can document but are not allowed to divulge their good fortune to anyone inside or outside the company. Why pay a multiple of the actual savings, and why require confidentiality about the payment?

---

[10]Information about typical scrap dealers is found at the Web sites for the David J. Joseph Company (http://www.djj.com/millservices/) and Schnitzer Steel Industries, Inc. (http://www.schnitzersteel.com/profile.asp). Find price quotes at the Demolition Scrap Metal and Salvage News Web site at http://demolitionscrapmetal-news.com.

[11]Russell Lamb, "The New Farm Economy," *Regulation* 27 (Winter 2003-2004): 10–15.

[12]Tom Horton, "42-Day Wonders," *Washingtonian*, September 2006, 66–80. A copy can be found at http://www.upc-online.org/broiler/9230842day.html.

Summary: Principles of Integration and Separation

A firm chooses vertical integration if doing so reduces costs below those it would incur in markets.[13] The costs include those of finding a trading partner, devising and enforcing an agreement, and evaluating the other party's performance. Previous chapters on contracts and organizations pointed to specific assets and uncertainty as forces determining the choice between them and markets. A firm without specific assets (for example, a farm on land that can grow numerous crops that sell in competitive markets) has little reason to integrate vertically with suppliers or customers or to form complex contracts with them. Its owner can easily switch among trading partners because it has made no relationship-specific investments that will lose value if a particular relationship ends. Specific investments increase value that can be protected by contracts or integration.

Uncertainty also affects the choice among markets, contracts, and integration because the ability to control and shift risk will vary with that choice. At least three dimensions of uncertainty can matter. First is its importance—the choice will vary with the probability of a loss and its expected size. Second are the possibilities for reducing ("mitigating") a possible loss, for example, by purchasing insurance or constructing a backup plan with an alternative partner. Third is the dimensionality of the risk. It is relatively easy to write a service contract with liquidated damages for a leased machine that can fail in only one way. If a machine can fail in many ways (and both you and I can take actions that affect the probability of failure), a contract to allocate the repair costs between us may be so costly to write and enforce that vertical integration that puts all responsibility on the owner may be superior.

Table 14-1 shows how different degrees of asset specificity and uncertainty can affect the choice of markets, contracts, or integration. One might measure an asset's specificity by the percentage of its cost that can be recovered if it is redeployed into its next most valuable use. Uncertainty increases with the variability of outcomes and the underlying degree of randomness in the environment that can affect a business relationship. If assets are relatively nonspecific, transactions will probably best take place in markets, and uncertainty will be even less of a problem if, insurance, derivatives, or other hedges are available. In general, the further to the east or south on Table 14-1 a combination of specificity and uncertainty lies, the more likely integration will be efficient. The entries on Table 14-1 are best viewed as shading into one another rather than as sharp dividing

TABLE 14-1 THE EFFECTS OF UNCERTAINTY AND ASSET SPECIFICITY ON VERTICAL ORGANIZATION

		DEGREE OF UNCERTAINTY		
		LOW	MEDIUM	HIGH
DEGREE OF ASSET SPECIFICITY	Low	Market Transaction	Market or Short-Term Contract	Long-Term Contract or Vertical Integration
	Medium	Market Transaction	Short-Term or Long-Term Contract	Long-Term Contract or Vertical Integration
	High	Market Transaction*	Long-Term Contract or Vertical Integration	Vertical Integration

*Assuming market offers possibilities for risk management like transactions in derivatives.

[13]This discussion follows Oliver E. Williamson, "The Vertical Integration of Production: Market Failure Considerations," *American Economic Review* 61 (May 1971): 112–23.

lines—for example, an asset with medium specificity will more likely be more efficiently transacted under a long-term contract than a short-term contract, the greater the underlying uncertainty.

Q. Vertical integration between two parties is more likely the more specific the assets are that are committed to their relationship. A contract is also more likely the more specific are the assets. Define a set of conditions in which a contract would be preferable to vertical integration for a given degree of asset specificity.

Vertical Mergers and Contract Restrictions

Mergers and Agreements

Chapter 8 showed that a vertical merger or an agreement between two vertically related firms might cut their costs and thereby make them two into a better competitive unit. Here we consider some cases that show how such a combination can be strategically useful even if it neither lowers transaction costs nor cuts the risks of opportunism.

Successive Monopolies Jones is a nondiscriminating monopolist who produces good A. Assume that his only cost is for input B, and it takes a unit of B to produce a unit of A. The top half of Figure 14-4 shows the market demand for A. If Jones somehow obtains B for free, his marginal cost is zero. He maximizes profit by producing 5 units of A and pricing them at $5 each. Unfortunately Jones's only source of B is Smith, who is also a single-price nondiscriminating monopolist. Assume that Smith's marginal cost is zero and there are no other users of B.

If Jones and Smith cooperate they maximize their combined profit when each produces 5 units and they split Jones's revenue.[14] If they cannot cooperate, Jones's demand curve for B is the marginal revenue curve for his output of A, shown in the bottom panel of Figure 14-4. He will pay no more for an additional B than his extra revenue from selling an extra A. Smith operates along MR_B, which is marginal to D_B. She maximizes profit by producing 2.5 units and selling them for $5 each. Jones now has marginal costs of $5 and maximizes profit by producing 2.5 units of A. Smith's profit is $\$2.50 \times 5 = \$12.50$ and Jones's is $\$7.50 \times 2.5 - \$5.00 \times 2.5 = \$6.25$. If Smith acts as a monopolist their joint profits are only $17.50 rather than $25.00. She, Jones, and consumers of A will all be worse off than if she and Jones had cooperated.

A and B are produced by *successive monopolies* that face the problem of *double marginalization*. If they operate independently their joint profits are smaller than if they cooperate because Smith maximizes her monopoly profit by operating on the curve that is marginal to Jones's marginal revenue. They can solve the problem by merging or devising a contract. If they merge, the new company's B division will transfer its output to the A division at its actual cost (zero) rather than the $5 Smith would have charged as a monopolist. If the two cannot merge, they can still reach an agreement. One possible form of agreement has Jones paying Smith only if she gives him all 5 units of B. Under such an agreement she would receive some amount between $12.50 (her stand-alone profit) and $20, because Jones's profit when Smith acts monopolistically is still $5.00.

[14]The exact division of the revenue between them will be determined by bargaining, but an even split is certainly possible.

FIGURE 14-4
Successive Monopolies

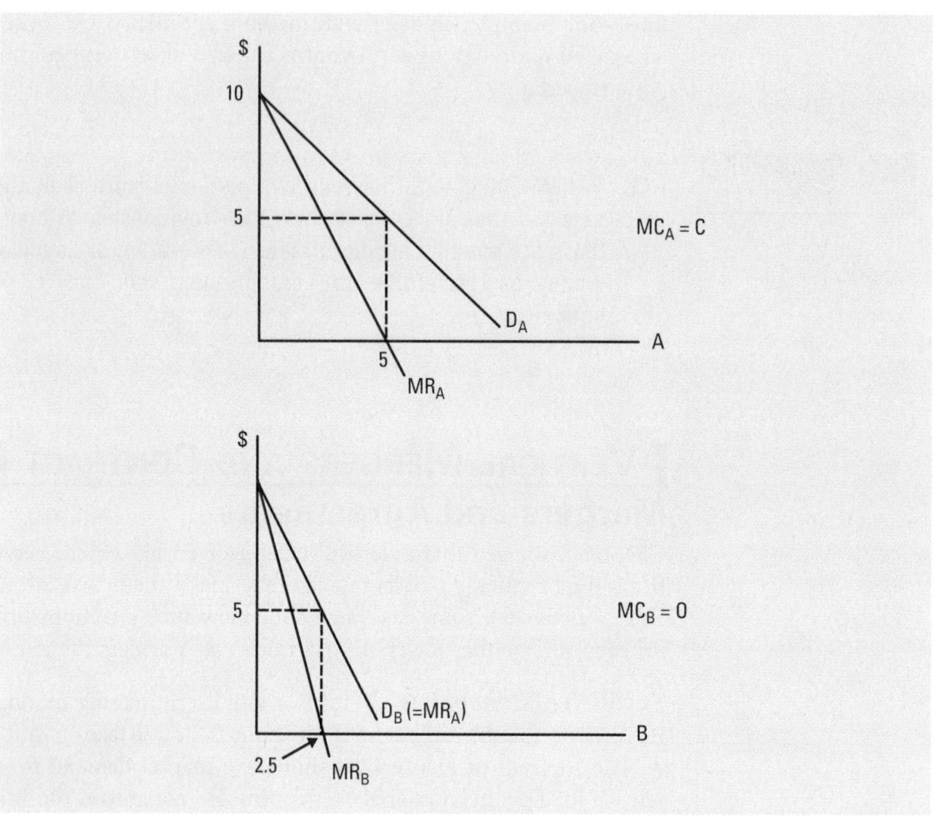

Q. Show that an equivalent way to induce the production of 5 units of output is to have Smith license Jones to be the only user of B. She charges Smith a license fee and then allows him to get as many units of B as he wants for free. (Assume that Smith has no opportunities to resell good B.)

Price Discrimination The Aluminum Company of America (Alcoa) had a near-monopoly in the United States during the first half of the twentieth century.[15] Its production patents kept costs well below those of any rival. Assume that Alcoa sells aluminum to two types of customers with different elasticities of demand. Aircraft producers are inelastic demanders because they have no raw materials as flexible, strong, and light as aluminum. Cookware makers have more elastic demands. Aluminum pots conduct heat well, but cooks can also use iron or copper to produce menu items of the same quality. Alcoa wanted to price discriminate but could not prevent cookware producers from ordering large volumes of aluminum and reselling some to aircraft manufacturers. The company solved its problem by vertically integrating into cookware production. Alcoa sold aluminum to its cookware subsidiary at a low price (its true marginal cost) and charged aircraft makers a high one. It offered aluminum to anyone willing to pay a high price, but that price allowed few cookware producers to compete.

[15]Martin K. Perry, "Forward Integration by Alcoa: 1888-1930," *Journal of Industrial Economics* 29 (September 1980): 37–53.

Avoiding Price Controls Most distributors and large users of natural gas buy it from producers or marketers and use interstate pipelines for delivery. Gas sells in a competitive market, and there are no controls on its price. The maximum rates pipelines can charge, however, are set by the federal government. Most of the time pipelines going to the same destination compete by discounting rates below the legal maximum. During peak periods, however, demand at the maximum price can exceed available capacity. A buyer willing to pay more has the option to arrange a "buy-sell" transaction with the pipeline. In a buy-sell the pipeline offers to resell gas it purchased in the market for a higher price than it paid. The pipeline bundles the gas with the transportation service, and an itemized bill will show that it charged no more than the allowed maximum for transportation. By integrating into gas production or contracting with a producer the pipeline evades the legal ceiling on its transportation charge.[16]

Obtaining Market Information Assume that your firm uses large amounts of some input, which you buy from several different producers without facing transaction costs or opportunism that might otherwise warrant vertical integration. The prices you pay are individually negotiated, but you may be at a disadvantage because you do not know the producers' true costs and may be paying more than you have to. To gain information, you might consider integrating into the production of this input, not just to obtain part of your supply but also to better estimate the costs of other producers.[17] Asimilar phenomenon is seen in franchising. A parent company like McDonald's may not be able to monitor franchisees' sales efforts, or it may disagree with them on what retail prices to charge. If the company owns some outlets and staffs them with employees, its management can better understand the behavior of its franchisees and can test operating techniques that might make the franchisees better competitors.

Vertical Restraints

Complementary Skills and Competition The steps in a vertical chain may require quite different resources and skills. Ford Motor Company designs, produces, and nationally advertises its cars, but an actual sale requires effort by a local dealer. The Coca-Cola Company advertises nationally, protects its secret formula, and distributes syrup to bottlers and fountains. Most bottlers are stand-alone companies that are responsible for local promotions, on-time deliveries, and for maintaining the quality of the bottled beverage. The corporate management of Hilton hotels must choose good locations, operate a reservation service, and coordinate customer loyalty programs. The manager of a particular hotel must employ a pleasant and efficient staff, keep the premises attractive, and make localized sales efforts. A manager salaried by headquarters may not be as motivated as one with a stake in the profits, and a manager from another city may not have the knowledge or connections to detect opportunities that a local person could. On the other hand, managers of individual hotels would probably do an inferior job of organizing advertising and reservations for the entire group.

In cases like these an agreement that assigns responsibilities to different parties could turn the organization into a stronger competitive entity than if all of the responsibilities

---

[16]You might ask why the government does not simply allow pipelines to charge market-level rates. The Natural Gas Act allows pipelines to recover no more than their costs plus a reasonable return for investors, but it does not forbid pipeline companies from having unregulated subsidiaries that may trade gas on whatever terms they can arrange with buyers.

[17]Kenneth Arrow, "Vertical Integration and Communication," *Bell Journal of Economics and Management Science* 6 (Spring 1975): 173–183.

were in the same hands. One common agreement is a *franchise contract* between a parent company (the franchisor) and the operator of a local outlet (the franchisee), specifying each party's duties and the structure of payments that will link them. Each of the 250 Johnny Rocket's restaurant franchisees must agree to honor all nationwide credit cards and display certain signage.[18] Johnny Rocket's parent reserves the right to be the exclusive supplier of certain items (for example, trademarked sauces) to its outlets, and to determine eligible wholesalers from which a franchisee may buy others.[19] Managers of franchises are required to take certain training provided by the parent prior to opening their outlets. The contract also limits a franchisee's ability to use corporate trademarks that might affect the fortunes of the entire chain.[20] (For example, the trademark cannot be used to support a political candidate.) The law refers to obligations and prohibitions in these contracts as *vertical restraints.*

Q. In the event a franchise agreement is terminated (for any reason) Johnny Rocket's requires the franchise holder to remove all signs and décor from the premises that could possibly identify them as the former home of a Johnny Rocket's. Why?

Free Riding Like all contracts, franchising is subject to risks of opportunism. These risks can be aggravated by the fact that a brand name has some properties of a public good. A hotel's or fast-food chain's name is valuable to both franchisees and the general public. Many customers might choose a franchised Johnny Rocket's over an unbranded restaurant on the basis of favorable prior experiences. An individual manager, however, might choose to cut costs by providing inferior food or service, secure in the knowledge that many customers are travelers who are unlikely to come back. A bad experience with one Johnny Rocket's, however, might give a customer the impression that others in the chain are also substandard, leading that customer to avoid that brand entirely. A full enumeration of all possible opportunistic behaviors may be impossible, but the success of the brand requires the parent company to be able to sanction franchisees who are not making the expected effort. It may be particularly hard to define effort in an industry where service quality is important, however. Johnny Rocket's contract simply tells the franchisee to follow procedures outlined in a company manual, but no manual can exactly specify what is meant by "courteous" or "prompt" service.[21] Incompleteness or ambiguity can also give rise to opportunism by a franchisor, who might try using such contract provisions to terminate a well-operated franchise in order to turn it into a profitable company-owned outlet.[22] There are limits, however, because a parent company that acts opportunistically often enough will acquire an unfavorable reputation, demoralizing existing franchisees and discouraging new ones from joining the organization.

[18]The basic contracts for a Johnny Rocket's franchise are downloadable at http://www.freefranchisedocs.com/johnny-rockets-Franchise-Agreement.html.

[19]Johnny Rocket's Franchise Agreement, Section 13.

[20]Johnny Rocket's Franchise Agreement, Section 16.

[21]Johnny Rocket's Franchise Agreement, Section 19.

[22]These are only examples of possible behavior and are in no way intended to describe the actual conduct of Johnny Rocket's or its franchisees.

Q. Why would Johnny Rocket's parent company want its manual for franchisees kept confidential? After all, if its contents were public, potential customers would have more accurate knowledge of what they could expect from a restaurant on their first visit?

The Structure of a Franchise Contract A franchise contract must reward sales efforts by the franchisee while acknowledging that any relationship between effort and results is inexact. The parent company can obtain sales figures but may be unable to evaluate the franchisee's actual efforts. Poor figures can reflect extraordinary effort in a bad location or weak effort in a good one. The contract must thus be structured to motivate the franchisee. Effort can also entail costs that the franchisee must have some expectation of recovering. An auto dealer with a sizable sales staff and a full inventory of parts has higher costs than one with few salespeople and no parts department. Franchise agreements often require that certain services be offered. In return the parent auto company can protect a dealer against free riding competitors by including contract terms stating that it will not open another dealership within a certain distance of this one.

Franchisor and franchisee are in a principal-agent relationship with the same types of monitoring problems and risks of opportunism we previously encountered. To lessen them, many franchise contracts have similar structures. First, the franchisee pays a fixed annual fee for the right to operate. Second, the franchisee pays a *royalty*, usually a monthly payment that averaged 5.1 percent of gross revenue in 2001 (the latest data available). Approximately 70 percent of franchisees also pay their parents a percentage of gross income for advertising, on average 1.7 percent for those with such an obligation.[23] Problems in measurement and monitoring may explain why the figures are percentages of gross rather than net revenue. A franchisee can understate profit by incurring costs (a company Cadillac) that do not improve the competitive position of either the outlet or its parent.[24] A few home-based franchise systems charge a flat royalty per month regardless of the franchisee's revenue or profit.

Q. What characteristics of home-based franchises make a flat monthly royalty superior to the usual arrangements described in the previous section? Explain for both the franchisor and franchisee.

Outsourcing and Refocusing

The Decision to Outsource

The logic of vertical integration is also the logic of de-integration, nowadays often called "outsourcing." It has grown steadily over the last half of the twentieth century in all industrialized nations. The highest percentage of U.S. business outsourcing is to other

[23]Percentages are from Roger Blair and Francine Lafontaine, *The Economics of Franchising* (New York: Cambridge University Press, 2005), 64 and 77.

[24]It is also possible for a mass franchisor to audit its outlets (because they use identical accounting procedures) and compare their performances. One economist argues that because auditing is easy the purpose of royalties on revenue is to get the most sales effort from a franchisee known to be in conformance with those parts of the contract that the parent can measure. See Paul Rubin, "The Theory of the Firm and the Structure of the Franchise Contract," *Journal of Law and Economics* 21 (April 1978): 223–33.

firms located in the United States. Imports of business services made up only 0.4 percent of gross domestic product in 2003. Foreign outsourcing is more important in economies that lack the skills and equipment to produce certain services for themselves. Figure 14-5 shows that in relative terms, India is among the largest international outsourcers, at 2.5 percent of its gross domestic product. If foreign outsourcing suddenly ended in all nations, the U.S. economy would take the world's worst hit in dollar terms, followed by the United Kingdom.[25] Foreign outsourcing is important in the information technology industry and a few others, but the trend that matters for management has been the growth of outsourcing *within* the economies of industrialized nations, in both manufacturing and service industries. About 30 percent of Japan's total manufacturing costs are currently outsourced, up from 20 percent as recently as the 1980s.[26] (There is no consensus figure on the overall percentage of outsourcing in the United States.)

Asset specificity and uncertainty are major factors in de-integration, but they act in opposite directions. A management's choice to outsource also depends on its ability to evaluate and compare external to internal performance. At the high end of comparability, many businesses use outside specialists to operate their cafeterias and provide janitorial services. These activities are common and standardized, and few investments on either side are specific to a relationship with a particular provider. Nonspecificity means that it matters little whether the firm or its outside janitorial supplier owns the brooms—if the brooms are owned by an outsider they will be equally productive in anyone's building, and if they are owned by the firm any janitorial service can use them. The transactions are also not costly to arrange. Many already-existing contracts have terms that can be easily adapted to a firm's relationship with its cafeteria operator. For services like these it is also easy to measure and compare a contractor's performance, which will

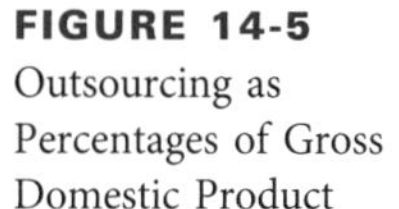
FIGURE 14-5
Outsourcing as Percentages of Gross Domestic Product

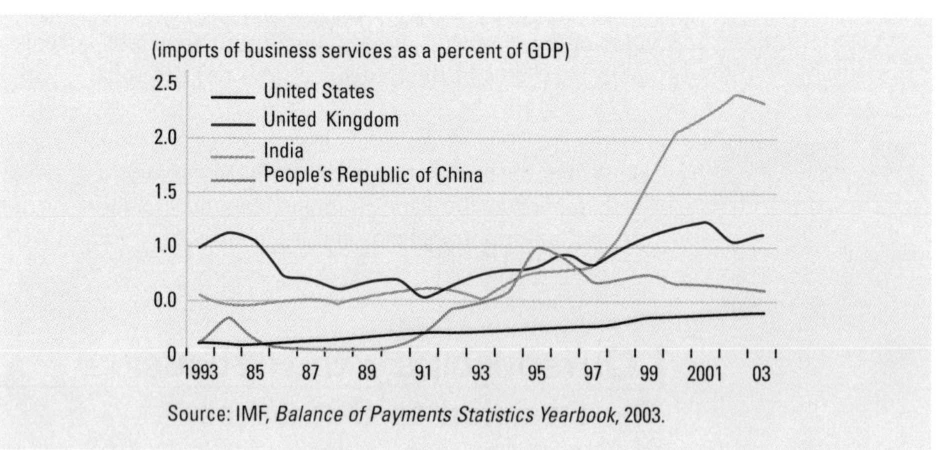

Source: IMF, *Balance of Payments Statistics Yearbook*, 2003.

[25]Mary Amiti and Shang-Jin Wei, "Demystifying Outsourcing," *Finance and Development*, December 2004, 36–39, http://www.imf.org/external/pubs/ft/fandd/2004/12/pdf/amiti.pdf; and "More Work Is Outsourced to U.S. than Away from It, Data Show," *Wall Street Journal*, March 15, 2004.

[26]"The Ins and Outs of Outsourcing," *The Economist* (U.S. Edition), August 31, 1991, 54. Manufacturing creates approximately 23 percent of Japan's gross domestic product. See Statistics Bureau Web site, "Statistical Handbook of Japan," Chapter 3: Economy, http://www.stat.go.jp/english/data/handbook/c03cont.htm.

be almost exclusively determined by the contractor's effort. Food quality or cleanliness will be under the control of the contractor and independent of other activities that the firm performs.

Q. There has been a very substantial increase in the percentage of businesses (of all sizes) that outsource their payroll check printing and recordkeeping. Give some reasons why you would expect this to happen.

Q. Compared with payroll, the percentage of businesses that outsource their information technology management is considerably lower. Explain why.

Change the task and outsourcing becomes more difficult. Assume that the design of your firm's products must constantly change if the firm is to maintain its edge over competitors. Design and engineering require contact with customers, intelligence about competitors, and familiarity with the details of your own manufacturing process. You are unlikely to outsource designing or manufacturing for several reasons. Many of the assets devoted to them will be quite specific, whether they be capital goods in your plant, intellectual property in your patents, or the intellects of people who are highly familiar with your customers. With so much specificity it will be hard to summarize in writing the scopes of your activities and the contractor's, as well as the rewards for success and the remedies for breach. The unavoidable incompleteness of an outsourcing contract will increase the risk of opportunism.[27]

Both parties can face uncertainty about the exact scope of the contractor's duties, which may also depend on what the firm's competitors are doing. These uncertain responsibilities can create difficulty in measuring performance and allocating costs and risks between the parties. It can be particularly hard to change a complex contract when unforeseen technological developments occur or unexpected events happen in the market. Instead, the gathering of market intelligence, development of products, and manufacturing are often a company's core competency and would be better managed internally than by an outsider.

Outsourcing, however, has both costs and benefits. Chapter 13 showed that new methods of risk management and new markets for trading risk have greatly increased its importance and complexity for many businesses. A small firm with a complex risk situation may prefer not to hire the high-priced personnel and software necessary to manage risk analysis in-house. Recently, however, it has become possible to contract with specialists who will perform daily (or more frequent) risk analyses and recommend transactions based on them.[28]

---

[27]Firms have long outsourced routine engineering activities that involve minor product designs or tests. A few firms in industries where technology changes rapidly have taken to outsourcing new product development. See "Outsourcing Innovation," *Business Week Online,* March 21, 2005. http://www.businessweek.com/magazine/content/05_12/b3925601.htm.

[28]For example, SunGard Corporation offers clients its web-based Kiodex Risk Management Workbench and other tools used to price a wide variety of commodity, interest rate, foreign exchange, and fixed income derivatives and to assess the interrelationships among their risks. The Kiodex web site is at http://www.sungard.com/kiodex/

Q. Give another example of a function that has become more complex, leading an increasing numbers of businesses to outsource it.

Some Trends to Explain

It is hard to estimate the overall importance of vertical integration in an economy, but evidence points to a general decrease since the 1970s. Firms encompass fewer stages of production, and market transactions are replacing activities that formerly took place in-house.

> The largest single employer in the country is not General Motors, but a temporary employment agency called Manpower Inc. The largest owner of passenger jets is not United Airlines, or any other major carrier, but the aircraft leasing arm of General Electric. American automakers have spun-off their in-house parts subsidiaries and outsourced the design and manufacture of entire automotive sub-systems to first-tier suppliers…[29]

> …In electronics, firms like Sanmina-SCI, Solectron and Flextronics specialize in assembling on contract electronic systems of all sorts… But they neither design nor distribute nor market the systems themselves… A major new trend in semiconductor manufacturing has been the rise of "fabless" [firms that] retain design, development and marketing functions but do not own their own manufacturing plants…. instead they contract out the actual manufacture of the chips to specialized "silicon foundries."[30]

Functions formerly undertaken within a firm are being replaced by transactions between firms, and they often cross national boundaries in the process. In 1998, 30 percent of the dollar value of a typical American cars (that is, brands first manufactured in the United States) originated in Korea, 17.5 percent in Japan, 4 percent in Taiwan and Singapore, 2.5 percent in the United Kingdom, and 1.5 percent in Ireland and Barbados. Only 37 percent came from the United States.[31] Outsourcing goes both ways. Today, the largest private employer in central Ohio is Japan's Honda Motor, which operates a major assembly plant there. Add in the fact that many of its components are domestic, and we lose a lot of reasons to call Honda a foreign company.

Statistics on international commerce point to the rise of de-integration. Trade in components of final goods (those sold to ultimate users) has grown faster than trade in the goods themselves.[32] Although U.S. firms are increasing their presence internationally,

---

[29]Timothy Sturgeon, "Modular Production Networks. A New American Model of Industrial Organization," *Industrial and Corporate Change* 11 (September 2002): 454. Manpower has 4.0 million "associates" who were placed into permanent, temporary, and contract positions around the world in 2005. See "About Manpower," http://www.manpower.com/about/about.cfm. The quoted text only applies to private employers—some governments have larger workforces.

[30]Richard N. Langlois, "The Vanishing Hand: The Changing Dynamics of Industrial Capitalism," *Industrial and Corporate Change* 12 (September 2003): 373.

[31]Pol Antras and Elhanan Helpman, "Global Sourcing," *Journal of Political Economy* 112 (June 2004): 553.

[32]Robert Feenstra and Gordon Hanson, "Globalization, Outsourcing and Wage Inequality," *American Economic Review* 86 (May 1996): 240–45; David Hummels, Jun Ishii and Kei-My Yii, "The Nature and Growth of Vertical Specialization in World Trade," *Journal of International Economics* 54 (June 2001): 75–96. The same holds true almost everywhere in Europe. See Emanuele Breda, Rita Cappariello and Roberta Zizza, "Vertical Specialization in Europe: Evidence from the Import Content of Exports," Bank of Italy Working Paper, 2008, Social Science Research Network Web site, http://ssrn.com/abstract=1290513.

between 1977 and 1999 their imports from foreign affiliates fell from 23 to 16 percent of total imports while those from unrelated suppliers rose.[33] Another measure of vertical integration is the average number of industrial sectors a firm operates in, which fell from 2.72 in 1979 to 1.81 in 1997.[34] As the growth of Manpower, Inc., shows, industries that supply outsourcing services have grown. Between 1972 and 1993, employment in the business services industry that supplies contract employees grew by 288 percent while non-farm employment rose only 50 percent.[35]

Why the Change?

If vertical integration is declining, either its costs must be rising relative to markets and contracts or its benefits must be falling. The available evidence supports both explanations.

Markets and Information In Chapter 3 we learned that markets reduced the costs of finding information about both prices and potential trading partners. Markets increase the likelihood of finding trades that create more economic value. Air travel and telecommunications reduce the costs of meeting others and moving goods, as well as transaction costs like credit checking, translation, and visual inspections. The changes have helped to establish markets where people need no longer actually meet. Many formerly localized markets are becoming national or global as it becomes cheaper to obtain, disseminate, and verify information at a distance. An increasing number of workers can provide services to residents of other countries without emigrating, because it has become so easy to maintain voice and electronic communications with them. Advances in computing and finance have brought new risk management techniques that make possible transactions that were once beyond peoples' risk tolerances.

Technological and social changes have lowered other costs of using markets. Prior to the 1980s shipping goods between inland locations on two continents generally required a complex sequence of journeys by rail, ship, and truck. Before containerization, transporting goods from a central Chinese city to a port cost three times as much as shipping them from the port to America.[36] Goods moving from Asia to Chicago often spent more time being unloaded and reloaded than they did in motion. This book's cover shows the future of international trade, a night photo of the port of Singapore, with containers and gantry cranes as far as the eye can see. Today, a manufacturer simply packs a standardized freight container that can stay sealed until it reaches its destination. The container first becomes a truck trailer, is later hoisted onto a railroad car and then a container ship. After crossing the ocean it undergoes another sequence of modal transfers, often without anyone ever seeing the contents.[37]

The growth of international commerce is standardizing both containers and contracts. Commercial laws are being harmonized and their terminology standardized for greater

---

[33]Antras and Helpman, "Global Sourcing."

[34]Joseph Fan and Larry Lang, "The Measure of Relatedness: An Application to Corporate Diversification," *Journal of Business* 73 (Oct. 2000): 629–60.

[35]Katherine G. Abraham and Susan Taylor, "Firms' Use of Outside Contractors: Theory and Evidence," *Journal of Labor Economics* 14 (July 1996): 394–424. Business Services is SIC code 73.

[36]Mark Levinson, *The Box: How the Shipping Container Made the World Smaller and the World Economy Bigger* (Princeton, NJ: Princeton University Press, 2006), 270.

[37]"The Container That Changed the World," *New York Times*, March 23, 2006.

ease of making contracts and settling disputes.[38] Agencies like the International Organization for Standardization (ISO) are creating common technical standards to improve exchangeability.[39] These standards include the ISO 9000 family of quality management and assurance procedures.[40] Standardization lowers the cost of obtaining information about the goods to be traded and the counterparties with whom you might trade. Finally, although some view it with concern, the costs of obtaining information and making tranactions are falling as English becomes the standard language of international business and computer-assisted translation becomes more accurate.[41]

Information, Scope, and Scale Figure 14-6 shows two long-run average cost curves. The first, $LRAC_1$, portrays a firm's costs before the arrival of inexpensive information technology (IT), such as personal computers and inexpensive telecommunications. As recently as the 1970s, most businesses that used computers had no choice but large and very costly mainframes. Only larger businesses could efficiently use machines with such high fixed costs, and a cost curve like $LRAC_1$ would only reach its minimum at the high output of Q_1^*. The coming of small computers and cheap communication lowers fixed costs and shifts the curve down to $LRAC_2$, which reaches its minimum at the lower output of Q_2^*. As industries adopt these less expensive, smaller-scale IT applications, the optimal size of firms will shrink.

Changes in technology and markets can facilitate the transfer of formerly internal activities to outsiders. Consider a small manufacturer choosing whether to fabricate certain

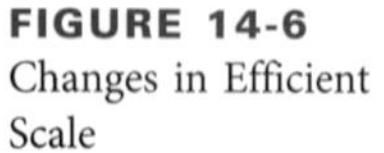
FIGURE 14-6
Changes in Efficient Scale

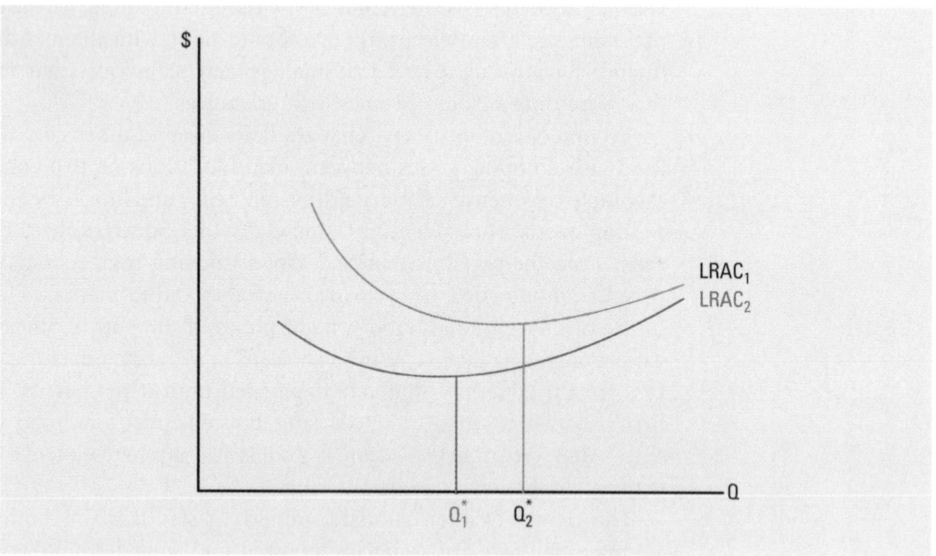

[38]To see how the change is taking place, check New York University Law School's Globalex Web site, http://www.nyulawglobal.org/globalex/Unification_Harmonization.htm.

[39]International Organization for Standardization Web site, "About ISO," http://www.iso.org/iso/en/aboutiso/introduction/index.html.

[40]International Organization for Standardization Web site, "Understand the Basics," http://www.iso.ch/iso/en/iso9000-14000/understand/inbrief.html.

[41]*World Englishes*, a scholarly journal, publishes studies on how the language is adapting to changes in demography, culture, and trading patterns. See http://www.blackwell-synergy.com/loi/weng. The text refers primarily to transactions between businesses. Anyone who wishes to mass market in China still has little choice but to understand its languages.

components of a product whose quality is critical for the product's success. If the firm makes its own components, however, it will be unable to realize the same scale economies as a specialized outside supplier. Newer technologies can make outsourcing possible by allowing the buyer to monitor a distant supplier in real time and to correct problems on the spot. If both parties use compatible software, the buyer may be able to directly load its desired specifications into the seller's equipment. Both parties' costs fall, and the ease of communication and monitoring cuts the risks of genuine errors and opportunistic behavior. Changes like these can simultaneously lower costs of internal and external coordination.[42] For example, if everyone uses compatible software, the user of a product can sketch proposed modifications in a graphic that the producer can simultaneously share among its engineering, production, research, and cost accounting departments, and with its own outside suppliers, if necessary.

Internal and External Coordination The drop in efficient scale shown in Figure 14-6 is not the only possible outcome of improved IT. The full effect of the new technology on a firm's size and scope will depend on what happens to the benefits of internal relative to external coordination. Some types of technology and software may decrease the costs of internal coordination and make larger firms more efficient. These include enterprise software (for example, SAP or Oracle), which centralizes much of a firm's data acquisition and management and allows the creation of standard and customized reports. Customer relations management software allows information sharing among market-centered departments such as sales, credit, accounts payable, and warehousing. Other types, like the shared design system described previously, may most strongly affect external coordination.

If IT increases the net benefits of external coordination by more than those of internal coordination, its vertical scope will shrink and so will its size.[43] IT first became a major investment for most businesses in the 1970s. Shortly afterward, the twentieth century's trend to larger business units began to reverse itself, both in the United States and other industrial countries.[44] In all but one major U.S. manufacturing industry (tobacco) the number of employees per plant declined during the 1980s, by an average of 18 percent. Value added per plant (revenue minus costs of material inputs) also fell, indicating that the typical plant encompassed fewer steps in its industry's vertical chain.[45]

---

[42]For more examples of internal and external coordination and the effects of new technologies, see Paul Milgrom and John Roberts, "The Economics of Modern Manufacturing: Technology, Strategy and Organization," *American Economic Review* 80 (June 1990): 511–28.

[43]If firm size is measured by the number of employees (a common practice), the effect of IT may not be clear. If computers are substitutes for labor, the firm's size will fall, and if they are complements (i.e., they make workers more productive), it will rise. For more on the distinction between internal and external coordination costs, see Erik Brynjolfsson et al., "Does Information Technology Lead to Smaller Firms?" *Management Science* 40 (December 1994): 1628–44; and Erik Brynjolfsson and Loren Hitt, "Paradox Lost: Firm-Level Evidence on the Returns to Information Systems," *Management Science* 42 (1996): 541–58. Their broad conclusion is that IT cuts the efficient size of firms.

[44]Michael Piore, *The Changing Role of Small Business in the U.S. Economy* (Geneva: International Labour Organization, 1986); and Tjerk Huppes, *The Western Edge: Work and Management in the Information Age* (Dordrecht, Netherlands: Kluwer Academic Publishers, 1987). Some research suggests that the rate of shrinkage of firms has dropped during the 1990s. See John Baldwin, Ron Jarmin, and Jianming Tang, "Small North American Producers Give Ground in the 1990s," *Small Business Economics* 23 (2004): 349–361.

[45]Bo Carlsson, David Audretsch, and Zoltan Acs, "Flexible Technology and Plant Size: U.S. Manufacturing and Metalworking Industries," *International Journal of Industrial Organization* 12 (September 1994): 359–372.

Chapter Summary

- In previous chapters we treated business firms as sets of relationships among suppliers of productive inputs. Firms could create economic value by establishing hierarchical organizations that operated by command and did not use markets.
- This chapter goes beyond organizational form to determine a firm's vertical scope. That scope will be the outcome of a comparison of the costs of transacting in markets with those of performing an activity internally.
- Other things being equal, the costs of using markets will be greater the more specific the assets necessary for a transaction and the greater the uncertainty about how those assets will be utilized. Specificity and uncertainty increase the risk of opportunistic behavior and increase the costs of contracting with outsiders.
- A firm may also change its scope as a market strategy rather than in response to changing organizational costs. Vertical mergers, for example can eliminate successive monopolies or facilitate price discrimination.
- If the activities in a vertical chain are dissimilar, the efficient form of organization may require that some steps in it be controlled by different persons or entities. Instead of vertical integration, contracts like franchise agreements may bind upstream and downstream firms.
- The success of a vertically de-integrated chain can require efforts at one stage that those at another stage cannot easily observe or evaluate. To elicit the desired behavior, vertical contracts may impose obligations that are superficially uncompetitive but allow the creation of greater economic value.
- Like decisions to integrate, decisions to outsource also depend on the relative costs and benefits of internal and external activities. Businesses are more likely to outsource when performance is easy to measure, alternative suppliers are available, and contracting is not costly.
- Beginning late in the twentieth century, firms in many industries have been shrinking their vertical scopes and relying more on markets for goods and services they formerly produced for themselves. There also appears to be a downward trend in size in a number of industries.
- Changes in information and communication technology have made transactions easier with outsiders and have increased the sizes of markets. In general, these changes have raised the benefits and lowered the costs of external transactions relative to internal provision of the same services.

Questions and Problems

1. In fast food we often see that a single franchisee owns all the outlets in a certain area that may be as large as a city. How does this increase the value that a franchise agreement is likely to create?
2. Some large coal-burning power plants are located at the mouth of a mine and have been designed to burn coal specifically extracted from that mine. Others are at a distance from mines. Coal can reach them by rail from many different mines, and they are not as dependent on a particular type of coal as mine-mouth plants. Why

do you expect that the owner of the mine-mouth plant is more likely to own its coal supplies than the owner of one located at a greater distance from mines?

3. Chapter 8 mentioned that DeBeers, the dominant firm in diamond mining and wholesale marketing, has until recently been unintegrated into any downstream activities. In the past few years, however, it has opened a handful of its own retail outlets on some of the world's most prestigious shopping streets. Does this chapter suggest any reasons why the company might have picked now to integrate itself into this type of retailing?
4. An auto manufacturer gives franchised dealers exclusive service territories, and the law allows dealers to set prices as they wish. Why might you expect the dealer and manufacturer to disagree about the price that should be charged? How might a manufacturer try inducing the dealer to set price more in accordance with its wishes?
5. Check that the calculations in the section on successive monopolists are correct.
6. The producer of a movie has sole rights to make DVDs of it and is thus a monopolist in that particular movie. Assume that Blockbuster Video also has a near-monopoly on retail rentals. The producer could charge Blockbuster $85 for the DVD and let it choose the rental price. Producers found, however, that it is more profitable to charge Blockbuster a low rate to purchase the video (about $8) and then require it to send them 40 to 60 percent of the gross revenue on rentals of that DVD. Explain why the revenue-sharing scheme is more profitable for both parties than the alternative.

   a. For what types of movies do you expect that the producer will insist on receiving 60 percent of the revenue rather than 40 percent? Explain.

   b. Might your previous answer be related to characteristics of the audience, for example, the importance of a younger and more computer-literate demographic that can more easily obtain illegal copies?

7. Why might McDonald's and its franchisees disagree on the proper retail price to charge? (Note: The answer is not the same as Question 4.) How do the incentives of the parent and its franchisees differ under a standard revenue-sharing franchise contract?
8. Why might you expect to see flat royalty payments in home-based franchises but revenue-based royalties in franchisees that operate from commercial buildings?[46] (Hint: Among the most popular home-based franchises are cleaning services offered to businesses, and delivery services for seniors who live at home.)

   a. Is your explanation consistent with the fact that franchised tutoring services often charge a fixed royalty per student enrolled?

9. How does a franchise contract in which the parent company supplies ingredients to a franchise holder reallocate risk between the parties, as opposed to the situation faced by a non-franchise business and its spot market suppliers?
10. One study compared the performance of a single company's franchised and company-owned fast-food outlets on health inspections.[47] It found that franchises received higher (i.e., better) average point scores on a standard rating form and

---

[46]See "Franchises and Business Opportunity Information," at http://www.franchisegator.com/.

[47]Roy Beheler, Seth Norton, and Kabir Sen, "A Comparison of Company-Owned and Franchised Fast Food Outlet Performance: Insights from Health Inspection Scores," in *Strategy and Governance of Networks*, ed. Gerhard Girard and Josef Windsberger (Berlin: Springer-Verlag, 2008): 113–25.

that their scores had a smaller standard deviation than those of company-owned outlets. Do these two facts surprise you? Why or why not?

11. One consequence of increases in business litigation over the past 20 years has been an increase in the percentage of lawyers who work as employees of firms rather than as independent practitioners. Explain why you might would have expected this increase in vertical integration to happen.
12. A small-volume foreign auto maker limits the number of its franchised dealers in the United States and gives them exclusive territories. There are also non-dealers who have no official connection with the manufacturer. They buy its cars overseas and sell them in the United States, a phenomenon sometimes called a "gray market." If you are a manufacturer do you necessarily want the gray market to cease to exist? Why or why not? How about if you are a franchised dealer?
13. Show that the joint profits of a franchisor and franchisee are maximized if their contract specifies that the franchisee pays royalties as a percentage of profit rather than a percent of sales. Because the franchisee pays a percentage of sales in most franchise agreements, do you conclude that existing agreements are inefficient?

Chapter Appendix

Successive Monopolies

In the top half of Figure 14-4, market demand for A is given by

(14.1) $$Q_A = 10 - P_A.$$

Jones's marginal revenue curve is his demand for B:

(14.2) $$MR_A = 10 - 2Q_A.$$

This crosses the horizontal axis (marginal cost = 0) at 5 units. Producing 5 units, however, would leave Smith with revenue of zero. Instead, she will maximize her profits treating (14.2) as the demand curve facing her. The marginal revenue curve for (14.2) is

(14.3) $$MR_B = 10 - 4Q_B.$$

Smith maximizes profit at 2.5 units of B, which sell for $5.00 each. Her profit is $12.50. Jones produces 2.5 units and sells them for $7.50 each. His profit is $18.75 − $12.50 = $6.25. Their joint profits are $12.50 + $6.25 = $18.75. If instead Jones gets B for free (its actual marginal cost) he will produce 5 units and sell them for $5.00 each, for a total profit of $25. Jones can pay Smith some amount over $12.50 and make the two of them better off than they were as successive monopolists.

Q. For this example, show that consumers are also better off with a single monopolist than they are with successive monopolies.

Chapter 15

Employment Relationships

Introduction

Big Blues

The photos below tell a story of corporate transformation. In 1985, IBM topped *Fortune* magazine's list of America's most admired corporations, chosen by a survey of top

FIGURE 15-1

Underwood & Underwood/CORBIS

ALY SONG/Reuters/Corbis

executives. It ranked fifth among the world's corporations in sales and first in profits.[1] From its modest beginnings in the 1920s, "Big Blue" (the corporate color, still visible in television advertising) went on to dominate mainframe computers, starting with System/360 in the late 1960s. IBM was a good stock to own and a great place to work if you did not mind conforming to strict dress standards and bureaucratic rules. In the top photo are IBM technicians in 1968, dressed in the company's traditional white (never any other color) shirt and narrow tie, working on the world's most powerful computer at the time. Today a $500 laptop has 20 times the speed and 25,000 times the memory.

At IBM pay was competitive and employment was secure through the 1980s. A high-performing employee could count on an upward ascent into management. Until the 1990s every President of the company had come up from an entry-level position. IBM took pride in the fact that it had never laid off any employees. Workers whose performance had sagged were simply shifted to less responsible positions, a level of security made possible by the growth of IBM's near-monopoly in mainframes.[2] But why would the company's shareholders acquiesce in an unwritten offer of security that might carry a high cost of keeping nonperformers on the payroll? In this chapter we examine employment from several vantage points. In particular we will examine why it is often a long-term relationship, and why some employers might choose to bear the costs of employment practices like IBM's.

After 1985, IBM's fortunes fell. Changing technologies had brought new price and performance competition to the mainframes, a slow-growing market even in the best of times. In the early 1980s IBM developed the ancestor of today's personal computer (PC), but instead of promoting it to home users the company marketed it primarily to businesses as a steppingstone to mainframes. The PC also abandoned IBM's previous practices of making its own components and writing its own software. Intel processors and Microsoft software opened the company to competition from inexpensive mass-marketed clones with the same parts and software. IBM's top management failed to adapt to upheavals in markets it once dominated, but it continued to avoid the layoffs, terminations, and restructurings that might have restored the company.[3] In 1990 its shares sold at half their 1985 price.

By 1993, IBM's directors finally understood that the company could no longer maintain its old ways. They decided to choose a CEO whose lack of ties with the company would allow him to force the reorganizations and downsizings that career executives could not or would not impose.[4] Louis V. Gerstner Jr. came from a background like no other IBM executive. He had a Harvard MBA and had previously served as CEO of American Express, later moving to RJR Nabisco as chairman and CEO. He instituted reorganizations that replaced decision-making processes based on compromises among lifelong employees with more market-oriented policies. In particular, he turned the company from one that centered on mainframes and related products to one that concentrated on solving problems for customers. Gerstner was the first CEO to upset other traditions—IBM would finally see mass layoffs and division closings. The

---

[1]Patricia Sellers, "America's Most Admired Corporations," *Fortune*, April 13, 1985. Paul Carroll, *Big Blues*, (New York: Three Rivers Press, 1994) covers IBM's problems and its response to them.

[2]Recall Chapter 7's discussion of IBM as a dominant firm facing a fringe of small competitors.

[3]Carol Loomis, "Dinosaurs?" *Fortune*, May 3, 1993.

[4]Inside directors (those holding executive positions in the company) were almost entirely shut out of the decision process, which was initiated by outside directors. Carol Loomis and David Kirkpatrick, "The Hunt for Mr. X: Who Can Run IBM?" *Fortune*, February 22, 1993.

change from monopoly to competition meant the company's survival would depend on unpopular decisions made by executive order.[5] "When you got a call from Lou," said a former manager, "it was never to hear a compliment."[6] Gerstner had, however, restored IBM's profitability with a new business model, one that did not even have a place for PCs. The bottom photo is Beijing in 2004, the year IBM sold its PC business to China's Lenovo.

What's Next?

Employment relationships are as important as family ties for many of us, whether we are employees or employers. "Self-employed" just means there is no boss between you and the customer. Our study of employment will illustrate how much light economics can shed on seemingly ordinary business relationships. The association of employer and employee usually begins in a market where they screen alternatives and try to find beneficial matches, but its subsequent unfolding takes place in the nonmarket environments of contract and hierarchy.

This chapter covers the following:

- The economic theory of labor supply shows how a person's desired working hours depend on the wage being offered and on personal trade-offs between income and the value placed on leisure. The economic theory of labor demand shows how an employer required to pay the market wage decides on the most profitable amount of labor to hire.
- Putting supply and demand together determines the level of wages and the volume of employment in the market. This theory also helps to explain wage differences among workers.
- A more general market model examines how potential employees search for positions and how employers search for persons to fill them. In equilibrium some job slots go unfilled for the short term and some workers may be unemployed.
- Investments in human capital, such as education or on-the-job training, improve productivity. A worker usually pays to acquire general skills that are valuable to many employers, and an employer bears the costs of specific training that only improve productivity in its own firm.
- The employment relationship has aspects of a contract, but it is usually an unwritten one that must change as time passes. Like many contracts, this one entails specific investments that can put each party at risk of opportunism by the other.
- A surprisingly large percentage of employment relationships are long-term. Pay can be structured to encourage workers to make efforts both early and late in their careers, and employers who value their reputations have incentives to keep even unwritten promises.
- Markets offer information about more choices and more potential trading partners, but it often pays employers to bypass outside markets and instead restrict their

---

[5]As you were warned in Chapters 1 and 8, in cases like this one it is important to be on guard against selection bias. At IBM, however, an important part of the turnaround appears directly attributable to Gerstner and policies that clearly originated with him. External factors such as changed market conditions were also unlikely causes of IBM's improved condition.

[6]Betsy Morris, "He's Smart. He's Not Nice. He's Saving Big Blue," *Fortune*, April 14, 1997.

search for candidates for promotion to those already employed; this is known as an "internal labor market."

- An employee is generally a member of a team, which makes her personal productivity hard to observe. Pay must be structured to induce and reward work effort, but the efficient type of pay arrangement varies with characteristics of the job.

MARKETS FOR LABOR

Supply

Wages and Hours Most people receive their incomes in return for supplying inputs into production. Landowners supply land, savers and investors provide funds, and workers provide labor services. Producers of material inputs, such as fuel and buildings, supply them in response to market prices. As usual we assume that suppliers of inputs wish to make themselves as well off as possible. Producers of material inputs attempt to maximize their profits, but workers are a harder case because they value both income and leisure time. A few find their jobs intrinsically enjoyable, but other jobs require physical or mental exertions that many workers find unpleasant. Income earned on the job is of little value to a worker without the time to enjoy the goods it can purchase. Income is the opportunity cost of leisure time and vice versa—an extra hour of leisure comes at the price of an hour's wages.[7] At the margin the trade-off depends on the number of hours already being worked. Someone working 10 hours a week might happily sacrifice another hour of leisure for the income, but one working 60 hours might insist on a higher wage in return for one more hour on the job. Figure 15-2 shows a person's supply curve of labor hours as an increasing function of the wage that person can earn.[8]

FIGURE 15-2
Individual Labor Supply

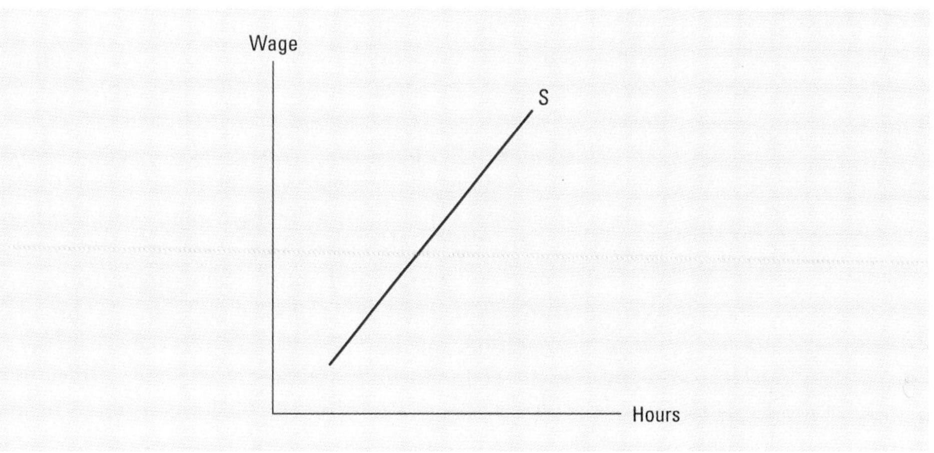

[7]For the time being, assume that workers are free to choose the number of hours they will work. Later we explain why full-time employment is the norm.

[8]It is possible that if the wage is high a person will choose to work fewer hours in response to a further increase in the wage. Although this backward-bending supply curve is a possibility, it is hard to find examples of this behavior by actual workers.

The use of "wage" in the previous paragraph was a deliberate simplification. Compensation can take other forms, such as employer-provided health insurance, a van-pool service for commuters, three weeks of paid vacation time, and discount lunches in the company cafeteria. Important parts of compensation over the more distant future are not directly related to one's current pay. Superior performance might earn you a bonus at the end of the year or put you in line for a major promotion, and accumulated time on the job may entitle you to a higher pension upon retirement. Other aspects of a job may be highly valued by some workers but not others. Tenure offers college professors a type of job security and pay insurance available in few other occupations. Some people require a premium to work at night while others welcome the opportunity. Child care has little value to a childless person and a substantial value to parents who both work. An employer can thus tailor its compensation package to attract workers with traits it believes will advantage it against competitors in the market for its output.

Q. Employer-provided health insurance obviously benefits workers (although possibly not as much as cash wages), and workers will surely prefer a plan that offers wider coverage. How might an employer tailor the rest of a pay package so that workers likely to use more medical care are not adversely selected into employment there?

Supply of Labor to the Market Understanding the supply and demand for labor requires us to be quite clear about the exact market we are analyzing. The opportunity cost of supplying labor depends on the worker's alternatives. Many people who compete with you as a supplier of labor in some markets will not compete with you in others. A pipefitter surely views other pipefitters as competitors for employment in the same labor market, but neither pipefitters nor contractors who hire them will think of an economics professor as a competitor. As time passes and adjustments such as changes in location become possible, some pipefitters will move from lower-wage areas to higher-wage ones. Two such areas may become a single market as wages move toward equality between them. For other analyses a more general geographic market may be best. If the oil industry is booming (and people cannot move instantly), average wages will rise in Houston relative to Indianapolis for both oilfield workers and for those who produce local goods that the migrants will buy. As a first approximation economists often assume that workers are identical and model demand and supply conditions in Houston. For other problems distinctions among skills are important. Estimating the impact of illegal immigration, for example, requires an analysis of the market for unskilled labor (where illegals compete with Americans) and the market for skilled labor (where they add little to supply but their presence might increase the productivity of skilled workers).

Human Capital and Long-run Supply Productivity may be an accident of birth, like a unique musical talent, but most people must incur costs to build up their earning powers. Your value to employers will depend in part on the skills you have chosen to develop, which economists call investments in *human capital.* Acquiring new skills or improving existing ones is an investment in the same sense as a business owner's decision to build a new plant. Both will generate income over a span of years, and both have an opportunity cost in the form of what the funds could have earned in their next best use. The investment cost of college consists of both direct expenses on schooling and the forgone wages of a high school graduate.[9] Investments in human capital can take many forms—education that provides a skill, doctor visits and vitamins that keep you healthy, and migration to an area with higher wages, to name just a few.

Investments in human capital take place under uncertainty. Attending college allows a student to build up "general" human capital—learning to write a readable paragraph or mastering math can raise productivity in almost any job a graduate might take. More specific choices are riskier, because future technologies and markets are intrinsically difficult to predict. The payoff to a major in petroleum engineering will depend on how oil markets evolve over the 40-plus years of a graduate's working life, and on how many others chose that major. The best jobs may be in industries that do not yet exist—think of computers in 1950, environmental specialties in 1970, or Internet services in 1990. When expected wages rise in one field relative to others, investment in human capital adds new specialists to those already trained. As in other competitive markets, the supply curve of labor is more elastic in the long run than in the short.

Q. Why should a person invest in general-purpose human capital as early in life as possible? Does the same hold for skills that are only valuable in a few industries? Explain the difference, if any.

Demand

The Employer's Objectives We start with a single employer's short-run decision. All of the employer's other inputs are fixed, and it can hire all the labor it wants at the market wage. The employer is also a price-taker in the market for its output. Disregard differences among workers and assume that there is a standardized unit of labor, the person-hour. Labor is the only variable input, so the number of person-hours employed determines output, and the amount of output produced find profit. Our job is to find the profit-maximizing amount of labor to employ.

The short-run production relationships of Chapter 4 reappear in Figure 15-3. As before, the upper panel shows that the employer's daily output (total product) increases as more labor is hired, and that it increases at a decreasing rate. The lower panel shows labor's marginal product, the extra output over the day from hiring an extra unit of labor (mathematically, the derivative of total product). Marginal product diminishes as additional labor is employed, because it is not a perfect substitute for the fixed inputs.[10] To see the impact of another person-hour on profit requires calculating the additional revenue it generates. The value of marginal product (VMP) of labor is its marginal product times the price of output. Because marginal product slopes downward, so does VMP, which appears in Figure 15-4. Hiring an extra person-hour increases the employer's

[9]Here we are disregarding the material from Chapter 11 on the controversy about whether higher education actually improves productivity or whether it merely provides a signal that the person with a degree is more desirable than one without one.

[10]Chapter 4 showed that at small outputs marginal product might be increasing, but for simplicity we now only consider the area in which it is decreasing.

FIGURE 15-3
Total and Marginal Products

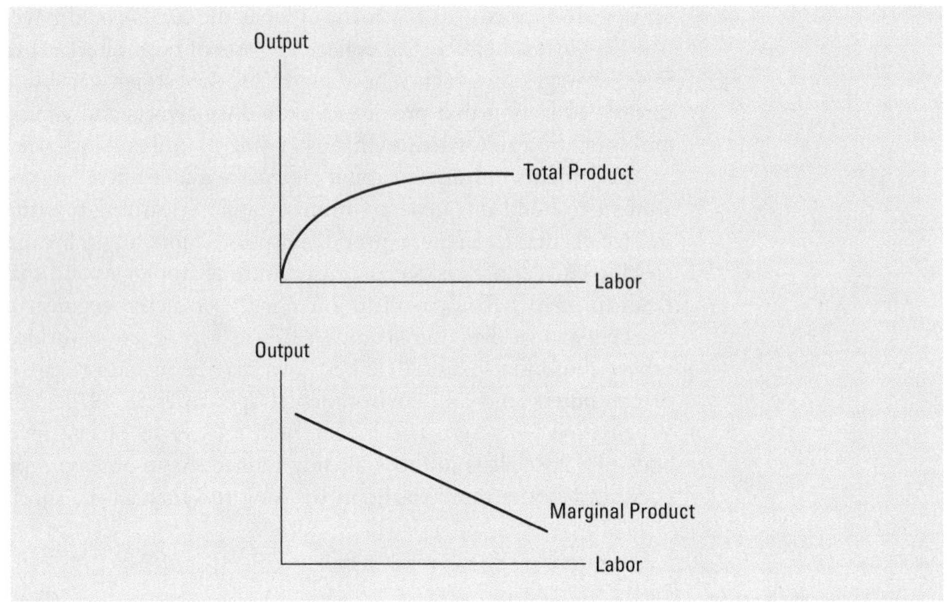

profit as long as VMP exceeds the wage. If the market wage is $11 per hour, the employer hires 77 person-hours. The wage bill is $847 ($11.00 × 77), but long-run survival requires that its revenue cover the costs of all its inputs. Funds available for fixed inputs equal the triangular area where VMP exceeds the wage, and profit is the amount left over, if any. Thus, VMP is an employer's demand curve for labor—it shows the profit-maximizing (or loss-minimizing) amount to hire at various market wages. If the market wage falls to $7, the 78th worker becomes worth hiring, as do all other workers up to the 111th. Each of the original 77 workers produces a $4 higher difference between VMP and the wage, and the 78th to 111th workers further add to the funds available to pay for fixed inputs.

Q. Explain why funds available to pay the fixed inputs are equal to the area of the triangle below VMP and above the wage.

FIGURE 15-4
Value of Marginal Product and Wage

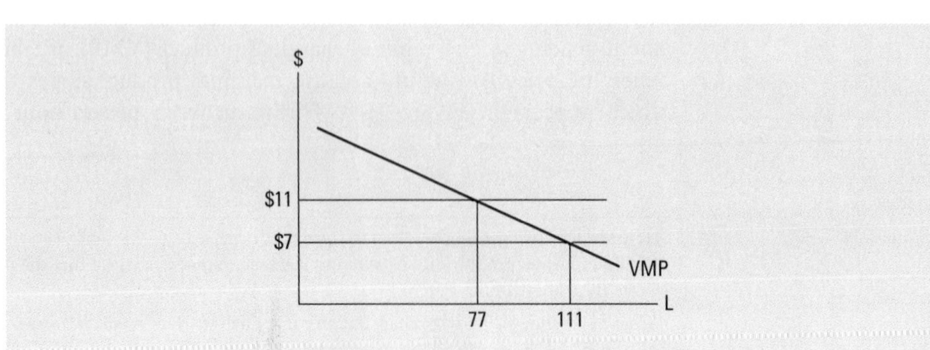

FIGURE 15-5
Shifts of VMP

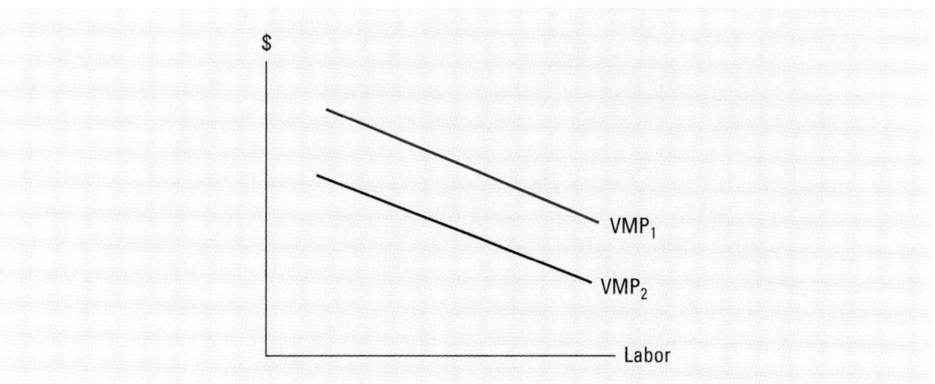

As in markets for goods and services, we distinguish slides along a stationary demand curve (i.e., changes in quantity demanded) from shifts of the curve itself (i.e., changes in demand). Looking at Figure 15-5, we see that if the price of output rises the entire VMP curve shifts upward from VMP_1 to VMP_2. At any market wage the employer will use more person-hours than before. Labor's VMP also rise with human capital. A worker can acquire *general* human capital that increases productivity by making investments such as formal education. Productivity may also increase with experience in a particular job. With experience the worker learns the employer's operating procedures, how to coordinate with coworkers, and how to do his own job more efficiently. The time and other resources (e.g., defective output produced during the learning process) expended in gaining experience is an investment in *specific* human capital. It renders the worker more valuable to this employer but not to others whose workplaces are operated and staffed differently. Thus, we expect that a worker will make most of her own investments in general human capital. If the employer makes these investments and the worker leaves for another job, the new employer would benefit from expenses made by the former one. Because human capital specific to this employer is not valued by other employers, the worker will not voluntarily invest in it and the employer must do so.

Second, workers and capital goods are often complements in production—increasing the amount or quality of equipment a worker can use will increase his productivity. An accountant in the days of hand-cranked adding machines spent a large fraction of the workday totaling columns of figures or performing long division with pencil and paper. Working with a computer frees up time formerly spent in routine calculations so he can use his skills to analyze financial documents. Jobs for operators of old-style adding machines vanish, both here and elsewhere in the economy. Since human wants appear to be unlimited, there are always jobs to be done, but there may be costs of finding them (including spells of unemployment) or acquiring the necessary skills. At the turn of the twentieth century, nearly half of the labor force worked on farms, but today only 2 percent of workers produce the groceries for a much larger population.

Q. Does human capital depreciate like physical capital equipment? Give some examples.

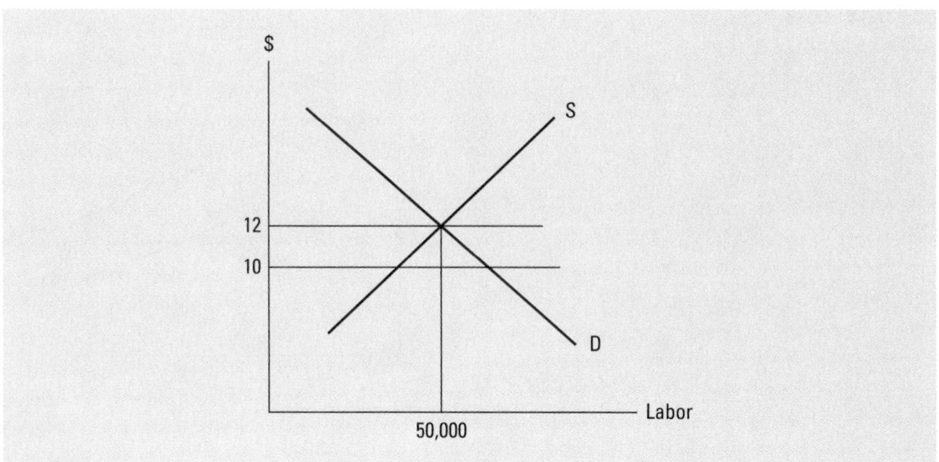

FIGURE 15-6
Labor Market Equilibrium

Labor Market Equilibrium

As we did for product markets, we can add up individual supplies of labor to get market supply. For our purposes it is sufficient to add the demand curves of employers in that market to get market demand.[11] Figure 15-6 shows market supply and demand, with equilibrium at a wage of $12/hour and 50,000 person-hours of labor employed. As in product markets, if a labor market is out of equilibrium wages and employment will move in that direction. If the market wage were $10 for some reason (say, just before the demand curve shifted upward), labor would be in shortage. Employers would offer more to fill vacant job slots, and as already employed workers learn (perhaps slowly) about higher offers from other employers, the wage for all workers would go to $12. The reverse reasoning would hold if the market were in surplus at an unsustainably high wage.

Shifts in demand and supply help in the analysis of many labor market phenomena at many possible levels of detail:

- We could explain long-term trends in average wages and employment by simplifying and treating workers and jobs as identical. If the underlying population is relatively unchanged, a general rise in educational levels raises productivity, and thus both wages and employment. Figure 15-7 shows that the old equilibrium of a $12 wage and 50,000 employed changes to a $15 wage and 60,000 employed.
- Computers and workers are complements in production. Workers with more computing power at their disposal have higher marginal products. Science fiction authors have written many stories about worlds where computers put everyone out of work.[12] Their error is to disregard the remarkable scope of human desires—if peoples' wants are unlimited, there are always other jobs to be done. Figure 15-7

[11]The market demand may not be the simple sum of demands because increased demands of all employers can affect wages and product prices. Additionally, in the long run employers will probably react to changes in market wages by changing the amounts of other inputs they use, which affects productivity and the demand for labor. See Steven Landsburg, *Price Theory and Applications,* 6th ed. (Mason, OH: Thompson Learning, 2005), 514–518.

[12]See, for example, Isaac Asimov, *I, Robot* (New York: Bantam Spectra, 2004).

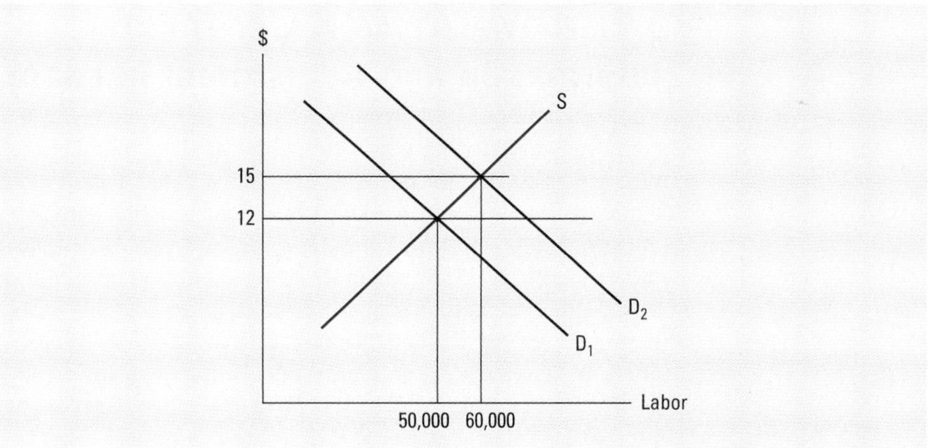

FIGURE 15-7
A Shift in Demand for Labor

also illustrates this point. As computers have made workers more productive, the demand for them shifts upward and their wages and employment increase.[13]

- Most illegal immigrants to the United States are unskilled workers. The end-of-chapter questions will ask you to explain why relatively unskilled U.S. citizens view their coming with alarm, but relatively skilled ones either favor it or show little concern.

What Supply and Demand Do Not Tell Us

So far so good, but there are many things about employment that supply–demand diagrams don't help us to understand. The familiar market diagram showed that labor markets contain forces that lead to equilibrium much like markets for other goods and services. Behind supply and demand, however, we treated labor like a commodity that traded in spot markets.

- First, we assumed that workers could easily learn about job vacancies and wages, and could move quickly and at low cost to push wages toward equilibrium. Without saying much about it, we treated all person-hours of labor as identical and any job vacancy as no different from any other.
- Second, we mentioned investments in human capital but did not explore their consequences. In a spot market there is little value to a buyer or a seller in maintaining a long-term relationship, because all goods traded in it are identical, as are all buyers and all sellers. Employer–employee relationships, however, often remain in force for a large part of the worker's adult life, despite the fact that few such relationships are governed by enforceable written agreements.
- Third, we did not ask why long-term employment is common, even though markets and technologies change over the years in ways that could not have been foreseen when a relationship began.

To analyze these and other questions, we must treat employment as a relationship governed by contracts and hierarchies.

[13]Timothy Bresnahan, Erik Brynjolfsson, and Loren Hitt, "Information Technology, Workplace Organization, and the Demand for Skilled Labor: Firm-Level Evidence," *Quarterly Journal of Economics* 117 (February 2002): 139–176.

Employment as a Contract

Information and Adjustment in Labor Markets

The assumptions underlying our basic supply–demand model are unlikely to hold completely in labor markets. Often, there are large numbers of possible buyers and sellers, but neither people nor positions are standardized. Different employers will attach different responsibilities and working conditions to a standard job title like "milling machine operator." Some possible candidates can be weeded out quickly, for example, if the employer insists on certain amounts or types of experience. But qualifying candidates themselves differ in both backgrounds and in personality traits that may matter for job performance. An unfilled position is costly for an employer who must devise workarounds that use existing employees. Filling a position with the wrong person is also costly. That person might be less productive than expected or might adversely affect the productivity of others, but replacing her can require a search as costly and risky as the one that originally brought her to the company.

Likewise, potential employees are aware that not all jobs are identical, and they too need to discover facts about alternative employers (including their identities) and the desirability of the wages and working conditions they offer. Prospective employees also bear costs. Those already on the job elsewhere incur the opportunity costs of search, such as sacrificed leisure time or expenses paid to agents. Except in extreme circumstances an unemployed person has other earning opportunities (which may be so inferior they are not further considered) and has prospects worth the cost of pursuing them. Workers engaged in a job search are the counterpart of unfilled vacancies, and flows of new searchers and vacancies end in matches to fill them.[14]

Generally, we expect to see a range (distribution) of wages rather than a unique equilibrium. By most measures labor markets adjust slowly to changes in supply or demand. Buyers and sellers must first detect those changes. Wages in a position are generally fixed and subject only to infrequent (often annual) reviews. If there is a general upward trend of wages (whether due to market changes or inflation) someone's pay may be higher or lower relative to the average simply because of the timing of reviews. Wages set in a particular employer-employee match may differ from those in others because of differing productivities, differences in working conditions, and localized employer market power, to name only a few possible reasons.

Matches and Contracts

Labor markets are characterized by high information costs to both employers and employees. In few other markets do individual attributes of buyers and sellers play such important roles. If all apples are identical and dependably available on the market, a seller's only concern with a buyer may be creditworthiness and a buyer's only concern with a seller may be deliverability. By contrast a labor market is a *matching market,* where the value a relationship creates will depend heavily on how well employees and employers meet each others' expectations. Either party can initiate the unmaking of a match, but only at a cost. After a separation the employer must find another worker and the employee a new position. In addition, the employer loses the value of firm-specific human capital it has invested in the worker and must invest again in his replacement. The

[14]In an average month 10 percent of all workers change employers, enter or leave the labor force, or enter or leave unemployment. Steven J. Davis et al., "The Flow Approach to Labor Markets: New Data Sources and Micro-Macro Links," *Journal of Economic Perspectives* 20 (Summer 2006): 3–26.

worker bears the costs of searching for a new employer, which will include those of the search itself and possibly lower wages at the outset of the new relationship.

Q. Why might we expect to see lower wages when an experienced worker begins a new employment relationship? Use human capital in your answer. Why do you expect to see little if any discount with a new employer when professors change jobs? Would your reasoning be the same for major league baseball players?

Some employment relationships resemble spot-market transactions. They are standardized, of short duration, and both parties understand the work required and the pay expected. In Southern California hardware store parking lots one often sees a cluster of people (some there illegally) seeking work as day laborers. In the morning contractors size them up as candidates for unskilled work like construction site cleanups. There is an unwritten convention that the worker be paid a promised amount in cash at the end of the day. Contractors often find such workers almost interchangeable and vice versa (opportunistic workers and contractors acquire bad reputations). A contractor with a two-day cleanup job can get it done equally well by one laborer working two days or two working for one day. Because the work is unskilled and on-the-job learning is unimportant, any possible long-term relationship between a contractor and a laborer creates no more economic value than does hiring a different worker each day.

Our earlier study of contracts told us how relationships that either party can terminate at will might be economically inefficient. Without the assurance of an enforceable contract one or both parties could invest too little in relationship-specific assets that increase the economic value their joint efforts can create. A written contract creates value, but the benefits must exceed the costs of forming and enforcing it. Only a handful of employment relationships are simple enough to be governed by written agreements. A professional sports team's expectations for a player are few enough (e.g., appearance at games and practices, being available to the media, rules for product endorsements) that a relatively short written document can spell out the parties' obligations in almost all imaginable contingencies. Sports contracts are also easy to write because they must follow standard forms previously negotiated by leagues and players' unions. They can still, however, include player-specific terms such as consumption perks or bonuses for hitting home runs or pitching winning games.[15] Market realities also constrain the parties' desires to act opportunistically—a team must contract annually with many players, who have their own reputations to maintain. Similarly, an actor's contract with a producer can be in writing because it only applies to a single movie or play, and basic contract provisions have evolved over time. Expiration dates can also be specified—actors in Broadway theaters generally sign "run of the play" contracts that obligate them to perform for as long as their show is being staged.[16]

Incompleteness and Opportunism in Employment

Incompleteness An employment relationship need not be memorialized in an enforceable contract, but even without one the parties become aware of each other's expectations and will likely attempt to meet them. The employer (or an agent we again call the "boss")

[15]Find the pay and special contract provisions of your favorite major league baseball player at http://mlbcontracts.blogspot.com/.

[16]To see the terms of some typical theater contracts, see the Actors' Equity Web site, http://www.actorsequity.org/AboutEquity/contracts.asp. Actors' Equity is the stage actors union.

may assign the employee a wide variety of tasks and monitor her performance. Changes in markets and technology change the set of possible tasks, some of which might not have existed at the start of the relationship—even the PC is only 30 years old. Mutual expectations give the employment relationship some aspects of one governed by a contract, but the need to accommodate change means that it must be a highly incomplete one. As with written agreements, incompleteness is more than just a response to high costs of negotiation. At the initiation of the relationship both parties are aware that the future will almost surely bring changes, and they cannot currently envision how they will react to these changes. If the relationship is worth maintaining they will have to respond to unforeseen events by reformulating the affected parts of their implicit agreement.

Efficiency Wages Employment is a principal/agent relationship in which the worker (agent) receives assignments from the employer or boss (principal). The principal benefits from the efforts of the agent, but he is unable to monitor everything she is doing or evaluate the quality of her efforts. Because random events affect the result, even after observing it the principal cannot conclude with certainty that success is an indicator of high-quality efforts. We previously learned that the principal's problems become particularly difficult if the agent is on a team whose members must work cooperatively but whose individual productivities are difficult to measure. In Chapter 10 we analyzed payment schemes such as contingency fees and capitation arrangements that align the agent's incentives with the principal's interests. These schemes, however, applied only to a particular lawsuit or medical procedure. We now seek pay arrangements that can induce ongoing effort by the employee.

One possibility is for the employer to pay an *efficiency wage* that is above the market level. A worker paid the efficiency wage and fired for loafing is unlikely to find another job that pays as much. If the increased disutility of extra effort (i.e., loafing less) is small relative to the gap between efficiency and market wages, the worker will make the effort. The employer will see higher productivity and will be able to reduce its costs of monitoring the worker, because the worker now loses more if caught loafing.

Table 15-1 gives a numerical example. (All figures are purely for illustration.) Assume that the going wage for this kind of labor is $10 per hour.[17] A worker who is caught loafing is fired, but if a new employer cannot easily find out about her work history she can quickly find another $10 per hour job. Her hourly output is worth $15. The employer must pay $3 of the remaining $5 to monitor the worker and has $2 left over for other costs and profit, if any. The disutility of an hour's effort to the employee is $5, so her net gain per hour is $5. Paying an efficiency wage can benefit both employer and

TABLE 15-1 EFFICIENCY WAGES

	MARKET WAGE	EFFICIENCY WAGE	DIFFERENCE
Worker output	$15.00	$20.00	+$5.00
Worker paid	10.00	14.00	4.00
Monitoring cost	3.00	1.00	−2.00
Residual for employer	2.00	5.00	3.00
Disutility of effort	5.00	7.00	2.00
Net benefit to worker	5.00	7.00	2.00

[17]To avoid complications that come when we consider the adoption of efficiency wages by more than one employer (this changes market output and wages), assume that either (1) other employers have lower monitoring costs or (2) this employer is the first to consider it, and disregard the reactions of others.

employee. As one possibility, assume that if the employer pays the employee $14 per hour she will work harder and produce $20 of output. If we assume that harder work adds $2 of disutility, the employee's net gain is now $7 instead of $5. If her lower motivation to loaf allows the employer to reduce monitoring from $3 to $1 per hour, the employer is left with $5 to apply to other costs and profit. Both are better off with the efficiency wage.

Q. In this example can we conclude that the worker under an efficiency wage will choose never to loaf at all?

This example works, but where might we actually see efficiency wages in operation? All else the same, they are more likely if monitoring is more costly. Alan Krueger of Princeton University compared wages in franchised fast-food outlets with those in outlets staffed by employees of the parent company.[18] He hypothesized that franchise owners had stronger monitoring incentives because their incomes are linked more closely to performance than those of supervisors on the parent company's payroll. Krueger found that earnings premiums for assistant and shift managers in company-owned outlets averaged 9 percent higher than for the same positions in franchises, and full-time crew workers earned an average of 2 percent more in company outlets. These differences may look small, but they might be evidence of efficiency wages paid at company outlets.

Monitoring costs may explain other market phenomena. In many cities the ratio of qualified applicants to job openings in fire and police departments exceeds that for desk-bound civil servants with similar qualifications. The larger queues at fire and police departments might be evidence of efficiency wages. Desk employees are more visible to their supervisors, which eases the task of evaluating them. Police and fire employees often work away from headquarters as individuals or small groups. The public values their on-the-job efforts highly and wants to see them making risky decisions without active supervision—pursuing an armed suspect or rescuing someone from a burning building. An efficiency wage might motivate these efforts if firing leaves a person with few options beyond working as a low-paid security guard.

Q. Assume that a new and cheaper monitoring method is developed, for example, television cameras that can track several workers at once rather than one-on-one observation by a supervisor. Do you expect that efficiency wages will become more or less common?

Two-sided Opportunism Both employers and employees can behave opportunistically. A worker who understands the high costs of replacing him may choose a lower level of effort than one who is more easily replaceable. Employers who cannot be bound by enforceable contracts might do likewise. Assume that when a new employee starts work at $15 per hour her boss tells her that good performance over the next year will earn her a raise to $17. She responds with high levels of effort but when the year is over she gets no raise. The boss might claim that the commitment was never made, and in any case this gratuitous promise is unenforceable in court. Incompleteness of the

[18]Alan B. Krueger, "Ownership, Efficiency, and Wages: An Examination of Franchising in the Fast Food Industry," *Quarterly Journal of Economics* 106 (February 1991): 75–101.

contract provides another reason: with no explicit standards for good-quality work, the boss can claim the employee did not perform as well as expected (but was nevertheless good enough to keep working at $15) or that the company's financial problems preclude giving the employee a raise, which might or might not be a lie. Employer opportunism has risks of its own—there are costs of replacing and training a new worker, and employees already on the job may make fewer efforts if management acquires a reputation for untrustworthiness. To further analyze the problem we next examine employment relationships that unfold over time.

Long-Term Employment

Wages and Productivity

Lifetime Paths All of the aforementioned difficulties in incomplete contracting and opportunism might lead you to a mistaken conclusion—that most employer-employee pairings are of short duration. In reality, long-term employment is common. In 1982, about 40 percent of workers over age 30 had jobs that would last 20 or more years. The changes that have pervaded the economy have hardly affected these figures. Just over half of men ending their careers in 1969 had been with a single employer for at least 20 years; the same was true in 2002.[19] Long-term workers tend to stay that way—once a person has 10 years' experience with the same employer, the probability of another 10 years exceeds 0.7. Women tend to have shorter tenures than men, but perhaps surprisingly blacks and whites enjoy equally durable employment relationships.[20]

Figure 15-8 shows the fundamental relationship that governs long-term employment.[21] Assume that an employee joins an employer at age 21, and both parties expect that the job will continue until he retires at age 65.[22] To simplify things, let's give them

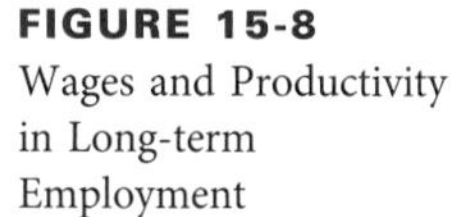
FIGURE 15-8
Wages and Productivity in Long-term Employment

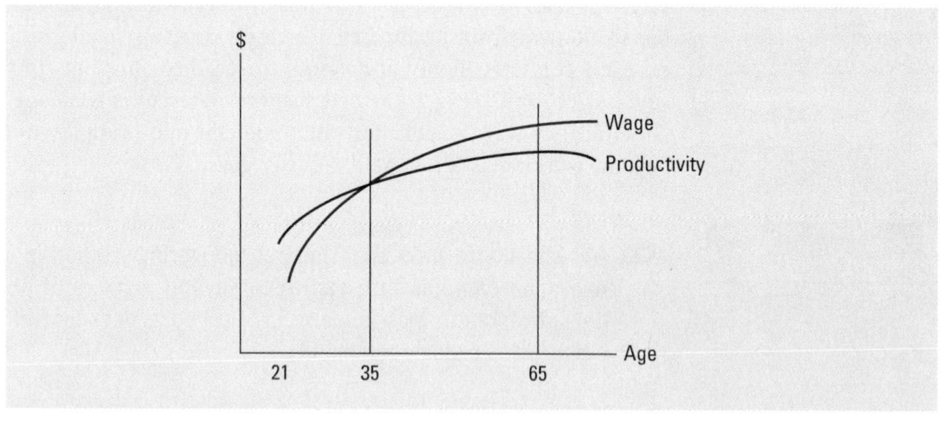

[19]Ann Huff Stevens, "The More Things Change, the More They Stay the Same: Trends in Long-term Employment in the United States, 1969-2002," National Bureau of Economic Research Working Paper, 11878, December 2005. http://papers.nber.org/papers/W11878. David Jaeger and Ann Huff Stevens, "Is Job Stability in the United States Falling?" *Journal of Labor Economics* 17 (October 1999, supplement): S1–S28.

[20]Robert E. Hall, "The Importance of Lifetime Jobs in the U.S. Economy," *American Economic Review* 72 (September 1982): 716–24. Changes in the methods of calculation alter some of these figures. See Manuelita Ureta, "The Importance of Lifetime Jobs in the U.S. Economy, Revisited," *American Economic Review* 82 (March 1992): 322–35.

[21]For data on these relationships see Katherine Abraham and Henry Farber, "Job Duration, Seniority, and Earnings," *American Economic Review* 77 (June 1987): 278–97.

[22]The employer's management may, of course, change over this period, but assume that any future management team will act to enforce the agreements made by their predecessors.

remarkable powers of prediction. First, they agree that the dollar value of the worker's productivity (value of marginal product per hour worked) will follow the curve shown in the diagram. Productivity increases as he gains experience on the job and comes to embody more firm-specific human capital. As he ages, firm-specific human capital increases more slowly, for many possible reasons. Aging makes it more difficult for most workers to adapt to new technologies, and past a certain age there may not be much firm-specific human capital left for him to absorb. Perhaps the job requires physical or mental skills that unavoidably deteriorate with age (heavy lifting or quick computations in your head), in which case productivity ultimately falls.

Figure 15-8 also shows the worker's hourly earnings over his life span. In our first model above the employer hired workers until the value of marginal product just equaled the market wage. This is a solution would occur in a spot market where a durable relationship produces few benefits to the parties. Here, however, there are costs of forming and ending the relationship, and both parties can gain from commitments (i.e., investments) specific to it. The relationship between the wage and productivity curves in Figure 15-8 shows an important aspect of the unwritten contract that governs long-term employment. As is typical in long-term job attachments, the worker's wage falls short of his productivity in the earlier years of employment but later rises above it.[23]

Characteristics of the Contract We must first explain the back-loading of wages in Figure 15-8—why they don't match productivity over the worker's years on the job, and why they exceed productivity only after some time has passed. Alongside the relationship between wages and productivity we need to explain why many employers require all workers to retire at a certain age, as shown by the vertical line at age 65. If mandatory retirement is illegal, employers can devise benefit packages that make retirement at that age a smart decision for the worker. Disregarding pensions, at age 65 both the worker's productivity to this employer and the employer's payments to her become zero. Why throw away a still-productive worker, particularly when replacing her requires the employer to bear the costs of finding and training her replacement?

The worker may prefer to act opportunistically (disregard employer opportunism for the moment) but still has no desire to bear the costs of searching for a new job if she is released after being caught loafing. The back-loading of wages means she will give up the premium pay that the relationship promises for her later years. To avoid these consequences she will attempt to avoid loafing during the early years or will loaf only if quite certain she will not be caught. The back-loading also induces effort during the later years of the worker's employment. As she approaches retirement age her wages are well above her actual productivity. Loafing during these years means losing high pay, and if she joins a new employer she will often start at lower pay. Her productivity for the new employer will be lower because she has little of that employer's firm-specific capital, and her remaining work years are too few to match the earnings she would have received by staying with the old employer.

The question is how long the later years can last. The employer and employee entered into an implicit contract when the worker was 21 years old. The employee understands the employer's retirement policy, and the employer can only break even if it terminates at a certain date.[24] For the worker in Figure 15-8 (and many others in the labor force), wages are at their highest level when she reaches retirement age. If so, she may wish to act

---

[23]Edward Lazear, "Why Is There Mandatory Retirement?",*Journal of Political Economy* 87 (December 1979): 1261–84.

[24]The calculation must use present values from the start of employment. See Lazear, "Why Is There Mandatory Retirement?"

opportunistically and attempt to continue working beyond the agreed-on date. The employer can resolve this problem (and avoid the appearance of discrimination) by announcing an ironclad policy—all workers retire at age 65, including those who could remain productive and valuable. Releasing the latter raises the employers' costs of replacement hires, but it saves costs associated with opportunism of workers seeking to extend their careers. Our model of long-term employment explains both back-loading of wages and mandatory retirement as methods of enforcing an unwritten contract. We next need to examine what might keep the employer from acting opportunistically.

Q. Give an example of a package arrangement that makes retirement at age 65 sufficiently attractive that most workers will voluntarily choose it. (Assume that you cannot let benefits shrink if the worker retires at a later age.)

Q. Does the logic of this section explain the common observation that workers released late in their careers will find it quite difficult to find work with new employers?

Employer Reputation and Enforcement A look at Figure 15-8 also suggests how the employer can profit from opportunism. If the employer's cost of investing in a new worker's firm-specific human capital is low, why not fire the employee just before his wage would go above his productivity? Hiring a replacement who mistakenly expects lifetime employment (and terminating him in the same way) could then raise profits. An employer who disappoints employee expectations in this way, however, can acquire a reputation as untrustworthy, which would disadvantage it in the competition for workers. New workers may be unwilling to start at low wages because they expect to be terminated early in their careers. Those currently employed will revise their estimates of the probability of dismissal upward, and possibly choose to exert less effort because the reward for it has become less certain.

There are, however, occasions when an employer known for long-term relationships will have good reason to fire a worker with seniority. Her productivity may have fallen for one of many possible reasons, or she may no longer follow orders as she once did. Other workers who see the event may not know whether it happened because the worker performed poorly or because the employer was opportunistic. If there is a risk that workers will misinterpret the firing of an unproductive worker, the firm's managers might incur costs to minimize the (groundless) loss of morale. Office floors in Japanese companies with reputations for long-term employment are often open, and executives do not have private offices. Executives work close to the center of the floor, where much important information originates and terminates, and subordinates are on the periphery. Instead of firing a poor performer some Japanese employers put his desk far away from the center, often near a window. Away from the action and with few responsibilities, this employee is one of the "window people," a living exhibit of employment security visible to the others.[25] Had he been fired his coworkers might have

[25]Joel Dreyfuss, "Fear and Trembling in the Colossus (Japan's Troubled Future)," *Fortune*, March 30, 1987, 32–42. Life at the window is often unpleasant. The person is sometimes given nothing to do and is not allowed to occupy himself with pastimes like games, or is given humiliating tasks (e.g., a man is asked to serve tea, which is normally a function for women).

misinterpreted his departure, and some employers find it important enough to maintain reputations that they will keep window people on the payroll. Similarly, IBM held to its no-layoffs policy for decades and reassigned workers whose productivity had ebbed to positions elsewhere in the company that carried little responsibility and few prospects for advancement.

Internal Labor Markets

Classifying Jobs and Setting Pay The wages of a worker in Figure 15-8 can increase with time spent in a given position, or with an upward move to a more responsible one. Promotions raise the question of why managements often restrict their searches to fill vacant positions to current employees, forgoing even a look at the many potential candidates outside the firm. A firm that limits its choices this way is said to utilize an *internal labor market.* We need to explain the sense of such a restriction, and how the appropriateness of an internal labor market depends on the position to be filled. Before doing so, however, we ask why large employers generally associate pay with positions rather than with a particular employee's performance.

Job positions and descriptions of their responsibilities are a relatively recent development. A small business in the nineteenth century might have employed a handful of people and assigned them to various tasks as was necessary—taking customers' money, sweeping the floor, helping unload a shipment of goods, and so on with no hierarchy or specialization among them. There is no good reason to give each of these persons a job title and no possible way to summarize their diverse responsibilities in a few words. Larger businesses, however, may formally limit the tasks to which specialist workers can be assigned and pay them in accordance with their responsibilities. A larger workforce has a wide range of specialized skills that are seldom easy to compare for purposes of setting pay. Market wages provide some guidance, but a long-term employment relationship also entails setting wages on the principles of Figure 15-8. It is equally hard to compare the productivities of individuals in a group that shares common skills or responsibilities, and if comparisons are made they often invite discontent and suspicions of employer favoritism. Finally, the firm's employees as a group (or at least those in a particular facility) are engaged in team production. All must supply effort if the team is to produce anything at all, and it is difficult or impossible to measure the contribution to output (marginal product) of any one team member. Job classifications and pay based on experience resolve some of these problems and allow management to avoid the difficult tasks of measuring and comparing the productivities of individual workers, while also giving experienced workers the higher wages they expect under their unwritten long-term employment contracts. Employers often give all workers in a certain job or skill category the same percentage increase in wages for the next year. Someone who performs adequately but never gets promoted to a new classification will still see the rising wages he expected when he signed on, and those with more seniority will earn more than those with less. Thus, a worker promoted to a more responsible position may find that some colleagues with lower-level job titles continue to earn more than she does.

Low-level Promotions An internal labor market facilitates comparisons between candidates for a promotion. Unlike outside applicants, their on-the-job conduct can be easily observed and their records are kept as part of ordinary company business. Other important information about an internal candidate would be hard to obtain for an external one—for instance, is he quick to take sensible action after an unexpected event occurs, and can he elicit effort from workers on his team. If several candidates look equivalent on paper, the experience of those currently in the higher position may improve the quality of the choice. The prime candidates for promotion to foreman may be workers currently in the department that the new foreman will supervise, and their recommendation will carry weight with whoever makes the final decision. Additionally, promotion from inside means the new foreman can hit the ground running because of firm-specific investments made during his prior years on the job.

Mid-level Promotions Information may be harder to process for higher-level promotions than for lower-level ones. Information about job performance and the characteristics of a good foreman is relatively objective, easily summarized, and readily available. Moving upward, the information becomes harder to evaluate, and those who choose the winner may not be certain what weights to place on the different bits of information that are available. Assume that a vacancy for plant manager has turned up and all of the prime candidates are currently foremen. The desirable skills and character traits of a plant manager are not always those of a good foreman. Instead of motivating and coordinating a small group of lower-level workers, the manager must coordinate the activities of a number of teams with very different responsibilities. Larger and more diverse responsibilities mean that she must know which work to delegate and who should perform which particular tasks. At the same time she must have the ingenuity and self-confidence to do things her subordinates cannot, like working around a major equipment breakdown or a supplier's failure to deliver. Looking upward in the organization she will be valued for the content and insight of her reports to higher management. Their limited information processing capabilities will be better used if she knows what *not* to burden them with. No one can foretell what tasks may come to matter. She might need to make friends with local officials to help dampen citizen concerns about traffic around the plant, and sometimes it really helps to discuss the matter during a round of golf with the mayor.

All candidates would like to convey information to the decision makers that make them appear more desirable than their competitors, and to conceal information that suggests the opposite. Candidate A may have good reason to tell them things about Candidate B that they do not know—that B often goes by the book when faced with situations where it would be better to act more creatively (which can also be risky), or that B has a drinking problem. Management must now consider ambiguous and possibly incorrect information rather than the more objective data that helped them choose the next foreman. Recipients of this information have good reason to question it, but they often also have few reasons to completely disregard it. Workplace politics can convey facts that help improve the choice. Part of the decision maker's skill is in deciding which of that information to take seriously.

Q. Do you expect that information gleaned through office politics will be more important in determining who will head the company's research lab or who will be in charge of its Washington lobbying office? Why?

High-level Vacancies Now assume that there is a vacancy in a position such as chief executive officer or chief financial officer. The board of directors' decision to use the internal labor market may not be a sound one, particularly if the vacancy arose because the last holder of the position was fired. There are, however, also some good reasons to search internally. Candidates with company experience have more knowledge of the its operations and the personalities involved. An insider who is promoted may make better-quality decisions because he is able to use factual knowledge and call upon a network of individual relationships accumulated over the years. These facts may also be reasons to fill the vacancy with an outsider. For example, the inside candidate may have spent much of his career building up a division that objective experts would agree should be closed or sold off because market conditions for its product have changed. The insider will understandably have sentimental attachments to this division and personal friends working there. These could get in the way of a decision that must be made if the firm is to free up resources for investments that will make it a better competitor in its other lines of business.

At the highest levels of decision making, current employees of the firm will require knowledge beyond that generated over years of employment. To make smart decisions the person will need to understand the markets the firm operates in and its competitors' strategies. This person's knowledge of the environment beyond the market, for example, contacts with government officials, may also have an important bearing on her firm's fortunes. In addition to knowledge about the world outside the company's doors, an ability to think abstractly might be important. A manager who knows general principles of corporate strategy (recall Lou Gerstner and IBM from the start of this chapter) may be able to make a firm more competitive whatever its actual line of business. Officers are more likely to come from outside than lower-level managers, and firms whose performance has been substandard are more likely to hire outsiders.[26]

Q. Do you expect that a firm is more likely to use an internal labor market to choose its next chief information officer or its next chief financial officer. Why?

Pay and Incentives

Designing Compensation Plans

Chapter 9 showed how pay arrangements can help align the incentives of principals and agents. A plaintiff with a once-in-a-lifetime lawsuit can elicit effort from her attorney using a contingency arrangement that awards the attorney a percentage of the amount won in court or settled, and nothing if the case is lost. A frequently sued defendant has experience that helps him to judge the efforts of his attorneys and understand the role of random events in determining the outcomes of cases. A defendant familiar with litigation will probably prefer to use lawyers who bill by the hour (or possibly employees). Our job now is to determine some more general principles of pay design in light of what we have learned about employment relationships.

Piece Rates The apparel industry includes many small firms that assemble garments from pre-cut pieces of fabric. A sewing machine operator assembles a single piece (e.g., a shirt) from start to finish and receives a predetermined amount for completing it. Piece rates are relatively rare in the economy, and their existence in this industry reflects certain characteristics of the assembly job and the work environment. First, it is easy to count the number of garments a worker completes and check their quality. Second, the job does not involve team production—an operator's effort translates directly into her own output. No worker's output depends on the efforts of other workers, and effort by one worker does not generate benefits for the others. Third, the worker's output is within

[26]Kevin Murphy and Jerold Zimmerman, "Financial Performance and CEO Turnover," *Journal of Accounting and Economics* 16 (January 1993): 273–315.

her control and is little influenced by random events, so she can count on a strong link between effort and pay. If a sewing machine malfunctions there are spares on hand, and uncontrollable incidents like power outages are rare.

Capitation payments by insurers to physicians are in some ways equivalent to piecework. They are fixed amounts for standard procedures like electrocardiograms or simple operations like a tonsillectomy. Capitation reduces the risk of opportunism relative to hourly pay if the insurer is unable to see the actual time a doctor spends on a procedure. An insurer can, however, observe a sample of actual cases and estimate the average time spent by the physician and the value of other resources needed. It is often easy to see the quality of the work that was done (e.g., the patient's tonsils are gone and there were no postoperative problems.) A physician sets the speed at which he will work, and for many procedures he will only rarely encounter time-consuming complications. Capitation does not perfectly align the incentives of doctor, patient, and insurer, however. A doctor may hesitate to treat unexpected complications that accompany a normally simple operation if he doubts he can recover the added costs. At the other extreme, a doctor might attempt to cut corners when performing simple procedures under capitation if he can save money increasing the patient's risk by a small amount.

Q. Most specialized construction workers (e.g., bricklayers, plumbers) are paid hourly wages, but a few sometimes receive piecework pay. Identify some specialties that might be paid on piecework and explain why. (Hint: Think about randomness in the work environment and storability of the output.)

Q. Health insurance plans that cover psychiatric counseling generally pay the doctor on the basis of hours spent with a patient rather than by capitation. Why? Does your answer also explain why insurers usually put a ceiling on the number of hours of psychiatric care they will cover?

Hourly Pay Unlike doctors and garment assemblers, most workers are on teams whose members must cooperate and work as a group. As happened with the barge haulers, team production makes an individual worker's productivity hard to observe because extra effort by a single worker will usually have little effect on the team's output. Workers on teams may have little choice about their effort levels, for example, if they are on an assembly line whose speed sets the pace for all of the workers.[27] Failure of equipment used by the team can occur at random and lower its output. Randomness can upset the expectations of risk-averse workers and weaken the correlation between effort and output. If so we would expect to see the pay of a team's members depend on the actual hours the group is present in the workplace, as opposed to piecework pay that allows random events to determine a member's income. Team members must work together, their output as a group is measurable, and it increases with the team's hours on the

[27]A worker on this line can, however, choose to be more careless, in which case the team produces more defective units. Specialization of tasks can make it easier for the boss to identify who was responsible for the problem.

job. A member working apart (e.g., after the others go home) is unlikely to add much to team output, so there is no reason to pay that worker for the extra time.

Hourly pay gives the worker a fixed amount regardless of the task assigned. Not having to repeatedly negotiate pay lowers the cost of moving workers between tasks. Little is likely to be lost on either side because it is generally hard to measure the value created by a particular worker in a particular task. If similarly difficult tasks carried different wages, workers' incomes would depend on reassignments beyond their control. These reassignments might themselves become objects of competition. If two equally attractive tasks carry different wages, workers will compete among themselves for the higher-paying one, and if they pay the same the workers will compete for the more pleasant one. These competitions eat up worker time at the sacrifice of total output; in other words, they create deadweight losses that are known as *influence costs.* If many employees can perform a task equally well the employer can reduce influence costs by setting rules that objectively determine who will get which assignments. Airline flight attendants get more desirable routes and working conditions (e.g., first class instead of coach) by seniority. A casino worker can deal cards equally well at high-stakes and low-stakes tables, but high-stakes players usually offer significantly higher tips. Management eliminates the competition to work at high-stakes tables by requiring workers to pool their tips and share them equally.

Q. At many universities three-hour classes that meet one night a week are often assigned to junior and part-time faculty. In schools that operate for profit, members of the night faculty are as likely as members of the day faculty to be full-time workers. Why the difference?

Fixed Salaries Lower-level team members receive hourly wages, but their supervisors are often on salaries that pay a fixed amount each month, independent of the hours they work. In part the difference is due to observability. The worker team often operates as a unit, in which it is easy to verify that a person is present and is making at least minimal effort. It is harder to enumerate a supervisor's responsibilities and measure his efforts. He is the go-to person for almost any problem that affects the workers' team—an unexpected accident, a malfunctioning machine, a rush order requiring extra hours, or a problem due to incompetence elsewhere in the company. There may be no one over the supervisor to accurately monitor his efforts in a real-time crisis. There are few expectations about the time he should spend making these efforts, and a person on hourly pay would have reasons to overstate them (if his effort cannot be observed) or exaggerate the complexity of the problem (if effort can be observed). The variety of a supervisor's possible tasks means he can only be evaluated over a longer period, in which he will succeed at some tasks and fail at others. The difficulty of inferring the supervisor's true competence from a short work record helps explain why rewards for superior performance usually come only with delays. Simply being a supervisor usually indicates that a person is on a long-term career path, and he will be motivated to make effort today for bonuses, promotions, and higher pay that he may not receive for some time to come.

Q. Why do wage workers receive time-and-a-half pay for overtime, but their salaried supervisors do not even get hourly pay for overtime. (Disregard the fact that some U.S. laws require premium pay for overtime hours. An overtime premium was common prior to enactment of these laws.)

TABLE 15-2 THE POSSIBLE INEFFICIENCY OF SHARE PAYMENTS

WEEKS WORKED	TOTAL CROP	VALUE AT $1/BUSHEL	VMP*	MARGINAL COST	PROFIT TOTAL	0.5 × VMP	FARMER PROFIT
1	100	$100	$100	$27	$73	$50	$23
2	190	190	$90	27	136	45	41
3	270	270	80	27	189	40	54
4	340	340	70	27	232	35	62
5	400	400	60	27	265	30	65
6	450	450	50	27	288	25	63
7	490	490	40	27	301	20	56
8	520	520	30	27	304	15	44
9	540	540	20	27	297	10	27
10	550	550	10	27	269	5	5
11	550	550	0	27	242	0	−22

*VMP = value of marginal product.

Shares and Commissions The contingency-fee arrangement for paying the plaintiff's lawyer in Chapter 10 exemplifies a common payment mechanism called a *share contract.* Salespeople on commission operate under share contracts, and sharecropping is a common mode of farming around the world. A sharecropper contracts with a landowner (who may supply other inputs, like seeds and fertilizer) to grow a crop on her land. The sharecropper gets a fixed percentage of the crop (quite commonly half) to sell in the market. The ubiquity of sharecropping seems hard to explain, because it is easy to show that other agreements would create additional economic value for the farmer and landlord to share.

Table 15-2 uses the short-run production model from Chapter 4 to analyze the sharecropper farmer's effort decision. As usual, extra weeks of work raise the farmer's output, but at a decreasing rate because land is fixed. If the crop sells for $1 a bushel, Column 4 shows the value of the farmer's marginal product (VMP). The farmer's marginal cost (outside wages forgone or value of leisure time) is $27 per week. If the farmer owned the land, he would work the 8 weeks for which VMP exceeds marginal cost and realize a profit of $304. But if he shares 50 percent of his crop with the landlord he stops working after five weeks, leaving both of them worse off with only $265 of profit to share instead of the $304 available after eight weeks of work. Sharecropping appears to leave money on the table that both parties could have enjoyed.[28] Likewise, the contingency percentage discussed in Chapter 10 does not fully align the incentives of the plaintiff and the attorney. An attorney who gets a 33 percent contingency loses 67 percent of the revenue that will result from an extra hour of work. For these percentages, the attorney will only work those hours that increase the client's expected recovery by three times the attorney's opportunity cost.

Let's consider four arrangements that make both the farmer and the landlord better off than sharecropping:

1. To induce the farmer to work weeks 6, 7, and 8, change the share he receives for each of them. A 60 percent share will induce work the sixth week, but the seventh will require a higher share and the eighth a still higher one.

[28]Remember that the value of the farmer's leisure time or alternative wage is already accounted for in the profit calculation.

2. The landlord might agree to pay the farmer a wage of $27 or more per hour that covers his opportunity cost. The farmer is no worse off than in his next-best employment, and the landlord gets every bushel of crop that covers the opportunity cost of obtaining it.
3. The farmer pays a market-determined lump sum to the landlord before starting production (or somehow finances it to postpone payment until harvest time). He then works all of the eight weeks in which VMP exceeds his opportunity cost.
4. The farmer purchases the land from the landlord and operates it as an independent business.

Q. In Option 1, what are the minimum shares required to induce the farmer to work the seventh and eighth weeks?

Q. In Option 3, what is the maximum the farmer would pay to use the land for one year?

Sharecropping can be economically efficient if the landlord can monitor the farmer's effort. In Table 15-2, eight weeks of work by the farmer produces a $520 crop, leaving the pair with $304 net of opportunity cost. The landlord can get eight weeks of work from the farmer by making an all-or-nothing offer—$152 (half of the $304 profit) along with recovery of his $216 opportunity cost if he works eight weeks and no recovery if he works fewer. The all-or-nothing contract, however, only works if the landlord can monitor the farmer's efforts over weeks 6 through 8, because otherwise the farmer has little incentive to make those efforts. Raising the farmer's share above 50 percent in weeks 6, 7, and 8 will have the same effect, but it will be difficult to set the values of these shares beforehand. The landlord may not accurately know how weeks of work translate to output, and random events (extremely low or high rainfall) can change that relationship. Randomness can also confound the all-or-nothing offer. In reality, landlords or their agents actively monitor most sharecroppers, and they sometimes have the power to renegotiate inefficient contract terms.[29] Likewise, a sliding contingency percentage will be hard to set because it is hard for the plaintiff to know the lawyer's actual opportunity cost and to predict what will happen to the likely winnings if the lawyer works an extra hour.

In the sharecropping example, if monitoring is costly Option 2 begins to look more reasonable, and indeed many farm workers are paid by the hour. Hourly pay, however, also entails monitoring because the farmer can overstate his hours or exaggerate his claimed efforts. A fixed wage also reallocates risk. The landlord offers the farmer a sure income (below the expected value of the risky crop) but no extra payment if the market price of the crop is high. The wage, however, also eliminates the farmer's risk of starvation. Contracting problems may explain why Option 3, fixed prepayment to the landlord, is rare. Farmers who live from crop to crop and do not own land that they can use as collateral will have difficulty obtaining loans on reasonable terms that may (or may not) be paid off at the next harvest. Option 4, of course, turns the farmer into the residual claimant (owner) of his own farm.

---

[29]Keijiro Otsuka and Yujiro Hayami, "Theories of Share Tenancy: A Critical Survey," *Economic Development and Cultural Change,* 37 (Oct. 1988), 31–68.

There are other ways to elicit effort in the face of risk aversion. Many salespeople get low base salaries they can survive on when times are bad, along with a percentage commission on each dollar of sales (possibly over some minimum amount). The salesperson and sales manager share the same observability problems as the farmer and landlord. The manager cannot shadow the salesperson on workdays, and even if possible, the manager may not observe her level of effort, which includes choosing prospects to be called on. Sales to a particular customer have a random element, but sales effort raises their expected value. Unlike the absentee landlord, sales managers can compare performance of, say, salespeople in nearby territories, but random events can still confound such comparisons.

Q. Identify some factors that will determine whether the salesperson gets a relatively high base pay and a relatively low commission, or vice versa? Do you know of any data that would allow you to test your explanations?

Tips Restaurant servers, taxicab drivers, bartenders, and a few others earn much of their incomes in the form of tips or gratuities from customers they serve. Most customers leave tips, but the amounts actually given vary greatly. Recipients usually work for businesses whose reputations depend on the quality of their service. A server can influence his tip by offering superior service or by encouraging the customer to spend more. (Most tipping recommendations specify a percentage of the total bill.) Tips resolve a combination of monitoring and incentive problems. The owner of an expensive restaurant has many responsibilities and cannot monitor all the servers in real time. Evaluating performance often requires the observation of subtle differences that the owner may not spot—for example, a good server seems to sense when customers want to place their orders and can quickly spot glasses that need refills. Tipping rewards the conscientious server for activities that increase the restaurant's goodwill but are likely to go unseen by the owner. This reasoning also explains why tipping is virtually absent from fast-food outlets, where customer service is highly standardized and other measures of performance (e.g., the time between order placement and delivery) are easy for managers to make and to compare with other franchise outlets.

Executive Compensation In Chapter 12 we examined principal/agent problems between shareholders and the top managements of publicly traded corporations. We saw transactions in the market for corporate control, like mergers and takeovers, that put existing assets under new management, but these are often costly or drastic and may not succeed. Large shareholders can influence boards of directors, but their roles in corporate governance are limited. A tender offer or proxy fight to replace directors is costly to wage, and the results are uncertain. A board can defend itself by seeking a rival acquirer, instituting poison pills that raise the costs of a takeover, or taking advantage of laws that facilitate resistance, among other strategies. The costs and uncertainties of using the market for corporate control make it important to build incentives into executive pay packages that can reduce principal/agent problems by better aligning the incentives of shareholders and managers.[30]

Both shareholders and managers will likely be risk-averse, but their abilities to control income risk generally differ. Most shareholders can match their risk exposures to their

[30]In Chapter 12 we considered the role of high severance pay as an inducement to managers not to resist an acquisition or takeover of their corporation.

preferences by diversifying among stocks and between stocks and other investments. An executive may have more limited opportunities because a large percentage of her income originates with the assets she manages. Losing a large fixed salary will be painful, perhaps enough so that a risk-averse executive will be reluctant to make risky decisions that diversified shareholders would want her to make. Resolving the principal/agent problem might then require a combination of a large fixed element of pay and another element that depends on the company's performance.

Performance-related pay can reward improvements in such measures of company performance as earnings relative to its own past or relative to others in its industry. Measures of performance should be within the control of executives, however. For example, normal growth in earnings should not be rewarded if the entire economy is prospering. The same holds for higher earnings that result from events over which the executive has no control, such as a fall in the world market price of oil. Likewise, earnings decreases should not be punished if their sources are beyond the company's control. A performance measure should also be resistant to manipulation by the people being rewarded for it. An executive's compensation might increase with the company's revenue from customers, but not with revenue from the sale of corporate assets when divestiture is not in the interests of shareholders.

Q. On some occasions it is in the shareholders' interest for management to divest some of a corporation's assets. How can a pay package be designed to reward only warranted divestitures?

Common alternatives to performance-based pay (sometimes used alongside it) are based on the market performance of the company's stock. One common form is the granting options to buy the company's stock in the future, usually at or below today's market value. An option usually vests (becomes exercisable) at some predetermined time, at which the executive can buy the stock and either hold it or resell it if the market price has risen.[31] As vehicles for performance-related rewards, options are less than perfect. Some famous corporate downfalls (e.g., WorldCom, Enron) are said to have resulted from risky executive decisions that would raise the values of options that they held. Before the rules changed in 2004, options made corporate accounting less transparent because they usually did not show up on financial statements as expenses. It is also possible that options produce low-powered incentives. The influence of a given executive on the value of her company's stock is hard or impossible to estimate, but even if that person's decisions caused an increase it would also benefit all of the other shareholders. Finally, once an option has been exercised and the executive has sold her shares it will have no continuing effect on her incentives to make better future decisions.[32]

A more recent line of research says that principal/agent problems are even more complex than described here. These complications may explain why some executive pay appears excessive and why rewards are often given for mediocre performance.[33] Law professors Lucien Arye Bebchuk of Harvard and Jesse Fried of the University of

---

[31]Even with a discounted price an option on a poorly performing stock can become worthless, in which case it is said to be "underwater."

[32]Brian Hall and Kevin Murphy, "The Trouble with Stock Options," *Journal of Economic Perspectives* 17 (Summer 2003): 49–70.

[33]Lucian Arye Bebchuk and Jesse Fried, "Executive Compensation as an Agency Problem," *Journal of Economic Perspectives* 17 (Summer 2003): 71–92.

California, Berkeley argue that shareholder election of corporate directors does not necessarily imply that they act faithfully in the shareholders' interest. Outside directors value reappointment (in which CEOs have an important say) because they typically earn high pay for the little time they spend preparing for and attending meetings.[34] If so, a director who wishes to retain his seat may approve a CEO's desired pay package, even if the amount exceeds what shareholders want and the incentives in it are weak. By the same reasoning, compensation packages can include attractive severance provisions for departing executives (including forgiveness of loans from the corporation), even if the executive is leaving because of poor performance. Other scholars have argued that seemingly excessive executive pay is actually determined in large part by market conditions, and that existing packages contain adequate incentives to align executive behavior with shareholder desires.[35]

Chapter Summary

- Employment is a complex relationship governed in part by markets, in part by contracts (generally unwritten), and in part by hierarchies.
- Labor markets are in some ways like those for other productive inputs. Like any other supplier of an input, a worker's desired hours are determined by comparing compensation with opportunity costs, which can be wages in another job or the value of the worker's leisure time.
- An employer's demand for labor depends on its productivity and on the price of its output. In the short run (i.e., with other inputs fixed), the employer's demand curve slopes downward.
- Equilibrium in a labor market occurs at the wage where demand equals supply. As in other markets, equilibrium has predictive content—a shortage or surplus generates pressures to move toward a new equilibrium.
- Both sides of a labor market usually face high information costs. An employer may reject an eligible candidate if it expects that additional search will soon bring a better match, and a worker may refuse an otherwise acceptable job offer for the same reason.
- Durable employment relationships are valuable to both employers and employees, because initiating or ending them entails costs. The employer must replace the worker, the employee must find a new position, and the employer must incur the costs of investing in the new worker's firm-specific human capital.
- Only seldom do detailed written contracts fully specify the obligations of both employer and employee. Usually the range of possible worker tasks is too large to put in writing, the worker's value in different tasks is hard to determine, and changes in markets and technologies will change the list of possible tasks.
- These contracting problems give both the employer and the employee potential incentives to act opportunistically, because each knows it will cost the other to form a

[34]Average director compensation in the 200 largest U.S. corporations was $152,626 in 2001. Enron's were paid $380,000 annually. See Bebchuk and Fried, "Executive Compensation," 73.

[35]John Core, Wayne Guay, and Randall Thomas, "Is U.S. CEO Compensation Inefficient Pay Without Performance?" *Michigan Law Review* 113, no. 6 (2005): 1142–85.

new relationship that replaces their current one. In reality, however, employment often lasts for decades. Although unwritten, an employment contract can be enforced by the employer's reputation.

- In long-term employment wages are frequently back-loaded, below the worker's productivity in the early years and above it in later ones. Back-loading induces effort in both the early years (because of the promise of higher wages later) and in the later ones (because the cost of worker opportunism is higher). It is often seen in combination with mandatory retirement.
- In a firm where team production prevails and employer-specific human capital is important, the classification of workers into job slots reduces the costs of evaluating productivity and adjusting pay. Such a firm may choose to promote persons through an internal labor market rather than considering outside candidates.
- Promotions in an internal labor market are made using both objective performance measures and subjective personal information. If knowledge of matters external to the firm and an ability to analyze internal situations objectively are both valuable, an executive position might best be filled by an outsider.
- Pay comes in forms that include piecework; hourly wages; monthly salaries; various forms of sharing, commissions, and tips; and compensation based on company performance. The efficient form depends on such details as the measurability of output, the importance of team production, the impact of random events on productivity, and the observability of effort.
- Executive compensation often takes the form of fixed base pay combined with pay that is sensitive to organizational performance. Such a package can diminish the principal/agent problem between shareholders and executives by inducing executives to take risky decisions in the interests of diversified shareholders that they would not otherwise have made.

Questions and Problems

1. If VMP is downward-sloping, marginal cost must slope upward. Explain why verbally, and then try it mathematically.
2. How does your analysis of VMP change if the employer is a monopolist producer of its output but a price-taker in the labor market?
3. Most illegal immigrants to the United States are unskilled workers. Use diagrams of labor supply and demand to explain why unskilled U.S. citizens will view their arrival with alarm but relatively skilled ones will either favor it or show little concern.
4. What happens to the employment decision if an employer is a price-taker in the market for its output but faces an upward-sloping supply curve of labor, that is, it can only hire additional workers if it raises the wages to its entire workforce? (Such an employer is known as a *monopsonist.)*
5. Use present-value arguments to show why you should usually invest in general human capital in your early years.
6. Under the U.S. Social Security system, workers must contribute 6.2 percent of their wages (up to a maximum you can disregard here) and employers must also contribute 6.2 percent. Using the supply and demand for labor in the entire economy, show that if the demand for labor is relatively elastic and the supply is

relatively inelastic then workers pay relatively more than their stated 6.2 percent, and if the elasticities are reversed their employers do so.

7. Most elementary and high school teachers have been women, both in the past and present. What sorts of changes in their labor market might explain the declines in student achievement and test scores that have been observed over the past 40 years?
8. An MBA degree increases the general human capital of its holder. My university has both day and night MBA curricula. Students in the day program almost always pay their own fees Those in the night program are typically older and work full time during the day, and their employers sometimes pay their fees. Payment by employers appears to be inconsistent with our reasoning about why students are more likely to pay for their general human capital. When might it be rational for an employer to pay? Why for night students?
9. Labor markets are "matching markets," in which prospective employees are ultimately matched with job vacancies, and the quality of the match has a large impact on its productivity.
   a. Economists and sociologists interested in family behavior now often speak of a "marriage market," in which prospective partners attempt to display their desirability and make matches on the basis of an information search. In what ways does a marriage market resemble a labor market, and in what ways does it not?
   b. Some marriage markets actually involve cash payments (i.e., dowries) from one partner's (usually the woman's) family to the other's. What might be the economic function of dowries? Could they be like insurance policies or performance bonds? (Check the discussion of engagement rings in Chapter 10.)
   c. We can also think of a market for admissions to selective colleges. Why don't such colleges simply sell space to the highest bidders? (Wrong answer: because only the wealthy will attend. Why is it wrong?)
   d. In the past 20 years, many colleges have chosen to use a standardized common application form that includes the same questions, essays, and so on. When might a common application improve the quality of matches? When might it lower that quality?
10. In the 1930s the movie industry operated under a studio system, in which a performer signed with a single studio for some period and promised to appear in a certain number of movies. What might have led to the decline of the studio system and its replacement by today's star system, in which actors are signed to appear in single movies rather than being attached to a single studio for multiple movies?
11. As noted earlier in this chapter, IBM fell on hard times during the 1980s and ultimately abandoned its no-layoffs policy in the 1990s, while also taking other cost-cutting initiatives. Its "Hundred Percent Club," however, remained in existence to reward superior salespeople with luxurious vacations that also included some company business. Consultants suggested that IBM could save millions by eliminating the practice, but IBM's management refused to do so.
   a. If you ran IBM how would you explain to shareholders why you chose to retain the Hundred Percent Club?
   b. Under what circumstances might you choose to reduce or eliminate it?
12. There are a handful of employee-owned firms in the United States. In them, committees of workers make decisions that professional managers would normally make (e.g., which markets to enter, how to price products, when to build a new plant). Workers on the committees also determine the pay of their coworkers and how to split profits among themselves. In light of this chapter's discussions of teams and compensation, give several reasons why you would not expect to see employee-owned firms surviving.

a. Perhaps the most important worker-governed firms in the United States are several lumber companies in the Pacific Northwest that have been in operation since early in the twentieth century. Oddly, recent economic research has shown that their workers are actually more productive than workers in comparable lumber firms that operate for profit. Before you look at the source in the footnote, imagine some reasons why this unexpected outcome might happen.[36]

13. Farm laborers in the United States are sometimes paid by piecework, for example, a fixed amount for each basket of fruit that they pick from an orchard. Looking at the shirt assembly example, explain the similarities and differences that might lead you to expect this type of payment. Why do you expect that piecework pay will be more common in orchards than in poultry farms or dairies?

14. Explain why the incentives of a share agreement might lead a landlord to buy high-quality seeds and fertilizer for the farmer rather than leaving the decision about their use in the farmer's hands.

15. Research on how supervisors rate employees who work under them has found that in some firms as many as 95 percent of all ratings are "good" or "outstanding."

a. Is this necessarily evidence that supervisors are loafing to avoid the effort of making finer determinations of performance?

b. As an executive would you necessarily prefer a ranking system that required you to call no more than 20 percent of your subordinates outstanding and no less than 10 percent of them poor? (Assume that you are trying to maximize shareholder value.)

c. Do you expect that supervisors in government agencies will rate relatively more of their workers highly than supervisors in otherwise similar for-profit businesses? Why or why not?

16. ABC Company pays members of its sales force commissions based on their dollar volumes, but XYZ Company pays its salespeople fixed monthly salaries. What characteristics of the company, its market, or the product it produces might make monthly salaries a good choice for XYZ but a poor choice for ABC?

17. QRS Company pays its executives a higher annual fixed base pay than TUV Company, but TUV makes a higher amount of its executives' compensation dependent on the performance of its stock. Assuming that their executives have the same attitudes toward risk, what differences between the companies, their markets, and their products might make a relatively higher base pay the right strategy for QRS, and relatively more performance-based compensation the right strategy for TUV?

18. The directors of Ace Airlines have decided to incentivize their 1,000 employees by issuing every one of them 200 shares of stock. (Assume there is no problem of equity dilution, because the company has 40 million shares outstanding.) Under what circumstances might you expect this program to produce better employee performance?

19. Most restaurant customers tip according to a percentage rule—between 15 and 25 percent of the bill. Diners who have dinner and a $20 bottle of wine usually pay the same percentage of the bottle price as diners who order a $100 bottle. Why, when the same efforts must be made to uncork and pour both bottles?

---

[36]Ben Craig and John Pencavel, "The Behavior of Worker Cooperatives: The Plywood Companies of the Pacific Northwest," *American Economic Review* 82 (December 1992): 1083–1105.

Chapter 16

Time, Risk, and Options

Introduction

Time and Risk

The image below will be familiar to anyone who has recently shopped for a major appliance. Figure 16-1 is an "Energy Guide," required by law on all new refrigerators, water heaters, dryers, and other appliances that consume large amounts of power. It is attached to a refrigerator whose list price at Sears is $979. According to the sticker this model will

FIGURE 16-1

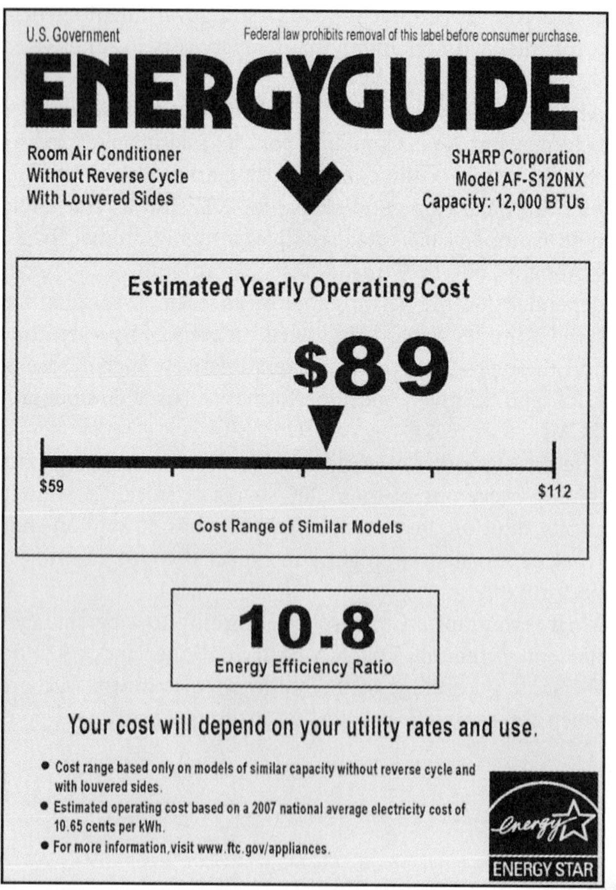

U.S. Government
Federal law prohibits removal of this label before consumer purchase.
ENERGYGUIDE
Room Air Conditioner
Without Reverse Cycle
With Louvered Sides
SHARP Corporation
Model AF-S120NX
Capacity: 12,000 BTUs
Estimated Yearly Operating Cost
$89
$59
$112
Cost Range of Similar Models
10.8
Energy Efficiency Ratio
Your cost will depend on your utility rates and use.
• Cost range based only on models of similar capacity without reverse cycle and with louvered sides.
• Estimated operating cost based on a 2007 national average electricity cost of 10.65 cents per kWh.
• For more information, visit www.ftc.gov/appliances.
ENERGY STAR

use $45 of electricity per year at today's average national price of $10.6 cents per kilowatt-hour. Sears sells another model (Energy Guide not shown) that retails for $849 and consumes $65 of power a year. Assuming their lifespans are the same, which should you buy to minimize the cost of keeping your food cool? The answer depends on your alternatives – we will soon see that if you can earn a high enough return on the funds you save, you should choose the less expensive model that consumes more power over its lifetime. (This need not require that you actually bank the money.) Understanding why requires that we introduce markets for borrowing and lending. The refrigerator comparison suggests other problems that might emerge as time passes. If you know that the cheaper model is more likely to break down (and there is no warranty), is there a risk of breakdown high enough to induce you to buy the more expensive one? In this chapter we model choices like the one between the refrigerators.

There may be more proverbs and sayings about time than any other single topic. Think about "time is money," "no time like the present," "time will tell," "can't turn back time," and "living on borrowed time." They reflect the many different roles time plays in our lives and our economic decisions. Some popular sayings are simply untrue, like "time heals all wounds." Others sound about right but aren't. "Never put off until tomorrow what you can do today" misses on two counts. First, you already know that it disregards the opportunity cost of allocating today's limited hours among different valuable activities. Less obviously, it neglects the benefits of being able to postpone a choice. You might, for example, commit yourself today to building a plant whose costs cannot be recovered if you abandon the project. Perhaps if you wait you will be able to obtain currently unavailable information about the prospects for success, such as future market conditions for your product or future costs of inputs required to make it. If that information is discouraging the delay means you still have an option not to undertake the project. You might be willing to pay a lot for the right to wait, and in this chapter you will learn how to calculate the amount.

For all of time's importance in our lives we have thus far paid remarkably little attention to it. Sometimes we neglected it as being an unnecessary complication. Of course it takes time for a business to acquire inputs, produce something, and then wait for payment. To see the logic of profit maximization more clearly, it helped to it to assume that time did not exist so that we could concentrate on the inputs and outputs themselves. Likewise to see the benefits of trade between two persons we did not have to include any details about borrowing or credit. Elsewhere we treated time as a learning aid rather than an actual duration. "Short run" and "long run" are handy ways to distinguish sets of inputs that a business may vary rather than statements about the passage of time on a calendar. In this chapter we add time and chance to our models:

- People have positive rates of time preference, the premium they place on earlier availability of goods. Persons with different rates of time preference will be able to arrange mutually beneficial lending transactions between themselves.
- Interest is the price premium (in percentage terms) a borrower pays for early availability and the reward to the lender for delaying consumption.
- The choice of an investment from a set of alternatives requires the calculation of present values that account for the opportunity costs of capital.
- Interest rates on loans will adjust to reflect expectations about inflation and considerations about the riskiness of individual borrowers.
- After learning or reviewing some basics of probability theory, we examine behavior in risky situations and show how to define and categorize peoples' attitudes toward risk.

- Markets will price investments so that those with higher risk will carry higher expected returns. Knowing this, we next show how to graphically portray an investor's attitudes toward risk, and how to determine which portfolios (mixes of investments) she prefers to alternatives.
- Having described investors' preferences we examine the portfolio choices the financial markets offer them and how the diversification investments reduces risk.
- Information is valuable because it helps to improve the confidence with which we can assess probabilities. The question of how much information to acquire before a decision depends on the costs of obtaining it and the benefits of reduced uncertainty.
- As people acquire information they update their prior beliefs about the probability of an event to account for the new information. This process, known as "Bayesian reasoning," allows us to compare the value of additional information with the cost of obtaining it.
- It is often worthwhile to postpone decisions until some relevant information materializes. Having that information reduces the zone of uncertainty reduces the likelihood of an incorrect decision relative to not delaying it. We will learn how to calculate these option values.
- We introduce financial options that give us rights but not obligations to buy something at a fixed price (i.e., call options) or sell it (i.e., put options). These have numerous applications in risk management, and economists have learned how to calculate their competitive market prices.
- We also analyze "real options" that show the value of postponing irreversible decisions, and how to calculate their values in situations that range from construction to lawsuits.

Borrowing and Lending

Positive Time Preference

Most humans have an innate preference for the present over the future. Offered the choice between a good that is available now and an identical amount of it at some future date almost everyone prefers immediate availability. You will voluntarily delay consuming it only if you are compensated for doing so. Your *positive time preference* is generally rational. Giving up something today in return for the same future amount loses you either the enjoyment of consuming it sooner or the income from investing its value in, for example, a loan to someone else. You might also, of course, not be around or able to enjoy it at the future date. People differ in their valuations of the present relative to the future. For ordinary goods, your valuation of A is the most you would pay for it over your next best alternative. Borrowing and lending are exchanges between the present and the future that people evaluate according to the same principles.

Let's begin with a loan to change your time pattern of consumption. Assume that you are fresh out of college and have a firm promise of a high-income job that starts next year. You understandably want to improve your standard of living today. Most loans are made in money, but to make things really clear assume that we are actually transacting the good that we will consume. You are willing to pay a premium in the future to have a six-pack of some beverage (actually, beer) in your hands today. You can of course buy it by forgoing some other use of today's income, but you also might try borrowing it. Consider me as a possible lender. I currently earn a high income, but I am near the end of my working years. Disregarding Social Security and pensions, during retirement I must live on income from previous investments. One such investment is to buy a six-pack today and lend it to someone who is willing to pay me a relatively large amount in the future in order to have it today.

That someone might be you. Our rates of time preference are both positive, but they differ. Each of us prefers to consume now rather than later, but our different future prospects make you more impatient than me. Assume that you are willing to pay for up to nine cans of the beverage a year from today if you can have six right now. I have a lower rate of time preference and would accept seven or more cans a year from now as compensation for parting with the six-pack today. Both of us benefit if in a year you pay me back between 7 and 9 cans. Assume that we strike a deal for eight. The interest rate on this loan is 33 percent per year. It is the percentage premium on present availability, expressed as a fraction of the amount loaned, that is, $(8 - 6)/6 = 0.33$, usually spoken of as a percentage but represented algebraically as a decimal.

This transaction illustrates several points:

1. Neither of us is acting irrationally. We are making an exchange that spans time, just as we can make an exchange that spans geography. Both of us became better off by our personal standards when we choose to alter the timing of our consumption.
2. Interest is not "the price of money," as it is frequently called. The price of a dollar today is a dollar, no more and no less. Interest is the price of earlier availability, expressed as a percentage of the amount loaned. Most loans are made in money because it is a medium of exchange. The borrower can spend it directly on goods, and the lender usually prefers repayment in cash. We used a commodity in our example to make it clear that this type of transaction beneficially rearranges the time patterns of both your consumption and mine.
3. Interest exists independently of any risk that you might default on the loan, and we assumed no such risk in the example. With risk the terms of our transaction will change—you might have to pay a higher interest rate or have someone else guarantee your loan. If I lend you money I might insist on collateral (possibly the title to the goods you are buying) that I could convert into cash in the event you default.
4. Interest does not exist because inflation might degrade the purchasing power of your repayment. Expectations of inflation will, however, affect the interest rate that I charge you.

Q. Chapter 3 introduced the concept of speculation with an example of a trade between your present and future selves in Figure 3-27. For simplicity, that discussion did not consider interest and time preference. How does your planned consumption pattern over the year change if you do consider those factors? Can you explain the change graphically?

Q. You lend me $400 today in return for a promise that I will repay $450 in a year. What is the implied rate of interest?

The Productivity of Capital, Present Value, and the Rate of Return

Loans for Investment in Capital Goods If you deposit \$10 in a bank account that pays 10 percent interest at the end of each year the money is on deposit, you will have \$11 a year from now.[1] Leaving that amount to grow for another year gives you \$11.00 × (1 + 0.10) = \$12.10, that is, the interest *compounds* over the two-year period with interest paid on the first year's interest. In general, let P be a payment made today (i.e., the deposit), i be the interest rate expressed as a decimal, and A_t be the amount today's payment grows to in t years. We have

(16.1) $$A_t = P(1 + i)^t.$$

Figure 16-2 shows the amount that \$10 grows to over various lengths of time. At 10 percent interest with annual compounding it becomes \$25.94, and in 20 years it becomes \$61.92. At 20 percent interest the \$10 grows to \$67.27 in 10 years and \$383.38 in 20 years.

The bank can pay interest to depositors because it receives interest on money that it lends. It is a *financial intermediary* between savers and borrowers.[2] Some loans will be made to people who wish to change the time shapes of their consumption, as in the six-pack example, but many will also be made to finance buildings, capital goods, inventories, and durable consumer goods, such as homes and vehicles. All of these have the

FIGURE 16-2
Compounded Value of \$10.00 at 10 and 20 Percent Annual Interest

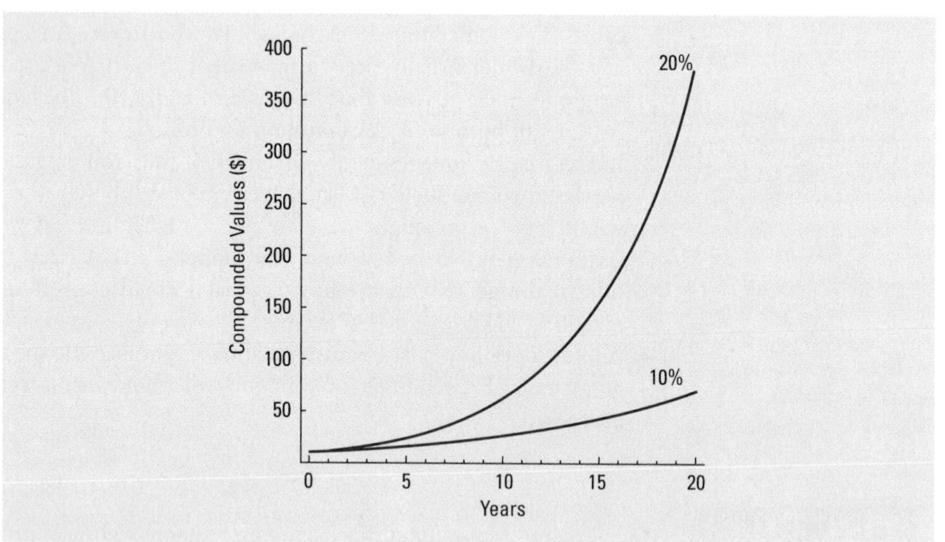

[1]For simplicity, we assume that all interest is paid at the end of the year. Interest, however, is often compounded at more frequent intervals. For example, if interest on the \$10 is compounded quarterly, you receive of 1/4 the annual interest percentage each quarter. At the end of three months you have \$1.10 × 1.025 = \$10.25, after six you have \$10.25 × 1.025 = \$10.506, in nine months \$10.506 × 1.025 = \$10.769, and in a year \$10.769 × 1.025 = \$11.038. In the limit, interest could be compounded instantaneously, in which case the \$10 grows over a year to $e^{1 + .10}$ = \$1.10517, where e is the base of natural logarithms. (For t years at i percent, the amount grows to e^{it}.) The differences between annual and more frequent compounding are minor for interest rates in the range most of us are familiar with.

[2]In this chapter we are interested in the responses of borrowers and lenders to interest rates and not in determining their actual level, which is primarily a topic in macroeconomics.

capability to provide their owners with income over the future.[3] We refer to purchases like these as *investments*. The proceeds of a loan might buy a drill press, which is a profitable investment if the sale price of its output covers the opportunity costs of all other inputs and interest on the funds loaned. A person who uses his own funds to buy the drill press still bears the opportunity cost of interest income that he is no longer earning.

Q. The interest rate your funds can earn for the next two years is 12 percent annually. To what value will your funds have grown at the end of the first year? At the end of the second year?

Present Values Assume that someone offers you a deal that requires an immediate payment. Specifically, she promises you $100 a year from today in return for $95 now. If you are certain she will pay your decision to accept the offer depends on your alternatives. If the best of these is 10 percent interest per year on a bank account, refuse her. Instead of the $95 she charges, all you need to deposit today to get $100 in a year is $90.91. At 10 percent interest it grows to $100 in a year, that is, $90.91 × 1.10 = $100.00. Thus, $90.91 is the *present value* (sometimes called the *discounted value* or *capital value*) of $100 that will be paid a year from now. You reject the offer of $100 in a year for $95 today because the bank promises the same amount for only $90.91 today. Figure 16-3 shows the decreasing relationship between the present value of a $100 payment a year from now and the interest rate at which that payment is discounted. In that figure the lower curve shows the present value of the same payment if it instead arrives two years in the future.

The present value principle holds for payments that come due at any time in the future. Let another person offer you a sure $100 two years from today in exchange for $80 today. If your best alternative is again a bank account that earns 10 percent per year,

FIGURE 16-3
Present Value of $100.00 to Be Received One Year (Upper Line) and Two Years (Lower Line) from Today

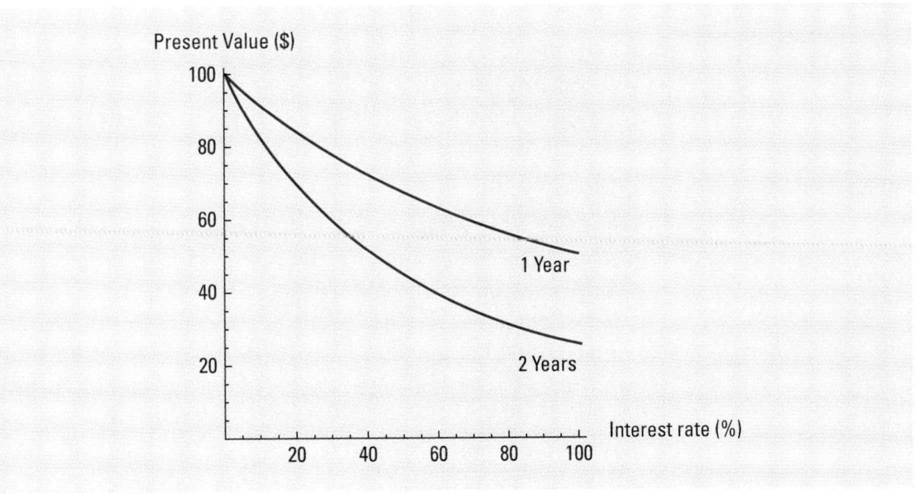

[3]Some durable goods like homes produce cash for the owner only if they are rented out. The rent that a home could have fetched in the market is a rough measure of the value of the services that the house produces for an owner who lives in it. The government estimates this "rental income of persons" and treats it as a part of national income.

FIGURE 16-4
Present Value of $100.00 Payment at Various Points in Future

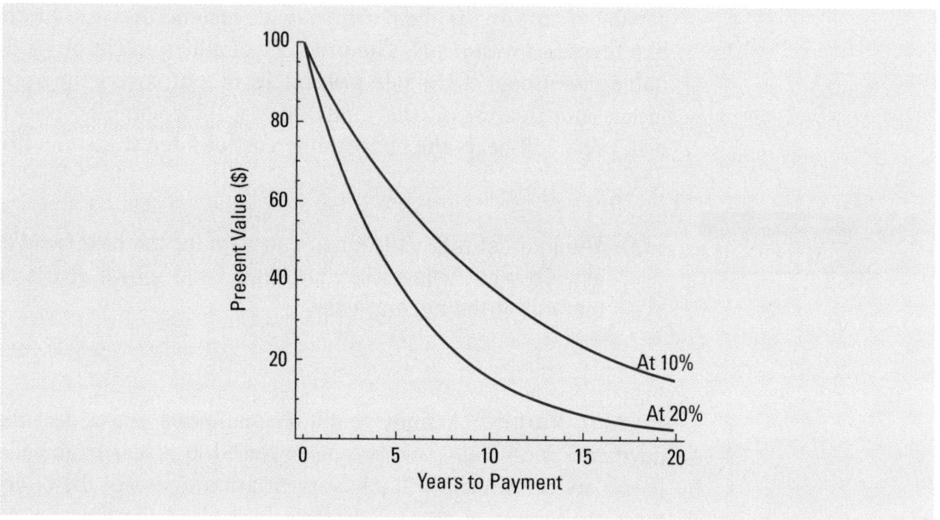

take the offer, because obtaining $100 in two years from the bank requires an $82.64 deposit today. In a year, that amount will have grown to $90.91, and in two years to $100. Rearranging the compound interest formula (equation 16.1) shows that $82.64 = $100.00/(1 + .10)^2. In general, the present value of a payment A_t that is due t years from today is

(16.2) $$P = A_t/(1+i)^t.$$

Figure 16-4 plots the present value of $100 to be received at various points in the future, at interest rates of 10 and 20 percent a year. The further in the future a payment is to come, the lower is its present value. The algebra of compounding indicates that present value falls more than proportionately with the length of the delay in payment.

Q. If the interest rate is 15 percent per year, find the present value of $444 to be received one year in the future. If the interest rate remains 15 percent, what is the present value of $444 to be received in two years?

Annuities and Bond Prices You may want to know the present value of a series of payments that are to come (or be made) at several dates in the future. For example, the present value of income created by a drill press is the sum of the present values of each year's net income over its life span.[4] An *annuity* is a set of equal annual payments. A two-year $100 annuity consists of two payments—$100 a year from today and $100 in two years. If your best alternative earns 10 percent per year the most you should pay for the annuity today is $100/(1.10) + $100/(1.10)^2 = $90.91 + $82.64 = $173.55. Turning the problem around, you can put $173.55 in the bank today and watch it grow to $190.91 in a year, from which you can withdraw your first $100.00. After you do that your account still contains $90.91, which grows to $100.00 during the second year. At the end of that year you take the $100 and close the account.

[4]If newer models make the drill press technologically obsolete its economic life span may be less than its physical life span.

Q. Price a two-year $100 annuity if the interest rate is 15 percent.

Q. Why does the text say that the most you should pay for the annuity is $173.55? Explain why you benefit if you can somehow get it for $160.

A longer annuity has a higher present value. Figure 16-5 shows how the value of a $100 annuity varies with its duration when discounted at 10 percent and 20 percent. What might be surprising is that its value does not increase without bound as the number of payments increases. A 10-year annuity discounted at 10 percent has a present value of $614.46, but an annuity that runs for 20 years is worth $851.36, only 38.6 percent more. A 40-year annuity has a present value of $977.91, only 14.9 percent greater than one that runs for 20 years. Discounted at 20 percent, a 20-year annuity's present value is $486.96, whereas one that lasts for 40 years is worth only $499.65. We can conclude that an infinitely long-lived stream of payments does not have an infinite present value. If a bank offers 10 percent interest on your deposit over all future years, the value of a $100 per year *perpetuity* is $100.00/0.10 = $1,000.00. You can derive this formula by summing an infinite series, or you can use easier logic. A thousand dollars deposited today grows to $1,100 in a year, after which you can take out the $100 interest it has earned. This still leaves your principal of $1,000 intact to earn another $100 over the second year, and likewise over all subsequent years. If the bank pays 20 percent, you need only deposit $500 to get $100 a year in perpetuity.

Q. What is the value of a $500 annual perpetuity if the interest rate is 12 percent?

FIGURE 16-5
Annuity Values, 10 and 20 Percent Interest

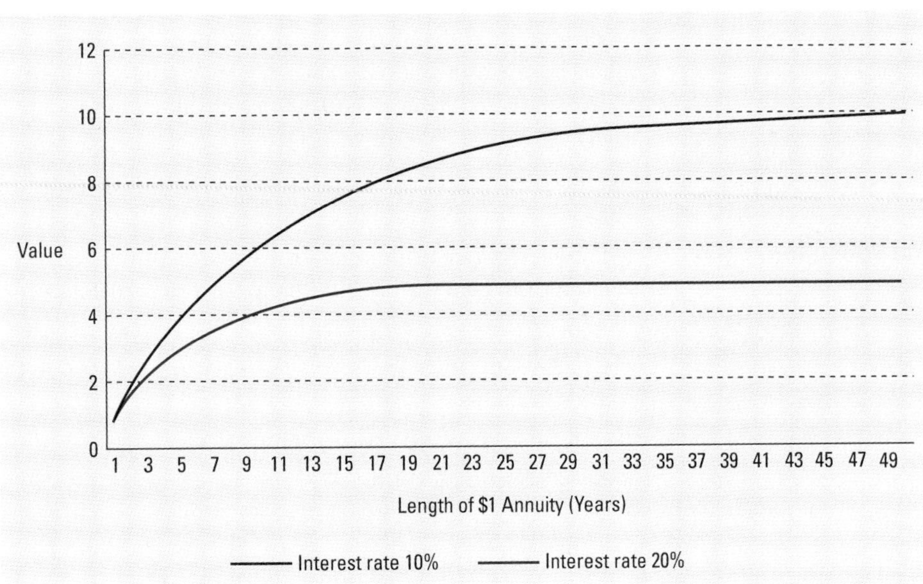

Q. Try deriving the perpetuity formula by summing an infinite series. For example, if the annual payment to the holder is A you want to sum $\sum_{k=1}^{\infty} A/(1+i)^k$

A bond is a legally enforceable promise to pay a defined stream of payments over the future. The simplest kind of bond is a pure *discount bond*, like a U.S. Treasury bill, often called a "T-bill." It obligates the government to pay $1,000 to whomever holds it at maturity, which can be three months, six months, or a year ahead of the issuance date.[5] The Treasury sells bills at regularly scheduled auctions for major brokers and banks. Disregarding all other costs, if banks are paying 10 percent a year on equally safe (i.e., federally insured) deposits, a one-year bill would be expected sell at auction for about $1,000.00/(1.10) = $909.91. A T-bill's promise of payment may be ironclad, but the value of the bill itself is not. Instead, its market price varies inversely with interest rates. Assume that immediately after you buy one for $909.91 the interest rate unexpectedly increases to 15 percent, where it will stay.[6] The bill is still a promise to pay $1,000 in one year, but now the alternatives have changed and its present value is only $1000/(1.15) = $869.57. If you sell your T-bill you will realize a capital loss because $869.57 is all anyone will pay for it. If, on the other hand, the interest rate permanently fell to 5 percent the day after you bought the T-bill, it would suddenly be worth $952.38.

Q. Why was it important that the interest rate increase unexpectedly? What would happen if everyone somehow knew in advance that it would rise from 10 to 15 percent in three months?

The same reasoning holds for *coupon bonds* that provide a stream of fixed interest payments each year. The simplest "vanilla" bond (as in ice cream) has a *par value*, usually a multiple of $1,000, payable a certain number of years from its issuance.[7] At the end of each year its holder gets a fixed payment, sometimes called the coupon amount.[8] A bond is thus a combination of an annuity that consists of coupon payments and a terminal payment of the par value. A newly issued 20-year bond with a coupon value of $1,000 and a par value of $10,000 has a value *P* given by

(16.3)
$$P = \sum_{t=1}^{20} \frac{1,000}{(1+i)^t} + \frac{10,000}{(1+i)^{20}}.$$

If the interest rate at the time of issue was 10 percent, the newly issued bond would sell for $10,000. Like the discount bond, its price varies inversely with the interest rate.

[5]Bonds of different maturities usually get different names. The Treasury's most common issues are *bills* that mature in a year or less; *notes* that run for two, five, or ten years; and *bonds* with 30-year terms.

[6]The figures in the text are only illustrative. Daily interest rate fluctuations of 50 percent are unheard of, and not all markets adjust instantaneously.

[7]Non-vanilla features might include interest rates that adjust to stay in line with changes in the market. The bond might be *callable*, that is, the issuer has the right to buy it back on predetermined terms, or it may be *convertible* into stock shares of the company issuing it, among many other possibilities.

[8]In earlier times bondholders actually cut coupons off of the bond itself with scissors and sent them to the issuer to claim their payments.

Q. Assume the interest rate is 5 percent at the time the bond in equation 16.3 is issued. Why will its price be $20,000?

Q. Explain in commonsense terms why if the interest rate in equation 16.3 remains at 10 percent the price of the bond will always be (near) $10,000. Why the qualifier "near"?

Net Present Value and the Analysis of Investment Assume that you are considering whether to construct a building, an activitity we will call "Project A." Further assume that there are tenants who have agreed in advance to lease space in it, so that you know with certainty the future cash flows it will generate. We can calculate the value of constructing it in the same way that we valued an annuity. If the building can be constructed instantly and lasts for two years, you give up P dollars today in return for payments net of operating costs of A_1 a year from today and A_2 two years from today. (For simplicity assume that all payments are made at year-end.) The two amounts can be positive or negative (e.g., a teardown cost in the final year might make A_2 negative), but here we assume both are positive. There are no subsequent payments or receipts, and the building has no scrap value. At discount rate i the *net present value* of the project is

(16.4a)
$$NPV_A = -P + \frac{A_1}{(1+i)} + \frac{A_2}{(1+i)^2}.$$

The alternative is construction Project B, which also entails spending P dollars today, but in return it gives you three years of net revenue in installments B_1, B_2, and B_3. Project B's net present value is

(16.4b)
$$NPV_B = -P + \frac{B_1}{(1+i)} + \frac{B_2}{(1+i)^2} + \frac{B_3}{(1+i)^3}.$$

Assume that P is $100.00; A_1 and A_2 are $100 and $45; B_1,B_2, and B_3 are $50, $40, and $70; and the interest rate is 10 percent. Insert these into equations 16.4a and 16.4b to get NPV_1 = $28.10 and NPV_2 = $31.10. Figure 16-6 shows the NPVs of the projects for interest rates between 0 and 0.5. If all you have available is $100, then invest in Project B, because it leaves you with more wealth than Project A. Just after you commit the $100 to Project B you could sell the stream of future payments for more than if you had just put the same amount into Project A. Project B is superior on the net present value criterion, but we need not have assumed that you are limited to spending only $100. If you can obtain another $100 at 10 percent (and the projects are not mutually exclusive), you should invest it in project A. The fact that its net present value also exceeds zero is another way of saying that undertaking both projects leaves you better off than had you only undertaken Project B. This project also adds to your wealth and leaves you better off than Project B alone. The NPVs of the two projects become equal at an interest rate of 0.134, i.e., 13.4 percent. If you can only undertake one of the projects, you will be wealthier with Project A if the interest rate is below 13.4 percent, and with project B if it is above that amount.

Q. Verify these calculations for Projects A and B.

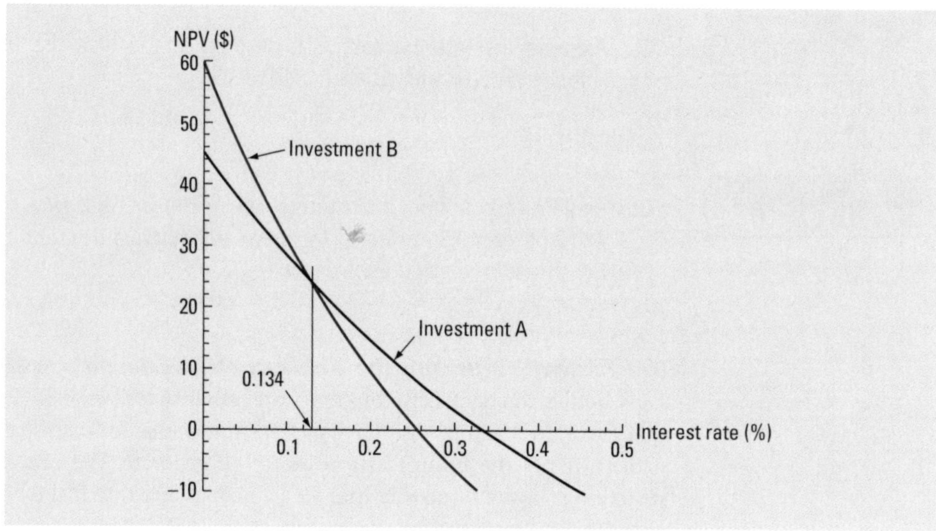

FIGURE 16-6
Net Present Values of Two Investment Projects at Various Interest Rates

The Right Refrigerator We are finally ready to choose our refrigerator. Recall that there were two models. Refrigerator A had a cash price (payable today) of $979 and required $45 per year of electricity to run. Otherwise equivalent refrigerator B sold for $849 and used $65 of power annually. For simplicity, assume that each has a fixed lifespan of 10 years, after which it has zero scrap value, and that you pay a single electricity bill at the end of the year. The interest rate is 10 percent. Then the net present value of costs for refrigerator A is

(16.5a)
$$NPV_A = \$979 + \sum_{i=1}^{10} \frac{\$45}{(1+0.10)^i} = \$1,255.51.$$

The corresponding figure for B is

(16.5b)
$$NPV_B = \$849 + \sum_{i=1}^{10} \frac{\$65}{(1+0.10)^i} = \$1,248.40.$$

After accounting for the opportunity cost of our funds, Refrigerator B is superior. But the choice of refrigerator changes with the interest rate. If it is 4 percent per year instead of 10 percent, we find that NPV_A = $1,343.99 and NPV_B = $1,376.21 At the lower interest rate, A becomes the better buy.

To see why the interest rate matters for your choice, let's use some easier numbers. Assume refrigerator A sells for $20 today and refrigerator B sells for $24, and each lasts for just a year. A requires $26 worth of power, and B requires $21, each payable in a year. The present value of costs for A is $PV_A = \$20 + \$26/(1 + i)$, and for B is $PV_B = \$24 + \$21/(1 + i)$. You can easily check that at an interest rate just above zero, B is the lower cost alternative, that at a very high interest rate A is the winner, and that at $i = 0.25$ they are equal. The opposite holds at low interest rates and your better choice is B. At high interest rates the choice of A reduces your wealth by less than the choice of B. Your decision depends on the price of the refrigerator, the price of electricity, and the interest rate.

Inflation, Default Risk, and Rational Behavior

Inflation Expectations of an inflation that will increase all prices will also affect interest rates on loans. Assume that both you and your lender (me) confidently expect that a dollar will be worth some percentage of its original value when the loan is due. I will insist on a repayment that compensates me for delayed consumption and the opportunity cost of investing elsewhere. That amount must allow me to purchase the same bundle of goods as if there had been no inflation. You will probably also accept the same adjustment because your money income and the values of your assets (those that are not fixed in dollars) will also rise with the price level.

To understand the calculation let's first assume that both of us mistakenly expected price stability and agreed on 10 percent interest for a one-year loan of \$100. Just after the money changes hands, however, a 20 percent inflation takes us by surprise. After you repay me in a year I will have real purchasing power of \$110.00/1.20 = \$91.67, measured in dollars of a year ago. Unanticipated inflation transfers wealth from the lender to the borrower. To compensate me for inflation and interest, you must return \$110.00 × 1.20 = \$132.00. If I lend you P dollars and prices inflate at an annual rate of π percent, I must receive

$$A_1 = P(1+i)(1+\pi), \tag{16.6}$$

The nominal interest rate on the loan will be $i + \pi + i\pi$. For interest and inflation rates in the normal range the third term will be small enough that we can often disregard it.

Q. Show that if you repay my loan at the end of T years I will recover purchasing power and interest if I get $A_T = P(1+i)^T(1+\pi)^T$.

Default Risk and Credit Rationing Assume you are a lender whose fallback option is making loans to safe borrowers that earn 10 percent per year and are never in default. There is also a population of higher-risk borrowers who will only repay the principal and interest with a probability of 0.9, that is, a tenth of the loans will be unrecoverable.[9] You can distinguish people who are bad risks from those who are good ones, but you cannot tell whether a randomly chosen bad risk will default. Because loans to the good risks at 10 percent are always a possibility, you will only lend to bad risks if your expected (i.e., mean) return on loans to them is at least as much as you can earn with certainty by lending to good risks. A year from today your expected revenue from lending \$100 must be \$110 for each type of risk. Let $\bar{i}$ be the interest rate on a risky loan. At the equilibrium value of $\bar{i}$ you will make the same expected revenue from a bad risk as you do with certainty from a good risk. Thus, $\bar{i}$ is the solution of $0.9 \times 100(1 + \bar{i}) = \$110.00$. A risky borrower with a default probability of .10 will have to pay 22.2 percent on a loan that a safe borrower would get at 10 percent. In a competitive market the realized returns on loans of different riskiness will tend to equality. A risky borrower who can increase the likelihood of repayment (e.g., by finding a cosigner or supplying collateral) will pay a lower interest rate.

Q. Verify the calculation that produces the 22.2 percent interest rate to risky borrowers.

[9]If you are completely unfamiliar with probability, read this material only after you become familiar with the "Frequencies and Probabilities" material on page 451.

How Do People Discount and Anticipate the Future? *Unexplained behavior in durable goods purchases.* People prefer goods now over equivalent goods in the future, but do they discount future payments and receipts in accordance with economic theory? Subjects in psychological experiments that involve short delays often appear to discount at extremely high rates.[10] Questions like "how much would you pay for a candy bar now rather than two hours from now" may tell us more about how a person reacts to immediate stimuli (is it before or after lunch time?) than about his borrowing behavior for a car or house. Some choices with longer-term consequences, however, are harder to explain. A consumer choosing a refrigerator should rationally compare discounted benefits with present costs, particularly since refrigeration and air conditioning account for 25 percent of a typical U.S. household's electricity bill. People can easily project their future expenses from an appliance's "Energy Guide," and compare them between models. Jerry Hausman of MIT has found that the present value of saving on power is often worth the higher initial cost, even if a buyer must borrow at rates as high as those on unpaid credit card balances (e.g., 18 percent).[11] On the other side, energy prices are subject to great random variation. If calculations based on today's power price poorly predict the savings buyers will realize, those who pay a premium for the refrigerator are locked into gambles that they would prefer to postpone. Kevin Hassett of Columbia University and Gilbert Metcalf of Tufts University showed that buyers in such situations may rationally purchase less expensive appliances that do not save the most energy.[12] Some other financial behavior is also hard to explain. Many consumers pay interest on debts that exceeds what they simultaneously earn on savings accounts. It is possible that they value liquidity, the ability to obtain cash when they want it on predictable terms. Nowadays, however, liquidity is relatively easy to come by thanks to developments like credit card cash advances and home equity lines of credit.

Foresight and Social Security. Investment behavior is an important element in the debate over privatizing Social Security, which would allow people to substitute purchases of stocks and other financial assets for a portion of their Social Security taxes. In part the debate is over whether people have the knowledge, self-control, and foresight to make rational retirement choices. If they have these abilities, some argue that they should not be forced into Social Security, whose returns are far below those of many financial markets.[13] If you are confused about your retirement options or have neglected to plan, you are in the distinguished company of several recent Nobel Prize winners in economics.[14] Harry Markowitz, formerly of the University of Chicago, shared the 1990 prize for research on risk discussed later in this chapter, but his own risk management is another story. He admits that he allocated his retirement funds in the same proportions between one high-return and one low-return investment for most of his adult life, contrary to the usual recommendations of financial planners. At age 77 he remarked that "In retrospect it would have been better to be more in stocks when I was younger." George Akerlof of the University of California, Berkeley shared the 2001 Nobel for his work

[10]For a discussion of extreme discount rates and their implications, see Matthew Rabin, "Psychology and Economics," *Journal of Economic Literature* 36 (March 1998): 11–46.

[11]Jerry A. Hausman, "Individual Discount Rates and the Purchase and Utilization of Energy-Using Durables," *Bell Journal of Economics* 10 (Spring 1979): 33–54.

[12]Kevin Hassett and Gilbert Metcalf, "Energy Conservation Investment: Do Consumers Discount the Future Correctly?", *Energy Policy* 21 (June 1993): 710–716. We learn how to calculate the value of delay in the section on option value later in this chapter.

[13]For a review of these and many other issues, see David Laibson et al., "Self-Control and Saving for Retirement," *Brookings Papers on Economic Activity* No. 1 (1998): 191–96.

[14]"Experts Are at a Loss on Investing," *Los Angeles Times*, May 11, 2005, 1. All quotes are from this article.

on asymmetric information that we discussed in Chapter 11. He kept most of his retirement funds in money market accounts whose average annual return is 2 percent.[15] "I know it's utterly stupid," he said. Princeton University's Daniel Kahneman shared the 2002 Nobel Prize for his research on errors in reasoning about probability discussed in Chapter 1. "I think very little about my retirement savings," he said, "because I know that thinking could make me poorer or more miserable or both." Of course, not all of the Nobelists dropped the ball. Stanford University's William Sharpe, the 1990 co-winner, founded a company that charges people to make retirement finance decisions for them.

Whatever the behavior of individuals, businesses of every kind now apply the insights of financial theory to investment choice and risk management. Virtually all major corporations now have a chief financial officer, and an increasing number have a chief risk officer, like those mentioned in Chapter 13. Businesses base their capital budgeting and related investment decisions on models of net present value, augmented to deal with uncertainty and calibrated to examine worst-case scenarios. Many issues that we neglected in order to make our basic points are intensely researched by real businesses. For example, instead of discussing the intricacies of calculating a company's cost of capital, we simply asserted that we knew the interest rate it should use to discount its future costs and revenues. Businesses increasingly apply the economics of finance and uncertainty in their operations in matters that include risk assessment, the valuation of information, and the pricing of options. We devote the rest of this chapter to these topics.

RISK AND DIVERSIFICATION

Some Basics of Probability

Frequencies and Probabilities Economists often model situations in which risks can be summarized by probabilities that various events will occur. Probabilities are long-run frequencies. When the weather forecaster in Chapter 1 announced a 30 percent chance of rain tonight, he could do so with some confidence because records show that it has actually rained on 30 percent of days with tonight's atmospheric conditions. We cannot know whether the next toss of a fair coin will show heads or tails, but on the basis of past experience we can confidently expect heads half the time. Heads and tails are the only two elements (we call them events) in a *sample space* that contains all possible outcomes of this rather simple exercise. Because either heads or tails must occur, we set the sum of their probabilities to 1. Experience says that the probability of a head, $\Pr[H]$, is .5, and so is the probability of a tail, $\Pr[T]$. This sample space is shown in Figure 16-7a as an equal division of a line of length 1.

Q. What is the probability that the side with three spots will turn up on a single roll of a standard cubical die (the singular of dice)?

Events A and B are *independent* if the probability that A will happen is the same regardless of whether or not B has happened. Tosses of the coin are independent because the probability that the second toss is a head is .5, regardless of whether the first toss was

[15] The long-term average for stocks is about a 7 percent return per year after adjustment for inflation. See Jeremy Siegel, *Stocks for the Long Run*, 3rd ed. (New York: McGraw-Hill, 2002).

FIGURE 16-7
Two Sample Spaces

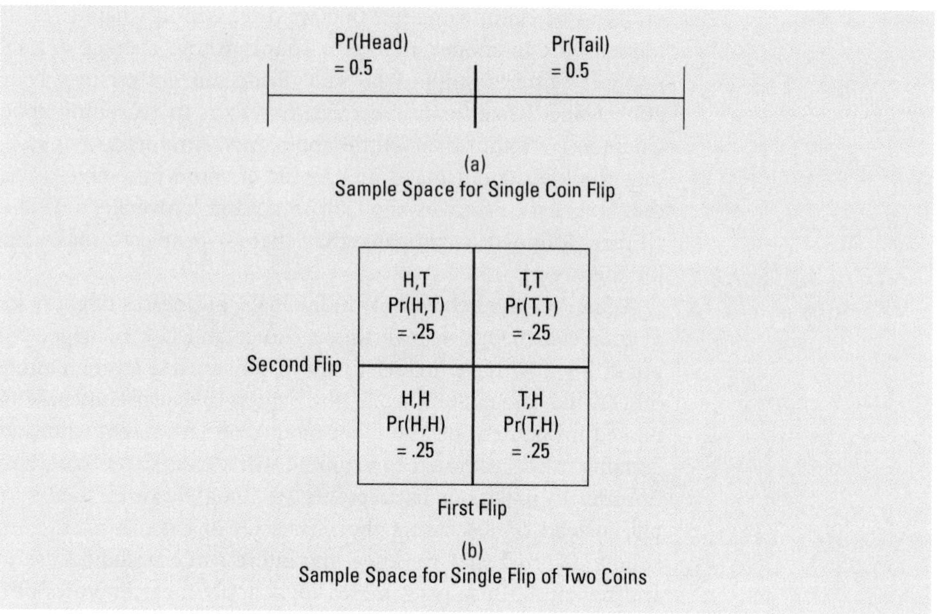

heads or tails. For two independent tosses, the sample space is the square shown in Figure 16-7b. Each side of the square is of length 1. The horizontal axis is the outcome of the first toss and the vertical is the outcome of the second. The sample space has four elements, (H,H), (H,T), (T,H), and (*T*,*T*), each with probability 0.25. Figure 16-8 shows a slightly more complex sample space. Assume that all points in the square are equally likely to be hit by a randomly thrown dart. Rectangle A's edges are 1/2 and 3/4, so the probability that a dart randomly thrown at the square will land in A is 3/8, i.e., 1/2 × 3/4. Rectangle B is 1/2 by 1/4, so the probability of your dart landing in B is 1/8. The area common to both A and B (sometimes called their intersection) is 1/4 unit on a side, so $\Pr[A \text{ and } B] = 1/16$. If A is entirely contained in B, $\Pr[A \text{ and } B] = \Pr[A]$. If A and B are disjoint (i.e., have no events in common), $\Pr[A \text{ and } B] = 0$. The probability that the dart will land in either A or B is:

$$\Pr[A \text{ or } B] = \Pr[A] + \Pr[B] - \Pr[A \text{ and } B]. \tag{16.7}$$

FIGURE 16-8
Probabilities of Combinations of Two Events

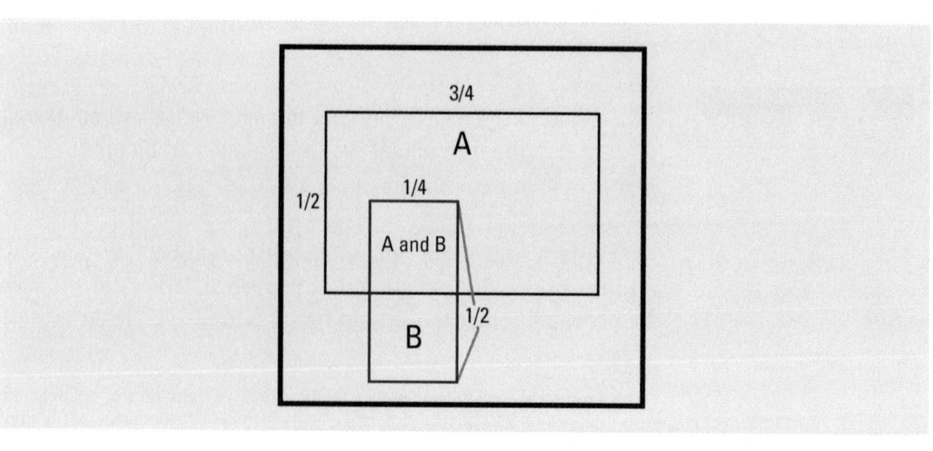

The last term is necessary to avoid double-counting the intersection of the two sets. In Figure 16-8, Pr[*A or B*] = 3/8 + 1/8 − 1/16 = 7/16. If A and B are disjoint, Pr[*A and B*] = 0 and Pr[*A or B*] = Pr[*A*] + Pr[*B*].

We are often interested in the probability of event A, knowing that B has occurred or will occur. This is the *conditional probability* of A given B, denoted $\Pr[A|B]$.

(16.8) $$\Pr[A|B] = \Pr[A \text{ and } B]/\Pr[B].$$

In Figure 16-8 $\Pr[A/B] = {}^{1/16}/_{1/8} = 1/2$. Only by coincidence will we see $\Pr[A|B] = \Pr[B|A]$. Here $\Pr[A/B] = {}^{1/16}/_{3/8} = 1/6$. We can define independence in terms of conditional probability. A and B are independent if $P[A|B] = P[A]$, which can be restated as $\Pr[A \text{ and } B] = \Pr[A] \times \Pr[B]$. The probability of one head and one tail in two sequential coin tosses is 1/2, because no matter which turns up on the first toss, the probability that the other will turn up on the second toss is 1/2.

Random Variables and Distributions A *random variable* is a function that takes on a defined value for every point in the sample space. For example, looking at the top left of Figure 16-9, random variable X_1 might be the number of heads that come up in two tosses. The probability of no heads, Pr[0], is 1/4, Pr[1] = 1/2, and Pr[2] = 1/4. We can also construct other random variables based on coin tossing and examine their distributions. At the top right of the figure is another random variable, X_2, defined as the number of heads in two tosses times twice the number of tails. Now we have Pr[0] = 1/2 and Pr[2] = 1/2. These are the *probability density functions* of X_1 and X_2. Each rectangle is one unit wide and has a height equal to the probability that the random variable takes on

FIGURE 16-9
Probability Distribution Functions

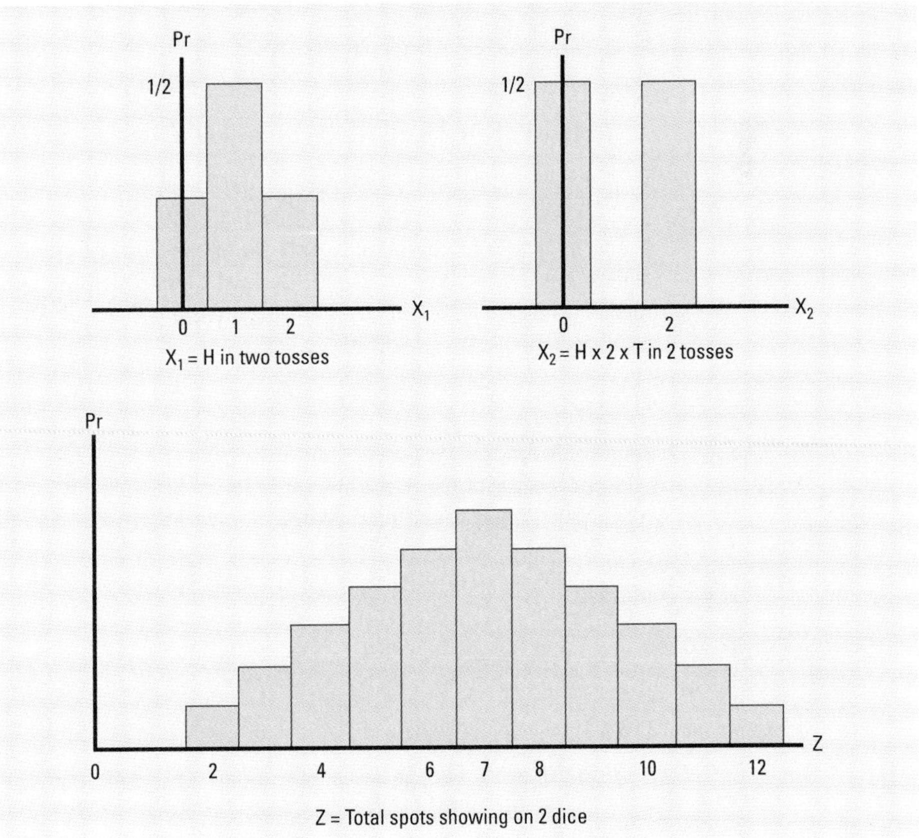

that value. The areas of the rectangles must total to 1, that is, all possible outcomes must be accounted for. We can draw other conclusions from the distributions. For example, the probability that X_1 is less than but not equal to 2 is 3/4. The bottom half of Figure 16-9 shows the probability distribution of Z, the number of spots that will show on a single throw of two six-sided dice. You should be able to check that the probabilities of 2 or 12 are each .028, the probability of 7 is .167, and the probability that they sum to 9 or more is .278.

Q. You have a pair of six-sided dice. Define random variable Y as the highest number showing on a toss of both. Graph its probability density function. Determine $\Pr[Y = 4]$ and $\Pr[4 \le Y \le 6]$.

Mean and Variance The *expectation* of a random variable X that can take on any of N possible values, X_i, is denoted $E[X]$ and defined as

(16.9) $$E[X] = \sum_{i=1}^{N} X_i \Pr[X_i].$$

The *mean* of X is defined as its expectation:

(16.10) $$\mu = E[X].$$

(μ is the Greek letter "mu.") We are often interested in expectations of functions of X. For a linear function,

(16.11) $$E[a + bX] = a + bE[X].$$

Because the constant a is independent of X, its expected value is a. Substituting bX for X in equation 16.8, $\sum_{i=1}^{N} bX_i \Pr[X_i] = b\sum_{i=1}^{N} X_i \Pr[X_i] = bE[X] = b\mu$. The mean number of heads in two coin tosses is 1, and the mean sum of spots on two dice is .028 × 2 + .056 × 3 + ... + .028 × 12 = 7. Both of these distributions are symmetric around their means. More generally, if two density functions $f(x)$ and $g(x)$ have means μ_f and μ_g, their weighted sum has a mean of:

(16.12) $$E[\alpha f(X) + \beta g(X)] = \alpha\mu_f + \beta\mu_g$$

where Greek letters alpha (α) and beta (β) are the weights.

Important aspects of risk are summarized in the range of values that X can take and on the likelihood of extreme values. The *variance* of X is defined as

(16.13) $$Var[x] = \sigma_X^2 = \sum_{i=1}^{N} \Pr[X_i]\ (X_i - \mu)^2.$$

(σ is the Greek letter "sigma.") Applying the definition of expectation, we can show that

(16.14) $$\sigma^2(x) = E[x^2] - (E[x])^2$$

A distribution with a larger percentage of its observations beyond a certain distance from the mean will have a higher variance. Because variance is a squared quantity, it increases more than proportionately with the "spread" of the distribution. If X_1 is the number of heads in two coin tosses, its variance is 0.5, If X_2 is twice the number of heads times the number of tails in two tosses, it variance is 4. More of the mass of the distribution of X_2 lies at a distance from its mean, even though the highest and lowest values of X in both distributions are the same. The variance of the sum of spots on a roll of two dice is 5.833.

Q. Can you derive equation 16.14? (If you have difficulty, almost any statistics book shows how.)

Q. Verify that the variance of the sum of spots on a roll of two dice is 5.833.

Attitudes Toward Risk

Expected Utility In Chapter 11 we explained how your expected gain in wealth could be positive, while at the same time your expected gain in well-being, which we call "utility," is negative. Here we go more deeply into the calculations and generalize the model. Assume your house (i.e. your wealth W) is worth \$100,000 and a fire would destroy all of its value. If the probability of a fire is .01 and full insurance is \$1,000 your expected wealth is the same with or without insurance. Buying it gives you

(16.15a) $$E[W] = -1{,}000 + (.99 \times 100{,}000) + (.01 \times 100{,}000) = \$99,000,$$

because you get \$100,000 back in the event of a fire. If you remain uninsured your expected wealth is

(16.15b) $$E[W] = (.99 \times 100{,}000) + (.01 \times 0) = \$99{,}000.$$

Whether or not you insure, your expected wealth is the same. If there are costs of writing the insurance policy and handling your claim you will actually pay more for it than your expected loss.

What you really care about is the change in your well-being (i.e., utility) if there is a fire. In Chapter 11 we saw that if you are a risk-averse person, your utility is related to your wealth by a curve like the one in Figure 16-10. The wealthier you are, the higher your utility, but the increase in utility ("marginal utility") from an extra dollar of wealth falls as your wealth rises. The person portrayed in Figure 16-10 is *risk averse*—willing to lose some wealth with certainty as an insurance payment to avoid putting the rest of it at risk. Figure 16-11 portrays a person who is *risk neutral.* Her marginal utility of wealth remains constant whatever its level.[16] Figure 16-11b shows a *risk preferrer,* whose marginal utility of wealth increases as wealth increases. As we will see, it is possible that at some levels of wealth you will be risk averse and at others you will be a risk preferrer.

Q. Jones is risk averse. This means Jones would never buy stock in a company whose earnings are uncertain. Right? Explain.

[16]In the diagram, zero wealth gives the person zero utility, but this is not necessary. For risk neutrality it suffices that utility increases linearly with income in the area of the possible loss.

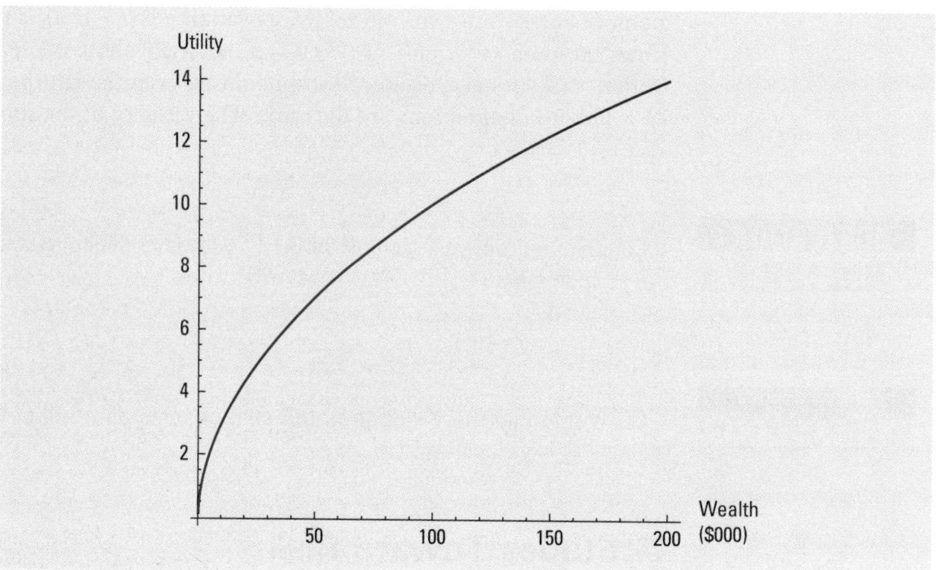

FIGURE 16-10
Utility and Wealth for a Risk-Averse Person

Insurance and Gambling Figure 16-12 shows why a risk-averse person will buy insurance. Utility is assumed to equal the square root of your wealth (in thousands of dollars). Because a graph with realistic probabilities would be hard on the eyes we let the probabilities of a gain and a loss both equal .5. You begin with $100,000, which has a utility of 10 units. The risk is that with probability .5 you will end up with $180,000, and with the same probability you will get $20,000. This is called a "fair gamble" because its expected dollar outcome is neither a gain nor a loss to you. The expected change in your utility, however, is negative: $100,000 gives you 13.41 units of utility and $20,000 gives you 4.47. The expected utility if you take the gamble is $(.5 \times 13.41) + (.5 \times 4.47) = 8.94$. It is the vertical coordinate of the midpoint of the straight line joining points A and B on $U[W]$. Relative to the 10 sure units of utility you get from $100,000 in hand, making the bet lowers your expected utility. We can also calculate how much you would be willing to pay for insurance. Your expected utility if you bet is 8.94 units, which is the same as the utility of a sure $79,920. You would pay up to $20,084 to avoid having to make the bet, and paying any smaller amount for such insurance would leave you better off.

Q. Explain why your expected utility from the gamble is the vertical coordinate of the midpoint of the line joining A and B. Then show how your analysis changes if the probability of an $80,000 loss becomes .25 and that of a win becomes .75.

Q. The expected utility of this bet becomes greater as the probability of gaining $80,000 rises relative to the probability of losing it. What probability will make you willing to take the gamble, even if you have the option of buying fair insurance?

FIGURE 16-11
Utility and Attitudes Toward Risk

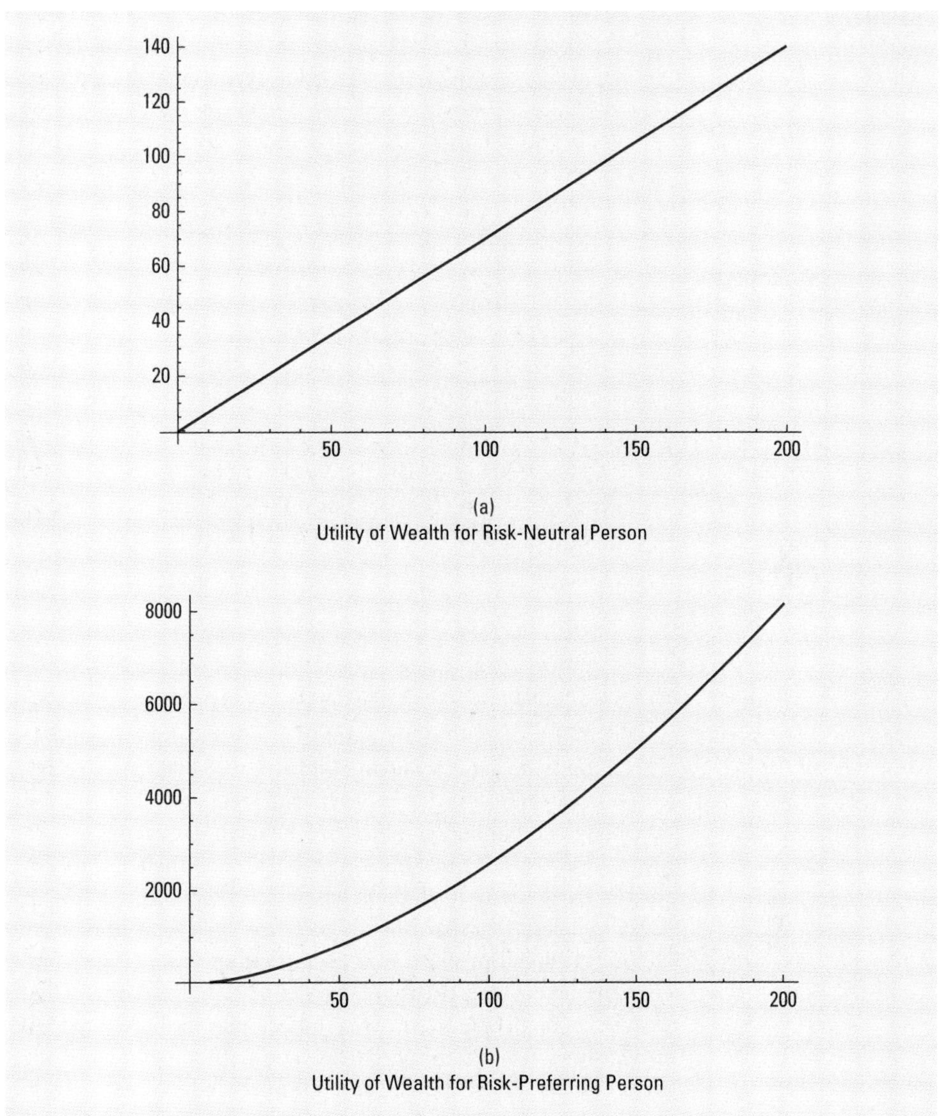

Risk aversion can explain why people buy insurance, and risk preference is a possible explanation for why they gamble. Figure 16-13 shows a person whose marginal utility increases at levels of wealth below \$50,000, but past that point his utility is that of a risk avoider and equal to the square root of his wealth. At the subsistence level of \$3,000 a move to \$4,000 makes only a small impact on his well-being. However, a rise from \$3,000 to \$40,000 so raises his utility that it is worth an *unfair* gamble that carries a negative expected value. With \$4,000 he remains a day laborer forever, but with \$30,000 he can open a business and adequately provide for his family.[17] Assume that the person in Figure 16-13 starts with \$25,000. He has a .5 probability of winning \$20,000 and an .5 probability of losing the entire \$25,000. Taking the gamble leaves him with an expected wealth of \$22,500, less than he started with. The \$25,000 he has at the start provides 2.2

[17]The New York State Lottery once advertised "All you need is a dollar and a dream."

FIGURE 16-12
Insurance Purchase by a Risk-Averse Person

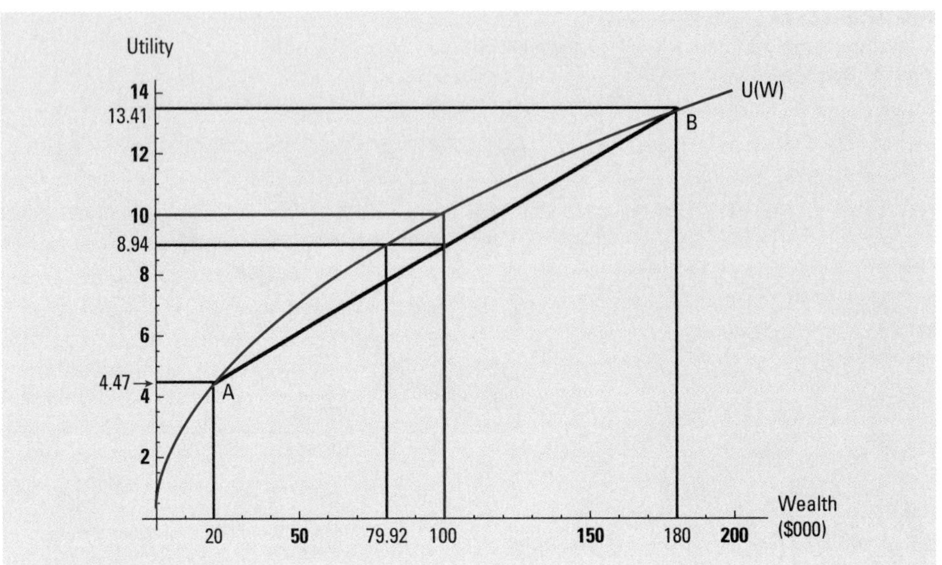

units of utility. Winning $20,000 would raise his wealth to $45,000, whose utility (5.7) is 3.5 units higher than $25,000. Losing $25,000 leaves him with utility of zero. The expected utility of the unfair gamble is $(.5 \times 0) + (.5 \times 5.7) = 2.85$ units, greater than the 2.2 units he gets by staying with the $25,000.

This reasoning can help us evaluate frequently heard opinions that poor persons who take long-shot unfair gambles are behaving irrationally.[18] The poor play lotteries and illegal "numbers" games out of proportion to their numbers in the population and their wealth, particularly in nations where social mobility is low. If you believe your situation is so hopeless that hard work will not raise you above poverty you might rationally choose the small promise of a lottery rather than resign yourself to a bleak life.[19] Whatever the actual degree of social mobility in the United States (a subject of much research), poor people are heavier lottery players here, too.[20] Wealth, rather than income, is relevant for determining participation. "Poor" students with temporarily low incomes buy very few lottery tickets, and so do retired people.

Risk preference may explain other interesting facts. Steven Levitt of the University of Chicago and Sudhir Venkatesh of Columbia University managed to obtain the account books of a gang that sold crack cocaine in Chicago. They found to their surprise that most street-level dealers lived with their mothers. Most of them apparently had such

---

[18]Other factors explain gambling by wealthier people. Luxury hotels and casinos in Nevada were not built to compete with lotteries. Many well-off people find gambling pleasurable enough that they are willing to accept a small expected loss as the price of an enjoyable vacation experience.

[19]Reuven Brenner, *History: the Human Gamble* (Chicago: University of Chicago Press, 1983), 6–11. Brenner says that lotteries in poorer countries appear to be marketed only to the poor, in which case they can be viewed as voluntary exchanges that redistribute wealth (at a high transaction cost) among that segment of the population. Whether a lottery should be marketed to the poor and whether the government should run it are largely normative questions.

[20]The top 10 percent of lottery players in the United States account for 50 percent of total spending. Blacks and Hispanics play more heavily than whites, and Catholics play more heavily than Protestants (why?). Charles Clotfelter and Philip Cook, "On the Economics of State Lotteries," *Journal of Economic Perspectives* 4 (Fall 1990): 105–119.

FIGURE 16-13
Rational Gambling by a Risk-Preferring Person

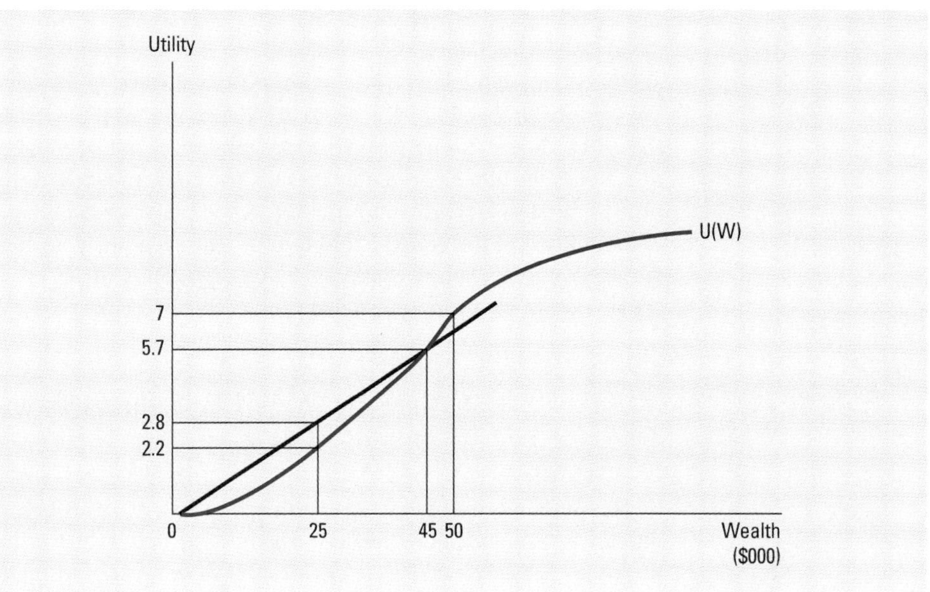

short and unrewarding careers that they did not earn enough to leave home.[21] However, they were willing to take an unfair gamble to attain a level of wealth that, however unlikely, would have been impossible to attain legally within their likely time horizons.

Q. If the gang's business is illegal, why would you expect its managers to keep an accurate set of account books?

Q. Only a small fraction of the U.S. public plays state lotteries intensively. Assume that each person in that group spends $1,000 per year on dollar tickets and other members of the public do not participate at all. Does it make sense for the lottery to cut operating costs by switching to a policy of selling only $100 tickets with the same expected return per dollar that the $1 tickets formerly had? Why or why not?

The Risk–Return Trade-off

Diversification Taken at face value, the proverb that you should not put all your eggs into one basket is not very helpful as a guide to how you should act in risky situations. If you stumble while carrying the basket you are indeed likely to break all of the eggs. Assume that the probability of a stumble on any given journey between the henhouse and your destination is .25. Putting all of a dozen eggs in one basket and making one trip leaves you with an expected nine eggs intact. If you choose to carry two eggs on six trips you will end up with exactly the same expected number of unbroken eggs as if you carried them in one basket. The real benefit of repeated trips with only a few eggs in each basket is not the expected number of eggs that arrive unbroken. It is the range of outcomes you can expect. If you

[21]Steven Levitt and Sudhir Venkatesh, "An Economic Analysis of a Drug-Selling Gang's Finances," *Quarterly Journal of Economics* 115 (August 2000): 755–89.

make six trips, the probability that you will stumble on every one of them is 0.25^6 = .000244. The probability that you will stumble on five trips is .004394, and on four it is .032959.[22] If you must eat at least six eggs to survive, taking six trips with two eggs apiece lowers your probability of death to .0376, the sum of these three probabilities. If you carry the entire dozen in one trip, your probability of not surviving is .25, nearly seven times higher. On the other side, assume that if you consume eight or ten eggs you will get enough nourishment to carry on a normal life. An eleventh or twelfth egg gives you relatively little extra utility and the added cholesterol might even put your health at risk. The six-basket strategy only gets you twelve eggs with a probability of $.75^6$ = .1780, but the last two eggs are not worth much to you so this is an acceptable risk.

Q. Explain the logic of using $.75^6$ = .1780 for the six-basket strategy.

Now instead of carrying eggs, think of a basket as an investment. Instead of growing like an investment, however, the eggs can at best stay constant in value by remaining unbroken. The six-basket strategy deals with the risk of losing too many. You have diversified your holdings (your portfolio) by putting them into several baskets, and in the process you have reduced the variance of your returns. The two extreme outcomes are the only ones you can get with the one-basket strategy, while the six-basket strategy yields a far higher probability of surviving. If you are risk averse that strategy leaves you better off in expected value terms. Our next job is to get a deeper understanding of the reduction in variance that diversification brings.

Q. Why might you not necessarily choose to make 12 trips with one egg each rather than 6 trips with two each?

The six-basket strategy carried an unstated assumption that the returns on the different baskets were independent, that is, the probability that you will fall on one of the trips is the same regardless of what might happen or has happened on the others. This need not be the case—if you stumbled with the first basket and twisted your ankle, you might be more likely to stumble on other attempts. Or possibly you made the first trip unscathed and now remember the portions of the path along which you should be particularly careful, which raises the probability of success on subsequent trips. Switching to more ordinary investments, Figure 16-14 presents three scatterplots of observations on two variables, X and Y. The points in the upper left plot (Figure 16-14a) are said to be *positively correlated.* They might, for example, show hypothetical annual returns in various years on stock shares in an oil producer (X) and a natural gas producer (Y). The scatter indicates nothing about which (if either) share price causes the other to move. Because oil and gas are substitute fuels in some applications, we expect that high gas prices will often accompany high oil prices, raising both stocks' returns. In some years both may have earned negative returns (none are shown on this graph), and in others the returns may have had opposite algebraic signs. The scatter of returns on X and Y is oriented from northeast to southwest. X and Y could also be negatively correlated, as in Figure 16-14b, with high values of one variable (gasoline prices) associated with low

[22]These calculations require use of the binomial distribution, which we did not discuss. It can be found in almost any statistics or probability text.

FIGURE 16-14
Positive (a), Negative (b), and Zero (c) Correlation

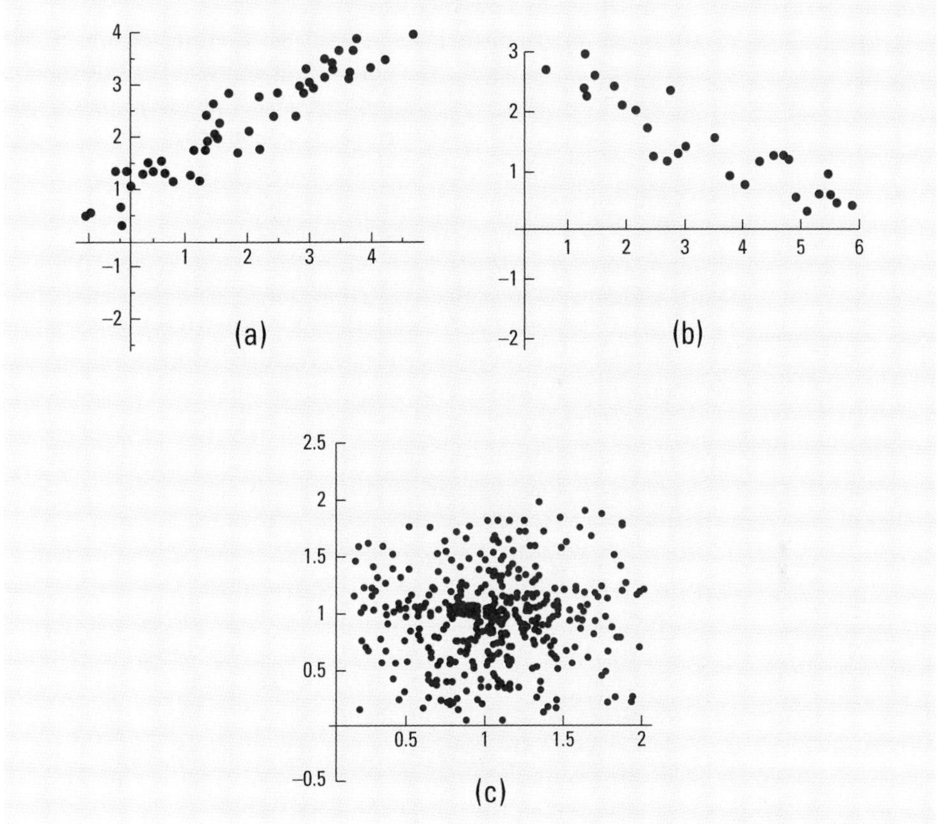

values of the other (tire sales). Finally, they might be uncorrelated, as shown in Figure 16-14c. None of the statistics thus far introduced can compute correlations like these. Disregarding Y, we could calculate the mean and variance of X, and vice versa. These means and variances tell us useful facts about X and Y taken by themselves, but they tell us nothing about whether X and Y might be positively correlated like in the various panels of Figure 16-14a.

To summarize the association between X and Y, we introduce the *correlation coefficient* between them, ρ_{XY}.[23] (ρ is the Greek letter "rho"). It measures the closeness of that association and tells us whether it is positive or negative. It is bounded by +1 and −1, and the closer it is to either extreme the higher the degree of association.[24] In Figure 16-13a, X and Y have a high positive correlation. (From the numeric data [not presented] we can compute $\rho_{XY} = 0.77$.) The X-Y combinations lie near an upward-sloping line, which need not pass through the origin. Obtaining a better understanding of why diversification cuts risk requires an expression for the variance of a weighted combination (as in a portfolio) of X and Y. To economize on notation, set $Z = \alpha X + \beta Y$. Then it can be shown that

(16.15) $$\sigma_Z^2 = \alpha^2\sigma_X^2 + \beta^2\sigma_Y^2 + 2\alpha\beta\sigma_X\sigma_Y\rho_{XY},$$

where σ_x, σ_y, and σ_z are the square roots of their variances, called their *standard deviations.*

[23]This exposition follows that of William F. Sharpe, *The Economics of Computers* (New York: Columbia University Press, 1969), 116–20.

[24]In this chapter all we want is an understanding of the size and sign of ρ_{XY}. Most statistics texts discuss its derivation, its properties, and how to calculate it.

The Investor's Preferences If two investments, X and Y, have equal risk, you will rationally prefer the one with the higher expected return. If they have the same expected return you will prefer the one with lower risk. The horizontal axis of Figure 16-15 measures the expected (mean) returns μ_x and μ_y (expressed as decimals) on two possible investments, X and Y. The vertical axis shows the variance of those returns. First look at X, whose mean returns are 5 percent (.05) a year with a variance of .07. Investment Y has both a higher expected return (.09) and a higher variance (.13) than X. Market forces will see to it that the mean and variance of the two stand in this relationship—a higher expected return will only be available to those willing to take on more risk.

Figure 16-16 allows us to derive some likely properties of your preferences for returns and risk, starting with investments X and Y from Figure 16-15. If another investment, W, has the same expected return and a higher variance than X, you will reject it unconditionally. If a fourth investment, Z, has the same variance and a higher expected return than X, you will always choose it over X. Thus, investments like W are clearly inferior to X, and investments like Z will always be chosen if X is the alternative. For X and Y the story is not as clear. You will rank X and Y in accord with your personal preferences regarding their relative abilities to help you attain your financial objectives. You may be nearing retirement and favor relatively steady (small variance) but low returns, in which case you might prefer X to Y. Or you might be starting out in adult life and willing to bear more risk for a higher expected return, preferring Y to X. Between those two, the 6 percentage point increase in your risk from holding Y might raise your return to a level that leaves you as well off as if you had been holding X instead. If this coincidence occurs, Y and X will be two points on a curve like I_1, which shows all of the combinations of risk and return that leave you as well off as at X. This is called an *indifference curve*, because you will be indifferent as to exactly where you are on it—someone else could just as well choose between Y and X for you.

If you are risk-averse your indifference curves are shaped like I_1, upward sloping and flattening toward the northeast. You require a higher expected return to compensate for greater risk, but the return needed to compensate you changes with the amount of risk you are already bearing. Starting from X, you may be just willing to accept 0.04 extra units of risk to enjoy an increase in your expected return from 5 to 7 percent, which would leave you at point U. If offered a further increase from 7 to 9 percent you will be willing to take on at most 0.02 added units of risk, leaving you at Y. Riskier investments are more likely to produce large losses, and risk avoiders place different values on equally-sized gains and losses. Figure 16-16 shows three of your indifference curves. A

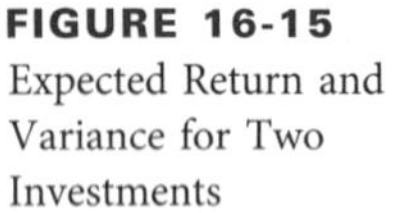

FIGURE 16-15
Expected Return and Variance for Two Investments

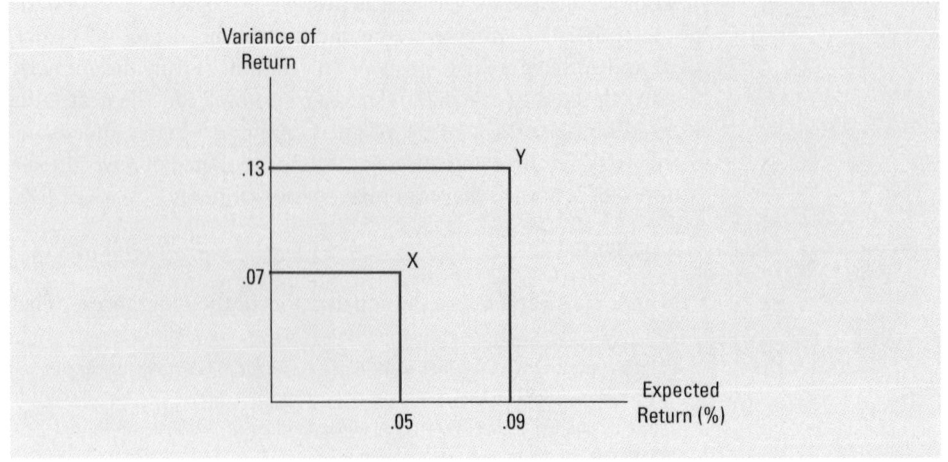

FIGURE 16-16
Preferences over Means and Variances of Investments

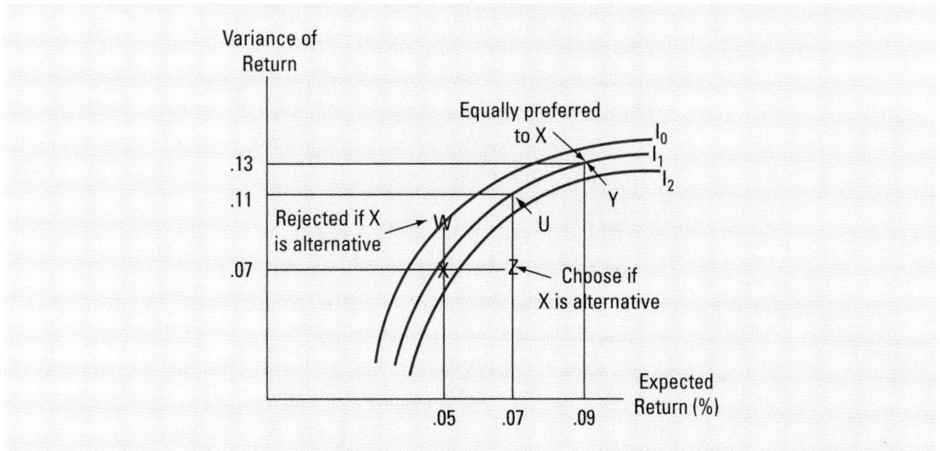

curve to the left of I_1, like I_0, consists of risk/return combinations that leave you worse off than I_1. To its right a curve like I_2 consists of points that leave you better off than I_1. Indifference curves can be drawn through all points in the quadrant, and any one of them will have the same shape as the three that are shown. Indifference curves cannot possibly cross—if they did it would mean that same risk/return combination gave you both a higher and a lower level of utility.

The Market Possibilities Assume that you have a fixed amount to allocate between investments X and Y, which are your only alternatives. X and Y may themselves be combinations of other investments, for example, mutual funds that hold a number of stocks. Your expected return on a portfolio with α percent of your funds in X and $(1 - \alpha)$ percent in Y (see equation 16.11) is $\alpha\mu_x + (1 - \alpha)\mu_y$. The variance of your returns when you hold X and Y in these proportions, $\sigma^2{}_p$, is given by a special case of equation 16.15. (Subscript P means "portfolio.")

(16.16)
$$\sigma_P^2 = \alpha^2\sigma_X^2 + (1-\alpha)^2\sigma_Y^2 + 2\alpha(1-\alpha)\sigma_X\sigma_Y\rho_{XY}.$$

Because α and $(1 - \alpha)$ are both between zero and one, their squares and products are smaller than the numbers themselves. Thus, diversification lowers the variance of returns on the portfolio. The gains also depend on the size and sign of ρ_{XY}. As an example, assume that $\mu_X = 0.02$ and $\mu_Y = 0.07$, while $\sigma_X^2 = .03$, $\sigma_Y^2 = .06$ and $\rho_{XY} = 0$. Figure 16-17 is a

FIGURE 16-17
Risk-Return Frontier

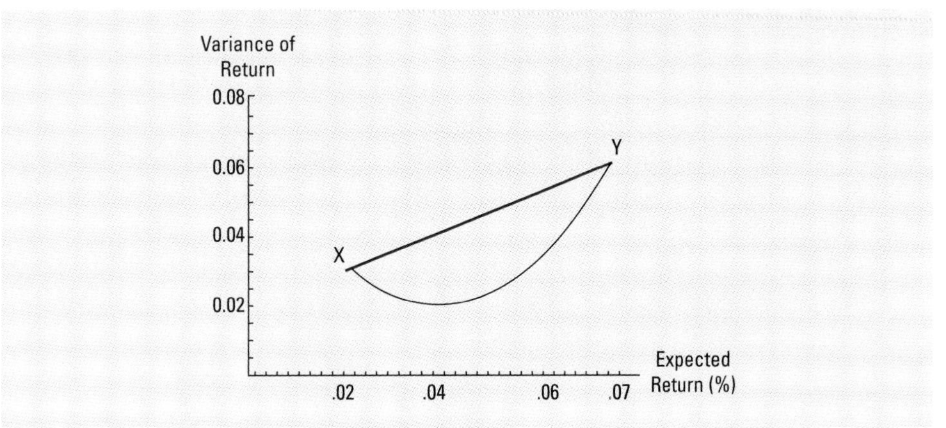

graph of equation 16.16 for these values as α varies. It is called the *risk-return frontier.* The leftmost point shows the mean and variance of a portfolio that consists of X alone, and the rightmost point shows them for Y alone. The variance of any mix of the two is given by equation 16.16, whose graph is the curved line between X and Y. The variance of a portfolio that mixes X and Y in a certain proportion is less than the proportionally weighted average of their individual variances, shown by the dotted straight line that joins X and Y. Diversification reduces risk even if the returns on X and Y are uncorrelated, as was the case with our original egg basket.

Figure 16-18 shows a set of risk-return frontiers for the same X and Y under different assumptions about their correlation. The frontier from Figure 16-17 (where $\rho_{XY} = 0$) lies in the midst of them, below those for which ρ_{XY} is positive and above those for which it is negative. The topmost straight line between the two investments shows the variance of a portfolio containing the two investments when $\rho_{XY} = +1$. When it equals +1 a high (or low) return on investment X is certain to be accompanied by a high (or low) return on Y. Because they are perfectly correlated, the variance of the portfolio is just a weighted average of their variances. The lowest frontier in Figure 16-17 is drawn for $\rho_{XY} = -0.8$. It's shape reflects the fact that a relatively low return on X is more likely to be accompanied by a relatively high return on Y than it is on any of the higher frontiers.

The Investor's Choice Indifference curves summarize your preferences, and the risk-return frontier summarizes the menu of alternatives available to you. You want to be on the rightmost (highest) indifference curve that the risk-return frontier allows you to reach. Figure 16-19 portrays the situation. If you are at point A on the risk-return frontier you can make yourself better off by shifting toward investment Y. If you are at B you could improve your situation by substituting lower-risk asset X for higher-risk asset Y. Your best choice is the portfolio P*, where the slope of the risk-return frontier equals the slope of I_1, the highest indifference curve you can attain. The division of the horizontal distance shows that about 75 percent of P* will be invested in Y and 25 percent in X. Figure 16-20 shows a person who is extremely tolerant of risk, as shown by his vertical indifference curves. They indicate that he simply wants to maximize his expected return, which happens on indifference curve I_2. His best portfolio, P**, consists entirely of the riskier investment Y. Buying any X at all would give a lower expected return.

Figure 16-21 shows a person whose preferences are at the other extreme—she has no interest in the size of her returns and only wants to minimize risk.[25] Her indifference

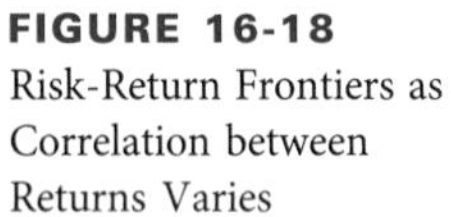

FIGURE 16-18
Risk-Return Frontiers as Correlation between Returns Varies

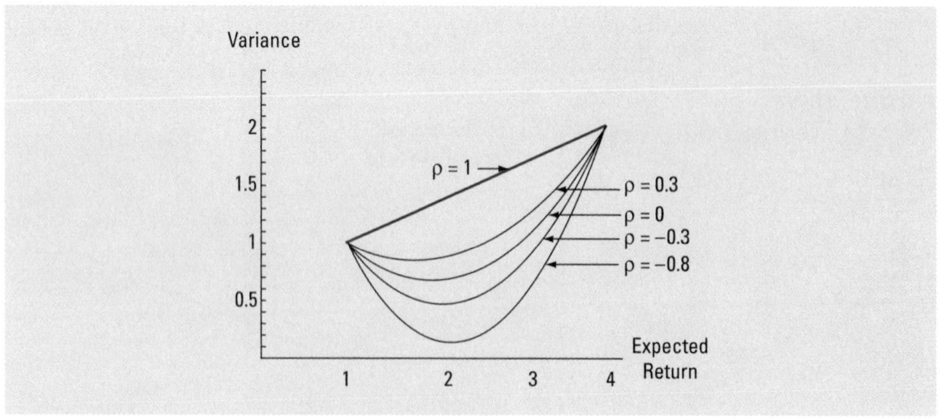

[25]This person might prefer some investment with a very low return and very low risk to either X or Y, but we are assuming that X and Y are the only two possible places to park her money.

FIGURE 16-19
Investor's Choice of the Optimum Portfolio

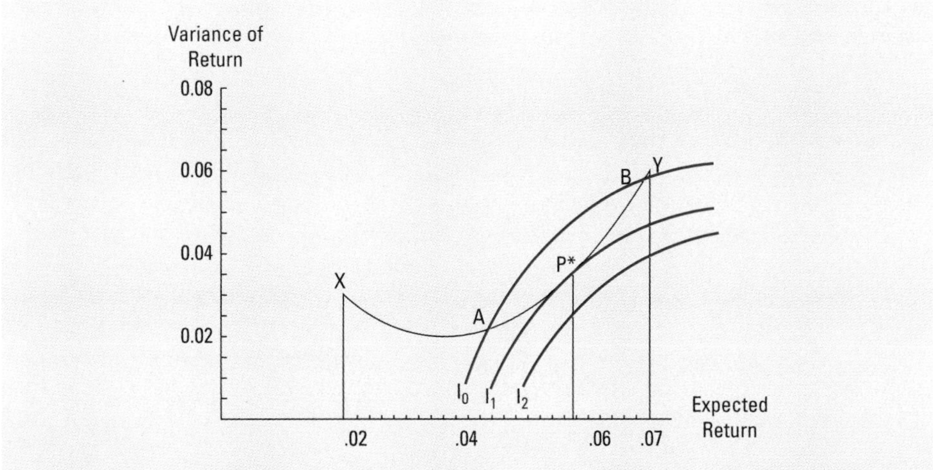

FIGURE 16-20
Optimum Portfolio for Investor Seeking only to Maximize Expected Return

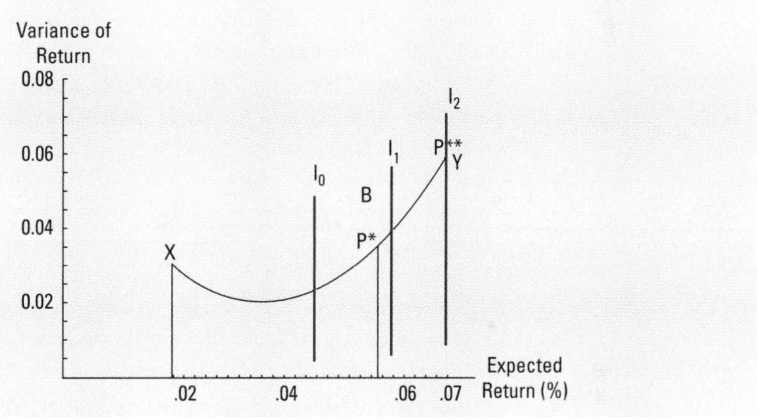

curves are horizontal—no increase in expected returns is large enough to compensate her for taking on any extra risk at all. She feels better off with portfolio P_2 on indifference curve I_1 than on I_0, where the best she can do is to hold portfolio P_1. It contains a mix of X and Y, but one with more X and less Y than P*, which the more risk-tolerant investor in Figure 16-20 chose. The investor in Figure 16-21 is probably too extreme to exist in reality, but she gives us a non-obvious insight: as long as the returns on X and Y are not too positively correlated, the portfolio with the minimum variance contains a mix of high-risk and low-risk assets. Even if you are an extreme risk avoider, your best choice is *not* always to hold only the asset with the lower variance. Instead, you can sometimes cut your portfolio's overall risk by investing part of it in the riskier asset.

THE VALUE OF INFORMATION

Risk and Uncertainty

Our models of risky choice thus far have assumed that people accurately knew all of the probabilities they face. In some situations they even knew the means and variances of distributions of random variables. If all such knowledge were there for the taking business decisions would be no more than algebraic exercises, only slightly harder to evaluate

FIGURE 16-21
Optimum Portfolio for Investor Seeking Only to Minimize Variance of Returns

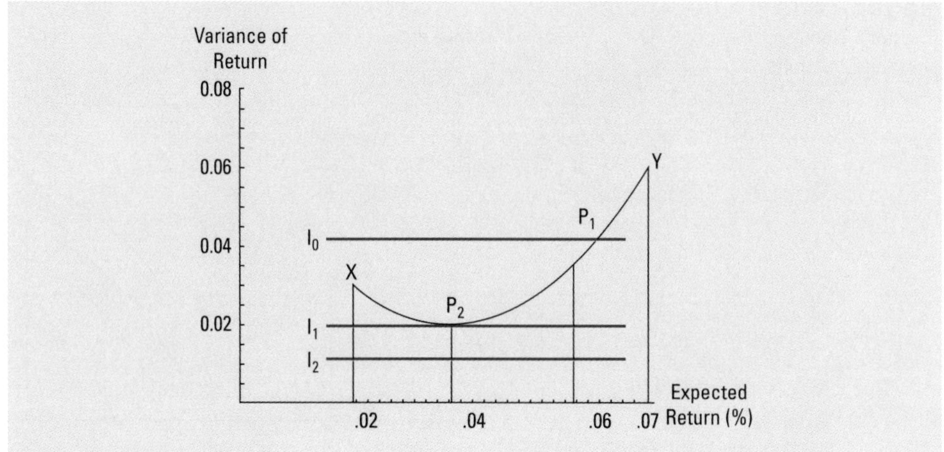

than probabilities of outcomes in a dice throw. Now we consider what happens if decision makers are ignorant, but we need to realize that like knowledge, ignorance is a matter of degree. The more accurately we know the probabilities of unfortunate events the better we can prepare for them, avoid them, or possibly prevent their occurrence. The more we know about the probabilities of fortunate events the more completely we can benefit from them. More or better data might improve the quality of your choices by providing you with more accurate estimates of a stock's expected return and its variance. Uncertainty would, of course, remain—past performance is no guarantee of the future.

Unfortunately, all too often in business (and personal) situations data that might improve the quality of our decisions simply do not exist. Personal experience is not always a reliable guide, but even it may be unavailable; there may be no comparable situations in your past that you can confidently generalize from. At the extreme, you are operating under *pure uncertainty*.[26] In our terminology, uncertainty differs from risk. In risky situations you have at least some information about probabilities and the underlying distributions of the possible outcomes of your choice. In situations of pure uncertainty, you have absolutely none.

As a practical matter, such extreme uncertainty seldom exists, and you will probably start your decision-making process with educated guesses about the probabilities of various events. You may not know the demand for a new product that you intend to test market, but the fact that you chose to go forward indicates that you believe its probability of success exceeds zero. If you take an opportunity to do some market research, you are implicitly indicating that you do not believe its probability of success equals 1.0, in which case you would confidently begin marketing without a test.[27] As a practical matter, you may well have more detailed beliefs (perhaps based on the success and failure of similar products) than that the probability of success is above zero and below one. You will start with a probability distribution of possible outcomes in mind, called a *prior distribution*, or simply a *prior*.

---

[26]The distinction between risk and uncertainty is due to Frank H. Knight, *Risk, Uncertainty and Profit* (New York: Augustus M. Kelley, reprint 1964).

[27]Because reasoning like this is always possible, some scholars argue that the concept of pure uncertainty should be abandoned because using it is more likely to confuse than enlighten. See Jack Hirshleifer and John G. Riley, *The Analytics of Uncertainty and Information* (New York: Cambridge University Press, 1992), 10.

There is some debate about the principles to use when forming a prior. What, for example, would you do if you somehow knew that the most profitable price for your product is $1, $2, or $3 but you have no grounds for favoring any one of the three. Some decision theorists recommend that in cases like this you use the *principle of insufficient reason* and attach probabilities of .33 to each of the prices being the right one.[28] Whatever your prior, you want a method that will help you reduce whatever uncertainty remains. The job has two aspects. First, you must try to devise tests whose results will allow you to reduce the zone of uncertainty. Starting from the prior probabilities of .33, the outcome of your market research might suggest that you consider changing these probabilities, a process called *updating*. Second, if such research is possible you must decide whether the reduction in uncertainty is worth the cost of undertaking it.

The Cost and Value of Information

The Parable of the Tycoon Decision makers often engage in research whose outcomes will help them update their priors. A famous tycoon has been said to do just this when he acquires control of a company he suspects is underperforming due to poor management. The tycoon's first action is to change its top management. If the firm's performance fails to improve he hires a new management. If the second management also fails, he sells the company. Soon we will put some numbers into this story, but first try to understand the tycoon's logic.

This person has a reputation for painstaking research before he decides to acquire a company. That research gives him reasons to hold a prior belief that it is a good company under bad management. He holds that belief strongly enough that he will pay a high acquisition cost and take on the risk of having to sell the company if he concludes that it is a loser. How might the tycoon decide whether the company is worth keeping? First, he picks a new management that his experience tells him is likely to be successful, but he understands that this team might actually be a poor one. Incompetent managers will be unable to fix a potentially good company, but there is also a probability that a good team will be unable to do the job either. All sorts of random factors (think personality clashes or misconduct by a third party) might intervene to make a good team fail.

If the first new management team succeeds, the story ends. But even if it fails the tycoon has acquired information he can use to update his prior. Good management teams have a high probability of success, and thanks to his experience the people he picked were likely to be good. These facts raise his estimate of the probability that the company is a loser. But there is still the possibility that the first team was a poor one, or that it was a good one but for some reason things went wrong. Selling the company is costly in two ways: beyond the direct losses (potential buyers will learn of his failed attempts and bid less for it), the company might actually still be a winner and he will forgo a long stream of profits by abandoning it too soon. After the first new management fails, the tycoon reduces his estimate of the probability that the company is a winner, but not to a number low enough to warrant an immediate sale.

Instead, he tries a second management team and keeps the company if it succeeds. Even if the second management fails it might still be a good company. The second management team might also be incompetent or competent but unable to do the job. Now, however, the tycoon has stronger reason to believe the company is a loser because not one but two management teams have failed to turn it around. A third management team might further reduce uncertainty but the tycoon has seen enough to conclude that the company should be

[28]For a fuller explanation of the principle of insufficient reason, see R. Duncan Luce and Howard Raiffa, *Games and Decisions* (New York: Dover Publications, reprint 1989), 284.

FIGURE 16-22
Value of Information about a Risky Investment

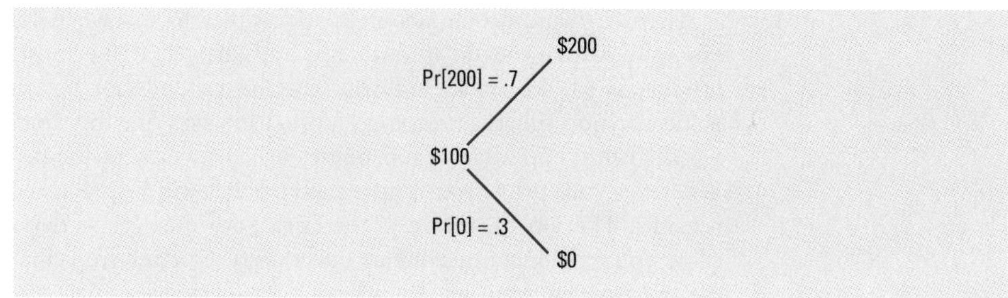

sold. The potential gain from a more accurate determination is not worth the added cost. The tycoon installs new management teams only as long as the marginal value of the additional information generated is worth the cost of installing them. After a few preliminaries we will be able to formulate his problem and examine the effectiveness of his two-management rule.

Determining the Value of a Test Figure 16-22 shows the possible outcomes of investing \$100 today. Tomorrow you will get either \$200 with probability .7 or \$0 with probability .3. Assuming that you are risk neutral over these amounts, the payoff's expected value is $-100 + (0.7 \times 200) + (0.3 \times 0) =$ \$40. If you have no better opportunities you should make the investment because its expected value is positive. Now assume that just before you commit the \$100, a reliable person offers to sell you a test for \$20 that will determine the outcome with certainty. Buying the test means you will only commit the \$100 if it says you will gain \$200. Your payoff will be $-20 - 100 + 200 =$ \$80 if the test is positive and −\$20 if it is negative. Because the test is perfectly accurate, the probability that it will give a result of \$200 is .7. Whatever the test result, if you buy it you lose \$20 with certainty. Your expected payoff if you buy the test is $-20 + 0.7 \times (200 - 100) + (.3 \times 0) =$ \$50. The expected payoff if you do not test is \$40, but if you test, the expected payoff, net of the cost of the test, is \$50. Thus, it pays you to buy the test as long as it costs less than \$30. The test is valuable because it reduces your uncertainty, and the value of that reduction is \$30.

Q. If the probability you will win \$200 is .9, explain why you will be willing to pay less for the test than if it is .7. What is that amount?

The test in the previous example was perfect, but most real ways to reduce uncertainty are only helpful. Exactly how helpful depends on the underlying probabilities and on the test's accuracy. Assume that you produce and market video games and have just received an idea from a designer outside your firm. That person has given you the code for an initial (or alpha) version of a first-person shooting game called *Invasion of the Economists.* You want to reduce your uncertainty about its ultimate market success. Readying the game for market will require \$200 for additional development expense. If the game is a flop, your revenue will be zero and you will write off the \$200, but if it succeeds you will receive \$700, which becomes \$500 after subtracting the development costs. From your experience producing and marketing games like this one you expect success with probability .3.[29] The initial prospects are unattractive, since in the current

[29]This is probably a high estimate relative to what is known about the actual success rates of such games.

state of your knowledge the expected payoff from further development is $-200 + (0.3 \times 700) + (0.7 \times 0) = \$10$, and you can (we assume) invest the $200 elsewhere for a higher return with certainty.

At the start you have no reason to believe *Invasion of the Economists* has a higher or lower probability of success than the typical game of this kind. You can, however, obtain additional information by retaining a group of hard-core gamers (so hard-core that they will work for free) who will play it, compare it with competitors, and report back on its prospects. Assume that they only say yes or no and do not provide any probability estimates. The entries in Table 16-1 are percentages that summarize their testing record. The testers seem biased toward optimism, because they think a larger proportion of games (45 percent) will succeed than actually do (30 percent). Very seldom, however, (only 5 percent of the time) do they give an unfavorable rating to a game that actually succeeds.

If you hire the testers and their opinion is favorable, the conditional probability that the game will be a market success is 25/45 = .56, and the probability that it will be a failure is 20/45 = .44. In the first case you receive $700, and in the second case you will get no revenue and will lose the $200 in development expenses. Your expected payoff if the test comes out favorably and you go ahead with the marketing is $-200 + (0.56 \times 700) + (0.44 \times 0) = \$190$. If the testers' report is unfavorable, the probability that the game will actually succeed after development is 5/55 = .09, and the probability that it will fail is .91. Your expected payoff is $-200 + (0.09 \times 700) + (0.91 \times 0) = -\$137$, and you will not market the game.

If there are no testers or you choose not to hire them, your expected payoff after the $200 development charge is $10. The test information does not perfectly predict success or failure, but it does allow you to revise your prior estimates of the probabilities of success or failure. If the testers' opinion is unfavorable, you lose nothing beyond what you spent for their services (we assumed for simplicity that they were free), and if their opinion is favorable you go to market and net back an expected $190. The probability of a favorable rating is .45, so your expected payoff from hiring the testers is $.45 \times 190 + .55 \times 0 = \$85.50$. Had you not commissioned the testing you would have abandoned the game. The expected value of testing the game and then only marketing it if you receive a favorable report is $85.50, less the $10 that you could have expected to earn just by going forward without the testers' opinion. Thus, $75.50 is the most you should pay for a test, and it is the value of the information that the testers generate for you.

Q. How does your decision to hire the game testers change if your prior estimate of the probability of the game's success is .2? Give a commonsense explanation, and then do the same for a prior probability of .8

TABLE 16-1 THE VIDEOGAME TEST

ACTUAL PERFORMANCE OF GAMES TESTED	TEST GROUP OPINION		
	FAVORABLE	UNFAVORABLE	ROW TOTAL
Success	25	5	30
Failure	20	50	70
Column total	45	55	

Bayesian Reasoning

Bayes's Theorem and an Example Our approaches to the previous problems exemplify a more general process called "Bayesian reasoning." If A and B are two events in the sample space, the definition of conditional probability says that

(16.17)
$$\Pr[A|B] = \frac{\Pr[A \; and \; B]}{\Pr[B]}, \text{ and } \Pr[B|A] = \frac{\Pr[A \; and \; B]}{\Pr[A]}.$$

Substituting, we obtain *Bayes' theorem*

(16.18)
$$\Pr[B|A] = \frac{\Pr[A|B] \; \Pr[B]}{\Pr[A]}.$$

Rather than events in the usual sense, let B be a hypothesis ("the company I just bought is a loser") and let A be some potentially relevant evidence ("new management failed to improve the company's performance"). You started with a prior that summarizes your beliefs about the probability that B is true, and now you have additional evidence. Should this evidence change your estimate of the probability that the hypothesis is true, and if so, how?

Before dealing with the videogame test and the tycoon let's exercise Bayes' theorem on a more transparent problem. A bag contains two coins. You know one is an ordinary coin with a head and a tail, but the other has two heads. You close your eyes, grab a coin, set it down without looking at the other side, and see a head. What is the probability that you chose the two-headed coin? Your prior is that the probability of the two-headed coin is .5, because you picked it at random. But you also know that three of the four sides that could have appeared are heads, and that the ordinary coin has only one of those three. Because heads are more likely on the two-headed coin, you might want to revise your prior probability of the two-headed coin upward.

Call the ordinary coin "HT" and the two-headed one "HH." Your hypothesis is that you picked HH. Before you see the result of your draw, you believe the probability of picking the two-headed coin is 1/2. The new evidence is E, the fact that the upturned side of the coin you drew is a head. By counting the possibilities you know that Pr[*E*] = 3/4. Applying Bayes' theorem and remembering that if you drew the two-headed coin the probability of turning up a head is 1:

(16.19)
$$\Pr[HH|E] = \frac{\Pr[E|HH]\Pr[HH]}{\Pr[E]} = \frac{1 \times \frac{1}{2}}{\frac{3}{4}} = \frac{2}{3}.$$

Your estimate of the probability that you drew the two-headed coin increases if you see a single head.

Q. Apply Bayes' theorem to show that if you draw a coin and see a tail the probability that you drew the normal coin is 1. (Obviously that probability equals one, but you are to show that Bayes' theorem gives you that result.)

More Examples *The videogame test.* In the videogame test problem earlier, your prior probability of the game's success, S, is .3. Your new evidence is a favorable report, F, from the testers. The probability that they will report favorably on a successful game is .25/.30. Unfortunately, they also mistakenly predict that a fraction of the failures (.20/.70

of them) will be successful. What is the probability that the game will be a success if you get a favorable report from the testers? You have

$$\Pr[S|F] = \frac{\Pr[F|S]\ \Pr[S]}{P[F]} = \frac{\frac{.25}{.30}\times .3}{.45} = .56, \tag{16.20}$$

the same as was calculated from the table. Bayes' theorem, however, can provide more "what-if" insights. First assume that the testers continue to report favorably on 45 percent of the games, but now a smaller proportion of those they favor actually turn out to be successes. In Table 16-2, only 44.4 percent of those they view favorably (i.e., 20 of 45) will actually succeed, and 55.6 percent (25 of 45) will turn out to be failures. This also changes the right-hand column of the table, because it implies that 10 percent of those they disfavor will also be successes. Applying Bayes' theorem, we find that Pr[S|F] is now $\frac{\frac{.20}{.30}\times .3}{.45} = .44$. If the testers are less accurate at spotting successes the revised estimate of the probability of this game's success will not rise by as much over the prior of .30. This is reasonable because now the testers are less accurate at spotting successes and failures.

Sequential replacement of managements. The tycoon's problem is an instance of a broader class of problems about *sequential searches* or *stopping rules.* Visiting auto dealers and getting price quotes from them is a common example of sequential search. The marginal benefit of seeing another dealer is your expected savings relative to the best offer thus far.[30] The marginal cost of seeing another dealer is largely the forgone value of your time. You can already guess that marginal benefit and marginal cost will determine the optimal number of dealers to visit. The tycoon faces a problem of this type. He will keep a newly acquired business only if it is a winner. The first management he installs, however, might be competent or incompetent. If the firm is a winner and the management is competent, it performs well and that's that. But continued poor performance could mean either a loser firm or incompetent managers. The tycoon might consider trying a second management. A winner company that was poorly managed last time might get good executives this time.

Two rounds might seem like too few to resolve the uncertainty, but the numbers might say otherwise. Begin by assuming that the tycoon really has some ability to identify undervalued firms, rather than just being lucky. That ability, however, is not perfect. Let the probability that a newly acquired company is actually good be .6. Further assume that the tycoon is also a fairly good judge of management teams. Any team he picks has a .7 probability of being competent enough to make a good firm perform well, but a competent team cannot make a bad firm profitable. The top half of Table 16-3 shows the initial situation. All figures in it are probabilities or percentages, but it's easier to think of 100 episodes with 100 different firms. In the first round, 70 percent get

TABLE 16-2 THE VIDEOGAME TEST WITH LOWER PROBABILITY THAT TESTERS JUDGE SUCCESSES CORRECTLY

	TEST GROUP OPINION		
ACTUAL PERFORMANCE OF GAMES TESTED	FAVORABLE	UNFAVORABLE	ROW TOTAL
Success	20	10	30
Failure	25	45	70
Column total	45	55	

[30]Assume that offers do not expire so you can revisit the lowest-price dealer you have seen thus far.

TABLE 16-3 MANAGEMENT TRIALS

	TRIAL 1: 100 FIRMS		
	MANAGEMENT QUALITY		
FIRM QUALITY	COMPETENT	INCOMPETENT	ROW TOTAL
High	42	18	60
Low	28	12	40
Column total	70	30	

	TRIAL 2: 58 FIRMS		
	MANAGEMENT QUALITY		
FIRM QUALITY	COMPETENT	INCOMPETENT	ROW TOTAL
High	12.6	5.4	18
Low	28	12	40
Column total	40.6	17.4	

competent management teams but only 42 of them (.6 × 70) are actually good firms. The remaining 18 winners received incompetent management teams and performed poorly. All 40 of the loser firms still lose, whatever the quality of their management teams.

After the first round the 42 well-managed high-quality firms are profitable and out of the picture, and 58 firms remain for a second try, shown in the bottom half of Table 16-3. Now the probability that a randomly selected firm is a loser has risen to 40/58 = .69. As before, the probability that a given management team is competent is .7. Of the 18 high-quality firms hidden among the 58, 12.6 get good management teams and the tycoon keeps them. Forty losers remain, alongside 5.4 winners that received incompetent management teams both times. With only two rounds of new managements (30 percent of which are incompetent) placed in the firms (40 percent of which are losers), the tycoon gets almost 95 percent of the cases right. His only mistakes are the 5.4 good firms that he will mistakenly sell alongside the bad ones.

Bayes' theorem gives another perspective on the tycoon. He holds a prior probability of .4 that a randomly selected firm is of low quality. A new management is competent with probability .7. Let L stand for low quality, and H stand for high quality firms. P denotes poor performance and G good performance. Then we have

(16.21)
$$\Pr[L|P] = \frac{\Pr[P|L]\ \Pr[L]}{\Pr[P]}.$$

The probability that a firm performs poorly, $\Pr[P]$, is the sum of the probabilities that it performs poorly because it is a loser and that it performs poorly although in reality it is a winner.

(16.22)
$$\Pr[P] = \Pr[P|L] + \Pr[P|H].$$

Substituting, equation 16.22 into 16.21 (the probability that a loser performs poorly is 1), we get $\Pr[L|P] = (1 \times .4)/[.4 + (.6 \times .3)] = .69$, the same as we derived from Table 16-3.

Q. Use Bayes's theorem to derive the probabilities found for the second management team.

Let's make a deal. A notorious Bayesian problem first emerged on television's classic game show "Let's Make a Deal."[31] After a series of preliminaries, host Monty Hall asks a contestant to choose which of three large boxes on the stage contains a valuable prize. The others hold junk. (One favorite was a live goat, sometimes a skunk.) The contestant receives no other clues, picks a box (call it Box A), but is not allowed to open it. The host then selects one of the remaining two (assume it is Box C) and opens it. The box he picks invariably contains junk. Because the host never selects the winning box we can safely assume that he knows all of their contents beforehand. The contestant is now asked if she wants to change her choice from Box A to Box B, and some contestants do so. Does it make a difference?

Most people's first feeling is that it makes no difference, but Bayes's theorem says that the contestant's expected payoff is higher if she switches. To see why, first note that if she picks Box A and stays with it her probability of winning can only be 1/3. Monty selects one of the two boxes that he knows both contain junk. Assume that it is Box C. Either Box A and C both contain junk or Box B and C do. If Box A actually holds junk, then after Box C is eliminated the probability that Box B holds the prize becomes 1/2. But if Box A contained junk Monty would have no choice but to pick Box C. If A is the winner, he would have picked Box C with probability 1/2. Switching from Box A to Box B raises the contestant's probability of winning to 2/3. From Bayes's theorem:

$$\text{(16.23)} \qquad \Pr[B\ wins|C\ has\ junk] = \frac{\Pr[C\ has\ junk|B\ wins]\Pr[B\ wins]}{\Pr[C\ has\ junk]} = \frac{1\times\frac{1}{3}}{\frac{1}{2}} = \frac{2}{3}.$$

If you are still not convinced that switching boxes makes sense, assume that there are 100 boxes and you originally picked box number 1. The host opens boxes number 2 through 99, which he knows in advance all contain junk. Now do you want to switch from box 1 to box 100?

Q. Assume all the conditions of the "Let's Make a Deal" problem, but now there are four boxes, one of which contains the prize. Again you pick a box, the host picks one, shows that it contains junk, and asks if you want to change your choice. What happens to the probability that you will win if you change your choice?

Q. If you still have problems with this reasoning, try programming a spreadsheet to duplicate a large number of plays of the three-box game, first with the contestant not switching her choice and then with the contestant switching. You will find that the latter wins more often.[32]

---

[31]Barry Nalebuff, "Choose a Curtain, Duelity, Two-Point Conversions and More," *Journal of Economic Perspectives* 1 (Fall 1987): 157–63.

[32]Or you can just play the same game: "The Monty Hall Problem," DecisionHelper.com; Web site, a companion Web site to *Decisions, Decisions: The Art of Effective Decision Making* by David A. Welch, http://www.decisionhelper.com/montyhall.htm.

Option Value

Economics and Options

We often encounter a tension between keeping our options open and making risky commitments. Economics is about choices at the margin, and here too there is a margin. What if instead of having to decide today you could buy the right to delay that choice? This right could be particularly valuable if your choice is irreversible. During the extra time you might uncover information that helps you better predict success or failure. If the information is unfavorable, you can choose not to make the commitment and leave your resources available for other uses. But time is also valuable—if the information is favorable the delay in committing your funds reduces the present value of your returns relative to investing earlier. Whether to buy the time requires comparison of the costs of delay and the benefits of additional information.

Options are everywhere. Some go by that name, such as those that give you the right to buy a share of your employer's stock at a prespecified price. If the stock's market price is below that level you will choose not to exercise the option and instead buy it in the market if you so wish. If the market price is above the option price you can turn an instant profit by selling the shares immediately after you buy them, or you may choose to hold them, and hope for still greater gains. If a potential new employer offers you a package consisting of a monthly salary and an option like this one, how do you determine the option's equivalent cash value? Without knowledge of that value you cannot compare this package to another employer's offer of a higher salary and no options. Another common option allows you to pay off the principal of a mortgage for a prespecified penalty, possibly zero. We see still another when a bond's issuer has the right to "call" it and pay the holder its principal before maturity. This right will be reflected as a discount (relative to an uncallable bond) on the value of the bond at the time of issuance. In another vein, outdoor goods seller L.L. Bean will refund the price of any item that you purchased, no matter how long ago, if you later deem that item unsatisfactory.[33] L.L. Bean is actually selling a package that consists of the item plus a non-expiring option to sell it back for the price you originally paid. Insurance policies have aspects of options, too. If you have fire insurance you have an option to sell the (destroyed) property back to the insurer for an amount specified in the policy.

Q. You can buy as much or as little electricity as you want per month for the same price per kilowatt hour. Explain why this is an option. Does your local supermarket sell options on groceries?

Q. What is the cost to your power supplier of issuing the option in the previous question?

Puts and Calls

A *derivative* is any financial instrument whose value depends on the value of some *underlying asset* (also called the "underlying" or "underlier"), for example a natural gas

[33] "Guaranteed: You Have Our Word," L.L. Bean Web site, http://www.llbean.com/customerService/aboutLLBean/guarantee.html?feat=ln.

futures contract whose underlier is the gas. An option is a derivative whose holder has the right, but not the obligation, to buy or sell a certain quantity of an underlying asset before a fixed expiration date.[34] Common underliers are commodities and shares of corporate stock. Other options are based on exchange rates, interest rates, or indexes like Standard & Poor's 500 stock-price average.[35] A *call option* (usually just referred to as a *call*) allows but does not require its holder to buy the underlying for a fixed amount known as its *strike price* (or *strike*) at any date on or before its expiration.[36] A *put option* (or *put*) allows but does not require its holder to sell the underlying at a preset strike price prior to expiration. An unexercised option becomes worthless upon expiration. Some options are customized two-party arrangements made in the over-the-counter markets, but a increasing variety now trade on organized markets like the Chicago Board Options Exchange (CBOE) and the New York Mercantile Exchange (NYMEX).[37] Options are particularly valuable to persons who either wish to profit from high variability in the market value of the underlier (usually called its *volatility*) or wish to purchase protection against it. The greater the volatility of the underlier's price the more likely that the option will go "in the money" before it expires.[38] A call option goes in the money if the price of the underlying exceeds the strike price, and a put goes there if the underlying's price falls below its strike price.

Options cannot eliminate risk—nature still determines whether this year's corn crop will be large or small—but options give people choices about which risks they will hold and help to price those risks they might wish to assign to others. The use of options to reduce uncertainty, like the use of futures contracts discussed in Chapter 3, is another instance of *hedging*. A corn farmer who holds put options gains certainty that he can sell his crop for at least the strike price. If the market price at harvest time is higher, the options will not be exercised. A cereal maker who turns corn into corn flakes can cap the price of corn she will be using by holding calls whose strike prices are at her desired cap. If the market price of corn exceeds the strike price, she exercises the options. If it is below the strike price, she buys in the spot market and lets the options expire. The farmer's and cereal maker's chosen strike prices need not be equal and will depend on their individual situations and expectations. Speculators with no interest in using the commodity will be counterparties to some option transactions. If the price of corn exceeds the strike price of the cereal maker's call, when she exercises it the speculator will either have to supply corn from his holdings or buy it in the spot market and resell it to her at a loss. In reality, very few options go to delivery and most are settled for cash. If the farmer no longer wants the put option's guaranteed purchase price he can sell it in the option market and take his chances on the spot price.

---

[34]Several comprehensive texts cover options. See, for example, John C. Cox and Mark Rubinstein, *Options Markets* (Englewood Cliffs, NJ: Prentice-Hall, 1985). At a more basic level, see Robert A. Strong, *Derivatives: An Introduction* (Cincinnati: SouthWestern Publishing, 2002).

[35]For an introduction to the S&P 500 and other index options, see the Chicago Board Options Exchange's *Understanding Index Options*, January 2001, at http://www.cboe.com/LearnCenter/pdf/understandingindexoptions.pdf.

[36]An option that can be exercised at any date before expiration is usually called an "American" option. A "European" call (or put) option allows purchase (or sale) of the underlying at the strike price only on its expiration date. (The names have nothing to do with their places of origin or use.)

[37]For more information, see the CBOE Web site at www.cboe.com and the NYMEX Web site at www.nymex.com.

[38]The most commonly used definition of daily volatility is $\sigma\left(\ln\left[\frac{P_t}{P_{t-1}}\right]\right)$, where P_t is price at day t, σ is the standard deviation of the expression in parentheses, and ln is the natural (base e) logarithm. To convert from daily to annual volatility, multiply by $\sqrt{252}$, where 252 is the average number of trading days in a year. For more on the definition and meaning of volatility, see "Volatility," at riskglossary.com, http://www.riskglossary.com/link/volatility.htm.

An option originates when someone *writes* it. The writer of a call option on a certain company's stock might be a large holder who does not expect its price to vary greatly before the option expires. (The corn speculator in the example may have written the option he holds, or he might have bought it in the options market.) If the writer holds shares of the stock or an actual quantity of the commodity when she writes the call option on it her position is said to be *covered*; otherwise, it is *naked*. If the stock's price comes to exceed the strike price, she will have to give up her underlying or buy it on the market when the holder chooses to exercise the call. If the stock's price does not pass the strike price, she keeps the money she received from selling the option she wrote. The buyer of the call is acting on his belief that the stock's price is likely to go above the strike before expiration. All of the uncertainty about the price of the underlying is still there, but the writer and purchaser are better off because both are holding risks they individually prefer. If the buyer's situation or expectations change, he can sell the option at a price determined in the market.[39] If the writer of the call comes to expect that the stock's price will rise above the strike price, she can buy it back or otherwise "unwind" (market jargon) her position, for example, by purchasing another call.

The Values of Puts and Calls *Just before expiration.* Let's begin by trying to find the value of a generic (again, "vanilla,") call option that is just on the brink of expiration. The one shown in the top half of Figure 16-23 has a strike price of $20. If the stock's current price is less than $20, the option is worthless because the stock can be bought in the market for less. If its market price is over $20, say $22, the option will be in the money, worth $2 just before it expires. Arbitrage will determine a price for it that leaves an investor indifferent between buying the stock outright for $22 and buying an option for $2 and then exercising it. The relationship between the price of the underlying and

FIGURE 16-23
Values of Call [Top] and Put [Bottom] Options Just before Expiration

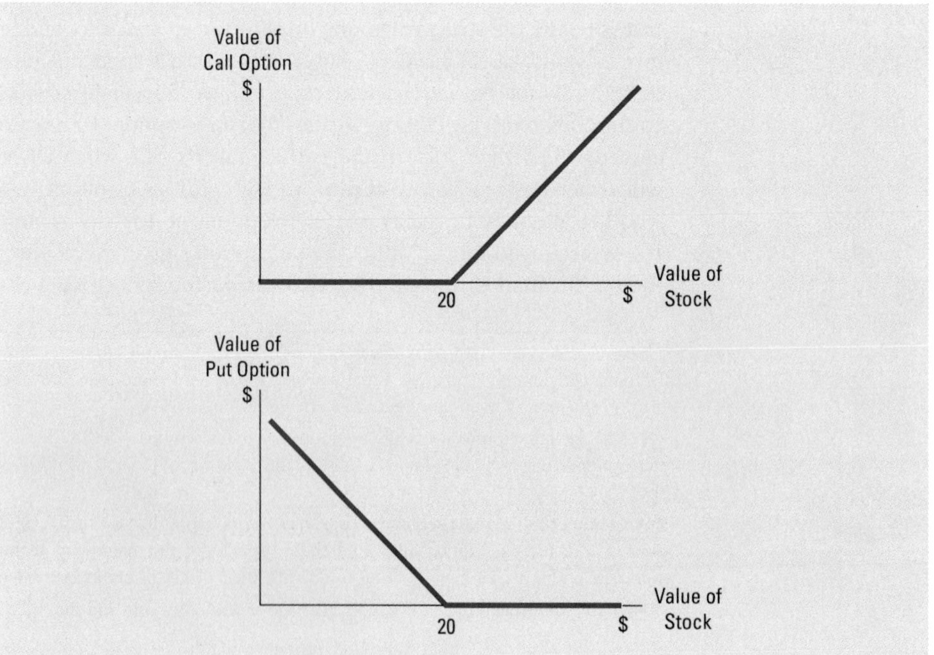

[39]For options traded on exchanges like the CBOE, the counterparty for all purchases and sales is the exchange itself, rather than an identifiable individual like in most over-the-counter markets.

the price of the call will be the angled line in the top half of Figure 16-23. It is flat and equals zero to the left of $20, and then it rises at 45 degrees. The same arbitrage principle determines the price of a put option just prior to expiration, shown in the bottom half of Figure 16-23. It will be worthless if the price of the underlying exceeds $20, since you can sell the stock in the market for more. Below that amount the put rises dollar-for-dollar with the difference between $20.00 and the price of the underlying.

Expiration further in the future—the determining factors. We cannot rely on simple arbitrage principles to value an option that has time to run before expiring. To see why, begin with Table 16-4. On June 24, 2005, a share of stock in Johnson & Johnson (J&J), the manufacturer of Band-Aids, Tylenol, and other medical products, sold for approximately $65. For about the same price you could purchase a share of Altria, the parent of cigarette manufacturer Philip Morris and brewer of Miller Beer. The table shows that day's prices of some call options on J&J and Altria. A January 2006 call on J&J (i.e., one that expires at the end of that month) with a strike price of $70 could be bought or sold for $1.40 on June 24, and one with a $75 strike was $0.40. A $70 January 2006 call on Altria sold for $2.90 that day, and one with a $75 strike sold for $1.30. A $70 January 2007 call on J&J could be bought for $3.90 in June of 2005, and a $70 call on Altria was $5.20.

To understand these price relationships we must first know the volatilities of the two stocks. The historical volatility of Altria's returns (annualized value of 0.215) is greater than that of J&J's (0.151).[40] Both companies face many uncertainties, but a single court decision in some tobacco-related case could impose massive losses on Altria. The company has, however, successfully defended itself in many lawsuits and is a party to a multibillion dollar settlement with federal and state governments that removes the threat of certain types of lawsuits. Favorable verdicts in some pending cases could remove much uncertainty about Altria's future prospects. The medical care market carries its own risks, but most of J&J's products sell in predictable markets and carry fewer legal risks than Altria's. Higher volatility means Altria's price is more likely to make a $5 move up to $70 (or down to $60) over a given time span than J&J's. Because Altria's calls are more likely to go in the money before expiration, investors will bid more for them ($2.90) than they will for similar options on J&J ($1.40). The prices of both stocks are less likely to cross a $75 threshold before next January than they are to cross $70, and both companies' $75 calls expiring that month accordingly sell for less than those with $70 strikes. Finally, both companies' January 2007 calls sell for more than January 2006 calls with the same strike price. An option with more time to expiration will be worth more than a similar one with less life remaining (disregarding the effects of discounting). The probability that the price of its underlier will move by enough to put the option in the money will be greater the longer the time that passes.

TABLE 16-4 STOCK PRICES AND CALL OPTION PRICES

	STOCK PRICE 6/24/05	PRICE OF JAN. 2006 $75 CALL	PRICE OF JAN. 2006 $75 CALL	PRICE OF JAN. 2007 $70 CALL
Altria	$65	$2.90	$1.30	$5.20
J&J	$65	1.40	0.40	3.90

[40]Both were calculated using the formula in footnote 43, using two years of daily closing data. The calculations did not adjust for dividends. The Black-Scholes formula requires that an annual volatility measure be adjusted for the time until the option's expiration date.

The Black-Scholes Formula Imagine that for some reason no one had ever discovered that the market price of a long-term bond would equal the present value of its payment stream. Further assume that people did, however, understand how to calculate interest on loans of a year or less. Many of them would shy away from issuing and buying long-term bonds, because no one would know how to determine whether a bid or asked price for a bond was in line with alternative investments. If long-term finance carried such great uncertainty some worthwhile projects might never be built, and the transaction costs and riskiness of all loans would be greater. The few longer-term bonds that did exist would be less liquid and would probably carry higher interest rates than if people knew how to determine what their prices would be in competitive markets where arbitrage was possible. Substitute "options" for "bonds" in these sentences, and you will understand how little economists understood about options before 1973. In that year economists Fischer Black and Robert Merton of MIT and Myron Scholes of the University of Chicago used their findings about arbitrage in volatile environments to derive a mathematical expression for the market price of an option—the price that would make an investor indifferent between holding the option and holding the underlying.[41] Economists and financial experts have since derived pricing formulas for many more complex types of options than simple puts and calls. In the process they have revolutionized our understanding of risk and made possible new tools for managing it.[42] During 2008, 9.36 *billion* option contracts of various types were traded worldwide, a larger number than the planet's population.[43]

The value of an option depends on its strike price, the current price of the underlying asset, the volatility of the underlying's price, the time to expiration, and the interest rate.[44] The Black-Scholes formula for the price of a European call option (one that can only be exercised on its expiration date) shown in Figure 16-25 includes all of these factors. Many other books explain the technical assumptions behind the formula, its derivation, and how to use and misuse it. Here all we need know is that it is the source of the relationships discussed here and shown in Figure 16-25. That figure shows how the prices of a call (top half) and a put (bottom half) calculated from the Black-Scholes formula vary with the price of an underlying stock.[45] Both are assumed to have strike prices of $25. Each curve corresponds to a different value for the volatility of the underlying. The numbers are different but the graphs illustrate the logic we used earlier to value options on Altria and J&J.

First, when the stock price is close to $25, say $20, the call's value exceeds zero even though the holder cannot exercise it profitably today. The option has value because if the stock is at $20 there is some chance that it will rise above $25 before the call expires. The further out of the money an option is, the closer to zero its price will be. Likewise, the

[41]Fischer Black and Myron Scholes, "The Pricing of Options and Corporate Liabilities," *Journal of Political Economy* 81 (May 1973): 637–54; and Robert C. Merton, "Theory of Rational Option Pricing," *Bell Journal of Economics and Management Science* 4 (Spring 1973): 141–83. Scholes and Merton were co-recipients of the 1997 Nobel Prize in Economic Science for this work. (Black's untimely death made him ineligible because Nobel stipulated that only living persons could win.)

[42]For an excellent and readable introduction to options, and risk in general, see Peter Bernstein, *Against the Gods: The Remarkable Story of Risk* (New York: Wiley, 1998), Chapter 18.

[43]Futures Industry Association, *Futures Industry Magazine*, Annual Volume Survey, March 2009, 17, http://www.futuresindustry.org/downloads/March_Volume.pdf.

[44]The text did not discuss the relationship between an option's price and interest rates. It can be shown that the value of a call rises with the risk-free interest rate, but an explanation requires some understanding of "put-call parity," which is beyond the scope of this discussion.

[45]Figure 16-24 also assumes one year to expiration and an interest rate of 10 percent. Calculations and graphics were made using software from Simon Benninga, *Financial Modeling* (Cambridge, MA: MIT Press, 1998), Chapter 19.

FIGURE 16-24 The Black-Scholes Formula

Let C be the value of a call option, with

S = current price of the underlying stock
K = the strike price
ln = natural logarithm [to base e]
r = interest rate
T = time to expiration
σ = standard deviation of returns on underlying stock
$N_1(d_1)$ and $N_2(d_2)$ = cumulative standard normal distribution functions.

Then

$$C = S\,N(d_1) - Ke^{-rT}\,N(D_2)\,,$$

With

$$d_1 = \ln\left(\frac{S}{K}\right) + \left(R + \frac{\sigma^2}{2}\right)T \Big/ \sigma\sqrt{T} \text{ and } d_2 = d_1 - \sigma\sqrt{t}$$

put option is worth little when the stock price is far above \$25, but if it is close to \$25 there is a higher probability of a further decline that will put the option in the money before it expires. Second, the value of an in-the-money option will exceed the difference between the stock's current price and the strike price. There is a probability that the stock will rise even higher before a call option expires (or fall further before a put expires), making that option potentially worth more. Only just before expiration will the option's value exactly equal the difference between the stock and strike prices. Third, at any stock price an option on a low-volatility stock will be worth less than a similar one on a higher-volatility stock that currently sells at the same price. The price of the more volatile stock is more likely to reach the strike price than that of a less volatile one.

The Diversity of Options Thus far we have only looked at simple puts and calls. As our theoretical knowledge of derivative pricing grows and risks become more complex, our abilities to devise and price new options also grow. A new specialty called financial engineering has arisen to design and determine those prices, often by extending the Black-Scholes formula.[46] Just a few of the many so-called exotic (i.e., the opposite of vanilla) options include the following[47]:

- *Compound options,* which give the holder an option to purchase or sell another option.
- *Barrier options,* such as a "down-and-out" call that becomes worthless before expiration if the price of its underlying falls below some value.
- *Lookback options,* which give the holder the right to sell (buy) the underlying at the highest (lowest) price it has attained over the life of the option.
- *Average options,* such as an "Asian" option that can be exercised upon expiration at a price equal to the average price of the underlying over its life span.
- *Contingent-premium options,* which, unlike ordinary puts and calls, need only be paid for (at a predetermined price) if they are actually exercised.

[46]For an introduction, see Salih Neftci, *Principles of Financial Engineering*, 2nd ed. (New York: Academic Press, 2008).

[47]For a far more comprehensive listing, see Michael Ong, "Exotic Options: the Market and Their Taxonomy," in *The Handbook of Exotic Options*, ed. Israel Nelken (Irwin, 1996), 3–44.

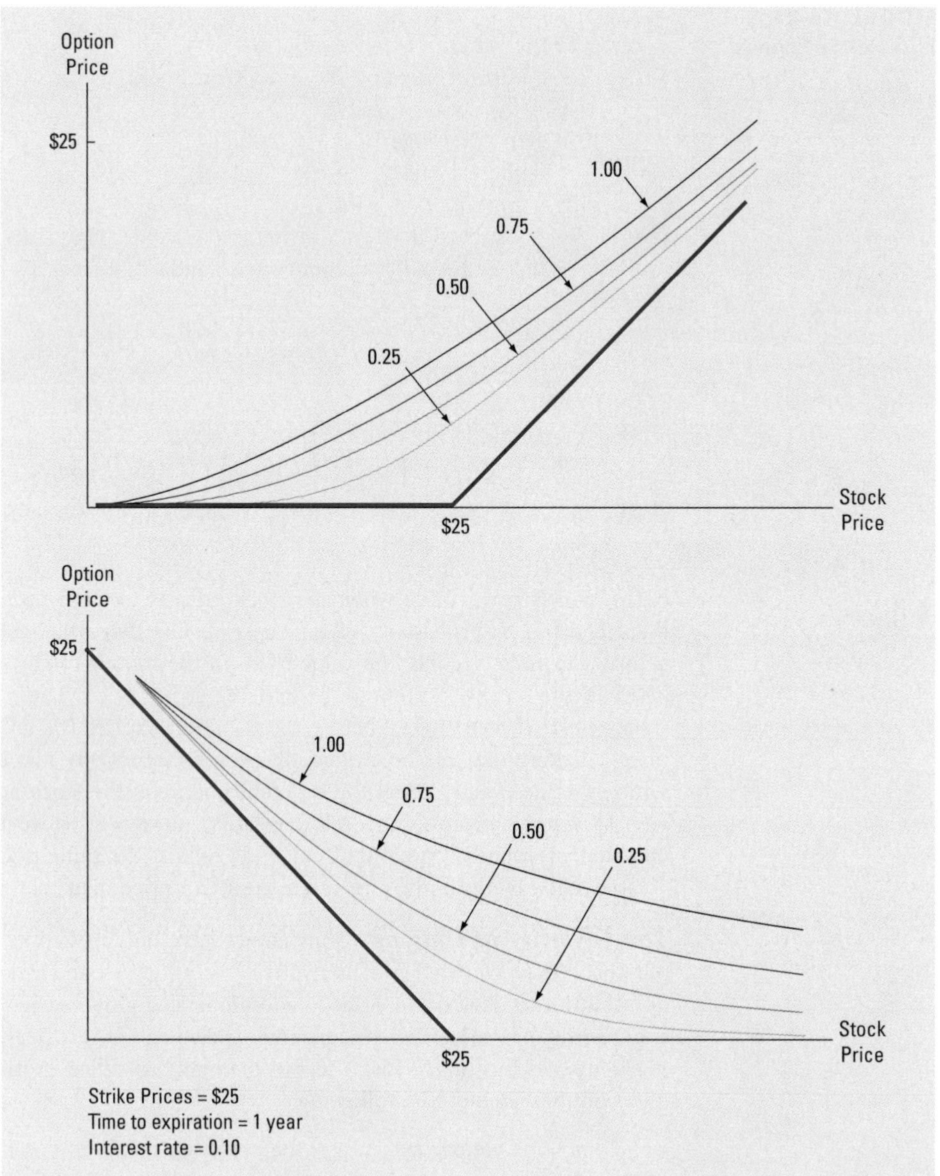

FIGURE 16-25
Black-Scholes Prices for Call [Top] and Put [Bottom] Options for Various Annual Volatilities

- *Basket and rainbow options*, in which strike prices and/or payoffs depend on the behavior of several underliers, for example, a call that can be exercised if some average of the prices of its components passes a critical level.
- *Leveraged options,* in which payoff is some multiple or power of the difference between the strike price and the price they are exercised at.

Try imagining situations in which options like these might be useful. You might, for example, want to buy a compound call option if you are bidding on a contract and need to lock in the price of some raw material that you will use if you win the job. At the time you bid, however, you do not want to hold the option itself because you might have to sell it at a loss if you do not win. Instead, you buy a compound option that you will exercise to buy the option you require if you win the contract and that you will let expire if you do not win it.

Irreversible Decisions and Real Options

Real Options Many decisions cannot be undone, either in part or in full. You cannot move a newly completed building to another site, and if you tear it down the salvage value will only be a fraction of its cost. The value of a building specially designed for making a particular product depends on both the price of its output and the costs of other inputs you must use. When you are deciding whether to build it a net present value calculation might show a loss if the market price of your output is low but a profit if it is high. Now assume that after a year passes you will (somehow) learn your product's long-term price with certainty. How much will you pay today for the right to postpone the start of construction until then, and to abandon the project if the price is low? An investment that you would reject on the basis of a net present value calculation might become worth undertaking when you account for the value of options embedded in it, such as the right to postpone construction. This right to postpone is an example of a *real option,* as opposed to a financial option like a call on a stock. Like a financial option, a real one gives you a right but not an obligation to do something in the future. Unlike market-traded options, real options are often unique to particular projects, and their strike prices are not always easy to uncover.

Real options have numerous applications.[48] For example, if you are building a plant that requires a large heat source for processing raw materials you can choose inexpensive equipment that can burn only natural gas, which has a volatile market price.[49] More costly equipment would be able to switch between gas and fuel oil, which also has a volatile price. What is the value of a real option embedded in a plant that can switch fuels, and what does that value depend on?[50] Looking at other decisions, a project whose size can be scaled up or down after construction may be worth more than one that you cannot alter. Oil in a storage tank and oil underground both have option values because you have a choice of when to use or extract them.[51] The right to prepay a home mortgage has option value. A plant that can be cheaply shut down for short periods can be worth more than one that must run continuously. High stock prices of new biotechnology firms may reflect the relative ease with which they can undertake and abandon research programs, compared with established pharmaceutical producers that operate on larger scales.[52] Going beyond markets, you might decide whether to file a lawsuit by treating it as an investment and seeing if the expected present value of your winnings is worth the cost. The right to settle or abandon the suit as information develops over the course of the case adds option value to it.[53] On a more somber note, there is an option value to flexibility in choosing the time to start a war and in making decisions to continue or abandon it.[54]

---

[48]Robert C. Merton, "Applications of Option Pricing Theory: Twenty-Five Years Later," *American Economic Review* 88 (June 1998): 323–49 contains many examples beyond those in this text.

[49]In this example we disregard the possibilities for hedging gas through the use of futures, options, or contracts.

[50]For a fuller discussion of examples like these, see Lenos Trigeorgis, *Real Options* (Cambridge, MA: MIT Press, 1996), 9–21.

[51]James L. Paddock, Daniel Siegel, and James Smith, "Option Valuation of Claims on Real Assets: The Case of Offshore Petroleum Leases," *Quarterly Journal of Economics* 103 (August 1988): 479–508.

[52]Simon Benninga and Efrat Tolkowsky, "Real Options: An Introduction and an Application to R&D Valuation," *Engineering Economist* 4, no. 2 (2002): 151–68.

[53]Bradford Cornell, "The Incentive to Sue: An Option Pricing Approach," *Journal of Legal Studies* 17 (June 1988): 377–99.

[54]Vincent Medina and Cyr-Denis Nidier, "Pricing War Within a Real Option Framework," *Defence and Peace Economics* 14 (December 2003): 425–35.

The Value of Postponing a Commitment Assume that you can build a plant instantly, and that your costs and revenues all come due at the end of each year.[55] Assume that the decision to build the plant is completely irreversible—it lasts forever, cannot produce any other good, and has no value as scrap. You can get \$8 million today to build it and in a year one of two scenarios begins. In the first your net revenue will be \$0.5 million annually forever. In the second, you get \$2 million a year forever. Each scenario occurs with probability .5. Finally, assume that you discount at 10 percent per year.

To begin, calculate the net present value of building the plant today. To calculate the present value of your expected profit, $E[\pi]$, you must weight each income stream by its probability and use the perpetuity formula discussed earlier in this chapter.

(16.24)
$$E[\pi] = -8 + 0.5\sum_{i=1}^{\infty}\frac{0.5}{(1.10)^i} + 0.5\sum_{i=1}^{\infty}\frac{2}{(1.10)^i}$$
$$= -8 + 2.5 + 10 = \$4.50 \text{ million}$$

Now assume that you have the option of waiting for a year, after which you will learn whether your future annual returns will be \$2 million or \$0.5 million. If they are \$0.5 million, the net present value of the project is

(16.25a)
$$\frac{-8}{1.10} + \sum_{i=2}^{\infty}\frac{0.5}{(1.10)^i} = -\$2.73 \text{ million.}^{61}$$

You avoid this loss by not building the plant. (Note that if you build you must use the present value of the construction cost.) If annual revenues are \$2 million, the expected net present value is

(16.25b)
$$\frac{-8}{1.10} + \sum_{i=1}^{\infty}\frac{2}{(1.10)^i} = \$10.91 \text{ million.}$$

If you can postpone construction until the uncertainty about revenue is resolved, you will be better off today by \$10.91 − \$4.50 = \$6.41 million. That amount is the value of the real option to delay construction.

The option value varies with the underlying conditions. The logic is similar to that used in determining the value of a financial put or call.

- *Greater range of outcomes*: Assume that the difference between good and bad revenues is larger than in the example, but expected value remains constant. If the revenues are \$0 and \$2.5 million, each with probability .5, the expected net present value of construction today remains \$4.5 million. The value of the option to delay construction for a year, however, increases. Recalculating equation 16.25b, the present value of profits when income is \$2.5 million per year is \$15.45 million, so the value of an option to delay rises to \$15.45 − \$4.50 = \$10.95 million. As a general principle, the greater the range of uncertainty that can be resolved, the higher the value of an option to delay. For these real option examples, this is analogous to a put or call rising in value with the volatility of its underlying.

---

[55]These assumptions are only made to keep the math manageable. For another example like this one, see Robert S. Pindyck, "Irreversibility, Uncertainty, and Investment," *Journal of Economic Literature* 29 (September 1991): 1110–48. For an estimate of the actual value of an option to delay construction, see Kyle Stiegert and Thomas Hertel, "Optimal Capacity in the Anhydrous Ammonia Industry," *American Journal of Agricultural Economics* 79 (November 1997): 1096–1107.

[56]To find the sum, note that it equals the value of 0.5 million in perpetuity, i.e., \$0.5/0.10 million less the present value of the first payment, i.e., \$0.5/1.10 million.

Q. Verify the calculations for the scenario with a greater range of outcomes.

- *Higher interest rate*: Going back to the original numbers, assume that interest will be 15 percent rather than 10 percent over the future. If you must build today, recalculating equation 16.24 yields expected profits of \$0.33 million. If you can defer construction for a year and build only if annual revenue turns out to be \$2 million, the present value of your expected profit stream is \$4.63 million. The option value of delaying construction is now \$4.63 − 0.33 = 4.30 million. A higher interest rate indicates a stronger preference for a given payment in the near future relative to the distant future, and the present value of the stream discounted at 15 percent is less than that of the same stream discounted at 10 percent.

Q. Verify the calculations for the higher interest rate scenario.

- *Longer delay in resolving uncertainty*: Assume next that all of the data are as before, but two years rather than one must pass before you know the future product price. The present value of expected profits if you build now is still \$4.5 million. Using equations 16.25a and 16.25b once more, the present value of the \$0.5 million payments in perpetuity starting two years from today is −\$1.65, and the corresponding figure for \$2 payments is \$9.92. The option value of a 2-year delay is thus \$9.92 − \$4.50 = \$5.42 million. Because the revenue stream is delayed, the value of a two-year delay option is less than that of a one-year delay option. The option value model also tells us the maximum premium you should pay for the right to resolve the uncertainty in one year rather than two.

Q. Check the calculations for longer delay in resolving uncertainty in the third bullet. Reconcile the outcome with the fact that a put or call that has a longer time to expiration will be worth more than one that expires sooner. How do these cases differ?

Chapter Summary

- Interest rates reflect peoples' preference for consumption goods that are available immediately (or sooner) over goods that are only available later. They also reflect the productivity of investment as savings are used to purchase capital goods that produce output over longer spans of time. Both the borrower and lender benefit from a loan for the same reasons a buyer and seller benefit from an exchange of goods.
- Interest is an opportunity cost. Investments that produce income over the future must entail forgone consumption in the present. Calculating net present values by discounting their future income flows allows us to compare investments by reducing them to a single number showing wealth that is gained or lost today. Discounting income streams and computing internal rates of return help us to account for the opportunity cost of capital.

- Interest is not the "price of money" but is instead the price of early availability. If inflation is anticipated, interest rates on money loans will adjust to ensure that lenders are paid back the actual purchasing power of the funds loaned.
- Just as people have differing preferences over goods, they also have differing tolerance for risks, which are summarized in measures of risk aversion. Transactions such as insurance and many other types of contracts (including derivatives) allow people to adjust their risk exposures.
- Markets assign values to possible investments that account for trade-offs between risk and return. Assets with higher risk will only find buyers if they offer higher expected returns.
- In all but extreme cases the diversification of an investment portfolio reduces the investor's risk. The optimal degree of diversification will differ depending on the relative values the investor places on risk and return.
- Better information improves the quality of decisions. In situations of uncertainty it does so by improving estimates of probabilities and the confidence one can have in those estimates. Information, however, also has costs, and the efficient amount to acquire depends on the costs and benefits.
- Bayes' theorem provides guidance on how to revise prior probabilities as new information is acquired. The degree of revision depends on both the probability of the information that was found and on what is known abut the probabilities of the data.
- The principles of net present value tell us that, other things equal, it is usually best to invest immediately if possible. If there is uncertainty it is sometimes better to postpone the investment until the uncertainty is resolved. The value of deferring an investment is its option value.
- Financial options are assets that give holders the right, but not the obligation, to make certain transactions at prespecified strike prices. They have become valuable tools for risk management, particularly in the years since option pricing models were developed.
- Real options involve decisions that are irreversible once they have been made. Generalizations of present value calculations can determine the value of postponing such irreversible decisions.

Questions and Problems

1. Electric utilities in California often make exchanges of power with utilities in the Pacific Northwest because their time patterns of consumption differ. California peaks in summer to meet air conditioning loads, and the Northwest peaks in winter because many homes and businesses use electric heating. If Southern California Edison delivers 1,000 megawatts of power to Seattle City Light in winter, the contract may specify that Seattle will return, say, 1,050 megawatts next summer. Although no cash changes hands, this transaction includes interest. Explain why.
2. Following are some compounding and discounting problems:
   a. Say \$177 grows to \$189 over a year at simple interest, that is, one annual payment and no compounding within the year. What is the implied interest rate?

b. Show that the present value of $189 a year from today at the interest rate you computed is $177.
c. At 12 percent simple interest, what does $230 grow to in two years?
d. What is the present value of $350 to be received in two years if the interest rate is 14 percent?
e. You know in advance that the interest rate your funds can earn for the next year is 12 percent, and 6 percent for the year after that. To what value do your funds grow in one year? In two years?
f. Same question as the last one, but now next year's interest rate is 6 percent and the following year's is 12 percent. To what value do your funds grow in one year? In two years? Why are both of your answers for the two-year calculation the same?
g. The interest rate is 12 percent per year. What is the present value of $500 to be received in one year? In two years?
h. You somehow know that next year's interest rate is 18 percent and the following year's will be 3 percent. Calculate the present value of $275 to be received two years from today.
i. Find the value of a three-year $45 annuity if the interest rate is 5 percent per year.
j. Find the value of a $70 perpetuity if the interest rate is 12 percent per year.

3. Lenders perceive that you are risky, so you must pay 12 percent annual interest to borrow from one of them. You only receive 6 percent on funds you have deposited in the bank. Do the opportunity costs of borrowing and using your own funds differ in this example? Explain why or why not.

4. The interest rate is 10 percent and you purchase the newly issued bond in equation 16.3 for $10,000. After you hold it for 16 years the market interest rate rises to 15 percent. Calculate the change in its price that results.

5. There are analogies between the value of a piece of land and that of a perpetuity. Assume that the land generates a fixed net income per year, i.e., the value of the crop it produces less the costs of production and maintaining the land's fertility. Then the market price of the land will approach that of a perpetuity. What will happen to that market price if annual property tax payments increase? If the current owners lose, can they recover any of that loss by selling it to a new owner?

6. Find the annual payments if the investments in equations 16.4a and 16.4b are transformed into annuities of two and three years, respectively. Then calculate the annual payments in a three-year annuity that has the same present value as the two-year payment stream in equation 16.4a.

7. Assume that I arrange a $100 loan from you at 10 percent real interest, and we both expect 20 percent inflation over the next year. What will the nominal interest rate be on that loan? Now assume that you lend me $100 to be repaid in two years and we both expect zero inflation in the first year and 20 percent in the second. Is the amount you will repay me the same as if we both expect 10 percent inflation in each year. If the amounts differ, why?

8. Go to "Approximating Social Security's Rate of Return, January 30, 2007," in *Political Calculations blog* and calculate the expected rate of return on your anticipated Social Security tax payments.[57]

9. If most people are risk averse, wages for jobs like high-rise construction and bartending will be higher than wages in similar but safer jobs. Yes or no? Explain.

---

[57]http://politicalcalculations.blogspot.com/2007/01/approximating-social-securitys-rate-of.html. This site contains a large number of calculators that produce net present values for a great variety of life decisions.

10. A family-owned business can borrow as much as it wants in the financial markets. If so, the family would have no reason to turn it into a corporation and issue publicly traded stock. Yes or no? Explain.
11. We can think of return on an investment as a "good" and risk as a "bad." Now assume that A and B are both goods, that is, more of A is preferable to less of it, and likewise for B. What do indifference curves between them look like?
12. There are two bags, each containing 100 ping-pong balls. Bag A contains 100 red balls and no black balls, and bag B contains 20 red and 80 black. You are blindfolded and reach into a bag. There is a .5 probability it is bag A and a .5 probability it is bag B. You draw a red ball. What is the probability that you drew the ball from bag A?
13. Do two variations on the tycoon problem with 100 firms. In the first, all numbers are the same as in the text, except the probability that a company is good is now .4 instead of .6. How many winner firms will be abandoned after two rounds of management trials? In the second variation, again use the same numbers as in the text, except the probability that a new management is competent is now .5 rather than .7. Again, how many winner firms will be abandoned after two rounds of management trials? What, if any, conclusions might you draw from these examples?
14. Try the following variant of the Let's Make a Deal game. Again one of the three boxes contains a prize, but now there are two players, 1 and 2. Assume Player 1 picks Box A and Player 2 picks Box B. The host (who again has perfect knowledge) opens Box B, which contains junk, and Player 2 leaves the show. Player 1 can either stay with Box A or switch to Box C. Using Bayes' theorem, show that now it does not pay Player 1 to switch, that is, the probability Player 1 will win with Box C is 1/2, the same as the probability Player 1 will win by staying with Box A.
15. If it is properly adjusted, a machine used to produce Good X produces 5 percent defective units of output. If improperly adjusted it produces 20 percent. You randomly pick a freshly produced unit of Good X and find that it is not defective. What is the probability that the machine is improperly adjusted?
16. Construct diagrams similar to those in Figure 16-23 for the net values of call and put options just before expiration when you must pay your broker a fixed commission to purchase an option. A *long straddle* is a transaction in which you simultaneously purchase a put and a call with the same strike price. Draw a diagram to show that you only profit if the price of the underlying asset at expiration is either well above or well below the strike price, but whether it is above or below does not matter.
17. Devise a hypothetical business situation in which buying a lookback call option on a commodity may be a sound strategy for you. How about a down-and-out call option?

Chapter 17

Conflict, Negotiation, and Group Choice

INTRODUCTION

Trials on Trial

In nations around the world a trial is the heart of the civil justice system.[1] If you are engaged in a dispute you probably find it reassuring that you can go to court if you cannot settle with your opponent. A trial gives both of you a public forum in which to state your cases and introduce evidence. The judge and jury are sworn to uphold the law and act impartially. Attorneys on both sides must follow elaborate rules to ensure fairness and protect your rights. You are indeed fortunate to have a right to a trial.

If you go to court the empty chairs below will soon be filled with jurors, a dozen people whom the court believes are your peers. Their decision may change your life and

Don Farrall/Getty Images

[1]This chapter does not cover criminal law. For a collection of articles on that topic, see Steven Levitt and Thomas Miles (Eds.), *Economics of Criminal Law* (Northampton, MA: Edward Elgar, 2008).

your opponent's. The jury will consist of people taken away from their everyday lives who have no particular interest in your dispute and no knowledge of your business. Your attorney can reject some potential jurors but those who survive may still be biased against you. Even if the jurors make their best efforts to understand both sides' cases their decision might be emotional rather than logical. Jurors whose formal schooling may have ended in eighth grade may be told to weigh the testimonies of opposing PhDs on highly technical issues.

The uncertainties of a jury do not vanish if instead you and your opponent agree to a bench trial by a judge alone. That person interprets the law every working day, but the law covers a lot of territory. The judge's mental powers are limited, but over the weeks she might try cases in areas as diverse as homicide, drunk driving, business contracts, toxic waste, and employment discrimination. Your business dispute may hang on facts that a well-educated judge cannot evaluate more accurately than less-educated jurors. Impartiality is hard to determine objectively, and your judge might be a political appointee who shares the philosophy of the governor who named her to the post. A judge may know more about the law than most jurors but is also someone whose opinions need not be accepted by 12 other people.

With all this in mind you might revise your thinking about trials. Instead of opportunities, they are evidence that the litigants and their attorneys have failed. Rational people will try to avoid them.[2] Failure to resolve a dispute means a courtroom where both parties may walk out worse off than if they had settled. Both will bear the costs of preparing for trial and presenting their cases. Long preparation times and crowded court schedules can mean delays during which the parties must still carry on their businesses. Going to trial compounds the uncertainty and has no obvious benefit. The two parties are throwing their dispute into the hands of people who cannot possibly know as much about their work as they already do. The law understands this and generally encourages negotiation to reach a settlement. People can privately agree to almost any settlement terms they both accept, but the law may not allow a judge to order them to do things that they might agree upon between themselves.[3] Negotiation is an important part of many ongoing business relationships, and the memory of a trip to court can make negotiations harder to manage over the long term.

In reality, plaintiffs and defendants usually avoid court. They manage to settle approximately 95 percent of all civil disputes that could have gone to trial. What happens is consistent with an economic model. Cases with more at stake are more likely to settle, as one expects if the parties are risk averse. So are suits that will entail higher court costs. Types of lawsuits that one side has a high probability of winning are more likely to settle than those in which there are more equal odds of victory.[4] Trials take place more often

---

[2]Samuel R. Gross and Kent D. Syverud, "Getting to No: A Study of Settlement Negotiations and the Selection of Cases for Trial," *Michigan Law Review* 90 (November 1991): 319–93. The title is a play on the mass-market book *Getting to Yes: Negotiating Agreement Without Giving In*, by Roger Fisher and William Ury (New York: Penguin Books, 1991). The title of this section is the same as that of a book which raises some of these issues, *Trials on Trial* by Gordon Tullock (New York: Columbia University Press, 1979).

[3]For example, assume that A is plaintiff in two related disputes with defendant B. As a condition of settling the first case they may agree that A will abandon the second. If only the first case is being tried the court must work exclusively on it and generally cannot force A to drop the second case.

[4]See Gary Fournier and Thomas Zuehlke, "Litigation and Settlement: An Empirical Approach," *Review of Economics and Statistics* 71 (May 1989), 189–95. Settlement can also mean abandonment of a suit that was brought largely as a bargaining chip. Defendants in private antitrust cases, for example, win such a high proportion of cases that actually go to trial that plaintiffs often settle for small amounts rather than incur the costs of a long-shot case.

in cases where the parties have greatly differing expectations about the outcome or asymmetric information about the facts.[5]

A large percentage of other disputes also settle. Negotiations between labor unions and employers overwhelmingly result in agreements rather than strikes. Like a trial, a union strike or an employer lockout only happens after negotiations have failed, and both sides bear the costs of that failure. During a strike the workers bring home no pay and the employer loses profit and continues to incur fixed costs.[6] In 2008, only 72,000 workers in the U.S. labor force of 155 million lost any hours at all to strikes.[7] Regular cycles of contract negotiation are integral parts of ongoing relationships between unions and managements. As we will see, repetitive negotiations differ in some important ways from one-time events like those that take place before a possible trial. Faced with a strike deadline, the union and management will also face negotiating problems quite unlike those of the trial lawyers.

Negotiation is a process in which parties initially in disagreement attempt to reach an agreement. In our earlier examples of two-party exchange the area of mutual benefits was generally easy to define. The negotiators in this chapter may have substantial problems just discovering the boundaries of the zone within which they can reach agreement, and then they must still settle on an outcome in that zone.[8] Exploring to find areas where both parties can gain becomes more important the greater the number of items they must agree on. Over the course of negotiation they may discover trade-offs among the various objectives that they had not previously noticed. Even agreeing to disagree on some aspects of their conflict while resolving other difficulties provides useful knowledge that might help the parties to better structure their future negotiations.[9]

Negotiation and Choice

Conflict and negotiation play fundamental roles in all of the social sciences. Sociologists examine agreement and disagreement within families and organizations, and political scientists analyze how they play out in governments. Anthropologists focus on commonalities and differences in business relationships and negotiations between societies. This chapter provides economic insights into the same subjects that will shed light on organizational forms and employer–employee relationships. In particular, we will focus on the following:

- We will review two-person exchanges and summarize the findings of lab experiments in bargaining. We will then see how bargaining between automobile buyers and dealers has changed between the 1960s and today, when information about markets is easier for customers to acquire.

---

[5]In some economic models these divergent beliefs lead to plaintiffs and defendants each winning approximately half of the trials, an outcome that may be little different from one determined by a coin flip. George L. Priest and Benjamin Klein, "The Selection of Disputes for Litigation," *Journal of Legal Studies* 13 (January 1984): 1–56; and Joel Waldfogel, "Reconciling Asymmetric Information and Divergent Expectations Theories of Litigation," *Journal of Law and Economics* 41 (October 1998): 451–76.

[6]Both sides may also have sources of income that they can rely on during the strike, for example, public assistance for workers and business interruption insurance for employers.

[7]U.S. Bureau of Labor Statistics, "Work Stoppages Summary," February 11, 2009, http://www.bls.gov/news.release/wkstp.nr0.htm. A single strike by the International Association of Machinists against Boeing Aircraft accounted for half of all lost workdays in 2008. Labor force data are from the 2009 *Economic Report of the President*, p. 327, http://www.gpoaccess.gov/eop/2009/2009_erp.pdf.

[8]Otomar Bartos, "Determinants and Consequences of Toughness," in *The Structure of Conflict*, ed. Paul Swingle, 46 (New York: Academic Press, 1970).

[9]John G. Cross, *The Economics of Bargaining* (New York: Basic Books, 1969), 4–5.

- We illustrate the possible outcomes of two-person bargaining and discuss how social customs and shared expectations lower the costs of reaching agreement, particularly in repeated bargaining situations.
- Multi-person negotiations are generalizations of two-person situations. With the concept of a "core" we can characterize situations in which no subset of a group's members can do better for itself by leaving the group than by staying with it.
- There are important distinctions between "private" goods consumed exclusively by one person and "public" goods that are concurrently consumed by all members of a group. If exclusion of non-payers is impossible, it will be difficult to learn a person's actual valuation of a public good.
- Sometimes private incentives will suffice to get public goods produced, but in other important cases (for example, national defense) a government with the power to tax must do so.
- In democracies voters ultimately determine governmental policies. In some situations the "median" voter is decisive, but in others a subset of voters can manipulate the process.

Negotiation: Some Theory and Data

Experiments

Figure 17-1 brings back the familiar situation of two-person exchange. Buyer Smith's valuation of some good or service is \$11, and seller Jones's opportunity cost is \$7. There are \$4 of potential benefits to share if they make an exchange, the sum of their producer and consumer surpluses. In the diagram \$7 and \$11 bound a "zone of agreement" in which the exchange will benefit both of them.[10] Negotiators sometimes call it "headroom." We expect the two parties to reach an agreement, but that region could just as well be called a "zone of conflict," where a dollar more of benefits for one means a dollar less for the other. The red vertical line at \$8.50 denotes one possible division, with \$1.50 going to Jones and \$2.50 to Smith. Jones's interest is in pushing the red line rightward and Smith's is in pushing it leftward. In the language of game theory, this prospective exchange is a *positive-sum* game. It is a game because each chooses offers and counteroffers, and the final outcome depends

FIGURE 17-1 Negotiation and Exchange

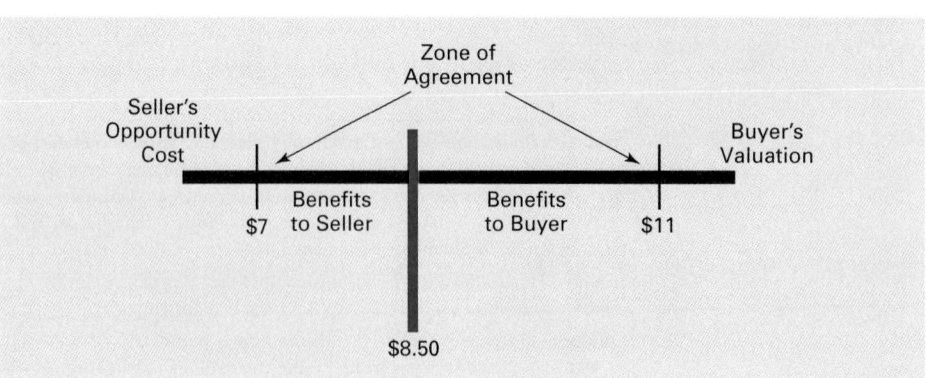

[10]This terminology follows that of Howard Raiffa, *The Art and Science of Negotiation* (Cambridge, MA: Harvard University Press, 1982), 46.

on both of their actions. Their benefits add up to $4, an amount they will forgo if they are unable to agree. If they have committed themselves to an exchange but have yet to agree on a price they are playing a *zero-sum* game. They will definitely share $4 of benefits but any gain for one is an equal loss for the other.

A buyer often can only guess the lowest price a seller will settle for, and the seller may be equally unsure about the highest a buyer will tolerate. Economists and psychologists have performed many bargaining experiments with underlying situations like the one depicted in Figure 17-1. In a typical experiment people are assigned at random to play the roles of buyers and sellers. Each party learns her own personalized opportunity cost or valuation but gets little or no information about what her counterparty's critical figure might be. Although the parties cannot divulge these figures to each other, nearly all pairs usually manage to strike bargains at mutually beneficial prices.[11] Average final prices are often near the halfway mark between valuation and opportunity cost. The distribution of these prices, however, usually has a high standard deviation, and significant percentages are close to the upper or lower boundary of the zone of agreement.[12] In most bargaining experiments researchers do not find significant relationships between the final prices and such personal characteristics of the bargainers as age, education, income, or gender.

Q. In bargaining experiments the personal characteristics of the bargainers seldom influence the outcome. Give two possible reasons why this might happen.

Negotiating Automobile Prices: Two Generations of Data

Lab experiments can provide insight, but we can also learn a lot from actual price quotations. The latter might tell us more about how price offers vary with market conditions, characteristics of buyers and sellers, and techniques of bargaining. Buying a car is a familiar experience, and most buyers shop more than one dealer. Nearly everyone seems to know that the legally required sticker price is often just a starting point for negotiation.[13] If face-to-face with the buyer, a dealer generally begins by offering less than the sticker price, with further declines as the bargaining goes on. Many people still buy their cars this way, but increasing numbers of buyers and dealers now transact online. The older and newer ways of negotiation have remarkably different outcomes that shed light on bargaining, and on how markets work when the institutions underlying them change.

---

[11]In a typical experimental session 96 percent of the pairs reached agreement in the expected range, 3 percent never got to an agreement, and 1 percent misunderstood the instructions and reached agreements outside the range. See Raiffa, *The Art and Science of Negotiation,* 48.

[12]Some other regularities are of potential interest. Average opening offers in such experiments are often close to the limits of the zone of agreement, and an amount halfway between their first offers (assuming that it lies in the zone) is often a good predictor of the final price. When subjects are given valuations and costs that are close to each other, for unknown reasons it often takes a larger number of offers and counteroffers to reach a final price. See Raiffa, *The Art and Science of Negotiation,* 48.

[13]The General Motors Saturn is the only car currently produced whose dealers sell at firm, nonbargainable prices. The typical transaction, however, still requires negotiation over the amount paid for a trade-in. As of 2009 it appears that GM intends to stop producing Saturns, but this probably reflects GM's poor financial condition rather than Saturn's pricing policy.

Surveys of Chicago Dealers, 1960 In the late 1950s and early 1960s, economists first used price quotes from auto dealers to analyze bargaining. Allen Jung of the University of Chicago sent three different persons to every Ford and Chevrolet dealer in the city (about 30 of each).[14] They were instructed to obtain prices from each dealer for the same model, identically equipped. In one experiment the first shopper was instructed to explain to the salesperson that he had just finished driving school, had no experience with cars, and would like to buy immediately from that particular dealer.[15] The second was told to act like a normal shopper but not to attempt to bargain after obtaining the dealer's first price. He (all were male) was also instructed to tell the dealer that he intended to see a number of other dealers before choosing. The third shopper was made familiar with the industry and trained to act very experienced. After getting the dealer's quote he would make a "final" offer well below the car's wholesale price, and then record the price the dealer quoted in response. Among other results, Jung found that:

- Price offers covered a wide range. The Ford's sticker price was $3,034 (remember, this was 1959), but no dealer held firm to that price. Actual quotes ranged from $2,875 (95 percent of sticker) to $2,495 (82 percent). Figures for the Chevrolet were comparable. Unless search costs are very high, it pays to shop more than one dealer.
- Variation in the offered price seemed to be random. Only one of the 58 dealers quoted the same price to all shoppers, and only eight quoted the same price to two of the three.
- No statistically significant differences were found between the mean prices offered to the naive Ford buyer ($2,610), the average buyer ($2,584), and the tough customer ($2,577). The same held for Chevrolets.
- The experienced buyer received a final offer on the Ford that averaged 2.4 percent below the initial offer. Dealers who quoted relatively high initial prices came down more in the final price than those quoting low ones, but the final average for tough customers did not differ significantly from averages quoted to others.
- Dealer characteristics had little or no influence on the prices they offered. No statistically significant differences were found in the average prices quoted by large, medium, and small dealers. Dealers in higher-income neighborhoods quoted the same prices as those in lower-income areas. There were no significant differences between the offers of new dealers and more established ones.
- In another study, Jung found no significant differences in the average quotes given to people who telephoned for a price and those who came into the showroom.[16]

The auto price data in some ways resemble those from controlled experiments. The actual figures vary widely in both, and in both they appear unrelated to the characteristics of the people performing the negotiation. Average prices were unrelated to the bargaining techniques they used. The buyer's information about the dealer's wholesale cost appears to have been unimportant, since average quoted prices were the same to buyers who knew that cost and buyers who did not. Auto dealers had no information about

---

[14]Allen F. Jung, "Price Variations among Automobile Dealers in Chicago, Illinois," *Journal of Business* 32 (October 1959): 315–26.

[15]After obtaining a price, this buyer would explain that he had to check it with his brother and leave the dealership.

[16]Allen F. Jung, "Price Variations among Automobile Dealers in Metropolitan Chicago," *Journal of Business* 33 (January 1960): 31–42.

previous prices offered to surveyors, and the distribution of their offers was similar to those found in experiments.[17] Jung's survey methods did not address one potentially important question: because all of his surveyors were white men he could not investigate whether women or minorities got significantly different quotes. For that we go forward 40 years.

Q. Give two possible reasons why dealers in higher-income neighborhoods might quote higher prices than dealers in low-income neighborhoods. Then give two possible reasons why those prices might be lower in high-income neighborhoods.

Discrimination and Internet Auto Sales, 2003 The growth of online auto purchasing has provided new insights into how information and personalities affect negotiations. As one example, Internet data have been used to analyze claims of discrimination in prices offered to women and minority group members. The pervasive randomness of quoted prices makes differences hard to measure, and researchers have disagreed about whether they exist at all.[18] If the differences exist they may reflect price discrimination based on differing elasticities of demand, rather than discrimination based on a customer's personal characteristics. If differences are due to price discrimination, otherwise identical men and women will get identical offers, but if they are due to gender discrimination the same individuals will get different offers. If more women than men have some trait that dealers associate with more inelastic demands, on average women will get higher prices. Those prices, however, are the result of more females having the trait in question, rather than simply being females.

Recent research has found that the use of Internet broker Autobytel.com favorably affects prices women and minorities actually pay.[19] The differences between prices paid by women and minorities and prices paid by others are smaller for those who use Autobytel.com than for comparable people who go directly to dealers.[20] The exact reasons are not yet clear. One possible explanation is that women and minorities have higher search costs, perhaps because low incomes, language difficulties, or stereotype-based discrimination limit their shopping areas. Fewer substitutes mean their demand elasticities for cars sold by a given dealer will be lower than those of people with wider shopping areas, and they will be charged higher prices. The Internet makes it easier to shop distant dealers while avoiding personal contact that could signal a higher willingness to pay. Autobytel.com appears to erase virtually all quoted price differences for those who use it, and it

---

[17]Even if the surveyor told the dealer about other offers, the dealer would have no good reason to believe they were true.

[18]Compare Ian Ayres and Peter Siegelman, "Race and Gender Discrimination in Bargaining for a New Car," *American Economic Review* 85 (June 1995): 304–21 (which found discrimination) with Pinelopi Goldberg, "Dealer Price Discrimination in New Car Purchases: Evidence from the Consumer Expenditure Survey," *Journal of Political Economy* 104 (May-June 1996): 622–54 (which found no discrimination).

[19]See the Autobytel Web site at http://www.autobytel.com/.

[20]Fiona Scott Morton et al., "Consumer Information and Discrimination: Does the Internet Affect the Pricing of New Cars to Women and Minorities?" *Quantitative Marketing and Economics* 1 (January 2003): 65–92. Using a database of individual sales, they found that blacks and Hispanics paid an average of 2 percent more for a given car than the remainder of the population. After accounting for lower incomes, education, and other demographic variables, that difference shrunk significantly. It approached zero for those who used the Internet.

appears to bring greater benefits to those who are at greater risk of discrimination in face-to-face bargaining.[21]

Models and Advice

The Benefits of Alternative Outcomes

Utility Possibility Frontiers In Figure 17-2, Jones and Smith are negotiating over a transaction that can potentially raise the utility that each of them enjoys. For expositional purposes we assume that their utilities are cardinal (i.e., numerically measurable). Downward-sloping curve UPF is the *utility possibility frontier* that shows the possible combinations of utility that an efficient bargain can get the two parties. When we studied production the efficient outcomes were on the boundary of the economy's production set, where more of one good required a reduction in output of the other. Figure 17-2 is an analogy—along the UPF Jones can only get more utility if Smith gets less.

Figure 17-2 also shows that if Smith and Jones cannot agree they both stay at their original utilities: 7 units for Jones and 9 for Smith.[22] These fallback levels are both safe havens and threats. Smith will reject any bargain that leaves her with fewer than 9 units, but if she walks away she will leave Jones at his fallback of 7. Neither can benefit by trying to make the other worse off than before the bargaining began, but both will benefit from any move toward the northeast. The distribution of these benefits will depend on the exact move. A move from the fallback to point A allocates relatively more of the benefits to Smith and less to Jones, and the reverse is true for a move from the

FIGURE 17-2 Utility Possibility Frontier

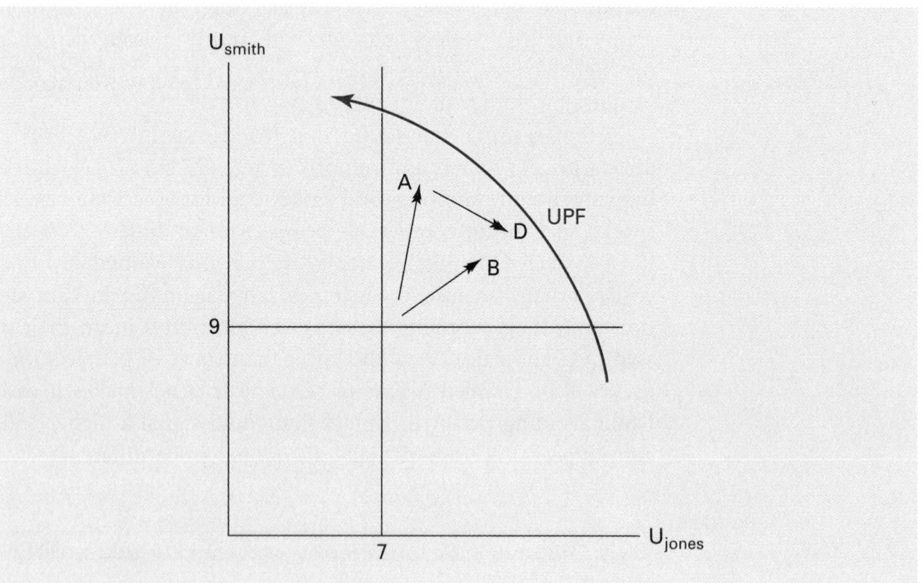

[21]Because dealers do not charge preannounced prices to walk-in customers, we cannot definitively conclude that Autobytel users get better bargains. Research on other Internet services finds that this is the case. For example, Internet users pay 8 to 15 percent less for term life insurance policies than direct shoppers. See Jeffrey Brown and Austan Goolsbee, "Does the Internet Make Markets More Competitive? Evidence from the Life Insurance Industry," *Journal of Political Economy* 110 (June 2002): 481–507.

[22]This is sometimes called BATNA, or the "best alternative to a negotiated alternative." See Fisher and Ury, *Getting to Yes.*

fallback to point B.[23] If Smith and Jones negotiate in steps and manage to reach A it becomes the new fallback, limiting future improvements to those that are to its northeast. Jones will not suggest and Smith will not accept a move from A to D, because it makes Smith worse off. If they are instead at B, a move to D can benefit both of them.

Telling the Truth Assume that Jones and Smith are exchanging a good. Jones will give it up for $15 or more and otherwise prefers to stay at his fallback utility of 7 units. If Smith's actual valuation of the good is $20, but she tells Jones she will not pay more than $12, Jones will walk away and leave both of them with unrealized gains. It is of course possible that as Jones makes his exit Smith will shout "Come back! My real valuation of the good is $20." Even if Jones comes back the chances for a durable relationship will diminish if Smith reveals herself at the outset to be a liar. There are no foolproof ways for one party to directly learn the other's opportunity cost or valuation. Assume that Jones says to Smith "Let's get this over with. Write down your valuation on a slip of paper, I'll write down my opportunity cost on another, and we will set a price halfway between them." Nothing about this technique suggests that either of them intends to tell the truth. We seldom encounter proposals like Jones's because they do not necessarily reduce the parties' perceived zone of agreement. Even after the negotiations are over there are few good reasons for one party to ask about the other's critical number, and even if the question is asked, there are few good reasons for a truthful response.

The UPF limits the possible moves Jones and Smith can make at different stages of their game, but it still does not tell us any details of what will happen. It does not suggest a theory that might help predict where two bargainers will end up, or how the point on the UPF that they finally reach might differ with their personal characteristics, or with the subject of their bargaining.[24] What the UPF can tell us is whether they still have room to make an even better deal than they currently have and the range within which they can strike that deal. More specific predictions are still beyond the powers of economics.

Q. Assume that we are bargaining over a small amount of money, say $10, and each of our utilities rise (fall) by one unit for each dollar we gain (lose). If we fail to reach agreement, the $10 vanishes. Draw the situation in a UPF diagram. Why do you expect that we will quickly agree on $5 each?

Norms and Focal Points

Norms The behavior someone else expects of you, and your expectation of that person's behavior, both depend on the details of the situation. When your expectations of each other are consistent the costs of negotiating will probably fall. You and the other person still have different outcomes in mind, but getting to an agreement will be easier if both of you already agree on how to structure your interactions. The mutually understood customs the two of you follow from experience are known as *norms.* As a first example, "good

[23]This sentence assumes that not only are Jones's and Smith's utility levels cardinally measurable, but that we can use them to directly compare increases in well-being, that is, an extra unit of utility for Jones has the same effect on him as, say, a 1.44 unit increase for Smith has on her. This is only done to make the text more readable.

[24]There are economic theories that predict the outcomes of some bargaining processes under particular assumptions. One example of such a theory appears in John Nash, "The Bargaining Problem," *Econometrica* 18 (September 1951): 155–62.

faith" bargaining is a legal term whose exact definition varies with the details of the transaction.[25] Negotiating in good faith is an example of a norm. For two parties negotiating over a purchase price (and no other terms of the transaction) good faith can mean the buyer never lowers the price she offers the seller, and the seller never raises the price he offers the buyer. A negotiator who changes an offer in an unexpected direction upsets the other's expectations and leaves the other to devise a response that may further slow their progress toward an agreement. In extreme cases an unorthodox or unexpected pattern of offers and responses might even put an end to the bargaining.

Some norms reflect long-standing relationships between the bargainers. Two electric utilities operating at different marginal costs can gain if the high-cost one cuts output and replaces it with power from the low-cost one. A common norm in these transactions is to split the savings, by setting the price halfway between the two companies' costs. Split savings is a workable norm because it ensures that each party will capture about half of the benefits, and a typical utility can find itself as a buyer on some days and a seller on others. Exchanges of power can last for as little as an hour, so the norm should also be easy to compute. Because the parties to transactions like these often know each other's approximate marginal costs there is little to be gained if one of them attempts to violate the norm by misrepresenting its costs.[26]

We can better appreciate the value of norms by looking at an activity where distrust is a norm. When you play poker you expect that the other players will sometimes attempt to mislead you by bluffing, acting like they have good hands when in reality they do not and vice versa. You can expect to win less from the others if you bet large amounts only when your cards are good and always bet small amounts or drop out when they are mediocre or bad. The others will soon learn your style of play and will bet less when they believe that you have a good hand. If at times you bet substantial amounts on questionable hands you acquire a reputation as untrustworthy, which makes you more of a threat to your opponents. They expect that a competent player will bluff, and this zero-sum game is more fun when everyone does it. A business negotiator whose bargaining tactics are intended to confuse others quickly acquires a considerably less favorable reputation.

Q. Illustrate a transaction with split savings graphically and show that it reduces the total cost of producing a given amount of electricity.

Focal points Before continuing, give an answer to the following: Imagine that you and someone else are currently at different locations in New York City. Both of you have been told that you will become wealthy if you can meet at noon tomorrow and no later, but before that time any contact between the two of you is impossible. Where will you go? (If you are unfamiliar with New York choose a meeting place in the area where most of your classmates live.)

How might you decide on a place? You might start with what you know about New York and about the other person, and then where that person is most likely to appear and then go there. Thinking backward a step you realize that the other person is probably using the same thought process and guessing about you. Your decision must be

[25]One definition of good faith is "a total absence of any intention to seek an unfair advantage or to defraud another party; an honest and sincere intention to fulfill one's obligations." Steven H. Gifis, *Law Dictionary* (New York: Barron's, 1975), 91. This definition leaves open the question of what fairness means.

[26]For more on split savings and negotiation over it, see Robert W. Hahn and Mark V. Van Boening, "An Experimental Examination of Spot Markets for Electricity," *Economic Journal* 100 (December 1990): 1073–94.

consistent with what you expect of the other person, and likewise for her expectations about you. As one possible exit from this whirlpool of guessing each other's guesses, an assumption that you are both familiar with New York might by itself lead the two of you to choose the same spot.

The choices match surprisingly often. Thomas Schelling of Yale University once asked a large sample of people in the New York area to choose such a spot.[27] More than half of them responded that they would go to the information booth at Manhattan's Grand Central Station. We call Grand Central a *focal point*, a clear standard that people use to coordinate their activities. New Yorkers' experience and knowledge of the city lead many of them to envision the station as a meeting point. As another example, assume that driving and highways are both recent inventions. There is no good reason for anyone to prefer driving on the right rather than the left side of the road. We can, however, expect that people will soon agree to use one side or the other out of a desire to avoid accidents, even if they never have a formal meeting or a vote on the issue. Laws can further strengthen the convention, and car interiors can be redesigned to increase safety once the choice has been set. In the United States, right-side driving is a focal point that extends to other activities.[28] Most strangers walking toward each other in the United States veer to the right if a collision appears likely, but in England, where they drive on the left side, the opposite is true.

Q. Construct a matrix for a two-person game where each chooses one side of the road. Show that there is no reason for either of us to initially prefer one side to the other. Why is a mixed strategy of choosing left and right each half of the time an inferior one?[29]

Sometimes a focal point greatly simplifies and shortens negotiations. As we saw earlier, one common outcome when two people bargain is a price halfway between their initial offers, even when each is uncertain about the other's opportunity cost or valuation of the good. Even if each person suspects that the other's offer is exaggerated, the midway point might still be focal simply because no other number stands out. Communication becomes more valuable if there is no obvious focal point at which bargainers can converge. Representatives of governments attempting to negotiate a complex international treaty present a different approach. They are more likely to attempt to convey information that others at the table will find relevant than are people bargaining over a car. In the treaty situation self-interested remarks by one country's representative may nevertheless contain important information that leads other countries' representatives to reconsider their stances.

---

[27]Thomas Schelling, *The Strategy of Conflict* (Cambridge, MA: Harvard University Press, 1960), 54–58. To be exact, most people surveyed were in New Haven, Connecticut, from which commuter trains regularly go to Grand Central Station. Schelling received the 2005 Nobel Prize in Economic Science for his work on this and related topics.

[28]Everything you ever wanted to know about the side people drive on is at "Why Do Some Countries Drive on the Right and Others on the Left," World Standards Web site, http://users.pandora.be/worldstandards/driving%20on%20the%20left.htm. The United Kingdom and Japan both came to drive on the left almost accidentally. See "Why We Drive on the Left in the UK," http://www.driving.co.uk/4a2.html and "Why Does Japan Drive on the Left," http://www.2pass.co.uk/japan.htm.

[29]For more on this see H. Peyton Young, "The Economics of Convention," *Journal of Economic Perspectives,"* 10 (Spring 1996): 105–22.

Time and Tactics

Extended and Repeated Negotiations *Time.* If the length of time before two parties reach agreement is of no importance then it does not matter whether they ever agree at all.[30] In reality, time does matter, and understanding its role may help distinguish better strategies from worse ones. First, decisions that involve future payments and receipts must consider their present values. Second, the value of a settlement may change with its calendar date. If the government wants to buy land for a national park, prolonged negotiations may allow landowners to harvest trees in the interim and lower its value to tourists. Third, the opportunity costs of bargainers can themselves be high, and so can the costs of deadlock, for example, when failed labor negotiations bring a strike that reduces both the employer's profits and the workers' incomes. Fourth, some negotiations will harm people in the future who are not here today to voice their interests. The ability to throw costs on them may increase the gains both sides can achieve in a negotiation today.[31] In wage negotiations between a government and public employees, for example, it is easy for citizens to see that immediate pay increases mean higher taxes soon. Citizens may be less able to foresee the more distant consequences of negotiating generous pensions for the same workers. An increasing number of governments and private employers are facing crises as high payouts of previously negotiated pensions begin to bind financially.[32]

Repeated negotiations. An automobile salesperson will probably never again encounter some particular customer he previously dealt with. After the two reach agreement today, neither has much reason to keep their relationship alive. Other negotiations occur repeatedly and may cover the same issue each time. An employer and union, for instance, may bargain annually over next year's wage increase. Because they can expect repeated negotiations over the same topic to continue negotiating over the same things they may develop norms for settling more quickly. Future negotiations may involve previously unencountered issues but experience on related matters can help the parties understand each other's positions on them. Patterns can cover space as well as time. A company with several plants that are heavy energy consumers may find itself in similar negotiations over fuel supply contracts with local sellers in different regions.

Noneconomic Factors Economics is just one of the social sciences that study conflict and negotiation. Like economics, none of them has a definitive model of them. Mass-market books purport to give helpful hints on how to win, but selection bias may render them unreliable guides. Authors often recount instances in which their favored tactics succeeded, but we seldom see studies that analyze a random sample of similar negotiations to see whether these claims generalize. The fact that the author's preferred tactic worked in a certain negotiation tells nothing about how other tactics might have performed, or whether that tactic works well in other types of negotiations. Data like the auto price quotes discussed earlier suggest few reasons to favor any particular bargaining strategy. Of course we should hardly be surprised that no one has yet found a definitively

[30]Cross, *The Economics of Bargaining,* 13.

[31]This is a positive statement about opportunities and not a normative one about the ethics of such tactics.

[32]San Diego's underfunding of government workers' pensions has brought national attention to the problem. "San Diego Seeks a Pension Savior," *Institutional Investor—Americas,* December 14, 2005. In May 2008, Vallejo (population 117,000) became the first California city to file for bankruptcy, largely the consequence of previously negotiated public employee pension plans. The current city government expects that bankruptcy will force the unions to renegotiate the plans. "Vallejo Is Largest California City to File Bankruptcy," Bloomberg.com, May 23, 2008, http://www.bloomberg.com/apps/news?pid=20601087&sid=a5mErpbjjNXY&refer=home.

superior bargaining technique. If one actually existed so many people would adopt it that any temporary advantages it offered would be lost.

The fact that we know little about the actual performance of different bargaining strategies does not imply that negotiators should choose them at random or that they should always use the same one. You may have psychological information about the other person's thought processes that can help you select a bargaining method or eliminate some from consideration. Some experts believe applying heuristics like those described in Chapter 1 might at times be advantageous.[33] The heuristics suggest that a person's receptiveness to an offer may depend on its context. For example, an availability heuristic might dissuade the recipient of an objectively good offer from accepting it. A plaintiff's lawyer who recently saw a news item about an extremely high jury verdict might mistakenly treat that memory as evidence that she should insist on a higher settlement than her client's case warrants. The defendant's lawyer might understand the appeal of the heuristic and take the initiative by being first to mention that case and explaining why it does not apply to their negotiation. Understanding attitudes toward risk may also help a bargainer. A plaintiff's lawyer may reject a defendant's settlement offer because he prefers a trial with a small probability of a very large win that has the same expected payoff as the offered settlement. A risk-averse defendant might respond by making the trial appear unattractive, perhaps by mentioning recent defendant victories in court that left plaintiffs with nothing.

Q. Give an example of a negotiating tactic based on a representativeness heuristic, as defined in Chapter 1.

Principals and Agents People often have good reason to entrust their negotiations to agents rather than doing the job themselves. If a dispute may lead to a trial, a lawyer who understands both bargaining and the law can be a valuable asset. Two such attorneys might be able to reach an agreement that the parties themselves could not. They might better understand their clients' legal situations and may share professional norms that can help them negotiate more expeditiously. A lawyer's experience with similar situations may allow her to better understand the range of likely settlements and estimate the probabilities of different outcomes more objectively than an emotionally involved client.

For all these advantages, the use of specialists like lawyers is still subject to the hazards of principal/agent relationships that we have discussed in many other contexts. The principal may have difficulties monitoring the agent's efforts, and asymmetric information may make it impossible for the principal to judge the quality of the agent's work. Even after a negotiation has concluded or a court has made its decision, the principal may still not know the agent's true quality, because the outcome may reflect both the agent's effort and random factors. The principal and agent can partially align their incentives by choosing payment schemes that induce the agent to make only those efforts that are likely to benefit the principal.

Negotiations offer principals some other opportunities to beneficially employ agents. Two parties may agree beforehand that if a dispute arises over an agreement they have made they will retain an arbitrator to resolve their differences and be bound by the arbitrator's decision. For more than 125 years, the New York Stock Exchange has required

---

[33]Examples like these and a fuller discussion appear in Russell Korobkin and Chris Guthrie, "Heuristics and Biases at the Bargaining Table," *Marquette Law Review* 87 (2004): 795–808.

brokers and customers who cannot reach agreements to settle by arbitration, with no future possibility that their claims will be reheard by a court.[34] In cases like these that entail highly specialized knowledge, both parties will often prefer a knowledgeable arbitrator to a uninformed jury whose judgment is less predictable. The relevant knowledge is not always technical. Professional mediators, for example, sometimes work alongside the parties' attorneys in divorce cases to help resolve emotionally charged issues such as child custody and support. Finally, judges in complex cases sometimes hire their own experts to inform them about technical issues and provide information on the environment that the litigants operate in.

Productive Coalitions

Characteristic Functions and the Core

A Two-Person Example In this section we generalize from two-person situations to larger groups. We introduce concepts that summarize the conditions in which individuals can mutually agree to form productive alliances. We begin with an alternative description of a game known as its *characteristic function.* That function gives the value each possible coalition of a group's members can create by operating independently. A coalition can distribute the benefits (e.g., profit) it creates among its members, who can leave the group if they find better opportunities elsewhere.[35] Jones (J) and Smith (S) hold complementary resources that enable them to produce more as a coalition than either can working alone. The first example has the characteristic function

$$V(J) = \$7, \quad V(S) = \$12, \quad V(J, S) = \$25. \tag{17.1}$$

If the value produced by every coalition is at least as great as the value producible by any of its sub-coalitions (here just Jones and Smith acting alone) the game is called *superadditive.*[36]

$$V(J, S) \geq V(J) + V(S) \tag{17.2}$$

Jones and Smith have good reason to reach an agreement. As long as Jones gets more than \$7 and Smith gets more than \$12, both are better off than when each acts alone (i.e., as a one-person coalition). Jones cannot insist on more than \$13 because doing so would leave Smith better off operating alone. But if Smith leaves the coalition her withdrawal forces Jones to work alone and earn only \$7.

Blocking Coalitions and the Core Let $W(Z)$ denote the value realized by members of a coalition made up of subset Z. Here we wish to find all W that satisfy

$$W(J, S) \geq W(J) + W(S). \tag{17.3}$$

These allocations are said to be in the *core* of the game.[37] In the core neither person can credibly threaten to withdraw from the coalition that consists of the entire group (here just the pair of them). The entire group is sometimes called the *grand coalition.*

[34] See New York Stock Exchange, "A Guide to the NYSE Marketplace," Chapter 3, page 13 at http://www.nyse.com/about/education/1098034584990.html.

[35] Here we measure value in money that can easily be transferred among members of a coalition.

[36] The mathematically rigorous notation is $V(\{J\})$ and $V(\{S\})$ to denote persons or sets of persons, but the text neglects this. A complete description also includes a statement that $V(\{\emptyset\}) = 0$, where $\emptyset$ is the null or empty set, that is, the one that contains no members.

[37] Most game theory textbooks introduce the concept of the core. For a more application-oriented exposition see Lester Telser, *Economic Theory and the Core* (Chicago: University of Chicago Press, 1978).

If instead Jones can make more working alone we say that he (a one-person coalition) can *block* some allocation of the value created by the entire group. The core is the set of all allocations that cannot be blocked.

The core of a two-person exchange model contains all allocations of money and the good that make both parties better off after trade. If Jones's opportunity cost is \$7 and Smith's valuation of the good is \$11, exchange of the good at any price within those bounds leaves them both better off. If the value of the pre-trade status quo is set at zero,

$$V(J) = \$0, \quad V(S) = \$0, \quad V(J,S) = \$4. \tag{17.4}$$

Any allocation of the \$4 that gives either of them at least a cent is in the core. For a given allocation, such as \$1 to Jones and \$3 to Smith, neither can credibly refuse to trade because doing so would make him or her worse off.

More Than Two Persons

More complex coalitions allow us to further explore the core. Start with a three-member group of individuals named 1, 2, and 3 for convenience. Define an *imputation* as a set (vector) of payoffs $X = (x_1, x_2, x_3)$, where group member i receives x_i. The total of individual payoffs in the grand coalition must equal the value the coalition earns; nothing is thrown away:

$$\sum_{i=1}^{3} x_i = V(1,2,3) \tag{17.5}$$

An imputation is *individually rational* if $x_i \geq V(i)$ for all i, that is, the gain to member i exceeds his payoff from operating alone. In our two-person example, Jones or Smith could block an allocation if he or she could do better alone. A two-member subset of the three people can also block an imputation if its members get more by withdrawing than by staying in the grand coalition. As before, the core of this game is the set of imputations that cannot be blocked by any coalition that consists of a subset of the grand coalition. In the core we have

$$\sum_{i \in S} x_i \geq V(S) \tag{17.6}$$

for all subsets S; no coalition does better for itself by staying outside.

Begin with a three-person group and characteristic function

$$\begin{aligned} &V(1) = \$0,\ V(2) = \$0,\ V(3) = \$0 \\ &V(1,2) = \$3,\ V(1,3) = \$2,\ V(2,3) = \$4 \\ &V(1,2,3) = \$6. \end{aligned} \tag{17.7}$$

To help with the graphics we introduce *barycentric coordinates.* In Figure 17-3, each edge of the equilateral triangle represents a payoff to one of the three players. Along the bottom edge we have $x_1 = 0$. Its value increases as we move upward parallel to that edge. Along the right-hand edge $x_2 = 0$, and along the left-hand edge $x_3 = 0$. Figure 17-3 shows the barycentric coordinates of several other points. All points on or within the triangle are potentially in the core. No points outside the triangle can possibly be in the core, because they would leave some person with a negative payoff that could be blocked by withdrawing from any coalition. The coordinates of any point on or inside the triangle always add to 6, the maximum achievable by the grand coalition.

Figure 17-4 lets us use superadditivity to find imputations that are in the core. One-member coalitions are not a problem: anyone who goes it alone stays on his or her edge

FIGURE 17-3 Barycentric Coordinates

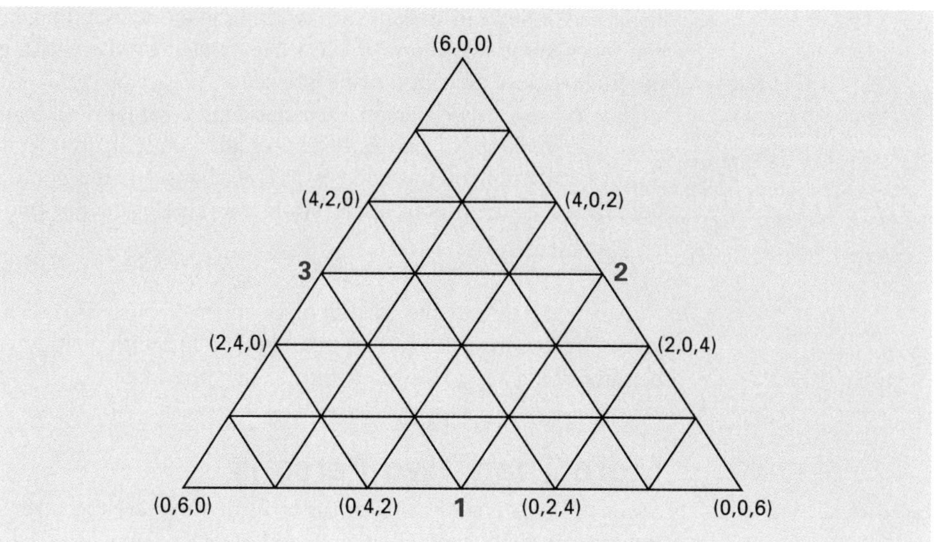

and receives zero. Next we find imputations that give a two-person coalition at least as much as its members can get by leaving the grand coalition. The region for which $X_1 + X_2 \geq 3$ consists of all points to the left of the line that passes through (\$0, \$3, \$3) and (\$3, \$0, \$3). Similarly, we can bound the regions in which $X_1 + X_3 \geq 2$ and $X_2 + X_3 \geq 4$. The intersection of these areas (along with a short segment of the lower axis) is the set of allocations in the core. For the possible core imputation (\$1,\$3,\$2) no one person will withdraw because doing so leaves that person with nothing. Likewise, no pair of players can do better for themselves. If 1 and 2 leave they get \$3, but staying gets them \$4. If 1 and 3 break away, they get \$2 instead of \$3, and 2 and 3 get \$4 for breaking away but \$5 if they stay. Allocations outside the core cannot be sustained. For example, 1 and 2 will be quite happy with their shares of imputation (\$3, \$2, \$1), which is more than their

FIGURE 17-4 Finding the Core

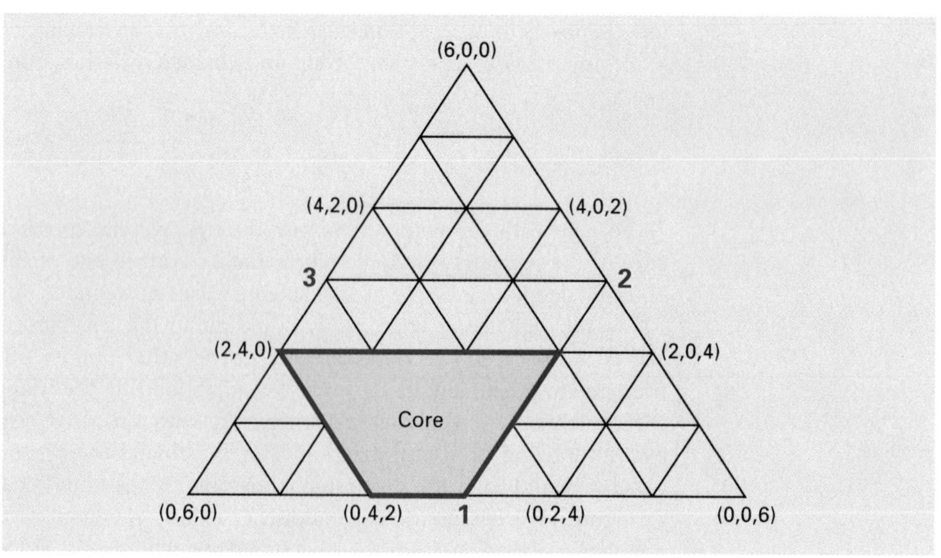

coalition could create by itself. The pairing of 1 and 2, however, will not last because 2 and 3 can team up to get $4 rather than $3. They can divide it so that 2 gets $3 rather than the former $2, and 3 gets $1 rather than receiving $0 as an outsider.

Q. You can also see that 1 and 3 will accept imputation ($3, $2, $1) because each is better off than being alone. Show that it pays for 2 and 3 to form an alliance that blocks this imputation.

Q. How would Figure 17-4 change if $V(1) = \$1$ rather than $V(1) = \$0$?

Empty Cores

An Example and a Comparison The core helps us analyze bargaining where agreement of all the parties (and all possible coalitions of them) is necessary. Any allocation in the core will leave no persons or coalitions worse off than if they went out on their own. The core, however, also indicates the limits of bargaining. Figure 17-5 shows an example in which the core does not exist, which we call an *empty core.* Assume that the characteristic function is

(17.8)
$$\begin{aligned} &V(1) = \$0, = V(2) = \$0, = V(3) = \$0 \\ &V(1,2) = \$4, = V(1,3) = \$4, = V(2,3) = \$5 \\ &V(1,2,3) = \$6. \end{aligned}$$

The three two-person inequalities are graphed as before. Attached to each boundary line is an arrow that extends into the zone where the inequality is not binding, for example, $V(1,2) > \$4$ to the northwest of the line joining (4,0,2) and (0,4,2). Nowhere on the diagram do all three of the inequalities simultaneously hold. To see why it matters,

FIGURE 17-5 An Empty Core

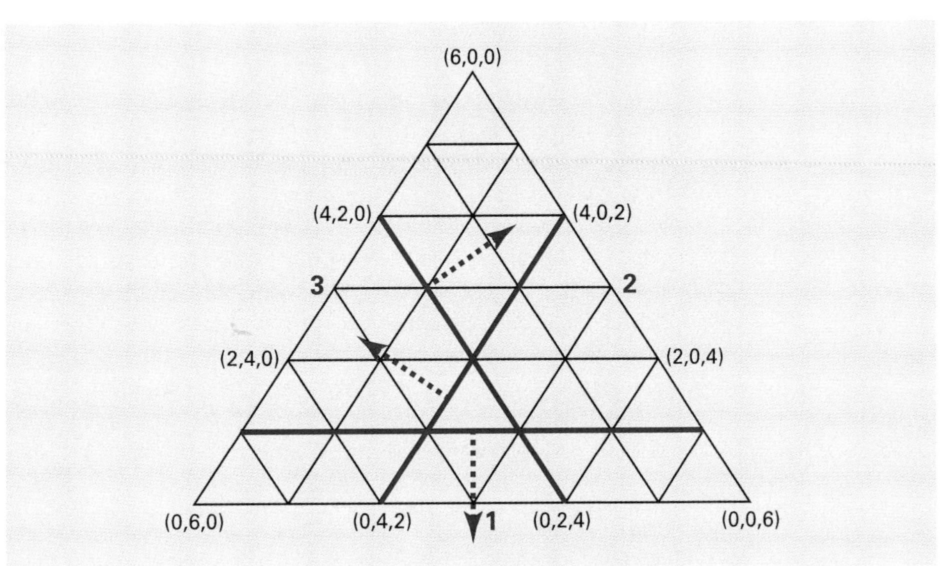

assume that 1, 2, and 3 start with imputation ($2.00,$1.00,$3.00), which satisfies the second of the two-person inequalities. The grand coalition will not hold because 1 and 2 will want to leave—if they stay the two make less than the $4 they could get as a two-person coalition. They propose an alternative of ($3.00,$1.99,$1.01), which makes them both better off than before. But now 2 and 3 together are only getting $3, less than the $5 they could get by leaving. They thus propose ($0.98,$3.01,$2.01), which gives them more than $5. Now, however, 1 and 3 together make only $2.99, which is less than the $4 they could make by withdrawing. Accordingly, they propose ($2.00,$1.00,$3.00), the same imputation we started with. When the core is empty, their proposals and counter-proposals can cycle without ever settling into an unblockable allocation. There is no set of side payments that the group's members can make among themselves that will not leave some coalition with a credible threat to exit.

Q. Provide a similar demonstration that the game 17.8 has an empty core by assuming that the coalition of 2 and 3 is the first to depart.

The differences between the core and empty core examples reflect the degree to which these persons' resources are complements that improve the productivity of working together in coalitions. Speaking loosely, with an empty core the value a two-person coalition can create is large relative to what an individual can do (zero in this example). The extra value from adding a third person to that coalition, however, is only a bit larger than the members of a two-person coalition can get for themselves. Relative to an empty core, a game with a core offers small gains to two-person coalitions (but they still beat going it alone) and large gains from adding a third person.

Q. Are the barge haulers in Chapter 12 playing a game with an empty core? What does this tell you about the possible need for a boss? About the difficulties of incentivizing the boss to maximize the team's profits?

A Market with an Empty Core The theory of the core brings new insights into oligopoly markets in which fixed costs are important.[38] In Figure 17-6 D is market demand. Assume that there is only one possible size of firm, with average and marginal costs AC and MC. Firm A already exists, with average costs that reach their minimum of $8 at an output of 70 units. This is more than half of the 110 units demanded at that price. If A is alone it will earn profits and attract competitors. But if Firm B opens up and has the same cost curves as A, the sum of their marginal costs will be the curve 2×MC. If they compete they cannot both break even. When each produces at the bottom of its average cost total output is 140 units, which can only be sold at a price where both take losses.

But if Firm A stops operating, Firm B has the market to itself and can recover all of its costs and turn a profit. Firm A, however, still has fixed costs and can recover some of

[38] For an example suggesting that airlines operate in a market with an empty core, see Lester Telser, "The Usefulness of Core Theory in Economics," *Journal of Economic Perspectives* 8 (Spring 1994): 151–64.

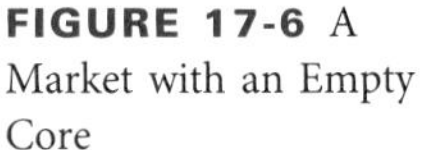

FIGURE 17-6 A Market with an Empty Core

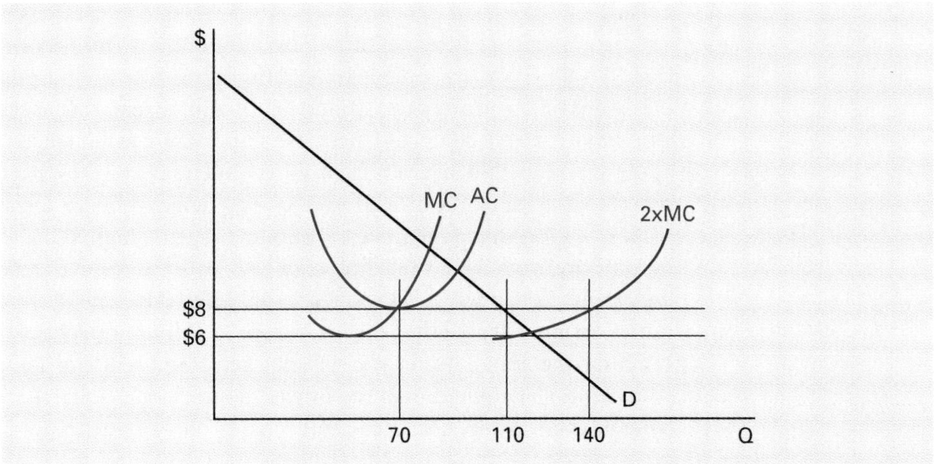

them if it begins to produce again. The added output drives market price down, but now the firms are back in the situation where neither breaks even. Whatever the situation at least one of them will want to change its output. To see the possible relevance of the example, assume that each of two airlines has fixed costs (the monthly lease on its planes) and must incur other costs to operate at a minimum level (at least ten employees at every airport to refuel the planes and handle baggage). Both will survive only if they can agree on how to schedule their operations or on which airports each will serve. Coordinating operations this way may make price fixing easier for them, but coordination may also be efficient in the presence of high fixed costs and adjustment costs.[39] A zero-profit equilibrium only exists in the unlikely coincidence that the sum of outputs at each firm's minimum average cost exactly equals quantity demanded by the market at that same price.

Q. Can you illustrate the correctness of the claim that a zero-profit equilibrium is only possible if the sum of all a firm's outputs at their minimum average costs exactly equals quantity demanded at that same price.

Public Goods and Voting

Public and Private Goods

The Public–Private Distinction Before this chapter almost every good or service we encountered had two characteristics that seemed so obvious we never even mentioned them. First, they were *excludable*. A person with property rights could exclude others from interfering with his ability to enjoy its benefits. Second, they were *rivalrous*. If this

[39]George Bittlingmayer, "Decreasing Average Cost and Competition: A New Look at the Addyston Pipe Case." *Journal of Law and Economics* 25 (October 1982): 201–29. The article uses adjustment cost data from the cast iron pipe industry to argue that collusion to allocate output among producers may have been economically efficient.

person used the good or service, it was unavailable to create benefits for others. Someone getting a manicure is by definition excluding others from receiving that manicure at that time. To purchase an apple is to acquire rights over it, and one person's bite of that apple is unavailable to others. Excludability and rivalry define what economists call a *private good.*[40] These characteristics have important consequences for markets. To enjoy the apple you must bid it away from other potential users by paying the seller a price that reflects your valuation of it. If everybody's demand curve for apples shifts upward price will rise. Producers will increase output by attracting resources from industries whose outputs are no longer valued as highly. If you are willing to pay up to $2 for an apple, and its market price is $1, you can only get the benefits by offering the producer as much or more than other buyers will pay. Telling a producer you will pay at most 10 cents for the apple means you will not get it and will end up worse off than if you had paid the dollar. Others may be buying apples for a dollar each, but their consumption benefits them alone, and they can exclude you from getting a bite.

Compare the apple with an over-the-air television broadcast. Anyone with a TV who lives within the range of the signal can enjoy the program. If another person with her own set moves into the area she can enjoy that program without in any way diminishing the enjoyment of other viewers. The broadcast is *nonrivalrous* because my enjoyment of the program does not leave any less of it for you. It is also *nonexcludable*, because there is no way to prevent someone with a set from watching the show. Nonrivalry and nonexcludability are the defining characteristics of a *public* or *collective* good. The fact that we call a good public does not necessarily mean it must be produced by the government. Private entities can produce public goods like advertiser-sponsored TV broadcasts. On the other side, governments also produce private goods—many municipalities sell electricity to local homes and businesses, and government-owned railway system Amtrak excludes unticketed passengers.

Q. Do you think higher education has attributes of a public good that warrant funding it through taxes? What might that good be? What if the only effect of the education is to raise your individual earning power?

Q. Does the U.S. Postal Service produce a public good? Why or why not?

Free Riders and the Revelation Problem We could expect that at least some private goods will be efficiently produced and allocated because a consumer unwilling to pay enough to cover its cost will be excluded from enjoying it. Public goods are different. Once a public good has been produced anyone can consume it without lowering the well-being of other consumers. If nonpayers benefit alongside payers my hope will be for you to pay so that I can *free ride,* enjoying the benefits without paying the costs. You will likewise hope that I pay for it. Unless we feel a sense of mutual obligation to pay (or can devise a system like television sponsorship) the public good will not be produced.

[40]For more on private and public goods see any textbook on public economics, such as Harvey S. Rosen, *Public Finance,* 7th ed. (New York: McGraw-Hill Irwin , 2004), 56–80.

For all the appeal of the free-rider argument, many producers of public goods receive enough in payments to make production worthwhile. Some are voluntarily funded by persons with a sense of obligation—members of a congregation may contribute enough so that even those who do not pay can benefit from attending a church's services. In other cases social pressure may play a role. The beekeeper of Chapter 9 produced a public good (pollination services) for all the farmers in the area. Here a nonpaying farmer might find himself ostracized from local society or unable to obtain help from neighbors in an emergency. Some public goods are financed voluntarily, but many are not.

Inducing Payment for Public Goods If voluntary provision does not suffice, there are three basic ways to fund the production of public goods. First, the public good can be tied with a private good. For example, sponsors of television broadcasts pay for advertising to sell their products, and they pay enough so that shows are produced. Organizations that provide public goods (think of an uncrowded country club golf course) can exclude nonmembers or require them to pay special charges. Many trade associations also produce both types of goods. They often have Washington, DC, offices that stay abreast of policy developments and attempt to introduce or influence legislation that affects their members. An association that successfully influences legislation produces a public good because the new law benefits those who have paid their dues to the organization and those who have not. Some members might want to free ride on others, but their dues might also buy them services that are unavailable to nonpayers.[41] Associations, for example often collect market data to which only dues payers have access, or it can advise them on policies that pertain to their individual companies.

Second, the law can make a public good excludable. For example, information that is embodied in a new invention has aspects of a public good. The concept of the integrated circuit is an idea that some developers applied to computer chips, others to cameras, and still others to electronic ignition systems for cars. Any person can use this underlying idea without detracting from the ability of others to use it. To encourage inventive activity and discourage free riding, inventors can apply for patents that will allow them to control unauthorized use of their inventions for 17 years. Technological developments can also make a good excludable. Cable and satellite television, for example, deliver signals only to those people who pay for required services and equipment.

Third, governments can supply public goods financed by taxes that citizens have little choice but to pay. The British Broadcasting Corporation's programming is largely funded by an annual tax on television sets, enforced by mobile squads that can detect unauthorized reception. The U.S. Army provides the public good of defense to all Americans, and a new resident gets the same protection others already enjoy. If many persons are affected and expenditures must be large, taxes may resolve the free-rider problem at reasonable cost, but there are also other ways to do so. People regularly form organizations similar to governments whose members are bound by legally enforceable agreements to pay for public goods. Today more than 50 million people live under homeowners' and condominium association agreements that were virtually unknown in 1960. The buyer of a residential unit agrees to pay certain fees for upkeep of the surrounding grounds and structures. Attractive surroundings are a public good that residents can enjoy equally, and they will also enhance the market values of all of their units.[42] Owners elect the association's government and give it powers to assess them for certain services.

---

[41]Mancur Olson, *The Logic of Collective Action* (Cambridge, MA: Harvard University Press, 1965).

[42]For evidence that homeowners' and condominium associations improve property values, see Amanda Agan and Alexander Tabarrok, "What Are Private Governments Worth," *Regulation* 28 (Fall 2005): 14–17.

Making Decisions by Voting

Why Vote at All? This simple question has puzzled economists and political scientists for a long time. Most of our models start by assuming that people act rationally and try to make themselves well-off in the face of constraints on their choices. In particular a person will seek out information only if its expected benefits to her exceed the costs of acquiring and processing it. This model helps us understand the behavior of shoppers but is greatly at variance with the behavior of voters. You are quite likely to shop more than one dealer for a car, but if you intend to maximize your utility, how much time is it best to spend informing yourself about candidates and ballot issues? An economist would probably respond that you should spend almost none—even in a small local election the probability that your vote could change the outcome is tiny, and even if it does your benefits from having Jones rather than Smith as county clerk are minimal. The probability that you will change the outcome of a presidential election in which 122 million people (the 2004 figure) vote is astronomically small.[43] An economist would almost surely call you foolish to bother informing yourself and then voting.[44]

But that same economist is about as likely to vote as other people of his socioeconomic status. Truth be told, we do not know why. Theory says that people with higher time costs (earnings) should be less likely to vote, but in fact greater percentages of high-income people than low-income people turn out at the polls.[45] On the other hand, some aspects of voter turnout appear quite rational. Government employees turn out in higher percentages than the rest of the population and are more likely to vote for candidates who support their interests.[46] More hotly contested elections in which a person's vote is more likely to matter draw higher turnouts.[47] It is easy to say that people feel a sense of duty to vote, and a person may wish to become informed for other reasons—Many people enjoy political discussions and some enjoy feeling superior to neighbors who did not vote. Noneconomic explanations, however, should also be able to explain other activities than voting: Why don't people who vote from a sense of duty also invoke that same sense to stay within speed limits, turn up for jury service, and avoid littering?[48]

The Relative Rarity of Voting Most people probably prefer democracy to dictatorship, but few can explain exactly why. If you could be certain that a dictator would always impose policies that you personally preferred (including ones like freedom of speech), you might well give up the right to vote rather than run the risk that a majority of your neighbors will sometimes prefer different policies. In reality, no matter what your preferences you will sometimes find yourself on the losing side. Yet most choices about private goods need not have winning and losing sides. Markets allow people who prefer

---

[43]"Voter Turnout in Presidential Elections, 1824–2004," The American Presidency Project Web site, http://www.presidency.ucsb.edu/data/turnout.php. In the United States, the calculation is further complicated by the presence of the Electoral College, which gives all of a state's electoral votes to the candidate who wins it, regardless of the number going to the losers. And even if your candidate for president wins, Congress may not go along with his proposals.

[44]Given the odds against your changing a presidential election, it is nearly as rational to write in your own name on the ballot as to vote for one of the party candidates. Gordon Tullock, "The Paradox of Not Voting for Oneself," *American Political Science Review* 69 (September 1975): 919.

[45]U.S. Census Bureau, *Voting and Registration in the Election of November 2000, Current Population Reports P20-502* (Feb. 2002), 7, http://www.census.gov/prod/2002pubs/p20-542.pdf.

[46]Elizabeth Corey and James Garand, "Are Government Employees More Likely to Vote?: An Analysis of Turnout in the 1996 U.S. National Election," *Public Choice* 111 (June 2002): 259–83.

[47]Yoram Barzel and Eugene Silberberg, "Is the Act of Voting Rational," *Public Choice* 16 (Fall 1973): 51–58.

[48]The author has several acquaintances who say they have not registered to vote because doing so puts them at risk of being called to serve on juries.

black shoes to have their choice and allow those who prefer other colors to get what they want. There would be no obvious gain to anyone (except maybe a few busybodies and colorblind people) from a system that required all Americans to wear shoes of whatever color a majority preferred. The differences that people settle by voting will more often involve public goods or decisions that, unlike shoe color, are not divisible. At any given time the United States can only have one president and an army of only one size. Voting governs our activities in only a few areas, such as governments and associations like clubs and labor unions. In addition, corporate shareholders vote for boards of directors and are sometimes asked to approve other actions like mergers.

Very few everyday decisions are the result of voting. Such important institutions as families, churches, and schools make most of their decisions administratively, without any votes of approval from those whom their policies will affect most heavily. Employees voluntarily put themselves under the control of supervisors who have some dictatorial power over their assignments and their pay. There are limits on supervisory powers, some set by law (e.g., discrimination, assignment to hazardous tasks) and others by local customs. Workers also have the sometimes costly option of quitting.[49] Now for the puzzle: Most of us support voting in various contexts because it lets a group (or society) express its preferences, although some of the electorate will of course disagree. But if voting is so desirable, why does it govern so few of our activities? We will soon uncover some difficulties. Seemingly clear concepts like "society's preference" turn out to have little meaning—depending on the details, any voting process can at times be manipulated to ensure that some particular outcome happens. And no voting process is strategy-proof—voters may have good reason to misrepresent their actual beliefs at the ballot box, so the results of a vote may not be a truthful summary of their preferences.

The Median Voter We begin with a simple situation. Assume that our small community will set aside some land for a public park, and that only one park can be built. It will be large enough to provide a public good—even if we all go at once, each of us can enjoy the open space without feeling crowded. Whatever sort of park is chosen, assume that each voter's tax to pay for it has already been set (e.g., by the market values of our homes for property tax). There are three possible park sites: one is a lakefront (Lake), one is in the Hills, and one is convenient to downtown (Urban).

There are three voters, A, B, and C, whose preferences are shown in Table 17-1. The symbol > indicates preference, for example, the top line shows that Voter A prefers Lake to Hills and prefers Hills to Urban. If all three are on the ballot and voters cast single votes for their first choices, Hills will win. Some other voting methods can produce the same winner. For example, in a *Borda count* each voter gives 3 points to his favorite site,

TABLE 17-1 PREFERENCES OF THREE VOTERS

VOTER	TYPE OF PARK
A	Lake > Hills > Urban
B	Hills > Urban > Lake
C	Hills > Lake > Urban

[49]There are a small number of worker cooperatives that determine their management policies by majority vote of their members. Although many economists had expected otherwise, this mode of governance has not led to inefficiency in the plywood industry, where worker-run firms compete with corporations. See John Pencavel, "The Behavior of Worker Cooperatives: The Plywood Companies of the Pacific Northwest," *American Economic Review* 82 (December 1992): 1083–1105.

two to his next-favorite, and so on. Under that procedure, Hills will win with 8 points, Lake will get 6 votes, and Urban will get 4. As another example, assume a two-phase election. People vote over two of the sites in the first round and the winner goes against the remaining choice in the second. If the first round is Lake versus Hills, Hills will win and then challenge Urban, where it wins again. You can show that Hills also wins regardless of which alternatives are voted on in the first round. Thus, Hills is the *median voter's* preference, that is, half or more of the voters' most desired outcomes are equal to or better than it and half or fewer are below.

Q. Show that Hills wins regardless of which pair is voted on in the first round.

The Importance of Institutions The voting procedures discussed so far are quite simple in comparison with those used by most legislatures. The three-person community voted directly on three alternatives, and we assumed that each person's taxes had already been set. We also did not allow the government to go into debt. Real public budgets are collections of many different sources and uses of funds. In U.S. legislatures committees determine individual items, but one vote of the legislature determines whether the entire budget passes or fails. The fact that representatives cast the votes rather than voters can further weaken the link between the preferences of voters and the outcomes they actually get, as we will see next.

Assume that the U.S. Congress is a single legislative chamber that has only three members. One represents New York, another Chicago, and the third Los Angeles. Each cares about his or her own city and has no interest in the condition of the others. They are debating a bill to give their cities cash grants for new mass transit facilities. Each city's project would generate $15 in benefits and cost $18. Assume that the costs are paid from a tax that will collect $6 per project from each city, whether or not it gets a project. As shown in Table 17-2, if the New York representative proposes a grant to her city alone, it will fail because New York gets $9 in after-tax benefits ($15.00 − $6.00), and the other cities get no benefits and are each $6 worse off. The same will happen if the only grant under consideration goes to Chicago. Now let the New York and Chicago representatives put each of their projects into a single law that must be voted up or down as a unit. The fourth row of Table 17-2 shows that New Yorkers' net benefits are now $3, equal to their $15 in benefits less the $12 they must pay for both projects, and so are those of Chicagoans. The law will be enacted because the alternative is no project and zero benefits for both cities. Bundling the two projects into a single proposal will win a majority, even though neither project passes its own cost-benefit test. Geographic representation allows Chicagoans and New Yorkers to benefit while Los Angelenos pay $12 in taxes and receive nothing in return. Political strategies like this one, sometimes called *logrolling*, superficially resemble some phenomena seen in markets with "bundling" like those we encountered in Chapter 6. In markets, however, the purchaser gets all of the

TABLE 17-2 BUNDLING PROJECTS IN LEGISLATION

CITY	NEW YORK	CHICAGO	LOS ANGELES	VOTE
New York only	$15 −$6 = $9	−$6	−$6	Fail
Chicago only	−$6	$15 −$6 = $9	−$6	Fail
Los Angeles only	−$6	−$6	$15 −$6 = $9	Fail
New York + Chicago	$15 − $12 = $3	$15 − $12 = $3	−$12	Pass

benefits and bears all the costs of what he buys. He would not pay $18 for something that gave him only $15 of benefits.

Voting Strategies and Outcomes

Intransitivity and the Impossibility Theorem In Table 17-3, the preferences of voters Alf, Bev, and Cal are nearly the same as those shown for three other voters in Table 17-1. Alf's and Bev's orderings are as before, but Cal's first choice is now Urban and his third is the Hills. This configuration of preferences leads to deeper questions about the meaning of group choice and the importance of voting institutions. To see why look first at the outcomes of pairwise majority votes:

Hills versus Lake: Lake wins
Urban versus Lake: Urban wins
Urban versus Hills: Hills wins

The first line says that the group prefers Lake to Hills, and the second says that it prefers Urban to Lake. But if Urban and Hills are on the ballot, Hills wins. It does so despite our earlier showing that Urban would carry a majority over Hills. Using the notation of Table 17-2, we have found that for this electorate

(17.9) $$\textit{Urban} \succ \textit{Lake} \succ \textit{Hills} \succ \textit{Urban}$$

This set of relationships is paradoxical—Urban defeats each of the other choices in pairwise comparisons, and then is itself defeated. Alf, Bev, and Cal each have a consistent ranking of the parks, but majority voting has produced an *intransitive* set of outcomes. There is no hope of determining what this particular electorate "really" prefers, because "preference" loses its meaning in situations like these.[50]

The effects of intransitivity go deeper. Again let Alf, Bev, and Cal vote in two rounds of pairwise elections. There are three possible ways to organize the elections, each with a different outcome:

- Lake and Hills are on the first ballot, and Lake wins.
- Lake then runs against Urban, and Urban wins.
- Lake and Urban are on the first ballot, and Urban wins.
- Urban then runs against Hills, and Hills wins.
- Hills and Urban are on the first ballot, and Hills wins.
- Hills then runs against Lake, and Lake wins.

Every person has the same number of votes, but any of them may be able to ensure that the electorate's choice is the one that he or she most prefers. For example, Alf can

TABLE 17-3 PREFERENCES OF THREE VOTERS

VOTER	TYPE OF PARK
Alf	Lake > Hills > Urban
Bev	Hills > Urban > Lake
Cal	Urban > Lake > Hills

[50]It does not help to have a single ballot with all three alternatives on it, because the three alternatives will end up tied and some other method will be necessary to determine a single choice.

do this by controlling the sequence of ballots, usually referred to as the *agenda.* To get his most preferred alternative, Lake, he runs Hills and Urban in the first round. After Hills wins it is pitted against Lake, which wins the second round.[51] The person who controls the agenda can control the outcome, which can be any of the three choices.

Of course it is possible that Table 17-3 is just a mathematical curiosity. After all, how often do we see three people so evenly divided in their preferences over three items?[52] We have many documented occurrences of the paradox in Congressional committees.[53] We might also ask whether agenda dependence is just a result of the voting system we chose, and perhaps some other type of voting will eliminate the problem. Unfortunately, our example is potentially relevant. Kenneth Arrow of Stanford University won the Nobel Prize in 1972 for work that included his "impossibility theorem" on collective choice. Speaking informally, the theorem says that it is impossible (not just difficult, but impossible) to devise a voting method in which the outcomes always have certain desirable properties for all possible sets of voter preferences.[54] Stated another way, any choice process that meets a small set of reasonable standards can sometimes run up against the problems described in the three-person example.[55]

Strategy-Proofness Individual voters or minority coalitions might affect an election's outcome in a second way. We have thus far assumed that individuals vote their true preferences; this is known as voting "sincerely" or "nonstrategically." Someone who prefers X to Y will always vote for X over Y if they are among the alternatives. The preferences shown in Table 17-3 also admit the possibility of strategic voting. Again assume that Alf is chairing the meeting and he manipulates the agenda by putting Hills and Urban on the first ballot to get his preferred outcome, Lake, on the second one. From Bev's standpoint Lake is the worst choice. She can get a better final outcome for herself by voting for Urban on the first ballot, even though she really prefers Hills. Her decision to vote insincerely makes Urban the first-round winner, and in the second round it beats Lake. Misrepresenting her preferences at the ballot box gives her a better outcome.

More than one voter can play at this game, and the possibilities become even greater if they can make side payments to each other. (This in effect happens in legislatures, where payments take the form of provisions that might be added to a law.) We left the story with Bev voting insincerely in the first round to get Urban for herself in the second. Urban, however, is the worst possible choice from Alf's standpoint, and it is still the second-worst from Bev's. Assume that Alf and Cal know before the voting starts that Bev intends to vote insincerely in the first round. Cal suggests a deal to Alf. Assume he knows that Alf would be a lot happier with Lake rather than Urban, that is, he would pay someone a lot (say $20) to change the outcome to Lake. Cal mentions to Alf that

---

[51]Notice we are assuming that Alf has fairly good knowledge of Bev's and Cal's preferences, which may not necessarily be true.

[52]For three persons and three alternatives under majority voting, if all possible preference configurations are equally probable then the intransitivity paradox will happen with probability .056. As the group size grows the probability of the paradox increases.

[53]See William Riker and Peter Ordeshook, *An Introduction to Positive Political Theory* (New York: Prentice-Hall, 1973), Chapter 4.

[54]The properties include such reasonable requirements as (1) if someone changes his or her preferences and ranks alternative X higher than before, the group choice rule cannot rank it lower; and (2) alternatives that are irrelevant will not change the group's choice. For a full list, see Kenneth Arrow, *Social Choice and Individual Values,* 2nd ed. (New Haven, CT: Yale University Press, 1963).

[55]Arrow, *Social Choice and Individual Values.* For an easier proof of the theorem and some questions about its significance, see Duncan Black, "On Arrow's Impossibility Theorem," *Journal of Law and Economics* 12 (October 1969): 227–48.

he places only a tiny premium (say $1) on getting Urban rather than Lake, because he is an indoor person and seldom goes to parks at all. They can now make a deal. Alf gives Cal $5, and Cal changes his first-round vote from Urban to Hills. Bev continues to vote strategically for Urban, and Alf votes his true preference for Hills. When first-round winner Hills goes against Lake in the second round, Lake wins, a situation that makes both Alf and Cal happier than if they had voted sincerely.

There are lots of ways to further complicate the story. Groups or legislatures may be able to get the same sorts of results with no need for money to change hands. Instead of giving Cal $5, Alf can promise that he will vote insincerely on some future matter that C values very highly but which will only win if Alf switches his vote. Different sequences of strategies and payments can make any of the three possible parks the final outcome, and none of them has any particular claim to be the group's choice over the others. This is particularly true because some of its members have willfully voted against their true preferences or paid or received money in hopes of getting better outcomes for themselves. As was the case with intransitivity and the impossibility theorem, we can show mathematically that there is no *strategy-proof* mechanism of collective choice that is always immune to misrepresentation of preferences by voters.[56]

Both the theory of the core and the theory of voting have a message that people in situations of conflict might usefully recall. The core suggests that there are times when large numbers of people can achieve agreements without a credible threat from holdouts. Voting theory posits that a majority vote by itself may indicate nothing at all about society's preferences. In most private good situations, voting is simply unnecessary and voluntary exchanges do a better job of giving people what they individually prefer. In those situations where voting does occur, it can have imperfections, just like markets might. People think of themselves rather than their communities, and their choices as a group can be inconsistent. There will be occasions when they can advance their individual interests by misrepresenting their preferences or purchasing each other's votes.

Chapter Summary

- The outcomes of bargaining are generally indeterminate and hard to link to characteristics of the buyer or the seller. There are important elements of randomness, but the comparison of auto price quotes from different eras shows that access to market-related information also affects outcomes.
- The utility possibility frontier shows the potential benefits to two bargainers and how to identify strategies that make them both better off. Norms and focal points can both lower the costs of negotiation and leave fewer benefits to go unrealized by the bargainers.
- The core of a multiplayer game is the set of non-blockable allocations, in which no subset of the players can make more for themselves by withdrawing.
- Private goods are rivalrous (my consumption is not available for you) and excludable (I can prevent you from consuming my good). Because public goods are nonrivalrous and nonexcludable, free-rider incentives make it difficult to accurately elicit peoples' preferences for them and to fund their production.

[56]Allan Gibbard, "Manipulation of Voting Schemes: A General Result," *Econometrica* 41 (July 1973): 587–601; Jean-Marie Blin and Mark A. Satterthwaite, "On Preferences, Beliefs, and Manipulation Within Voting Situations," *Econometrica* 45 (May 1977): 737–63.

- There are situations where private production of public goods is feasible, such as when the public good is produced jointly with a private good. There are, however, important cases like defense that generally must be funded by taxes.
- Voting for elected officials and government policies can sometimes bring outcomes that are consistent with the preferences of the median voter. In other situations the voting process is manipulable, either because the person who sets the agenda can control the outcome, or because voters can individually gain by misrepresenting their true preferences.

Questions and Problems

1. Construct a model (at least a verbal one) to determine how many price offers a buyer should obtain before buying from the dealer who quotes the lowest price. Does your model predict that the buyer will see more dealers if a car purchase takes up more of her wealth?
2. In Jung's studies there were no significant differences in prices quoted by large, medium, and small dealers. Is this an outcome you would have expected? Why or why not? What characteristics of the market make it more likely that a dealer will quote prices at random rather than stick with a single one, or will choose prices that vary with the perceived characteristics of individual customers?
3. What sorts of assumptions might produce a utility possibility frontier that was upward-sloping over part of its length? Would two bargainers ever want to end up on the upward-sloping portion? Explain.[57]
4. Let's revisit the ultimatum game of Chapter 1. Assume that both of our utilities vary directly with our money holdings, that is, a person with \$4 gets 4 units more of utility. The experimenter gives me \$10 for free and I choose an amount, say \$3, to give you. You can accept the gift, leaving me with \$7, or you can reject it and leave both of us with zero dollars.
   a. Draw the utility possibility frontier under these assumptions, and show how to illustrate a possible division of the \$10.
   b. Then show graphically how your rejection of some proposed division leaves us both worse off. Explain why you might choose nevertheless to reject it. Does your explanation make sense if you and I both know we will never play the game again?
5. Graphically illustrate a situation in which an agreement between two utilities to split the savings on a power purchase yields a highly unequal distribution of the benefits of the transaction.
6. Is it possible to bluff in chess, where, unlike poker, all pieces are visible and all rules are known to both players?[58]
7. The characteristic function of a game with players 1, 2, and 3 is the following:

$$V(1) = \$0, = V(2) = \$0, = V(3) = \$0$$
$$V(1,2) = \$2, = V(1,3) = \$2, = V(2,3) = \$1$$
$$V(1,2,3) = \$5.$$

   Graphically determine its core. Then pick an imputation outside of the core and show that it can be blocked.

[57]See David Friedman, "Many, Few, One: Social Harmony and the Shrunken Choice Set," *American Economic Review* 70 (March 1980): 225–32.

[58]See Robert Byrne, "Chess; A Bluff That Is Called Can Bring Disaster," *New York Times*, September 6, 1981, http://www.nytimes.com/1981/09/06/arts/chess-a-bluff-that-is-called-can-bring-disaster.html.

8. The characteristic function of a game with players 1, 2, and 3 is the following:

$$V(1) = \$0, = V(2) = \$0, = V(3) = \$0$$
$$V(1,2) = \$5, = V(1,3) = \$6, = V(2,3) = \$7$$
$$V(1,2,3) = \$8.$$

   Show that it has an empty core.
9. Is it possible that elementary education produces a public good but higher education does not? Explain.
10. Explain why the LoJack example from Chapter 9 is about a public goods problem. Be sure to exactly identify the public good being discussed.
11. Some economists have argued that requiring people to pay for television programming is inefficient because nonpayers are unable to enjoy shows they could have watched without degrading the enjoyment of other viewers. In which ways does this argument make economic sense? In which ways does it not?[59]
12. We said that an uncrowded country club golf course has aspects of a public good. Why? Is it still a public good if it becomes crowded and people's games are slowed down?
13. Why might you expect that higher-income people have higher voting turnout despite their higher opportunity costs of time? Do you expect that higher-income or lower-income people will vote more heavily by absentee ballot?
14. Construct an example of three persons voting among three issues by a Borda count (3 points for most favored, and so on) that turns out to be intransitive.

---

[59]This was an important controversy in the days when the Federal Communications Commission was formulating policies affecting cable (and later satellite) television. Compare Jora Minasian, "Television Pricing and the Theory of Public Goods," *Journal of Law and Economics* 7 (October 1964): 71–80; and Paul Samuelson, "Pitfalls in the Analysis of Public Goods," *Journal of Law and Economics* 10 (October 1967): 199–204.

Glossary

A

Acquisition A process in which one company gains a controlling interest in another, either by purchasing a sufficient amount of its stock or by directly purchasing its assets.

Adjustment Clause Also known as an escalator provision, changes the contract price in accordance with fixed rules to reflect changes in the market price of the good under contract.

Adverse Selection In insurance markets, the possible tendency of persons with above-average risks to purchase fuller coverage, thereby leaving insurers with higher payouts than income from premiums which are set on the basis of population averages.

Affordable Housing Law Laws in some California cities which require builders of expensive new houses to build lower priced houses on some percentage of their land.

Agenda In models of voting, the sequence in which various issues are voted upon. The Impossibility Theorem says that in certain circumstances a person who can control the agenda can control the outcome of the group's voting.

American Option One that may be exercised at any time prior to its expiration date.

Annuity A stream of given duration of equal annual payments.

Arbitrage Simultaneous purchase of a good at a low price and sale at a higher price elsewhere to profit from the difference. Arbitrage results in prices becoming equal, net of the cost of transferring the good.

Ascending-Value Auction An auction in which bidders sequentially bid higher prices for some object, with the high bidder winning it. *Descending-value auctions* may be held to determine who will supply some good at the lowest cost.

Ask Price Price a seller will accept for some good. Also called asked or asking price.

Asymmetric Information Situation in which one party holds economically valuable information that he cannot or will not convey to a *counterparty*. Failure or inability to convey the information will affect the economic value that could be created by the relationship.

Availability Heuristic One that is used to predict the likelihood of an event on the basis of the easiest example that can be found.

Average Cost Total (fixed plus variable) cost divided by output.

B

Backward Induction Method of solving a multiperiod game by starting from a player's best choice in the final round and using it to determine best choices in earlier periods.

Barrier to Entry An institution or practice that raises the costs of competitors entering a market relative to those of existing sellers, for example large capital requirements or established brand names. A barrier need not necessarily harm consumers, as when a brand name connotes dependable product quality.

Bertrand Oligopoly One in which each producer chooses price on the assumption that other producers will maintain their prices unchanged.

Bid Price Price a buyer is willing to pay for some good.

Block Holder A large shareholder, sometimes capable of influencing corporate decisions despite not holding a position of formal authority.

Blocking Coalition In a game, the subset of players who can veto a proposed allocation and do better for themselves by leaving the rest of the players.

Board of Directors A group of people elected by corporate shareholders to oversee management of a corporation. The composition of a board is determined by the corporation's charter and by-laws.

Boilerplate Slang for provisions in a contract or other legal document that are routine and often generally applicable to all contracts of a certain type.

Bond A financial instrument that obligates its issuer to make a defined stream of payments over the future.

Bounded Rationality Decisions are boundedly rational if they are as rational as possible given the limited availability of information and limits on the decision maker's ability to process it.

Breach of Contract Breach occurs when a party to a binding contract fails to perform or interferes with the other party's performance under the contract.

Bundling Goods or services that are sold as a unit (bundled) rather than being priced separately.

Business Interruption Insurance Insurance that allows recovery of lost profits and fixed expenses in the event that the normal activities of a firm are interrupted for specified reasons.

Business Judgment Rule A legal principle stating that any court must presume that a management decision was made in the interests of shareholders, absent strong evidence to the contrary.

Buy-and-Hold A market in which the only way to speculate is to increase or decrease one's holdings of a good. No derivatives or forward transactions are possible.

C

Call Option A financial instrument that allows its holder to buy the underlying asset for a predetermined *strike price* on or before its expiration.

Callable Bond One whose issuer can repurchase it on predetermined terms prior to maturity.

CalPERS The California Public Employees Retirement System, responsible for pensions and health insurance of retired employees.

Capital Gain An increase in the value of an asset relative to its purchase price.

Capitation Principal/agent payment arrangement in which the agent receives a fixed amount regardless of effort required to perform the service for the principal.

Cardinal Utility A hypothetical measure of a person's well-being that carries a numerical value, e.g., my cardinal utility in situation A might be 2.44 units, while in situation B it would be 3.75 units.

Cartel An agreement among producers to reduce output and maintain higher prices than if they had been competing.

CEO Acronym for Chief Executive Officer.

CFO Acronym for Chief Financial Officer.

CIO Acronym for Chief Information Officer.

Coasian Reasoning Associated with economist Ronald Coase, studies relationships between legal rules, transaction costs, and economic efficiency.

Cobb-Douglas Function A production function of the form $Q = AF^{\alpha}K^{\beta}$. Q is the quantity of output produced, F and K are inputs, and A, α, and β are positive constants.

Coinsurance Provision in an insurance policy that allows recovery of only a certain percentage of a loss, intended to control *moral hazard*.

Commodity Charge See *Two-Part Pricing*.

Comparative Advantage Producer X has a comparative advantage over producer Y in good A if it is the lower marginal cost supplier of A. X may still have a comparative advantage in A even if Y has a higher total productivity than X (an "absolute advantage") in all goods, including A.

Competition A process that occurs whenever a scarce good is to be rationed among potential holders. It can take many forms, including exchange offers, violence, standing in line, politics, and others.

Competitive Fringe See *Dominant Firm Model*.

Complements Two goods are complements if they must be used together in order to produce a desirable good, e.g., flour and eggs that make a cake. Two inputs into production can also be complements if increasing one of them increases the *marginal product* of the other.

Complete Contract One that assigns rights and responsibilities for all possible situations that might arise in the relationship governed by it. It is generally impossible or very costly to construct a truly complete contract.

Compounding Paying interest on a sum that includes both the original amount and interest previously paid on the amount.

Conglomerate A firm whose units are engaged in unrelated lines of business.

Consumer Surplus A measure of the benefits a consumer obtains from being able to trade at a market price. It is the difference between the consumer's valuation and the market price, summed over all units purchased.

Contingency Payment A type of *share payment* in which a principal and agent agree that the agent will get a fixed percentage of the value that the agent creates for the principal.

Contract An enforceable set of promises to take certain actions over the future.

Co-Operative A non-profit organization jointly owned by producers (or sometimes by consumers) and operated for the owners' benefit.

Co-Payment Provision in an insurance policy that reduces payment for a loss by a fixed amount, intended to control *moral hazard.*

Core In a game, the set of allocations that cannot be "*blocked*" by some subset of the players who can do better for themselves by leaving the group of players and operating for themselves.

Corporation A legal and contractual mechanism for creating and operating business for profit, using capital from investors that will be managed on their behalf by directors and officers. A corporation's shareholders are its residual claimants.

Counterparty A party with whom someone contracts to trade.

Coupons Claims attached to a *bond* that entitle the bondholder to *interest* payments when due.

Cournot Oligopoly Also known as Cournot-Nash, a model in which each producer assumes that others will maintain their current output levels in response to any change in its own output.

Cover Charge See *Two-Part Pricing.*

Covered A *call option* is said to be covered if its writer holds the *underlying* asset at the time it is written.

CRO Acronym for Chief Risk Officer.

Cross-Elasticity The cross-elasticity of demand for good X with respect to the price of good Y is the ratio of the percentage change in the amount of X purchased to the percentage change in the price of Y that induced it. X and Y are substitutes if their cross-elasticity exceeds zero, and complements if it is less than zero.

Customer Charge See *Two-Part Pricing.*

D

Damages Amounts that must be paid by a party that has breached a contract to the nonbreaching party.

Deadweight Loss A loss of benefits to consumers and/or producers in a market that is gained by no one.

Death Spiral A consequence of *adverse selection,* in which higher rates for high-coverage insurance lead low-risk policyholders to abandon it, leaving suppliers of it with fewer policyholders who are of higher risk on average.

Deductible In insurance, a fixed amount for which the insurer is not responsible. A policy holder can only file claims for amounts above the deductible.

De-Integration Reducing the scope of activities in a chain of production that take place within a single firm.

Demand Also called a demand curve, the relationship between the quantity of some good or market service a consumer wishes to purchase and its market price. All else equal, at higher prices the consumer will be willing to purchase fewer units of it. A point on a given demand curve is called the quantity demanded at some price.

Derivative A financial instrument whose value depends on the market price of some other good, known as the underlier or underlying good. Futures and options are examples of derivatives.

Dilution Decreasing the per-share value of a company's stock by issuing excessive amounts of new shares.

Discount Bond One without *coupons,* whose market price will equal the *present value* of its *par value.*

Discounting Calculating the *present value* of a future payment.

Disutility The opposite of *utility*, a subjective measure of the unpleasantness an individual associates with some activity such as working.

Diversification Incorporating a variety of investments in one's portfolio, which cuts risk by reducing the variance of the portfolio's overall return.

Dividends Payments to shareholders from corporate profits, distributed in proportion to shares held.

Division of Labor Specialization of workers to individual tasks that increases their productivity as a team.

DOD Common acronym for U.S. Department of Defense, in charge of its armed forces.

Dominance Solvable A game is dominance solvable for its *Nash Equilibrium* if that equilibrium can be found by iteratively eliminating dominant strategies of the players.

Dominant Firm Model A market model with a dominant firm whose output decisions can determine market price, but whose choices are constrained by the supply responses of a *competitive fringe* of small price-taking sellers.

Dominant Strategy In game theory, a dominant strategy is one that is a player's best choice regardless of the choices made by the other players.

Double Marginalization A problem encountered in situations of successive monopoly. When each of the upstream and downstream producers acts as a monopolist, they realize lower total profits than they could realize if they were operated as a single unit through integration or by contract.

Downstream Refers to a later stage in a production process.

E

Economic Efficiency A situation in which a given set of inputs is producing the most valuable bundle of output possible, or in which a given bundle of output is produced by the least-cost bundle of inputs.

Economic Good One that a person prefers to have more of rather than less.

Economic Inefficiency A situation in which a given set of inputs is not producing the most valuable bundle of output possible, or in which a given bundle is not being produced by the least-cost bundle of inputs.

Economic Institutions Arrangements or structures in a society within which competition and exchanges take place.

Economic Value The difference between a seller's *opportunity cost* of some good or service, and a buyer's *valuation* of it.

Economics The study of goal-oriented choices that must be made under constraints othat result from scarcity of resources.

Efficiency Wage One that is set above the market level in order to lower the cost of monitoring an employee and increase that employee's productivity.

Elastic A demand curve is elastic if its elasticity exceeds 1 in absolute value. If so, an increase in market price yields a decrease in total spending on the good by buyers.

Elasticity of Demand Along a given demand curve, elasticity is the ratio of a (small) percentage change in quantity demanded to the percentage change in price that induced it.

Elasticity of Supply Along a given supply curve, elasticity is the ratio of a (small) percentage change in quantity demanded to the percentage change in price that induced it.

Elimination Heuristic Decision rule that suggests choosing the first alternative that fails to satisfy one of a sequence of tests.

Empty Core A game for which no core exists is said to have an empty core.

Equilibrium A market is in equilibrium at a price that equates supply and demand. All producers who wish to do so can sell their desired outputs at the equilibrium price, and all buyers can purchase their desired amounts.

Event Market A market in which people place bets on alternative outcomes (e.g., of an election). Those who bet on the winner share the amounts bet on the losers.

Exclusive Dealing A *vertical restraint*, for example between a retailer and manufacturer, that prohibits the retailer from carrying any brand other than that of the manufacturer.

Exclusive Territory A *vertical restraint* that guarantees one party (for example a franchised automobile dealership) that it will be the sole entity with rights to sell that brand in a certain area.

Exotic When discussing options, the opposite of *vanilla.*

Expansion Path In an isoquant isocost diagram, the line traced out by the tangency points between isoquants and isocosts at least-cost production for each output level.

Expectation Damages A type of liquidated damages for breach of contract, in which the breaching party must pay the nonbreaching party an amount that would have made the nonbreaching party as well off as if the contract had not been breached.

Expected Value The sum of all possible outcomes of some risky choice multiplied by their individual probabilities, also known as the mean of those values.

External Benefit or Cost See *Externality.*

External Coordination Coordination between two activities that results from the efforts of separate firms.

Externality Also known as an external benefit or cost. An increase or decrease in the wealth of some party not otherwise connected with an economic activity, as a result of that activity.

F

Facilitating Practices Industry practices (e.g., preannouncements of price changes) that may make it easier for sellers to compete less aggressively and to maintain higher prices.

Fallback In negotiation, the situation a party will be in if negotiations fail or do not take place. Two parties' fallback positions bound their *zone of agreement.*

FERC Acronym for U.S. Federal Energy Regulatory Commission, which has jurisdiction over interstate pipelines, sales of high-voltage electricity, and federally-owned hydroelectric facilities.

Final Good One that is sold to ultimate users after passing through various vertical stages.

Financial Intermediary Institution such as a bank that makes loans from funds placed on deposit with it.

Firm A set of written and unwritten agreements among suppliers of inputs used in production.

First Possession A legal rule granting ownership of some type of object to the first person who seizes it.

First-Price Auction One in which the winner of a good is the high bidder, who must pay that bid to obtain it. This also holds for the low bidder in a procurement auction.

Fixed Charge See *Two-Part Pricing.*

Focal Point A standard people use to coordinate their activities.

Forex Market Worldwide network of banks and other financial institutions where transactions in foreign exchange, i.e., various national currencies, take place.

Formal Authority Relationship between persons or departments as portrayed on an organizational chart, which may differ from the actual pattern of *informal authority.*

Forward Price A price agreed on today by a buyer and seller for delivery of some good at a particular date in the future.

Franchise Contract One between a parent company and an independently owned franchisee that describes their rights and responsibilities. Limitations it places on their behavior are known as *vertical restraints.*

Free Cash Flow Cash generated by a business after all prior claims on it have been met, which may be distributed to shareholders or reinvested in the company.

Free Rider A person who receives benefits without paying for them, most often in connection with production of a *public good.*

FTC Acronym for U.S. Federal Trade Commission, which has jurisdiction in antitrust law, unfair practices, false advertising, and other areas.

Functionalization An organization with departments specialized in different functions such as sales and production is said to be functionalized or *U-form.*

Futures Contract A standardized financial instrument (a *derivative*) that commits the purchaser (seller) to take delivery (deliver) of some amount of a commodity at a given future date. The price is set today by supply and demand on a futures exchange.

G

Game A model in which several players choose strategies. The payoff to each player depends on both his choice and the choices made by the others.

General Human Capital Human capital that increases worker productivity in nonspecific employment situations, e.g., general education in language and math. Employees will generally bear the costs of investing in it.

Governance The legal and institutional environment within which transactions take place. This book is organized around three basic modes of governance: markets, contracts, and hierarchies.

H

Hedging Taking a position to protect oneself against price risk. One can, for example, purchase a futures contract or a call option today to lock-in a future price for some good.

Heuristics Mental rules of thumb and shortcuts that are used to simplify more complex calculation and decision-making processes.

Hierarchy A command-based organization in which prices do not serve to allocate resources as they do in markets.

HMO Acronym for Health Maintenance Organization, a prepaid group health insurance plan that provides members with a certain set of medical treatments.

Holdup Opportunistic behavior dependent on asset specificity, in which one party to a transaction threatens actions that will reduce the value of those assets unless the other party acquiesces to the first party's demands.

Horizontal Merger One that puts the assets of two firms that produce the same good or service under common ownership.

Human Capital Skills and knowledge embodied in a worker, whether *general* or *specific.*

I

Imputation A possible set of payoffs to the players in a game.

Income Elasticity of Demand The ratio of a percentage change in quantity of a good purchased to the percentage change in income that induced it. If income elasticity is positive, the good is called normal. If it is negative, the good is called inferior.

Incomplete Contract One that does not assign rights and responsibilities for all possible situations that might arise in the relationship governed by it. The opposite of a *complete contract.*

Indifference Curve A graphic portrayal of those combinations of two goods that give a person the same level of *utility*. One or both of the goods can be a "bad," that a person wishes to avoid.

Inelastic A demand curve is inelastic if its elasticity is below 1 in absolute value. If so, an increase in market price yields an increase in total spending on the good by buyers.

Inferior Good A consumer's desired quantity of an inferior good to purchase decreases as income or wealth increases.

Inflation A general increase in all prices in the economy, including wages, at equal percentage rates.

Influence Costs Those that arise from competition among an employer's workers for desirable positions or assignments.

Informal Authority In contrast to the *formal authority* shown on a chart, the actual relationships prevailing among persons and departments in the organization.

Inside Directors Members of a corporate board of directors who hold positions within the company.

Institutional Investor An organization such as an insurer, mutual fund, charitable endowment, or bank, that pools funds from numerous sources for investment purposes.

Intangible Asset Literally, one that cannot be physically touched, such as a respected brand name or a patent that may increase the value of a business.

Intensive Refers to the relative amounts of inputs used in production. If the inputs are labor and capital, production is labor-intensive if it uses a relatively high ratio of labor to capital, as compared with some other production activity.

Interest Percentage premium on present availability, expressed as a fraction of the amount loaned.

Intermediary Some individual or organization that lowers the cost of an exchange between two parties.

Intermediate Good One intended for further processing before it becomes part of a final good that will be sold to its ultimate user.

Internal Coordination Coordination of two activities in a vertical chain by the management of a single firm.

Internal Labor Market A firm considering candidates for promotion may restrict itself to persons that it currently employs, in which case it is said to use an internal labor market.

Intransivity A type of inconsistent behavior, here in the context of voting. Although each citizen may have transitive preferences where A is preferred to B, B to C, and A to C, the electorate as a whole may have intransitive preferences, and in some cases, we will see a sequence in which it prefers A to B, B to C, and C to A.

IPO Acronym for Initial Public Offering, generally for shares of corporate *common stock*.

Isocost A line showing all possible bundles of inputs that can be purchased for a given total cost, at market prices for them.

Isoquant A curve showing all of the possible combinations of inputs that are capable of producing the same level of output.

IT Acronym for information technology, e.g., computers.

L

Law of Large Numbers Mathematical statement that (under certain conditions) a large random sample from a population will on average have the same statistics (mean, variance, etc.) as the population.

Law of One Price States that only one price can prevail in market equilibrium. Multiple prices would give rise to arbitrage that drives them toward a uniform value.

Learning Curve A relationship that generally shows lower average costs for a good the larger the total amount that has been hitherto produced. Also known as a progress curve.

Lemon Slang for a car with mechanical defects that will be costly to remedy.

Leverage A firm is said to be more highly leveraged if it has a higher ratio of debt to equity (stock) finance than some comparable firm.

Leveraged Buyout (LBO) Attempt at a *takeover* financed by debt issued against the taken-over firm's assets.

Limited Liability A situation in which a person's financial liability is limited to a fixed amount, for example when a shareholder in a bankrupt corporation is responsible only for the value that he invested in it.

Limited Partnership A type of partnership with two classes of partner. General partners have decision-making power and are residual claimants, while the potential liabilities of limited partners are capped at the amounts they have invested.

Liquidated Damages A class of legal remedies for breach of contract in which the breaching party pays the nonbreaching party in cash.

Liquidation Terminating the existence of a firm by selling its assets and paying off its liabilities with the proceeds of the sale.

Liquidity An asset is said to be liquid if it can be sold quickly for a predictable price. A market is said to be liquid if individual transactions can generally be made in it without greatly affecting market price.

Logrolling The bundling of otherwise failing initiatives into a single piece of legislation that will pass.

Long A market participant who has obligated himself to take delivery of a good in the future is said to be long or to hold a long position.

Long Run In models of production and cost, the time span following the short run, during which the firm can vary all inputs. In models of markets, the time span after the short run during which sellers can enter and leave the market in response to profits and losses.

M

M-Form An M-form firm is divisionalized, typically along product or geographic lines. Operating decisions are made within the divisions while strategic decisions are made by management on the basis of information it obtains from the divisions.

Marginal Cost A cost that can be avoided if a different choice is made. The marginal cost of (for example) producing an extra unit of a good is the additional cost thereby incurred, or that can be avoided if the unit is not produced. Mathematically, it is the derivative of total cost.

Marginal Product The added output produced by the addition of one more unit of a variable input, all other inputs remaining the same.

Marginal Revenue Additional revenue received by a seller for selling an extra unit of output. For a price-taker seller, it equals market price. Marginal revenue of a single-price monopolist is the combined effect of selling an additional unit (which raises revenue) and reducing the price on all units produced. Mathematically, it is the derivative of total revenue.

Marginal Utility Increase in a person's utility from acquiring an extra unit of some good, or possibly a dollar of increased wealth.

Marginal Valuation Maximum amount a person will pay in order to obtain an extra unit of some good or service.

Market Demand The horizontal sum of demand curves of all consumers in a market, i.e., total quantities demanded at various possible market prices.

Market Power A seller has market power if it faces a downward-sloping demand curve for the good or service it produces. The more and better the substitutes for the seller's product, the more elastic is that demand curve.

Market Protocol A set of rules that parties to a transaction in a given market will generally follow, e.g., ascending-value auction is one of many auction protocols.

Matrix Form Also known as MX-Form, is an organization simultaneously divisionalized by product and geographic activities.

Median Voter The person whose most preferred position on an issue splits the population, half preferring more than his position and half preferring less.

Merger The legal union of two corporations into a single entity, the shares of the new entity replacing those of both companies.

Merger Guidelines Regulations of the U.S. Department of Justice and Federal Trade Commission used to determine when they will judge that a merger does not significantly increase market power of the merged firm.

Mitigation If a contract is breached, the non-breaching party will in some cases only be able to collect liquidated damages if it can show it has undertaken mitigation efforts to minimize the harm it has suffered due to breach.

Mixed Bundling Offering customers the choice of purchasing goods individually or purchasing them as a bundle. Ordinary bundling does not allow the former option.

Mixed Strategies A game player chooses his particular strategy from a set of them in accordance with probabilities that are determined by the choices of other players, which may also be mixed strategies.

Model A representation of some aspect of reality, simplified to emphasize relationships between variables of interest to the researcher and predictions that can be derived from those relationships.

Monopsony A market characterized by a single buyer, who has some power over the price at which others supply to him.

Moral Hazard Incentive of an insured person to behave in ways that raise the probability of a claim, relative to the probability if not insured.

Most Favored Customer A provision in a sales agreement with a particular customer stating that if any other customer gets a lower price from the seller then this customer will also get that price.

N

Naked A *call option* is said to be naked if the writer does not hold the *underlying* asset at the time it is written.

NASDAQ Short for National Association of Securities Dealers Automated Quotations, is an electronic stock maket that currently lists approximately 3,800 companies. More shares trade on NASDAQ than any other exchange in the world.

Nash Equilibrium Solution of a game in which each player chooses his best strategy, given that all other players are also choosing their best strategies.

Natural Monopoly An industry is a natural monopoly if a producer's long-run average costs always decrease with its size. A larger firm can serve the entire market with lower average costs than any smaller competitor.

Net Present Value The algebraic sum of costs and income from an investment project, all discounted to the present.

Norm A generally accepted social convention about how one ought to behave.

Normal Form A matrix representation of a two-person game, in which the (i, j)th element represents the payoffs if player 1 chooses strategy i and player 2 chooses strategy j. The definition can be generalized to more than two players.

Normal Good A good whose desired consumption increases with a buyer's income or wealth.

Normative Economics Statements about economic phenomena that make judgments about their desirability.

NYMEX The New York Mercantile Exchange, where futures contracts in metals, minerals, and fuels are traded. NYMEX recently merged with CME Group, which also owns the Chicago Board of Trade and Chicago Mercantile Exchange, where futures are also traded.

NYSE Acronym for New York Stock Exchange.

O

Oligopoly A market supplied by a small number of sellers, each large enough to change market price by changing its own output.

OPEC Short for Organization of Petroleum Exporting Countries, a group of oil producing nations who attempt to coordinate their outputs in order to maintain high world oil prices.

Opportunism Attempting to gain an advantage by bending or breaking the rules underlying a transaction.

Opportunity Cost The most valuable alternative foregone when a choice is made.

Ordinal Utility A measure of personal well-being that allows one to rank a situation as more preferred or less preferred than some other.

Outside Directors Members of a corporation's board of directors who do not hold positions within the corporation.

Outsourcing A business outsources when it chooses to obtain some good or service from an outsider rather than produce it for itself.

Over-the-Counter (OTC) Market A venue for trading nonstandardized goods, as opposed to an organized exchange in which (for example) identical shares of stock or identical futures contracts change hands.

P

Partnership A form of business whose owners, known as partners, make its decisions and share in its profits or losses according to rules they have set. In general, each partner has *unlimited liability*.

Par Value Face value of a bond, to be paid at maturity.

Perpetuity An annuity that continues for all future years.

Piece Rate Payment of a worker on the basis of the amount of output he produces.

Poison Pill An anti-takeover defense that makes it difficult or impossible for a potential takeover organization to gain control of a company's board of directors, or that automatically creates a less valuable company when an outsider acquires some percentage of its shares.

Portfolio The set of assets held by an investor.

POS Acronym for Point of Sale, for example scanners that transmit retail sales data to manufacturers in real time.

Positive Economics Statements that attempt to describe economic phenomena objectively, i.e., without making value judgments about them.

Positive Time Preference General desire of individuals for earlier rather than later availability of goods. Persons with different rates of time preference can arrange mutually beneficial lending transactions between themselves.

Possessory Right A legal right to engage in a particular act or prevent others from engaging in it, often used in connection with property.

Present Value Amount today that will grow at interest to equal a specified amount to be paid at a future date.

Price Ceiling A maximum legally allowed price in some market. A ceiling price that is set below the equilibrium price will give rise to a shortage.

Price Discrimination Sale of otherwise identical goods or services by a monopolist at prices that differ depending on customers' individual elasticities of demand. Customers with higher elasticities are charged lower prices.

Price Floor A minimum legally allowed price in some market. A floor price that is set above the equilibrium price will give rise to a surplus.

Price-Taker A seller is a price-taker if it can sell as much or as little as it desires without affecting the market price. The same holds for price-taker buyers.

Principal/Agent Relationship One in which a principal contracts with an agent who will perform certain tasks specified by the principal. In general the principal cannot monitor all of the agent's activities, and the actual outcome may include random elements.

Private Equity Shares in a corporation that are not publicly traded, often as a result of purchases by a single entity.

Private Good A good characterized by exclusivity in consumption and the ability to exclude nonpayers from its benefits. In certain ways the opposite of a *public good.*

Producer Surplus A measure of the benefits to a price-taker producer from being able to sell at a market price, equal to the difference between price and (marginal) opportunity cost for each unit produced.

Production The act of transforming resources into goods or services that are more valuable.

Production Function Mathematical relationship showing maximum possible output that can be produced from various bundles of inputs.

Production Set The set of all possible bundles of outputs that can be produced using a given bundle of inputs.

Property Rights Rights to use something in a defined manner, possibly including rights to sell or transfer it.

Propitious Selection Also called advantageous selection, in which lower-risk people are more likely to be insured than high-risk ones.

Proprietorship A business owned by a single person (a "sole proprietorship") with the exclusive right to enjoy its profits and obligation to bear its losses.

Prospectus An offer to sell securities containing information about the business issuing them and its plans.

Proxy Fight An attempt, generally organized by shareholders, to vote in directors other than those endorsed by the current board of directors. Proxy is the term used for vote.

Public Good A good characterized by concurrent consumption in which all consumers share equally, and from which it is impossible to exclude nonpayers. In certain ways, the opposite of a *private good.*

Pure Strategy A situation in which a player in a game makes a single choice of strategy and plays it with certainty.

Put Option One that allows its holder to sell the underlying asset at a predetermined *strike price* on or prior to its expiration.

Q

Quantity Demanded A point on a given demand curve. Generally, if the market price of a good or service rises, quantity demanded will fall.

Quantity Supplied A point on a given supply curve. Generally, if market price rises, quantity supplied will rise.

Quid Pro Quo Agreed-upon concessions made by both parties to a contract.

R

Rational Behavior Choices intended to move the decision maker toward some goal.

Reaction Function A function showing how duopolist A's best choice varies with duopolist B's choice. Equilibrium occurs where A's and B's reaction functions intersect.

Real Option One based on real rather than financial assets, and often involving irreversible investment decisions.

Recognition Heuristic A decision rule that says if X is recognized and Y is not, one should conclude that X is more likely to be the correct answer for some particular type of question.

Regulation Q A regulation of the Federal Reserve that prohibits the payment of interest on certain types of bank deposits.

Reinsurance The transfer of insurance risk to another insurer.

Reliance Investment One made pursuant to a requirement specified in a contract, typically specific as regards the parties' relationship.

Remedy An action that a party that has breached a contract is ordered to undertake, in order to undo the consequences of breach. The most common orders are for cash payments, known as liquidated damages, and for specific performance, that forces the breaching party to fulfill its obligations.

Remittances Payments from wages earned by foreigners working in another country, sent to their relatives in the home country.

Rent Seeking A type of competition in which bidders for some governmental benefit (e.g., a monopoly) waste economic resources as they compete to obtain that benefit.

Reopener Provision Clause in a contract specifying that in the event some external event happens certain parts of it become open for renegotiation between the parties.

Representativeness Heuristic A heuristic that estimates a probability on the basis of easily available data ("representativeness") rather than the entire relevant population.

Requirements Contract A *vertical restraint* requiring a downstream firm (for example, a fast-food franchise) to purchase all of its food requirements from an upstream seller specified in the contract.

Residual Claimant The person in a hierarchy who receives the income that remains after accounting for all of the organization's costs.

Residual Demand In a *Dominant Firm Model*, residual demand is the demand curve facing the dominant firm after the output of the competitive fringe is subtracted from market demand.

Resource In a resource-based model of a firm, an asset (possibly an intangible one) that confers competitive strength or weakness on the firm.

Returns to Scale Summarize how output changes for equal percentage changes in all inputs. Returns to scale are increasing if increasing all inputs by x percent yields an output increase greater than x percent. They are constant if output increases by exactly x percent, and decreasing if it increases by less than x percent.

Risk A situation in which the decision maker knows the probability distributions that are important for his decision, to be distinguished from *uncertainty*.

Risk Averse A person is risk averse if he refuses to take "fair" gambles, defined as those with expected returns of zero.

Risk Neutral A person is risk neutral if he is indifferent between taking and not taking a "fair" gamble, defined as one with an expected return of zero.

Risk Preferrer One who will pay to take an unfair gamble, defined as one with a negative expected return.

Risk-Return Frontier The combinations of expected returns and risk (standard deviation or variance of *portfolio* returns) that are available in the market.

Royalty Payment One specified as a certain percentage of income. Examples include arrangements in franchising and book publishing.

Rule of Reason The standard used in antitrust law that requires a court to balance the favorable and unfavorable effects of some activity on competition.

S

Salary Fixed payment to a worker, often monthly, that is independent of actual hours worked or tasks undertaken.

Sarbanes-Oxley Act 2002 federal law that imposes additional disclosure requirements on corporations and requires management verification of financial statements.

Sealed-Bid Auction One in which each bidder writes down a single bid to purchase a good and seals it in an envelope prior to a deadline. When the envelopes are opened, the high bidder wins. Generally, no rebidding is allowed.

SEC Acronym for U.S. Securities and Exchange Commission, which has regulatory jurisdiction over most markets for corporate stock and bonds.

Second-Price Auction One in which the winning bidder pays the bid of the second-highest bidder. In a procurement auction, the low bidder will receive the amount bid by the second-lowest bidder.

Selection Bias Source of errors in inference that result from a sample of observations that are nonrandom—relevant data may be unavailable or the data may have been chosen in a way that resulted in the bias.

Self-Contained Unit Within an M-form organization, a specialized operation that manages some activity that affects several divisions, using information supplied by the divisions and its own staff.

Self-Insurance Setting aside reserve funds in order to cover some potential loss, as an alternative to purchasing an insurance policy in the market.

Share Contract One in which the worker, for example a *sharecropper*, is paid a pre-set percentage of output or revenue from sale of the output.

Sharecropping An arrangement in which a landlord hires a worker to farm his land in return for a fixed percentage of the crop.

Short A market participant who has obligated himself to deliver a good in the future is said to be short or to hold a short position.

Short Run In models of production and cost, the time span during which some inputs are fixed, while others are variable. In models of markets, the time span during which the number of sellers is fixed.

Shortage A market is in shortage if price is held below its equilibrium level, in which case there will be frustrated buyers who cannot find sellers at that price.

Signal An action a person can take that provides information about her that is otherwise unobservable.

Smith, Adam Generally acknowledged as the founder of modern economics, his 1776 book *The Wealth of Nations* remains the basis for much of the subject's fundamentals.

Specific Asset (Specific Investment) One that is most valuable in a particular economic relationship, and cannot be redeployed to some other use without losing value.

Specific Human Capital Human capital that only improves productivity in a worker's relationship with a particular employer. Employers will generally bear the costs of investing in it.

Specific Performance A remedy in which the party that has breached a contract must perform as the contract requires, and is not, for example, allowed to substitute money payments to the nonbreaching party.

Speculation Holding a position in some good with the intent of liquidating it in the future at a profit. Both buyers and sellers may be speculators.

Spot A cash trade for immediate delivery of some good, said to take place in a spot market.

Stackelberg Duopoly A two-seller oligopoly model in which one acts as the leader and the other as follower, with each taking into consideration the other's best choice when making its output decision.

Staggered Board A corporate board of directors whose members have terms that expire at different dates, making it more difficult to change its composition quickly in connection with a *takeover*.

Stock Option A grant to a corporate executive that allows her to purchase shares of the company's stock, typically at a price below their market price.

Strategy One of the possible choices available to a player in a game.

Strategy-Proofness In models of voting, there is no voting mechanism that will always be strategy-proof, meaning that under any rules for voting there will be cases in which some person can obtain a more preferred outcome for herself by not voting her true preferences.

Strike Price The price at which the holder of a *put* or *call option* may exercise it.

Subchapter S Corporation One with under 35 owners, each of whom has unlimited liability and whose shares are not tradeable. Profits are passed through directly to the income taxes of the owners.

Substitutes Two goods are substitutes if they can provide the same service for a consumer, e.g., sugar and honey can both serve as sweeteners. The same holds for inputs used by a producer, e.g., nails and screws are sometimes substitutes for fastening.

Successive Monopolies A monopolist who supplies an input and another monopolist who turns it into output. If their activities are not coordinated, *double marginalization* implies that the pair of them will realize lower profits than if they are integrated into a single firm or linked by contract.

Sunk Cost A cost that, once incurred, cannot be altered or recovered by any choice made today.

Supermajority Requirement A corporate charter provision or by-law stipulating that some minimum percentage of shares voting (over 50) is required for changes in corporate policy.

Supply Also called a supply curve, the relationship between the quantity of some good a price-taker supplier wishes to produce and its market price. All else equal, at higher prices a producer will be willing to supply more units of it. A point on a given supply curve is called the quantity supplied at that price.

Surplus A market is in shortage if price is held above its equilibrium level, in which case there will be frustrated sellers who cannot find buyers at that price.

T

Take In a contract, the amount of a good that the purchaser may choose to have delivered.

Takeover An attempt to gain control of a corporation and install a new board of directors in the expectation of increasing its value.

Target A firm at risk of *acquisition* or *takeover*.

Team A collection of individuals who cooperate in some type of production. They are assumed to own different resources, and their individual contributions to the team's output cannot generally be identified.

Technical Efficiency Production is technically efficient if for a given bundle of inputs, output is at its maximum possible level.

Tender An offer to purchase shares of a company from existing shareholders for a price above their current market value, usually in connection with a takeover. Shareholders who sell are said to "tender" their shares.

Termination Clause A provision in a contract specifying that it will terminate if certain events happen. If termination is triggered, the parties remain free to continue operating under the contract if they prefer to do so.

Thin Market One with a small number of buyers and sellers, in which few transactions take place and often cannot be made on short notice.

Tie-In Goods A and B are tied if the purchase of A (the *tied* good) is required as a condition for a customer to purchase B (the *tying* good).

Total Product In models of short-run production with one variable input, total product of the variable input is the total output that results from various amounts of that input.

Transaction Costs Those costs incurred in arranging and fulfilling transactions (e.g., delivery), as opposed to costs of producing a good or service itself.

Trigger In game theory, a commitment by Player A to choose a certain strategy in the event Player B makes some particular choice. Variants include a *grim trigger*, in which A will play that strategy forever, and a *forgiving trigger*, in which A plays it for a finite number of periods.

Two-Part Pricing A pricing scheme that charges a customer a fixed amount (often called a fixed charge, customer charge, or cover charge) for the right to purchase a good, and a separate amount (often called a commodity charge) for each unit actually purchased.

U

UCC Acronym for Uniform Commercial Code, an attempt to standardize laws pertaining to business relationships throughout the U.S. Parties to a contract often choose the UCC as a default that will apply to all items not otherwise discussed in their contract.

U-Form Firm One organized along functional lines, with separate departments for individual aspects (production, sales, etc.) of the business.

Uncertainty A situation in which the decision maker has no prior estimates of the probabilities of importance for her decision, as distinguished from *risk*.

Underlying Asset Also called underlier, the asset upon whose value a *derivative* is based, for example a share of stock or a commodity.

Uniform Delivered Prices A practice in which a seller charges the same price to all of its customers, even if there are different costs of transporting its good to them.

Uninsured Motorist Type of provision in automobile insurance policies that pays policy holder in event of a hit-and-run accident or one involving a driver without insurance.

Unit Elastic A demand curve is unit or unitary elastic if its elasticity equals 1 in absolute value. If so, an increase or decrease in market price leaves total spending on the good unchanged.

Unitization Contract In oil or gas, an agreement among parties with rights to access an underground deposit that they will coordinate exploration and production activities to maximize the value of the oil or gas recovered.

Unlimited Liability A situation in which a person has liability for all of an organization's debts, as occurs in a sole *proprietorship*.

Upstream Refers to an earlier stage in a vertical production chain.

Utility A subjective measure of a person's well-being.

Utility Possibility Frontier Line representing the possible combinations of *utility* that two individuals can reach by negotiation. Utilities are assumed *cardinally* measurable.

V

Valuation The maximum that a person will voluntarily pay rather than go without some good or service.

Value of Marginal Product A worker's marginal product multiplied by the price of output, equals the additional revenue an employer receives from hiring that worker.

Vanilla A financial instrument is "vanilla" if it contains no special features, only the generic ones that define it. A bond that is *callable* is not vanilla.

Vertical Agreement One between firms at different stages of production, for example a franchise contract between a parent company and an independent locally owned retailer of its product.

Vertical Integration A firm is vertically integrated if it controls several stages of production of some good or service, for example manufacturing and retailing.

Vertical Merger A merger between two firms that operate at different stages of production of some good or service, for example one between a raw material supplier and a firm that processes that material.

Vertical Restraint Also known as a vertical restriction, a term in a vertical agreement that requires or prohibits certain action by one of the parties, for example one that prohibits a franchised automobile dealer from selling any other make of car.

Volumetric Dependence Characterizes a production process in which volumes must match very closely between stages, and holding of inventories is very costly.

W

Warranty Assurance, generally written, that a product will meet certain specifications, and that if it does not the seller will take remedial actions.

White Knight A corporate management whose jobs are threatened by a takeover may respond by looking for an alternative takeover organization that intends to treat them better. The alternative is sometimes called a white knight.

Williams Act 1968 federal law imposing disclosure requirements on persons making cash *tender* offers for corporate stock in connection with possible *takeovers.*

Winner's Curse In auctions with incomplete information, the bidder with the most optimistic information may put in the highest bid. Because the information is only observed with error, that person may end up paying more than the actual value of the object.

Workers' Compensation Insurance (held by employers or supplied by government) that guarantees payments to replace wages for employees injured in workplaces.

X

X-Inefficiency Increase in production cost that results from using larger quantities of inputs than are necessary to produce a given quantity of output at minimum possible cost.

Z

Zero-Sum Game One in which one party's loss equals the other party's gain.

Zone of Agreement In negotiations, the set of outcomes that make both parties better off than their fallbacks.

Index

D

N

O

T

U

V

W

X

Y

Z